# Fostering the Growth of High Ability: European Perspectives

# Creativity Research

## Robert S. Albert, Series Editor

# Fostering the Growth of High Ability: European Perspectives

edited by
Arthur J. Cropley and Detlev Dehn
University of Hamburg

 Ablex Publishing Corporation
Norwood, New Jersey

Printed in the United States of America

Library of Congress Cataloging-in-Publication Data

Fostering the growth of high ability : European perspectives / Arthur
    J. Cropley and Detlev Dehn, eds.
        p.   cm. — (Creativity research)
    Includes bibliographical references and index.
    ISBN 1-56750-241-5 (cloth). — ISBN 1-56750-242-3 (pbk.)
    1. Gifted children—Europe—Psychology.  2. Gifted children—
Europe—Counseling of.   3. Creative ability in children.  4. Gifted
children—Education—Europe.   I. Cropley, A. J.   II. Dehn, Detlev.
III. Series.
BF723.GF67    1996
155.45'5'094—dc20                                                    96-15631
                                                                      CIP

Ablex Publishing Corporation
355 Chestnut Street
Norwood, New Jersey 07648

# Contents

## IV. Talent in Sport

## V. Creativity and Curiosity

# Foreword

The chapters in this book all appeared originally in the *European Journal for High Ability*. They are reprinted here in order to make them available to a North American readership. They cover basic concepts in the study of giftedness, cognition and problem solving, musical talent, counseling. The authors come from a dozen different countries including not only the United Kingdom, Germany, Holland, France, Italy and Sweden—"mainstream" countries with a strong Western European cultural and educational tradition with which North Americans will be familiar—but also Russia, Ukraine, Croatia, Poland, Hungary and the Czech Republic, nations which have just emerged from a period of domination of ideas by a social-political tradition known to North Americans only in the abstract,

The book gives many insights into thinking on giftedness in Eastern European nations: The "philosophy" of efforts to foster the development of gifted individuals in the former German Democratic Republic (East Germany) or the former Soviet Union is spelled out in the first section of the book. Cognitive approaches to giftedness or issues in promoting musical talent, as they are seen from a Polish point of view, are discussed in relevant sections. Intense interest in fostering sporting talent is reflected in chapters from Hungary, including the idea that sporting performance can be enhanced by appropriate psychotherapy. The role of school is presented from the point of view of (former) East Germany, Poland, and (former) Yugoslavia. These examples illustrate the source of the book's claim to offer broader perspectives and stimulating ideas for North American readers.

The *European Journal for High Ability*, from which the following chapters are taken, is published by *the European Council for High Ability*. With effect from January 1, 1996 the name of the Journal has been altered to *High Ability Studies*. The journal sees as its purpose providing a forum for the exchange of ideas on both practice and research. It publishes in English reviews of the literature, descriptions of projects, research reports, book reviews and similar material. An important aspect is that high ability is understood not only as intellectual giftedness but also as giftedness in sport, fine arts, music and the like. The journal has an international orientation, and publishes papers from both Western and Eastern Europe, North America, Asia and South East Asia. The contents of this book reflect both the breadth of coverage of the journal and also the geographical variety of its contributors.

The journal is published with the assistance of the German foundation *Bildung und Begabung*. The editors have also received substantial help from the *Computer Centre of the University of Hamburg*, as well as from *Psychologisches Institut II* of the university, and we are grateful to these institutions for their support. *Ablex Publishing Corporation* has shown vision and creativity in helping us to make available to North American readers material with which they would otherwise have no contact, and we appreciate this greatly.

—**Arthur J. Cropley**
**Detlev Dehn**
**University of Hamburg 1996**

# Section 1

## Basic Concepts

# 1

# A Broader View
# of Giftedness

**Arthur Cropley**
**Detlev Dehn**

*University of Hamburg, Hamburg, Germany*

Recent years have seen substantial changes in the conceptualization of giftedness: incorporation of gifts in areas other than those emphasized in school, emphasis on qualitative aspects (patterns and structures rather than levels), and acceptance of the importance of noncognitive factors in giftedness (e.g., motivation, self-image, feelings). A further broadening has involved steadily increasing emphasis on creativity, which is seen as interacting with conventional intelligence to yield "true" giftedness. Fostering of giftedness requires encouragement not only of schoolhouse skills, but also of creativity, intense interest, prolonged effort, the feeling of not being alone, and the joy of achieving.

Traditionally, the notion of giftedness has focused on the cognitive domain (e.g., feats of memory, exceptional achievement on learning tasks, outstandingly clever thinking, etc.). In particular, giftedness has been associated with school settings or school-like situations. This approach to giftedness often has been expanded somewhat to include performances in music, the fine arts, and, perhaps surprisingly, chess. More or less parallel to interest in outstanding performance of the kind just described has been an interest in exceptional sporting performance, although these two areas, the cognitive, on the one hand, the sensorimotor, on the other, usually have not been discussed in a single context; apart from exceptions such as the conferences and symposia of the European Council for High Ability, books and conferences on gifted education and related topics rarely have concerned themselves with the teaching and learning of, for example, skill in putting the shot or swimming, whereas coaches of outstanding athletes have seldom concerned themselves with the fostering of talents in chess or music. A major tendency in recent discussions, however, has been a broadening of the definition of giftedness to include not only "schoolhouse" giftedness, but also nonschool giftedness. This tendency has been greatly facilitated by increased interest in not only the cognitive aspects of gifts and talents, but also the personal, affective, and motivational elements. An example is to be seen in discussions of self-concept and attitudes in high academic achievement as well as in record-breaking athletic performances (Süle, 1990). Another example is to be seen in the area of leadership: Many recent discussions emphasize the need for gifted individuals to use their gifts and talents in an ethically desirable way, applying them not, for instance, to self-aggrandizement and personal enrichment, but to the solution of societal problems such as poverty, prejudice, or environmental destruction (see Cropley, Urban, Wagner, & Wieczerkowski, 1986, for several relevant papers).

In the cognitive domain there has been a move away from a quantitive (How much of some particular skill does a particular gifted person possess?) to a qualitative approach (What kind of abilities constitute giftedness? How are they organized and how do they interact with each other?). It has been suggested that even traditional cognitive tests should be used to define, not level of ability but pattern of organization, for example, "cognitive structure." Allied with this development has been an increasing emphasis on cognitive processes, especially on the activities that define them and the mechanisms that direct, accelerate, or decelerate, and guide them. Among others, achieving insight or developing heuristics for solving problems have been investigated.

The metacognitive approach to giftedness (see, e.g., Sternberg, 1985) emphasizes elements such as the selection of "good" problems, the distinction between promising lines of attack and dead ends, the evaluation of partial solutions or the identification of more promising alternative lines of attack when evaluation shows that progress to date has not been satisfactory.

Noncognitive approaches to the defining of giftedness emphasize motivation, values and attitudes, and personal characteristics, such as self-image: Great expertise requires not only skills and abilities, but also fascination for a particular area, a feeling that it is worthwhile to dedicate oneself to this area, and confidence in one's own ability to master the area in question. The achievement of exceptional expertise also frequently requires investment of large amounts of energy (see also later discussions). Amabile (1983) discussed a number of these factors. Finally, it has become apparent that giftedness has a strong social element: The society or its subgroups play a major role in deciding which achievements will be regarded as prodigious and valuable (and hence talented), which, by contrast, will be dismissed as crackpot, dangerous, subversive, destructive, or even criminal (and hence not talented). This aspect recently has been emphasized by Sternberg (1985).

## CREATIVITY AND GIFTED ACHIEVEMENT

Sternberg and Lubart (1992) took the view that outstanding gifted achievement always involves going against the mainstream and requires "contrarianism" (p. 41), which is closely relatated to creativity. The view that creativity is a major aspect of giftedness has, in fact, been evident for most of the period of modern creativity research. The "Sputnik shock" of the late 1950s led to a period of national soulsearching in the United States, and to the conclusion that the country's educational system had failed to produce enough gifted scientists, mainly because of its lack of emphasis on creativity. The wave of creativity research that followed set the stage for intense interest in the topic on a worldwide basis. The late 1970s saw the emergence of a second wave of research that is still continuing. Once again this was largely set in motion by renewed interest in fostering creativity. In retrospect, it is apparent that, from the very beginning, creativity was seen as an element in high academic achievement. The purpose of the initial education act on creativity in the United States was production of scientists and engineers capable of matching the achievements of their counterparts in the Soviet Union.

Studies such as Gibson and Light's (1967) investigation of scientists at Cambridge university, which showed that many of them had IQs under 130, a traditional cutoff point for identifying giftedness, indicated that intelligence alone was not sufficient for outstanding achievement. In a major review of research on IQ and creativity, Milgram (1990) showed that, despite occasional findings to the contrary, IQs and similar scores do not predict real-life creativity adequately. Apparently, talented achievement demands something more than simply high IQ.

Wallach and Kogan (1965) showed that children high on both intelligence and creativity did particularly well at school. In studies of both schoolchildren in Canada and also university students in Australia, Cropley (1967a,) showed that, although the highly intelligent-low creative subjects obtained good marks, they were consistently outstripped by students high on both characteristics. This superiority of achievement among people combining conventional intelligence and creativity became more pronounced as the level of education increased (i.e., from seventh grade to first year university to final year university to honors level studies). In a longitudinal study in the Federal Republic of Germany, pupils of very high intelligence but without corresponding creativity surpassed those merely high on creativity, but in all other cases those higher on creativity achieved better (Sierwald, 1989). As Facaoaru (1985) showed in a study of engineers in Romania, talented achievement depends on a combination of conventional abilities (good memory, logical thinking, knowledge of facts, accuracy, etc.) and creative abilities (generating ideas, recognizing alternative possibilities, seeing unexpected combinations, having the courage to try the unusual, etc.). This combination defines "true giftedness."

Probably the best known attempt to depict the interaction of creativity and high conventional intelligence in talented performance is Renzulli's (1977) "three ring" model: He depicted intelligence, creativity, and "task commitment" as three overlapping circles, each of the constituent elements defining a necessary but not sufficient condition for giftedness. The area in which all three circles overlap defines giftedness. The three ring model has been extended by Mönks, van Boxtal, Roelofs, and Sanders (1986), a group of Dutch researchers, who included a fourth dimension, the social environment. They showed, for instance, that underachieving gifted youngsters had a negative self-concept. A further extension of this model is to be seen in the results of an investigation carried out in Finland (Ruth & Birren, 1985). By taking the unusual step of including elderly people in a cross-sectional study of creativity at various age levels, these authors were able to demonstrate the importance of biological factors in creativity, especially those affecting speed of information processing and memory. Adapting their findings for the present purposes, it can be said that they showed that intellectual giftedness requires a rich store of information to which there is free and rapid access (usually regarded as an essential characteristic of conventional intelligence), allied with the capacity to find novel ideas, and willingness to express them (usually thought of as creativity). Applied to nonintellectual domains such as sport or music this would mean that talented performance requires technical skill that can rapidly be adapted to a given situation, plus capacity and willingness to try the new, try the old in new situations, work out new approaches, and so on.

The question that arises now is that of how creativity and intelligence interact to produce giftedness. An early approach was that of MacKinnon (1962), who proposed the threshold theory. In essence, this argues that a certain minimum level (threshold) of intelligence is necessary before creativity is possible. Bringing out a different aspect of the same idea, McNemar (1964) pointed out that high IQ is no guarantee of creativity, but a low IQ means that it is impossible. Guilford and Christensen (1973) took a somewhat different position, suggesting that there is a "one-way relationship" between creative potential and intelligence, that is, an IQ test provides an indicator of the upper limit for performance, but does not indicate the likelihood of creativity. Their interpretation is based on the argument that IQ indicates the extent to which an individual possesses relevant information and can call it out of storage upon demand. If a person does not have access to information, there is nothing to be retrieved and divergently processed. A more dynamic interpretation along similar lines is to regard the individual as a communication channel. Channel capacity, in the sense of an upper limit on the number of "bits" of information that can be assimilated, is intuitively compatible with the concept of intelligence, whereas the versatility and extent to which an individual can manipulate, reorganize, and recombine those "bits" is compatible with the notion of originality, creativity, or divergent productive thinking.

Of particular interest is the conceptualization of creativity as a *qualitative* aspect of mental functioning: Over 25 years ago, on the basis of data showing substantial correlations between creativity test scores and IQ scores, as well as between "creativity" and "intelligence" factors, Cropley (1969) described creativity as a "style" for applying intelligence, rather than as a separate ability; more recently, Gardner (1983) referred to creativity as the highest *form of application* of intelligence, and Runco and Albert (1986) defined it as *intelligence in action*. Horn (1988) distinguished between two basic styles of reacting to novelty, the one involving avoidance, the other attraction. In essence, the "style" approach argues that people may deal with situations requiring intelligence either by trying to reapply the already learned, concentrating on proven tactics, and relating the new situation to the familiar, or by searching for the novel, backing intuitions, taking a chance, and so on.

Simonton (1988) advanced what he called the "chance configuration" model of genius. He concluded that achievement of gifted products involves production of a large number of associations, more or less randomly or blindly, and the chance occurrence of "configurations"—happy combinations that represent just what is needed to solve the problem in question. The gifted achiever is especially good not only at producing associations, but also at recognizing that a configuration has occurred, and grasping that it offers a solution. Weisberg (1986) examined self-reports and case studies of famous creators and combined this information with data obtained in experimental studies. He concluded that creative production arises not from random combinations, but from "chains" of ideas connected associatively in a long series of strictly logical small steps, for which knowledge of the field is vital.

## NONCOGNITIVE FACTORS
## IN GIFTED ACHIEVEMENT

However, an analysis based on thinking alone cannot offer an adequate explanation of the achievement of gifted products. Studies of famous gifted individuals of the past have confirmed that, among other things, *motivation* plays an important role. For instance, Cox's (1926) retrospective studies of geniuses of the past such as Newton, Copernicus, Gallileo, Keppler, and Darwin showed clearly that in addition to high intelligence these people were marked by tenacity and perseverance. In a similar vein, Biermann (1985) concluded, on the basis of a study of outstanding mathematicians of the seventeenth to nineteenth centuries, that fascination with the subject matter and consequent extreme motivation was one of the major features of his subjects. Hassenstein (1988) also commented on the obsessive nature of the work of gifted individuals, whereas Goertzel, Goertzel, and Goertzel (1978) showed the importance of motivation in their case studies of historical figures.

One of the early findings in studies of talented mathematicians, scientists, architects, painters, and writers already mentioned was that these people seemed to possess special *personality characteristics* that set them off from less creative colleagues: flexibility, sensitivity, tolerance, sense of responsibility, empathy, independence, and positive self-image. Heinelt (1974) studied school children identified on the basis of test scores as highly creative, and came to the conclusion that they were significantly more frequently than uncreative youngsters introverted, self-willed, intellectually active, flexible, and possessed of wit and a sense of humor. Reviewing a substantial number of studies in this area, Farisha (1978) concluded that a relationship between personality and creativity is one of the most consistently emphasized findings in the literature.

Related to studies of personality and creativity are investigations emphasizing interactions with other people, that is, *social factors.* Heinelt's (1974) study showed, for instance, that school children identified as creative tended to remain aloof from their classmates and preferred to work independently. They were often socially isolated and unpopular, and this phenomenon was associated with a tendency to feel superior to their classmates or even to be arrogant. Other studies (e.g., Neff, 1975) showed that creative youngsters are often uninterested in making a good impression on others or in conforming. Being creative involves thinking or behaving differently from others, otherwise the element of originality would be missing. Consequently, creative individuals must display "the courage to create" (Motamedi, 1982): they must risk the censure and rejection often associated with failure to conform. Anderson and Cropley (1966) studied the reactions of school children in situations where a number of alternative courses of action were possible, and concluded that they were guided by social "stop rules" that forbade most reactions in favor of the socially approved one. Societies have "filters" (Fromm, 1980) through which not only behaviors but also ideas must pass, and carry out constant "surveillance" (Amabile, Goldfarb, & Brackfield, 1990) in order to detect and deter deviance.

Feist and Runco (1993) drew attention to a further noncognitive element in creativity—*feelings and emotions*. According to these authors, emotion is one of the least studied areas in the creativity literature, although recent work (e.g., Russ, 1993; Shaw & Runco, 1994) may well contribute to correcting the imbalance. In a study involving successful engineers and physicists, Shaw (1989) identified several feelings and emotions that are of major importance for creativity: *Fascination, self-confidence, frustration* (in case of blockages), *intuitions, excitement*, and *satisfaction*. The participants in Shaw's study made little mention of feelings such as the joy of competition or pleasure of aggression, perhaps because these are socially undesirable, perhaps, as would be pleasant to imagine, because negative feelings are less important in creativity.

Emerging from the considerations just outlined is a more comprehensive definition of giftedness than in the past. It is not confined to school-related activities, but also involves areas such as sport and leadership. It derives not merely from possession of a high level of cognitive skill, but also involves the nature and organization of abilities, and is best regarded as a process. The nature, direction, and speed of this process partly depends on cognitive factors, but is also strongly influenced by personality and motivation, and has strong social elements, including, among other things, an ethical dimension and an important communication aspect. Finally, it is possible to adopt the apparently paradoxical position that anybody is (at least potentially) capable of high level performance, even if only a few actually display it. Howe (1990) went so far as to argue that with trust in themselves and sufficient effort (e.g., practice), most people are capable of high achievement.

## FOSTERING DEVELOPMENT OF TALENTS

Gifted performance is related to gender (e.g., superior performance of boys in mathematics; lower incidence of women among famous scientists, writers, artists, and so on; lower activity of women in "everyday creativity"), birth order (e.g., higher proportion of Nobel prize winners among first born; higher proportion of later borns among artists, poets, or actors) and age. Despite criticism over the years, the classical study of Lehman

(1953) on age and peak performance is still widely supported (see Lindauer, 1993). Simonton (1988) gave many examples of famous people from the past. The age at which peak performances occur differs somewhat from discipline to discipline, mathematicians tending to become famous particularly early, but it is generally true that most outstanding achievements occur between 30 and 40, somewhere around 40 being the most productive age. Nonetheless, many famous talented people continue to produce until well into later life: Darwin, Freud, and Einstein became famous in their twenties and remained active into their seventies. Those who start youngest seem to continue longest. Mumford and Gustafson (1988) offered a model that helps to make sense of the apparent discrepancy between the findings that peak performances occur young and that productivity often persists into old age. They distinguished between two forms of productive creativity, "major" and "minor" creativity. Significant breakthroughs (major creativity) tend to occur up to about 35–40, broadening and consolidation (minor creativity) after that.

Concentrating on "ordinary" people who had not become famous for outstanding performances, various authors (see Cropley, 1994 for a summary) have concluded that there is a curvilinear relationship between creativity as measured by test scores and age up to about 30, for instance, increasing scores until about age six, a trough between about six and 16, and again increasing scores until about 30. After 30 there is a steady decline. Cropley concluded that this pattern results from aspects of cognitive development (e.g., passage from the preoperational to the operational stage), the influence of school norms (emphasis on logic and accuracy), social pressures (the demands of the job), and physiological factors (e.g., reduced speed of thinking with increasing age).

What are the factors that determine whether or not a particular person develops high levels of expertise and displays extremely capable levels of performance? Many of the findings underlying the conventional wisdom are derived from the application of psychological tests with school children. Recently, biographical and autobiographical studies of living or historical gifted individuals have come to play a more important role in investigating the developmental conditions for the emergence of gifts and talents. Such studies are by no means new, and many examples existed before World War I. However, after a period of neglect the last few years have been marked by a resurgence in case studies of exceptional achievers such as famous personalities of the past, Nobel Prize winners, or Olympic gold medalists, persons rated as exceptional by their colleagues, and the like (see Simonton, 1988; and Weisberg, 1986, for examples). These have been extremely fruitful, as they have contradicted a number of common beliefs about gifted individuals. Many talented people do not show exceptional performance at an extraordinarily early age, despite the existence of exceptions such as Mozart. Achieving success often is a very long process: famous pianists, successful scientists, and even Olympic swimmers typically require 15 years or more of intense effort before they are accepted as gifted (see Elshout, 1990, for a relevant discussion). During much of this time their performances may be merely good average or only somewhat above average. However, because of the personal and motivational factors already discussed, some stick at it and eventually become outstanding. If intense dedication commences at about 15–20, it is apparent why peak performances frequently come at 30–40.

What is clear is that the development of talents does not involve the automatic emergence in a more or less preprogrammed way of God-given potentials. On the contrary, outstanding achievement involves a process that may or may not reach a successful conclusion—it is possible, for instance, to speak of unrealized talents. (It is also possible to identify talents that have emerged from apparently unpromising beginnings.) Quite apart from the possible possession of inborn advantages involving the sense organs, the central nervous system, or other physical features, the development of talents depends on the circumstances of life. It also depends on the individual's personality, values, interests, self-image, motives, and so on, and these are themselves shaped by the circumstances of life.

Necessary for the development of gifts and talents is *opportunity* (contact with a particular field, its contents, activities, materials, etc.). In most cases *long and concentrated practice* also is necessary—case studies have shown that very few gifted individuals succeeded without this element. *Fascination with an area*, motivation to dedicate oneself to the area, belief in oneself as capable of high levels of achievement, and the like, are not only important prerequisites for willingness to practice (possibly for thousands of hours), but are themselves partly acquired through crucial experiences provided by the environment. As various studies have shown, *contact with models or mentors* is of great importance (e.g., Bloom, 1985): These people may be parents or siblings, teachers, coaches, and the like. They display the skills of the area of giftedness, the values and attitudes associated with it, and the self-image required for success. They need not themselves be gifted—the "crystallizing" person is sometimes someone in a humble role, such as an elementary school teacher.

The fact that the emergence of gifts and talents involves a developmental process guided by "environmental enablers" raises special problems for children from disadvantaged backgrounds: Not only for social outgroups such as the poor or immigrants, but also for groups from whom giftedness usually is not expected, or who by virtue of some special characteristic are denied contacts with a field, opportunities for practice, interactions with crystallizing persons, or other crucial experiences (e.g., girls, the physically handicapped, the sensorily handicapped). Not only may a stigma or a handicap limit contact with environmental enablers, but it may also inhibit recognition of an emerging potential (e.g., because of prejudice or even a well-meaning desire to "protect" the child in question), and thus further reduce opportunity, introducing a downward spiral of unrealized potential. The problem of recognizing gifted potential in groups such as those just mentioned has received intensive interest in recent years (e.g., Baldwin, 1985), and is one of the most important issues in contemporary gifted education.

## IDENTIFICATION

In keeping with the early, very simple definition of giftedness as high conventional intelligence, identification of the gifted and talented has been, and still is, dominated by intelligence tests, high IQ being taken as a sign of giftedness. Although a number of writers have argued for an extension of the mental test approach by incorporating creativity tests, research has shown that only moderate progress has been made: Intelligence tests still predominate (see McLeod & Cropley, 1989). In any case, use of creativity tests represents only an improvement of the existing, cognitively oriented, socially biased approach. More recently, some authors have called for "identification by performance" (Shore & Tsiamis, 1986). The basic idea is simple: Children who display high achievement are deemed to be gifted and are offered special forms of provision. If this approach were limited to high marks in traditional school subjects, however, it would be fraught with problems. For instance, young children would scarcely be identified at all, since they have had no chance to display high achievement. The well-known correlation between home background (social class, ethnic origin, mother tongue, and the like) and school marks would mean that identification would be limited almost exclusively to children from the dominant social class (usually middle class speakers of the official language of the society in question). For these reasons, "performance" must be understood as something more than school grades.

The extended definition of giftedness already discussed provides many ideas for the redefinition of "performance", and hence offers new impulses for identifying the gifted. Unusual skill or high levels of talent can be expanded to include content areas going beyond those of the traditional classroom (e.g., photography, music, debating, and the like), or even lying outside the school altogether (e.g., hobbies and clubs, sports organizations, part-time work, etc.). Furthermore, "performance" need not be confined to finished products, but can be expanded to include noncognitive aspects: intense interest in a field of endeavor, sustained effort stretching over months and years, willingness to make sacrifices in pursuing an interest, confidence in oneself as capable of "making it," willingness to stand up for something in the face of peer group pressure, and similar properties. The areas of activity need not be those conventionally prized in the dominant social group; indeed, in the case of youngsters from outgroups (the social underclass, migrants, native speakers of "foreign" languages—in many cases these are the same people, since there is a strong interaction among the three conditions), it is important that they are not. What is important in identifying the gifted is exceptional performance in areas of activity prized by the social subgroup to which a particular child belongs: naturally, excellence in conventional schoolhouse areas should not be devalued, but interest should be expanded in the way just outlined (see McLeod & Cropley, 1989).

Another approach is "identification by provision" (Shore & Tsiamis, 1986): Children who wish to take part in special provision for the gifted and talented (or whose parents or teachers nominate them) are admitted to such provision. If they flourish, they have, in fact, identified themselves (i.e., this is a variant of identification by performance), if they do not do well in "the gifted program" they have demonstrated its inappropriateness for them, and can return to normal provision. Children "identified" by provision succeed about as frequently as youngsters identified by other procedures, such as IQ testing. This raises the question of the usefulness of parent, teacher, even self-nominations for identifying the gifted. Self-selection, especially through performance as outlined earlier, as well as nomination by parents is not significantly less accurate than identification via test procedures—although both approaches have substantial weaknesses. Traditionally, the ability of teachers to identify gifted children has been sharply criticized, on the grounds that they tend to identify boys, conformers, and generally likable youngsters at the expense of girls, quiet, self-effacing children and troublemakers. However, large-scale studies have shown that when teachers are given a clear definition of the properties they are looking for and a certain amount of training, they can select with a satisfactory degree of accuracy (see Denton, 1986).

## GIFTED EDUCATION

Identification of gifted children has no point unless it leads to special treatment aimed at facilitating the development of gifts and talents. Once again, the expanded definition of giftedness already outlined provides guidelines for such special provision. In order to promote the acquisition of high levels of expertise, it should offer opportunities for intensive work in a particular area. In addition, however, it should promote interest in the area, conviction of its importance and worth, familiarity with the values and ethics of the area, confidence in one's own ability to do outstanding work, and willingness to make long and sustained effort to achieve such success.

Traditionally, discussions of special provision in schools have distinguished between "acceleration" (completing the work specified in the curriculum in less time than foreseen) and "enrichment" (going into material more deeply than foreseen). Speeding up by covering contents quickly or entering school, high school. or university early may simply mean that a child finishes a program at an early age, leading, for instance, to people graduating from university at 13, 14, or 15, or receiving a PhD at 18, 19, or 20. However, in school settings typically it involves children spending time in a "resource room" or with the "gifted" teacher: The activities then carried out typically involve a more intensive treatment of the standard material, often accompanied by attempts to promote creativity. Thus it is apparent that acceleration and enrichment are, for all practical purposes if not in theory, two sides of the same coin.

More recent work on special provision for gifted children has emphasized other forms of organization in which the acceleration–enrichment dichotomy has become blurred. For example, elementary schools may cooperate with secondary schools to allow gifted pupils to spend some class time with agemates in subjects where they are working at the "normal" level, possibly with an enriched intensity, some with older students, where the gifted pupil has shown a thirst for acceleration. Outstanding examples of such patterns of special provision involve youngsters who may be in fifth or sixth grade in, let us say, mother tongue and social studies, in grade 11 or 12 in chemistry and biology, and in third year university in mathematics and physics. Other organizational forms of special provision include cooperation between schools and industry (e.g., highly motivated students work in a firm's laboratory at weekends or during their vacations), Saturday schools, and vacation camps. Such forms of provision meet a number of objections to acceleration, such as removal of a child from social contact with agemates, and offer great promise.

A second area in which there have been marked changes in gifted education in recent years involves the definition of who is a teacher: not only may schools invite successful practitioners to give talks to pupils, but contact between gifted youngsters and such people may go beyond occasional visits, to include regular opportunities to work with them (e.g., at the practitioner's place of work), intense tutoring from such people (for instance at weekend seminars or vacation camps), or even establishment of an informal or sometimes formal mentorship. (Practitioner and pupil plan a project together and the child carries it out under the watchful eye of the expert, who provides advice, encouragement, criticism, concrete help, collegial feedback, and the like.) Such contacts are particularly important in helping gifted youngsters develop not only skills but also attitudes, values, and identity, and, perhaps most important, a feel for the ethics and brotherhood–sisterhood among practitioners of a particular discipline. In view of recent research on the role of a crystallizing person in the childhood of people who later became highly successful, this latter aspect should not be undervalued.

One difficulty with these measures, however, is that they require a high level of cooperation among segments of the education system, and are possible only when administrators and teachers are flexible. In many cases the readiness to act is missing. In some Western European countries' Education Ministries, teachers' unions and even teachers are opposed to special provision for the gifted on ideological grounds: In 1985 the Minister of Education of the state of Hamburg drew a comparison between contemporary interest in gifted education and that of the Nazi regime (without mentioning that the Nazis actually banned gifted education on the grounds that it was inconsistent with their ideology), whereas a few years later the Minister of Education for the Australian State of Victoria announced that gifted education would be introduced only over her dead body.

Recent political events in the countries of Central and Eastern Europe raise a number of interesting issues. Communist regimes were generally strongly in favor of gifted education (even if the political status of the parents played a major role in deciding which children were identified as gifted). Several of these countries had well-developed systems of special schools (including the Soviet Union), as well as organized and effective holiday camps and children's villages, university clubs for children gifted in special subjects, and the like. Although participation in competitions at national (such as the national science, language, and music competitions in Germany) or international level (e.g., Mathematics Olympics) was by no means restricted to the former Communist countries, they supported such forms of special provision for the gifted with great vigor. It remains to be seen if these traditions will be maintained and strengthened under new governments, or if they will be swept aside in the course of the reforms currently taking place.

## REFERENCES

Amabile, T. M. (1983). *The social psychology of creativity.* New York: Springer.

Amabile, T. M., Goldfarb, P., & Brackfield, S. C. (1990). Social influences on creativity: Evaluation, coaction, surveillance. *Creativity Research Journal, 3,* 6–21.

Anderson, C. C. & Cropley, A. J. (1966). Some correlates of originality. *Australian Journal of Psychology, 18,* 218–227.

Baldwin, A. Y. (1985). Programs for the gifted and talented: Issues concerning minority populations. In F. D. Horowitz and M. O'Brien (Eds.), *The gifted and talented: Developmental perspectives* (pp. 223–250). Washington, DC: American Psychological Association.

Biermann, K.-R. (1985). Über Stigmata der Kreativität bei Mathematikern des 17. bis 19. Jahrhunderts [Indicators of creativity in mathematicians of the 17th to 19th centuries]. *Rostocker Mathematik Kolloquium* [Rostock Mathematics Colloquium], *27*, 5–22.

Bloom, B. S. (1985). *Developing talent in young people.* New York: Ballantine.

Cox, C. M. (1926). *Genetic studies of genius: The early mental traits of three hundred geniuses.* Stanford, CA: Stanford University Press.

Cropley, A. J. (1967a). *Creativity.* London: Longmans.

Cropley, A. J. (1967b). Divergent thinking and science specialist. *Nature, 215,* 671–672.

Cropley, A. J. (1969). Creativity, intelligence and intellectual style. *Australian Journal of Education, 13,* 3–7.

Cropley, A. J. (1995). Kreativität [Creativity]. In K. Pawlik & M. Amelang (Eds.), *Differentielle Psychologie* [Differential psychology]. vol. 2, Enzyklopädie der Psychologie [Encyclopedea of psychology]. Göttingen: Hogrefe.

Cropley, A. J., Urban K. K., Wagner, H., & Wieczerkowski, W. (Eds.). (1986). *Giftedness: A continuing worldwide challenge.* New York: Trillium.

Denton, F. C. J. (1986). Identifikation durch Lehrer [Identification by teachers]. In W. H. Wieczerkowski, H. Wagner, K. K. Urban, & A. J. Cropley (Eds.), *Hochbegabung, Gesellschaft, Schule* [Giftedness, society, school] (pp. 172–184). Bad Honnef: Bock.

Elshout, J. (1990). Expertise and giftedness. *European Journal for High Ability, 1,* 197–203.

Facaoaru, C. (1985). *Kreativität in Wissenschaft und Technik* [Creativity in science and technology]. Bern: Huber.

Farisha, B. (1978). Mental imagery and creativity: Review and speculation. *Journal of Mental Imagery, 2,* 209–238.

Feist, G. J., & Runco, M. A. (1993). Trends in the creativity literature: An analysis of trends in the Journal of Behavior (1967–1989). *Creativity Research Journal, 6,* 271–286.

Fromm, E. (1980). *Greatness and limitations of Freud's thought.* New York: New American Library.

Gardner, H. (1983). *Frames of mind: The theory of multiple intelligences.* New York: Basic Books.

Gibson, J., & Light, P. (1967). Intelligence among university scientists. *Nature, 213,* 441–443.

Goertzel, M. C., Goertzel, V., & Goertzel, T. C. (1978). *300 eminent personalities.* San Francisco: Jossey-Bass.

Guilford, J. P. (1950). Creativity. *American Psychologist, 5,* 444–454.

Guilford, J. P., & Christensen, P. R. (1973). The one-way relation between creative potential and IQ. *Journal of Creative Behavior, 7,* 247–252.

Hassenstein, M. (1988). *Bausteine zu einer Naturgeschichte der Intelligenz* [Elements of a natural history of intelligence]. Stuttgart: Deutsche Verlags-Anstalt.

Heinelt, G. (1974). *Kreative Lehrer—kreative Schuler* [Creative teachers—creative students]. Freiburg: Herder.

Horn, J. L. (1988, August). *Major issues before us now and for the next few decades.* Paper presented at Seminar on Intelligence, Melbourne, Australia.

Howe, M. J. A. (1990). *The origins of exceptional abilities.* London: Blackwell.

Lehman, H. C. (1953). *Age and achievement.* Princeton, NJ: Princeton University Press.

Lindauer, M. (1993). The span of creativity among long-lived historical artists. *Creativity Research Journal, 6,* 221–239.

MacKinnon, D.W. (1962). The nature and nurture of creative talent. *American Psychologist, 17,* 484–495.

McLeod, J., & Cropley, A. J. (1989). *Fostering academic excellence.* Oxford: Pergamon.

McNemar, Q. (1964). Lost: Our intelligence? Why? *American Psychologist, 19,* 871–882.

Milgram, R. (1990). Creativity: An idea whose time has come and gone? In M. A. Runco & R. S. Albert (Eds.), *Theories of creativity.* Newbury Park, CA: Sage.

Mönks, F. J., van Boxtal, H. W., Roelofs, J. J. W., & Sanders, M. P. M. (1986). The identification of gifted children in secondary education and a description of their situation in Holland. In K. A. Heller & J. F. Feldhusen (Eds.), *Identifying and nurturing the gifted* (pp. 39–66). Bern: Huber.

Motamedi, K. (1982). Extending the concept of creativity. *Journal of Creative Behaviour, 16,* 75–88.

Mumford, M. D., & Gustafson, S. B. (1988) Creativity syndrome: Integration, application, and innovation. *Psychological Bulletin, 103,* 27–43.

Necka, E. (1986). On the nature of creative talent. In A. J. Cropley, K. K. Urban, H. Wagner, & W. H. Wieczerkowski (Eds.), *Giftedness: A continuing worldwide challenge* (pp. 131–140). New York: Trillium.

Neff, G. (1975). Kreativität in Schule und Gesellschaft [Creativity in school and society]. Ravensburg: Maier.

Renzulli, J. S. (1977). *The enrichment triad model: A guide for developing defensible programs for the gifted and talented.* Wethersfield, CT: Creative Learning Press.

Runco, M. A., & Albert, R. S. (1986). The threshold theory regarding creativity and intelligence: An empirical test with gifted and nongifted children. *Creative Child and Adult Quarterly, 11,* 212–218.

Russ, S. W. (1993). *Affect and creativity: The role of affect and play in the creative process.* Hillsdale, NJ: Erlbaum.

Ruth, J.-E., & Birren, J. E. (1985). Creativity in adulthood and old age: Relations to intelligence, sex and mode of testing. *International Journal of Behavioral Development, 8,* 99—109.

Shaw, M. P. (1989). The Eureka process: A structure for the creative experience in science and engineering. *Creativity Research Journal, 2,* 286–298.

Shaw, M. P., & Runco, M. A. (Eds.), (1994). *Creativity and affect.* Norwood, NJ: Ablex.

Shore, B. M., & Tsiamis, A. (1986). Identification by provision: Limited field test of a radical alternative for identifying gifted students. In K. A. Heller & J. F. Feldhusen (Eds.), *Identifying and nurturing the gifted* (pp. 93–102). Bern: Huber.

Sierwald, W. (1989, September). *Kreative Hochbegabung—Identifikation, Entwicklung und Förderung kreativer Hochbegabter* [Creative giftedness—Identification, development and education of the creative gifted]. Paper presented at 2nd Meeting of the Section Educational Psychology of the German Psychological Society, Munich.

Simonton, D. K. (1988). *Scientific genius. A psychology of science.* Cambridge: Cambridge University Press.

Sternberg, R. J. (1985). *Beyond IQ: a triarchic theory of human intelligence.* New York: Cambridge University press.

Sternberg, R. J., & Lubart, T. I. (1992). Creative giftedness in children. In P. S. Klein & A. J. Tannenbaum (Eds.), *To be young and gifted* (pp. 33–51). Norwood, NJ: Ablex.

Süle, F. (1990). Imaginative psychotherapy in the psychological care of top athletes. *European Journal for High Ability, 1,* 162–165.

Torrance, E. P., & Hall, L. K. (1980). Assessing the further reaches of creative potential. *Journal of Creative Behavior, 14,* 1–19.

Wallach, M. A., & Kogan, N. (1965). *Modes of thinking in young children.* New York: Holt, Rinehart and Winston.

Weisberg, R. W. (1986). *Creativity.* New York: Freeman.

# 2

# The Public's Responsibility to Promote Excellence

## Sebastian Coe

*The Sports Council, London*

Despite the many systems—political, social, and cultural—in the world, achieving excellence is a common goal. It should not be confused with elitism or simply success, but involves experts, leaders, even heroes: people who set standards and serve as examples to others, in sport, the arts, business, and technology. The pursuit of excellence provides motivation; it sets targets and goals, not only for nations but also for personal development. The crucial issue is that of how a society can ensure that all citizens have the chance to fulfill their potentials. What is needed is an environment in which excellence can flourish through provision of incentives, tools and equipment, teaching, and support. In all of this, education plays a vital role. It must provide an appropriate climate of challenge, the necessary resources, opportunities for assessment and stocktaking, and, finally, competition.

## INTRODUCTION

The theme I wish to develop is that of excellence—the way it is developed, the part it plays in our lives, and its wider social importance. By excellence, I do not mean elitism, with its connotations of superiority. Nor do I simply mean success, although often that may be a part. My starting point is the dictionary definition of "an action, characteristic or feature, etc. in which a person excels." It is a crucial and timeless concept, and a vital part of our lives.

I have been, and remain, an active sportsman and many of my conclusions have been drawn from my own experiences. Since 1977 I have competed internationally, and in visiting most countries of the world I have become aware of the great variety of different systems and creeds around this planet, and of ways in which excellence can be promoted through them. However, I am also an administrator in British and international sport, currently as Vice Chairman of the British Sports Council, and member of the Athletic and Medical Commission of the International Olympics Committee. In those capacities, I am used to acting as a communicator (not least in working with the media and their particular demands), trying to provide the means by which individuals can work toward fulfillment. It is important to stress, however, that although my expertise is in the world of sport, my concerns about excellence range widely, encompassing all fields of study and development toward achievement.

## THE DEVELOPMENT OF EXCELLENCE

Every age and every community needs its heroes, its experts, who are the leaders of opinion and action. They are the people who set and raise standards, and who provide examples for the young and the not so young. To all of us, they are the people who represent us in the world outside our own walls. Without Constable, for example, there might never have been an English school of landscape painting. Before Hillary and Tensing Everest looked unclimbable, and without Marie Curie we might never have begun to find the treatment for cancer with radium. Excellence is part of the kind of national or local pride that motivates education and industry, stirring the mind and the blood. It provides goals, yet it is constantly changing them, because by definition excellence is about doing better than before. For me, however, excellence also is about personal development, about achieving a personal best, fulfilling potential. There is excellence in all of us. And we must never despair of finding it. Jean Guiton said that "Originality exists in every individual, because each of us differs from the others; we are all primary numbers divisible only by ourselves." However hard to find, I want to secure the opportunities for all individuals to find their originality—whatever it is—and in whatever form.

Recently I was at Cambridge University, taking part in a unique event, the great court run. In this, runners attempt to race round the perimeter of Trinity College courtyard (about 400 meters) before the ancient clock finishes chiming twelve. I was deeply conscious of the surroundings, the refined environment of tradition and excellence, in one of the world's oldest universities. Later, in that precious environment, I was privileged to meet a rather special man, Professor Stephen Hawkings. He has one of the world's finest brains, in a body confined to a wheelchair. He cannot speak, save with the aid of a computer, which also enables him to write. His physics text, *A Brief History of Time*, has captured the imagination of many thousands of people. His life shows that the old and the best can be complementary, so long as there is a readiness to adapt.

Therefore, we must never be deflected in the search for excellence by even such terrible problems, but keep on making provision for it to develop. The vital potential is in all of us, to excel in something, even though we cannot all perform on the regional, national, or world stage. And although we cannot be clever beyond our capacities, we can still strive to reach our limits, to perform at our best. Thus, I see excellence as a broad church, open to all. There is such a church in every village and town, and also there are great cathedrals in the world.

## COMPETITION

Of course, the world is a smaller place than it used to be. Thanks to the communications explosion we have much better information in both quantity and quality, and accordingly, a better understanding of each other. Perhaps we are even more like each other in culture, because so many things are now the same wherever you go. We eat each other's food, enjoy each other's entertainment, and we even speak each others' languages.

Just one result of these developments is that competition has become more intense. Thus, in spite of the market being more crowded because it is more open, the potential rewards are also greater, because of the simpler and quicker delivery of information. However, all of us sink or swim according to our ability to anticipate and make change. A striking example of the way the enduring qualities of tradition can be used in flexible and innovative ways is the Swatch phenomenon. After some years of a downturn in business their watches are seen on wrists and lapels everywhere. The Swiss watch industry is (dare I say it) once again ticking over nicely!

Competition is both the carrot and the stick. It is the target and the touchstone, the motivation and the measure. Excellence is about doing and being better, and competition is of positive importance in getting there. We should neither shirk it, underrate it, nor malign it. Although for some children, and in some fields, competition would be both unnecessary and inappropriate, that is no reason to deny the greater, more universal truth of its value as a spur to and a test of excellence. We should not be overprotective. So much has been achieved because of the desire to compete. Witness the race to the South Pole, the space race to be first to the moon, the dramatic story of the discovery of DNA, the double helix. And, talking of races, my career might not have been quite the same without Ovett, or Cram, or those tantalizing targets of world records.

## PROVISION FOR EXCELLENCE

The most practical consideration for self-development is education. For those of us concerned with individual excellence, it is the area to concentrate on. Of course, educational systems, methods and priorities can be very different, and it was Cicero who said that "Natural ability without education has more often raised a man to glory and virtue than education without natural ability." But good education implies adequate resources, opportunity, and competition, and those crucial factors must vary with the activity or field of study. In sport, for example, facilities and competition are vital, whereas in many types of research it is resources that are essential.

Education is now a major issue on many political agendas, and on such issues everyone is an expert and a critic. I favor a basic national curriculum, covering the right topics and skills for the future, as long as there is the flexibility to give the potentially gifted the different kind of teaching that they need within the system. John F. Kennedy said, "A child miseducated is a child lost." I believe those words have particular force where gifts and excellence are at stake. Without the right facilities, many forms of excellence simply will not develop. This applies not only to the playing fields and stadia of sport, but also to the roots of modern civilization and progress, such as equipment for the laboratory, books in the library, musical instruments for the band or orchestra, and the hardware or software of this computer age.

We all get a thrill when we hear that a promising young violinist has been given a Stradivarius. We wish there were more instruments to give, and more youngsters with the talent to merit them, so that the "Stradivarii" of every discipline somehow could be provided for those who can best use them to exploit their own potentials, surely for the general good. The state cannot be the sole provider, however. Even today excellence can be helped by patronage. A present day Mozart would have to look for what we now call sponsorship from business and industry. And he would be right to do so. There is also the crucial role of the voluntary sector, where people come together to help themselves.

I am making a plea for funding, in the hope that what is needed for the development of excellence can be made available. I know only too well that it takes money to provide time and space to train and practice, to fund trips, for learning, for competition, and to pay for facilities and equipment. Although money is hard to come by, especially public funds, deserving cases are not, and the competition for funds is just one of the hurdles to be overcome in the pursuit of excellence. In my administrative roles I am too often in the position where I have felt myself torn between allocating funds to equally deserving contestants. However, sometimes persistence pays. In 1985 I chaired the British Olympic Review, which was set up to help people to train and develop for Olympic competition. Because our case for more money was clear and well presented we were successful in getting it from both government and private sponsorship. But the politician in me knows that you cannot expect that sort of result very often. For the pursuit and support of excellence there always is the need to have a good case and to make it as well as we can. We have a duty to seek a proper share of communal resources for this important goal.

## PUBLIC RESPONSIBILITY

Philosophers have long wrestled with the duties and needs of society and how best to meet them. They have seen that people come together in communities for companionship and mutual protection, as well as for necessities, and that to attain these benefits they are prepared to accept certain rules and restrictions. Yet people must be free. The early political thinkers, such as Rousseau, saw personal development as one of the essential freedoms. Freedom is the vital component for self-expression and the exercise of talents. I will not say that without freedom excellence is impossible, because we all know of inspiring examples of achievement against the climate of the times. Indeed, that very defiance of restriction can be the prime motivator of talent and excellence. People can and will break through terrible odds to achieve their own version of excellence, with its satisfactions and rewards.

Those who achieve excellence are to some extent representatives of their own community or the society where it was nurtured. Such people may be physically representative in activities like sport, but they also mirror a way of life, and as such, can be powerful advertisements for their own culture and products. Boris Becker, for example, represents the youth of West Germany; Pavarotti is for many the embodiment of Italy, a land of song and glorious tenors; Pele was Brazil. For America, I choose Gershwin and Ellington.

How can a society ensure that every one of its citizens has the opportunity, support, and encouragement to seek and fulfill his or her potential? Some of the answers depend, of course, on its nature, that is on politics. Comparing results in all fields shows that different political creeds can work in different ways, and that they also can hinder in different ways. Although in the end the seeds of excellence must lie in the individuals themselves, we cannot afford to be complacent. Society has a vital duty to provide the framework, the tools, the teaching and support, and even the incentive, to enable its people to develop themselves and their abilities to their fullest possible potential. It is a criterion by which I would judge any government or political system.

In the nebulous area that I will call simply "the prevailing atmosphere," opinions are encouraged or directed. An atmosphere that fosters the development of talent is the hardest to define, or even describe. It comes from incentive and encouragement and it takes many forms, whether capitalist or communist, the latter clearly shown in East German sporting success or the Russian domination in chess. This support may be in the recognition of either individual or group achievement. It is found in the mix of social policies for all the things I have been discussing, based on the kind of social goals and ideals that leaders express. All that is underlined by the lessons of tradition and history, and the way they are remembered or forgotten. The concern for excellence lies, in sum, in the prevailing values of society. Yet obviously, we cannot and must not base our thoughts and plans entirely on the role of the state. Governments can do too much, interfering to cramp the vital spirit and spark. Sometimes, talent needs to be left entirely to its own devices in finding its parameters and goals.

It is difficult, isn't it? You see in the end I have no firm blueprint for success, to develop that excellence we all treasure and seek. The great and the good cannot be foreseen, and although some may thrive on adversity, no one would wish to create it in order to force out some unknown rare talent. We cannot stimulate the worst to beget the best. Rather, we must seek to create the right positive conditions. I have sought to identify the key ones, and have suggested that in order to reach them we must argue for constructive policies and press for a fair share of national and international resources. Whatever the underlying reasons, excellence also can be partly the outcome of personal duty fulfilled, if we can get things right the rewards glitter. Efficiency experts sometimes tell us "The best is the enemy of the good." Well, it is nice to have the good, but let us go for the best.

# 3

# Facilitating the Development of Talents

**Manfred von Ardenne**

*Dresden, Germany*

World class pioneering achievements are a nation's most valuable asset. They arise from the efforts of talents—people of extraordinary ability. The vital task of fostering the emergence of such talents requires a concentrated effort covering the entire lifespan. Significant factors are parents, contemporaries, and teachers, as well as media, the societal atmosphere, and contact with great social and scientific issues. These must act together to produce talents with, not only the ability, but also the dedication to achieve.

## Talented People and the Future of Europe

**A**s a consequence of the rapid rise of competition from Japan in important areas of the world market since World War II, little imagination is required to predict that very difficult economic struggles are in store for future generations in Europe. It is only necessary to consider China and other far eastern countries, wherein combinations of cheap labor and large numbers of hard workers have developed into prime industrial nations, and the foreseeable commencement of world market level production in today's Third World. Europe will be able to overcome these assaults and retain a sufficient standard of living only if it arms itself for this conflict in time, that is, very soon. Its chief weapons for this are likely to be found in the field of "cybernetic creativity" (Hans Sauer) that is, in the cultivation of intellectual creativeness closely intertwined with the complex requirements of the day. The elements of such creativity are people with inborn or acquired extraordinary abilities, people I call *talents*.

Increasing the incidence of talents is, therefore, a crucial problem in Europe. A fundamental difficulty in solving this problem under present conditions should be mentioned at the outset. It arises from the contradiction of life in an affluent society and the old proverb, "necessity is the mother of invention". We have to rediscover forms of life not lacking in the pressures that inspire creative deeds—necessity and a struggle for existence.

## Support for the Development of Talents

One characteristic of many talented people is that they attract attention by exceptional precocious achievements. Given the same initial situation (stored knowledge and experiences) young people, with their high energy level, are equipped a priori for the accomplishment of particularly great achievements. This is why gifted youngsters should be introduced to the great open questions of their day as early in life as possible. A very effective method that requires little time is to convey inspiring impressions (experiments, observations from nature, particular technical achievements) from their chosen future vocation to intelligent children at the receptive age between about 8 and 12 years. In this way the emergence of talents can be fostered. Often, such an intense experience will set a child's mind on a chosen subject area. The child passionately studies everything connected with this field, but neglects other subjects in school. It is then the duty of the educational lawmakers and teachers to make sure that such pupils are not disadvantaged by this onesidedness but rather, that it is beneficial to further education in their chosen field. This suggestion for increasing the number of talents stemmed from reading numerous biographies of successful personalities and scientists. The origin of later genius is often to be found in intense impressions at the age of 8 to 12.

## Identification, Selection and Fostering of Talents

The present generation of national leaders, parents, teachers, university lecturers, scientists, researchers, developers, and heads of industry have a decisive contribution to make to increasing the incidence of talents, namely in the identification, selection and fostering of talents.

The three phase plan shown in Tables 1 to 3 is the result of an attempt I undertook, in connection with the conferring of an honorary doctorate by the *Pädagogische Hochschule* K. F. W. Wander, Dresden in 1982, to summarize the combination of measures to be undertaken in solving this complicated educational problem. In these tables, the left hand column shows that a favorable environment stimulates exceptional achievement during the three educational phases: at school, at university (college or polytechnic), and perhaps even in autodidactic education. During these three phases, the stimulation to strive for exceptional achievements must be enhanced by an environment that is, preferably, partly structured by the talented persons themselves. Above all, optimal methods must be developed for identifying and selecting exceptionally talented people at an early age. This leads to the questions of who selects and how can talented youngsters be recognized? I believe that an important characteristic is demonstrated when young people pose conspicuously unusual questions. Finally, all measures furthering the ability and achievement of those selected should be organized systematically during all three phases of education. Limiting myself to a few particularly essential points, the following can be said:

### *The first phase:*
The following factors and measures are among those that, to a large extent, foster the development of talents during youth and schooldays:

- The parents' exemplary influence and support for the child's specific interests.
- Focusing of attention on former and current leading figures in the fields of science and technology, that is by means of impressive biographies and television programs.

**TABLE 3.1**
**Three Phase Plan to Form a Creative Scientific Elite—First Phase**

| Phase of Development | Encouragement to Strive for Individual Exceptional Achievements | Selection of Extraordinary Talents | | Measures to Foster Ability and Achievement |
|---|---|---|---|---|
| | | Who Selects? | Characteristics of Talents | |
| 1. School | 1.1 Parents' exemplary influence and support for child's interests. Respect for achievements of the child or youth. | 1.2 Teachers with flawless character. | 1.3 Noticeable interest invariably shown in the same fields. | 1.4 Support for one-sided talents. Criteria for admission to higher education do not depend only on high average marks. Main criteria are in basic subjects of future vocation. Exceptional regulations, no strains on leisure time that do not further talent development. More effective use of skipping classes. Support for groups of friends with the same subject interests. Right to participate in teachers' assessment (democracy in school). Special classes for highly talented students at university. Creation of special schools. Featuring achievements (see 1.1). Improved knowledge of teachers in developmental psychology and leadership. Support by means of challenge. |
| | Featuring recent leading figures in the fields of science and technology (e.g. Einstein, Koch, Nernst, Röntgen, Warburg, Joffé, Hahn, Barkhausen, Bohr, Hertz, Laue, Curie, Kurschatov, Diesel, Tupolew, Lohmann, Amundsen, Wegener, Hilbert). Featuring present day leading figures (Eigen, Kolff, Rompe, Mothes, Stubbe). | Successful scientists or technicians. (Examination of suggestions from school community.) | Increasing amount of clever questions. Outstanding achievements with the following characteristics: imagination, creativity, ability, motivation to achieve and perseverance in one or in few subjects. | |
| | Regular experimental lectures on science on television and films on discoveries, inventions, and so on. Featuring exceptional performances in the school setting or in mass media. | | | |
| | Leisure time to be used mainly to become familiar with the chosen scientific and technical field. | | | |

- Emphasizing exceptional performances at school, or even in the mass media, in order to convey a sense of achievement to the selected persons. They have to realize that achieving more than others is worthwhile!
- Providing a favorable environment during the school phase, thus allowing talents plenty of time to become intensively involved in their future vocational field, by working with their hands, carrying out experiments, studying, and talking with likeminded friends.

The question of who selects is very important. Here, measures must also be elaborated and enforced at the basic level to put theoretical recommendations into future oriented practice. All supportive measures should take into account the following aspect that has already been mentioned briefly: youth has to fight. Things ought not be made too easy for young people at the beginning. They should not be given large salaries right from the start. Pay rises should always have to be fought for by high achievement. The weapons that lead to genuine ability in life are only developed by fighting. One conclusion should be drawn immediately. Admission to university or college education should not be made dependent on the average of the marks for all subjects. In the future, those who have conspicuously good marks (only) in the subjects connected with their future vocation should be especially designated and supported by special provisions. This feature should also become a preferred decisive determinant in the selection of people of talent. Early action along these lines will strongly increase the probability and frequency that genuine talents will be put on the desired track.

### The Second Phase:
During their studies at universities, colleges, or polytechnics, measures must be elaborated for a select circle of students to counteract the anonymity in education. At the beginning of this century, a professor was in charge of only a few students and maintained a personal relationship with them (weekly tea parties). Max Planck had only ten students at his famous lecture on thermodynamics in 1925, which I was lucky enough to experience. Nowadays a professor is often faced with 200 students. This is why it is of the utmost importance that measures should be introduced that gather selected highly able students with the same specialized interests around their professor during their course of studies. I found measures like these being

## TABLE 3.2
### Three Phase Plan to Form a Creative Scientific Elite—Second Phase

| Phase of Development | Encouragement to Strive for Individual Exceptional Achievements | Selection of Extraordinary Talents | | Measures to Foster Ability and Achievement |
|---|---|---|---|---|
| | | Who Selects? | Characteristics of Talents | |
| 2. University, Polytechnic College | 2.1 Highly talented people with the same specialized interests to be brought together locally during the course of studies. Mutual stimulation to attain the best possible achievements. Discussions, participation in exploring the most worthwile subjects for research, personality formation regeneration (literature, music, visual arts, philosophy, sports). | 2.2 Particularly successful scholars, researchers, and originators, including the retired. Distinct disregard of careerists in favor of genuine achievers! | 2.3 Science pursued for its own sake and not because of rewards. Scientific enthusiasm and passionate search for knowledge. Contributions to discussion lucidity, creativity, and profundity. "The last to leave the institute at night". | 2.4 Grouping talents around exemplary personalities with considerable life achievements. Favoring development of scientific schools around exemplary personalities. Drawing talents with the same bent together into groups of fewer than 10 students and organizing intensive individual attention from successful teaching personalities. Providing contacts with research tasks with unusual prospects. Enrolling in subjects of own choice. |
| Autodidactic studies | Following occupation with basic subject, permanent practical studies orientated to the changing tasks of the day, clearing the way for the development of talents with nonacademic backgrounds (equal status, delegation of important responsibility, etc.). | | | |

introduced at the private university of Witten-Herdecke, Germany, during a visit there recently.

I had the pleasure of personally meeting the great nuclear physicist Arnold Sommerfeld in Munich. Sommerfeld was an outstanding teaching personality and author of several classical textbooks. This great personality attracted the most talented students in Europe, students interested in nuclear physics who instinctively recognized Sommerfeld's considerable importance. These highly talented students met together with Sommerfeld in Munich. It was not so much Sommerfeld's lectures or teaching that led almost all of these students to later becoming Nobel Prize winners, but most probably the advantageous interaction among them that brought results that changed the face of physics. They would remain at the end of these lectures, often until late at night, in keen discussion and surpassing each other intellectually. Those days with Sommerfeld were an exceptionally productive period.

Similarly, significant processes occurred for the same reasons with Max Born, in Göttingen, and Abraham Joffé in Leningrad. These facts should lead to systematic support for establishing schools around a leading personality with, for example, not more than 20 to 30 students.

Allow me to mention some further experiences. Not all talented people follow a strictly academic career. I knew, for example, an outstanding theoretical electrotechnician by the name of Küpfmüller. He was completely self-educated. Without having attended university, he acquired so much knowledge and ability that he was finally able to write his famous textbook and become head of research at Siemens. We should not, therefore, place obstacles in the way of an outstanding autodidact but, where special circumstances demand it, provide support.

### The third phase:

Permanent postgraduate studies are often made necessary by the demands of day to day work. These studies are very effective because their results can be put into practice immediately and concrete examples are more easily understood than abstract didactic examples. Continual studying as a hobby has become indispensable for the utmost development of talents. Science and technology are currently subject to far more considerable changes in structures, and in their elements and methods, than in the first half of this century. Consider, for example, the case of electronics. The changes in this field since

**TABLE 3.3**
**Three Phase Plan to Form a Creative Scientific Elite—Third Phase**

| Phase of Development | Encouragement to Strive for Individual Exceptional Achievements | Selection of Extraordinary Talents | | Measures to Foster Ability and Achievement |
| --- | --- | --- | --- | --- |
| | | Who Selects? | Characteristics of Talents | |
| 3. Post-graduate activity | 3.1 Willingness of the mass media to not only tolerate, but want a creative intellectual elite, and to honor them by giving them prominence. Assessment and placement of talents according to their specific achievements, not their level of education, and so on. Support of lifelong continuous studies in line with the changing tasks (daily ad hoc studying as a hobby, publications and compilation of knowledge as steps to success). Linking one's own work to the important questions of the day. Cooperation with a world class researcher for several years (example later Nobel Prize winners Krebs, Ochoa, and Lippmann in the institute of Nobel Prize winner Otto Warburg). Granting unusual trust and high level of responsibility to deserving talents. Rewards for achievement and willingness to take risks. Favoring personnel in the special field. Creation of a forum to promote and discuss pioneering ideas and results (journals, television). | 3.2 Eminent personalities. Academy of Sciences and the Research Council. Scientists and organizers with wide industrial experience. Politicians who regard the ability of the candidate as the factor for selection. | 3.3 Conspicuous results and success at work. Dissertations, publications, patents, achievements, and so on, that are far from mediocre. Many good ideas. Positive attitude to other people's achievements. | 3.4 Support for talents showing good dispositions regardless of educational course. Adaptation of environmental conditions to favor development. Organizing small institutes or autonomous departments according to the wishes of the person to be supported. (Securing their creative collaboration. Example: Kaiser Wilhelm Institutes of Berlin between 1912 and 1933.) Creating conditions for work by delegating organizational tasks and establishing a good internal and external working atmosphere. Varied measures to improve working morale, such as drastically reducing the report system. Top world class results and harmony with our economic structure should be fostered with more courage to take risks, by quick decisions in constructive talks with few partners (setting free capacities by means of profile changes; thinking of the whole; careful evaluation and judgement by experts, etc.). |

1925 have ranged from valves to transistors to integrated circuits—What a transformation! When the rapid development of modern electronics began, it would have been impossible to design a curriculum that would have had any direct relevance to modern microelectronics. This example shows that researchers and developers who wish to achieve anything of significance have to, under present circumstances, continue their studies after completion of university education permanently, until the end of their professional career. Studying as a lifelong hobby must therefore become mandatory.

### Stimulation of Creativitity

Finally, some aspects should be dealt with that, when taken into consideration, can significantly stimulate creativity in talents. These include the basic intellectual attitude that there is much still to be invented and designed, and that everything already in existence can be improved upon. An inexhaustible source of new discoveries is to be found in the observation of nature. The wisdom of nature, by virtue of its evolutionary development over inconceivable periods of time, is boundless. Of what significance can the greatest human wisdom be in comparison? All that remains for us is to listen attentively and in deep modesty to the divine wisdom of nature.

Nature on this planet has developed by evolution over many millions of years, a space of time that humans can scarcely conceive of. Research geniuses such as Charles Darwin and, as a more recent example, Manfred Eigen have attempted to unveil the secrets of evolution and even of the complicated living organism. In the course of their work, they discovered several "principles for the mode of selection of the superior." But in spite of these endeavors, the human intellect only just touches the surface of what nature accomplished over long periods of time and of how this was done. The famous words of Charles Darwin on completion of his book "The Origin of Species" explicitly warn us to be extremely modest when dealing with this issue. He said: "I shudder when I think of the origin of the eye!"

Knowing that the observation of nature is one pathway to making discoveries and finding and forming new things, researchers should realize that, in the interest of progress, everything must be done to extend and improve the observation of nature by increasingly sophisticated means. Quantitative exploration by measurement is the outstanding method that has generated thousands of great discoveries that have helped to shape modern human life and extend the limits of knowledge and ability further. These concurrences were accompanied by both the creation of increasingly sensitive and accurate measurement instruments, and the development and perfection of many types of sensors. Numerous instrumental devices and procedures for visually observing nature emerged. The optical microscope came first, followed, in more recent times, by the transmission electron microscope and the scanning tunnel electron microscope. The human field of vision even reached atomic dimensions. Each use of these instruments in the pioneering days of electron microscopy meant a glance into hitherto unknown worlds of the microcosm. In addition, methods of analysis emerged, in particular electron beam microsondes, that facilitated research into microscopically small structural elements of the nonliving and living world. Highly sensitive detection methods using unstable and stable isotopes enabled far reaching insights into the complicated processes of nature in the fields of biochemistry, biology, and medicine. If the sensitive and precise devices of sophisticated modern measurement and analysis are applied with imagination, intelligence and tenacity, high level results and discoveries are almost bound to ensue.

Otto Warburg, Nobel Prize winner (twice) and teacher of five Nobel laureates, was once asked which important event in his life most influenced his very successful career. He replied: "The confrontation with genius at an early age". Warburg's father was a physicist and president of the Imperial Laboratory for Physics and Technology in Berlin. Friends of the family included Planck, Lummer, and Einstein. The young Warburg experienced how Planck deduced the "constant of action h" from Lummer's measurements of radiation (observation of nature by means of measurement)—a discovery that marked the entry into the nuclear age. This experience led Warburg to introduce measurement to biochemistry, thus becoming the architect of modern biochemistry. This is a prime example of how creativity can be stimulated by eminent models and by measuring observation of nature. Being given responsibility and independence, as well as experiencing success through its acknowledgement at work, in scientific circles, and also sometimes in public (mass media) are considerable incentives for creativity development.

The older generation can, and should, make a crucial contribution towards talented persons' success and, thus, to their support, by providing astute advice on their choice of subjects.

Topics with extraordinarily good prospects of success are the still unanswered questions of the day and, to a lesser extent, present day industrial und scientific requirements. Well chosen topics characteristically tend to offer advantages not only in one, but in many directions (multivalence). Among the basic requirements for good subject recommendations are a precise knowledge of the international state of the art, harmony with raw materials and national resource conditions, and ecological compatibility.

The frequency of significant creative achievements will, in the future, also be determined by the degree that talented people succeed or are enabled to rationalize intellectual work. I am referring here to the use of computers that are able to store extremely large amounts of information, and to significantly more efficient artificial intelligence machines (with human language input and output) that are still being developed.

A recently published book (Ardenne, Musiol & Reball, 1988) also deals with rationalizing intellectual work. Creative achievements frequently emerge from the intelligent application of one or more effects. The book " Effekte der Physik und ihre Anwendungen" (Effects in physics and their application)—the result of ten years work—was produced with contributions from 90 authors with the aim of helping talented people in a new way. The individual effects and phenomena are each dealt with as a whole, and facilitate immediate rational use. In addition to historical footnotes and further bibliographical references, information is provided on the facts, measurable and theoretically derivable characteristic values, and functional correlations, but, in particular, on the application of the specified effects.

These reflections express, in part, experience accumulated during 65 years of struggling for research results. I hope that my thoughts contribute to national and organizational pioneering actions wherein the frequency of emergence of talented people in the Europe of the future will be significantly increased.

## REFERENCE

Ardenne, M. von, Musiol, G., & Reball, S. (1988). *Effekte der Physik und ihre Anwendungen [Physical phenomena and their application]*. Berlin: VEB Deutscher Verlag der Wissenschaften.

# 4

# The Nature
# and Development
# of Giftedness
## A Longitudinal Study

**Kurt A. Heller**

*Ludwig Maximilians University of Munich, Munich, Germany*

Following a short discussion of conceptual and theoretical problems of giftedness, the methodological foundations and selected results of a (at the time of writing) four-year longitudinal study are presented. This study is based on a multidimensional concept of giftedness: intelligence, creativity, social competence, musical ability, and psychomotor ability (or practical intelligence). Both academic achievements and leisure activities, as well as cognitive and motivational personality factors and school and family socialization conditions relevant to giftedness, were studied. During the second project phase developmental aspects and achievement analyses of gifted and normal students aged six to 18 years were the central aspects of the study. Finally, methodological problems in the identification of gifted children and adolescents as well as consequences for the nurturing of giftedness are discussed.

## THE PSYCHOLOGICAL CONCEPT OF GIFTEDNESS

Broadly conceptualized, "giftedness" can be defined as the totality of personal (cognitive, motivational) potential and sociocultural conditions for learning and achieving (Roth, 1968). The development of giftedness is understood as resulting from the interaction of internal (personal) dispositional factors and external sozialization factors. The term is used in psychology both to describe (ability concept) and to explain (qualitative category). These two conceptualizations stem from different research paradigms: (a) nomothetically oriented psychometric studies that attempt to measure quantitative inter- and intraindividual differences in ability; (b) idiographically oriented information processing approaches in modern research on problem solving that try to determine qualitative (thought) process components. A third conceptualization is of immediate practical importance: (c) "giftedness" in the sense of psychological aptitude or demands. Here giftedness is considered to be a person's disposition or characteristic profile with regard to particular demands for learning or achievement (i.e., school, university, or career planning).

Whereas the psychometric conceptualization of giftedness is directed at general or differential abilities (verbal, quantitative, technical–constructive, or musical abilities, factors etc.), in the cognitive psychological approach, elementary information processing units are measured as conditional components of gifted activities. Although in more recent research on giftedness cognitive psychological approaches have been favored over psychometric research approaches, both research paradigms contribute in their specific way to an understanding of giftedness. One cannot easily be substituted for the other. From process–analytical research on giftedness, important information about conditions that nurture or inhibit the development of giftedness is expected. On the other hand, status–diagnostic (psychometric) results still are considered to be the essential basis of all types of prediction about achievement and success. Diagnoses of giftedness thus serve an important function in nurturing personality, for example, in individual developmental counseling or intervention (cf., Heller, 1987, 1989). Both conceptual and practical solutions often can be achieved only when psychometric and cognitive psychological information processing or rather experimental thought process and problem-solving approaches are combined. In an analogous fashion, the necessity for differential curricula and school environments specific to types of giftedness is emphasized in modern educational psychology (e.g., Feldhusen, 1985; Gallagher, 1985; Tannenbaum, 1983).

Giftedness also belongs to the so-called hypothetical construct concepts (cf., McCorquodale & Meehl, 1948) whose definition depends on the theoretical framework being employed. This also holds true for related concepts such as intelligence or creativity. Construct concepts are popular in psychology; researchers hope for information about particular behavioral expressions of the personality in the sense of causal factors. For example, exceptional achievement in a foreign language or in mathematics may be attributed to corresponding verbal or quantitative abilities. At the same time, motivational and sociocultural causal factors can be more or less involved in the manifestation of achievement. It becomes clear that every concept of giftedness also includes relatively complex behavioral phenomena and depends on the use of it (cf., Hany, 1987; Heller, 1989; McLeod & Cropley, 1989; Sternberg, 1990).

Inasmuch as psychologists claim a difference between intelligence and giftedness, the concept of giftedness may be analogous to aptitude, for example, giftedness in learning to play a musical instrument, facility in learning foreign languages, high achievement in fine arts or in sciences, and so on. The assumption is that there are different forms of giftedness that can be categorized according to specific behavior and achievement areas. As an example, we present a model of giftedness (Heller & Hany, 1986, p. 70) in Figure 4-11; see also Gardner (1983).

Gagné (1985), who also favors a multidimensional model, differentiates between general and specific gifts on the dispositional side and domain specific talent forms on the behavior or achievement side. The assumption of mediating factors (referred to as "catalysts" by Gagné) is also interesting (e.g., personality factors such as motives, interests, and attitudes, and socialization factors such as family and school). Mierke (1963) also referred earlier to aiding and supporting factors of intelligence in his theory of giftedness. Heller, Rosemann, and Steffens (1978) introduced so-called "moderators" as mediating variables for the explanation of predictor–criterion relationships in their prognostic study of counseling on the kind of school to attend.

We define "giftedness" as the individual cognitive, motivational, and social possibilities for attaining excellence in one or more areas (cf., Figure 4-1). Thus, in this study, we used a multidimensional concept of giftedness. The achievement behavior is seen as the product of the predictors giftedness, personality, and environment (cf., Figure 4-2). The Munich model of giftedness includes five (research) dimensions that can be related to particular achievement areas (Figure 4-1).

Giftedness arises in the areas of intellect, creativity, social competence, artistic (musical) ability, or psychomotor ability.

The individual dimensions of giftedness correspond to particular academic and nonacademic achievements.

In addition to cognitive abilities, various noncognitive personality characteristics (such as motives, interests, work and learning style) are involved.

Family and school are the central focus with regard to socialization factors.

FIGURE 4-1.    The division of giftedness and achievement with information about talent factors and performance areas.

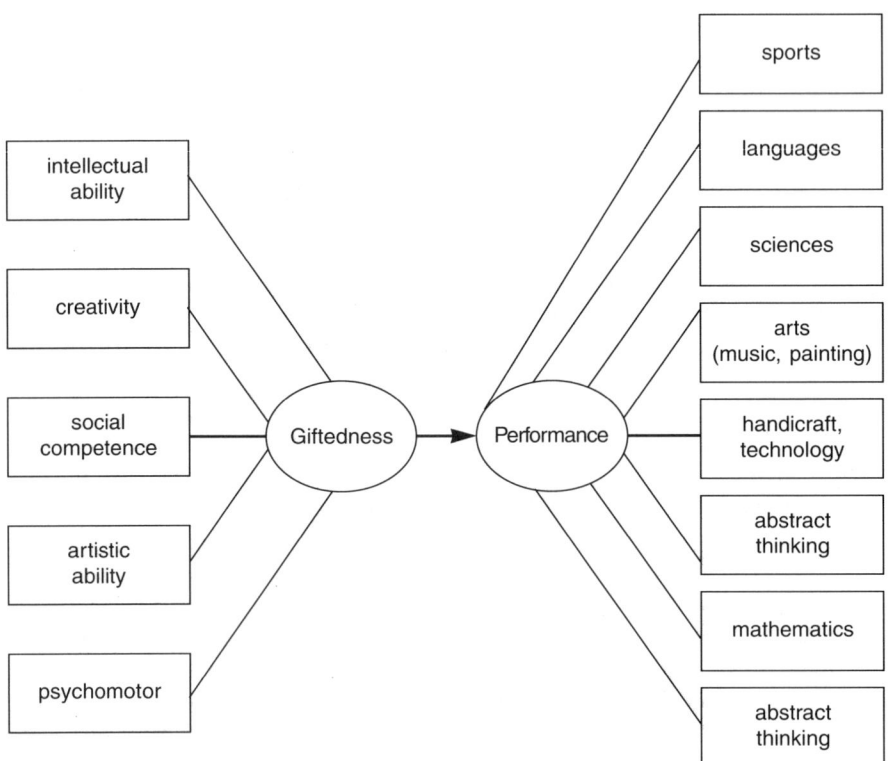

FIGURE 4-2. Multifactorial causal model of giftedness. *Personality characteristics:* Achievement motivation (hope of success, willingness to exert oneself), locus of control (quest for knowledge, coping skills). *Giftedness factors:* Intelligence, creativity, social competence, artistic (musical) ability, psychomotor ability. *Environmental characteristics:* Stimulation in the home environment, parental educational level, number of siblings and birth order, city versus country origin, school climate, critical life events, role expectations regarding "giftedness," performance demands at home, success and failure experiences.

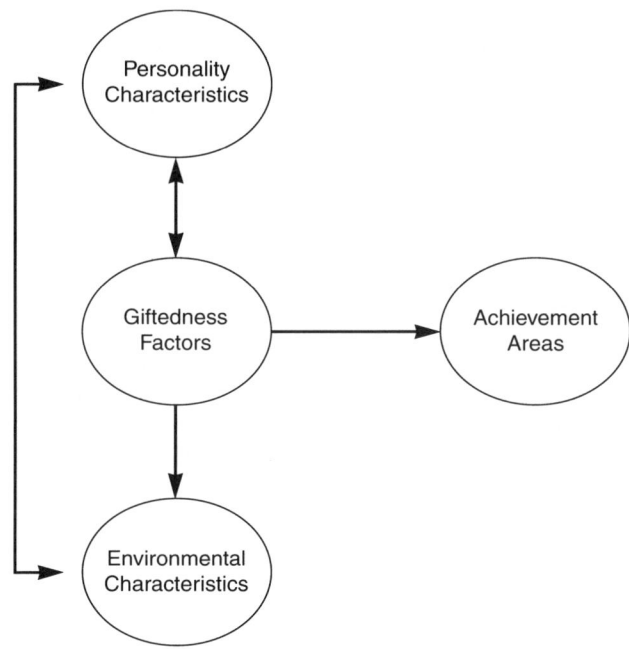

## PROJECT PHASE ONE

### Goals

1. The development and evaluation of a differential diagnostic instrument for the identification of highly gifted children and adolescents for various forms of giftedness.
2. The observation, description, and analysis of the interrelationship of potential for giftedness and actual performance, in which, along with cognitive and noncognitive personality preconditions, situational or social contextual conditions also are included in the investigation.

## Research Design

Starting from a large multiregional sample with six age cohorts between six and 16 years (who were eight and 18 at the time of study completion), data were collected on (highly) gifted students during three periods between 1986 and 1988. The study is characterized as a longitudinal cross sectional design. The entire sample design is shown in Figure 4-3.

The most important information sources, the research variables, and the measurement instruments are summarized in Table 4-1.

There were two stages in the selection of the sample:

> In the first step, teachers of more than 26,000 students were requested to rate their gifted to highly gifted students according to the five dimensions of giftedness as compared to their peers.
> In the second step, about 30% of the original sample were given achievement tests and differentiated questionnaires in order to identify the top 2–5% of the students.

## Results

The following results from the first research phase (1986–1987) are available (cf., Heller, 1990).

1.  The five factors intelligence, creativity, psychomotor ability–practical intelligence, social competence, musical ability were found to be independent dimensions of giftedness. The hypothesis that there are *domain-specific forms of giftedness* was confirmed.
2.  The measurement instruments (see Table 4-1) for determining cognitive and noncognitive personality characteristics of the gifted as well as relevant conditions of the social learning environment are reliable, even at extreme levels of giftedness. A particularly useful strategy was the use of intelligence and achievement test items for the gifted that are normally solved by students one to three years older.
3.  There were clear differences between the gifted and nongifted (i.e., average) students in every domain of giftedness. The intellectually or academically talented (so-called "schoolhouse gifted," according to Renzulli) were characterized by their good grades; they were not only better than the

FIGURE 4-3.   Sample design of the Munich Longitudinal Study of Giftedness (see also Steffens & Perleth, 1990, pp. 76–78).

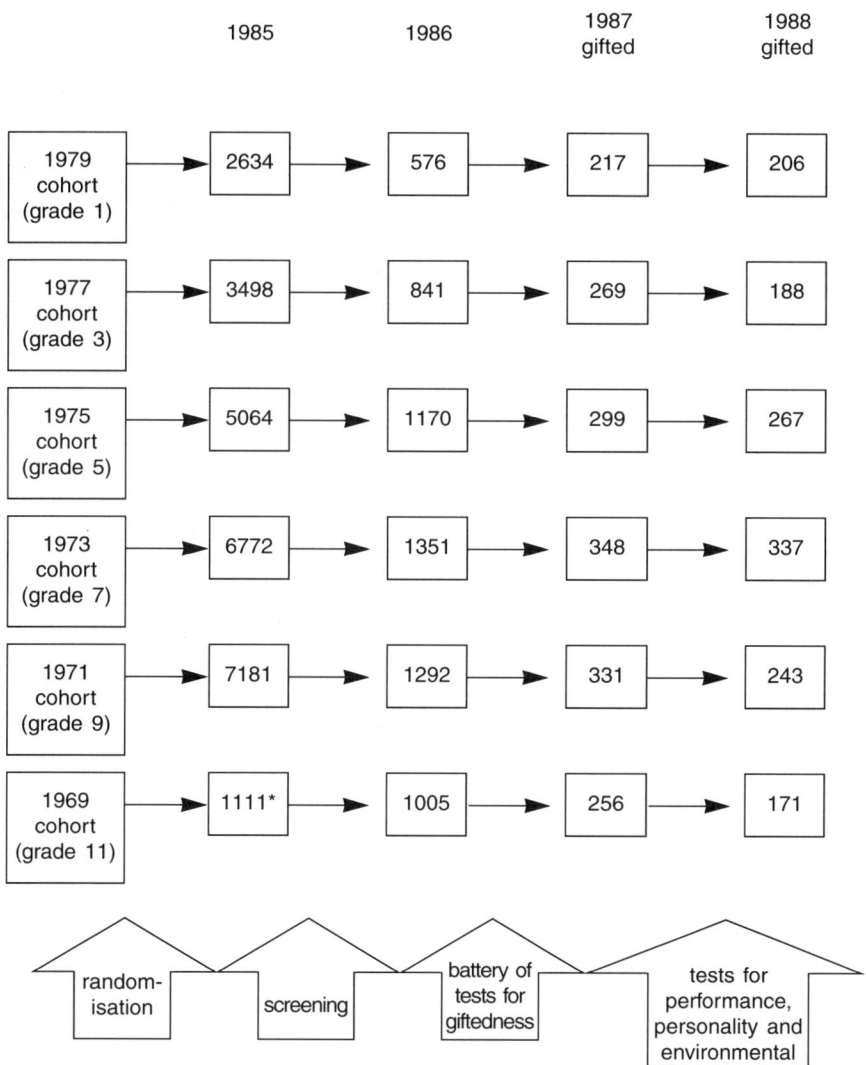

*Total evaluation without screening (since the 11th grade in academic secondary schools consists of the most gifted students)

creative (so-called "creative-productive" according to Renzulli), but also than the socially or practically gifted. The creatively gifted, on the other hand, were better in art and literary areas, the socially gifted in social areas.

TABLE 4-1
**Information Sources and Measured Variables of the Munich Longitudinal Study of Giftedness**

| Variables | Information Sources | |
| --- | --- | --- |
| | Student's Psychometric Scores | Teacher Ratings |
| Intellectual dimension | Tests<br>   KFT (German CAT by Heller, Gaedike<br>      & Weinlader, 1985)<br>   ZVT (Numbers Connection Test by) Oswald<br>      & Roth, 1978 | Teachers' checklist<br><br><br>Grades |
| Creativity dimension | Tests<br>   VWT (Unusual Uses according to Guilford)<br>   VKT (Verbal Creativity by Schoppe, 1975)<br>   Questionnaire<br>   GIFT (Group Inventory for Finding Creative<br>      Talent by Rimm, 1980) | <br><br>Teachers' checklist<br>T-Cre |
| Social competence dimension | Questionnaire<br>   Social Competence | Teachers' checklist<br>T-SC |
| Psychomotoric | | Teachers' checklist<br>T-PM |
| Art (music) dimension | | Teachers' checklist<br>T-Mus |
| Noncognitive personal characteristics | Questionnaires<br>   TfK (Thirst for Knowledge by Lehwald<br>      & Friedrich, 1987)<br>   HS (Hope of Success)<br>   FF (Fear of Failure)<br>   Anxiety<br>   Self-Concept<br>   Attribution<br>   Learning Styles<br>   MAI (Munich Activity Inventory) | |
| Environmental characteristics | Questionnaires<br>   Critical Life Events<br>   Family Climate<br>   School Climate | |

4. Multiple gifted were seldom found in our sample (*n* = 1800). However, students (from six to 16 or later 18 years) who were both intellectually and creatively gifted were superior to all other students in important achievement areas. The *diagnosis of giftedness should, therefore, not continue in a unidimensional manner*, for example, using a (single) IQ cutoff score (also see Sternberg, 1990).

5. Particularly capable students are characterized by the following: drive for achievement, willingness to exert them-

selves, perseverance, thirst for knowledge, research drive, inventiveness, and self-assurance.

## PROJECT PHASE TWO

### Goals

During the second project phase, the actual longitudinal study, the focus was on developmental psychological aspects and analyses of (academic) achievements. The main goals of this project phase were

1. Determination of the prognostic validity of the instruments used during the first (1986), second (1987), and third (1988) measurement periods to identify gifted students (first to twelfth grade).
2. Determination of the validity of the typological conceptualization of giftedness as well as interactions between different types of giftedness and achievement at various age levels.
3. Evaluation of the effects of personality and environmental factors on the achievement of gifted students based on our causal model (see Figure 4-2).
4. Observation, description, analysis, and explanation of the course of development in gifted children and adolescents (experimental and control group design) with regard to changes in characteristics in cognitive and noncognitive areas.
5. Determination and analysis of interactions among giftedness, achievement, personality, and environment over the course of time.

### Results

Numerous individual results cannot be reported because of the limited space here; for more details see Hany (1990) and Perleth and Sierwald (1990). The following results should be of particular interest with regard to practical identification and nurturing of gifted children and adolescents (also see Heller & Perleth, 1988).

Most of the test–retest coefficients for the variables of giftedness and motivation are in the central range, that is, between

.50 and .70. In order to determine the stability of the scales used in both forms (the students were given the parallel form during the second measurement period) of the German version of the Cognitive Abilities Test, the KFT (Heller, Gaedike, & Weinländer, 1985; also see Steffens & Perleth, 1990), the correlations between the first and the third measurement periods were calculated separately. The corresponding coefficients are almost all higher than those between the first and second measurements.

The correlational analyses of prognostic validity indicate that general intelligence (KFT total score) is an especially good predictor of academic achievement. The various KFT dimensions show, as expected, domain-specific variations in the relationships to German, mathematics, and English grades. Although the teacher checklists were very good predictors of academic achievement, no statistically significant relationships were expected or found between the other tests of giftedness, that is, social competence, psychomotor ability, and academic performance.

Multiple correlation coefficients between the various predictors were determined at measurement one (variables of giftedness, teacher checklist variables, and motivation variables) and the criterion variables at measurement two (achievement variables) in order to answer the question of predictability of domain specific achievements. Achievement and teacher checklist scores for academic secondary school students only were considered, in order to avoid confounding school specific judgment systems (the frame of reference for teachers is, in my experience, naturally their own type of school). Because of the problems of colinearity within the predictor set, the standardized regression coefficients should not be over interpreted. As a whole, however, the results on prognostic validity indicate that the data do not contradict the causal model of achievement behavior, but rather are in good agreement with it. Analyses supported the hypothesis of various types of giftedness, but definite characteristic clusters of the gifted were not found; the contrary was the case (see Steffens & Perleth, 1990).

With regard to the association of family characteristics (style of upbringing, values, discipline, etc.) with the adolescents' activities, only partial negative effects—for example in the eighth graders—of parental control could be determined. An association of intelligence with literary and artistic activities in the eighth grade was also found. Family characteristics, such as cultural interest or joint leisure time activity planning, are apparently correlated with students' activities in art and literature. There was an interesting interaction between parental control and intelligence. Whereas highly intelligent students from families with a low level of control were more active in literary areas, average students tended to develop more activities when they perceived their parents as controlling.

In the area of social activities, a negative influence was found for intelligence in older students (from the tenth grade). This perhaps is not overly surprising. An interaction was also found with regard to "control": In average students, parental control had a more positive effect on adolescents' social activities; in the highly intelligent adolescents, however, the situation was almost reversed. Taken as a whole, the gifted students seemed to be less influenced in their personality development by the family climate than the average students.

Since similar results were found regarding school climate variables such as achievement pressure, cooperation, and disturbances in the classroom, the conclusion seems to be that gifted adolescents are more resistant to environmental influences than their average peers. This is consistent with recent theoretical assumptions that gifted children are much more likely to influence their social environment actively or change it to suit their needs. Such suppositions are supported by statements made by parents. They often complain about their gifted children's undying thirst for knowledge and explorative drive, about their individual, almost stubborn, behaviors or work styles, and so on. It may very well be true, then, that gifted adolescents are better able to cope with systematic stresses in the family or at school simply because they are "more mature" and have a larger number of coping strategies available.

In following sections, more detailed results about the relationship between giftedness and noncognitive personality characteristics as well as various (academic and nonacademic) achievement variables will be presented. Finally, some sex-related differences will be reported. The best 6–10% of an age cohort will be referred to as "gifted," the best 3–5% as "highly gifted," and the top 1–2% as "extremely gifted." The data analysis was completed by my coworkers, Ernst Hany, Christoph Perleth, and Wolfgang Sierwald.

Selected typical characteristics of various groups of gifted will be presented here for the tenth grade (academic secondary school) students of this study. In the intelligence group, academic self-concept in the highly gifted was significantly higher than in the gifted or normally gifted group. This is in agreement with the results of a Dutch study (Mönks et al., 1986). No differences were found between the three groups of gifted with regard to general self-concept, again in agreement with Mönks et al. Despite the expected lower tendency to external causal attributions in the highly to extremely gifted, the various groups of intelligence, unexpectedly, did not differ with regard to other motivation variables (thirst for knowledge, assurance of success vs. fear of failure). By contrast, the average and gifted students could be clearly differentiated from the highly and extremely gifted students in their learning styles. The latter scored significantly lower on the scales "planning and organizing of work" and "control of motivation" (in the sense of Kuhl, 1983). Apparently the highly and extremely gifted have no problems with homework, so that they do not need the usual (simpler) techniques for coping with it. In addition, it was found that the highly gifted prefer to work alone and not to cooperate in groups with classmates.

The differences in characteristics were less pronounced in the creativity groups. The older adolescents could be differentiated by their academic self-concept as well as by motor control and the motivation variables "hope for success" and "thirst for knowledge." These differences were not significant, however.

In contrast, the gifted underachievers clearly were quite different from the gifted achievers. The term "underachiever" is used here to characterize students who achieve much less well than could be expected on the basis of their intelligence. That is to say, in comparison to "achievers" (in school performance), they do not live up to their potential. The underachiever profile corresponds to that found in the literature on the subject. Underachievers generally tend to be more anxious, and their thought processes are more easily disturbed in stressful situations. They seem to attribute success more externally and failure more internally (stable), that is, they attribute the latter to what they see as their lack of ability. The academic self-concept, that is, the subjective conviction of one's personal ability to perform academically, is clearly poorer than that of the academic achievers. This is also true of their general self-concept and their motivational control. They obtained low scores on the achievement motivation scales with regard to the variables "hope of success," a high score on "fear of failure." Their motivational structure is, therefore, very unfavorable.

Finally, certain sex-related results are of particular interest. They are summarized as follows.

1.  Girls were less frequently judged by their teachers to be the best in intellectual abilities and more frequently in musical abilities.
2.  The results of the tests of giftedness frequently were sex-dependent: Girls had, on average, poorer scores in the area of intellectual abilities, especially with regard to quantitative and practical-technical abilities. If the total score on a (differential) intelligence test is used as selection criterion, for instance, to form the sample in a scientific study or in talent searches for gifted programs, the sex-specific selection effect will be apparent in the area of intelligence. The girls, however, were superior to their male peers in their information processing speed and verbal creativity.
3.  It is striking that, according to our results, girls' giftedness declined steadily with increasing age or continued schooling as compared with the boys'. Since this statement is based solely on cross-sectional evidence at this point, possible cohort effects need to be eliminated before it is possible to speak with certainty about systematic developmental effects.
4.  Girls were somewhat superior to the boys in academic achievement, except for mathematics and physics accomplishments, where the boys showed better performance. With regard to extracurricular activities or accomplishments, a sex-role distribution is apparent: Girls were more frequently represented in musical-artistic domains, whereas they were seldom found in scientific-technical activities.
5.  Several sex-related effects were found with regard to the prediction of academic achievement. In some aspects different predictors are necessary for prognosis of very good to exceptional academic achievements for girls than for boys. Above and beyond this, test items that were primarily developed for boys, were too "difficult" for girls, whereas many girl-specific items were too easy for the boys. Independently of clarifying whether girls employ other problem-solving strategies to obtain excellent performances (which could not be measured here), the problem of test fairness thus arises.
6.  Highly gifted girls tended to demonstrate fear of failure rather than confidence of success. Of course, methodological artifacts cannot be completely eliminated. Girls perhaps

are more likely than boys to admit to anxiety in such group studies.

7. Initial evaluation of data on sex-related differences in environmental variables, here a family climate questionnaire, indicates that no notable differences between girls and boys were found regarding self-perceived family climate. However, additional analyses are necessary before final conclusions can be drawn about environmental influences on sex roles.

8. Extracurricular activities and achievements take place in both sexes when similar conditions exist. The more active girls tend to be closer in level of activity to other girls than to active boys. Obviously girls are not as well able as boys to turn achievements in scientific–technical areas into social recognition.

## CLOSING REMARKS AND ACKNOWLEDGMENTS

The complete methodology and the research results, which obviously could only be presented here in an abbreviated form, will be published (in German) as a book (cf., Heller, 1991). Here the tests and questionnaires used for the identification of the highly gifted students described along with the developmental psychological findings will be concerning special measures for the highly gifted. A follow-up study of the forms and conditions of metacognitive development has been running in cooperation with the University of Leipzig (Prof. Dr. Gerhard Lehwald) since 1989, and is supported by the Volkswagen Foundation.

The research project presented here was financed by the German Federal Ministry for Education and Science (BMBW) in Bonn (Grant number B 3570.00 B). This manuscript was written during an Academy Scholarship from the Volkswagen Foundation (1989–1990). I am also grateful to Colleen S. Browder, who assisted me in the translation of this manuscript.

## REFERENCES

Feldhusen, J. F. (Ed.). (1985). *Toward excellence in gifted education.* Denver: Love.

Gagné, F. (1985). Giftedness and talent: Reexamining a reexamination of the definition. *Gifted Child Quarterly, 29,* 103–112.

Gallagher, J. J. (1985). *Teaching the gifted child* (3rd ed.). Boston: Allyn & Bacon.

Gardner, H. (1983). *Frames of mind. The theory of multiple intelligences.* New York: Basic Books.

Hany, E. A. (1987). *Modelle und Strategien zur Identifikation hochbegabter Schüler* [Models and strategies for identifying gifted students]. Unpublished doctoral dissertation, University of Munich, Munich, West Germany.

Hany, E. A. (1990). Identifikation hochbegabter Schüler [Identification of gifted students]. In K. A. Heller (Ed.), *Formen der Hochbegabung im Kindes- und Jugendalter* [Forms of giftedness in children and adolescents] (pp. 39–200). Göttingen: Hogrefe.

Heller, K. A. (Ed.). (1987). Hochbegabungsdiagnostik [Diagnosis of giftedness]. *Zeitschrift für Differentielle und Diagnostische Psychologie, 8* (special issue).

Heller, K. A. (1989). Perspectives on the diagnosis of giftedness. *The German Journal of Psychology, 13*, 140–159.

Heller, K. A. (1990). Goals, methods, and first results from the Munich Longitudinal Study of Giftedness in West Germany. In C. W. Taylor (Ed.), *Expanding awareness of creative potentials worldwide* (pp. 538–543). Salt Lake City, UT: Brain Talent-Powers Press.

Heller, K. A. (Ed.). (1991). *Formen der Hochbegabung im Kindes- und Jugendalter* [Forms of giftedness in children and adolescents]. Göttingen: Hogrefe.

Heller, K., Gaedike, A.-K., & Weinländer, H. (1985). *Kognitiver Fähigkeitstest* (KFT 4-13+), 2nd ed. [Cognitive Abilities Test, CAT]. Weinheim: Beltz.

Heller, K. A., & Hany, E. A. (1986). Identification, development and achievement analysis of talented and gifted children in West Germany. In K. A. Heller & J. F. Feldhusen (Eds.), *Identifying and nurturing the gifted* (pp. 67–82). Toronto: Huber.

Heller, K. A. & Perleth, Ch. (1988). Formen der Hochbegabung bei Schülern. Aktuelle Ergebnisse einer Längsschnittstudie [Forms of giftedness in students. Recent results of a longitudinal study]. In B. Grillmayer, W. Hübl, & A. Pusch (Eds.), *Needed the gifted.* Report of the European Conference from September 26–28, 1988 in Salzburg (pp. 56–61). Salzburg: Landesschulrat/Päd.Institut.

Heller, K., Rosemann, B., & Steffens, K. (1978). *Prognose des Schulerfolgs: Eine Längsschnittstudie zur Schullaufbahnberatung* [Prediction of student success: A longitudinal study of educational guidance]. Weinheim: Beltz.

Kuhl, J. (1983). *Motivation, Konflikt und Handlungskontrolle* [Motivation, conflict and action control]. Berlin: Springer.

Lehwald, G., & Friedrich, G. (1987). Entwicklungspsychologische Probleme der Früherkennung von Begabungen [Developmental psychological problems in the early recognition of giftedness]. *Psychologie für die Praxis* (Special issue, pp. 5–12).

McCorquodale, K., & Meehl, P. E. (1948). On a distinction between hypothetical constructs and intervening variables. *Psychological Review, 55*, 95–107.

McLeod, J., & Cropley, A. (1989). *Fostering academic excellence.* Oxford: Pergamon Press.

Mierke, K. (1963). *Begabung, Bildung und Bildsamkeit* [Giftedness, education, and educability]. Bern: Huber.

Mönks, F. J., van Boxtel, H. W., Roelefs, J. J. W., & Sanders, M. P. M. (1986). The identification of gifted children in secondary education and a description of their situation. In K. A. Heller & J. F. Feldhusen (Eds.), *Identifying and nurturing the gifted* (pp. 39–65). Toronto: Huber.

Oswald, W. D., & Roth, E. (1978). *Der Zahlenverbindungstest* (ZVT) [Connect-the-Numbers-Test]. Göttingen: Hogrefe.

Perleth, Ch., & Sierwald, W. (1990). Entwicklungs- und Leistungsanalysen zur Hochbegabung [Developmental and achievement analyses of giftedness]. In K. A. Heller (Ed.), *Formen der Hochbegabung im Kindes- und Jugendalter* [Forms of giftedness in children and adolescents] (pp. 201–451). Göttingen: Hogrefe.

Rimm, S. (1980). *Group inventory for finding creative talent* (GIFT). Watertown, WI: Educational Assessment Service.

Roth, H. (Ed.). (1968). *Begabung und Lernen* [Giftedness and learning]. Stuttgart: Klett.

Schoppe, K.-J. (1975). *Verbaler Kreativitätstest* (VKT) [Verbal creativity test]. Göttingen: Hogrefe.

Steffens, K., & Perleth, Ch. (1990). The structure of cognitive abilities in highly and moderately gifted young people. *European Journal for High Ability, 1,* 76–84.

Sternberg, R. J. (1990). What constitutes a "good" definition of giftedness? *Journal for the Education of the Gifted, 14,* 96–100.

Tannenbaum, A. J. (1983). *Gifted children: Psychological and educational perspectives.* New York: Macmillan.

# 5

# Gifted and Talented Children

## The Nature of Giftedness, Screening, and Development

**Alexey Matyushkin**

*Institute of General and Educational Psychology,
Moscow, Russia*

The intensive restructuring of Soviet society has led to the decision to establish the National Centre of Creative Giftedness to lead theoretical and applied research on the nature of giftedness both in children and adults. The development of a gifted person is viewed as an ideal model of normal development. The psychology of giftedness includes investigations into the nature of creativity and creative personality growth; the structure and dynamics of general ability and special capacities; the psychophysiology of individual differences; psychogenetic studies. Applied research involves educational practices based on creative problem discovery and problem solving. General giftedness is viewed as primarily expressing itself in problem sensitivity and sensitivity to nonstandard ways of solving problems. It also involves a high ability to anticipate and forecast the future. The integral components of giftedness are considered in terms of an evaluation function based on the individual's perspective, and intellectual and emotional "standards." Special abilities are viewed as emerging against the framework of general giftedness.

## THE IMPORTANCE OF EDUCATIONAL PROVISIONS FOR THE GIFTED AND TALENTED

Early screening, education, and counseling of gifted and talented children is a task that should be carried out as a first priority in any system of education. Socialist societies can advance by fostering development of creative potential in every aspect of social and economic life.

In spite of numerous controversial issues, medical and behavioral sciences have shown repeatedly that we have to acknowledge the existence of differences in creative potential in children in order to explain differences in individual progress in learning. Unfortunately, contemporary preschool and school education hold strongly to the image of the *typical* student, whereas vocational and professional training aim to train a *standard* specialist—overlooking the urgent need of society for diverse abilities. Much money is spent providing for the needs of less able children, but far less is spent on special programs for the gifted and talented. Research should aim at discovering the essentials of giftedness and showing how to create an appropriate environment that would provide for the fullest realization of creative potential in every child. I see learning and the development of the gifted and talented as an approximation to the *ideal* model of universal creative growth in human beings. Research and educational practice have demonstrated that talent may be blocked and often wasted at any developmental stage. Special psychological help is needed to facilitate realization of a creative personality.

## SOVIET RESEARCH ON GIFTEDNESS AND CREATIVITY

Governments should support research on giftedness and creativity as experiences in other countries have shown. In Russia at the stage of *perestroika* conditions were favorable for intensifying research on giftedness and implementing the findings, thus developing a system of special schools on the basis of sound knowledge.

In Russia numerous studies have been carried out on the psychological foundations of creativity (Rubinshtein, Ponomarev, Kedrov, Tihomirov, Brushlinsky), on the psychology of general and specific talents (Leites, Teplov, Krutetsky, Ignatyev), and on the psychology and psychophysiology of individual differences and abilities (Teplov, Nebelitzin, Golubeva, Rusalov)—the ontogenetic basis of individual differences. Didactic principles and educational programs for individualized instruction have been developed. Very significant research has been done by Zaporotzets, Elkonin, Lisina, Venger, Davidov, and Podyakov on the psychological principles of creative development in preschool and elementary school, on the principles of problem solving in education (Brushlinsky, Kudravtzev, Lerner, Mahmutov), and on *developing education* (Davidov). However, the material accumulated in educational research never has been used for educating the gifted and talented.

## THE PSYCHOLOGICAL STRUCTURE
## OF GIFTEDNESS

The psychological structure of giftedness coincides with the basic structural elements that are peculiar to creativity and to the creative development of the individual. The manifestations of creative development are varied. They express themselves in early childhood in the form of rapid development of speech and thought; early involvement in music, drawing, reading, and counting, and in curiosity and activity.

Cognitive needs that constitute the psychological basis of a dominant content motivation probably are the most general characteristic, as well as a structural component of the creative potential of the child. The domination of content motivation over other types of learning motives is expressed in the creative child in the form of investigatory activity. It reveals itself in lower thresholds or higher sensitivity for new stimuli (Sokolov, Horn, Berlyne, Golubeva, Danilova, et al.), for the novelty of a situation, or for the discovery of the new in the already known. Cognitive or content motivation also reveals itself in a high level of selectivity of the child in the area of the unknown being investigated, the child's preferences for colors, sounds, forms, and so forth. Stable selectivity is one of the necessary conditions for the development of special abilities.

Investigatory activity permits the child's discovery of the surrounding world, transformation of the unknown into the known, creative generation of images, and stabilization of sensory and perceptive patterns (Zaporotzets, Venger). These constitute the initial and basic knowledge of the child. General investigatory activity is characterized by its relative extent and its stability. It also reveals itself in the gifted child as broad curiosity (Berlyne, Lisina) about anything that is subjectively unknown to the child. Investigatory activity is terminated by the acquisition of new knowledge and a general understanding of the area of investigation. The opposite type of development is based on the domination of achievement motivation and other needs that permit only the degree of investigatory activity necessary to satisfy the need for food, safety, and so forth. Investigatory activity directed by these types of primary needs stops as soon as the needs are satisfied.

In the course of the creative development of a gifted child, by about 3–5 years of age, investigatory activity is transformed into higher forms. The child asks questions in a self-directed way and discovers new problems to investigate. The range of this type of activity expands as means or tools to explore not only facts but also causes, connections, and consequences. As the child attempts to answer questions, the answers determine the selectiveness in the child's creative self-directed learning. Later, at about 5–6 years of age, problem finding becomes the main structural component of giftedness and creative growth in the talented child. It provides for a continuous openness in the child to the new and unknown. It is manifested in the search for contradictions and dissimilarities, in self-directed questions, and in the discovery of problems. Each failure brings forth another cognitive problem, generates investigatory activity, and creates the basis for another stage in the individual's development.

The process of creative search and exploration thus consists of solving problems, and the discovery of new elements and their relations to each other. In many cases these not immediately visible relations are hidden by previous knowledge, by stereotypes in thought, and by rigid attitudes. The difficulty in discovery of the new manifests itself in the task of overcoming habitual approaches to the problem. Solving a seemingly unsolvable problem constitutes what is known as an act of creation. Data that do not relate directly to the problem might result in *indirect products of activity* (Ponomarev), or *lateral forms of thought* (De Bono).

Originality also is a necessary structural element of giftedness. It expresses the extent of dissimilarity, novelty, inventiveness, and unexpectedness of the new solution as compared to standard solutions. Originality is determined by the following factors.

1. transformation of a given problem into one's own, personal problem;
2. emergence of the individual's own position with regard to the problem that is being solved; and
3. rejection of the standard, obvious hypothesis.

Originality has its origin in the act of challenging what is commonly accepted, of what has become a truism.

General giftedness is characterized by rapid discovery of solutions. Finding solutions always is a process of reaching some intellectual goal or the answer to an independently formulated question. This involves a number of consequent transformations. Choice of the way to discover the unknown and of intermediate goals and questions is essential (Tihomirov). This choice is determined by the extent of anticipation or prediction (Brushlinsky) of the optimal steps in finding the solution. The depth of anticipation therefore is another basic structural element of general giftedness. One of the American theories of giftedness is based on this integral characteristic of giftedness (Torrance).

In Soviet psychology and psychophysiology the universal significance and role of anticipation has been described by Bernstein, who studied the phenomenon in relation to every goal-oriented act of behavior. However, his work has not achieved due recognition and is still interpreted only in the context of the *development of physical movements*. A number of diagnostic tests and special methods (e.g., for measuring intellectual capacities) have been constructed on the basis of the notion of the *depth of anticipation*, and projective methods for predicting the possibility of anticipating the desirable future have been developed, both in experimental research and in real-life situations. These tests have universal relevance and can be extended to include evaluation of the ability to predict the visual form of objects, the trajectory of movements, or even social events. In the latter case, not only the cognitive but also the creative potential of the individual is characterized.

The final basic structural element of giftedness is the function of evaluation, a *measuring* function of all psychological structures. In child and developmental psychology the function of evaluation has been described by Zaporotzets, who formulated the principal role of this function as based on perceptive, intellectual, and emotional patterns. In Western psychology this function was studied particularly by Bartlett. Guilford mentioned evaluation as a specific aspect of creative thought. Many of Piaget's phenomena and methods of diagnosis are based on this fundamental factor. Essentially, all complex psychological structures fulfil the role of *measurements* or *measures*, with the help of which human beings attempt to evaluate their environment, other people, and themselves. Aristotle defined Man as the *measure* of all things. The evaluations emerge in the form of emotional standards, and determine esthetic and moral preferences. They also emerge in perceptive and intellectual standards and determine the individual's estimates of the significance and credibility of ideas. Choices and decisions are taken on the basis of evaluations. The ability to evaluate includes in itself the possibility of understanding both one's own reasoning and also the behavior, thoughts, and actions of others. High ability to evaluate provides the gifted child with a sense of self-reliance, self-control, confidence, and trust in one's own abilities. It leads to independence, nonconformism, and other intellectual and personality traits.

In summary, the following are the basic structured components that constitute the psychological foundation for creative development.

1. domination of cognizing or content motivation;
2. investigatory creative activity that aims to discover the unknown, to formulate problems, and to solve problems;
3. possibilities for reaching original decisions;
4. the ability to predict and anticipate; and
5. the ability to create ideal standards that would provide a basis for esthetic, moral, and intellectual evaluation.

All these factors make up the integral structure of the phenomenon of giftedness and they manifest themselves at every stage of individual development. A number of diagnostic methods used in Western psychology allow screening for some of these factors.

In the preceding sections I have avoided a commonly accepted Soviet approach, which views giftedness as the manifestation and development of general and specific abilities. I did this purposely, in order to present the notion of giftedness as a facet to creative development. This does not, of course, mean underestimating the achievements of Soviet psychology. Neither do I ignore the debate that took place between Leontjev and Rubinstein in 1959. At that time the discussions and debates were complicated by a number of methodological difficulties and did not result in constructive decisions. However, there always has been a dominant tendency in Russia toward an integrative approach to the study of giftedness. Important examples are the unique longitudinal research of Leites or the research of Shadrikov in 1984. One such integral approach implies that giftedness or talent should be understood as the most general aspect of creative development in the child. The other special abilities, in my view, develop out of this underlying source, provided that they reach the level of creative productivity in science, technology, and culture. Therefore, research done on the psychology of creativity is the basis for the investigation of giftedness. This approach may help to overcome the one-sided perception of high ability as predominantly intellectual (Piaget); it allows for the description of giftedness as a premise of creative personal growth. The creative personality would be able not only to create the new and discover new laws but also to achieve self-expression and self-discovery in the arts, literature, and daily life.

This approach to giftedness implies that all theoretical knowledge in the area should be used to provide psychological support for the gifted and talented. This in turn means a methodological shift from purely academic research, indicating the presence or absence of giftedness, to the practical implementation of scientific findings through the provision of specially organized *lessons on creativity* in schools, the improvement of the psychological qualifications of teachers of gifted and talented children, and the provision of psychological counseling to the parents of gifted children. The reform of compulsory and vocational schools in Russia that is now taking place is an expression of the urgent necessity for creation and implementation of differentiated programs in schools.

I have managed only very briefly to scan new prospects and challenges that emerge from the focusing of attention on the problems of giftedness in education and educational psychology. Western psychology has already had an effect on the practice of education through the development of manuals and instructional materials (some of them have been published recently in translation into Russian: see e.g., *Questions of Psychology*, 4 [1988]). To achieve better results and more effective research in the area, Soviet psychologists should work together with outstanding scientists all over the world and participate in the activities of the World Council for Gifted and Talented Children and the European Council for High Ability. This would help gifted and talented children, and help to develop a better future for all.

# 6

# Developing Talented Children: Problems and Experiences

**László Balogh**

*Kossuth Lajos University, Debrecen, Hungary*

**Kálmán Nagy**

*Bethlen Gábor Elementary School, Törökszentmiklós, Hungary*

A project in the seventh and eighth grades aimed at providing the best possible school conditions to promote development of the abilities of children aged 13–14. The children's activity was founded on two main psychological and pedagogical principles: adequate motivation and individual differentiation. The children's development was monitored by means of intelligence and personality tests. The main results were as follows: There was a pronounced improvement in the performance tasks, but no significant development in verbal tasks; the role of inner motives had greatly increased, but the pupils had become more tense and impatient by the end of the school year. Necessary alterations in the project are outlined.

## INTRODUCTION

For a long time experts have disagreed on the most fruitful method of fostering the development of children. One camp says that this aim can be achieved most effectively at the school the child otherwise attends, that is, it is not necessary to segregate talented school children into separate schools. The other side holds the view that separate schools for nurturing talents should be set up and high ability students educated in these, in order to quicken their progress. For several reasons, we support the first view in principle, that is, we are convinced that the school the child goes to, the natural school environment, can provide the best possibilities for developing talents. At the same time it is true also that an intensive development of abilities depends on both personal and material circumstances, and if either of these is missing the child is not able to evolve to the utmost. Unfortunately, in Hungary too, conditions in schools leave something to be desired. What is more, even developing the basic skills presents problems. Among the reasons are lack of qualified teachers, lack of classrooms, the large number of children in one class, and the lack of educational materials and equipment—just to mention the most important reasons. In such conditions the abilities of a great number of children remain latent, that is, these valuable assets are lost.

Taking all this into consideration, it is necessary to collect the students who seem to be gifted and provide suitable conditions to promote their abilities to the highest possible level. This was the motive that led the headmaster of the Bethlen Gábor Elementary School, Törökszentmiklós, to recruit a group of seventh form students from 14 elementary schools from the town and its surrounding area, and launch an experimental program aimed at developing the children's abilities in the school year 1987–1988. A class of 20 children (a number sufficient to comprise one class) was formed on the basis of nominations of the schools the students attended. Since the number of applicants was 20 altogether, no selection was possible. As there was one dropout, a total of 19 children remained in the project.

## THE PROJECT

### Aims

As mentioned, the primary aim was an intensive development of the children's abilities by all available pedagogical means. Beside this general aim, it was our direct intention to prepare the seventh and eighth form students to achieve as well as possible in secondary school. In addition, the aim involved the task of developing the children's personalities (e.g., self-knowledge, adjustment, morality, behavior, etc.), in accord with the view that without a highly developed personality it is hard to further abilities.

## Organizational Framework of the Project

The students' morning and afternoon activities were organized into a unit. The main task was that the children should carry out the requirements of the curriculum at the highest level possible, but there was also opportunity for them to expand their abilities during extracurricular activities once special abilities became manifest in their achievement. The morning activities ran in accordance with the school curriculum; in the afternoon, however, work went on in special subject areas aimed at nurturing talent. There were eight of these that function as frames for developing abilities:

> mother tongue;
> mathematics;
> science;
> drawing, esthetics;
> singing, music, esthetics;
> Russian language;
> German language; and
> computer sciences.

In the morning the students worked together during lessons, in the afternoon they worked in separate groups. Each student was given tasks individually, an approach that had many advantages; it made it possible to go deeply into the subject matter of the class, practice it, gain more knowledge, and raise or maintain interest in the field in question. Table 6-1 shows the distribution of activities in a two-week period.

In addition to providing suitable conditions for skill development, these frames ensured that the students' relationships to others were stabilized. Obviously this was promoted also by spare time activities and by the fact that 11 students out of the 19 lived together in the student hostel.

**TABLE 6-1**
**Distribution of Activities**

| Odd week | | Lessons (Mornings) | | |
|---|---|---|---|---|
| Monday | Tuesday | Wednesday | Thursday | Friday |
| Math | Biology | Biology | History | Math |
| German | Math | Physics | German | German |
| History | Spelling | Math | Geography | Geography |
| Russian | Technical ed. | Homeroom | Math | Chemistry |
| Spelling | Literature | Literature | Russian | — |
| — | Phys. ed. | Phys. ed. | Phys. ed. | — |
| | | Extracurricular Activities (Afternoons) | | |
| Math | Computer science | Russian | Science | — |
| Mother tongue | Drawing, esthetics | Singing, music | German | — |
| **Even week** | | **Lessons (Mornings)** | | |
| Monday | Tuesday | Wednesday | Thursday | Friday |
| Geography | Physics | Biology | Math | Math |
| German | Math | German | Physics | German |
| History | Literature | Technical ed. | German | Spelling |
| Russian | Homeroom | Technical ed. | Russian | Chemistry |
| Spelling | German | Chemistry | Chemistry | Literature |
| — | Phys. ed. | Phys. ed. | Phys. ed. | — |
| | | Extracurricular Activities (Afternoons) | | |
| Math | Computer science | Russian | Science | — |
| Mother tongue | — | Singing, music | German | — |

## Pedagogical and Psychological Principles

During the project we had two main considerations in mind: how to motivate the children properly and how to achieve individual differentiation. It is well known that in evolving talents what kind of relationship the child has to the activity in question is crucial. If the activity is not in harmony with the aims of the individual, it is hard to believe that high skill levels will be formed. The basis for mobilizing inner energies is enthusiastic involvement with the material. We tried to create the appropriate motivation and identification with the learning activity, by means of the following principles.

> The children's self-activity played a central role in the project. Independent work had a strong motivating effect and was interwoven with rich emotions.

The teachers were encouraged to motivate the children positively rather than use negative incentives.

Feedback to the students after task solutions was stressed in motivation. Assessment of and information about the results inspired their achievement, too.

Another important factor in motivation was the raising of the level of aspiration. This was brought about as a result of the arrangement of incentives, and largely depended on achievement in the given field.

The teacher's personality in motivation was considered to be a decisive factor; consequently, permanent self-education and further education of teachers were important elements of the whole project.

In order to ensure an appropriate background to the activity it was primarily important that the students should be able to form a positive self-image and develop self-esteem.

In addition to the inspiration from solving tasks individually we also relied on motivation provided by group activities.

In addition to suitable motivation, the other main issue is differentiation in the childrens' activities. This is also an essential condition for evolving abilities, as children capable of different achievements are together in the same class. This was proved both by assessments in subjects and by scores on intelligence tests. Table 6-2, which follows, summarizes of the distribution of children according to their IQs, using scores on the Hungarian standardized version of the Wechsler intelligence test.

There were possibilities for differentiated work during the lessons, but it was most clearly manifest in the afternoon periods. During the morning lessons differentiation was ensured mainly by allowing children to solve tasks at different levels, in the afternoon activities by giving them tasks most suitable to their individual abilities.

TABLE 6-2
Distribution of Participants According to IQ

| | | |
|---|---|---|
| Average | (91–109 IQ) | 2 |
| Above average | (110–120 IQ) | 6 |
| Very high | (121–130 IQ) | 4 |
| Extremely high | (+ 131 IQ) | 7 |

## RESULTS

Three kinds of examination were conducted at the beginning and the end of the school year.

> The students did subject tests;
> They were tested on intelligence tests; and
> They filled out personality questionnaires.

The aim was to measure the influence of the pedagogical development work by means of objective psychological procedures. By taking into consideration the results, pedagogical work may be made more purposeful and there is greater opportunity to differentiate the amount of influence exerted on each student.

We are concerned here with the results of two of the areas in which data were collected: intelligence and personality test scores. The reason why we do not intend to analyze the results of the subject tests is that almost all the students (85–97%) did well in every subject at the end of the school year; apart from these general data only very special subject problems could crop up during an analysis of students' shortcomings, and we are less concerned with these here. The scores on intelligence and personality tests show more of the general tendencies of the students' development. In the examination of intelligence we used the Hungarian standardization of the Wechsler intelligence test. In addition to measuring the general IQ it also examines the structure of intelligence, so that it can be used to measure the level of different abilities. There are two main types of task: five verbal and five performance tests. Table 6-3 indicates the types of task and shows differences between scores at the end of the year and those at the beginning.

What important consequences can be drawn from this Table?

1.  At first glace it is striking that there was a pronounced improvement in the performance tests, whereas in the verbal tests there was hardly any change. The total data also give evidence of this, as the mean Performance IQ score increased from 123.8 to 129.7 ($p < 0.05$).
2.  The results show that the students' work based on their individual activity was fruitful. Similarly, the fact that the difference in achievement in the subtest information was significant indicates that the way knowledge was transmitted to the children had been successful.

TABLE 6-3
Scores on Intelligence Subtests

| Subtest | Mean Difference | Standard Deviation | Probability |
|---|---|---|---|
| Verbal tasks | | | |
| Information (memory, associative readiness, interest) | 0.94 | 1.54 | 0.05 |
| Comprehension (practical knowledge, generalization of experiences) | 0.21 | 2.57 | ns |
| Digit span (perception, memory) | −0.68 | 2.31 | ns |
| Arithmetic (comprehending problems, picking out the essential points, arithmetic functions) | 0.94 | 2.06 | ns |
| Similarities (abstraction) | 0.47 | 2.58 | ns |
| Performance tasks | | | |
| Coding (perception, psychomotoric quickness) | 1.21 | 1.75 | 0.01 |
| Picture arrangement (visual perception, causal relations) | −0.47 | 3.00 | ns |
| Picture completion (visual perception, part–whole relations) | 2.10 | 2.80 | 0.01 |
| Block design (analysis–synthesis, transfer, spatial orientation) | 1.26 | 1.24 | 0.001 |
| Object assembly | 0.84 | 3.28 | ns |

3. The lack of improvement in Verbal IQ (120.9 vs. 120.3) indicates that more attention should be paid to language education.

4. Poorer results in the subtest Digit Span are an indicator of tiredness and loss of concentration at the end of the year. The large number of programs might be the cause here, so care should be taken in this area next year.

5. The significant changes in the performance subtests 6, 8, and 9 indicate a considerable improvement in analytic–synthetic activity, which is an important element of mental abilities.

In the personality examination the California Psychological Inventory was used. Its 480 items are arranged into 18 scales. The test is meant to analyze the basic dimensions of a normal personality. Significant differences between test scores at the beginning and the end of the year cast light on the development of the students' personalities.

1. There was a considerable decrease in the students' self-control; they became more tense and more impatient by the end of the year. This may be connected with the heavy work load mentioned earlier.
2. The value placed on creating a good impression also decreased. At the end of the year the children attached less importance to how others reacted to them. This is a sign of the development cf autonomy.
3. The role of outside incentives in achievement decreased, whereas that of internal incentives increased. This indicates the success of the motivational work of the teachers.
4. Ability to win respect, general well-being, sense of responsibility, and flexibility all developed. The children became more mature in comparison to the beginning of the year. The responsibility they felt for their own future became more pronounced.
5. The values of the following scales decreased: sociability, disposition, tolerance, and feeling of unity. This might be an indicator of problems in relationships among children in the class.

We intend to investigate this by means of sociometric examinations, and to plan necessary steps on this basis. Probably, increased rivalry means that the children do not pay enough attention to one another. Unfavorable boy–girl relationships also may be influenced by the characteristics of the age group, that is, adolescence. These results also point to the necessity of taking greater care in developing the students' personality, otherwise distortions may follow, that, in the long run, are likely to have unfavorable influences on the evolution of the childrens' talents. In addition to the teachers' observations, regular measurements can be of help here.

The personality tests also were filled out by the teachers at the beginning of the school year, as their personalities are essential factors in developing the students, and we had to know what values they possesed. Table 6-4 gives the mean scores on some important personality traits, putting the teachers' and the children's data side by side.

It is only natural that the superego functions should be more developed among teachers, although they approximate the average. Their strong self-control, conformism, and relative inflexibility are conspicuous. These last two features also support the

TABLE 6-4
Significant Differences between Teachers' and Children's Personality Traits

| Trait | Teachers | Children |
|---|---|---|
| Self-control | 63.19 | 51.09 |
| Self-acceptance | 48.40 | 42.13 |
| Sense of responsibility | 56.57 | 50.36 |
| Tolerance | 53.11 | 44.56 |
| Achievement by conformity | 57.86 | 51.47 |
| Achievement by independence | 55.49 | 46.70 |
| Flexibility | 41.90 | 50.60 |

view that teachers taking part in the project need permanent self-development and regular consultations. Further education was underway among teachers last year, too, and this year even further new aspects will be added to the agenda.

## PERSPECTIVES, FURTHER TASKS

This year another seventh form was started. We had a greater opportunity for selection, as we could choose the 20 students in the class from among more than 40 applicants. While arranging the program for the new class we took into consideration the experiences of the previous year, and we are going to conduct tests at both the beginning and the end of the year. Considering experience to date we have modified the program for the first experimental class (the eighth form at present), making three essential alterations.

1. It is not compulsory for everyone to attend each subject area, but is optional according to interest and capacity. This option has already taken place: Three children have chosen four subject areas, six have chosen three, two areas have been chosen by nine students, and one area by one.
2. The teachers at the local secondary school also are taking part in the activities during the afternoon periods.
3. We are striving to ensure more opportunities for individual work, thus permitting further differentiation.

The children will complete the subject matter in three terms instead of four, thus permitting us to concentrate on more in-

tensive development of their special abilities in the fourth semester. In order to carry this out we need further experience.
We are going to continue observing how graduates from the experimental class achieve in secondary school and later, as success or failure will only manifest themselves in the children's
achievements in later years.

# 7

# The Early Development and Education of Highly Able Young Children

**Joan Freeman**

*University of Middlesex, London, England*

Because the very early development of abilities is vitally affected by personal relationships, research emphasis has shifted away from the quasi-experimental situation to the more natural home context. This has resulted in the rejection of some limiting ideas of very early potential, and particularly appropriate for the highly able, concern with young children's own awareness of what they do. The educational conclusions are that infants who develop and learn with speed and ease need a wide variety of activities, with parents who are aware and responsive, especially in play and verbal interaction. They also need both the appropriate material provision and facilities for practice to develop specific skills.

## INTRODUCTION

There are two different aspects to this chapter. The first touches on some exciting new knowledge about early development, and the second on the process of educating the highly

highly able young child. My immediate problem is how to combine this duality to use each to enhance the other. I am taking the early years to mean those from birth to around the start of school; this implies that, although the home will have the lion's share of influence, the preschool and first tastes of school are also included. The meanings of the two words, development and education, are so intertwined that it is hard to disentangle the more natural process of development from the influences of education. However, because extremes tend to be more easily distinguishable, focusing on high ability can help to separate the two. The study of those people who are the most outstanding, for either part or all of their lives can highlight the potent sources from which each individual, of whatever ability, will emerge.

Because learning is so often a matter of establishing shared understandings between individuals, the development of the intellect and its creative use are vitally affected by personal relationships. Development stems particularly from the infant's ability to assess the capacities and predict the behavior of other people. Normally, the first learning relationship is with mother, then with both parents, brothers and sisters, and eventually with school, and so forth. However, babies are born with a wide range of abilities and tastes, and any interaction between them and others has to include their respective intellectual capacities and personalities. Mental skills, then, are part of the whole child, so that the way an individual approaches an intellectual problem can be seen to change considerably with the social context. This is discernable in an individual's cognitive style— the manner in which individual people employ their intellectual abilities.

Most psychological research on the development of intellectual life has been carried out in an experimental way, either with infants in a clinic or children in classrooms. It has most often been concerned with how they interact with an exceptionally ordered physical world, which follows clear rules—one not much in evidence at home. Such designs are supposed to keep the measurement "pure," to avoid contaminating it with the influence of the child's personality or the social environment. But that is like trying to measure the behavior of a fish without regard to the water it swims in.

Looked at *in situ*, the picture can be very different. Take the gifted, for example; many of their so-called "typical" behaviors are in fact heavily influenced by circumstances, and are not specific to their exceptional ability. In the first Gulbenkian study, children seen as gifted by their parents were compared with those of the same measured ability but unlabeled as gifted. A statistically significant proportion of the labeled children were seen to have more health problems of a "nervous" nature, such as poor sleep and asthma, and this was described as being the case from their infancy. Careful analysis of home visits and interviews with parents about their lives showed that there was almost inevitably a wider cause for children's emotional discomfort than a high level of intellectual potential (Freeman, 1979).

Increasing interest in early development over the last decade has caused psychologists to shift their research strategies away from the more experimental to a more natural means of measurement. For instance, in separate works, Bryant (1974) and Donaldson (1978) reworked Piaget's original observations in a manner more relevant to the child's logic and language. They provided their subjects with a greater chance of success, which altered the age parameters of the then-recognized stages of intellectual development. This changed methodology in research includes

1. A more positive approach—rejecting previously accepted limits to discover what infants can actually do. For example, acceptance of age boundaries made it pointless to teach a child beyond its recognized capacity—remember "reading readiness"—but in fact, children are now successfully taught in advance of their "stages."
2. Focus on real-life situations—taking the observation of children out of the quasi-experimental situation into the home, thereby recognizing the importance of the developmental context.
3. Attempting to understand the children's own awareness of what they do. This means that children are not only measured by others, but are involved in the measurement situation, spoken to, and asked about how they see things. This approach is particularly appropriate for the highly able.

## EARLY DEVELOPMENT

Babies start to learn how to cope with their environments from birth. Indeed, there is some evidence that demanding infants trigger special family attention and resources, and that this extra attention can stimulate and speed up their intellectual development. However, the option is not open to all babies. Interaction is the key. It is only in families where the parents themselves are good communicators that the baby's demands are likely to be beneficially effective. This implies a decidedly active role for the baby that positively involves the parents too (Newson & Newson, 1974).

Not only can newborns' personality features be recognized, such as preferences for taste and sights, or the fact that some babies demand more attention than others, but communication is now seen to be dynamic (in its limited way) from birth. Nonverbal conversations between the mother (normally) and baby begin from day one. Such a conversation may be started when mother looks at baby, then baby catches her eye. She leans forward and says "Who's a lovely baby then?" The baby purses his or her lips and coos. She copies. Baby does it again. And so on until interest wanes. By this means the style of the mother–baby relationship may well have been initiated and set by the time the pair leave the hospital. Clear evidence of a built-in ability to interact at birth has been demonstrated by many researchers. Butterworth (1980), at Southampton, showed how newborns can turn toward a sound. From two months a baby can follow a pointing finger, then soon after that look to where someone else is looking. This apparently insignificant information provides considerable counterevidence to the Piagetian idea of the baby's total egocentricity. Even tiny babies can alter their own viewpoint to that of someone else.

However, it seems that from the very earliest days attentiveness is not so much related to future IQ scores as to socioeconomic status. Kagan and his colleagues, starting with 33 four-month-old infants, followed them for 10 years. They concluded that the children's outcomes, in terms of IQ and reading ability, bore a closer relationship to their parents' status in life than to the infants' own qualities (Kagan, Lapidus, & Moore, 1979). It is known how vital the first year is, how important it is to speak and listen to a baby. In fact, there is no lack of evidence that the style parents use in bringing up their children is highly effective in the child's eventual intellectual development and outlook.

Early environment has a decided effect on verbal development, as Tulkin (1977) found in New York. His sample of children under three years old, who had enjoyed a high quality of communication with their mothers both verbally and nonverbally from birth, showed better intellectual progress than children who had not been given that amount and quality of input. They played for longer times with the toys he gave them, were less distractable, more easily soothed, had better perceptual discrimination, and—eventually—had higher IQ scores. In a London study, Tizard (1985) found that when children were learning to read, those who read out loud to their parents at home had markedly higher reading attainments than those who did not.

In attempting to identify gifted babies, Lewis and Michalson (1985) devised tests to analyze developmental skills. They started with three-month-olds, and when the children were remeasured in conventional ways at six years of age the tests were found to have predicted high level verbal skills but not quantitative skills. It was concluded that as "different skills develop along different paths," in order to make early predictions of giftedness it is necessary to focus on a particular area.

Infant development is swift. The Harvard Project (White, 1985) discovered that toward the end of the second year an infant has made considerable progress toward adult stability, and has

1. a full array of social skills;
2. two-thirds to three-quarters of all the language he or she will ever use in ordinary conversation for the rest of his or her life, including: a receptive vocabulary of about a thousand words; and all the primary grammatical elements in the native language;
3. many lifelong attitudes toward learning; and
4. thinking skills.

I would also add

5. A basic awareness of the self—for good or ill.

The Harvard group claims that progress is "at-risk" from between 7 to 36 months, because this is a time that is particularly sensitive to lack of good stimuli. They reported that not more than 1 in 10 children gets sufficient input at that time for the fulfillment of potential. How much more true this must be for the development of special gifts and talents.

## EMERGENT GUIDELINES

As the evidence stands, the verdict is still not proven. It is not yet possible to identify with certainty gifted infants, those who will grow up to give consistently superior performances on any measures or in any field of endeavor. However, in an upside-down way there are pointers for identifying the "at-risk" gifted infant. The variables to watch out for are pre- and perinatal problems, and family and socioeconomic status. Nonetheless, there are some guidelines from work with children who later proved to be highly able that make it possible to identify the kind of very early home preparation that helped their potential to flower.

1. Stimulation alone does not provide an impetus for intellectual growth and can simply be confusing if it is not meaningful to the child. For example, loud clashing noises and screaming can be detrimental, whereas normal background music seems to be irrelevant.
2. Little ones need a variety of activities and experiences, most importantly through parents who are responsive to their child in play and conversation. Verbal abilities clearly are related to family verbal interaction.
3. Material provision of learning materials is essential.
4. Specific skills, including verbal skills, have to be positively taught, and children must be given opportunities to practice them.

### Enhancing the Early Education of the Highly Able

Although working with the highly able does help to identify pertinent factors in educating all children, the gifted themselves do have special educational needs. These come from the highly able child's capacity to learn more quickly and in greater depth, which parents and teachers so often see and encourage, sometimes to the curtailment of the children's all-round development. Possibly this is owing to an overemphasis in education on the accumulation of knowledge, to the detriment of the more creative aspects of development. The poignant effects of academic pressure were demonstrated in the follow up to the Gulbenkian Research Project, which looked at the children 10 years later when they had become young adults. The urge to scholastic excellence seemed to affect boys more than girls, and scientists most of all. The considerable study time required to win scholarships and prestige took a heavy toll on young persons' formation of nonacademic skills, and in some cases appeared to have given the brilliant young men a lifelong social handicap, with its attendant misery (Freeman, 1994). It may not be possible to do much with a child's personality, but it is possible to ease emotional blocks before they become too strong to shift. In all educational processes there is some conflict between the two natural yet opposing tendencies in children and adults—either to open up to the world or to seek the security of a closed familiar world.

According to Rogers (1969), the atmosphere that best facilitates learning is one of security; this implies the freedom to be oneself and demands sufficient self-confidence to take risks in the threatening unknown of new learning and creative thinking. Jung (1964) described how people often erect psychological barriers to protect themselves from "the shock of facing something new," because of a "deep and suspicious fear of novelty," which he called "misoneism." Children (and adults) can modify their anxiety in new learning situations by using strategies of analogy—making the unfamiliar familiar—by means of play. However, the scholarly, conforming child can find the anxiety overwhelming, and so may only accept learning that seems to be safe, that is, from a safe source, such as a teacher, and thus question little. However, with emotional support and guidance all children are better able to develop their learning skills to cope with and generate their own ideas and sense of self.

## Imaginative Play

However intelligent, a young child's natural approach to a new experience is one of play—a wonderfully flexible and creative aspect of intellectual development. Play is an activity that is not obviously goal directed. It may merely recreate what has been observed, but it is imaginative when the child brings in novel settings, times, and characters. Educators can use the level of children's play as an assessment guide to their development. Play can be seen from either a cognitive or an emotional perspective, although, of course, there is overlap between the two. Piaget (1962, 1971) saw it as vital to the developing intellect in the process of assimilating new information into the old. Emotionally, it is a social learning tool, and can also be a cathartic activity for young and old. Children use it to comprehend social behavior by replaying what they have seen others do, as well as in coping with their own fears and fantasies. When the quality of children's imaginative play is poor, it is a matter for real concern.

It is a sad truth that parents and teachers who are ambitious for an intellectually highly able child can place too much emphasis on measurable achievement, and may regard play as a "waste of time," prohibiting it until formal learning—the real business of the day—is finished. Even very young gifted children often are unconsciously perceived as quasi-adults, with little need for play, so that the only approved provision for learning experiences they receive are relatively sophisticated and often "bookish." Yet Bloom (1985), in his investigations of talented young people, found play with a musical instrument to be an essential early basis if there were to be really outstanding performances later. However, this is not to dismiss the equally essential hard work of learning and practice. It cannot be assumed that all children play freely and imaginatively; cross-cultural studies indicate that in some cultures, as with culturally disadvantaged children, it hardly ever occurs. Even among children who have facilities and encouragement, there are very different levels in the frequency, amount, and quality of play. However, the connection between early imaginative play and future creativity has not been satisfactorily measured.

The conditions for good play are the same as those for good learning.

1. an educational atmosphere in which there is permission to experiment, whatever the outcome;
2. emotional support;
3. the relevant learning materials; and
4. a living cultural tradition from which to draw and on which to build.

Sometimes the teacher has to encourage a child to risk doing what is disapproved of at home—and provide a "license" to play. For example, children with play difficulties at first may have to be encouraged to play with simpler, more babyish toys. Virtually all places of care and education for young children provide the means for play—in the reading and telling of stories, imaginative games assisted by the provision of dressing-up clothes, unstructured boxes, packing cases, and so forth, which lend themselves to use as a variety of props. However, the teacher's attitudes and personality are equally important in facilitating creative play. Higher up the age range, schools are more likely to channel play into the more rigid lines of competitive sport.

The intellectually highly able can be encouraged in their playful use of both their imaginative and conceptual abilities. This list has been adapted from one by Kaplan (1980).

1. *Content:* Introduce new ideas and take up the child's own from the play experience, and suggest generalizations and principles from there. For example, the play might be imagining life as a robot, from which the child could be encouraged to generalize to possible changes in lifestyle because of improved technology—a look into the future.
2. *Processes:* Introduce higher-level thinking and research skills during play. For example, a bright preschool child might be building a tall shaky tower of wooden blocks. The adult then could discuss the problems of constructing the tower, as a way of teaching problem-solving and thinking skills.
3. *Product:* Help the child to form new constructs by listening to the description of what she or he has learned from the play experience. The child could be asked to talk about new ideas from the play with others, and perhaps devise a game from it.
4. *Affect:* Children can learn more about themselves from their play experiences, discovering their own abilities, interests, and needs, as well as finding out about the others they play with and their relationships with them.

## CONCLUSIONS

The highly able have certain educational needs for their full development which begin at birth and go beyond the acquisition of knowledge. Though these needs are the same as those of other children, they are sometimes overlooked in the education of the very bright. In early childhood, both the acquisition of knowledge and its creative use are furthered by the same general environmental influences—encouragement, example, and educational facilities. But as children get older, the influences which benefit these two aspects of their intellectual functioning are not identical, and at times may even be contradictory. Whereas creativity needs emotional freedom to flower, high scholastic achievement often obliges emotions to be held in check. The question for educators of the highly able, therefore, is how to blend the two. The answer, I believe is in the playful, questioning approach.

There is a quality of playfulness in questioning and searching for ideas, enjoying their contradictions, and rearranging them into experimental combinations (Medawar, 1969; Piaget, 1962). Einstein (Einstein & Infeld, 1938) described how he delighted in his research, once writing that if he had regarded it as work he would never have succeeded. The spirit of playful enquiry helps creatively gifted people avoid taking themselves too seriously, providing a vital flexibility to look at things from many angles. By encouraging children to ask questions, it is possible to help keep their natural curiosity alive, stimulate their imagination and sense of adventure, and at the same time keep the learning process enjoyable (Landau, 1985).

An environment in which the exceptionally able child can fully prosper must be belanced, implying enough time with other people to form good social relationships and take part in a variety of activities. It is the very essence of pupils' gifted behavior that is at risk through conformity to social desirability. The area is a sensitive one, in which not only is a creative child's contribution too easily diminished, but pupils who feel obliged to subdue their own personalities in that way may also find their self-concepts damaged. The three guidelines offered here are really very simple—in words if not in actual practice. To enhance the education of the brightest young children, parents and teachers should

> promote the development of self-confidence for courage;
> encourage playful enquiry in an environment of mental freedom; and
> give permission to keep an open mind—in both children and educators.

## REFERENCES

Bloom, S. (1985). *Developing talent in young people.* New York: Ballantine Books.

Bryant, P. (1974). *Perception and understanding in young children.* London: Batsford.

Butterworth, G. (1980). A discussion of some issues raised by Piaget's concept of childhood egocentrism. In M. V. Cox (Ed.), *Are young children egocentric?* London: Batsford.

Donaldson, M. (1978). *Children's minds.* London: Fontana.

Einstein, A., & Infeld, L. (1938). *The evolution of physics.* New York: Simon & Schuster.

Freeman, J. (1979). *Gifted children: Their development in a social context.* Baltimore: University Park Press; Lancaster: MTP Press.

Freeman, J. (1994). Gifted school performance and creativity. *Roeper Review, 17,* 15–19.

Jung, C. G. (1964). Approaching the unconscious. In C. G. Jung (Ed.), *Man and his symbols.* London: Aldus Books.

Kagan, J., Lapidus, D. R., & Moore, M. (1979). Infant antecedents of cognitive functioning: a longitudinal study. In S. Chess & A. Thomas (Eds.), *Annual progress in child psychiatry and child development.* New York: Bruner Mazel.

Kaplan, S. N. (1980). The role of play in a differentiated curriculum for the young gifted child. *Roeper Review, 3,* 12–13.

Landau, E. (1985). Creative questioning for the future. In J. Freeman (Ed.), *The psychology of gifted children.* London: Wiley.

Lewis, M., & Michalson, L. (1985). The gifted infant. In J. Freeman (Ed.), *The psychology of gifted children.* London and New York: Wiley.

Medawar, P. N. (1969). *Induction and intuition in scientific thought.* London: Methuen.

Newson, J., & Newson, E. (1974). Cultural aspects of child rearing. In M. P. M. Richards (Ed.), *The integration of a child into a social world.* Cambridge: Cambridge University Press.

Piaget, J. (1962). *Play, dreams and imitation in childhood.* New York: W. W. Norton.

Piaget, J. (1971). *Structuralism.* London: Routledge and Kegan Paul.

Rogers, C. R. (1969). *Freedom to learn.* Columbus, Ohio: Merrill.

Tizard, B. (1985). Social relationships between adults and young children, and their impact on intellectual functioning. In A. Hinde, A. Perret-Clermont, & J. Stevenson-Hinde (Eds.), *Social relationships and cognitive development.* Oxford: Clarendon Press.

Tulkin, S. R. (1977). Social class differences in maternal and infant behavior. In P. H. Leiderman, S. R. Tulkin, & A. Rosenfield (Eds.), *Culture and infancy.* New York: Academic Press.

White, B. (1985). Competence and giftedness. In J. Freeman (Ed.), *The psychology of gifted children.* London: Wiley.

# 8

# The Role of Personality in the Regulation of Gifted Children's Development

**Lidia A. Germikova**

*Institute of Psychology, Ashkhabad, Turkmenia*

Experiments on problems of development of abilities have been carried out for five years with pupils in different age groups. The basis of the approach was development of psychodiagnostic approaches that would help in speeding up the development of cognitive activity in children with ordinary abilities. Gifted children display a high level of self-regulation, master complicated psychological processes faster, react positively to novelty and complexity, and can differentiate more clearly. Teaching of gifted children is carried out in the Small Academy of Sciences, where programs on the development of interests and abilities take account of each specific pupil's characteristics. Gifted children can predict the future better; their plans are directed to the future. They are interested in renewing society, because their aims are more motivated by a strongly developed future perspective. Further work requires coordination with the International Council on Children's Talents and Gifts, especially regarding teacher training programs involving the study of special endowments and their development.

## INTRODUCTION

The national system of education of the Turkmenistan, indeed of the former USSR in general in the present period of reorganization, is faced with the task of fostering development of the creative potential of gifted and talented pupils and students. The work of many Soviet psychologists, such as Rubinstein, Teplov, Platonov, Kovaljev, Myasitshev, Leites, Lomov, Brushlinsky, Krutetskoi, Artemjeva, Rusalov, and others has convincingly shown that in attacking this problem attention should be paid both to innate aspects of abilities as well as to their conditioning by the surroundings, including education.

The aim of Teplov (1985), an eminent investigator of abilities, was basic in the investigations: "Although I have rejected understanding abilities as innate, I do not reject the idea that innate abilities and inclinations are the basis of the development of abilities in most cases." In fact, the personality factor, the individuality factor, is basic in defining gifts and talents. Issuing from this is the further problem of the personality regulation of gifted children's development. The definition of "ability" itself requires consideration of its relation to individual differences.

In worldwide psychological science there are two developed fields that are of particular relevance: differential psychology and differential psychophysiology. The representatives of these disciplines deal specially with individual differences in abilities and gifts. Nowadays, issuing from accumulated foreign and also local experience, there is a need to create a special program by regions, providing for intensive investigations and applying the accumulated practical experience to the fostering of gifted and talented children. In connection with this, the International Council on Children's Talents and Gifts plays a progressive role. It is important to note that timely special psychological help and assistance for gifted and talented children could promote the maximum use of the abilities of these persons.

There is a great deal of debate on the abilities problem. There are different approaches; particularly, the general psychological or the individual psychological. I will concentrate here on the personality regulation approach. The general psychological approach takes the view that any manifestation of a person's potentialities is a manifestation of that person's abilities; the premise is that a person is able, if he or she can carry out any activity. At the center of attention is one question—how to develop the potentialities of all the people up to the level of the gifted and talented. According to the individual-psychological approach, a personality's uniqueness is expressed by his or her abilities. The personality regulation approach derives from the position that a person is the owner of his or her abilities and has a right to perfect them. Corresponding help concentrates on the individual, his or her potentials. The main point in the personality regulation approach is the need for accurate psychodiagnosis.

For five years an investigation has been carried out annually in Turkmen schools with pupils aged from seven to 15. The comparative study has involved two groups of pupils, differing considerably according to level of ability development (according to expert ratings). Individual aspects of personal self-regulation have been defined, particularly the content of self-education aims and the conditions of their realization. Findings indicated that 60% of children in the group of seven–eight-year-olds are more interested in the development of sensations and perceptions; 90% engaged in many kinds of activity, beginning with games and including different variations of labor or professional activity. The pupil group aged from nine to 12 paid the most attention to the development of memory, speech, and will (80%); the group of 12–15-year-olds to the perfection of emotions and feelings (75%) and to thinking development (92%).

The development of the cognitive, volitional, and emotional processes often manifests itself in the individual plan of self-education. An investigation of 50 children (25 with ordinary abilities and 25 gifted) showed that the cognition of 80% of the gifted children was speeded up; in 70% it was marked by the predominance of interest in the future. Children were motivated by purposes, not only in the sphere of short-term perspectives, but, basically, by future plans. The gifted children consciously took up the task of developing their capacity to make complicated demands on their cognitive activity, their moral self-expression. The aims of the self-education of less gifted children (60%) related basically to the present time and partly to the immediate future. This group (70%) paid more attention to compensating for their personal defects with the aim of enriching and complicating cognitive activity related to some definite short-term perspective.

It is possible within the differential-psychological approach to abilities to distinguish between two approaches: personality-activity and function-genetic (Iljin, 1987). The special feature of the personality-activity approach is consideration of abilities, as with other psychological phenomena, from the position of activity (as an explanation of ability genesis). Abilities are defined as properties (or the whole complex of properties) of the personality that influence the efficiency of activity. This approach has been refined during the last 30 years, with some questions related more to the first part of the definition: What properties of the personality or its peculiarities should be regarded as abilities? There are two methods of deciding this question. Some authors (the minority) consider some separate property of a person as defining ability, the whole complex of personal properties and peculiarities as the abilities. Kovaljev (1970) regarded the totality or synthesis of the properties of the personality, manifested in meeting activity demands, as abilities. Of gifted and talented children, 60% have many-sided abilities, but with a definite tendency to manifest them in a particular direction.

In Turkmenistan, the problem of gifted and talented children is handled in a one-sided way. More attention is paid in schools to the fostering of mental abilities. Gifted children have the possibility of studying at special musical or sports schools, or at schools with specialization in mathematics, foreign affairs, or military studies. In the Academy of Sciences (AS), there is a Small Academy of Sciences (SAS) that focuses on teaching children from different schools in various areas of knowledge. The pupils of the psychological section are 40% gifted and talented, determined by testing their reactions to novelty and complexity. Fostering motivation and growth of self-regulation of gifted and talented children is natural in the SAS; in the ordinary schools the children very often are left to their own resources, because the teaching staff believe that they do not need any help. Within the AS gifted children are attached to skilled, talented scientists, who help to formulate the scientific program of developing interests and abilities, and to define the main direction orientation of gifted children.

Great attention is paid to the study of the level of working ability, endurance, and persistence. With this aim children are given tasks for the month. The way in which they are completed, and peculiarities and special difficulties are registered in a diary. About 70% of the gifted children complete their tasks. However, psychological work, which is more tedious, is necessary to examine the motives for their behavior. Lack of clear communication between teacher and gifted pupil very often manifests itself in nonunderstanding of the aims and tasks of teaching. Gifted children more often resist dictated norms and rules and group and intragroup orientations against different styles of leadership.

The adaptation period in higher education, including SAS, is more difficult for gifted children than for ordinary ones. For this reason, working out the nature of personal interests is the first task. Some 55% of gifted children are able to express the goals of their self-education. In Turkmenistan the transition to differentiated study is extremely important, but the shortage of appropriate textbooks for gifted children and the shortage of teaching materials hamper this process. During the present reorganizational period, the most progressive form of work with gifted children is their inclusion in the management of teaching. The development of the ability to predict future development in any branch of industry, agriculture, and so forth is emphasized in the lessons in the SAS. The tasks for the gifted are at an adult level, and are varied in order to permit the manifestation of different kinds of gifts, and show the children's perspectives for the future. Methods of teaching leadership skills appropriate for children lead to difficulties, so that nowadays in Turkmenia the approach of Matyushkin and Sisk (1988) is used.

At present, in the Republic, attention is being paid in school to the free advancement of the child, but only in a few schools, because in general work on development of gifted children in the ordinary, mass schools is poor, and talented children usually are lost in the total mass. At schools Nos. 32 and 12 in Ashkhabad, the educational methods of Canada, the United States, and Holland have been adopted, especially registration of individual peculiarities of the cognitive style of pupils. In the Central Advanced Training Institute for Teachers interesting investigations are being conducted, in which the persons being trained are developing programs for gifted children in competitions to develop textbooks for children gifted in the various subjects (mathematics, history, language). The pupils of the SAS also are accustomed to this work, for instance, helping to evaluate this or that program based on a particular textbook. However, in the Republic there is no member of the International Council on Children's Talents and Gifts, and this, naturally, limits access to new, foreign advances in practical work with gifted children. Greater contacts with the World Council for Gifted and Talented Children are needed. We are interested especially in the problems of preparing creative teachers, who are capable of leading gifted children, working out programs and textbooks for lessons with gifted children (enriched programs), carrying out scientific investigation of the problems of the gifted, conducting comparative international investigations of the nature of giftedness, and arousing public interest in the problems of the gifted ("defence of gifted children").

In general, it is important to note that a radical reorganization of the system of teaching gifted children is needed, especially at the preschool age (at present, teaching of three to four languages is introduced in kindergarten). It is desirable that the natural gifts of the child should not be inhibited by reorganizational processes, namely, bureaucratic obstacles. An important task is also that of reorganizing the system of teaching in order to reveal talents, and at the same time achieve earlier qualified recognition of the existence of gifts, not allowing either intuition or obsolete selection criteria to play a role. An integrated conception is required for developing the creative personality, issuing from the efforts of scientists all over the world and guiding psychological–diagnostic thinking both of educators and teachers, as well as of children. Appropriate suggestions include exchange of specialists, holding of discussions, carrying out of cross-cultural investigations in schools in different countries, including Turkmenia. Contacts with the scientists of other countries are desirable, and the issuing of joint publications of both a theoretical, as well as applied nature is desirable. Such joint efforts of Soviet and foreign investigators should promote the solution of general problems—in complete realization of the creative potential of people all over the world.

## REFERENCES

Iljin, E. P. (1987). Abilities. Problem: Two approaches to its decision. *Psychological Journal, 8* (2), 37–47.

Kovaljev, A. G. (1970). *Psychology of personality.* Moscow: Prosvetshenie.

Matyushkin, A. M., & Sisk, D. A. (1988). Gifted and talented children. *Questions of Psychology, 4,* 88–97.

Teplov, B. M. (1985). *Selected works.* Moscow: Mysl.

# SECTION II

## Cognition and Problem Solving

# 9

# Levels of Mind

## A Multilevel Model of Intellect and Its Implications for Identification of the Gifted

**Edward Necka**

*Jagiellonian University, Kraków, Poland*

Contemporary theories of intelligence seek to relate certain behavioral or psychometric traits to information processing. It is believed that the study of basic information processing characteristics will enhance understanding of more complex behavioral traits. The present chapter presents a new theoretical framework that should help to interpret findings obtained within this approach. The proposed model assumes that human intellect is determined by elementary cognitive functions that operate at four distinct levels: biological, formal, heuristic, and pragmatic. Thus, the question of what intelligence is (or creativity, etc.) may be answered in four different ways, depending on the level under consideration. At present, numerous incomplete theories that refer only to one particular level are competing with each other. Consequently, it is not possible to agree upon concepts and instruments suitable for identification of the gifted. The aim of the proposed framework is to provide a theoretical background for future reconciliation and synthesis. Apart from this, some practical suggestions concerning identification of the gifted are proposed and evaluated.

## INTRODUCTION

The word "identification" appears to be as controversial as it is fundamental in the gifted education terminology. There seem to be two reasons for this. First, it is not always certain that the identification phase is necessary and advisable from the social and political standpoint, since it may originate from, and result in, elitist views of giftedness and talent. Second, it is not clear whether identification is efficient. Diamonds pass through the holes in the "riddles" too often for educators and researchers to feel satisfied with procedures for identification and selection of the gifted. Both problems sometimes lead to the far-reaching conclusion that no identification process is necessary; instead, it is argued, help and beneficial instruction should be provided for all children, as if all of them were gifted. The first objection is a question of values and I do not intend to discuss it here. The second one pertains to the question of pragmatics of gifted education; I want to take this as the topic of my chapter.

The pragmatics of identification are involved strongly in the problem of validity and reliability of measurement procedures and instruments, primarily psychological tests. However, what I want to discuss here is a theory of intellect rather than empirical results obtained with various psychological instruments. The main thesis amounts to the assertion that the concept of intelligence needs clarification, since it is now looked at from many different perspectives, and is based on many different kinds of data. In fact, the term "intelligence" refers to phenomena that may be observed on four distinct levels of human information processing. Thus, it is impossible to achieve consensus regarding definition of intelligence, and—particularly important from the present point of view—it seems to be difficult to design valid and reliable instruments that permit identification of intelligent people. An ideal nonexistent instrument would measure all aspects of human intellectual ability pertaining to all levels of processing, but obtaining such an instrument requires first concentrating on the very notion of intelligence as a multilevel phenomenon.

# A MULTILEVEL MODEL OF INTELLECT

The essence of the modern approach to intelligence consists in looking for processual foundations of general mental ability, instead of building up structural models of abilities. In other words, the task is to relate high-level achievements in intellectual tasks (both psychometric and real-life) to certain parameters of human information processing. Four distinct levels of processing are involved in such analysis, and so four corresponding definitions of intellectual giftedness may be formulated.

## Level I: Intelligence as Efficiency of Brain Functioning

At the most basic, biological level of analysis, intelligence is being related to certain parameters of brains functioning. Speed of neural transmission, or nerve conduction velocity, sometimes is suggested as a prerequisite of general intelligence, although empirical results are not consistent (Vernon & Mori, 1989; Wolski, Necka & Rychlicka, 1990). Moreover, it is not clear in theory why speed of neural transmission might be important for intelligent behavior. Some authors (e.g., Eysenck, 1987) therefore propose that efficiency rather than speed should be treated as the basis of general mental ability. The errorless transmission of nerve impulses characteristic for highly able people, Eysenck argues, makes their reactions more accurate in any task, including complex intellectual problems; at the same time, it makes their mean reaction time shorter as compared to less intelligent persons. In effect, a negative correlation between choice reaction time and IQ is observed, but this does not mean that speed is in any way necessary for intelligence; rather, it is a kind of side effect of errorless processing of impulses.

Efforts to define intelligence as efficiency of brain functioning have been supported additionally by psychophysiological evidence, showing that average evoked potentials (AEP) of gifted people differ from those obtained from the less gifted in terms of regularity and complexity of EEG waves (Eysenck, 1986). Together with the RT/IQ data already mentioned, this evidence corroborates the view that the biological level of analysis is indispensable for understanding the nature of human intelligence.

## Level 2: Intelligence as a Formal Parameter
## of Working Memory

Brain function is by no means the only level of importance, however. The second one refers to "mind" rather than "brain," that is, to psychological processes that determine intelligent functioning. These processes are regarded, however, from a purely formal, that is, content free, point of view. In other words, it is the mode of processing rather than the actual information being processed that matters. From this point of view, it seems worth examining whether some formal parameters of the human central executive mechanism may constitute the basis for intelligence at this level of analysis.

The nature of this central executive mechanism still is disputed, but there are at least two possible candidates: (1) attention as conceived by the so-called resource theories (e.g., Hunt & Lansman, 1982; Kahneman, 1973); and (2) working memory (Baddeley, 1986; Jensen, 1987). Both "candidates" possess a very interesting attribute, namely, they show limited capacity to process a great amount of information at the same time. In other words, the central executive mechanism responsible for human thinking and problem solving is likely to be overloaded by the necessity to process too much information simultaneously. Intellectual tasks that measure level of intelligence are particularly likely to cause such an overload, since they are complex, multifaceted, and require that many different chunks of information be kept in mind simultaneously.

It is interesting that theoreticians are not eager to draw the only logical conclusion from this state of affairs: that intelligence depends on capacity of working memory (or attention, depending on the specific theoretical model). Rather, these findings stress the importance of speed of processing. It is argued (e.g., Necka, 1990a; Vernon, 1987) that, since the system is likely to be overloaded by the influx of information, it is particularly important for an intelligent person to be quick, because speed is the efficient way to "outwit" the system of limited capacity, that is, to perform all necessary mental operations *before* the vital information is lost or forgotten. In this way, speed of processing is promoted to being a necessary condition for intelligence rather than a side effect of some more basic phenomenon, like errorless neural transmission.

There would be no need to "outwit" the system with the use of speed, however, if other formal parameters of information processing were well developed. In my own research (Necka, 1990b), I employed two elementary cognitive tasks in order to measure independently three formal parameters of working memory: speed, capacity, and retention capability. Correlations of capacity and retention capability with psychometric measures of intelligence lay between .30–.40, whereas correlations of speed with intelligence were lower (.20–.30), although they were still statistically significant. When all other variables were removed through partial correlation analysis, however, speed appeared to be completely insignificant as a correlate of IQ; capacity and retention capability, on the other hand, preserved their significance as partial correlates of intelligence. It seems probable, therefore, that intelligence is determined by some formal parameters of working memory or attention, although much effort is needed to establish the list of significant parameters of this kind. However, even before this work is done, intelligence may be defined in terms of well-developed formal parameters of human information processing.

## Level 3: Intelligence as an Appropriate Strategy

At the third level of analysis intelligence seems to be connected with strategic choice and planning. Different tasks may be executed in different ways, depending on individual preferences, on the one hand, as well as on an individual's ability to plan properly his or her cognitive activity, on the other. Undoubtedly, some ways of executing complex cognitive tasks can be considered more "intelligent" than others in terms of accuracy, efficiency, speed, or flexibility. Thus, people possessing the ability to choose and execute good strategies should be regarded as intelligent. The main feature of cognitive strategies amounts to the fact that they are mostly task dependent, and therefore qualitative in nature. For instance, some people may choose to trade speed for accuracy in simple cognitive tasks, whereas others may prefer to be fast rather than accurate. Similarly, some tasks may be executed either visually or verbally, and the choice of visual or verbal strategy is a matter of individual preference. As can be seen, strategies differ from one another in terms of unique, qualitative characteristics, in contrast to formal parameters, which are entirely quantitative in nature; for example, speed, capacity and so forth, which are *less* or *more* developed.

Knowledge about strategic aspects of intelligence is scarce.

Sternberg's (1985) notion of metacomponents looks very promising in this respect, but the empirical evidence he supplied to illustrate this notion is not so convincing as that referring to other aspects of the "triarchic" theory of intelligence. Hunt (1980) suggested that intelligence may be connected, not with any specific strategy, but with ease of flexible change of strategy in response to a task's requirements. Data obtained in my laboratory (e.g., Chawarski & Necka, 1989; Necka, Storki & Woiski, 1990) indicate that intelligent people—in contrast to less intelligent ones—pay more attention to, as well as deal better with, novel tasks and situations than familiar ones. Taking all this evidence into account, it can be concluded that, at the third level of analysis, intelligence may be defined as efficient planning and accurate execution of mental processes with the help of appropriate strategies of information processing.

**Level 4: Intelligence as Appropriate Judgment**

The fourth level at which intelligence may be regarded refers to the world of values. It is axiology rather than psychology that usually deals with this sphere of problems. The literature on abilities introduces notions like evaluation and judgment particularly rarely, with very few exceptions, such as Guilford's (1978) SOI model. Why do I propose to introduce them, then? First, I share the ever-stronger conviction that giftedness should not be restricted to intelligence especially to so-called "general intelligence." For instance, giftedness may refer to traits like creativity or wisdom, which are closely related to the category of judgment. Although creativity is widely studied and appreciated in research and education projects on gifted children, the same cannot be said about wisdom. I am convinced that we should study gifted children's ability to make decisions about complex, obscure, and fundamental issues of practical life, that is, their wisdom (Baltes & Smith, 1990). Even in the realm of intelligence traditionally viewed, it is worth asking if appropriate judgment constitutes one of its vital aspects. For instance, intelligent people may be better than less intelligent ones in terms of their ability to judge if the problem at hand is worth solving, or if the information that they can use is relevant to this problem. Intelligence might then be defined at this level as an ability to judge things properly.

## IMPLICATIONS FOR IDENTIFICATION
## OF THE GIFTED

If it is agreed that intelligence is a multilevel phenomenon—and I have tried to show that it is—this fact should be taken into account when new identification procedures and instruments are created. First, the illusion still shared by many theoreticians and practitioners that it is possible to measure giftedness by means of a single ideal instrument, for example, a psychological test, must be abandoned. It is possible to conceive of tests of almost everything, but I can hardly imagine a test measuring an ability to judge things properly, for instance. What should be done, I believe, amounts to assessing children's potential in terms of their individual profiles based on phenomena connected with every level of analysis. An important side effect is likely to occur, namely, abandonment of the simplistic "yes or no" conception of intellectual giftedness. Second, differentiated criteria should be applied in assessing giftedness at different ages, and in different groups. Level four may not be suitable for infants and minority groups, in contrast to level one, which comprises more basic and "culture free" phenomena. For instance, it would be quite objective (although expensive!) to diagnose efficiency of brain functioning in terms of EEG analysis. Certain behavioral methods based on reaction time tasks might be of equal validity if adopted for diagnostic purposes. The differentiated approach is likely to result in much more sound and reliable decisions concerning identification than is the case at the confusing and frustrating present.

## ACKNOWLEDGMENT

This chapter was supported by grant No. RPBP.III.29 "Human Creative Activity" from the Ministry of National Education.

## REFERENCES

Baddeley, A. (1986). *Working memory.* Oxford: Clarendon Press.
Baltes, P. B., & Smith, J. (1990). Toward a psychology of wisdom and its ontogenesis. In R. J. Sternberg (Ed.), *Wisdom: Its nature, origins, and development.* New York: Cambridge University Press.
Chawarski, M. C., & Necka, E. (1989). *Intelligence and dealing with novelty: Adaptation to unexespected changes in task's require-*

*ments*. Jagiellonian University, Institute of Psychology, Technical Report Mo. RPBP.III.28/1989/1.

Eysenck, H. J. (1986). The theory of intelligence and the psychophysiology of cognition. In R. J. Sternberg (Ed.), *Advances in the psychology of human intelligence*. Vol. 3. Hillsdale, NJ: Erlbaum.

Eysenck, H. J. (1987). Speed of information processing, reaction time, and the theory of intelligence. In Ph. A: Vernon (Ed.), *Speed of information processing and intelligence*. Norwood, NJ: Ablex Publ.

Guilford, J. P. (1978). *Natura inteligencji czlowieka* [The nature of human intelligence]. Warszawa: PWN.

Hunt, E. (1980). Intelligence as an information processing concept. *The British Journal of Psychology*, *71*, 449–474.

Hunt. E., & Lansman, M. (1982). Individual differences in attention. In R. J. Sternberg (Ed.), *Advances in the psychology of human intelligence*, vol. 1. Hillsdale, NJ: Erlbaum.

Jensen, A. R. (1987). The g beyond factor analysis. In R. R. Ronning, J. A. Glover, J. C. Conoley, & J. C. Witt (Eds.), *The influence of cognitive psychology on testing*. Hillsdale, NJ: Erlbaum.

Kahneman, D. (1973). *Attention and effort*. Englewood Cliffs, NJ: Prentice-Hall.

Necka, E. (1990a). Reaction time and intelligence. *European Journal for High Ability*, *1/2*, 211–221.

Necka, E. (1990b, September). *Intelligence as determined by speed, capacity, and retention capability of working memory*. Paper presented at the IVth Conference of the European Society for Cognitive Society, Como, Italy.

Necka, E., Storki, E., & Wolski, P. (1990). How does a knight know which frog is to be kissed: Analogical reasoning with metaphorical and odd concepts. *Personality and Individual Differences*, *11*, 101–103.

Sternberg, R. J. (1985). *Beyond IQ: A triarchic theory of human intelligence*. Cambridge: Cambridge University Press.

Vernon, P. A. (1987). New developments in reaction time research. In Ph. A. Vernon (Ed.), *Speed of information processing and intelligence*. Norwood, NJ: Ablex.

Vernon, P. A., & Mori, M. (1989, June). *Nerve conduction velocity: A physiological correlate of intelligence and speed of information processing*. Paper presented at the IVth Meeting of the ISSID, Heidelberg, Germany.

Wolski, P., Necka, E., & Rychlicka, A. (1990). Interhemispheric transmission time (IHTT) and intelligence. *Polish Psychological Bulletin*.

# 10

# Pulling Yourself Up by Your Own Thinking

**Philip Adey**

*University of London, London, United Kingdom*

This chapter concentrates on the metacognitve aspects of materials produced by the Cognitive Acceleration through Science Education project. A set of activities for promoting higher level thinking skills in adolescents emphasizes the development of metacognitive understanding of the reasoning patterns students use to solve problems. (Other psychological elements built into activities were focused on the reasoning patterns of formal operations, the use of cognitive conflict, and conscious effort to make transfer from the activity content to wider contexts.) Examples are given, and the long-term results following a two-year trial are reported. Although it is not possible to isolate statistically the specific contribution of encouragement of metacognition to the gains in cognitive development in science that were demonstrated, it is argued that the children's development of the ability to think about the nature of their own thinking was a critical contributor to success, without which the effectiveness of other aspects of the activities could not have been realized.

## COGNITIVE ACCELERATION

I should start by admitting that my interest in high ability children is to use them to set a standard to which all children can aspire: My work has been concerned with raising the ability of all children. Since the early 1980s Michael Shayer and I have been tackling a problem that we identified during the 1970s. The problem was that the school curriculum, at least in science, was making demands on the abilities of average pupils that they were not in a position to meet. Specifically, although the curriculum demanded formal thinking, we found (Shayer & Adey, 1981) that only about 30% of 16-year-olds could demonstrate the use of formal operations. Thus, secondary school students who were formal thinkers could be described as "able."

The social and historical origins of a curriculum system that builds in failure for a majority of its students need not be further discussed here, except insofar as one obvious "solution" to the problem—to make the curriculum material easier—was not politically acceptable and not (if some other solution could be found) desirable on educational grounds. The other "solution," of course, is to raise the level of ability of the pupils. This statement immediately begs questions about what counts as ability, which will no doubt continue to exercise the gifted children lobby as much as it has in the past. When I use the term ability, I certainly mean much more than "amount of learning" or "amount of knowledge." I mean something like the ability to learn, or the ability to process information effectively. The scale of ability (in this sense) that I have found useful as a set of operational descriptions of levels of information processing capability is derived from Piaget's descriptions of stages of cognitive development. A person using formal operations is able to handle a number of variables at once, to use hypotheses as a basis for planning, and to classify and organize material flexibly in different ways for different purposes. This person thus is able to make the most of any learning experience that comes his or her way. In the Cognitive Acceleration through Science Education (CASE) project, the immodest goal was set of raising significantly the proportion of the secondary school population of England and Wales who could use formal operational thinking. The purpose of CASE was to try to make many more children "able"—a perfectly respectable aim if one takes a criterion rather than norm referenced definition of "able."

Reviews of the literature (Adey, 1988; Goossens, 1989) on

cognitive acceleration suggest certain features that, if built into an intervention programe, should maximize its chances of bringing about long-term effects on the general ability of subjects. These features include

> the preparation of students to a state of perceptual readiness through concrete experiences that provide the necessary vocabulary and familiarize them with the terms of reference of the problem;
>
> focus on the schemata of formal thinking (control and exclusion of variables, ratio and proportionality, probabilistic thinking, correlation, combinations, compensation, classification, equilibria, and the use of formal models);
>
> the presentation of problems that induce cognitive conflict;
>
> the transfer of thinking strategies developed within the context of the special lessons to other areas of science, to other parts of the curriculum, and to everyday life; and
>
> the encouragement of metacognition.

In this chapter I will concentrate on the role that metacognition played in the intervention program, report something of the results, and invite the reader to speculate on the relative contribution of metacognition to those results.

## METACOGNITION

Sternberg (1985) described executive cognitive processes such as deciding what components of intelligence to use in solving a particular problem and how to combine different components as "metacomponents," which are "highly general across tasks involving intelligent performance and . . . in a large part responsible for the appearance of a general factor in mental ability tests" (p. 13). He went on (p. 23) to equate the executive function of information processing theorists with metacognition, although it is possible to question the distinction between the conscious awareness and direction of thought processes characteristic of metacognition in its usual meaning with the largely unconscious executive function that must select and apply cognitive processes appropriate to each problem. Indeed, the whole point of concentration on metacognition as a route to increasing performance is to make conscious, and therefore more directly controllable, processes that are assumed to occur naturally.

Nickerson, Perkins, and Smith (1985) characterized expert performance like this.

> Experts not only know more, they know they know more, they know better how to use what they know, what they know is better organised and more readily accessible, and they know better how to learn more still (p. 101).

They go on to describe the objective of metacognition as

> to make one a skilful *user* of knowledge; and utilisation of the term metcognitive skills serves to remind us that more is undoubtedly involved in this than simply giving one some new information about cognition (p. 103).

They emphasize the potential of learners' paying attention to their own thinking processes.

> The training of such skills, if done effectively, should have considerable payoff. In particular, inasmuch as these skills are very general, a successful effort to improve them should beneficially affect performance on a wide range of tasks (p. 104).

In spite of such hopes, however, they cannot report strong evidence that the development of metacognition (nor of any other strategy, for that matter) leads to the development of general academic performance.

Larkin et al. (1980) have charted the role played by strategic knowledge in marshaling the semantic knowledge that is undoubtedly needed to be an expert problem solver. They warn that, because of this semantic knowledge load, there is no quick and easy way to become an expert, but nevertheless propose that the development of strategic knowledge about one's own processes of retrieving data and using it effectively is an essential step from being a knowledgeable novice to being an expert ". . . it is only after one has solved a problem that one can learn most effectively how one should have solved it."

The alternative frameworks school of thought (e.g., Champagne, Gunstone, & Klopfer, 1985) tends to rely on students becoming conscious of their own conceptualizations, so that they can compare and contrast them with the scientists', conceptions that the instruction is aiming to develop in the students. The contrast between what perceptual evidence is telling them and what they currently believe can have no impact unless what they already believe is well articulated. In this sense, metacognition is seen as an essential prerequisite to the process of conceptual development.

Perkins and Salomon (1989) build on such findings and analyses to propose a model of context dependent general thinking skills. This recognizes the need for a semantic knowledge base for expert performance, but supposes that general thinking strategies developed within one domain context should be generalizable to other domains, provided that specific effort is made to bring together context specific knowledge with general strategic knowledge. "General cognitive skills can be thought of as general gripping devices for retrieving and wielding domain-specific knowledge . . ."

In the next section I will describe how such ideas of metacognition were applied to the particular program devised for the CASE experiment.

## CONTEXT AND EXPERIMENT

The project group chose to work in ordinary secondary comprehensive schools in Britain, and in particular within the science curriculum. The subjects were pupils aged about 11+ and 12+ at the start of the experiment. A set of 30 activities were designed that incorporated the features outlined in the first section, and these activities were introduced to teachers through a series of one-day workshops followed up by school visits during which lessons were observed and discussed afterward with the teacher. This in-service training activity is important since it could not be expected that the psychological foundation of the teaching strategies proposed would become immediately accessible to teachers through the printed material alone. It is important especially in relation to metacognition, since of all the features this was the one that could least explicitly be written into the printed materials, and therefore most in need of introduction through discussion and practice with the teachers.

The form of metacognition that the intervention program sought to promote was to make pupils think about their own thinking process, to reflect on difficulties and successes they had had with problems, to discuss with each other how they solved, or failed to solve problems, and to accrue understanding of the vocabulary of reasoning so that they could more easily transfer reasoning patterns from one context to another. One example of the way that pupils are encouraged to reflect on their thinking process in this material occurs in an activity on classification. This is the last activity of a set of simple classification exercises in which students have put animals into groups (according to their own criteria), arranged a variety of foodstuffs on the shelves of a larder, sorted some chemicals two ways (by color and by solubility), and so on. Now they are asked to consider the classifications that they have done, and to reflect on which was the most difficult for them, and why, and which was the easiest, and why. Furthermore, they compare their feelings about which was difficult, and so forth, with other groups, and discuss why some groups found some activities difficult and others found the same ones easy. In this way, students become accustomed to reflecting on the sort of thinking they have been engaged in, to bring it to the front of their consciousness, and to make of it an explicit tool that is then more likely to be available for use in a new context.

In the in-service training workshops and on-service visits to schools, a classroom atmosphere was encouraged in which students talked to each other about how they solved problems. "What were you thinking about when you did that? How did you get that answer?" "Ask Susan over there, she seems to have a different way of doing it," and so on.

Such reflection on their own problem solving processes is crystalized by the use of appropriate terminology. Thus very early in the program students become familiar with terms such as *variable*, and *relations between variables*. Later, they learn to recognize a proportionality problem, and to use the word *proportionality* in describing it and similar problems. This is a specialist application of what Vygotsky (1978) describes as the use of language as a mediator of learning. The language of reasoning mediates metalearning. Recognizing a problem as "proportionality" or "classification" in one context is the essential precursor to recognizing those types of problems in all contexts, which in turn is a necessary precursor to solving them. The explicit bridging to other contexts is the final aspect of this chain of developing, abstracting, and generalizing reasoning.

Details of the results are available elsewhere (Adey & Shayer, 1990; Shayer & Adey, 1992), but a brief summary will be given here. The experimental trial of the materials may be represented on a timeline.

**Sept 1985    July 1986    July 1987    July 1988    July 1989**
←period of CASE intervention→

|═════════|═════════|─────────|─────────|

Pupils'   12+          13+          14+          15+
  age:

Tests: **Pretest          Post tests      Delayed post tests  GCSE**

Nine classes in eight schools completed the program presented in the preceding. These classes were taught CASE lessons (Adey, Shayer, & Yates, 1989) at the rate of one every two weeks instead of a regular science lesson, for a period of two years. In each school, matched control classes were identified that did not use CASE lessons.

The pretest was a measure of cognitive development (Science Reasoning Tasks, Shayer et al., 1978). Parallel measures were applied at the posttest and delayed posttest points, immediately after and one year after the end of the intervention period, respectively. At these points we also obtained measures of the students' achievement in science, and at the delayed posttest point, of their achievement in mathematics and a foreign language as well. The GCSE is the General Certificate of Secondary Education, a public, externally set examination taken by the great majority of 16-year-olds in Britain. We looked particularly at GCSE results in science, mathematics, and English.

Of these measures, the ones where the experimental group made significant gains over the control group were

the posttests of cognitive development;
the delayed posttest of science achievement; and
GCSE science, mathematics, and English.

Of these, the first is the minimum signal of success of the program that one would hope to achieve. That there was no gain in science achievement immediately after the intervention, but that such a gain appeared one year later, may be explained in two ways. First, the experimentals lost 25% of their regular science curriculum time during the intervention period, so the fact that they did no worse than the controls at science achievement may be taken as a positive sign. Second, if children are taught how to learn, then results cannot be expected to occur exactly in parallel with the intervention process. In other words, if through some intervention program success in promoting students' ability to comprehend and learn new material is achieved, it is not until the intervention has been concluded and its effect has reached its maximum that there is any point in starting to observe the subjects' capacity for learning new material.

The gains in science GCSE grades by those who, two years previously, had concluded the *Thinking Science* programme is impressive evidence of the longevity of its effects, but can still be interpreted in terms of the development of domain-specific thinking strategies. However, the fact that the experimental group also performed significantly better in mathematics, and especially in English, argues for a far more general effect of the intervention program on the thinking skills of the learners. This looks like the holy grail of cognitive psychologists: long-term far transfer.

## CONCLUSION

The problem that remains is that of ascribing the effect found to the development of metacognition, rather than to any of the other features that formed the foundation of the Thinking Science activities outlined in the first section of this chapter. This is impossible. The data do not permit being certain what proportion each of the features contributed to the overall effect. Perceptual readiness is more in the nature of preparatory work for the potentially "accelerating" features, and bridging is a mechanism for transferring general thinking skills now developed to new contexts. It can be proposed further that concentration on the schema of formal operations simply provides a context within which the "accelerating" mechanisms may operate. However, both cognitive conflict and metacognition remain as candidates for the honor of being the most effective mechanism for bringing about the development of thinking skills that can be generalized to learning in a wide variety of domains. In the end, the nature of this study, as a pragmatic, large-scale empirical experiment intended to improve the ability of average students in ordinary schools, rather than as a laboratory-based academic psychological one, must be recognized. In such a study, a successful outcome may be welcomed in its own right, even if it is not clear just how that outcome was achieved.

## REFERENCES

Adey, P. S. (1988). Cognitve acceleration—review and prospects. *International Journal of Science Education, 10* (2), 121–134.

Adey, P. S., & Shayer, M. (1990). Accelerating the development of formal thinking in middle and high school students. *Journal of Research in Science Teaching, 27* (3), 267–285.

Adey, P. S., Shayer, M., & Yates C. (1989). *Thinking science: The curriculum materials of the CASE project.* Basingstoke: Macmillan.

Champagne, A. B., Gunstone, R. F., & Klopfer, L. (1985). Effecting changes in cognitive structures among physics students. In L. H. T. West & A. L. Pines (Eds.), *Cognitive structure and conceptual change.* Orlando, FL: Academic Press.

Goossens, L. (1989, September). Training scientific reasoning in children and adolescents: a critical review and quantitative integration. Paper presented at Third European Conference for Research on Learning and Instruction, Madrid.

Larkin, J., McDermott, J., Simon, D. P., & Simon, H. A. (1980). Expert and novice performance in solving physics problems. *Science, 208,* 1335–1342

Nickerson R. S., Perkins, D. N., & Smith, E. E. (1985). *The teaching of thinking.* Hillsdale, New Jersey: Erlbaum.

Perkins, D. N., & Salomon, G. (1989). Are cognitive skills context-bound? *Educational Researcher, 18* (1), 16–25.

Shayer, M., & Adey, P. S. (1981). *Towards a science of teaching.* London: Heinemann Educational Books.

Shayer, M., & Adey, P. (1992). Accelerating the development of formal thinking in middle and high school students II: post-project effects on science achievement. *Journal of Research in Science Teaching 1, 29,* 81–92.

Shayer, M., Wylam, H., Küchemann, D. E., Adey, P. S., Yates, C., & Bond, T. (1978). *CSMS Science Reasoning Tasks.* Slough: NFE.

Sternberg, R. J. (1985). *Beyond IQ: a triarchic theory of intelligence.* Cambridge, Cambridge University Press.

Vygotsky, L. S. (1978). *Mind in society.* Cambridge, MA: Harvard University Press.

# 11

## The Structure of Cognitive Abilities in Highly and Moderately Gifted Young People

**Karl Steffens**

*University of Cologne, Cologne, Germany*

**Christoph Perleth**

*Ludwig Maximilians University of Munich, Munich, Germany*

In order to assess the structure of cognitive abilities in highly and moderately gifted young people, data from the Munich Longitudinal Study of Giftedness were analyzed by conventional factor analysis. In the total group as well as in the subsample of the moderately gifted, a three-factor solution was obtained that subsequently was confirmed by a LISREL analysis of the same data. In the subsample of the highly gifted, a two-factor solution was obtained by conventional factor analysis and confirmed by a LISREL analysis. Contrary to the opinion voiced in the statistical literature that in groups formed on the basis of some cutoff value the reduced variances and covariances will lead to factorial artifacts, we argue that the factors obtained can be interpreted meaningfully. We were also able to predict, on the basis of the two-factor solution, the occurrence of specific types of highly gifted youths.

## INTRODUCTION

This chapter presents some results on the factor structure of cognitive abilities in highly and moderately gifted youths. As a measure of cognitive abilities the *Kognitiver Fähigkeitstest* (KFT—Cognitive Abilities Test) was used, an intelligence test developed by Heller, Gaedike, and Weinländer (1985) on the basis of the Thorndike Cognitive Abilities Test. The test is made up of 11 subtests that are classified into three test parts: verbal (V), quantitative (Q), and nonverbal (N) (see Table 11-1). The KFT responses being factor analyzed in our study were taken from a larger set of data collected in the context of the Munich Longitudinal Study of Giftedness (see, e.g., Heller & Hany, 1986). This study was initiated by Heller in 1985 and aims at

> developing adequate instruments for identifying gifted youths;
> making explicit the determinants of their scholastic achievement; and
> observing them grow over a period of three (and possibly more) years.

To identify the highly gifted youths, a three step screening procedure was employed (see Figure 11-1).

In the first phase, random samples of about 5000 students were taken from six different age cohorts. These were rated then by their teachers on the following five dimensions deemed to be relevant to the definition of high ability.

> intellectual abilities;
> creativity;
> social competence;
> artistic abilities; and
> psychomotor abilities.

In a third step, those students allocated to the top 10% by their teachers were give a large battery of tests, the results of

TABLE 11-1
Subtests of the Kognitiver Fähigkeitstest*

| Subtest Label | | Tapping Thurstone Factor (s) | |
|---|---|---|---|
| V1 | word meaning | V | verbal comprehension |
| V2 | sentence completion | V | verbal comprehension |
| V3 | word classification | V, R | verbal compr., reasoning |
| V4 | word analogies | V, R | verbal compr., reasoning |
| Q1 | math problems | R,V,N | reas., verb.compr., number |
| Q2 | comparing sets | N | number |
| Q3 | number series | R,N | reasoning, number |
| Q4 | constructing equations | N | number |
| N1 | classifying figures | R,S | number, space |
| N2 | symbolic analogies | R | reasoning |
| N3 | composing figures | S | space |

*Adapted from Heller et al., (1985).

which were used to select samples of highly and moderately gifted youths (with each $n$ approximately equal to 150) from each cohort (for details, see Heller & Hany, 1986). The total sample of 1313 then was divided into two parts: the lower 90% ($n = 1175$; moderately gifted) and the upper 10% ($n = 138$; highly gifted). In order to obtain a sample of moderately gifted comparable in size to that of the highly gifted, we drew a random sample from the lower 90% that yielded a subsample of 115 moderately gifted youngsters (see Table 11-2 for means and standard deviations in each subsample).

In order to explore the cognitive structure of the highly and moderately gifted youths, we took the KFT responses from the 1974 cohort. In the Munich study the KFT was given in two parallel forms, both as short versions that included the subtests V1, V2, Q2, Q4, N1, and N2. Since the two KFT forms differ in item difficulty, the responses were transformed into z-scores separately before being analyzed. The respective correlation matrices show that the KFT subtests correlated substantially in the total as well as in the subsample of the moderately gifted (see Table 11-3).

## THE FACTOR ANALYSIS

One of the customary ways of exploring people's cognitive structures is by means of factor analysis. Analyses of KFT re-

FIGURE 11-1.   Screening procedure for the identification of highly gifted youth (from Heller & Hany, 1986).

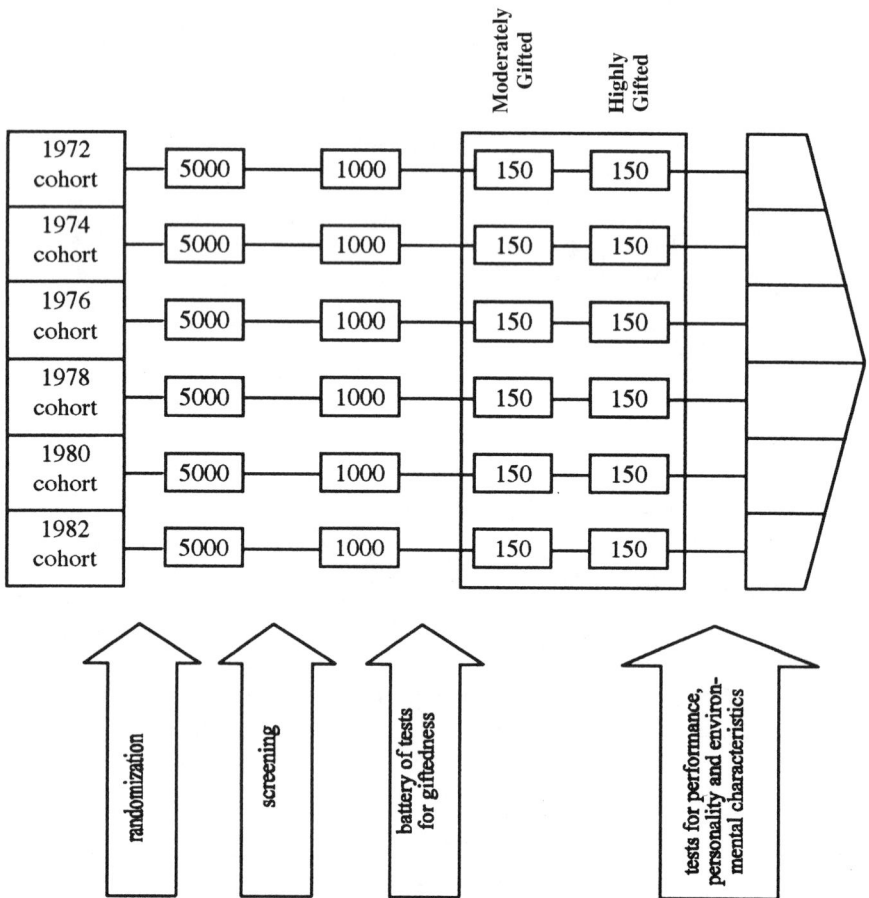

sponses usually yield a neat three-factor solution if one of the more common procedures (principal axis factor analysis followed by varimax rotation, e.g.) is employed, with the subtests of each test part loading on a different factor (see, e.g., Steffens, Hospelt, & Heller, 1983). The same applies to our data: In the total sample as well as in the subsample of the moderately gifted, the order of the eigenvalues of the corresponding correlation matrix suggests a three-factor solution (see Table 11-4).

In recent years it has become possible to test statistically the hypothesis that the obtained factor structure is in accordance with the data. To be more specific, one can test the hypothesis

TABLE 11-2
Means (M) and Standard Deviations (SD)
in the Two Subsamples

| Subtest | Moderately Gifted | | Highly Gifted | |
|---|---|---|---|---|
|  | M | SD | M | SD |
| V1 | .026 | .940 | 1.160 | .521 |
| V2 | −.065 | .928 | 1.015 | .506 |
| Q2 | −.206 | .942 | 1.234 | .647 |
| Q4 | −.175 | .961 | 1.040 | .935 |
| N1 | −.260 | .998 | 1.001 | .391 |
| N2 | −.183 | 1.098 | .788 | .307 |

TABLE 11-3
KFT Intercorrelations

| Subtest | Total Sample | | | | | | Subsample of Moderately Gifted | | | | | |
|---|---|---|---|---|---|---|---|---|---|---|---|---|
| V1 | 1.00 | | | | | | 1.00 | | | | | |
| V2 | .68 | 1.00 | | | | | .66 | 1.00 | | | | |
| Q2 | .48 | .44 | 1.00 | | | | .38 | .30 | 1.00 | | | |
| Q4 | .27 | .25 | .47 | 1.00 | | | .13 | .19 | .41 | 1.00 | | |
| N1 | .35 | .34 | .33 | .28 | 1.00 | | .29 | .32 | .20 | .18 | 1.00 | |
| N2 | .41 | .44 | .45 | .32 | .52 | 1.00 | .44 | .51 | .39 | .25 | .47 | 1.00 |

TABLE 11-4
Three-Factor Solution for Total and Subsample
of Moderately Gifted

| Subtest | Total Sample | | | Subsample of Moderately Gifted | | |
|---|---|---|---|---|---|---|
|  | F1 | F2 | F3 | F1 | F2 | F3 |
| V1 | .77 | .22 | .25 | .86 | .20 | .17 |
| V2 | .75 | .26 | .19 | .64 | .38 | .15 |
| Q2 | .33 | .22 | .69 | .25 | .13 | .75 |
| Q4 | .11 | .22 | .55 | .03 | .17 | .50 |
| N1 | .19 | .63 | .20 | .17 | .65 | .13 |
| N2 | .27 | .65 | .30 | .31 | .69 | .28 |

that the correlation matrix reproduced by the parameters of the
model (i.e., factor loadings, communalities, and, possibly, factor
correlations) is identical with the original correlation matrix.
With this kind of factor analysis, that is, confirmatory factor
analysis as opposed to exploratory factor analysis of the more

conventional type, it is possible to estimate the parameters of the model by maximum likelihood or some alternate method and fix one or more parameters to some specific value (e.g., set a factor loading equal to zero). This is quite meaningful, since factor analytic results are usually interpreted by looking for the highest loading of each variable and ignoring the other loadings (thereby implicitly setting these equal to zero). A confirmatory factor analysis will indicate whether this is an admissible procedure or not. This kind of factor analysis can be carried out elegantly with the LISREL program developed by Joereskog and Soerbom (1984), which, by the way, does not exhaust all of LISREL's many possibilities. The equality of the original and the reproduced correlation matrix may then be tested using a Chi-Square test (minimum of the fitting function times $n - 1$). Goodness of fit (GFI) indices also are calculated—these may be interpreted as measures of variance accounted for.

In the case of our data, we were able to confirm the three factor solutions obtained by exploratory factor analytic methods (cf., Table 11-5). The Chi-square value for the total sample is significant (Chi-square = 27.3; $df$ = 6; p < .01; goodness of fit = .99), but this is not surprising, considering that this value is obtained by multiplying the minimum value of the fitting function by $n - 1$. With a sample of 1313 every model but a perfect one will yield a significant Chi-Square value. The Chi-square value for the subsample of the moderately gifted is far from sig-

TABLE 11-5
LISREL Three-Factor Solution for Total and Subsample
of Moderately Gifted

| Subtest | Total Sample | | | Sample of Moderately Gifted | | |
|---|---|---|---|---|---|---|
| E | E1 | E2 | E3 | E1 | E2 | E3 |
| V1 | .84 | .00 | .00 | .78 | .00 | .00 |
| V2 | .82 | .00 | .00 | .84 | .00 | .00 |
| Q2 | .00 | .00 | .85 | .00 | .00 | .83 |
| Q4 | .00 | .00 | .55 | .00 | .00 | .50 |
| N1 | .00 | .64 | .00 | .00 | .54 | .00 |
| N2 | .00 | .81 | .00 | .00 | .88 | .00 |
| **Factor Correlations** | E1 | E2 | E3 | E1 | E2 | E3 |
| E1 | 1.00 | | | 1.00 | | |
| E2 | .64 | 1.00 | | .67 | 1.00 | |
| E3 | .64 | .65 | 1.00 | .48 | .54 | 1.00 |

nificant (Chi-square = 5.7; *df* = 6; *p* = .46; goodness of fit = .98), and the goodness of fit measures are quite acceptable in both cases. We did, however, have to allow the factors to correlate, which indicates that the model might be elaborated by implementing a second-order factor.

## THE PROBLEM OF COMPENSATORY COVARIANCE

These results are not unexpected. They say nothing, however, about the structure of cognitive abilities in the highly gifted. Our gifted sample consisted of students whose total KFT score (summed over the six KFT subtests) lay above a 90% cutoff value. What will happen to the variances and covariances of the KFT subtests in this group? We would expect the standard deviations and the correlations among the subtests in the subsample to differ from the corresponding standard deviations and correlations in the total sample: The subsample variances will be smaller and the subsample correlations will be negative. This phenomenon becomes understandable if we think about how people are selected for the high group: They will either have high scores in all subtests, or high scores in one or more and lower scores in others, that is, a low test score in one or more subtests will be compensated for by a high score in others, thus yielding negative or compensatory covariance between subtests (cf., Kalveram, 1969, 1970; Stelz, 1982).

This is exactly what happened to the covariances between the KFT subtests in our subsample of the highly gifted: Most of the corresponding correlations were negative, and the standard deviations were, of course, smaller than their counterparts in the total sample (see Table 11-6). It is not difficult to imagine that a factor structure different from what we have seen up to now would be yielded by these correlations. This is indeed the case, and it remains to be seen whether it is an artifact, as is claimed in the relevant literature, or whether the factor structure obtained from the group of the highly gifted can be interpreted, and whether there are means of validating this interpretation.

The order of the eigenvalues of the correlation matrix given in Table 11-6 suggests a two-factor solution. An exploratory factor solution (principal axis factor analysis followed by varimax rotation) is given in Table 11-7, along with the corresponding LISREL estimates. Again, the confirmatory factor analysis done with the LISREL program substantiates our exploratory findings,

TABLE 11-6
Means, Standard Deviations and Correlations in the Subsample
of the Highly Gifted

| Subtest | M | SD | Correlations | | | | | |
|---------|------|-----|------|------|------|------|------|------|
| V1 | 1.16 | .52 | 1.00 | | | | | |
| V2 | 1.02 | .51 | .26 | 1.00 | | | | |
| Q2 | 1.23 | .65 | −.01 | −.05 | 1.00 | | | |
| Q4 | 1.04 | .93 | −.28 | −.26 | .06 | 1.00 | | |
| N1 | 1.01 | .39 | −.14 | .03 | −.20 | −.05 | 1.00 | |
| N2 | .79 | .31 | −.17 | −.23 | .08 | .11 | −.02 | 1.00 |

TABLE 11-7
Two-Factor Solution for the Subsample
of the Highly Gifted

| | Exploratory FA (PAFA and Varimax) | | Confirmatory FA (LISREL) | |
|---------|------|------|------|------|
| Subtest | F1 | F2 | E1 | E2 |
| V1 | .56 | −.17 | .52 | .00 |
| V2 | .54 | .08 | .55 | .00 |
| Q2 | −.09 | −.32 | .00 | .86 |
| Q4 | −.47 | −.09 | −.48 | .00 |
| N1 | −.05 | .64 | .00 | −.23 |
| N2 | −.33 | −.08 | −.34 | .00 |

although the Chi-square value was not significant (Chi-square = 7.2; $df$ = 9; $p$ = .62; goodness of fit = .98). To help the reader get a better idea of the factor analytic results, we have depicted the two-factor solution as a configuration of points (the KFT subtests) in a two-dimensional (factor) space (see Figure 11-2).

Our interpretation of the two axes (factors) is based on our understanding of what kind of problem solving might be used by the highly gifted when responding to the KFT items. It seems to us that the two verbal subtests V1 and V2 require more of some kind of specific (knowledge-based) problem solving, whereas subtests Q4 and N2 may activate more general problem-solving tactics. This difference between specific and general problem solving bears some resemblance to Cattell's distinction between crystallized and fluid intelligence: N1 at the one end of the second axis may measure productive thinking, in contrast to Q2, which probably taps productive thinking. This is certainly reminiscent of Guilford's classification of mental operations, which includes the distinction between divergent and convergent thinking.

FIGURE 11-2.    Graph of the two-factor solution for the highly gifted.

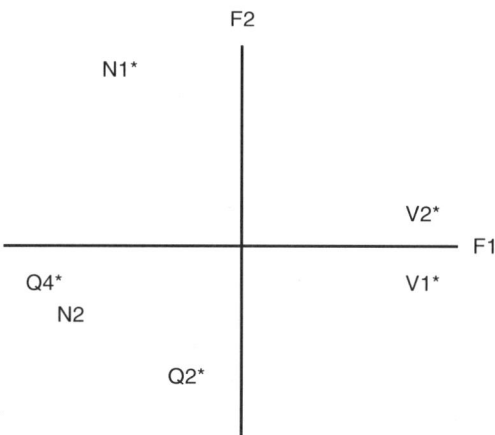

The question now is whether there is any evidence in support of our interpretation. In the final section of this chapter we will suggest an indirect way of validating our conclusions concerning the factor structure of the highly gifted.

## FACTOR STRUCTURE AND TYPES OF HIGHLY GIFTED YOUTHS

Looking at the graphical representation of the two-factor solution, we see that the KFT subtests form a number of groups or clusters. It follows from this specific configuration of subtests that there must also be a number of different groups or types of highly gifted subjects. Obviously, N1 and Q2 belong together, in the sense that they both have high loadings on the second factor. Their loadings are, however, of opposite signs, that is, their relation is a compensatory one. We should, therefore, have people in our sample who obtained high scores on N1 and low scores on Q2 (type 1) and vice versa (type 2). N1 and Q2 are independent of the other subtests. There, we find V1 and V2 in one cluster and Q4 and N2 in another, that is, the relation of V1 and V2 is a conjunctive one, as is that of Q4 and N2. The relationship between V1/V2 on the one hand and Q4/N2 on the other is, however, a compensatory one. Therefore we expect two other groups or types of highly gifted youngsters: those who score high on V1 and V2 but not on Q4 and N2 (type 3) and vice

TABLE 11-8
Expected Types of Highly Gifted Youths

|        | V1 | V2 | Q2 | Q4 | N1 | N2 |
|--------|----|----|----|----|----|----|
| Type 1 | —  | —  | 2  | —  | 1  | —  |
| Type 2 | —  | —  | 1  | —  | 2  | —  |
| Type 3 | 2  | 2  | —  | 1  | —  | 1  |
| Type 4 | 1  | 1  | —  | 2  | —  | 2  |

versa (type 4). If we let 2 denote a high score and 1 denote a low score, the four types we expect to show up among the highly gifted look like the ones depicted in Table 11-8.

In order to test our hypothesis concerning types of highly gifted, we transformed the KFT responses into binary data (below/above the subsample mean) and carried out configural frequencies analyses on these figures. Configural frequencies analysis (CFA) is a procedure developed by Lienert (cf., Krauth & Lienert, 1973; Lienert, 1988) to test whether one or more of the possible combinations of values of binary (or n-ary) variables occur in a given sample with a frequency significantly different from the expected frequency (i.e., given the interrelations between the variables as they are). Any such combination or configuration whose observed frequency differs significantly from its corresponding expected frequency constitutes a type, according to Lienert. In short, Lienert's configural frequencies analysis is a method for scanning the data for the existence of types of persons, each type being defined by a specific response pattern. There are numerous examples of fruitful applications of this method (cf., Lienert, 1988). We ourselves, for instance, applied CFA successfully to some of the teachers' ratings recorded in the context of the Munich Longitudinal Study to identify types of highly gifted youths (Steffens, 1989). The results of our first CFA done in the present study are given in Table 11-9. We selected the configurations with the highest Chi-square value, or, to be more specific, those configurations whose Chi-square values were statistically ($p = .05$) significant. For each configuration, the observed frequency $f_o$, the expected frequency $f_e$, the corresponding Chi-square value, its probability level $p$, and $\mathbf{Q}$, a measure of practical significance, is given.

In our opinion, the CFA results give substance to our claim that there are students of the type we postulated earlier. The first configuration—111212—for instance, is type 4 (V1/V2 vs Q4/N2), the second—221121—type 3. With this type, however,

TABLE 11-9
Configurations with the Highest Chi-Square Values

| Configuration | $f_o$ | $f_e$ | Chi-Square | $p$ | Q |
|---|---|---|---|---|---|
| 111212 | 5 | 1.49 | 8.22 | .004 | .026 |
| 221121 | 7 | 2.55 | 7.79 | .005 | .033 |
| 222111 | 6 | 2.33 | 5.77 | .016 | .027 |
| 221211 | 6 | 2.40 | 5.39 | .020 | .027 |

we also find the compensatory relation Q2 versus N1. Evidently the types we postulated can occur simultaneously. In order to clarify this issue we decided to form three classes of types, each class constituting an agglutinated type in the terminology of Lienert, that is, a composite of types or configurations (see Table 11-10).

The three agglutinated types are

Q2 versus N1 compensatory type (with V1/V2 and Q4/N2 in a conjunctive relation);

V1/V2 versus Q4/N2 compensatory type (with Q2 and N1 in a conjunctive relation); and

complex compensatory type (V1/V2 versus Q4/N2 and Q2 vs. N1).

It is the complex compensatory type that occurs with the highest frequency ($f_o$ = 21) in our subsample of highly gifted youths; the corresponding Chi-square value of 19.3 is (with four degrees of freedom) significant ($p$ < .001). A second type, the V1/V2 versus Q4/N2 compensatory type, can be observed also, but with a smaller frequency.

In conclusion, we find that there are students in our sub-sample of highly gifted youths who compensate for (relatively) low scores in a number of KFT subtests by achieving high scores in other subtests. This is, however, not done on a random basis; on the contrary, subtest specific abilities or problem-solving strategies are used in a conjunctive or compensatory manner in a way that we were able to predict from the results of our factor analyses. The results of the configural frequencies analysis serve at least partially to validate the factor analytic results. Notwithstanding these conclusions, our interpretation of the factor structure in the subsample of highly gifted youths is, no doubt, still amenable to more substantial forms of validation.

## TABLE 11-10
### Agglutinated Types

| | V1 | V2 | Q2 | Q4 | N1 | N2 | nc | fo | $\chi^2$ | p |
|---|---|---|---|---|---|---|---|---|---|---|
| **Q2 Versus N1 Compensatory Type** | | | | | | | | | | |
| Type 1 | — | — | 2 | — | 1 | — | 11 | 32 | 5.1 | n.s. |
| Type 2 | — | — | 1 | — | 2 | — | 14 | 32 | 11.2 | n.s. |
| | | | | | | | 25 | 64 | 16.3 | n.s. |
| **V1/V2 Versus Q4/N2 Compensatory Type** | | | | | | | | | | |
| Type 3 | 2 | 2 | — | 1 | — | 1 | 2 | 3 | 1.2 | n.s. |
| Type 4 | 1 | 1 | — | 2 | — | 1 | 2 | 8 | 8.7 | < .05 |
| | | | | | | | 4 | 11 | 9.9 | < .05 |
| **Complex Compensatory Type** | | | | | | | | | | |
| | 2 | 2 | 2 | 1 | 1 | 1 | 1 | 6 | 5.7 | < .05 |
| | 2 | 2 | 1 | 1 | 2 | 1 | 1 | 7 | 7.8 | < .05 |
| | 1 | 1 | 2 | 2 | 1 | 2 | 1 | 4 | 3.2 | n.s. |
| | 1 | 1 | 1 | 2 | 2 | 2 | 1 | 4 | 2.6 | n.s. |
| | | | | | | | 4 | 21 | 19.3 | < .001 |

# REFERENCES

Heller, K. A., Gaedike, A. K., & Weinländer, H. (1985). *Kognitiver Fähigkeitstest KFT4-13+.* Weinheim: Beltz.

Heller, K.,A., & Hany, E. (1986). Identification, development and analysis of talented and gifted children in West Germany. In Heller, K. A. & Feldhusen, J. F. (Eds.), *Identifying and nurturing the gifted* (pp. 67–82). Toronto: Huber.

Joereskog, K. G., & Soerbom, D. (1984). *LISREL IV. Analysis of linear structural relationships by the method of maximum likelihood.* Uppsala: University of Uppsala.

Kalveram, K. Th. (1969). Kompensatorische Kovarianz als Beispiel fuer einen Selektionseffekt. Oder: Wie man aus positiven Korrelationskoeffizienten negative macht. *Archiv für die gesamte Psychologie 121,* 255–265.

Kalveram, K. Th. (1970). Probleme der Selektion in der Faktorenanalyse. *Archiv für die gesamte Psychologie 122,* 223–230.

Krauth, J., & Lienert, G. A. (1983). *KFA. Die Konfigurationsfrequenzanalyse und ihre Anwendung in Psychologie und Medizin.* Freiburg: Alber.

Lienert, G. A. (Ed.). (1988). *Angewandte Konfigurationsfrequenzanalyse.* Frankfurt: Athenaeum.

Steffens, K. (1989). Zur typologischen Differenzierung Hochbegabter: Eine Konfigurationsanalyse auf der Basis von Lehrerurteilen. *Psychologie in Erziehung und Unterricht, 36,* 114–119.

Steffens, K., Hospelt, Ch., & Heller, K. A. (1983). Zur Faktorstruktur des KFT 4-13. Eine hypothesentestende Untersuchung unter Verwendung der konfirmatorischen Maximum Likelihood Faktorenanalyse. *Zeitschrift für Differentielle und Diagnostische Psychologie 4*, 149–162.

Stelz, I. (1982). *Fehler und Fallen in der Statistik.* Bern: Huber.

# 12

# Moral Reasoning in Gifted Adolescents

## Cognitive Level and Social Values

**Ornella Andreani Dentici**
**Adriano Pagnin**

*Istituto di Psicologia dell'Università, Pavia, Italy*

In a population of 1141 students attending the last year of secondary school (age 17–19) in three towns of North, Central, and Southern Italy, who were tested using four ability tests, we studied responses to six moral dilemmas, comparing subjects of low, average, and high ability by means of analysis of variance and cluster analysis. Two groups of very high (5% of the total sample) and extremely high (2%) students were individually interviewed in order to explore the motivation for their choices. The gifted showed, as expected, more responses at the formal level (greater choice of items concerning general and abstract principles, greater support for law and social contracts, more coherence), but in the average and lowest groups we found a more sentimental, humanitarian orientation, with a sympathetic attitude toward other people's feelings, which can constitute the base for a more intuitive, but not inferior morality.

## INTRODUCTION

Moral reasoning, as a part of social abilities, is an important but not as yet well studied component of abilities to be investigated in the gifted. Its importance is self-evident. From a cognitive point of view it is interesting to compare the sequence of stages in logical development with the stages in moral reasoning and the development of social cognitive processes in making moral evaluations; from the social educational point of view it is essential that the most intelligent people use their superior thinking capacity in making decisions, in behavior, in comprehending, interpreting, and anticipating the needs of other people.

The study of morality by psychologists may concern the area of thinking, behavior, and emotions (roughly, this division corresponds to the approaches of cognitive developmentalists, of social learning theorists, and of clinical psychologists and psychoanalysts). Our chapter refers to the first area. We assume that moral reasoning is an essentially cognitive ability, although it cannot be reduced to learning social standards or internalizing norms, because it is strictly connected with emotional (i.e., feelings of guilt) and behavioral (praise or punishment for actions) aspects. In this perspective, gifted children should have more opportunities to acquire and process relevant information and to restructure conceptions of social norms, as well as to justify them by reference to values. Superiority in reasoning abilities should correlate with superiority in moral reasoning, but, on the other hand, sensitivity to emotional stimuli and reactivity to environmental pressure might lead to development of a kind of moral reasoning based more on personal needs and values than on general, abstract principles.

Following Rest (1983), we distinguish between four major components of moral behavior.

1. interpreting the situation in terms of how people's welfare is affected by possible actions of the subject;
2. figuring out what the ideal moral course of action would be;
3. selecting among possible outcomes in deciding what is actually to be done; and
4. executing and implementing a plan of action.

In our research we have tried to explore the first three components, leaving the fourth for the future. The first two components are more strictly related to cognitive processes, because they require the capacity to interpret complex and novel situations, sensitivity to others' needs and welfare based on social cognition, anticipation of the consequences of actions, internalization of social norms (e.g., equity, reiciprocity, social responsibility), which regulate community life and coordinate the needs of different individuals in a general form.

We have made use of the model of moral development proposed by Kohlberg (1969), in which he hypothesized clearly differentiated stages of moral judgement structured in the same developmental sequence as intelligence operations: Each new stage employs more differentiated, reversible, and equilibrated operations, and has a higher degree of generality and abstraction. However, we used a procedure more similar to Rest's Defining Issues Test, because it takes into account criticism of employing an excessively strict stage model, the variability among subjects in the same stage, the influence of the content of problems, and so on. We were not interested in placing subjects in a definite stage, but in using Kohlbergian concepts as a grid for ordering and classifying moral expressions.

The objectives of the study reported here were as follows:

- to study the relationship between ability level and moral judgment;
- to compare gifted subjects with average and low intelli-gence subjects in strategies for solving moral problems; and
- to analyze the processes by which solutions to moral dilemmas are reached and the values that orient behavior.

## METHOD

We devised a test of moral judgment that presents six dilemmas focusing on values of human life and social norms. Dilemmas were preferred because they do not require a "correct" solution, but need a process of reasoning about a conflict between values or norms, as long as both are relevant for the subject. The problems concern three private and three public situations (abortion, euthanasia, embryo implants; kidnapping, racial prejudice, bribery). Each dilemma is followed by eight items, which present two prototype responses (opposite in value orientation) for each of four stages of moral development. We considered only four stages, excluding the two extreme stages (the lowest preconventional and the highest postconventional), as the lowest is less typical in subjects of the age we studied and the highest (stage 6 according to Kohlberg) is regarded as very rare by Kohlberg himself, and has been subjected to much criticism by many authors.

The stages considered were

- preconventional (Kohlberg's stages 1 and 2): the rule is a way to avoid punishment or harm and to satisfy one's needs and interests;
- lower conventional (Kohlberg's stage 3): the rule is a way to feel good and to meet expectations of the social group;
- higher conventional (Kohlberg's stage 4): the rule expresses the priority of a general social point of view and is considered as necessary, overcoming conformity to small group standards; and
- postconventional (Kohlberg's stages 5 and 6): the rule expresses a more abstract point of view, referring to meta-rules or abstract general principles to solve conflicts between specific different norms.

Subjects were asked to express their level of agreement on each item by using a five-point scale.

## Subjects

We examined 1141 students attending the last year of secondary school (aged 17–19), males and females, from middle-sized towns in three different areas of Italy (North, Central, and Southern Italy: Pavia, Siena, Salerno), and from three different types of school (Classical, Technical, and Professional) (see Tables 12-1 and 12-2).

In three sessions, four ability tests were administered to the subjects in order to measure verbal reasoning, abstract reasoning, mathematical reasoning, and semantic reasoning. In addition, the test of moral reasoning, referred to as the "Social Reasoning Test," was administered. On the basis of the results in the ability tests three groups of subjects were formed: low subjects (scored at less than the 25th percentile on at least three tests), average subjects (scored between the 25th and 75th percentiles on at least three tests), high subjects (scored higher than the 75th percentile on at least three tests).

### TABLE 12-1
### Sample by Sex and Town

| Town | Males | | Females | | Total | |
|---|---|---|---|---|---|---|
| | n | Percent | n | Percent | n | Percent |
| Pavia | 179 | 16 | 187 | 16 | 366 | 32 |
| Salerno | 274 | 24 | 224 | 20 | 498 | 44 |
| Siena | 158 | 14 | 119 | 10 | 277 | 24 |
| Total | 611 | 54 | 530 | 46 | 1141 | 100 |

### TABLE 12-2
### Sample by Schools

| School | Pavia | | Salerno | | Siena | | Total | |
|---|---|---|---|---|---|---|---|---|
| | n | Percent | n | Percent | n | Percent | n | Percent |
| Classical | 135 | 12 | 174 | 15 | 110 | 10 | 419 | 37 |
| Technical | 82 | 7 | 127 | 11 | 31 | 3 | 240 | 21 |
| Professional | 149 | 13 | 197 | 17 | 136 | 12 | 482 | 42 |
| Total | 366 | 32 | 498 | 44 | 277 | 24 | 1141 | 100 |

### TABLE 12-3
### Distribution of Subjects by Test Scores

| | Low | | | Medium | | | High | | |
|---|---|---|---|---|---|---|---|---|---|
| | Male | Female | Total | Male | Female | Total | Male | Female | Total |
| Pavia | 13 | 29 | 42 | 59 | 49 | 108 | 51 | 28 | 79 |
| Salerno | 27 | 63 | 90 | 72 | 57 | 129 | 48 | 29 | 77 |
| Siena | 14 | 7 | 21 | 49 | 47 | 96 | 33 | 30 | 63 |
| Total | 54 | 99 | 153 | 180 | 153 | 333 | 132 | 87 | 219 |

Finally two extreme groups were constructed: very high subjects, who scored higher than the 90th percentile on at least three tests (63 subjects, corresponding to about 5% of the total sample) and extremely high subjects, who scored higher than the 90th percentile on all four tests (23 subjects, corresponding to about 2% of the total sample). The selected subjects were more generally gifted than students with specific talents. Most of them attended classical schools (Lyceum), although some attended technical schools. There was a significant prevalence of males. In the final step, 15 very high subjects and 10 medium and low subjects were interviewed in depth. The same dilemmas and the same prototypical answers were used as initial stimuli, but the motivation for choices was explored and discussed.

## Analysis

Differences between groups were analyzed by analysis of variance, taking as factors level of ability, sex, and town. Hierarchical cluster analysis was then performed on the total sample and on selected groups, because of the interest in empirical grouping of the items, apart from the classification in Kohlbergian stages. Qualitative analyses of individual interviews were carried out by means of content analysis.

## RESULTS

### Differences by Sex and Town

There were significant differences between the sexes and among towns, which showed that level and type of response are not only related to the level of ability of individuals, but are also influenced by group and cultural values. In fact, the differences can be referred to as involving a general way of facing the specific contents of dilemmas in the two sexes and in the different towns. In females there was a more marked defence of life values, as indicated by much stronger opposition to abortion (dilemma 1) and much stronger defense of a hostage's life (dilemma 2). There was also stronger respect for civil rights as seen in stronger opposition to racism (dilemma 5) and stronger opposition to bribery (dilemma 6). In males, by contrast, there was a "harder" trend in defence of their own rights, both individually, as they were more favorable to abortion, especially if the fetus was seen as an obstacle to personal development (dilemma 1) and also socially, as they were more inclined to favor strict intervention against criminals, even if this were harmful to an innocent person (dilemma 2). There was also a more realistic trend in the field of social conformity and economic interests as shown by less condemnation of racism when supported by economic considerations (dilemma 5), and less condemnation of bribery, if this were seen as necessary (dilemma 6).

There were also significant differences by geographic area. In the Southern sample (Salerno) there was a more negative orientation toward abortion (dilemma 1), greater concern about other people's judgment, and a stronger view of bribery as inevitable (dilemma 6). By contrast, less conservative trends were found in Siena, a mostly left-wing town in political terms. For instance, there was defense of the right to abortion (dilemma 1) and defense of the right to individual choice in euthanasia (dilemma 4).

## Cross Comparisons between Levels of Ability

There was a clear response set of agreement among low ability subjects, a state of affairs that influences the appearance of the results: on most items low ability subjects scored higher than high subjects. In spite of this, however, clear differences emerged between low–average subjects and high–very high subjects according to the contents of dilemmas and to the levels of moral judgment. With regard to contents, low and average subjects showed a more "sentimental humanitarian" orientation, according to which common feelings and traditional roles were supported. For instance, there was stronger objection to abortion (dilemma 1), stronger objection to police intervention in case of risk to the hostage's life (dilemma 2), and a more favorable outlook on "natural" rights and duties of the mother in the story about the embryo transplant (dilemma 3). Greater importance was given to other people's opinions as in family opinion and people's opinions in the story on euthanasia (dilemma 4), people's attitudes in the story on racial prejudice (dilemma 5), and the common situation in the story on bribery (dilemma 6). In terms of formal levels, such subjects showed high approval of items concerning practical issues and immediate benefits, which can be classified as preconventional in the Kohlbergian sense (see e.g., dilemma 4), higher approval of items relating to social roles (i.e., as mother) and to the search for people's approval, which can be classified as lower conventional in the Kohlbergian sense.

In the selected samples, by contrast ("very high" and "extremely high" subjects) there was greater agreement on items concerning individual rights, as shown by acceptance of abortion (dilemma 1) and support of the right to decide about one's own life in the story on euthanasia (dilemma 4), greater support for social rights as defined by laws or contracts, including higher approval of police intervention against criminals, even if risky as in the story on kidnapping (dilemma 2), and greater stress on the importance of keeping a contract voluntarily signed in the story about the embryo transplant (dilemma 3), and greater choice of items concerning general and abstract principles as criteria for approving–disapproving of actions, particularly in the euthanasia story, the racial prejudice story, and the bribery story.

In terms of formal levels, such subjects displayed higher approval of items concerning abstract and general principles, which can be classified as postconventional in the Kohlbergian sense, and higher approval of items concerning respect for law and contracts, which can be classified as advanced conventional in the Kohlbergian sense.

## Dimensions of Moral Judgment

Further analysis (multivariate) showed that the subjects' answers could be organized into clusters that did not coincide with formal levels alone, but combined content and formal aspects. There was a basic stability in such clustering, both in the total sample and in its main sections. The main clusters into which the items were divided involved human rights and a humanitarian orientation, with many high-level items (advanced conventional, post-conventional) being present, defense of the law or approach to the law, with conventional items being present, defense of personal benefits and avoidance of personal risk of punishment, with many low-level items (preconventional or lower conventional) being present.

Beyond this basic structure, specific characteristics could be found in the clustering of the highest subjects, compared with the lowest ones. In the "very high" subjects the first cluster ("human rights") was characterized mainly by postconventional and advanced conventional items, concerning general principles of social life. The second cluster ("legal rights") emphasized both social and economic individual rights, and the third cluster ("immediate benefit") combined personal utility with other people's agreement, being totally defined by preconventional and lower conventional items. The items against abortion fell into a separate cluster: They defined a specific moral area (possibly a religious one), different from general principles and human rights.

In the "low" subjects, by contrast, the first cluster was defined as "sentimental humanitarism," as it consisted of items from all levels, emphasizing not only problems of "right," but also common feelings; in this cluster items against abortion are also included, in particular, the ones that focus on mainly emotional aspects. The cluster seems to be more affective than formal. The second cluster combined the defense of individual interests with freedom of choice in problems of life: Freedom is not part of general human rights, but a personal right. The third cluster, "immediate benefit," combined avoiding punishment and willingness to accept people's opinion with pro-abortion items: in particular, the ones that focus on utility aspects, where abortion is not seen as a problem of "right," but as a reaction to an obstacle. The fourth cluster, "defense of order," involved agreement with police intervention against criminals, and is different from other problems of respect for the law. The fifth cluster, "a mother's feelings," is related specifically to the story about the embryo transplant, and concerns the items that support the traditional role of the mother. From our data, it seems that a clear distinction between formal levels of judgment can be found only among higher subjects, whereas more pragmatic and content centered trends prevail in lower subjects.

## Individual Interviews

Individual interviews were carried out to investigate how subjects cope with the task of giving judgements on the dilemmas. The qualitative analysis of the material identified two main tendencies, which confirm and clearly state the previous results.

> Answers are organized according to a small number of basic orientations, selected in relation to the general value issues elicited by the contents of the stories.
> Such basic trends are quite different in high ability subjects than among average and low ability subjects. In average and low ability subjects humanitarian feelings and sensitivity to a specific human situation were found, but there was little attention to general principles and little sensitivity to logical coherence, as well as avoidance of the most critical aspects of dilemmas, and a reduction of these to conventional references (even if contradictory). In the highest ability subjects there was attention to coherence in reasoning, reference to general principles, discussed in relation to the specific aspects of the dilemmas, and an attempt to agree on such principles, based on values–ideologies reconciled with personal interests and need for achievement. This latter was seen, for instance, in rejection of abortion (because of reli-

gious values), reformulation of achievement in terms of
personal maturity (dilemma 1) or in rejection of racial
discrimination, but analysis of the story in terms of the
economic efficacy of the choices (dilemma 5), or finally
in rejection of bribery, but differentiation between ideal
values and practical, unfair reality.

In addition, in the highest ability subjects some logical
"routes" clearly emerged, including a *value-centered approach*
in which the story is first analyzed by deciding what kind of values are central and primary: pragmatic economy, efficacy—typical of the "public" stories—or ethical life, freedom—typical of the
"private" stories. In the story of the embryo transplant, for instance, "to give one's own body is prostitution," and consequently the woman is condemned; in the story on abortion, professional achievement is contrasted with the importance of being
parents and living according to life-oriented values, even in times
of trouble, and abortion is rejected as a responsible choice; in
the story on euthanasia, compromise is seen as unacceptable.

According to the *role-centered orientation*, the story is analyzed deciding first of all which point of view is to be assumed.
This may imply a refusal to make judgments, on the grounds
that what is right differs according to different roles: For instance, in the story on kidnapping, it is maintained that the
roles and duties of the hostage's family differ from those of the
authorities. This may lead to a "relative" judgment, choosing
the role with which it is easier to identify oneself; as, for instance, the physician or the patient in the euthanasia story. In
the *logic-centered approach* the story is analyzed by looking for
a hierarchical order in the justification of actions. There is
greater attention to the formal aspects of stories and items, and
less to value aspects. The choices are according to their justifications and there is a search for logically necessary ties. In
the kidnapping story, for instance, the decision of the police is
necessarily tied to not letting the crime go unpunished, or, in
the story on racial prejudice, the defense of economic rights is
seen as not necessarily tied to a defense of discrimination.

## CONCLUSIONS

The results, drawn both from quantitative and qualitative data,
suggest a two-level model of moral judgment.

A more intuitive one, typical of average and low subjects, in which some basic principles and immediate feelings are applied to situations, with few problems of coherence and justification. "Common" morals are applied to many everyday life events. These are largely traditional and linked to social consensus. There is little search for logical foundations, although the presence of contrasts or contradictions leaves space for individual adaptation.

A more formal one, typical of the highest ability subjects, in which there is a search for coherence and justification. Judgments are organized by levels very near to those proposed by Kohlberg. Situations are analyzed carefully, and various general principles are applied. Intuitive judgments are present, but these are harmonized with the specific aspects of situations and other principles. There is recourse to strategies in connecting different principles to each other, and in combining concrete needs with principles. There is a precise attempt to defend personal interests without leaving the area of moral judgment, and to find justifications not inconsistent with general principles. This may lead not only to more intellectual and verbal sophistication of judgment, but also to attempts to find new orientations yielding greater coherence between principles and actions.

Both levels can lead to moral behavior, but they present different dangers.

The intuitive level may lead to opportunistic, utilitarian judgments, and is unreliable because it is based on emotional, sympathetic attitudes that may be biased by prejudice or personal relationships.

The formal level may be founded on ideological premises (or even religious) and may sometimes be a rationalization of indifference and cruelty (see revolutions, Holy Inquisition).

The type of moral reasoning of the gifted is not necessarily to be seen as yielding "better" personal and social consequences: In fact, greater logical coherence of the gifted may lead to greater flexibility and innovation in morals and in social behaviors prior to social and ideological transformations, but often it can neglect the immediate feelings and moral inhibitions that usually control everyday life behaviors in common people in a fairly acceptable way.

## REFERENCES

Kohlberg, L. (1969). Stage and sequence: the cognitive developmental approach to socialization. In D. A. Goslin (Ed.), *Handbook of socialization: theory and research.* Chicago: Rand McNally.

Rest, J. (1983). Moral development. In P. Mussen (Ed.), *Handbook of child psychology, vol. 3.* New York: Wiley.

# 13

# Problem Finding

## Discovering and Formulating Problems

**Gerard M. Brugman**

*Rijksuniversiteit Utrecht, Utrecht, The Netherlands*

Research and theory on problem finding are scarce. This can be ascribed to difficulties in the operationalization of the concept and to neglect of the importance of this essential link in the problem-solving cycle. A similar lacuna, however, is not found in early research in the field of problem solving. In problem solving four types of components can be distinguished: cognitive (sensitivity to problems and formulating the problem), motivational (effectance motivation and curiosity), emotional (wonder and surprise) and, finally, personality components (tolerance for ambiguity, stimulus reduction, and self-confidence). Selective encoding, combining, and comparing can be regarded as essential elements of the cognitive component. With respect to the developmental aspects of problem finding, emphasis is laid on the importance of competence motivation and the quality of attachment as determinants. The educational implications are unequivocal: Problem solving and problem finding must have equal positions in curricula. For the time being this means that education will have to pay more attention to problem finding.

## HISTORICAL OUTLINE

Although there appears to be growing interest in problem finding at the moment (Dillon, 1982; Gardner, 1984; Getzels & Csikszentmihalyi, 1976; Perkins, 1981; Sternberg, 1984), this is a revival: The traditional researchers in the field (Claparède, 1933; Dewey, 1933; Rossman, 1931) paid considerable attention to the phase preceding the solving of a problem. Dewey (1933), for example, recognized two steps in the problem-solving cycle: (1) a state of doubt, cognitive confusion, frustration, or awareness of the problem; and (2) an attempt to identify the problem, involving a global definition of the aims to be achieved and the gap to be bridged in the particular problem situation. The term "problem situation," by the way, might be considered a forerunner of the concept "problem space," which was introduced by Newell and Simon (1972) in the 1970s. Somewhat less explicit, although clearly present, problem finding appears in Wallas' (1926) widely known quadripartite division of the (creative) problem-solving process: (1) preparation; (2) incubation; (3) illumination; and (4) verification. In elucidating the first step, Wallas stated that no definite answer can be expected to any problem unless it is clearly formulated in advance. Discovering and solving are the poles of one and the same continuum. Nevertheless, problem solving has received virtually all the attention of researchers, and research and development of theories in the field of problem discovering are extremely scarce.

Two exceptions, however, ought to be mentioned: Guilford and Torrance. Guilford's general problem-solving model (1977) contains the constituent processes "activation of attention" and "problem sensitivity and structuring." In his Structure-of-Intellect model the factor CMI (Cognition of Semantic Implications) is referred to as the "sensitivity to problems" factor. Torrance, who has been active in the field of creative thinking since the early 1960s did not direct all his attention to just one pole of the problem-solving cycle, judging by his description (Torrance, 1962) of creative thinking as involving "sensing gaps."

In the majority of studies, however, the traditional starting point for research is the given problem. It is true that Newell and Simon (1972), in their standard work on problem solving, devoted space to an orientation phase in the problem-solving process; however, this phase involved orienting processes with regard to a certain problem. One explanation for this lacuna in the research tradition or, in other words, the unilateral interest despite the good example set by the early cognitive psychologists, might be found in the fact that problem finding is a phenomenon that is difficult to come to grips with in research. The same is true for other equally intangible factors in the field of creative thinking, such as "illumination," "intimation," "intuition," "inspiration," and "incubation." These phenomena, however, are not totally intangible. Olton (1979), for example, carried out an ingeniously designed experiment on "incubation." It requires the necessary inventiveness to operationalize these factors that are as important as they are intangible. Getzels and Csikszentmihalyi (1976) attempted to measure problem finding in art students—this study will be discussed further in a later paragraph. A second possible reason for the lack of studies and theory development on problem finding might be found in educational practice: Education has been—and in most cases still is—aimed at the teaching of problem solving. It will, therefore, be no surprise that researchers have concentrated on this educational aim. On the other hand, problem finding is regarded as essential for progress by those who practice science themselves. Einstein, for instance, wrote:

> The formulation of a problem is often more important than its solution, which may be merely a matter of mathematical or experimental skill. To raise new questions, new possibilities, to regard old problems from a new angle, requires imagination, and marks real advance in science (see Zuckerman, 1983, p. 241).

Mackworth (1965) moved one step ahead by arguing that scientific progress is no more than a function of the ability to formulate new and verifiable ideas. Although this statement may sound too optimistic, researchers in the field of human cognition and education itself should take the tenor of Mackworth's statement to heart, particularly in view of the status Claparède (1933) assigned to problem finding, namely, that of the motor of the problem-solving process.

## PROBLEM FINDING

A common aspect of almost all descriptions of problem finding is alertness to discrepancies between incoming information and existing knowledge, among elements of knowledge themselves, or among the incoming information units themselves. In other

words, there is a high degree of sensitivity to paradoxes, missing links, and a permanent distrust of "natural" things. The motivational and emotional aspect of the concept is stressed in
most descriptions: Problem finding refers to an irrepressible
will to get to the heart of the matter, or the "infantile voracity
for 'becauses' and the naive hope that there are real answers to
every question" (Koestler, 1969, p. 456), combined with the refusal to accept the obvious. Relevant concepts are curiosity with
explorative behavior in its wake (Berlyne, 1970) and "effectance
motivation," which is the need to get control over the environment (White, 1959), or emotional components, such as wonder
and surprise. A heuristic function could be ascribed to the emotional factors: This element will be dealt with later, in view of its
developmental aspects and its educational implications. Also,
there is frequent mention of personality traits like tolerance for
ambiguity, self-confidence, openness to new information, strong
competence motivation, and stimulus reduction, which involves
a tendency toward finding new stimuli. Finally, problem finding
is viewed as the ability to convert "intuitively felt" discrepancies
into basically verifiable hypotheses. This element is comparable
with the fourth and last step in Wallas' model (1926): Verification also involves the explication of what is "intuitively felt," in
this case the solution to the given problem.

In view of the preceding, problem finding might be described
as the ability to detect discrepancies (problem sensitivity) and
to explicate felt problems (problem formulation), involving
strong intrinsic motivation. An essential element of problem
finding, as has already been pointed out, is problem sensitivity.
This element will be worked out in the following. Sternberg's
componential theory of intelligence (1984) contains important
starting points for a further analysis of this element. Sternberg
assumes three types of cognitive process: (1) performance components—the (actual) basic cognitive operations; (2) knowledge
acquisition components (selective encoding, combining and
comparing of information); and (3) metacomponents, which control the former two categories. One of the metacomponents
Sternberg mentions is "recognizing the essence of the problem
to be solved." This involves an insight into the nature of performance and knowledge acquisition components, and placing
them in the right order. It is these knowledge acquisition components that lead to the core of problem sensitivity. In Sternberg's model three knowledge acquisition components are distinguished.

1.  Selective encoding: For instance, the discovery of penicillin by Fleming. Observing a fungi culture he noticed that nearby bacteria had been destroyed, probably by the fungi. This example immediately leads to the concept of serendipity. It is often quoted as an example of finding something one was not looking for. Serendipity might be regarded as a successful marriage between shrewdness and coincidence; the emphasis is mostly laid on the latter. This concept, in other words, is part of the broader concept of problem finding.
2.  Selective combining: Darwin's theory of evolution is said to be a product of the fitting into a coherent system of a large number of data. The data were known separately, but needed to be combined. Selective combining also is found in Mednick's description of "creativity" as the connecting of elements that apparently are not related. Thus conceived—although there are numerous descriptions of creativity and most of them are considerably broader (Brugman & Dudink, 1977)—creativity might be viewed as an element of problem finding.
3.  Selective comparing: Kekulé's discovery of a specific chemical structure on the basis of a metaphor—a snake biting on its own tail.

In Figure 13-1 the elements of problem finding mentioned earlier are represented: cognition, personality, motivation, and emotion.

To put it differently, the three components mentioned earlier form essential elements of problem sensitivity: the ability to pick out the proper piece of information from the total and relate this selection to the proper elements in the knowledge base. An important aspect in this has to be added, that is, daring to make "lofty generalizations based on humble cues" (Koestler, 1969, p. 456). This involves a willingness to take risks. The personality trait "tolerance for ambiguity," which has already been mentioned, is closely related to this and can be regarded as a necessary prerequisite for problem sensitivity, being a permanent condition for cognitive anarchy.

**Research on Problem Finding**

There has been little research in the field of problem finding, because of operationalization problems and the lack of demand for studies in this area. Operationalizations that can be found

FIGURE 13-1.    Structure model for problem finding.

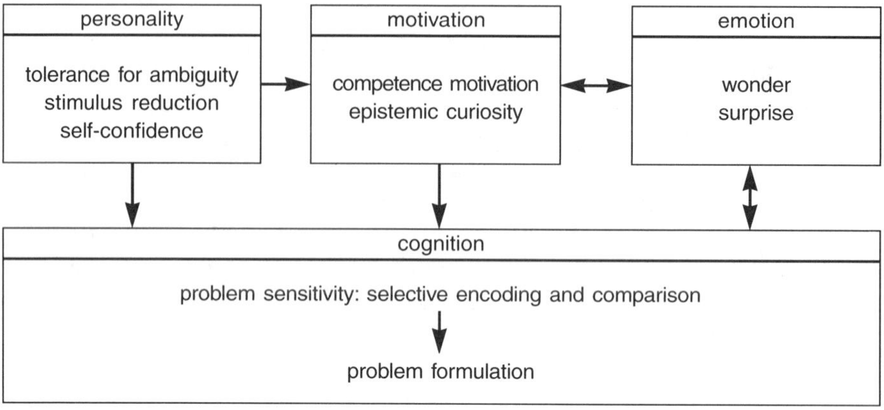

in the literature concern constituent aspects of problem finding, such as curiosity and the asking of questions, as well as
attempts to encompass the concept in its entirety.

Illustrations of the latter are the studies by Getzels and Csikszentmihalyi (1976) and Dillon (1988). The former studied the
relation between problem finding, problem solving, and artistic
success (the latter measured over a period of 7 years) with a
group of 31 art students. The drawback to this study is the operationalization of the concept of problem finding. The subjects
were asked to draw a still life: In the studio drawing materials
were available, as well as a number of divergent objects. The
task consisted of choosing a number of objects, making a composition out of them and drawing this composition. There was
no time limit; subjects stopped when they were satisfied with
the result. The researchers assumed that a more extensive exploration of the objects, the manipulation of many objects, the
selection of a unique combination, and a long "delay of closure," that is, that part of the working time in which the final
structure is not yet visible, would be indicative of a high level
of problem finding. In other words, there were four problem-
finding variables: the number of manipulated objects; the nature of the exploration of the objects; the uniqueness of the
chosen combination; and that part of the working time in which
the final structure was not yet visible. There was also an overall measure. The four variables were scored by experts. Problem-solving variables were the originality and the aesthetic
value of the final product. Also taken into consideration was the

subject's artistic success over a period of seven years, as scored by the same experts.

The correlations among problem finding, problem solving, and artistic success were substantial, particularly in view of the homogeneity of the sample (all subjects were advanced art students), the subjectivity of the measures (with the exception of manipulation and exploration), and the operationalization of problem finding. As for the latter, the actual manipulation of the displayed objects by no means excludes the possibility of mental manipulation. The performance of the task "produce a still life by means of the given objects" is a rather poor type of problem finding in the light of the description given in the previous paragraph. This is more a case of problem solving, and a strong correlation between two operationalizations of problem solving is not surprising.

A completely different operationalization can be found with Arlin (1975). Her study with 60 female students focused on the question whether problem finding can be regarded as a fifth Piagetian stage of cognitive development. This hypothesis led to the prediction that problem finding would be found only among those who had already attained the formal operational stage. Problem finding was operationalized by Arlin as the asking of questions concerning a collection of 12 objects (among others, a wooden cube, a pair of scissors, and a piece of red cardboard).

An important criticism of the research report is the absence of arguments that support the choice for the product dimension of Guilford's Structure-of-Intellect model as a means of weighting responses. Although the sequence—unit, class, relation, system, transformation, and implication—shows an increasing complexity, the use of this weighting system does not do sufficient justice to differences in the quality of the responses. With regard to the hypothesis that problem finding is characteristic of postformal thinking, Arlin could find only partial confirmation: The correlation between the formal operational tasks and problem finding was .31 ($p < .05$), but in replication studies (Cropper, Meck, & Ash, 1977; Dillon, 1988; Fakouri, 1976; Kramer, 1983) the cell "high score on problem finding/low score on formal operational tasks" turned out not to be empty after dichotomization of both variables. The data do not allow judgments on Perkins' statement (1981) that problem finding is more a way of using problem solving, that is, a cognitive style dimension, than a separate cognitive skill. The correlation can be interpreted in two ways: (1) problem finding is a skill that can only develop if the level of problem solving has reached a minimum value, probably in the sense of a threshold hypothesis; (2) problem finding is a cognitive style—the only thing that matters is whether or not this style is used in a certain way.

## Developmental Approaches

From a developmental perspective, a good deal of work already has been done on problem finding, although mainly in neighboring fields. The research tradition and development of theories on curiosity (Berlyne, 1968, 1970) and the asking of questions (Isaacs, 1945; Piaget, 1952) offer some useful information about the way in which the skill of discovering and formulating problems develops. Departing from the structure model presented earlier, curiosity might be viewed as a motivational component of problem finding. Berlyne (1968) divides epistemic curiosity into specific and diversive exploration. The former refers to the search for information under conditions of uncertainty: The individual tries to remove the feeling of dissatisfaction caused by lack of information by attending to those environmental aspects that can fill the gap. This might also be called a reactive sort of curiosity. Diversive exploration, on the other hand, encompasses many activities that can be placed under the heading of "play." It is directed to stimuli with characteristics such as novelty and complexity. According to Berlyne, this latter type of exploration forms the motivational basis for problem finding, whereas specific exploration would serve as the motivational basis for problem solving. This urge for exploration might be considered as resulting from the need mentioned earlier to be able to control the environment by gaining insight into it: "competence motivation" (White, 1959). However, even in the early stages of development babies show evidence of this need to control their environment. Papoušék (1967) states that they do so by comparing incoming information with an internal standard. If expectations and reality do not correspond, the standards need to be improved.

One of the shortcomings of many studies on curiosity is that they focus primarily on information features that evoke exploratory behavior: information with optimum levels of novelty and complexity. Problem finding, however, also involves what Koestler (1979) calls "an acuity of perception and a gift for seeing the banal objects of everyday experience in a sharp individual light." This amazement at the exceptional in everyday experience is strongly linked to the personality trait "tolerance for ambiguity" mentioned in the structure model. Maw and Maw (1971) found that this variable accounted for 10% of the variance in curiosity with children. With regard to problem finding, tolerance for ambiguity not only refers to tolerating what is multiply interpretable, but also to deliberately looking for it. This supposes self-confidence or lack of fear of the unknown. Vidler (Ball, 1977) found a negative correlation (−.15, $p < .05$) between curiosity and fear. Within this framework one might think of the phenomenon attachment. Studies on the relationship between exploration and attachment (Hughes & Noppe, 1985) suggest a strong positive correlation in children between secure attachment and interest in exploring the environment. To put it differently, safe attachment might be viewed as a necessary prerequisite for explorative behavior and curiosity, and also for the development of tolerance for ambiguity. Curiosity and the urge for exploration, in their turn, would provide the material and motivational basis for the discovery and formulation of problems. Further explorative behavior can be considered as self-reinforcing: satisfaction resulting from searching and the (possible) discovery itself.

Finally, the role of knowledge in this matter can be mentioned. Bruner (1961) argued that "discovery, like surprise, favors the well-prepared mind." There has to be at least knowledge before the individual is able to discover discrepancies, inconsistencies and the like. On the basis mentioned, the developmental relations can be represented as follows (see Figure 13-2).

Curiosity can manifest itself as the asking of questions. Consequently, research on the asking of questions is a useful source of information about the developmental aspects of problem finding. Piaget, for instance, described the developmental process of asking questions. To put it briefly, from the second half of the second year of their lives children spontaneously start to ask questions about the names of things. In the third year the classic "why and when" questions arise. Only in the sixth or seventh year do questions on explanations in terms of cause or effect with regard to physical objects appear, together with questions on justifications for rules and habits. In this sense the asking of questions can be regarded as the product of the knowledge base that is present and also as the motor for further exploration or further questioning. Children generally appear to experience serious difficulties in asking effective questions. They often hardly understand instructions, and need

FIGURE 13-2.    Developmental relations between cognitive, motivational, and personality variables.

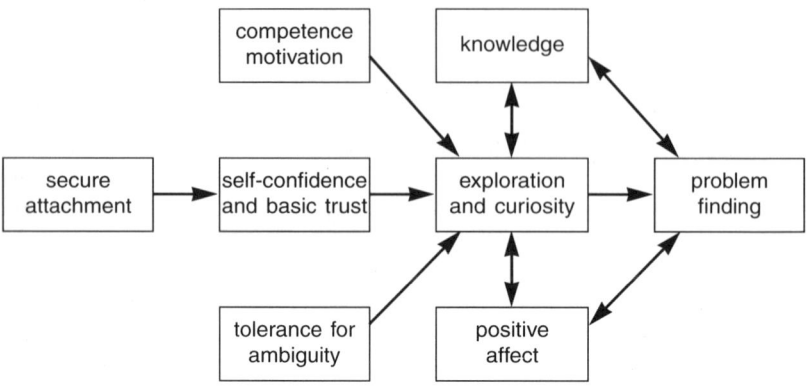

a considerable amount of steering to put their questioning behavior on the right path.

The protocol fragment that follows, from a preliminary investigation (Brugman, 1983), may serve as an illustration. Children were asked what things they would want to know, supposing there was someone who was able to answer all questions. Here follows the fragment from an eight-year-old.

Subject: "Well, eh, if you are then able to conjure up money, I would ask how you do that." The test leader repeats the question: "What would you want to know?" Subject: "For example, you can ask if you may have a house of your own, if you may have a piece of land to build a brick house yourself, you can also ask, eh, well, yes, that there will be cross country in America or bicycle races." The test leader corrects again and gives an example himself. Only then does the subject hesitatingly get going. Subject: "Why animals are mostly brown. They are mostly brown, look. A rock-goat and the like." (The subject points at a somewhat yellowed wall chart in the back of the classroom). Subject: "Also why people always . . . well, I don't know, but . . . that it is always summer, and also always winter, and that it is always longer, a whole year, winter, just like that . . . why you are not grown up immediately." And after a long silence the subject gave up. Subject: "I don't know anything else." This session did not even last four minutes. The major part of it was filled with silence. In this preliminary study it was possible, though, to demonstrate a clear relation between age (range: 7–12 years) and the number of questions asked. It turned out to be impossible to obtain a satisfactory score for the quality of the questions.

Isaacs (1945) went much more deeply into the why questions than did Piaget. She distinguished a number of categories: why questions with an expressive, a justificative, an informative, and an epistemological function. In problem finding, the latter two categories especially are important. Epistemological questions are said to be the result of the confrontation with contradictions or deviations, with the unexpected and the bizarre and, finally, with differences and contrasts. Informative why questions arise out of uncertainty about the function and the goal of objects and events. What is left unsaid, however, and this is also true for other categorizations of question types, is the problem of how individuals determine these contradictions, aberrations, and the like.

Although Piaget's studies on children's questioning behavior offer little more than a description, the concept of "equilibration," which is central in his theory of cognitive development, can serve as a point of departure for investigating sensitivity to contradictions, which is the core of problem finding. The concept "disequilibrium" is closely related to concepts like "conceptual conflict" (Ball, 1977), "perceptual discrepancy" (Hebb, 1949), "effective surprise" (Bruner, 1973), and "état équilibre instabile" (Claparéde, 1911). These are often regarded as the motor of question asking, curiosity, or problem finding. These notions have in common that expectation patterns based on cognitive schemata do not match incoming information, with the result that cognitive equilibrium is disturbed. This might lead to an effort to restore equilibrium by means of appropriate steps, such as explorative behavior or asking questions. However, as has already been stated in another context, here too there is a starting point for the wilfull and deliberate evoking of a disequilibrium, as is the case with problem finding: Contradictions are looked for, natural things are contested (Getzels & Csikszentmihalyi, 1976).

Neither are the considerations of the Piagetian Arlin adequate for explaining the core of problem finding. Formal operational thinking implies that reality is considered as one option out of an endless universe of possibilities. From this viewpoint it is possible "to question the question." In other words, it is not so much that there are qualitative differences with regard to the required cognitive operations as that there are differences in content. For the time being it seems more sensible to place

problem finding in the framework of the concept "décalage hor-
izontale" of formal operations. A second objection to Arlin is
the age indication that is implied. She marks problem finding
as typical "adult thought." This would mean, in the first place,
that children are excluded and, in the second, that the number
of adults reaching the problem-finding stage would be minimal,
in view of the fact that only a limited number of adults function
at a formal operational level (Birren & Schaie, 1985).

This is not an "argumentum ad misericordiam," but shows
the necessity of distinguishing levels of problem finding, with
Arlin's fifth stage at the peak of the hierarchy. Explorative behavior might be placed at the base of this hierarchy, as well as
questions about the names of objects and why questions, if Piaget's earlier studies on children's questioning behavior are
taken as a starting point. A study by Dillon (1988) addressed
the problem of different levels of problem finding. He made a
distinction between three levels: the recognition of evident, existing problems; the discovery of implicit questions; and the
highest level, the invention of potential problems. The relationship he found between these three levels was only moderate. In
contrast to Arlin's data, he found that problem finding and
problem solving were not closely related: The weakest relationship between finding and solving was found at the highest levels of finding and solving. In other words, the developmental
process runs from asking questions about the why of something to Arlin's metalevel; asking why something is as it is, or
Dillon's invention of potential questions. Problem finding is regarded as a function of the quality of the knowledge base and
of the cognitive level of development. Riegel's elaboration of Piaget's theory, the dialectical model of cognitive development,
probably yields the best approach. Like Arlin, Riegel (1973,
1975) assumed a fifth stage in cognitive development. This
stage would be characterized by the integration of the previous
four stages and by "disequilibration": The focusing on contradictions, and the deriving of pleasure from challenging the obvious. There is, however, no empirical evidence to support his
theory. As a consequence, the final conclusion must be that the
empirical as well as the theoretical output is poor.

**Educational Implications**

The question remains of the extent to which something as apparently important as problem finding can be stimulated in the

light of the conceptual, empirical, and theoretical knowledge
outlined earlier, as well as the not always equally impressive effectiveness of stimulation programs in the field of problem solving (e.g., Ausubel, Novak, & Novak, 1978). In every case research is available in which attempts were made to make
children more sensitive to discrepancies, uncertainties, and the
like. Torrance (1970), for example, has developed a program—
Reading 360—in which children have to look for contradictions
in texts. Although the program did not lead to an increase in
the quantity of the questions the children asked, it did result
in an increase in their quality. There were fewer questions on
verifying something to which the answer was already known; on
the other hand there were more questions concerning discrepancies in the text.

Coie (1973) confronted children with an apparatus that broke
the laws of gravity (a wheel that, once set free, drove up a slope
instead of rolling down it). The most important finding in this
study was that discrepancies made subjects use their intellectual capacity to a maximum. Suchman (1961) developed a
physics program based on similar starting points (confronting
children with discrepancies) and Doblaev (1957) trained children to ask arithmetic questions. He presented data without
explicating the question, which he did as follows: What can you
conclude on the basis of these data? Doblaev argued that this
sort of problem teaches pupils to "pose the solving question
while solving the problem by the synthetic method." Finally,
similar suggestions were made by Brown and Walter (1988) in
the field of mathematics education.

Although research is scarce, some suggestions that can be
deduced from the literature will be made for stimulating problem finding in education. The common denominator is that the
whole problem-solving cycle should be dealt with in education.
This means that not only ready-made problems should be offered, as is usually the case today. Pupils have to learn not only
to solve problems, but also to discover and formulate them.
This requires more from the teacher than "departing from natural curiosity." It also requires more than "linking up with the
children's world." In the first place it is not necessary to have
pupils discover everything by themselves that has already been
discovered. Second, curiosity has to be nourished: The breed-
ing ground is made up of knowledge and skills, whereas—to
take an agricultural metaphor—the fertilization consists of the
confrontation with conflicting information.

This might be clarified by a simple example. In a lesson on factors influencing the location of urban settlements, the pupils might be asked to point out on a map favorable locations for settlement. Next, they might be confronted with the actual settlement locations. This is what the teachers' task is about: They have to transmit knowledge as well as create doubt by giving information that disturbs cognitive equilibrium. The aim is to start a process by which pupils develop more sensitivity to problems and become more sensitive to conflicting information, and are less inclined to accept things unquestioningly. The pleasure deriving from challenging natural things might be the motor that gets this process going. This pleasure would be the moving spirit that maintains the behavior. Natural curiosity, in other words, is no more than a sufficient condition for learning to discover and formulate problems. It is noteworthy that Meacham (1990), in his provoking discussion on wisdom, which he defines as an epistemological position between certainty and doubt, attributes to children youthful wisdom that they lose in the course of development. The cause of that loss may be found in current educational practice.

All this does not mean that the teacher would no longer be allowed to present problems to the pupils. If, however, problems are presented, they should be formulated in such a way that there is enough space left for pupils to discover and formulate subproblems on their own (Doblaev, 1957; Puskin, 1977). Space should be created for problems different from those described by Getzels and Csikszentmihalyi (1975): The problem is known to the teacher and the pupil, the method of solving is given, the teacher already knows the solution, and the pupil has to find that solution. The mental function that is often appealed to in such cases is the mnestic one. In terms of Van de Geer's taxonomy (1957), the emphasis in education frequently is laid on problems in which reaching the solution requires digging up from memory the appropriate method. The degree of difficulty of the problem lies in the amount of information rather than in having to discover the crucial implications of the information. The problems presented in education not infrequently are interpolation problems: They have a clearly defined initial and final situation (Dörner, 1974; Mackworth, 1965). In terms of Guilford's Structure-of-Intellect Model they mainly require convergent production—moving along well-trodden paths by means of a detailed route description on the road to the one and only correct end station, which is known in advance.

It must be admitted that there is a large number of problems for which such an approach is the most efficient and most desirable one. However, education also has to prepare pupils for clearing themselves paths through a dense wood, on the road to unclear final destinations. If education takes to heart its task—which can be described in the broadest sense as "fostering effectively the long-term acquisition of meaningful and useful bodies of knowledge and of developing appropriate intrinsic motivations for such learning" (Ausubel, Novak, & Novak, 1978, p. 404), then attention will have to be paid to the latter. Summarizing the previously mentioned yields the following general suggestions.

1.  More than has been the case in the past, education will have to pay attention to the complete problem-solving cycle: In the present situation this means more attention to problem finding.
2.  More attention should be given to the emotional–motivational aspect, which is the motor of the process.
3.  Natural curiosity and the drive for exploration provide an insufficient base for problem-directed education: Curiosity has to be fed by means of, for instance, conflicting information.
4.  Transfer of knowledge is a necessary condition for detaching this curiosity from the immediate satisfying of needs, from the here-and-now, and for its restructuring in the direction of a need for knowledge acquisition as a goal in itself: It concerns intrinsically motivated learning.
5.  Transfer of knowledge is a goal in itself as well as a necessary condition for the development of a cognitive orientation; static knowledge is not the point in this transfer of knowledge.
6.  Problems presented to the pupils have to be as diverse as possible with regard to the method of solving, the degree of difficulty, and the nature of the initial and final situations: In the present educational situation, this implies more attention to problems with an open initial and final situation.
7.  Parents and teachers have to stimulate the asking of questions; they also have to try to answer the questions calmly and conscientiously.
8.  According to Berlyne (Krumboltz, 1968) the intellectual hunger of children is highly underestimated; within this framework he refers to the misconception that attaching

weight to pupils' interests would imply the offering of tempt-ing material. He points, however, to the importance of new, surprising, incongruent, and complex stimuli.

To conclude, a historical comment linked to a desideratum: In the past the following priorities were established in education.

1. transferring basic knowledge and skills;
2. delivering problem solvers; and
3. training creative thinkers.

In the future, education should not be aimed so much at turn-ing out problem finders as at offering educational programs in which all elements are equally represented.

## REFERENCES

Arlin, P. K. (1975). Cognitive development in adulthood: a 5th stage? *Developmental Psychology*, *11*, 602–608.

Ausubel, D. P., Novak, J. D., & Novak, H. (1978). *Educational psychol-ogy*. New York: Holt & Rinehart.

Ball, S. (Ed.) (1977). *Motivation in education*. New York: Academic Press.

Berlyne, D. E. (1968). Curiosity and education. In J. D. Krumboltz (Ed.), *Learning and the educational process*. Chicago: Rand McNally.

Berlyne, D. E. (1970). Children's reasoning and thinking. In P. H. Mussen (Ed.), *Carmichael's manual of child psychology*. New York: Wiley.

Birren, J. E., & Schaie, K. W. (1985). *The handbook of the psychology of aging*. New York: Van Nostrand & Reinhold.

Brown, S. I., & Walter, M. I. (1988). Problem finding in mathematics ed-ucation. *Questioning Exchange*, *2*, 123–131.

Brugman, G. M. (1983). *Het meten van weetgierigheid*. Internal publi-cation, Rijksuniversiteit Utrecht.

Brugman G. M., & Dudink, A. (1977). *De vraag naar creativiteit*. Mep-pel: Boom.

Bruner, J. (1961). The act of discovery. *Harvard Educational Review*, *31*, 21–30.

Bruner, J. (1973). *Beyond the information given*. New York: Norton.

Claparède, E. (1911). *Psychologie de l'enfant*. Geneva: Librairie Kündig.

Claparède, E. (1933). La génèse de l'hypothèse. *Archive de Psycholo-gie*, *24*, 92–94.

Coie, J. D. (1973). The motivation of exploratory strategies in young children. *Genetic Psychology Monographs*, *87*, 177–196.

Cropper, D. A., Meck, D. S., & Ash, M. J. (1977). The relation between formal operations and a possible fifth stage of cognitive development. *Developmental Psychology, 13*, 517–518.

Dewey, J. (1933). *How we think.* New York: Heath.

Dillon, J. T. (1982). Problem finding and solving. *Journal of Creative Behavior, 16*, 97–111.

Dillon, J. T. (1988). Levels of problem finding versus problem solving. *Questioning Exchange, 2*, 105–115.

Doblaev, L. P. (1957). Thought processes involved in setting up equations. *Izvestiya, 80*, 175–233.

Dörner, D. (1974). *Die kognitive Organisation beim Problemlösen.* Bern: Huber.

Fakouri, M. (1976). Cognitive development in adulthood: a fifth stage: a critique. *Developmental Psychology, 12*, 472.

Gardner, H. (1984). *Frames of mind.* London: Heinemann.

van de Geer, J. P. (1957). *A psychological study of problem solving.* Unpublished dissertation at the University of Leiden.

Getzels, J. W., & Csikszentmihalyi, M. (1975). From problem solving to problem finding. In I. Taylor & J. W. Getzels (Eds.), *Perspectives in creativity* (pp. 90–116). Chicago: Aldine-Atherton.

Getzels, J. W., & Csikszentmihalyi, M. (1976). *The creative vision: a longitudinal study of problem finding in art.* New York: Wiley.

Guilford, J. P. (1977). *Way beyond the IQ.* New York: Creative Educational Foundation.

Hebb, D. O. (1949). *The organization of behavior.* New York: Wiley.

Hughes, F. P., & Noppe, L. D. (1985). *Human development across the life span.* New York: West.

Isaacs, S. (1945). *Intellectual growth in young children.* London: Routledge & Sons.

Koestler, A. (1969). *The act of creation.* London: Hutchinson.

Koestler, A. (1979). *Janus, a summing up.* New York: Vintage Books.

Kramer, D. A. (1983). Post-formal operation. A need for further conceptualization. *Human Development, 26*, 91–105.

Krumboltz, J. D. (Ed.) (1968). *Learning and the educational process.* Chicago: Rand McNally

Mackworth, N. H. (1965). Originality. *American Psychologist, 20*, 51–66.

Maw, W. H., & Maw, E. W. (1971). Nature of creativity in high and low curiosity boys. *Developmental Psychology, 7*, 325–329.

Meacham, J. A. (1990). The loss of wisdom. In R. J. Sternberg (Ed.), *Wisdom, its nature, origins, and development* (p. 181–211). Cambridge: Cambridge University Press.

Newell, A., & Simon, H. (1972). *Human problem solving.* Englewood Cliffs, NJ: Prentice-Hall.

Olton, R. M. (1979). Experimental studies of incubation. *Journal of Creative Behavior, 13*, 9–22.

Papoušék, H. (1967). Experimental studies of appetitional behavior in human newborns and infants. In H. Stevenson, E. H. Hess, & H. L. Reingold (Eds.), *Early behavior* (pp. 249–277). New York: Wiley.

Perkins, D. N. (1981). *The mind's best work.* Cambridge: Harvard University Press.

Piaget, J. (1952). *The origins of intelligence in children.* New York: Routledge & Kegan Paul.

Puskin, V. N. (1977). Intentioneel handelen als cognitieve activiteit. *Voprosy Psichologii, 5,* 74–86.

Riegel, K. F. (1973). Dialectic operations: the final period of cognitive development. *Human Development, 16,* 346–370.

Riegel, K. F. (1975). Toward a dialectial theory of development. *Human Development, 18,* 689–700.

Rossman, J. (1931). *The psychology of the inventor.* Washington: The Inventive Publication Company.

Sternberg, R. J. (Ed.). (1984). *Mechanisms of cognitive development.* New York: Freeman & Co.

Suchman, J. R. (1961). Inquiry training. *Merrill Palmer Quarterly, 7,* 147–169.

Torrance, E. P. (1962). *Guiding creative talent.* Englewood Cliffs, NJ: Prentice-Hall.

Torrance, E. P. (1970). The creative teacher at work. *Reading Monographs 360.* Boston, MA: Ginn & Company.

Wallas, A. (1926). *The art of thought.* New York: Harcourt.

White, R. W. (1959). Motivation reconsidered; the concept of competence. *Psychological Review, 66,* 297

Zuckerman, H. (1983). The scientific elite: Nobel laureates' mutual influences. In R. S. Albert (Ed.), *Genius and eminence* (pp. 241–252). New York: Pergamon.

# 14

# Expertise and Giftedness

**Jan Elshout**

*University of Amsterdam, Amsterdam, The Netherlands*

The thesis of this chapter is that to be gifted means being able to go through the developmental curve from novice to expert more rapidly. Central in growing expertise are the building up of pattern recognition capabilities, schema formation, proceduralization of the knowledge base, and the development of a multistrategy control structure. However gifted the person, in most domains this development takes thousands of hours of hard work. For this reason the contribution to success of sheer intellectual ability is hypothesized to be overshadowed by the personal and situational characteristics that have been found to differentiate between actually (not potentially) creative and less creative persons, for example, an early, passionate, personal interest in a domain.

## INTRODUCTION

By generally accepted definition an expert is someone who has spent 5 years or more working in some particular field of activity. It is possible to speak of the expert in general, because there are many commonalities between experts operating in different domains: science, the arts, sports, and even cooking. In all such domains excellence can only be gained by actively working on skills and knowledge for thousands of hours. Expertise is easily recognized. Everyone marvels at the ease and assurance of experts, at their mastery and creativity, whether they are writers, athletes, or mathematicians, and we forgive them their superior ways and demands for high pay.

## THE PSYCHOLOGY OF POTENTIAL VERSUS THE PSYCHOLOGY OF ACTUAL EXPERTISE

The concepts of expert and of expertise are natural and easily assimilated constructs. Nonetheless, it was only recently that psychology became interested in expertise and experts. For the greater part of this century it was most interested not in expertise and excellent performances per se, but in personal ability or potential to excel. The emphasis lay on the potential instead of the actual. Actual performance can be observed and measured, but ability is a contruct abstracted out of the raw givens of actual performance. Put into the form of a rough formula: observed performance, how good someone actually is, is a function of potential, past opportunity to learn, and past and present motivational state. To get a good measure of potential, both the other factors must be kept constant. That was what I meant when I said that ability has to be abstracted: ability, giftedness, intelligence, talent are all dispositional constructs. They share the fact that they cannot be directly observed. A process of abstraction is necessary. This entails certain experimental and conceptual procedures to ensure that estimates of the potential of people are not obscured by differences in opportunity, experience, and schooling, nor by differences in interest and motivation. This abstract nature of concepts such as ability makes them difficult. At least part of the controversial nature of the concepts of giftedness and intelligence stems, in my view, from their abstract nature. That, for instance, someone who is less intelligent may perform intellectually better than someone of greater ability (because the latter is younger) is not easy to grasp. Compared with expertise, intelligence certainly is not a natural and easily assimilated construct.

### Two Strategies for the Study of Potential

Psychology has followed two strategies for studying ability without the inference of differences in motivation and previously acquired knowledge. The first strategy is to give subjects tasks of such short duration that most find them challenging: This is done to ensure optimal motivation. The second is to use tasks that may be called "knowledge lean," especially lean of the sort of knowledge that is dependent on explicit formal schooling. Tasks that ask for no knowledge at all obviously are difficult to construct, but tasks that demand only knowledge that everybody has had equal opportunity to acquire can be found. Every child has tried to put on its trousers over its head at least once, and failed. Only some children can explain later why they failed. According to the reasoning of psychology, this must reflect differences in the potential to understand and profit from experience.

These two strategies of abstraction took psychologists far. Tests of intelligence constructed according to these principles allow predictions that are far from trivial. It can be predicted, for instance, that of two children who perform at the same level on a test, although they are of different age, it will be the younger who will go further and profit more by instruction, who will show more transfer of learning, and so on (see Sternberg, 1985, for a general overview). The study of thinking too, has greatly profited from these strategies of abstraction. In the 1970s this approach culminated in the monumental work of Newell and Simon on human problem solving (Newell & Simon, 1972). Problem solving or productive thinking was described as a process of searching for a goal, in which the problem is decomposed step by step into more manageable subproblems, until a level of decomposition is reached where a particular person can proceed without difficulty. This view of problem solving as a goal-directed search (in a space of obstacles, a process governed by heuristic rules for looking for the weakest spot at any time) has been very influential and successful to this day. In the last few years Newell's group has expanded the 1972 theory in a way that is meant to incorporate human learning, in what is now proposed to be a universal theory of general human intelligence (Laird, Newell, & Rosenbloom, 1987).

For all this success in abstracting away the influence of differences in experience, schooling, and motivation, psychology has had to pay a price, namely that of generalizability. To keep experience a constant is one thing, but to keep it a constant at such a low level as is done by concentrating on puzzle solving means that the whole area of knowledge acquisition and knowledge application in problem solving is left in the shadows.

## The Complexity of Expertise

It is obvious that problem solving in real life—think of medical diagnosis as an example—heavily involves experience and formal knowledge. The point is how readily the theory of problem solving—studied in the form of knowledge lean puzzle solving—can be expanded to cover real-life problem solving too. Psychology therefore had to face the question whether puzzle solving is just a simplified form of real life problem solving, or a qualitatively different form.

The first to raise this question within the Newell-Simon tradition (outside critics never took studying puzzle solving seriously to begin with, for many different reasons) was Simon himself (Anzai & Simon, 1979). In the late 1970s he published a study on learning puzzle solving, for example, learning to do a puzzle better by doing it several times. His conclusion was that gaining expertise by repeatedly doing was in itself a knowledge lean process just as much as puzzle solving itself. In the same period he studied physics problem solving, posing the question whether problem solving in such a complex knowledge rich domain could be described in terms of the same theory of goal directed search that had proved successful for simple puzzle solving (Bhaskar & Simon, 1977). Simon's conclusion was that it could. In his view real-life problem solving was not qualitatively different from puzzle solving. Both involve goal directed search, a process of approaching the solution step-by-step, the choice of steps being guided by the same general heuristics. Only the operators used, the means that are applied, differ. Each problem area has its own domain specific operators and with real life problems there are simply a great many more specific operators than with laboratory puzzles. Thus, the generalizability of Newell and Simon's theory was deemed to have been saved: The complex arises in a simple way out of the simple.

However, somehow Simon was too late! The genie of interest in real-life problem solving was out of the bottle. Many took their point of departure from the work of de Groot on the thought and perception of chess grandmasters. Grandmasters are experts who have spent several thousand hours analyzing chess positions: De Groot's intuition—it was just after World War II—was that thinking and perceiving cannot be totally different processes, each governed by its own set of principles. There had to be a common ground (de Groot, 1946, 1965). It was in the context of this intuition that de Groot was struck by the remarkable speed with which chess experts take in a new complex chess position presented to them. De Groot relates an anecdote of an American grandmaster glancing in passing through the window of a chess cafe and noting that in a game going on there White would lose in one move! So, the expert "sees" in a glance what the less experienced have to compute in a slow process of deliberate thought.

Later, in the 1960s, such feats of expertise were brought under the heading of pattern recognition. Pattern recognition occurs when a number of perceptually distinct elements (e.g., pieces on a chess board) become recognized as one whole (as one new element) by virtue of the elements having been elaborately processed as a whole. Thus, a certain configuration of chess pieces that repeatedly turns up in different games and is repeatedly analyzed as a whole can end up as an old friend, a known identity, recognized at a glance. Later research has show that chess experts (during their thousands of hours of study) have developed a repertoire of several tens of thousands of such identifiable patterns of chess pieces. The development of pattern recognition is a feat of both perception and memory. People come to see as a whole what in their knowledge base has come to be one concept, one node of meaning. What holds for chess holds for other fields of expertise as well, although the patterns that are to be formed need not be figural but may be symbolic or semantic in nature. The general phenomenon of pattern recognition can be diagnosed when there is fast, automatic, and effortless recognition of an identity that a person without expertise has to discover after a slow process of effortful deliberate cogitation.

The advantages of pattern recognition to the expert are obvious. What takes neither time nor effort will leave the mind (the working memory!) free for deliberate thought that perhaps would have been impossible otherwise. Furthermore, the recognized pattern is a direct point of entry (retrieval cue) to other information that comes to be associated with it (in the memory store). For instance, once a person is able to recognize the sequence of symbols one, two, one as the number 121, the information that 121 is the square of eleven and divisable by eleven only and so forth can be organized around it, and all this information is at the person's disposal—again without explicit computation. The essence of pattern recognition is the formation of wholes out of what are discrete elements to the beginner.

When the perceptual is less important and the pattern is of a more conceptual nature, the pattern is called a "schema." Everyone has a great many patterns and a great many schemata available. The expert in any particular domain not only has a great many more relevant schemata and patterns that can be recognized, but also these structures are also of an intellectually higher level. They are more intelligent, so to speak, and that in two different ways: The schemata of the expert are both more operational, more geared to being used in the actual practice of solving problems, and they are based on deeper understanding of the subject matter. Someone who starts out learning in some realistic domain, say that of medical diagnosis, typically starts out having a large amount of recently acquired theoretical knowledge, in the present example, a large amount of knowledge about the structures and workings of the body and what can go wrong with them. It proves to be very difficult to use such a vast store of book learning in actual medical diagnostic problem solving (Boshuizen, 1989). Each patient presents the student with a great many specific data of potential importance—background data, medical history, complaints, laboratory data—that have to be connected to medical theory, resulting in one or more possible explanations.

Connecting the specific (this patient's particular pain) to the general (all the theoretically possible causes of such pain) is very difficult. Boshuizen observed that medical students in the course of several years of experience form schemata that help the making of this connection. These schemata—called illness scripts—connect patterns of patient data to certain descriptions of particular malfunctions. Thus, the doctor can have an AIDS script, a pancreatitis script, and so on. Each script details a description of a particular illness in the form of a causal chain and its posssible variations. (Often one particular patient's history functions as the nucleus around which the schema is organized.) In the later stages of gaining expertise these illness scripts are more operationalized (or compiled). This means that the chain of causal reasoning no longer fully comes to mind—the expert seems to jump to conclusions. To give an extreme example: The patient is a young male, out of work, so that his pain in the right side posssibly stems from pancreatitis—the expert omits the step of chronic alcohol overconsumption and its physiological effects. This may seem a strange and perhaps even dangerous evolution, because reasoning by association is certainly one of the least intelligent forms of reasoning. Indeed, rushing to conclusions is typical beginner behavior (Elshout, 1987). It has been called "pseudoexpert" behavior. The point is, of course, that the shortcut is only as good as the longer chain of reasoning from which it is derived. The expert has mastered the links of the chain, whereas the novice just leaps by association. Daily functioning is full of shortcut behavior that essentially amounts to stimulus–response activity. For instance, if the temperature indicator of some device turns into the red zone, some wheel or knob must be turned to the left: indicator red, wheel left. There is great mental economy in such shortcuts. Typical for novices is that the shortcut is all there is, leading to the problem that they will be in great trouble when the temperature indicator remains in the red after the wheel has been turned to the left.

Characteristic for experts, on the other hand, is that they use shortcuts, but are able at all times to revert to principled reasoning based on deep understanding. Experts know what makes the temperature of the device go up, how that makes the indicator move, and why it is important that the temperature stays within certain limits and how turning the wheel to the left closes a valve, thus cutting the fuel supply, and so on. Both the shortcuts and the deep understanding behind it are typical of expertise in any field. To sum this up: The expert has more levels of functioning than the less expert and is able to switch. The availability of a vast number of patterns of information that can be recognized as old friends, the structuring of knowledge about the domain into schemata that bring together the conceptual and practical aspects of the domain, the possibility of switching between levels of elaboratedness and attention, from the S-R level to real explicit know why, all this makes the expert at work qualitatively different from the not so expert of the same level of intelligence and motivation.

A last good illustration of this phenomenon is provided by the work of Crombach, de Wyckersloot, and Cohen (1977). They had a judge of the Dutch High Court evaluate some cases in civil law while thinking aloud. The thinking aloud protocols started out with a great deal of unintelligible mumbling interspersed with many silences. After a while, however—so to speak, after the deed was done—the reasoning became more explicit. From the protocols Crombach concluded that at this very high level of juridical expertise a verdict is first reached on the basis of a fast process of pattern recognition, of recognizing the present case as a case of a certain well-known legal variety; and only then, after the deed is done, a process is started of painstakingly constructing a justification of the verdict already reached "intuitively." Staff members of a Faculty of Law, also studied, worked the other way around, starting with an elaborate analysis and a process of systematic elimination that culminated in reaching the verdict. When gaining more and more experience results in such a drastic turn around in the direction of proceeding, first from justification to verdict, later from verdict to justification, the hypothesis that the expert differs from the beginner in a quantitative way only must be rejected. The expert has become a different animal, so to speak, not just a bigger one.

## There Is More to Growing Expertise than Passage of Time

All the many studies on the development of expertise thus far have concentrated on the cognitive side of expertise. I am not aware of any study that also looked at the affective and motivational aspects of growing expertise. I believe, however, that there is material to go on. In the 1960s and early 1970s there was great interest in identifying people with potential for scientific and technological creativity. This was part of the Sputnik effect. Because researchers were in a hurry, they could not wait for the outcome of longitudinal studies—which would have been the methodology of choice. The next best approach was to study scientists with about equal experience, and to correlate measures of their scientific excellence (judged creativity, number of publications) with self-ratings on relevant aspects of personal functioning and with scores on tests of cognitive abilities. To state the results briefly, the following pattern of relationships was consistently found: Scientific excellence goes together with an early and deeply felt interest in a particular scientific field, somewhat higher intelligence, a liking for intellectual challenge, persistence, intellectual independence, and a very high level of socalled professional self-confidence. The excellent may be any sort of neurotic, but as far as their particular field of expertise is concerned, they are fully convinced of their ability to excel again and again (Taylor, 1964).

I return now to the development of expertise of any type. As research paradigm I choose a developmental design, subjects starting from the same point on the long road to expertise, the level of expertise reached being measured after certain amounts of opportunity to learn, equal for all. This longitudinal design obviously is different from that of the creativity studies. Still, I am fully confident that the level of expertise reached after a fixed amount of time will prove to have the same correlates as scientific excellence: the more intelligent, the more deeply interested, the more accepting of challenge, the more confident, the more intellectually independent, the more persistent a person is at the start, the further the process of pattern and schema formation, of both schema compilation and conceptual deepening, will have run their course during a given period of time.

In other words, what I propose is that expertise is the same as excellence. It has the same causal background. One part of this is opportunity, the opportunity to learn for thousands of hours, to really master a domain. The other part is what the person brings to it: the ability to profit from this opportunity and, very important, to keep this opportunity going. If a person leaves the field—no expertise, no excellence. In the experiment I have proposed, the experimental treatment is not something like giving subjects a booster shot of vitamin C, passively taken. Instead it is a matter of more than 5000 hours of training. That is real life! Most subjects will drop out of the experiment, those who stay will have become experts. They could also be called "gifted." The implications of what I have said for the concept of giftedness are evident: To be gifted is to have what it takes to survive and enjoy and profit from years of intensive study. Certainly, in this light, giftedness will prove on analysis to be "a many splendored thing" as Guilford pointed out about creativity.

## REFERENCES

Anzai, Y., & Simon, H. A. (1979). The theory of learning by doing. *Psychological Review*, *86*, 124–140.

Bhaskar, R., & Simon, H. A. (1977). Problem solving in semantically rich domains: an example from engineering thermodynamics. *Cognitive Science*, *1*, 193–215.

Boshuizen, H. P. A. (1989). *De ontwikkeling van medische expertise.* Meppel: Krips Repro.

Crombach, H. F. M., de Wijkersloot, J. L. & Cohen, M. J. (1977). *Een theorie over rechterlijke beslissingen.* Groningen: Tjeenk Willink.

Elshout, J. J. (1987). Problem solving and education. In E. de Corte (Ed.), *Learning and instruction.* Oxford: Pergamon.

de Groot, A. D. (1946). *Het denken van de schaker.* Den Haag: North Holland.

de Groot, A. D. (1965). *Thought and choice in chess.* Den Haag: Mouton.

Laird, J. E., Newell, A., & Rosenbloom, P. S. (1987). SOAR: an architecture for general intelligence. *Artificial Intelligence, 33,* 1–64.

Newell, A., & Simon, H. A. (1972). *Human problem solving.* Englewood Cliffs, NJ: Prentice-Hall.

Sternberg, R. J. (1985). *Beyond IQ: A triarchic theory of human intelligence.* New York: Cambridge University Press.

Taylor, C. W. (Ed.) (1964). *Widening horizons in creativity.* New York: Wiley.

# 15

# Intellectual Abilities and the Use of Metaphors in Solving Problems

**Anna Rychlicka**

*Jagiellonian University, Kraków, Poland*

Little is known about the use of metaphors in problem solving. In this study, a group of 20-year-olds attempted to solve problems with the help of different kinds of metaphors (apt vs nonapt; remote vs literal). Different kinds of metaphors were valuable for different aspects of problem solving and for people of differing levels of creativity, but the use of metaphor did not depend on level of intelligence. Literal metaphors did not impede creative thinking, as long as they were apt.

## INTRODUCTION

An important element of the creative thinking group's work, attempting to solve a problem with the use of synectics (Gordon, 1961), is ability to invent apt and remote metaphors (or analogies, as some would say), that is, metaphors that accurately describe the problem put to the group during the session. Apart from synectics as a specific creativity technique, there is the general question of the extent to which metaphors and analogies help people to think up creative ideas. This probably depends on some traits of metaphors or analogies themselves, and individual characteristics of the problem solver. It is not known, however, which metaphors and analogies are most creativity stimulating, nor what kind of individual is most likely to profit from them while solving a problem. It may be that a metaphor by individual interaction takes place, but the question needs research before it can be answered.

The aim of this study is to gather data that would permit an answer to the preceding questions. First, it is important to know how far the ability specific to trained synectics groups is accessible to a private person solving a particularly difficult problem for the first time for him- or herself. It is of great interest to investigate whether people are able to make use of metaphors to help them grasp a problem and solve it in a creative way, the process being similar to the Gordon (1961) method. It is also interesting to ask how far a clumsy, mundane metaphor disrupts the process of thinking about a problem. Second, there is the important question of what kind of metaphor makes understanding the problem easier, and whether the same metaphor makes finding a creative solution to the problem easier. In other words, do the two different stages of problem solving—understanding the problem and producing ideas for a solution—require exactly the same kind of metaphor and if not, what relationships exist? Answers to these questions might be important not only for creative thinking groups but also for educators interested in construction of new, creativity centered curricula, which should contain metaphors and analogies in order to facilitate the processes of teaching and learning.

The hypotheses in my experiment concerned the functions of various types of metaphors for understanding and solving problems, as well as the influence of intelligence and creativity—as individual traits—on the use of different types of metaphor. First, it was assumed that literal metaphors make understanding of the material easier, because of the closeness of object and representation. The second hypothesis concerned features of remote metaphors, that is, those characterized by substantial semantic distance between the topic and the representation. Schon (1979) defined the generative metaphor as one that creates new understanding or casts new light on its object. The remote metaphor fulfills the condition of generativity; this is the reason why it should be an excellent starting point for a creative solution to a problem. Third, it was hypothesized that nonapt metaphors (i.e., those showing little resemblance between the topic and the representation) block the process of approaching the solution because of the lack of appropriate representation of a problem. Fourth, it was assumed that there is a connection between level of intelligence and creativity on the one hand, and the ability to use metaphors of various types on the other. Intelligent and creative persons should more frequently utilize the information contained in the metaphor, find more relationships between a given metaphor and a given task, and give solutions more directly connected with a metaphor.

## METHOD

### Subjects

Students in their first year in the Jagiellonian University psychology department were investigated, 11 men and 37 women, about 20 years in age on average.

### Materials

The materials used in the experiment consisted of four real-life technical problems. The first one concerned the technology of connecting broken fiber nets. The second referred to designing a valve without the transient state. The third problem required the invention of new methods for defining the speed of enlargement of a crack in a metal under pressure. The fourth problem concerned a method for measuring the quantity of gas flowing in a thin channel between two chambers of different pressure levels. The problems had been solved previously with the aid of synectics during creative thinking training sessions.

Metaphors used in the experiment also originated from the creative thinking sessions. The metaphors were judged by three competent judges with regard to two independent features: aptness and remoteness. These definitions refer to mutual relations between the vehicle (tender) of the metaphor and its object. The object is, in this case, the problem presented to a subject, whereas the vehicle is the metaphorical description of the problem. The vehicle is close to the object if both are easy to associate with each other, and it is apt if it expresses well what is most important in the object. Thus, four groups of metaphors were used: apt and remote, apt and literal, nonapt and remote, and nonapt and literal. This way, each problem had four metaphors, which differed with regard to aptness and remoteness.

Metaphors used in the experiment also can be divided in another way. The apt and literal metaphor is the one that is related to the defined object both formally (syntactically, i.e., with structural resemblance between the problem and the metaphor) and substantially (i.e., semantically). Such a metaphor occurs when the problem of repairing the broken fiber lines is compared with repairing a broken telephone line. In metaphors of this kind similar vocabulary is applied, but the resemblance goes deeper into the structure of the object and the vehicle. In other words, the vehicle possesses some features of the object and their common space is substantial. Thus, the apt and literal metaphor is connected with its object both syntactically and semantically, whereas the apt and remote metaphor preserves the syntactical connection only (see Gentner, 1983). The nonapt and literal metaphor is connected with the object only semantically because, although preserving substantial convergence, it does not express the object's structure suitably. The tender of the nonapt and remote metaphor has no connection with the object, or connections are only superficial.

**Procedure**

Each of the participants in the experiment was given a description of each of the four problems prepared for the research, along with the instructions. The presentation of each problem involved simply formulating it as a one-sentence task for the subject. A metaphor describing a problem was also provided, along with a question aimed at checking the level of a subject's understanding of the metaphor. A subject had to "map" a problem with the metaphor, so that he or she could answer the question of why both structures resembled each other. The next task of the subject also concerned mapping, and consisted in indicating further similarities between the problem at hand and the proposed metaphor. The third task was to try to solve the problem, whereas the possibility of using the metaphor attached to the problem was not mentioned.

The subjects were divided into four groups. The sequence of presentation of the tasks was the same in each group; only the metaphors proposed were changed. Tasks were rotated over metaphors of different types, so that a subject could receive all four kinds of metaphor but with different problems. For example, in the first group the first task contained the apt and remote metaphor, the second the apt and literal metaphor, and so on. In the second group, the first task was described with the apt and literal metaphor, the second with the nonapt and remote metaphor, and so on.

To test the last two hypotheses, Raven's Progressive Matrices and the Creative Thinking Test were administered. The latter is an original instrument for measuring a subject's potential creative abilities. The test yields information on several characteristics of this potential: the number of answers (fluency), the number of categories in answers (flexibility), and the level of the metaphoricity of the answers. The administration of the Test of Creative Thinking and the Raven's test took place at different times from the main experiment.

## RESULTS

The following dependent variables were taken into consideration: (1) mapping, that is, the quality of the answer to the question that tested the understanding of the metaphor; (2) the number of elements mapped independently by a subject (or the number of resemblances between the object and the vehicle found by a subject); (3) the number of elements mapped in a unique way, that is, found only by one subject; (4) the number of solutions given to the task; (5) the number of original solutions, that is, unique ones in the whole sample; (6) "traces of metaphor", that is, whether solutions given to the problem were based on the metaphor or not (assessed by judges); (7) elaboration of solutions, that is, whether they were rough or sophisticated, superficially or thoroughly described.

Intelligence and creativity constituted two between-subjects independent variables. The measures, Raven's Matrices and the Creative Thinking Test, were used to divide subjects into three groups: low, middle and high, according to the distribution of results in the sample. Multivariate analysis of variance (MANOVA) was applied in order to test the hypotheses. It appeared that

1. Quality of the first "mapping" answer was better in the case of literal metaphors (Mean = 1.72 on the 0-1-2 scale) than in the case of remote ones (Mean = 1.22, $p < .001$). Other factors proved insignificant in this case.

2. The number of elements mapped independently by subjects was determined by their creativity level. Highly creative people mapped 2.92 elements on average, whereas the middle group produced only 1.70 elements, and the lowest group 2.01 elements. This effect is significant beyond the .05 level. Also it appeared that highly creative subjects were particularly productive if they were provided with remote metaphors, although these were useless for low and medium groups. This creativity × remoteness interaction was significant at the .05 level.

3. Highly creative people also produced the greatest number of unique mappings. For instance, the low fluency group gave .61 original mappings on average, whereas the medium group produced 1.06 original mappings, and the high group as much as 1.48 such mappings ($p < .004$). A similar pattern may be observed in the case of flexibility and metaphoricity as measures of the creative potential, with $p < .003$ and $p < .06$, respectively. In addition, highly creative people were particularly original in their mappings in the case of nonapt metaphors, the interaction being significant at the .001 level. If apt metaphors are taken into consideration, no significant differences seem to have occurred between various creativity levels. The factor of remoteness was also significant ($p < .001$), this time in favor of remote metaphors (1.33 originally mapped elements on average), and not the literal ones (.77 originally mapped elements). It may be said that the open-ended task was tackled with the use of remote metaphors, whereas the closed-ended one led to the use of literal metaphors (see point 1).

4. Highly creative people produced the greatest number of ideas in response to the instruction that the problem should be solved on their own. The average numbers are: 2.21 for the high group, 1.07 for the medium group, and 1.31 for the low group ($p < .005$). It should be stressed that creativity was not assessed here with the fluency factor but with the metaphoricity of responses, so that the relationship under discussion is not as obvious as might seem at first glance.

5. The aptness × remoteness interaction proved significant ($p < .05$) if the number of unique solutions were taken into

consideration as a dependent variable. Remote metaphors made subjects think of basically the same number of original (i.e., unique) ideas, no matter whether they were apt or not, whereas literal metaphors appeared useful only if they were apt. In fact, the apt and literal condition was the best in this respect. The nonapt and literal condition, on the other hand, produced a significant decrease in the level of originality. In other words, to be original one should apply either apt and literal or simply remote metaphors; at the same time, one should avoid nonapt literal metaphors. Non-apt metaphors seem to be particularly harmful for medium creativity subjects. Neither low nor high creativity groups suffered in this condition, although the medium creativity group performed quite well if provided only with apt metaphors ($p = .05$ for this creativity $\times$ aptness interaction).

6. Generative metaphors may reflect themselves, to some degree, in solutions produced by subjects. These "traces of metaphors" appeared very often; however, literal metaphors appeared to be better in this respect, since their judged index of resemblance between metaphor and solution was .24, on average, compared to .21 in the case of remote metaphors (the 0-1-2 scale was applied, $p = .007$).

7. No interesting relationships were found concerning the level of elaboration of ideas produced by the subjects.

## CONCLUSIONS

As was hypothesized, the kind of metaphor as well as some individual traits of the problem solver are important factors determining the efficiency of metaphorical transfer in creative problem solving. However, detailed analysis of the present results leads to several concluding remarks. First, the use of metaphor does not seem to depend on level of intelligence; creative abilities are much more important in this respect, especially in interaction with aptness and remoteness of metaphor. Second, different stages of problem solving seem to require different types of metaphor. Correct understanding of the problem at hand (see point 1: quality of the answer to the closed-ended question) is best stimulated by literal metaphors, whereas original reformulation of the problem (number of mapped elements and number of *originally* mapped elements) probably requires remote metaphors. Third, literal metaphors do not impede original thinking, as might seem intuitively to be the case, provided they are apt. If they are not, the production of original ideas is hindered and remote metaphors should be preferred. Although these findings are preliminary, they suggest some ideas concerning the use of metaphors in teaching, instruction, and problem solving. However, the problem requires more detailed research, particularly field studies.

## ACKNOWLEDGMENT

Preparation of this chapter was supported by grant No. RPBP.III.25 from the Ministry of National Education to Professor Jan Strelau.

## REFERENCES

Gentner, D. (1983). Structure mapping: a theoretical framework for analogy. *Cognitive Science*, 7, 155–170.

Gordon, W. J. J. (1961). *Synectics: The development of creative capacity.* New York: Harper and Row.

Schon, D. A. (1979). Generative metaphors: a perspective on problem setting in social policy. In A. Ortony (Ed.), *Metaphor and thought.* Cambridge: Cambridge University Press.

# 16

# Teaching Inductive Thinking to Highly Able Children

**Karl Josef Klauer**

*University of Aachen, Aachen, Germany*

Two criteria were used to identify highly able kindergarten children: assessment by teachers and an IQ $\geq$ 115 on Raven's Progressive Matrices. In this way, 16 highly able children were found, matched pairwise according to age and IQ, and then randomly allotted to two treatment conditions. In one condition the children were trained using a program for fostering inductive thinking, whereas the children in the other condition continued their normal kindergarten activities. Based on a new theory of inductive reasoning, the training was expected to have a positive effect on intelligence test performance. Results showed that all of the trained children outperformed their matched counterparts. It was concluded that, even with highly able children, the level of cognitive functioning can be improved, and that training of inductive thinking is an effective means to this end.

## INTRODUCTION

The last decades have brought a great diversity of attempts at fostering the cognitive development of children, attempts that have already been critically evaluated by several authors such as Nickerson, Perkins, and Smith (1985), Resnick (1987a), or Schwebel and Maher (1986). For this reason it seems to be advisable to begin with some aspects that led to the proposal of one more training conception.

## DIFFERENCES BETWEEN GOOD
## AND POOR PERFORMERS

Differences between the performance of experts and novices have been studied in various fields of expertise during the last two or three decades. The studies of de Groot (1965) and Chase and Simon (1973) on the differences between highly skilled and novice chess players are among the most influential ones. One major finding is that experts outperform novices right from the inception of their play, and that they have stored "chunks" of moves that they are able to recognize, recall, and apply very quickly. Chi, Glaser, and Rees (1982) as well as Chi, Feltovich, and Glaser (1981) found large differences between expert and novice physicists: High-knowledge physicists categorize problems in ways different from those of low knowledge people. They obviously perceive in some way "deeper" structures, and are less influenced by superficial attributes of the task.

Similar results have been found with problem solving. Putz-Osterloh (1981) compared the ways in which successful and less successful subjects solved intelligence test items of the Raven test. She found, even in early phases of the solution process, differences between the two groups, indicating that some determinants of success and failure are already operative in the first steps of problem solving. Comparable results when comparing the performance of older and younger children led Siegler (1985) to the conclusion that it is the *encoding phase* in which success and failure are determined.

Another point that seems worth taking into consideration is the almost too self-evident difference in performance time between experts and novices. Simon and Simon (1978) found experts to be about four times faster than novices, a result that has been confirmed several times, at least with respect to the general tendency.

Now, looking at high intelligence versus low intelligence people, it might be no coincidence that they reveal similar differences to those that have been found between experts and novices. Intelligent persons tend to conceive a task or problem in such a way that their first steps are already better than those of less able persons, and they arrive at an adequate solution not only more often but also faster. There seems to be, however, a substantial difference between experts and highly intelligent persons: Experts have become experts by a long process of learning and practice, in short by experience, and most people think that intelligence cannot be acquired this way, that intelligence cannot be conceived of as expertise in a certain field of mastery.

Putting this last aspect aside for the time being, it is interesting to ask why it might be possible that some persons encode problem situations in a better way than others from the start. Why are some people able to process incoming information not only faster but also more adequately? And why are they able to choose the proper actions faster and to execute them more precisely and more quickly than others do? To answer questions like these, one should keep in mind an empirically well-confirmed assumption of modern cognitive psychology: Perceptions are not only determined by the stimulus configuration but also by the cognitive structure of the perceiver. If two persons perceive the same situation or problem differently, it is the difference in their cognitive structures that accounts for such a result. If, however, one person conceives a certain class of problems systematically better than the other, there must be relevant differences in their cognitive structures.

Which kind of problem-relevant differences in cognitive structure are suitable to explain large amounts of the performance differences between experts, novices, high and low intelligence people, good and poor problem solvers? One possible answer is simply their knowledge. The one who knows the answer to a question can respond very quickly and absolutely correctly. This is, however, a trivial case, because hardly any thinking processes have to come into play except retrieval processes. However, it is no longer a trivial case if one person knows the *basic structure* of a class of problems very well and is able both to identify this basic structure in given problems and to perform the steps required to solve the problem. A person having this kind of *generic* knowledge and able to apply it first to identify given problems and then to solve them accordingly has a substantial advantage as compared to a person lacking this kind of knowledge. Such knowledge makes it possible to recognize, right from the beginning, a problem as an exemplar of a well-known class of problems and to solve it in a straightforward and reliable manner. This kind of knowledge permits solving a problem of this type like an expert, or an excellent problem solver, or a highly intelligent person.

An important point is that the processes of identifying basic structures in different contexts and adapting the transformational (problem solving) processes to the varying contexts should be highly automatized (Frederiksen, 1984). Automatization ensures very fast processing, high quality results, and little demand on mental resources. Automatized processes are performed rapidly, easily, and almost error free. The impressive way some people, such as experts or good problem solvers or highly intelligent persons, are able to solve certain problems can be explained to a large extent by automatization processes of the variety just described. Therefore, one might ask whether it would be possible to induce the ability for high-level performance by deliberately promoting automatization processes. If this should prove to be the case, the next question to arise is which kinds of processes should be automatized in order to foster intelligent performance.

## WHICH CONTENT IS OPTIMAL
## FOR A TRAINING PROGRAM?

In order to foster general intelligence, it is a fascinating idea to look for processes that enter into every kind of intelligent behavior. Many people are convinced that the factor $g$, general intelligence, cannot come to light throughout the great variety of cognitive processes because different intellectual tasks demand different kinds of processes. Therefore, they speculate that general intelligence becomes apparent through metacognitive processes accompanying every act of deliberate cognitive processing (Perkins & Salomon, 1989). In accordance with this view, a great deal of research has been performed to examine whether or not metacognitive heuristics have so far-reaching an influence. In the meantime, however, many researchers are more and more skeptical.

Resnick (1987b) argued that psychometric research has demonstrated the existence of a great deal of evidence in favor of general intelligence, but she insists that the search for a general problem-solving strategy has not been very successful. Moreover, Lohman (1986) brought together accumulating evidence that teaching metacognitive components might even be detrimental instead of helpful.

Another important approach has been initiated by Feuerstein and his coworkers (Feuerstein, Rand, & Hoffman, 1982; Feuerstein, Rand, Hoffman, & Miller, 1980). His instrumental enrichment program consists of an unusually large number of content-free tasks enabling the students to learn and automatize a substantial number of basic cognitive processes. Processes practiced are, for instance, spatial relations, temporal or familial relations, comparisons, number relations, classification and categorization, syllogisms, and so on. Most of the tasks are sampled from well-known intelligence tests, so that a close relationship between training and test material is guaranteed. Moreover, Feuerstein stresses the idea of bridging the gap between content free training and content bound problems in everyday life or school by systematically applying the acquired procedures to various fields and contexts.

Although this program seems to be valuable in some respects, it does not fit into the mainstream of modern problem-solving research. According to the latter, it is quite clear that problem solving depends to a large amount on the availability of relevant knowledge. No content-free practice of certain processes can compensate for the lack of a piece of knowledge if it is an indispensable prerequisite. This is the reason why many researchers in the field of cognition and problem solving stress the importance of concrete knowledge. From the point of view of these researchers, it would be advisable to dispense completely with content-free training and to adhere to teaching of a solid knowledge base, establishing in this way a domain-specific expertise. Such a conception implies a certain renunciation of the possibility of fostering by training a more or less general problem-solving ability, and it is interesting to discover that this rather pessimistic view originated from problem-solving research.

Another stream of modern cognitive psychology stresses analogical thinking as an important source for transfer of training (Gentner, 1983, 1989; Gick & Holyoak, 1983; Holyoak, 1985; Klauer, 1989a; Vosniadou & Ortony, 1989). With analogical thinking, the subject is able to recognize a basic structure or chunk or schema or paradigm in a different context (Phye, 1989). This is achieved by comparison processes, that is, by processes of identifying similarities and differences. As soon as a problem situation can be recognized as representing a special case of a well-known basic structure, the given problem can be formulated in terms of this basic structure. A person who really masters the basic structure is able to perform the required steps within this structure and to transfer it analogically to the problem at hand.

It is clear that analogical transfer does not occur automatically. Students need to be taught and they even need adequate practice. Once students have automatized it this way, they will be able to both recognize and handle it immediately and in different contexts. Fortunately, it can be expected that bright students would not need as much teaching and practice to automatize a basic structure. With highly intelligent students, often only one appropriate teaching act or one good example might be sufficient to automatize such a basic idea.

On the other hand, it is clear that one such thinking schema is of limited use because it applies only in a very limited range of problems. This disadvantage, however, can be overcome. Teaching not only one but a certain number of such paradigms of thinking will lead to a correspondingly widened area of application. The idea underlying my research during the last 5–10 years has been to teach a small number of interrelated paradigms of thinking, paradigms encompassing a central part of cognitive processing, particularly of intellectual functioning. I am speaking of inductive thinking, which has been traced back to six basic paradigms of thinking, and which is known to represent the core of general intelligence.

## INDUCTIVE THINKING

From the very beginnings of modern psychometric research in intelligence, psychologists have been interested in inductive thinking. It consists of discovering regularities and order within seeming disorder, and in detecting irregularities in a seemingly ordered field. Psychologists have invented different item formats to test these abilities. Thus, they make use of analogies, number series, categorization, or discrimination tasks. The idea recently put forward amounts to the assumption that all of these and even some other tasks require the subject to perform a certain group of mental processes. The postulated processes essentially consist of comparison processes. Comparing means nothing more than discovering similarities and differences, or—more precisely—identity and difference. As a result of such a process, both commonalities and differences are uncovered. This process of comparing can be applied to different objects, to apples, or human beings, or natural numbers. With inductive thinking, however, it is not a case of the objects as whole entities being compared to one another. That would be a more or less holistic comparison procedure. Inductive thinking requires analytical comparisons instead. It is not objects as wholes that are compared but attributes of different objects and relations between objects.

Comparing attributes of objects means comparing them, for instance, with respect to their color or form or weight or material. Comparing relations between objects means such activities as, for instance, finding out which one is larger or heavier or younger, and so on.

Uncovering similarities and differences with respect to attributes of and relations between objects is a very important mental process. In modern logic, attributes are conceived as predicates having one argument, that is, they can be asserted of one object. Relations, however, are conceived as predicates with two or more arguments, that is, they are asserted of at least two objects. The relation "is greater than" thus can only be attributed to two objects, the one being greater than the other. Realizing that attributes and relations are predicates, namely predicates with one and predicates with more than one argument, implies an important consequence. Since there are no other predicates than those with one and with more than one argument, with attributes and relations all possibilities of talking about objects are exhausted. This demonstrates the far-reaching influence of inductive thinking as it is conceived in the present theory.

Going one step further, inductive thinking can become more specific, so that it is possible to arrive at a few basic thinking paradigms encompassing all kinds of inductive thinking. To this end, a look at the following definition in the form of a mapping sentence might be helpful.

According to Table 16-1, inductive thinking varies along three facets, the first two of them being the core facets and the last one being the content or material facet. This latter one could, of course, be conceived of differently, for instance as historical, mathematical, linguistic, geographical, and so forth, material. In that case, inductive thinking would be applied to subject matter as it is encountered in schools. It thus becomes clear once again that inductive thinking can be applied to various fields, and that the present conception has a strong bearing on school-related learning.

### TABLE 16-1
### Definition of Inductive Thinking

**Inductive Thinking Consists in Discovering Regularities by Finding Out**

| Facet A | | Facet B |
|---|---|---|
| $a_1$ Similarity (Sim.) | | $b_1$ Attributes |
| $a_2$ Difference (Diff.) | with respect to | $b_2$ Relations |
| $a_3$ Sim. & Diff. | | |

| Facet C | | |
|---|---|---|
| | $C_1$ Verbal | |
| | $C_2$ Pictorial | |
| within | $C_3$ Numerical | Material |
| | $C_4$ Geometric–figural | |

For the present purposes, however, facet C has been conceived in such a way that the mapping sentence defines a universe of test items usually found in intelligence tests. The core facets A and B constitute, if suitably combined, exactly six types of items that are differentiated by different processes of inductive thinking. The six item forms are given in Table 16-2.

These basic item forms require six types of thinking processes, all of them being variants of one or more general processes. Some algorithms have been constructed showing the basic pattern of processing that can underlie all of these variants and that specify the processes required by each of the six item forms (Klauer, 1989b). In this way, one general paradigm can be differentiated into six interrelated paradigms of inductive thinking. The family tree, so to speak, of these paradigms is depicted in Figure 16-1.

The figure shows that the solving process is differentiated according to the fact that attributes or relations are to be com-

### TABLE 16-2
### The Six Item Forms of Inductive Thinking Tasks

| Profile | Name | Abbreviation | Characterization |
|---|---|---|---|
| $a_1b_1$ | Generalization | GE | Similarity with attributes |
| $a_2b_1$ | Discrimination | DI | Difference with attributes |
| $a_3b_1$ | Cross-classification | CC | Similarity and difference with attributes |
| $a_1b_2$ | Recognizing relations | RR | Similarity with relations |
| $a_2b_2$ | Discriminating relations | DR | Difference with relations |
| $a_3b_2$ | System formation | SF | Similarity and difference with relations |

FIGURE 16-1.    Family tree of inductive thinking paradigms.

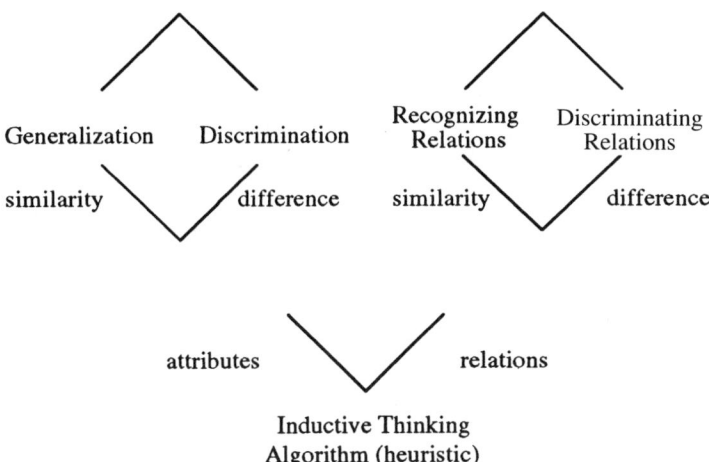

Generalization    Discrimination    Recognizing    Discriminating
                                    Relations      Relations

similarity              difference    similarity            difference

attributes              relations

Inductive Thinking
Algorithm (heuristic)

pared, and that similarities or differences or both are to be detected. Thus, a branch of attributional tasks and a branch of re-
lational tasks result. Moreover, it reveals the corresponding
tasks in both branches, for instance, that Generalization in the
left branch corresponds to Recognizing Relations in the right
branch and so on.

## PARADIGMS OF INDUCTIVE THINKING

The six classes of tasks represent six paradigms of inductive
thinking. Therefore, items of these classes can be used for
teaching the paradigms. How this might be possible will now be
demonstrated. The following examples are taken from the training program for 10- to 12-year-old children and from the Raven
Progressive Matrices Test.

    The upper part of Fig. 16-2 shows a house with windows.
Some of them are embellished with flowers. There is a certain
order to be detected, making it possible to find out how many
flowers belong to each window. The order is plus 1 in the rows,
but plus 1 and plus 2, consecutively, in the columns. The lower
part of the diagram shows the price list of an icecream shop
where some prices are not legible. They can, however, be in-
ferred from the relationship holding within the rows (plus 1 DM)
and columns (plus 0.50 DM). Although both pictures, the one
with the flower house and the one with the ice cream, are taken

FIGURE 16-2.   Examples from the training program for
10- to 12-year-old children.

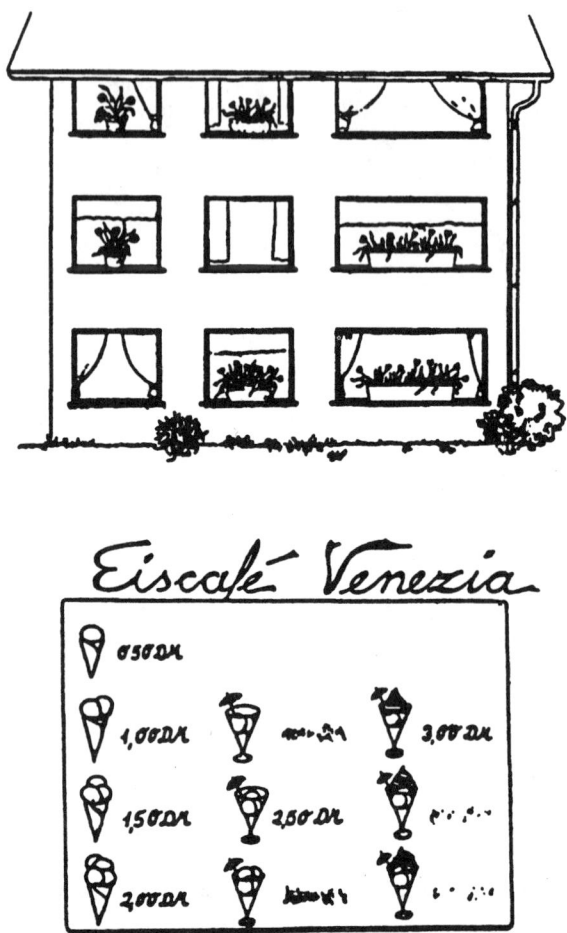

from very different areas of content, they reveal the same basic
structure. It is the same structure that can be found in Fig. 16-
3, a test item taken from the Raven test. The basic structure
underlying all of these tasks can be depicted abstractly as has
been done in 16-4. One relation holds within the rows, the same
or another one holds within the columns. This basic structure
also can be realized only partially so that different test items
result, as has been additionally depicted in Fig. 16-4. The series
and the analogy are examples that can be conceived of as partial realizations of the basic structure, the matrix. Item formats

FIGURE 16-3.    Example from Raven's Matrices.

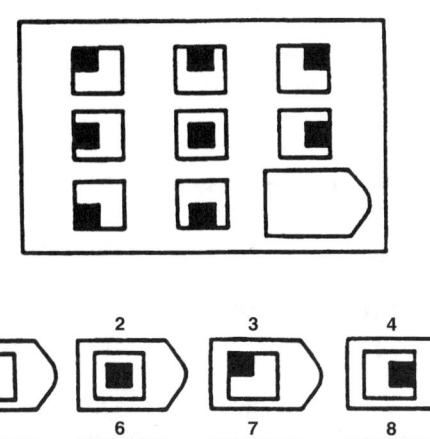

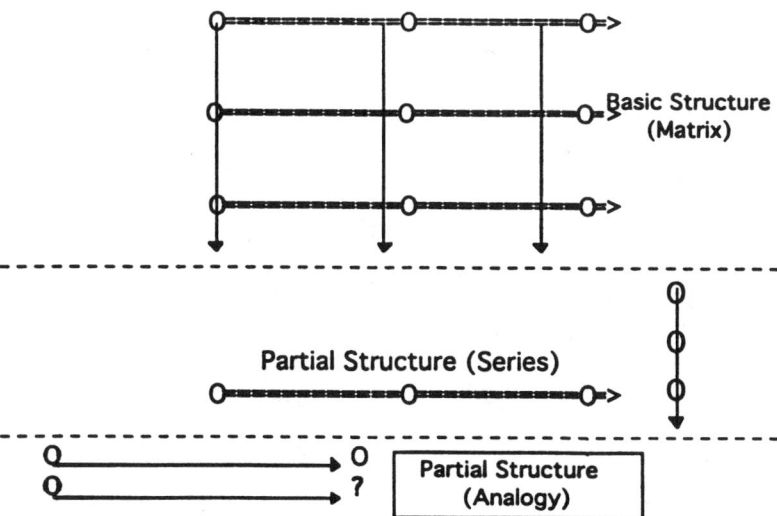

FIGURE 16-4.    Basic structure underlying the tasks.

such as the matrix, the analogy, and the series often are encountered in intelligence tests.

All of them can be solved by the same procedure, namely by
finding out that the same relation holds between corresponding
pairs of elements. The relations between the pairs can be in-

duced by a process of systematic comparing, as can be shown with the house in Fig. 16-2. It can be conceived as an arrangement of several series tasks. The same holds true for the ice cream shop in Fig. 16-2, which deals with an arrangement of numerical series, and for Fig. 16-3, where abstract figural series are given.

Figure 16-5 offers another example of a part of the basic matrix structure being dealt with now. Taking only the first two rows into consideration involves an analogy task. To solve it, the relationship between the pairs of a row is needed. However, to decide which animals have to be put into the third row, it would be necessary to find out the relationship between pairs in the columns, too.

All of these tasks can be solved in a very similar way by looking for the relationship between corresponding pairs. The tasks provide enough information for inducing the relationship. Therefore, it seems justified to assume strong transfer of training from one task to the other. This is obviously not the case, at least not under normal conditions. Children—and even adults—do not spontaneously recognize the same basic structure underlying these different kinds of tasks. This is particularly true if the tasks use elements from different content domains as, for instance, flowers or human beings or animals or prices or geometrical figures or numbers, and so on.

FIGURE 16-5.    Basic matrix structure.

A training program has to take these problems into account. Consequently it is necessary

> to teach the basic structure, the paradigm, in such a way that children can understand it;
>
> to teach how such a structure is to be solved;
>
> to teach recognizing the basic structure under different conditions, in various disguises; and
>
> to teach how the problem-solving procedure can be adapted to different content domains.

This is done for every one of the paradigms dealt with when teaching for inductive thinking. The different paradigms that are to be taught make it necessary to look for an adequate allotment of space to the different paradigms and an adequate number and distribution of repetitions within each of the paradigms. The first program, *Training Children to Think I* (Klauer, 1989c), attempted to find appropriate solutions. A summary of experimental results with normal or mentally retarded children is given in Klauer (1990b). The test of its effectiveness with bright kindergarten children will now be depicted.

## THE TRAINING EXPERIMENT

In order to identify bright kindergarten children a double procedure was used. A child was regarded as highly intelligent when the kindergarten teacher rated him or her as bright, and his or her Raven IQ was equal to or higher than 115, that is, one standard deviation above the mean. This is a widely recognized identification procedure (Feger, 1988; Heller & Feldhusen, 1986; Rost, 1989). The kindergarten teacher was asked to name the bright children, who were then tested with Raven's Progressive Matrices test. The children fulfilling the criteria were randomly allotted to a training and a nontraining control condition. The training condition consisted in a daily training session of 15–20 minutes continuing for about 15 sessions. The training took place on a one trainer-one trainee basis. The training program mentioned was used as training material. After each training session the child went back to his or her kindergarten group. During this time, the control children continued their normal kindergarten activities. A few days after the last training session all the children were retested. Both pretest and

post test were administered on an individual basis. The person
who administered the post test did not know whether or not the
child had been trained.

Table 16-3 shows the ages and IQs of the 16 children and how
they were matched to form eight pairs. The youngest child was
four years and four months old, the oldest six years and eight
months. The IQs ranged between 116–139. The mean IQs of
both groups were fairly high, indicating that highly intelligent
children had been found. The mean IQ of both groups combined
was 128.5.

In Table 16-4 the raw scores which the children achieved with
the Raven test are listed. The pretest, post test, and raw gain

### TABLE 16-3
### Ages and IQs of the Matched Pairs of Trained
### and Control Children

| Pair No. | Trained Children | | Control Children | |
|---|---|---|---|---|
| | Age | IQ | Age | IQ |
| I | 4.10 | 139 | 4.7 | 126 |
| II | 5.11 | 119 | 4.4 | 121 |
| III | 5.3 | 139 | 5.3 | 139 |
| IV | 5.1 | 139 | 5.6 | 130 |
| V | 5.4 | 125 | 5.4 | 122 |
| VI | 6.8 | 116 | 5.8 | 116 |
| VII | 5.8 | 127 | 5.10 | 125 |
| VIII | 6.0 | 134 | 5.10 | 139 |
| Mean (M) | 5.7 | 130 | 5.4 | 127 |
| Standard Deviation (s) | 0.7 | 9 | 0.7 | 8 |

### TABLE 16-4
### Raven Raw Scores and Raw Gain Scores

| Pair | Training Group | | | Control Group | | | Gain$_T$-Gain$_C$ |
|---|---|---|---|---|---|---|---|
| | Pretest | Posttest | Gain | Pretest | Posttest | Gain | |
| I | 28 | 32 | 4 | 21 | 18 | −3 | +7 |
| II | 23 | 26 | 3 | 20 | 18 | −2 | +5 |
| III | 23 | 25 | 2 | 23 | 21 | −2 | +4 |
| IV | 25 | 32 | 7 | 26 | 24 | −2 | +9 |
| V | 23 | 25 | 2 | 22 | 23 | 1 | +1 |
| VI | 23 | 30 | 7 | 20 | 24 | 4 | +3 |
| VII | 24 | 29 | 5 | 26 | 26 | 0 | +5 |
| VIII | 28 | 33 | 5 | 30 | 30 | 0 | +5 |
| M | 24.63 | 29.00 | 4.4 | 23.50 | 23.00 | −0.5 | 4.90 |
| s | 2.20 | 3.30 | 2.0 | 3.55 | 4.04 | 2.3 | 2.42 |

scores are depicted in that table. On average, a trained child gained 4.4 points, whereas a nontrained control child lost half a point.

The effect size ($d$) of the training was calculated according to the formula below. As can be seen, a correction for pretest differences was included:

$$d_{corr} = d_{post\ test} - d_{pretest}$$

$$\text{where } d = \frac{M_T - M_C}{S_p}$$

$T$ = training group, $C$ = control group; $S_p$ = pooled standard deviation.

Effect size ($d$) represents the mean difference between training and control group in terms of the control group's standard deviation. Thus, $d = 1$ results if the training group outperforms the control group by one standard deviation. Cohen (1977) speaks of a large effect if $d = 0.8$. The present data yielded a corrected $d_{corr}$ of 1.24. This is a remarkably high effect size. In a large experiment, Feuerstein obtained effect sizes from 0.22 to 0.24. In terms of IQ, the training group's mean improved from 130 to 137, whereas the control group's mean dropped from 127 to 126. Before the training, the difference between the means of the two groups was three IQ points, after training the difference had increased to 11 IQ points.

Using the raw gain scores and Wilcoxon's test for paired differences, the significance of the difference could be tested; as can be seen from Table 16-5, it was statistically significant ($p < 0.01$, two-tailed test). This is a result of the fact that with every pair of children the trained child improved more than the nontrained control child. Such a result indicates that the training effect of the program is reliable. Unfortunately, there was no op-

### TABLE 16-5
#### Raven Raw Gains and Wilcoxon Test*

| Pair | I | II | III | IV | V | VI | VII | VIII | M |
|------|---|----|----|----|----|----|-----|------|-----|
| Training | 4 | 3 | 2 | 7 | 2 | 7 | 5 | 5 | 4.4 |
| Control | −3 | −2 | −2 | −2 | 1 | 4 | 0 | 0 | −0.5 |
| T–C | 7 | 5 | 4 | 9 | 1 | 3 | 5 | 5 | 4.9 |
| Rank | 7 | 5 | 3 | 8 | 1 | 2 | 5 | 5 | |

*T = 0; $p < 0.01$ (two-tailed test).

portunity to retest the children after a longer period of time in order to see how long the effect remained stable. However, results with normal children showed that the effects dropped with time, but were still statistically significant after four months and, in another experiment, even after seven months (Klauer, 1990a).

## CONCLUSIONS

Although only 16 children were included in this training experiment it was possible to demonstrate a significant improvement among the trained children: The training yielded a fairly high effect size. Moreover, this result is by no means singular. In a recently published review (Klauer, 1990b) I was able to demonstrate the results of 15 other experiments using an intelligence test as the dependent variable. Only in four cases were there no statistically significant training effects, whereas in the remaining 11 experiments the differences were significant. The mean effect size of 0.71 was smaller than that in the present experiment, but in three cases even larger effect sizes than the present one were found. Thus, it is evident that the result presented here is part of a series of experiments using different kinds of subjects, from mildly retarded to highly gifted children, and using different kinds of intelligence tests, which yielded similar results. This body of evidence leads to the conclusion that the training procedure is effective in fostering cognitive functioning.

The next conclusion that can be drawn deals with the present theory of inductive thinking and its presumed relationship to general intelligence. There is strong evidence in favor of the assumption that the processes of discovering similarities and differences, both with attributes as well as with relations, have a direct bearing on the processes underlying general intelligence—if both are not identical. This connection might be reason enough to persuade educators to make more use of the processes of inductive thinking, that is, of uncovering commonalities and differences between attributes of objects and between relations among objects.

A final conclusion is that obviously it is possible to improve intellectual functioning even of highly able children by a suitable training program. Although the effect size was large, there is no reason to suppose that bright children can be trained more effectively than other children, nor is there any reason to assume that they are less susceptible to a training program. It is, however, a matter of educational objectives and values whether or not cognitive education of bright children is stressed. I think it is very important to help already bright and even gifted children to develop their potentialities fully. On the other hand, I think it is equally important to realize that noncognitive as well as cognitive factors make their indispensable contributions to a worthwhile life.

# REFERENCES

Chase, W. G., & Simon, H. A. (1973). Perception in chess. *Cognitive Psychology, 4*, 55–81.

Chi, M. T. H., Feltovich, P. J. & Glaser, R. (1981). Categorization and representation of physics knowledge by experts and novices. *Cognitive Science, 5*, 121–152.

Chi, M. T. H., Glaser, R., & Rees, E. (1982). Expertise in problem solving. In R. J. Sternberg (Ed.), *Advances in the psychology of human intelligence*, vol. 1 (pp. 7–75). Hillsdale, NJ: Erlbaum.

Cohen, J. (1977). *Statistical power analysis for the behavioral sciences.* New York: Academic Press.

de Groot, A. (1965). *Thought and choice in chess.* The Hague: Mouton.

Feger, B. (1988). *Hochbegabung* [Giftedness]. Bern: Huber.

Feuerstein, R., Rand, Y., & Hoffman, M. B. (1982). *The dynamic assessment of retarded performers.* Baltimore: University Park Press.

Feuerstein, R., Rand, Y., Hoffman, M., & Miller, R. (1980). *Instrumental enrichment: An intervention program for cognitive modifiability.* Baltimore: University Park Press.

Frederiksen, N. (1984). Implications of cognitive theory for instruction in problem solving. *Review of Educational Research, 54*, 363–407.

Gentner, D. (1983). Structure mapping: A theoretical framework for analogy. *Cognitive Science, 7*, 155–170.

Gentner, D. (1989). The mechanisms of analogical learning. In S. Vosniadou & A. Ortony (Eds.), *Similarity and analogical reasoning* (pp. 199–241). Cambridge: Cambridge University Press.

Gick, M. L., & Holyoak, K. J. (1983). Schema induction and analogical transfer. *Cognitive Psychology, 15*, 1–38.

Heller, K. A., & Feldhusen, J. F. (Eds.). (1986). *Identifying and nurturing the gifted.* Toronto: Huber.

Holyoak, K. J. (1985). The pragmatics of analogical transfer. In G. H. Bower (Ed.), *The psychology of learning and motivation*, vol. 19 (pp. 59–87). Orlando, FL: Academic Press.

Klauer, K. J. (1989a). Teaching for analogical transfer as a means of improving problem-solving, thinking, and learning. *Instructional Science, 18*, 179–192.

Klauer, K. J. (1989b). Paradigmatic teaching of inductive thinking. In H. Mandl, E. De Corte, N. Bennett, & H. F. Friedrich (Eds.), *Learn-

*ing and instruction in an international context*, vol. 2.2 (pp. 23–45). Oxford: Pergamon Press.

Klauer, K. J. (1989c). *Denktraining für Kinder I*. Ein Programm zur intellektuellen Förderung. [Training children to think I. A program for fostering intellect]. Göttingen: Hogrefe.

Klauer, K. J. (1990a). Denktraining für Schulanfänger. Ein neuer Ansatz zur kognitiven Förderung [Training preschoolers and first grade children to think: A new approach to fostering cognitive development]. *Praxis der Kinderpsychologie und Kinderpsychiatrie, 39*, 150–156.

Klauer, K. J. (1990b). A process of inductive reasoning tested by the teaching of domain-specific thinking strategies. *European Journal of Psychology of Education, 5*, 191–206.

Lohman, D. F. (1986). Predicting mathemathanic effects in the teaching of higher-order thinking skills. *Educational Psychologist, 21*, 191–208.

Nickerson, R. S., Perkins, D. N., & Smith, E. E. (1985). *The teaching of thinking*. Hillsdale, NJ: Erlbaum.

Perkins, D. N., & Salomon, G. (1989). Are cognitive skills context-bound? *Educational Researcher, 18*, 16–25.

Phye, G. D. (1989). Schemata training and transfer of an intellectual skill. *Journal of Educational Psychology, 81*, 347–352.

Putz-Osterloh, W. (1981). *Problemlöseprozesse und Intelligenztestleistung.* [Processes of problem-solving and intelligence test performance]. Bern: Huber.

Resnick, L. B. (1987a). *Education and learning to think*. Washington, DC: National Academy Press.

Resnick, L. B. (1987b). Instruction and the cultivation of thinking. In E. de Corte, H. Lodewijks, R. Parmentier, & P. Span (Eds.), *Learning and instruction* vol. 1 (pp. 415–442). Oxford: Pergamon Press.

Rost, D. H. (1989). Zum Thema "Hochbegabung" [On the topic "Giftedness"]. In Der Oberkreisdirektor des Kreises Neuss (Ed.), *Bundesmodell Begabtenförderung im Kreis Neuss* [National model for promoting giftedness in the Neuss region] (pp. 5–30). Mönchengladbach: Kühlen.

Schwebel, M., & Maher, C. A. (Eds.) (1986). *Facilitating cognitive development: International perspectives, programs, and practices.* New York: Haworth.

Siegler, R. S. (1985). Encoding and the development of problem solving. In S. F. Chipman, J. W. Segal, & R. Glaser (Eds.), *Thinking and learning skills*, vol. 2 (pp. 161–185). Hillsdale, NJ: Erlbaum.

Simon, D. P., & Simon, H. A. (1978). Individual differences in solving physics problems. In R. Siegler (Ed.), *Children's thinking: What develops?* (pp. 325–348). Hillsdale, NJ: Erlbaum.

Vosniadou, S., & Ortony, A. (Eds.). (1989). *Similarity and analogical reasoning.* Cambridge: Cambridge University Press.

# 17

# Achievement Motivation of Intellectually Gifted Students when Confronted with Challenging and Unchallenging Tasks

**Colleen Neitzke**

*Bad Homburg, Germany*

**Una M. Röhr-Sendlmeier**

*University of Bonn, Bonn, Germany*

Two groups of gifted adolescents solved two similar intelligence tests with differing levels of task difficulty in reverse order. Under both conditions the performance level on the less complex test was much lower, a result not observed in a control group of average intelligence. Behavioral observations revealed that the low performance of the gifted students was combined with lack of effort. This performance pattern is discussed with respect to recent postulates of achievement motivation theory, which emphasize the impact not only of the achievement motive, but also of the informational value of a given task for evaluating own level of ability. It is argued that the perceived informational value of the easier test was not high enough to create an incentive for the gifted students to perform at the highest possible level.

## INTRODUCTION

Research on gifted underachievers has focused attention on a population whose overall academic performance in achievement situations is lower than can be expected, given their extremely high level of cognitive ability (Whitmore, 1980; Wolf & Gygi, 1981; Yewchuk, 1986). Numerous causes and correlates of underachievement in gifted children and adolescents have been studied to date, but the actual measurement of the relationship between cognition, motivation, and performance has not received sufficient attention (van den Bercken, 1989). In this chapter, an empirical study is reported that approaches this neglected area of research. It focuses on the controlled investigation of underachievement on an unchallenging intellectual task.

## METHOD

As part of an investigation on the educational situation of 32 gifted tenth grade students at a German comprehensive school (*Gesamtschule*), the stability of their fluid intelligence over the previous five years was measured (Neitzke, 1988). Intelligence test results were available for these students from fifth grade (group 1) when all fifth graders at their school had been assessed with the CFT2 (Weiss, 1972), a German adaptation of Cattell's Culture Fair Intelligence Scales. Those 32 students who had achieved an IQ score of 130 or higher were included in this study. The CFT2 test version is normed for school children aged between 9–15 years. It consists of two parallel subtests of four groups of items each.

In tenth grade, when the students' average age was 15 years and eight months, the CFT20 test version (Weiss, 1980) was chosen for measurement. A number of considerations led to this decision. The construction of the CFT20 is based on the

CFT2, but it is normed for school children of all ages as well as adults without academic education. It is the most frequently used culture fair test in school and counseling settings in Germany. The students were tested in small groups of about 10 at a time. During the testing the instructor and an assistant observed independently that most students completed the sets of items long before the assigned time was up. The information that they could use the excess time to check their answers was ignored. Instead, they demonstrated boredom by yawning, playing with their pencils or gazing out of the window. There were no serious disruptions, however, so that those adolescents who did use all the available time were not disturbed.

Because of these unexpected behavioral observations and based on recent postulates of achievement motivation theory that have drawn attention to the interaction of cognitive ability, perceived level of task difficulty and performance (e.g., Meyer, 1984; Trope & Brickman, 1975; for details see the discussion that follows), the hypothesis was formulated that the intellectually gifted students would do better on a more difficult test. A similar, but more complex test version, the CFT3 (Weiss, 1971), was administered to the same group seven weeks later. This test is normed for adolescents from 14 years of age upward, university students, and adults with an academic education. The students were informed that the results of the first test had shown that it had been too easy for them. Therefore, a more difficult test, which was usually given to upper high school and university students, would be more appropriate.

In order to control for confounding effects that may have influenced the results of group 1 on the CFT3 owing to previously solving CFT20, it was decided to administer the two tests in reverse order to another group of intellectually gifted students. In addition to the first hypothesis it was postulated that students of average intellectual ability would show no difference in their performance on the two test versions. A total of 125 tenth grade students at the same school were given the CFT3 a year later (Klein, 1989). Twenty-two gifted adolescents whose IQ scores were 130 and above were identified (group 2). A control group of 21 students with IQ scores between 85 and 115 (group 3) was selected. The students' average age was 15 years and nine months. The CFT20 was administered seven weeks after CFT3. In addition, the students were asked to fill out a standardized personality inventory focusing on self-estimation of learning capacity and study behavior, the *Arbeitsverhaltensinventar* (AVI; Thiel, Keller, & Binder, 1979).

## RESULTS

The findings of this study concern

1.  a comparison of the fifth and tenth grade intelligence test results obtained for group 1;
2.  a comparison of the intelligence data—total results and subtest scores—obtained with the CFT20 and CFT3 for all three groups of tenth grade pupils;
3.  behavioral observations of these groups while solving the CFT20 and CFT3; and
4.  self-estimation results on the AVI scales for groups 2 and 3.

1.  Comparing the intelligence scores of group 1 from fifth grade with those obtained on the CFT20 and CFT3 in tenth grade, the statistical analysis revealed that the CFT20 results were significantly lower than those from the CFT2 in fifth grade ($t$ (31) = 8.28, $p < .01$). Whereas in fifth grade the average IQ had been 136.3, in the CFT20 testing in tenth grade the students reached an average IQ of 120.8. Based on the CFT3, however, there was no significant difference in measured intellectual ability between tenth grade and fifth grade ($t$ (31) = 0.64, ns). The CFT3 mean IQ (135.2 points) was almost identical with the average score in fifth grade.
2.  The difference in the total mean scores of the CFT3 and the CFT20 were statistically significant for both groups of gifted tenth grade students, that is, their scores on the more difficult test were much higher than those on the easier one. The intellectually average adolescents showed no significant difference in their two test results, although they, too, obtained somewhat higher scores ($p < .10$) on the CFT3 (see Table 17-1).

An analysis of the respective performance patterns on the two subtests for each of the three groups and both tests (see

**TABLE 17-1**
Scores on the CFT3 and CFT20 in Gifted and Average Students

| Group | N | CFT3 | | CFT20 | | $t$ | df | $p$ |
|---|---|---|---|---|---|---|---|---|
| | | M | SD | M | SD | | | |
| Gifted group 1 | 32 | 135.2 | 9.5 | 120.8 | 10.9 | 8.28 | 31 | <.01 |
| Gifted group 2 | 22 | 134.5 | 10.2 | 123.4 | 12.5 | 4.02 | 21 | <.01 |
| Control group | 21 | 106.4 | 7.4 | 101.8 | 13.0 | 1.86 | 20 | ns |

TABLE 17-2

Subtest Scores on the CFT3 and CFT20 of Gifted Students and Average Students

| Group | N | Test | Subtest 1 M | Subtest 1 SD | Subtest 2 M | Subtest 2 SD | t | df | p |
|-------|---|------|----|----|----|----|----|----|----|
| Gifted group 1 | 32 | CFT20 | 123.3 | 7.4 | 118.3 | 6.7 | 2.82 | 31 | <.01 |
|  |  | CFT3 | 135.1 | 6.2 | 135.6 | 7.8 | −0.22 | 31 | ns |
| Gifted group 2 | 22 | CFT20 | 125.2 | 13.8 | 116.5 | 11.1 | 3.02 | 21 | <.01 |
|  |  | CFT3 | 130.2 | 9.9 | 132.9 | 14.4 | −0.71 | 21 | ns |
| Control group | 21 | CFT20 | 104.3 | 11.9 | 100.1 | 11.7 | 1.88 | 20 | ns |
|  |  | CFT3 | 107.4 | 8.1 | 105.1 | 10.8 | 0.76 | 20 | ns |

Table 17-2) revealed that for both groups of gifted students scores on the second subtest of the CFT20 were significantly lower than on the first one. No such statistical effect was found for the control group, but there also was a tendency ($p < .10$) for higher scores on the first of the two subtests of the CFT20. None of the three groups showed a significant difference in the mean subtest scores of the more difficult CFT3 test.

3. The observed patterns of achievement behavior of both groups of intellectually gifted adolescents were practically identical. Two independent instructors each recorded that during the administration of the CFT20 the gifted students regularly completed the test items long before the time was up and subsequently demonstrated boredom as described. When solving the CFT3, however, the majority of the gifted adolescents worked with concentration and diligence. Only a few finished the tasks before the time was up and tended to behave as indicated, but to a negligible degree. The average ability students worked diligently on both tests, concentrating on the tasks until the time was up and showing no signs of boredom.
4. On the AVI scales the intellectually gifted students (group 2) estimated themselves significantly higher than the average ability students (group 3) in three dimensions: reflexive thinking as opposed to impulsive thinking ($t(41) = 2.77$, $p < .01$), learning by insight as opposed to stereotyped factual learning ($t(41) = 2.14$, $p < .05$) and confidence in their achievement potential and satisfaction with their achievement level ($t(41) = 2.63$, $p < .05$). They experienced significantly less fear of failure ($t(41) = 2.76$, $p < .01$). It should be noted, however, that the mean scores of the control group were well within the average range of each of these dimensions.

## DISCUSSION

Both the longitudinal and cross sectional data show that the CFT20 has very low validity for identifying intellectually gifted adolescents. Its use may, in fact, lead to a considerable under-estimation of a bright pupil's level of intellectual ability. Only administration of the more complex CFT3 standardized for older and academically educated individuals made it possible to de-scribe the outstanding fluid intelligence of group 1 as stable over a five-year period. Assessed with the CFT20 alone, the tenth grade students of both gifted groups would have been classified as intelligent, but by no means gifted. It is important to note that the scores attained by these students on the CFT20 were, on the whole, well above average. Under normal circum-stances a score at this level on an achievement test would not lead to the recognition that it might represent underachieve-ment; that is, educators might not realize that a gifted student is performing at much lower than his or her optimal level. Be-havioral observations, used as a source of additional diagnostic information when interpreting the scores, may counteract this danger.

Not only the total test results on the CFT20 as compared to the CFT3 reveal underachievement. The fact that for both gifted groups the mean scores of the second subtest of the CFT20 were significantly lower than those of the first subtest contradicts the expected performance pattern according to the test manual. Be-cause of a learning effect, higher scores usually are obtained on the second subtest. In the manual it is also suggested that this subtest gives a more reliable measurement of intellectual ability than the first one (Weiss, 1980). Taking the behavioral observa-tions during the test situations into account, the opposite ef-fect—found in this study for gifted students—is interpreted as a measure of their declining motivation to solve intellectually un-challenging tasks. On finding the tasks too easy in the first sub-test, these adolescents were not inclined to make an appropri-ate effort to solve the items of the second subtest.

The nonsignificant difference between the mean subtest scores of the CFT3 is similarly interpreted as a measure of the motivational effect of an appropriately complex task for intel-lectually gifted students. The CFT3, on the whole, seems to be a more valid instrument for assessing intellectual giftedness, al-though the observation that a few adolescents also demon-strated boredom while solving this test suggests that its ceiling also is too low for some intellectually outstanding students. The control group of students with average intelligence neither showed significantly lower total test results on the CFT20 as compared to those on the CFT3, nor much lower scores on the second subtest of the CFT20, nor any demonstration of boredom while solving this test. This implies that the underachievement reaction caused by the CFT20 is primarily shown by an intellectually gifted population. The tendency of the control group to perform at a lower level on the CFT20 and its second subtest as well, however, indicates that the CFT20 also may lead intellectually average students to underachievement to a certain extent.

The findings of this study confirm the need for an achievement motivation theory that can account for the interaction between level of cognitive ability, level of task difficulty, and level of performance. The basic postulates of traditional achievement motivation theory (e.g., Atkinson, 1964; Heckhausen, 1968, 1980) seem inadequate to account for this interaction. According to traditional theory, human beings strive to maintain or improve their own level of competence in areas of endeavor that have certain subjective and objective standards for evaluating performance. Cognitive, affective, and behavioral actions aimed at this goal are guided by the achievement motive (Murray, 1938). This motive has two functions for the maintenance of self-system. The first is to satisfy the need to strive for success. The second, dominated by the need to avoid failure, is to protect the self-system from negative feedback about a low level of competence. Achievement behavior that is dominated by the need to strive for success is demonstrated by a concentrated effort to perform at the highest possible level. Achievement behavior that is dominated by the need to avoid failure is demonstrated either in avoidance behavior or in exaggerated and highly stressful efforts to complete the task.

The behavior of the gifted pupils observed during the administration of the CFT20 cannot be explained by these postulates alone. Considering the relatively low level of difficulty of this test, success, represented by a very high score, would have been a likely outcome, considering that the conditions for optimal achievement motivation were met. These students had scored relatively high on "confidence in achievement potential" and "satisfaction with level of performance" on the AVI, which underlines their success orientation and their experience of success in achievement situations. They also had relatively little fear of failure in comparison with the control group. There-fore, on the basis of the postulates of traditional theory alone, the students should have exerted an optimal amount of effort to perform at the highest possible level. They should, for instance, have used the extra time to check their answers. Instead, they demonstrated lack of effort. During the administration of the CFT3, however, the same students made a much more concen-trated effort, striving for success and performing at the highest possible level.

More recent postulates that extend achievement motivation theory to include information seeking variables seem more ad-equate to explain the different reactions in solving the two in-telligence tests. According to this expanded theoretical frame-work (e.g. Heckhausen, 1968; Meyer, 1984; Trope, 1986; Trope & Brickman, 1975), the quality of the evaluation of the "own level of ability" also depends on the informational value of the task. An optimal amount of information is gained from tasks that have a subjectively perceived median level of difficulty. Such tasks are preferred by success oriented individuals; they represent a challenge, since success or failure are equally pos-sible. Tasks that are too easy or too difficult give information about the task, but not about the level of competence. Failure oriented individuals, that is, those who mainly strive to protect their self-system and less to improve their competence, tend to choose tasks that are either too difficult or too easy for them. The resulting success or failure then can be attributed to the level of task difficulty (Weiner, 1975). The self-estimates of the gifted students reveal that they were aware of their well above average intellectual abilities and had little fear of failure. Thus, their lack of effort while solving the CFT20 can be explained satisfactorily only by the fact that this test version provided too little challenge to their competence.

According to more recent achievement motivation theory (Heckhausen, 1968; Meyer, 1984; Trope & Brickman, 1975), sub-jective information about the level of task difficulty is provided by three aspects of the task situation:

1.  the perception of the degree of effort needed to complete the task successfully;
2.  the evaluation of one's own ability to perform successfully on a particular task, based on experience with similar tasks; and
3.  the evaluation of the level of task difficulty according to an objective norm (information about the norm population), an

individual norm (own standards of performance), and a social norm (observed performance of other individuals).

For the gifted students, these sources of information about the relatively low level of task difficulty of the CFT20 seemed to have had an influence on the lower level of achievement behavior. Firstly, the experience that the items of the first subtest did not demand a great deal of effort (individual norm) indicated that the level of task difficulty of the whole test was too low to offer an incentive to improve or maintain the personal level of competence. The amount of effort that was mobilized to perform on this test was progressively reduced during the course of the test administration. This accounts for the lower scores in the second subtest. Second, the observation that many other students also completed the tasks early activated the development of a social norm concerning the low level of task difficulty.

The higher performance on the CFT3 may be owing to the opposite effects with regard to the perception of the degree of effort required to solve the tasks and to the perception that the other students concentrated on this test. The explanation given to the students that this test was appropriate for university students and adults, that is, informing them about an objective norm, may have created an incentive to invest greater effort to perform well.

The definition of the discrepancy between the total mean scores of the two tests and the mean scores of the two subtests of the CFT20 for the gifted pupils as a measure of motivational reaction to an unchallenging task can thus be explained theoretically as a reaction to lack of diagnostic information about own level of ability supplied by the items of the CFT20. This test did not offer sufficient information about own level of ability to warrant extra effort in the gifted population.

## REFERENCES

Atkinson, J. W. (1964). *An introduction to motivation.* Princeton, NJ: Van Nostrand.

Heckhausen, H. (1968). Achievement motivation research: Current problems and some contributions towards a general theory of motivation. In J. W. Arnold (Ed.), *Nebraska Symposium on Motivation* (pp. 103–174). Lincoln, NE: University of Nebraska Press.

Heckhausen, H. (1980). *Motivation und Handeln.* Berlin: Springer.

Klein, B. (1989). Zur Situation intellektuell hochbegabter Schülerinnen und Schüler an einer Gesamtschule. Unpublished Master's thesis, University of Bonn.

Meyer, W.-U. (1984). *Das Konzept von der eigenen Begabung.* Bern: Hans Huber.

Murray, H. (1938). *Explorations in personality: A clinical and experimental study of fifty men of college age.* New York: Oxford University Press.

Neitzke, C. (1988). Die Situation von potentiell hochbegabten Schülern und Schülerinnen im 10. Schuljahr an einer Gesamtschule in Abhängigkeit von Rechtschreibleistungen und Tutoreneinschätzung. Unpublished Master's thesis, University of Bonn.

Thiel, R., Keller, G., & Binder, A. (1979). *Arbeitsverhaltensinventar (AVI).* Braunschweig: Westermann.

Trope, Y. (1986). Self-enhancement and self-assessment in achievement behavior. In R. Sorrentino & E. Higgings (Eds.), *Handbook of motivation and cognition* (pp. 350–378). New York: Wiley.

Trope, Y., & Brickman, P. (1975). Difficulty and diagnosticity as determinants of choice among tasks. *Journal of Personality and Social Psychology, 31,* 918–925.

van den Bercken, J. H. L. (1989). Intelligence and motivation in cognitive performance: Some methodological considerations. In F. Halisch & J. H. L. van den Bercken (Eds.), *International perspectives on achievement and task motivation* (pp. 165–182). Amsterdam: Swets & Zeitlinger.

Weiner, B. (1975). *Die Wirkung von Erfolg und Misserfolg auf die Leistung.* Bern: Hans Huber.

Weiss, R. H. (1971). *Grundintelligenztest, Skala 3, CFT3 (Cattell/Weiss). Handanweisungen für Durchführung, Auswertung und Interpretation.* Braunschweig: Westermann.

Weiss, R. H. (1972). *Grundintelligenztest, Skala 2, CFT2 (Cattell/Weiss). Handanweisungen für Durchführung, Auswertung und Interpretation.* Braunschweig: Westermann.

Weiss, R. H. (1980). *Grundintelligenztest, Skala 2, CFT20 (Cattell/Weiss). Handanweisungen für Durchführung, Auswertung und Interpretation* (3rd. rev. ed.). Göttingen: Hogrefe.

Whitmore, J. R. (1980). *Giftedness, conflict and underachievement.* Toronto: Allyn & Bacon.

Wolf, J., & Gygi, J. (1981). Learning disabled and gifted: Success or failure? *Journal for the Education of the Gifted, 4,* 199–206.

Yewchuk, C. (1986). Gifted/learning disabled children. Problems of assessment. In A. J. Cropley, K. K. Urban, H. Wagner, & W. Wieczerkowski (Eds.), *Giftedness: A continuing worldwide challenge* (pp. 40–48). New York: Trillium Press.

# 18

## Developing Problem-Solving Skills

**Dorien J. de Tombe**

*Delft University of Technology, Delft, The Netherlands*

Some complex societal problems, such as sudden changes in Eastern Europe or the problem of AIDS, are very hard to handle. Even defining the problem is difficult. Managers and experts often lack the knowledge and training to handle these kinds of problem, although the problems require intensive effort. Education typically offers few opportunities for learning how to handle them. Research on artificial intelligence mostly focuses on problems in stable situations that have been solved already, and ignores as-yet-unsolved problems in rapidly changing situations. Before a problem can be solved, it has to be defined: System dynamic modeling can be a powerful tool for doing this. Defining the kind of problem discussed here also requires teamwork: Managers and experts can learn to define a complex problem in a special learning environment involving cases embedded in free form games.

### MANAGING COMPLEX SOCIETAL PROBLEMS

Some of the complex societal problems of the last decade are pollution, the exponential growth of cities, sudden changes in Eastern Europe, and AIDS. Living in a modern society and being surrounded by high technology, people easily could be misled into believing that it is possible to solve all kinds of problems. However, the new and sometimes unexpected problems of the last decade have made it clear that some of them are very hard to handle. Knowledge, know-how, skills, and all the technology seem to be insufficient, and even professionals can offer no answer. There is evidence from various sources that it is very hard to define, let alone solve, these kinds of problems (Schön, 1983). Nonetheless, they require answers. As early as 1979, Botkin warned that there is a growing gap between the complexity of life and the capacity to deal with it. He called this "the human gap" (Botkin, Elmandjra, & Malitza, 1979).

Reflecting on the latest developments in Eastern European countries makes it clear that old models based on earlier situations do not function any more. In the post-communism situation of today nobody knows what is going to happen and how things are going to develop. Situations change very quickly, old strategies no longer work, and old managers are replaced although new ones are not accustomed to doing their work. The planned economy and the old communism seem to have failed, but alternatives are uncertain. In theory it is possible to change to a democracy combined with a market economy, but not many people in Eastern Europe have much idea of what a market economy really is and how a democracy works. Moreover, people must learn to use democracy. Copying the models of the Western capitalist countries may lead to a disaster. Sometimes the situation is unstable and could even become explosive. Even though the policymakers and economists do not know the answers, ways of planning and guiding the new situations must be found.

## DO CHILDREN LEARN PROBLEM SOLVING IN SCHOOL?

In school, children are educated to become fruitful members of society. They should be able to make a living, be reasonably socialized, and be able to deal with things like bureaucracy. These are broad, often implicit learning goals. The school as the major institution of education operationalizes these broad goals into smaller learning goals, dividing these into different disciplines, disciplines into domains, domains into subjects, and subjects into paragraphs. In this way it is possible to focus on the special problems of a particular subject, such as being able to read at a certain level. Most educational systems focus on strictly divided subjects, like history, economics, or physics, although there are some educational systems that try to overcome the domain gap by focusing on interdisciplinary issues instead of separate subjects.

## WHAT IS WRONG WITH THE USUAL TEACHING METHODS?

The object of teaching mostly is transmission of some small part of some domain of knowledge. Students learn the facts and rules of the subject. They are trained to solve the very specific problems of that subject by applying specific domain-related problem-solving methods. Teaching subject after subject is very efficient for the training of specific skills in that part of the domain, but is not the ultimate learning goal. The subject taught is not a goal in itself, although it often looks like one.

In training small subtasks in different domains, teachers hope that transfer will occur from the learning environment to the complex problems of everyday life, but these often contain aspects of different domains. They involve complexity, uncertainty, and vagueness. Research at the university of Nijmegen showed that the everyday life of a teacher has 55 different aspects, whereas in teacher training almost all the attention and time go to learning content or didactic aspects, but none to the everyday life aspects of the teachers' work. Unfortunately, educators often forget to put the artificially divided domains back together into learning situations in which the students can be trained in all aspects of a problem. For many socially relevant situations, knowledge and experience on how to handle these kinds of problems is missing. Real societal problems often are complex, multifaceted, and hard to define. Dealing with these kinds of problems differs greatly from what is required for the well-defined problems solved in school (Brown, Collins, & Duguid, 1989).

## TEACHING PROBLEM SOLVING IN THE LAST THREE DECADES

During the last three decades psychologists and learning theorists frequently have discussed the question of problem solving techniques. Should domain-specific knowledge be taught, or general heuristics for problem solving. In the 1950s and 1960s the answer was that teaching general problem-solving techniques is the best way to spend teaching time. Support came from the field of chess: Domain-specific knowledge is needed, but is not of decisive importance, since basic rules also lead to good play (Perkins & Salomon, 1989). This inspired researchers on artificial intelligence to build a program called "The General Problem Solver" (Newell & Simon, 1972). However, on looking more closely at the nature of the chess game, it was noted that the chess masters used not only general heuristics but also a great deal of domain-specific knowledge (schemata) (Chase & Simon, 1973). Having established this, artificial intelligence research switched from building general heuristics to building expert systems. Expert systems help (beginning) experts to enhance their domain knowledge by focusing such knowledge on very specific problems in the domain.

However, what is to be done with atypical problems? Research showed that experts confronted with atypical problems in their field not only use domain knowledge, but also switch to general heuristics closely related to the domain in order to solve problems. Thus, it looks as though domain-specific knowledge and general heuristics related to the domain would form a good combination. Some proof for this comes from the field of reading comprehension. Palinscar and Brown improved the reading comprehension of poor readers with their reading method "Reciprocal Teaching" (Baker & Brown, 1984; Palinscar, 1986). The reason for the success of the program is that not only reading comprehension is taught, but also metacognitive skills close to the domain. These metacognitive skills can be regarded as general domain-related heuristics. However, reading is a metacognitive skill, and that could have caused at least some of the transfer.

## GENERAL HEURISTICS

Are there also general heuristics that are not domain-related? These would be a great help in solving problems going beyond a single domain, as is the case with complex societal problems. In the field of artificial intelligence and cognitive psychology there are two programs that claim to be general heuristic problem-solving instruments. One program is ATC* (Adaptive Control of Thought) (Anderson, 1983). ACT* is a model of cognition in which stored task knowledge can be procedurally compiled. It represents knowledge as production systems. Although it purports to be a general psychological theory of the learning of skills needed to produce the observed behavior, and to be a skill-independent problem-solving instrument, it can solve only small problems, such as geometry proofs and translations of English into French (Boden, 1988). The other program is SOAR (State Operate And Result) by Allen Newell (Laird, Newell, & Rosenbaum, 1987), who is seeking to find a general theory of cognition. SOAR is a psychological model of natural intelligence combined with expert systems of artificial intelligence, based on the power of production systems. A single set of mechanisms is thought to be capable of producing all human cognitive behavior. The basic idea of the program is that human beings are regarded as information-processing systems. It uses a machine metaphor; if the production rule fits, it fires. SOAR is a developing system capable of general intelligence, and can handle a great number of the small artificial intelligence problems. The program is a combination of specific knowledge and general heuristics, based on the problem space hypotheses of Newell and Simon (Newell & Simon, 1972). The problem space is the space in which the solution of the problem can be found. In the problem space hypotheses all problem solving can be described in terms of systematic (analytic or heuristic) search in a problem space. It is very interesting that both programs can learn. Rules are reinforced or strengthened as long as they are not found to lead to errors. When learning occurs, the program can reach conclusions more rapidly.

These two computational theories both claim to offer a unified theory of cognition, but it is too early to tell if this is true. A unified theory means integrating and explaining all the different small-scale cognitive theories: This level has not yet been reached. Although these are very interesting instruments, they can cope with only well-defined problems in a well defined problem space, which have already been solved. Unfortunately, these are not the ill-structured problems that society is confronted with.

## ATTEMPTS TO IMPROVE THE TEACHING OF PROBLEM SOLVING

Bruner stated that education does not succeed in teaching problem solving even to the most intelligent children (Bruner,

1973). Recent research on Dutch education shows that little attention is given to problem solving. Where there is training in problem solving it is more a matter of applying rules to well-defined structured problems than an exploratory or creative activity in solving ill-structured problems. According to Schank, "the educational system has created an environment in which students are scared to explore creative hypotheses because of their fear of failure. This cultivates a belief in a single 'correct' solution to a problem" (Schank & Edelson, 1989). Bruner (1973) argued that giving more attention to discovery learning would enhance the problem-solving capacity of children. From the perspective of artificial intelligence, attempts have been made to use the computer for training problem solving in children. Papert (1980) sought to enhance the problem-solving capacity of children by giving them a stimulating and inviting exploration world, the microworld of Logo, a self-organized learning environment. Schank and Edelson (1989) would like the computer to be used as a friend, whom one can ask questions, as adults did when they were young. Education should give more attention to asking questions instead of giving answers. Unfortunately, however, when attention is given to problem solving in education, it is to problem solving within a domain, not to interdisciplinary real-life problems in changing situations.

## WHEN IS A PROBLEM SOLVED?

A problem can only be solved when it is recognized as a problem. Whose problem is it, and who are the ones who are going to solve it? Subsequently, the question can be asked: Is it possible to solve this problem, and when is it solved? Problems solved for one group can be the start of problems for others. A solved problem often is the beginning of a new problem. For many social problems there are no solutions in the form of a final and objective answer, and many must be resolved over and over again. Not all ill-defined problems can be translated into well-defined ones, since ill definition is more than lack of data and relevant information. Problems that are very hard to define are called "wicked" problems—it is uncertain whether or when these are solved. When a wicked problem is defined, it has been "tamed" (Rittel & Webber, 1973). Another aspect is complexity. A common general heuristic in solving a complex problem involves dividing it into subproblems (Newell & Simon, 1972), but the question arises of how dividing a problem into subproblems relates to complexity? Complexity cannot be eliminated by dividing a problem into pieces and putting them together later on. Complexity is a part of the problem.

## DEFINING COMPLEX INTERDISCIPLINARY PROBLEMS

Before the process of solving a problem can be started, the problem must be "set." Problem setting involves defining the problem space, and defining the scope of the problem. This involves defining the domain(s), the persons involved, the aggregation level, and the timespan of the problem. Knowledge and experience on how to handle this kind of problem often is missing. It is not always clear which domains, which fields, and which people are involved. Defining problems transcending domains is not a single person's job, but demands knowledge of various domains. Consequently, several specialists of differing expertise must work together to set the problem. Selecting the team is the first step in defining the problem. This is done on the basis of a mental model of the problem formed by the people who select the team. Selecting experts is directly related to the defining of the domains. Depending on which domains are involved, experts are invited to join the problem-setting team. Choosing people and selecting the domains can be a circular process. While clarifying which domains are involved, some experts may leave or join the group. Selecting people also depends on which point of view is chosen for setting the problem. Selection of certain people yields a conceptual model of the problem, but excludes certain solutions.

First the domains have to be defined, and then the level of aggregation, in order to determine whether the problem is defined on the micro-, meso-, or macro level. Subsequently, the countries, organizations and people involved, followed by the time scope of the problem, can be defined: Is it a problem that needs to be handled directly, immediately, or can it wait? Is it a problem of the past that is still having an effect, or is it a problem that is going to play a role in the future? On this basis, it can be decided whose responsibility it is to deal with the problem. By talking with each other people can make their mental idea of the problem more concrete. The starting point often is a vague idea about the problem, a vague mental model. Starting from this it is possible to look for data on the problem; finding these can lead to changes in the mental model. On the basis of this changing model, it is necessary to look for further data to connect the mental model to reality. Making a mental model thus is a circular process linking model and supporting data.

To make a conceptual model of the problem up-to-date, data concerning the latest developments in the different domains are needed: Data about the latest developments in technology, new political movements, the financial situation of the country, the possibilities of joint ventures, new government rules, latest medical developments, and so forth. Although not all data will be available, the problem setters should try to make the conceptual model of the problem as complete as possible. In order to be able to start handling the problem, the whole group of problem solvers should share more or less the same conceptual model—there need not be a complete consensus, but at least some kind of agreement on what the conceptual model of the problem is. Formulating this model of the problem can be the first step in solving it.

When the problem has been defined, it is possible to ascertain whether the whole problem or a part of it can be modeled in some kind of computer-aided decision support system, such as making a causal model of the relations and data flow of the entities, variables, and parameters. It can be a static or a system dynamic model such as a simulation on the computer. A simulation model makes it possible to form a picture of the consequences of various interventions. System dynamic modeling also can offer some support in the phase of analyzing complex problems. This approach focuses on cause–effect loops that make it possible to see whether one object has a positive or negative effect on another.

## A CONCRETE EXAMPLE—DEFINING THE AIDS PROBLEM

In defining a problem, often it is necessary to start with a rather vague idea of what it looks like: In the case of AIDS, some vague notion of how people get AIDS and how the disease develops. There also may be some vague ideas about what can be done to prevent the epidemic or slow down its spread. The four major points in the development of the disease depicted in Figure 18-1 offer a starting point for system dynamic modeling.

FIGURE 18-1.    The development of AIDS as a starting point for system dynamic modeling.

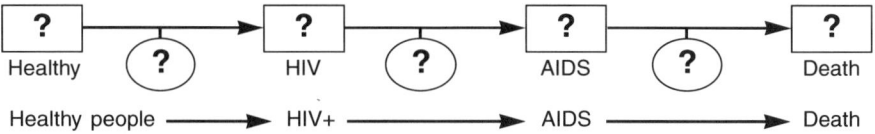

This simple model can serve as the start for discussions in the expert team. Talking about the model can make it clear that more information is needed for its formulation. Up-to-date data are needed to relate the model to reality, such as how many people are seropositive, time between infection and full blown AIDS, and percentage of healthy people who become infected with the AIDS virus. With the new data the model will become more detailed and more complicated. During this process it can become apparent that the problem-setting team needs additional experts, such as an educationalist to deal with the area of sexual education for safe sex in schools. Drawing a graphic model helps structure the problem by making it possible to concentrate on special aspects of it. A dynamic model makes clear the way in which the several parts of the problem influence each other, and permits simulations of future developments of the system.

The visualization involved in this model makes it easier to see what part of the problem is being referred to and where in the model data are missing. Handling complex problems demands knowledge of various domains, so that specialists with differing expertise must work together to set and solve the problem. This can cause serious communication problems because of the context boundness of each expert's knowledge and the colliding interests of participants. Each participant's view is colored by his or her own experience, culture, position, discipline, and language. Having a mutual graphic perception of the problem can help focus on the same issue. The model can function as a mutual language for talking about the problem (see Figure 18-2).

Defining a problem is directly related to handling it. This is clearly seen in the defining of the AIDS problem. The first notion of AIDS in the United States was that a large number of young homosexual men were dying of diseases that seemed to be caused by an immune deficiency: the first definition of the AIDS problem was that it was a homosexual disease and therefore a homosexual problem, even though there were already

FIGURE 18-2.    Graphic perception of the problem.

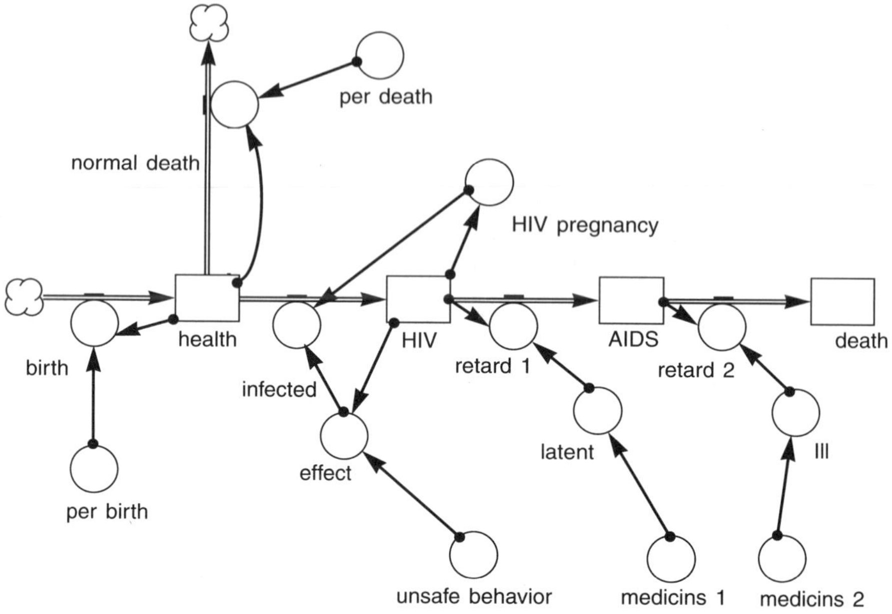

signs that the same virus was causing deaths in Africa among heterosexuals. Defining the AIDS problem as a homosexual disease and a homosexual problem in a puritanical society like the United States has caused a great deal of trouble that probably could have been avoided.

> Homosexuals are not very popular in the United States. The Moral Majority was not eager to help fund research for a homosexual disease. Some people even held the opinion that the promiscuity of homosexual men is reprehensible, and that they thus deserve this kind of punishment.

> By defining AIDS as a homosexual disease, people who did not regard themselves as homosexual were encouraged to think that they were immune to it.

> A great deal of US scientific research is made possible by special funding by the government, the states, or companies. Initially, the government regarded special funding for research on a homosexual disease as unacceptable to the electors. Companies did not want to connect their names with homosexuality. The consequence was

that funding of research for this new medical phenomenon and social problem was scarce in the beginning.

## TRAINING AND TRANSFER

Experts and managers who must solve these kinds of problems need training in defining complex domain transcending problems. What kind is needed? The most frequently used teaching methods in school are embedded in a one-to-one situation, whether it is one teacher and one student or one teacher and one group or classroom. For setting and handling complex problems, experience with cooperative problem setting is necessary, with problems that are undefined or only vaguely defined—data and knowledge are missing. The other vital element is training with whole problems, so that experience with complexity will be gained.

In order to enhance transfer to reality, the training situation must be as realistic as possible (de Tombe, 1990). By taking an actual case as a prototype of a real complex problem, a case in which the people involved can use their domain-specific knowledge and problem-setting methods in combination with their own commonsense knowledge, a learning situation approximating the natural setting can be reached. In this way a group of experts in the building field, for instance, should be trained with cases involving building new factories or new houses. A group of experts and managers in the field of health care should be trained with health care problems. These cases can be imbedded in a game, in which the complexity of the whole problem can be taken into account. The game into which the case is built discourages the people being trained from becoming too serious and too realistic. In a game it is possible to try out several strategies without causing serious problems, since mistakes do not have the impact they have in real life. On the other hand, a game can be used to generate a certain degree of tension and impose some constraints.

## A SPECIAL LEARNING ENVIRONMENT

A free-form game is a game with as few rules as possible where, in a nonthreatening situation, people can learn to practice defining complex cross-domain problems. A free-form game gives the participants the opportunity to experience the context boundness of each other's knowledge. This is the personal knowledge of each participant, the knowledge that is colored by experience, culture, position, and discipline from whose standpoint he or she considers the problem. Beside this, the participants may have divergent interests and different levels of power. In playing a free-form game it is possible to learn to deal with hidden agendas and divergent interests, become aware of blind spots in personal knowledge, experience the changing of levels from an outsider's viewpoint to that of an insider, and appreciate the complexity of the problem. It is important to recognize not only the boundaries of one's own knowledge, but also the boundaries of knowledge in the field. In defining the problem it is important to be aware that there are two kinds of knowledge: knowledge of facts and rules, universal, time-invariable knowledge, and context-dependent knowledge.

In order to obtain the full benefit of the training, the trainees should be able to act in accordance with their own capacities and interests. In a free-form game with a special case as a problem-defining item, the problem space should not be narrowed by the teacher by defining the space in which to search for a solution. The trainees should be encouraged to try to define the problem space themselves. In this kind of free-form game the game operator has the role of a facilitator. In education there is too little attention to problem setting and solving. If people are to set and handle complex societal problems, they need training with these kinds of problems from an early age; not only very intelligent children, but all children.

## REFERENCES

Anderson, J. A. (1983). A spreading activation theory of memory. *Journal of Verbal Learning and Verbal Behaviour*, 22, 261–295.

Anderson, J. A. (1989). Psychology and intelligent tutoring in artificial intelligence and education. In D. J. Bierman, J. Breuker, & J. Sandberg (Eds.), *Artificial intelligence and education.* Amsterdam: IOS.

Baker, L., & Brown, A. L. (1984). Metacognitive skills and reading. In R. Pearson (Ed.), *Handbook of reading research.* New York: Longman.

Boden, M. A. (1988). *Computer models of mind, computational approaches in theoretical psychology.* Cambridge: Cambridge University Press.

Botkin, J. W., Elmandjra, M., & Malitza, M. (1979). *No limits to learning: Bridging the human gap.* Oxford: Pergamon.

Brown, J. S., Collins, A., & Duguid, P. (1989). Situated cognition and the culture of learning. *Educational Researcher, 18,* 32–42.

Bruner, J. S. (1973). *The relevance of education.* New York: The Norton Library.

Chase, W. C., & Simon, H. A. (1973). Perception in chess. *Cognitive Psychology, 4,* 55–81.

Laird, J. E., Newell, A., & Rosenbloom, P. S. (1987). SOAR: An architecture for general intelligence. *Artificial intelligence.* Amsterdam: Elsevier.

Newell, A., & Simon, H. A. (1972). *The theory of human problem solving.* Englewood Cliffs, NJ: Prentice-Hall.

Palinscar, A. S. (1986). Reciprocal teaching. In ASCD (Association for Supervision and Curriculum Development), *Teaching reading as thinking.* Washington, DC: NAK Production Associates.

Papert, S. (1980). *Mindstorms.* New York: Basic Books.

Perkins, D. N., & Salomon, G. (1989). Are cognitive skills context-bound? *Educational Researcher, 18,* 16–26.

Rittel, H. W. J., & Webber, M. M. (1973). Dilemmas in a general theory of planning. *Policy Sciences, 4,* 155–169.

Schank, R., & Edelson, D. J. (1989). Discovery systems. In D. Bierman, J. Breuker, & J. Sandberg (Eds.), *Artificial intelligence and education.* Amsterdam: IOS.

Schön, D. A. (1983) *The reflected practitioner.* New York: Jossey Bass.

de Tombe, P. I. (1990). Manager training environment for setting complex problems. In D. F. Anderson, J. D. Richardson, & J. D. Sterman (Eds.), *System Dynamics '90* (pp 280–293). Boston, MA: The System Dynamics Society.

# Section 3

---

# Musical Talent

# 19

# Measuring Musical Talent Using the Complex Unity of a Piece of Music

**Harry T. Conrad**

*Asendorf, Germany*

Usually special factors thought to correlate with music are taken as tools for measuring musical ability: pitch, rhythm, and musical intelligence. It is expected that these tests will differentiate between people. Here elements of an approach to using the unity of music itself for differentation are offered, based on the hypothesis that a musical composition might, in a later stage of development, not only correlate highly with validated ability tests but also, because of its closeness to real life, make a positive contribution to the further development of musical ability tests.

## INTRODUCTION

The original "Seashore Measures of Musical Talents" were published in 1919, followed by a revision in 1939 (Seashore, 1939). Until recently there had been no further development of this procedure, despite the fact that music science, especially the systematic branch, has taken steps in the direction of a more empirical approach (see Füller, 1974). Those active in musicology give good reasons why they believe, up to this point, that a test of musical talent would be of no value. Two typical arguments are given here as examples.

1.  Seashore's Test measures only basic functions of the human perception system, such as pitch, loudness, rhythm, timbre, and tonal memory. Although these capacities are *conditio sine qua non* in musical talent, there are too many additional dimensions that have to be taken into account to justify the name "Musical Talent Test." A particular problem is the complexity of music as a dynamic system with ever-changing parameters. If the "Seashore" capacities only are considered, neither music nor musical talent are being discussed.
2.  Even if measurement of musical ability were possible, what would such a test be good for? This test would have nothing to do with the chances of a musician in his or her career. Sociopsychological variables are a major determinant of these chances. It might well be better to test whether a musician has management qualities; this might be a better indicator of later success.

Nevertheless, it might be possible to find theoretical and empirical evidence to solve the complexity problem, and to make clear what such a test could be good for.

Thousands of students in Germany dream of a professional career in music. On the assumption that at least 51% of the total variance of all the parameters responsible for later success as a professional is attributable to musical talent, a musical talent test could indicate the existence of a precondition that everybody who wants to have any chance at all in music would have to fulfill. A career as a pop singer might be much more influenced by other (sociopsychological) variables, and for this reason the present approach will be limited to the classical branch.

Students must be aware that only an estimated 5–10% of each year's output have a chance of getting a job, as there are not enough jobs as musicians in Germany (e.g., jobs in an orchestra, as a singer, a pianists, or a teacher). Far from being too low, this estimate may even be too high. The classical branch is a very good example of the effects of multicultural and international competition. Musicians from United States, Japan, Korea, Austria, Australia, France, Italy, and the former USSR, Poland, and Hungary are applying for jobs in Europe, especially Germany. Music education in the United States and Japan is much better than in Germany. Evidence is to be found in all well-known opera houses on the continent: in top positions are the soprano from Korea, the tenor from the United States and the bass from the former USSR, whereas a reasonable number of people from these countries work as orchestra musicians and in the chorus. Even more evidence is found in famous summer camps, like the Summer University "Mozarteum Salzburg" in Austria, a place where highly able music students can establish the extent to which they possess the necessary qualities. The representation of Germans is extremely low; very often German students are not permitted by their teachers to go to such camps. As a very negative result, many students believe themselves to be gifted for a musical career, whereas their talent is not even good enough to be accepted for participation in such a summer camp.

Thus, such a test could have at least one function: To give students some help in deciding if there is at least a chance of reaching the basic professional standard. This professional standard is set by the professionals themselves, by those active as opera singers, orchestra musicians, and conductors. Under the assumption that the variables that determine such a "Basic Professional Standard Music Test" (BPSMT) do not correlate too highly with the social aspects, it might be possible to find a way of measuring these variables.

## THEORETICAL BACKGROUND

A music student should be able to understand music, for instance, the complexity of a certain piece. If a conductor is listening to music, his or her specific talent is shown by the capacity to listen to all the "lines" the composer created; the violins, the trumpets, a combination of both. In his or her mind the conductor has the full context of the music. He or she may hear, just before it is played, the solo violin in combination with this context. There is an interaction between orchestral sound and specific lines of music. To integrate the system given in written codes (partitur, score) the conductor will come up with a specific and personal interpretation. A very important quality (which needs to be quantified as a variable) of a professional therefore might be the capacity to receive more information from a piece of music than a nonprofessional, who may only have the capacity to listen to one line of violins, or even to listen to the general musical sound alone, what is called here the "context" of the music. The person may even possibly not understand anything at all: What is then heard is "noise."

Complexity of a piece of music, being a variable of musical talent, will be able gradually to differentiate between students and professionals. Talent is thought of as something anybody possesses to some degree. This approach involves thinking of music as a stimulus system with a specific grade of complexity, complexity defined here as the structure of the basic musical context (for instance, the harmonic systems within a piece)— the basic system—and the sum of interacting and parallel ongoing subsystems (e.g., the music lines of different instruments). Processing music would thus involve parallel, continuous interactive systems, as described by Rumelhart and McClelland (1986).

A specific musical piece—the total stimulus system input— activates the listener's combined emotional and cognitive systems through the basic structures and processes related to emotional reactions and through the interacting and parallel subsystems related to integrating emotional and cognitive data. As a continuous parallel interacting system is involved, there is continous interaction between the level of context (basic system) and the subsystems, and vice versa. Activation through the basic system is nonspecific in the sense described by Magoun (1963), and involves the limbic system, the emotion center, and the ascending reticular activating system (ARAS) (Rosenzweig & Leiman, 1990; Werbik, 1971). There is specific (additive, individual) activation through the subsystems. (Reference is made also to the theory of short-term memory and the importance of rehearsal, as sublines of music are repeated very often in a heterogeneous mode [Atkinson & Shiffrin, 1968].)

The level of activation resulting from an individual complex musical input is detemined by "pacer level." Any complex musical stimulus configuration gives a certain emotional activation status to the individual. Under the condition that all stimuli of that complex system can be completely recognized by the individual, he or she is said to have reached the pacer level, the maximum possible input activation the specific individual can arrive at. The activation level of an individal, when listening to music at a certain time, must be very near to the total available output activation capacity of the music if the level of that individual's activation is to be changed positively, with a resulting positive emotional reaction (Berlyne, 1950, 1955, 1960, 1964; Dember & Earl, 1957). If the complex musical stimulus (CMS) does not nearly match the pacer level of an individual, the person will not react, or will react negatively to the music. Whether the individual pacer level is below the level of complexity of the music or above it does not make any difference. The person will reject the music, and the reaction will be negative as a function of pacer difference.

The relationships of pacer level (PL) to other variables are as follows (see Dember 1956a,b; Dember, Earl, & Paradise, 1957).

1. If the difference between the specific level of complexity of a complex musical stimulus and the maximum capacity for emotional arousal of an individual reaches a minimum, then this person's activation status reaches a maximum.
2. If the level of emotional arousal and the complexity of the music stimulus are not at least similar, then a negative emotional reaction (rejection) occurs. The degree of rejection grows with dissimilarity. Actually, only a limited part of the complex musical stimulus contributes to the individual activation status.
3. $GA_i$ is the level of emotional arousal of a person $i$, $CMS_j$ a complex musical stimulus of a specific grade of complexity $j$, EK the environmental influence on activation status and Dc the contribution of difference in activation status, measured by the Seashore test differences. The following function gives the actual level of emotional activation of an individual while listening to a piece of music.

$$GA_i = CMS_j * PL2_i + EK * PL_i + Dc$$

The figure on the following page (Figure 18-1) that, for simplicity's sake, does not take account of EK and Dc, shows that

1. $PL_i$ of a subject must be greater than a certain level by not less than 1/2 of a standard deviation if the music is to start its intensive activation work. For a first trial, a CMS of middle level is preferable.
2. If $CMS_j$ is very high, this influences only a high PL.

The model requires strong changes in EK and Dc, if they are to influence the basic function $GA = CMS * PL2$. Nevertheless,

FIGURE 19-1.   The influence of complex music stimulus on pacer level.

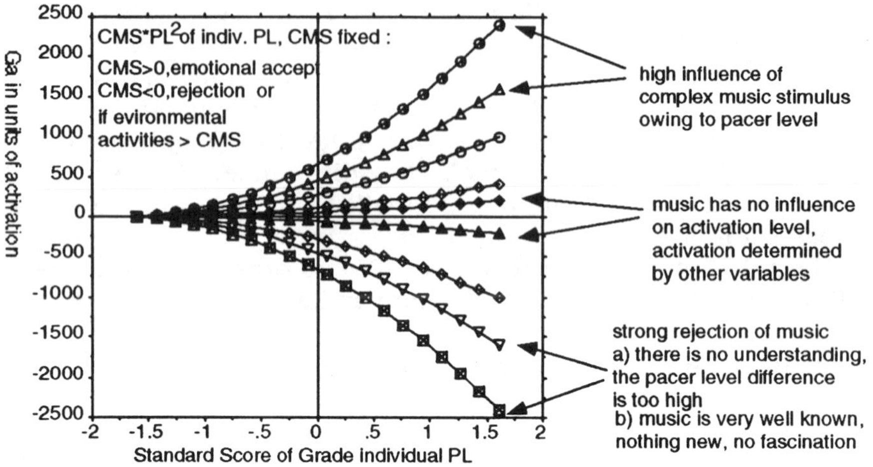

this is possible. If you listen to music while learning or reading you have such a case. Even when CMS = PL, music will not influence your activation state very much, as it is influenced much more by your actual studies. In this case EK becomes stronger and the angle of climb is going to be reduced. Dc might not exert much influence in general, as it could be expected that any student of music would reach the standard Seashore found for professional musicians. Nevertheless, this factor can be of tremendous influence for the one or the other student.

These hypotheses are also valid in the case of a complex language stimulus (CLS). The difference when CMS is compared with CLS is that the basic system is equivalent only for a certain time, because in music there is always the chance of changing the basic system within one context. Thus, the subsystems are very different. In language there is in general only one dominant subsystem line (which communicates the actual meaning to the partner) and several nondominant language lines that, although they exist and are sometimes as numerous as in music, do not come to dominate within the same context. In music, any dominant line can become nondominant, and this can change all the time music is going on. Shannon and Weaver (1949) described in their communication model the "transmission of signals" in a way analogous to the presented concept of "dominant line" and "nondominant lines." These are also defined in the broadened communication model of Hermann as "nonverbal components" (see Spada, 1990).

## EXPECTED OUTCOME OF THESE THEORIES

Assuming that testing conditions remain constant and that CMS and CLS have the task of transmitting a specific message, CMS will

1. arrive much faster at the pacer level of the basic system, and activate the emotional basic system of the person more intensely compared with CLS. If $GA_i - GA_{CMS}$ is at a minimum, then $GA_{CMS}$ is significantly higher than $GA_{CLS}$;
2. give additional impetus to the activation of arousal (combined emotional and cognitive system activation) resulting in the forced accelerated activation described in the quadratic function, if CMS is more complex owing to PDP (see footnote); and
3. not or only in reduced degree reach the pacer level (PL) of any individual ($i$), if $PL_i$ is significantly higher than $PL_{CMS}$. There is a threshold distance to the CMS and the activated data processing difference between CML and CMS approaches zero.

These theoretical results give grounds for anticipating complications: specifically, that for a given CMS there is the following theoretical activation model (Figure 19-2).

The $x$-axis gives the specific pacer level of any individual beginning with 0 and ranging to the maximum pacer level at $PL_{max}$. Only subjects near $PL_i$ will reach the maximum level of activation. In the case of minimum understanding (CML is significantly higher than $PL_i$), activation is low, as well as in the case where CML is significantly lower than $PL_i$. The function differentiates between individuals only from 0 to the actual $PL_{max}$ level.

This problem can be solved empirically. A series of "CMS items," that is, pieces of music must be found that correspond to the maximum pacer level of professionals. Variance would be at a minimum in this case (see Figure 19-3).

In the case of a complex language stimulus (CLS) it is pos-

FIGURE 19-2.    Theoretical activation model.

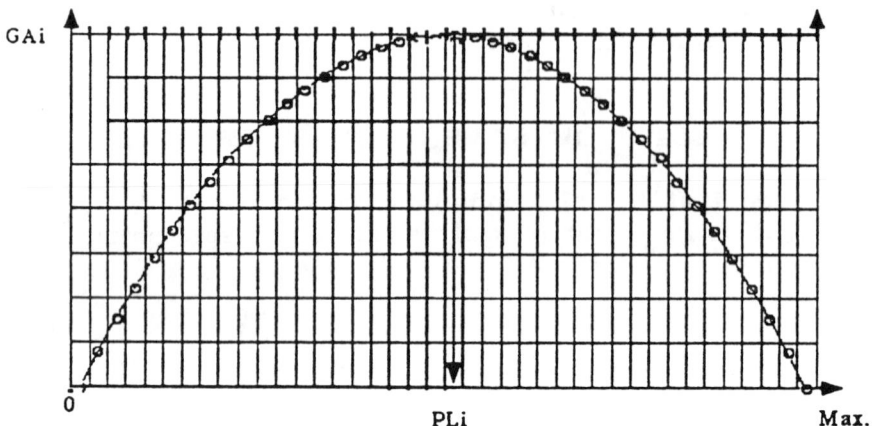

tulated that the degree of activation (GA) would be constant. If this is true, then CLS offers a scale, as CLS activation could be compared with CMS activation. For professionals, it is hypothesized that $GA_{CMS} - GA_{CLS}$ would be at a minimum. In this case it would—for a CMS corresponding to professional pacer levels—only be necessary to look at the function from 0 to A ($PL_{prof}$) as shown in Figure 19-3 (CMS 2). As can be seen, all the subjects outside A will have a pacer level below the professional standard.

## PROCEDURE

### Measurement of Change in Emotional Arousal

By "activation" is meant here the combined emotional-cognitive system. Emotional activation, modulated by cognitive operations, would ideally be measured directly. Unfortunately, however, physiological instruments still do not measure much more than the fact that there is some degree of emotional activation under very artificial conditions (Machleidt, Gutjahr, & Mügge, 1990). Consequently, a questionnaire requiring answers on a seven-point Likert scale (from 0 to 6) was constructed to measure the degree to which individuals judged specific adjectives as appropriate for describing the music input. The questionnaire contained 58 adjectives designed to measure emotional activity in response to CMS and CLS. The adjectives were taken from a list developed by Hevner (1936, 1937) and Lienert (1989).

FIGURE 19-3.   Model of a series of "CMS items" in relation to the pacer level of professionals.

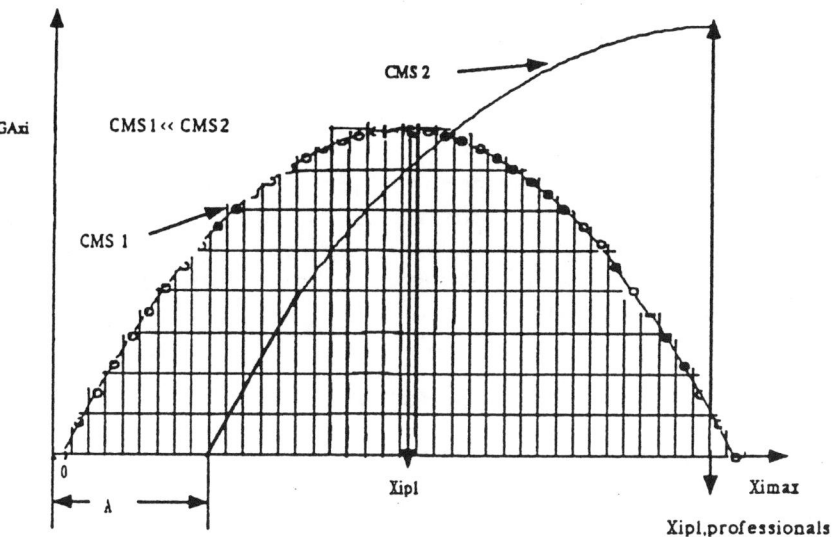

CMS1 << CMS2: The complex music stimulus "1" is much smaller then the complex music stimulus "2" but both are on a continuum, given by the range of total activation.

Subjects who were only able to understand the basic system combined with one subsystem line would make similar judgments of CMS and CLS, that is there would be a high correlation between the two. If CLS has a "meaning" different from that of CMS, the correlation would approach zero.

## CMS "Marriage"

Grieg's work "Hochzeit auf Troltaugen" (op. 65, no. 6. Disc, stereo 2535177, Deutsche Grammophon, "Nordmark Orchester," conductor Heinrich Steiner) was presented to 104 students of psychology at the University of Hamburg, nine pupils from a school of low educational level and musical interest, 14 students of music at the Academy of Music in Hamburg, 34 students of music at the University of Hamburg, and a teacher of music (piano) at the Academy. This was carried out with stereo equipment consisting of an Aiwa recorder (Type F3060) and two Victor loudspeakers (Type 2*70 Watt max.) in a laboratory at Hamburg University, in order to have the same conditions for all subjects. After listening to the music for exactly three minutes the subjects had to rate the applicability of each adjective one after the other (the sequence had to be strictly followed) and under slight time pressure.* Naturally there was no comment on the music at all, and those subjects who indicated that they knew the music were eliminated before the evaluation.

## CLS "Marriage"

The terms "Hochzeit" (marriage) and "Universität" (university) were presented as verbal stimuli to 197 students of psychology and 32 students of music science at the University of Hamburg. Naturally, this was a new sample, although the 58 items of the questionnaire were the same in all cases.

## RESULTS

### Rating Problems

Figure 18-4 shows the similarity of the rating profiles (means of the group ratings for each adjective) for language ("marriage") and music, and the dissimilarity of these for music and language ("university"), as well as between the language terms. It also shows arousal differences even in this case of middle complexity. These differences occurred even though the activation and pacer levels were not high.

### Clusters and Scales

Of interest at this point is the question of the content of the adverb list. A cluster analysis of the 58 adjectives indicated that they defined five clusters.

Hevner (1937) concluded that all her adjectives measured emotion, but Hoffmann (1986) gave evidence of cognitive elements, and the present interpretation is based on this point of view. In the present content, "cognitive" implies a process of

---

*Here I applied the theory of parallel interacting data processing (PDP) combined with theory on the limbic system to develop the hypothesis that after a few minutes of listening the context of the basic system as well as the subsystem lines would build up a sufficient grasp of the piece—existing at that specific cycle—to give an overall judgment of the "total" music. This means that it was not important for the judgments that the adjective item list was completed in a set sequence. Many scholars of music will disagree, especially because PDP processes are not yet well known.

FIGURE 19-4.    Profiles for the verbal concepts "marriage" and "university," and for the musical stimulus.

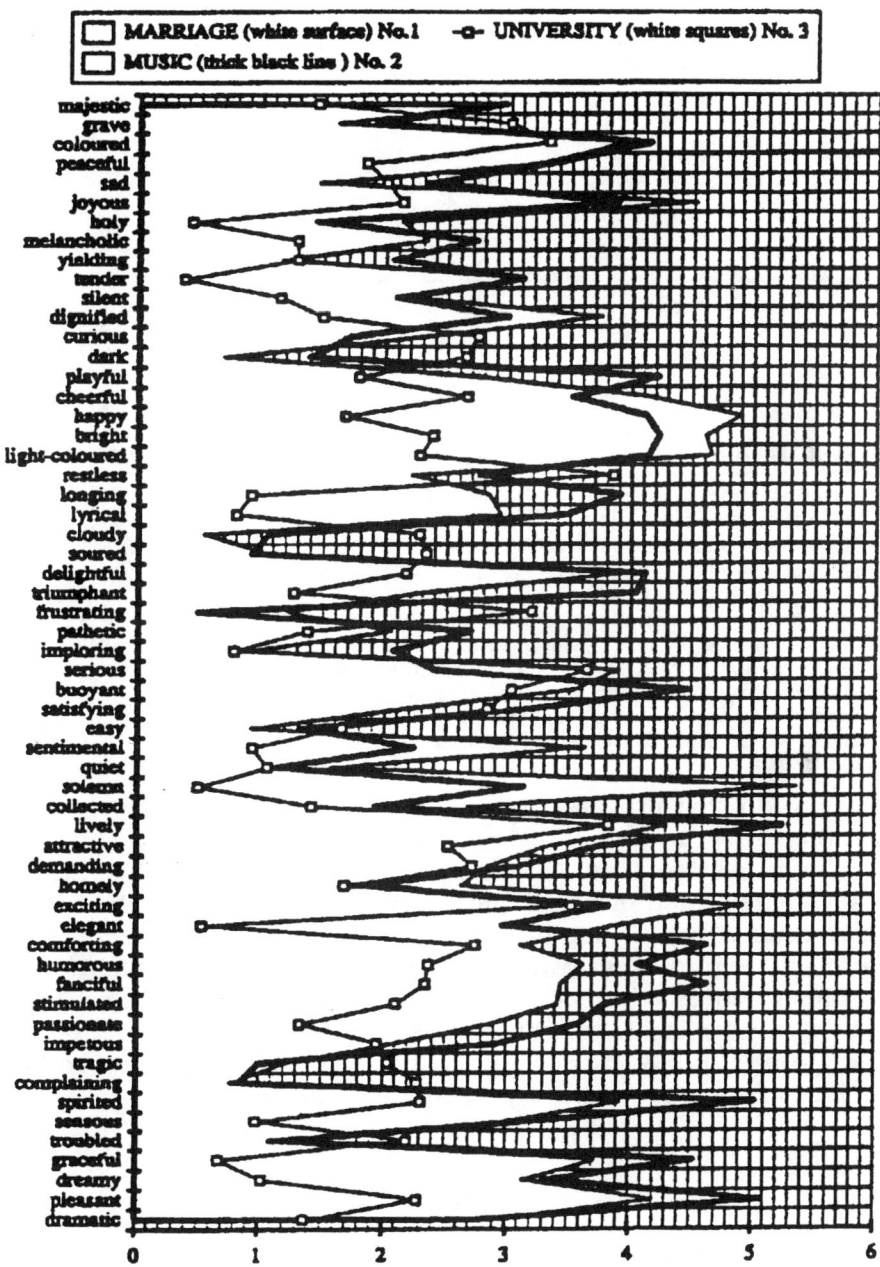

### TABLE 19-1
### Clusters Defined by the Adjectives

| Cluster | Title | Defined by Adjectives |
|---|---|---|
| Cluster I | Cognitive activation | Pleasant, graceful, spirited, fanciful, humorous, comforting, buoyant, triumphant, delightful |
| Cluster II | Emotional activation | Dreamy, sensous, lyrical, longing, stimulating, exciting, attractive, passionate, demanding |
| Cluster III | Cognitive introversion | Tender, peaceful, solemn, dignified, majestic |
| Cluster IV | Emotional rejection | Melancholy, sad, grave, yielding, serious, imploring, pathetic |
| Cluster V | Cognitive rejection | Curious, holy, cloudy, frustrating, complaining, tragic, troubled, dark, quiet, collected |

### TABLE 19-2
### Scores of Groups on the Five Scales*

| Type of Activation | Group | | | | | | | |
|---|---|---|---|---|---|---|---|---|
| | MAR | UNI | PSY | MUWI | KON | RAK | BGB | 4 DF |
| Cognitive activation | 3.487 | 2.308 | 4.030 | 3.675 | 3.841 | 5.040 | 3.740 | 3.175 |
| Emotional activation | 3.132 | 1.769 | 3.553 | 2.676 | 3.852 | 4.000 | 3.556 | 3.750 |
| Cognitve introversion | 3.422 | 1.286 | 3.087 | 2.831 | 3.235 | 2.286 | 2.857 | 1.667 |
| Emotional rejection | 1.945 | 1.913 | 2.312 | 1.815 | 2.459 | 1.714 | 2.286 | 3.286 |
| Cognitive rejection | 1.387 | 1.936 | 1.193 | 1.083 | 1.220 | 0.333 | 1.636 | 2.750 |

*MAR = CLS; UNI = CLS ("University"); PSY = CMS (psychology students); MUWI = CMS (music students); KON = (conservatory students); RAK = 43-year-old female piano teacher; BGB = 26-year-old male with high musical talent; 4 DF = 18-year-old female of low musical ability. The high musical talent of individual BGB as well as the low ability of 4 DF were ascertained via estimates over time of their teachers.

evaluation that provides information to emotional centers, such as the limbic system.

The adjectives can be regarded as measuring five "scales," each represented by the items defining the cluster. Each subject had thus given a judgment on positive or negative emotional arousal, cognitive activation, and introversion (see Table 19-1).

Mean scores of the various groups are shown in Table 19-2. There were significant difference between the mean scores of the groups ($F = 8.23$, $p < .001$). Correlations among the profiles of the various groups are presented in Table 19-3.

## DISCUSSION

The comparison of group means confirmed that the complex language stimulus (CLS, marriage) and the complex music stim-

TABLE 19-3
Correlations Among the Groups

| Group | Group | | | | | | |
| | CLS MAR | CLS UNI | CMS PSY | CMS KON | CMS RAK | CMS BGB | CMS 4 DF |
| --- | --- | --- | --- | --- | --- | --- | --- |
| CLS MAR | 1 | | | | | | |
| CLS UNI | −0.173 | 1 | | | | | |
| CMS PSY | 0.939 | 0.105 | 1 | | | | |
| CMS KON | 0.933 | −0.004 | 0.987 | 1 | | | |
| CMS RAK | 0.839 | 0.339 | 0.965 | 0.933 | 1 | | |
| CMS BGB | 0.907 | 0.158 | 0.987 | 0.978 | 0.982 | 1 | |
| CMS 4 DF | −0.133 | 0.657 | 0.191 | 0.210 | 0.380 | 0.291 | 1 |

ulus (CMS, students of psychology) differed from the control CLS (university), confirming the basic hypothesis. Furthermore, there was an extremely low correlation between CLS and MAR/UNI ($r = -0.17$). The correlation between the profiles of the person 4 DF, who was of very low musical ability, was also very low ($r = -0.13$). Thus, for low complex capacities this method was shown to be appropriate. According to the theoretical assumption, gifted persons may need a piece of music of higher complexity if pacer level is to be activated. The results for psychology students representing the "normal music listener," the BGB and RAK persons, and the music academy group, here representing "gifted" individuals, indicate that the expected very high correlation among psychology students between CMS and CLS reflects the stereotypic meaning of the language term: marriage. Music evokes practically the same feelings as the language stimulus in these people. This is in accordance with expectations; the next step is to find the appropriate CMS and the real professionals for further development of the approach presented here.

## REFERENCES

Atkinson, R. C., & Shiffrin, R. M. (1968). Human memory: a proposed system and its control processes. In K. W. Spence & J. T. Spence (Eds.), *The psychology of learning and motivation: advances in research and theory*, vol. 2 (pp. 89–195). New York: Academic Press.

Berlyne, D. E. (1950). Novelty and curiosity as determinants of exploratory behavior. *British Journal of Psychology, 41*, 68–80.

Berlyne, D. E. (1955). The arousal and satiation of perceptual curiosity. *Journal of Comparative and Physiological Psychology, 48*, 238–246.

Berlyne, D. E. (1960). *Conflict, arousal and curiosity.* New York: McGraw-Hill.

Berlyne, D. E. (1964). Uncertainty and conflict (contact between information theory and behavior theory concepts). *Psychological Review, 64*, 329–339.

Dember, W. N. (1956a). Response by the rat to environmental change. *Journal of Comparative and Physiological Psychology, 49*, 93–95.

Dember, W. N. (1956b). *The psychology of perception.* New York: Holt, Rinehart & Winston.

Dember, W. N., & Earl, R. (1957). Analysis of exploratory manipulatory and curiosity behaviors. *Psychological Review, 64*, 91–96.

Dember, W. N., Earl, R., & Paradise N. (1957). Response by the rat to differential stimulus complexity. *Journal of Comparative and Physiological Psychology, 50*, 514–518.

Füller, K. (1974). *Standardisierte Musiktests* [Standardized music tests]. Frankfurt: Diesterweg.

Hevner, K. (1936). Experimental studies of the elements of expression in music. *American Journal of Psychology, 48*, 246–268.

Hevner, K. (1937). Expression in music: A discussion of experimental studies and theories. *Psychological Review, 47*, 186–204.

Hoffmann, J. (1986). *Die Welt der Begriffe* [The world of concepts]. Weinheim: Beltz.

Lienert, G. (1989). *Test analysis* (4th ed.). Weinheim: PVU.

Machleidt, W., Gutjahr, L., & Mügge, A. (1990). *Grundgefühle, Phänomenologie, EEG-Spektralanalytik* [Analysis of exploratory, manipulatory and curiosity behaviors]. Heidelberg: Springer.

Magoun, H. W. (1963). *The waking brain* (2nd ed.). Springfield, IL: Thomas.

Rosenzweig, M., & Leiman, A. (1990). *Physiological psychology.* New York: Random House.

Rumelhart, D. E., McClelland, J. L., & PDP research group (1986). *Parallel distributed processing.* Cambridge, MA: MIT Press.

Seashore (1939). *Measures of musical talents.* New York: Psychological Corporation.

Shannon, C., & Weaver, W. (1949). *The mathematical theory of communication.* Urbana, IL: University of Illinois Press. (Dt. Übersetzung: Dr. Dipl. Ing. Dressler. (1976). München: Oldenbourg.

Spada, H. (1990). *Allgemeine Psychologie* [General Psychology]. Bern: Huber.

Werbik, H. (1971). *Informationsgehalt und emotionale Wirkung von Musik* [Information content and the emotional effects of music]. Mainz: Schott.

# 20

# Early Signs of Talents and Special Interests in the Lives of Young Musicians

**Michael J. A. Howe**

*University of Exeter, Exeter, England*

**John A. Sloboda**

*University of Keele, Newcastle, England*

This chapter reports findings from an investigation of the childhoods of young musicians that provides indications of musical talent and unusual liking for music in the earliest years of life. Forty-two students aged 10–17 attending a highly selective specialist music school were interviewed and encouraged to talk about significant events and experiences in their early musical lives. The parents of half the students were also interviewed. In 50% of the children there was some evidence of spontaneous early musical activity, in the form of either singing or picking out tunes on an instrument. However, the students who were most exceptional were no more likely than the others to have displayed special talents at a very early age. In addition, a number of parents reported that their child had shown an unusual degree of interest in music while still very young. The findings have implications concerning the possible existence of innate gifts and talents.

## INTRODUCTION

In some outstandingly able adults it is clear that evidence of the individual's exceptionality was present from early childhood. Opinion is divided, however, on a number of issues concerning early signs of being exceptional. For instance, there is little agreement about the actual proportion of outstandingly competent people who display clear signs of being exceptional in early childhood. There is a similar lack of agreement concerning the extent to which the early development of talent is an essential precursor of mature achievements, and opinions even differ on the question of whether such precocious development actually is desirable.

In the field of musical abilities early signs of special talents appear to be relatively common. The biographies and autobiographies of great musicians contain numerous accounts testifying to individuals already being exceptionally able musicians while they were still young children. For instance, there are various accounts of Mozart's childhood feats (Hildesheimer, 1983), there is Stravinsky's story of how, at the age of two, he astonished his parents with his skilful limitations of the singing of peasant workers he had heard locally, and there is Artur Rubinstein's recollection of how, as a young child, he would refuse to speak but was always willing to sing, and mastered the piano with very little effort despite the fact that he came from a non-musical family (Hargreaves, 1986; Howe, 1982, 1990a; Shuter-Dyson and Gabriel, 1981; Sloboda, 1985). There is also some evidence that by no means all those children who display exceptional early musical talents go on to become musicians of distinction (Sloboda, 1990).

Unfortunately, most of the evidence is anecdotal, and often it is less than reliable because it depends upon people's memories of events that occurred many years before the information was collected. A rare exception is provided by some findings obtained by Sosniak (1985a, 1990). She conducted an interview-based study, in which she talked to 21 exceptional young American pianists, all of whom had been finalists in a major international competition. In most cases she also interviewed their parents and their first music teachers. Sosniak was able to talk to these exceptionally accomplished musicians (and the people who played a close part in their early training) while they were still under 40 years of age. Hence the period of time between the individuals' early childhoods and the time at which they were interviewed was reasonably short. As a result, her findings appear to provide a source of evidence about the events of musical childhoods that is more reliable than most of the other data that are currently available.

Perhaps surprisingly, very few of these outstandingly accomplished young musicians had shown any clear signs of being exceptional while they were still very young. That is not to say that they did not make good progress, but this only occurred after the child had received plenty of opportunities and lots of encouragement, and had spent a considerable amount of time learning and practising musical skills. Sosniak (1990) reported that the large majority of these eventually exceptional individuals were not obvious prodigies as young children. In fact, even after they had been studying the piano for seven years or so, although they had by then achieved high standards as performers, they were still as likely to do poorly at the competitions they entered as to win. As young children they did not demonstrate abilities significantly beyond those appropriate for their age, and they did not show unusual promise right at the start of the lengthy process of developing talent. Moreover, there were similar findings in other areas of expertise. Sosniak (1985b) estimated that by the age of 11 or 12 years no more than 10% of individuals who will eventually reach the very highest levels of achievement in their chosen field have developed to a point at which confident predictions can be made about their eventual success.

Sosniak's findings appear to contradict the widespread belief that early signs of exceptionality are characteristic of outstanding musical performers. Her results seem to confirm the suspicion that some biographical and autobiographical recollections of very early indications of musical genius have been influenced by selective recall of events that typically occurred many years prior to the account being written. However, it is possible to question the reliability of Sosniak's data. For a start, her main sample was very small (21 subjects), and her musicians were all pianists. Also, although the length of time that had elapsed between early childhood and the time at which the interviews took place was shorter than is customary with biographical forms of evidence, in reality the data about early childhood were not actually obtained by Sosniak until 30 years or so after the events had taken place. This leaves considerable room for memory lapses to occur. To be really confident about the reliability of the evidence it would be necessary to reduce this period of time very considerably.

This was achieved in an investigation of the early childhood training of 42 highly capable young musicians involving students aged between 10 and 17 years of age, who were in most cases removed by less than a decade (compared with the 30-year intervals in Sosniak's study) from the beginning of their musical instruction. Parents of half the subjects were also interviewed. The investigation examined numerous aspects of early musical development. It concentrated both on obtaining quantitative measures of significant childhood events in the early lives of young musicians (Sloboda & Howe, 1991) and on reporting the children's own (qualitative) perceptions of their early musical experiences (Howe & Sloboda, in press a, b).

In this chapter quantitative and qualitative findings of the investigation by Sloboda and Howe that have some bearing on questions concerning very early signs of special talents are reported. What signs of exceptional ability were present at a very early age? Were such indications rare, as Sosniak found, or do the present findings contradict hers? In addition to any signs of special early ability, were there any indications of unusual interest in things musical at a time when the children in the study were still very young?

## METHOD

In all, 42 students and the parents of 20 of them participated in the study. All the students, who were aged between 10 and 17 years, attended Chethams School of Music, in Manchester, England. Chethams school specializes in musical education, devoting about one third of each child's time tabled activities to music, and admits students on a highly selective basis following auditions designed to assess their musical skills and their potential for future progress. Most of the students were boarders at the school. There were equal numbers of male and female participants. The majority were from middle-class backgrounds, but in 11 cases the father's occupation was manual worker or nonexecutive office worker.

As far as possible the sample was stratified and balanced for age, ability, and the primary instrument studied. Thus there were roughly equal numbers of younger (13 years or less) and older (at least 15 years) male and female players of piano, violin, cello, wind instruments, and brass instruments. In each of these subcategories half the subjects were described (by the school staff) as being exceptionally able at music by the very high standards of the school.

Each child was interviewed separately by one of the two authors. The duration of the interviews varied between 25 and 50 minutes. The interviews, which were of a semistructured nature, included a number of specific questions (see Sloboda & Howe, 1991 who provide further details that are not essential for the purposes of the present report). However, a substantial proportion of the questions permitted open-ended responses: The children were encouraged to talk freely about any aspects of their early musical experiences, and were asked to draw attention to significant events that had not been addressed by the questions.

## RESULTS

### Indications of Unusual Very Early Ability

Children and their parents were asked about their earliest spontaneous involvement of any sort with music. It was anticipated that answers to this question would indicate the presence of any very early signs of unusual ability. However, in 21 out of the 42 children neither they nor their parents could recall anything to remark upon. In six children (14%) there was evidence of early singing activity, such as reproducing songs in toddlerhood. In 15 cases (36%) there had been early experimentation at an instrument, with the child picking out tunes prior to the time any formal instruction had begun.

These data suggest that, on the one hand early signs of exceptionality were more common in our sample than in Sosniak's, but that on the other hand, half of the children provided no evidence at all of being unusually talented musicians before the time at which they began to have formal instruction. Thus the findings broadly agree with Sosniak's in suggesting that many if not most of those individuals who reach unusual standards of musical proficiency by late childhood displayed no remarkable abilities in the earliest years. Moreover, there was a surprising absence of differences in this respect between the children who (at the time of the study) were judged to be exceptionally able and those who, although sufficiently unusual to compete successfully for admission to the very selective specialist musical school they attended, were not judged to be exceptional. That is, those children who had displayed signs of being specially talented when they were still very young were no more likely to be judged excellent when they were older than those children who had displayed no early signs of excep-tionality.

On their own, these quantitative findings provide a rather scanty picture of the possible early precursors of musical excellence. Greater richness of detail is supplied by some of the observations of the children and their parents. For example, a substantial minority of the parents interviewed in the present study did report early childhood incidents suggesting that the child in question had already acquired certain musical skills at a very early age, in the absence of formal training. In a number of cases the skills took the form of the ability to pick out simple tunes.

In order to protect anonymity, only minimal information is provided here concerning the individual participants whose remarks are quoted. In the following extracts from the transcribed interviews, Y denotes a respondent aged 13 years or younger, O denotes 15 years or older, and M and F refer to male and female subjects, respectively. P denotes "parent of . . . ."

> (PYF) Somebody gave her a plastic recorder, and she managed to pick out tunes on it. She was four then. And I bought a recorder, a plastic recorder from Mothercare, and started to teach her. But she was far too quick and I thought she would benefit from proper lessons from somebody other than a parent. So that's why I enrolled her.

> (YF) My mum told me this story of when I went, when I go to parties I used to sit on the piano and just mess around and things. I used to get the plastic trumpet things and play with them as well, because I liked playing with trumpets when I was younger . . . it was just a few noises, you know. I used to know which, because some people didn't know the difference between notes, say if it was a semitone apart, I could tell. I knew that very young.

> (OF) [at age three] I remember watching the telly and I heard this music and we used to have a little upright piano that was my

mum's but I played it and the first thing I ever did was to go up to the piano and I worked out the tune I had heard on the telly. Just kept prodding my finger down and playing it, very out of tune but it was nearly the actual thing and then me mum asked me if I wanted to do the piano. And I said "Yes, yes, go on."

*(POF)* She just sat at the piano on her own. What she actually did was when she was very small she used to pick out tunes as the children usually do, and she used to imitate her elder sister, she was rather upset about lessons. And much to her elder sister's disgust, she was rather upset about it at the time I seem to remember, because X could just sit and play with two hands what [her sister] had been studying for ages and getting lessons. Which is really, I suppose I realised she was musical from that. She was about four then.

*(POF)* She obviously just had that facility where she could hear something and she was able to put it together on the piano both hands, because she would be able to hear it in her head. She must have been able to get the chords and things right. Most musical people I think can do this, but it was the first experience I've had of it, and she thoroughly enjoyed it. She's quite a good ear, she can spot a note out of tune even though to my ears it sounds perfectly alright, which is galling.

*(POM)* The first inclination we ever had was just his auntie— my auntie, great auntie—bought him a little organ when he was about 4 for a Christmas present. And everyone said hit these numbers—play by numbers—if you press the numbers on the keyboard it will play a tune. X just went up to it and played a tune, started playing anything, any tune he listened to he could go straight back and play it.

*(POM)* He was given a toy piano, when he was 2 or 3 and he used to play that. There was obviously a sort of interest in music. We were given a very old piano and he used to play tunes on it, long before he had lessons. He could actually pick out tunes himself, when he was 3, 4, or 5.

In other instances the signs of very early ability took the form of an ability to sing or whistle in tune.

*(POF)* She's always been able to sing in tune from a very, very early age. As soon as she could talk she would sing. She would sort of sing nursery rhymes and sing, quite nicely, in tune. So she's always been able to do that. And showed signs that she en-

joyed singing. I've got a 13-year-old son who is completely different, he has no musical ability whatsoever, likes pop music and
that's about it.

(POM) Interviewer: And you didn't at that time feel that he had
any particular talent? Parent: No, we didn't know whether he did
or not, he could whistle fiendishly, he was almost a virtuoso of
the mouthpiece. He was obviously musical, he had rhythm, he
had a sense of pitch. He could whistle basic in tune, so all the
basic ingredients were there, yes, but I suppose that we think
that's natural because that's what the Suzuki method, not that
we're particular advocates of the method, but it supposes that
everyone has a sense of rhythm.

It has been established that children's subsequent remem-
bering of events that took place in the first three or four years
of their lives is highly unreliable. Therefore, it is probably wise
to assume that parents' memories of these years are more accurate than those of the children themselves. However, even in
the parents, it is not inconceivable that memories of a child's
first years have been influenced by a knowledge of subsequent
events. As one parent remarked:

(PYF) I did think there was something special about X but you
would tend to as a mother, be a bit wary of that—everybody
thinks their child is absolutely marvellous.

## Signs of Unusual Early Interest in Music

Even in those cases where the parent reported no signs of unusual musical ability in earliest childhood it was quite common
to find that either the child or a parent gave some indication
that music had held an unusual attraction for the child from an
early age. As with the remarks recorded in the previous section,
there is always the possibility that memories of an individual's
early childhood have been affected by knowledge of subsequent
developments. All the same, the frequency of parental reports
suggesting that the young child had an above-average interest
in or sensitivity to musical sounds is impressive.

(PYF) At the nursery class, the nursery school that she went
to, they said that she was always messing around with all the musical instruments, you know, the trumpets and making music.

*(YF)* My mum said I used to go round the house singing my head off and whistling and things like that and when I couldn't whistle I used to say "Mum, how can I whistle, please can you teach me?"

*(PYM)* When he was a toddler I always remember he was given one of these Fisher-Price record players . . . I can remember we commented on the fact that he loved this little instrument and it was always on you know with these little tunes, they were always on and it was noticeable that he did enjoy this particular toy, and then we went, when he was about 4, 5, we went to a friend's home and they had a little Bon Tempi organ, a 12-key organ, and he used to like to go round to this particular house so that he could get on this little organ, so consequently we bought him one for Christmas. He would be about 4. And he played this organ and played it and he used to get very simple, basic tunes out of it. But it was a definite melody there, and he played this thing 'til it absolutely collapsed in heaps. So then we moved on to a bigger organ on a stand. It was still a kiddies' type of organ, but it had chords on it, and he got hours of enjoyment out of this . . . . And other people noticed his enjoyment of music and when he did go to primary school the teaching staff there, they picked it up as well, so whenever the children had concerts and what have you, he was sort of picked to play the instrument rather than perhaps a speaking part.

In some of the instances the child's awareness of and liking for music was probably prompted, and certainly encouraged, by the salience of music in the family home.

*(PYM)* Well, he was exposed to music obviously immediately. He came into a musical household and was obviously exposed to it which was very important right from the beginning. And he, I can remember, he showed a very keen interest in instruments and music right from the beginning, really, right from whenever he became interested in anything at all. And I actually remember him very well sitting on the piano stool when he must have been about, what, this must have been nine months, something like that, and just banging on the piano keys and singing with the piano, singing to his own accompaniment. He certainly had a taste for it, which was quite interesting. So, I mean he was very aware of music right from the beginning and very keen to partake in his own way from the very beginning. And I think that was basically because he thought everyone did that, I mean it was quite amazing . . . you see I've got this tape of when he was about 9 months old, banging on the piano and he's singing the Grand Old Duke of York. And ac-

tually obviously it's just fistfuls of notes with hands literally banging on the piano, but it makes a lot of sense, what he was doing,
in his own way. So, I mean, it wasn't an important thing at the
time but when we listen to the tape now it's rather intriguing.
There's something there, right from the beginning. Yes, he'd make
instruments himself when he was just crawling around on the
floor, I mean he actually made a bassoon out of cardboard tubes
and things like this. He just wanted to be involved all the time. We
gave him an old trumpet which he smashed up in the end, but
when he used to play he used to play with that.

(POM) From when he was a toddler really it started to show.
Looking back we had a car, and one of the back seats was up-
holstered. They looked like enormous piano keys, and he used to
kneel and pretend to play them. And that was going back to when
he was only about 18 months.

However, in at least one instance the child seems to have become strongly attracted to music without the parents making
any deliberate efforts to encourage this. Many infants are
calmed by sounds (Hargreaves, 1986), but it is unusual for an
infant to be as selectively affected by music as this child was.

(PYF) Looking back now, it was quite obvious from the start that
she was quite interested in music. She would sit as a tiny baby in
these bouncy chair things, we thought watching the television, but
it wasn't watching, it was just listening to the music, because when
it went onto dialogue, she started to create. And she would always,
she never played with toys, she always wanted to dance or sing or
clap rhythms to tapes. Spend all afternoon going through hundreds
of "Miss Polly had a Dolly" and "Baa baa black sheep" and action-
rhyme type things .... She always enjoyed rhythm and music.
When we went to church, she would scream blue murder during
the sermon, but as soon as there were hymns, she would be quiet.
She was obviously enjoying that.

## DISCUSSION

In common with Sosniak's results, the present findings show
that not all highly accomplished musicians display clear indications of exceptional musicality in early childhood. Unlike her,
however, we found that there was some evidence of early exceptionality in as many as half the young musicians we examined. Also, in a substantial number of cases it is clear that even

when early signs of musical ability as such were absent, the child, when young, was unusually interested in musical sounds, or seemed particularly attracted to musical experiences. Clearly, in a number of cases the child's enthusiasm for music was influenced by the kinds of opportunity and the amount of encouragement that one or both parents provided, but even when account is taken of that fact, the degree to which certain young children are attracted to musical events is striking, as is the sheer extent to which children, even when very young, differ in their liking for musical events and activities. Of course, when a young child does show a distinct preference for musical stimuli, as in the final example quoted earlier, it is likely that the parents will encourage that interest. Consequently, any connection observed between a child's early attraction to music and the same child's later musical ability may bear the imprint of the parental intervention that is prompted by the child's early signals. Thus, not all the links that connect early attraction to music and mature musicality are within the child alone.

The current findings have some bearing on the perennial and controversial question of whether or not exceptional musicianship depends on the individual possessing some kind of innate musical talent or aptitude. Attention has already been drawn to the fallacy of assuming that the sheer existence of verbal expressions of that kind makes it inevitable that such qualities do actually exist (Howe, 1990b). Furthermore, certain "natural experiments," such as the one in which remarkable degrees of musical competence were gained by substantial numbers of orphan girls at the *la Pietà* academy in eighteenth century Venice, suggest that the apparent absence of innate musical propensities need not rule out the possibility of a child gaining remarkable musical expertise (Howe, 1982, 1990a; Koldener, 1970; Kunkel, 1985). Nevertheless, the present finding that substantial numbers of talented young musicians have from a very early age displayed some sign of either special aptitude for music or an unusual degree of interest in music suggests that the possibility that certain individuals are in some way or other predisposed to becoming exceptional musicians, either innately or from a very early age, cannot be ruled out definitely.

If any quality, tendency, or predisposition in certain children that corresponds to the notion of an innate talent or aptitude does exist, what form or forms might it take? This question has not received as much attention as it deserves: The statement that an aptitude (innate or otherwise) exists does not assist efforts to understand the origins of an ability unless some effort is made to specify the form that the aptitude takes and to designate the precise way in which its effects are actually exerted. There are a number of possibilities. These range from e.g., special cognitive mechanisms or other structural differences to innate differences in ability to learn or remember, or differences in sensitivity to sounds, or unusual rhythmic tendencies (Howe, 1990a). However, scientific research has produced little direct support for the view that individuals who eventually become outstandingly able musicians are born with special powers. Indeed, in the case of the most frequently mentioned candidate for the role of an innate ability that could facilitate the acquisition of musical abilities by certain individuals but not others—"perfect" pitch perception—there is strong evidence that the ability is not in fact innate but learned, although it is much more likely to be learned in early childhood than in later life (Brady, 1970; Sloboda, 1985).

If it is true that predispositions present at birth or soon afterward affect the likelihood of an individual becoming highly accomplished at musical skills, the possibility should not be dismissed that such predispositions may not take the form of abilities as such or even of qualities that directly contribute to abilities (as unusual auditory sensitivity might, for instance). It is just as likely that an individual may be marked from birth (or very soon after) by attributes that essentially are a matter of temperament, mood, or personality, which can affect the likelihood of being attracted by and attending to musical stimuli. Such attributes could have just as strong an influence on the likelihood of a young child gaining musical skills as the presence of directly relevant abilities would have. There is some evidence that small differences in infants' early preferences can trigger off differing responses that eventually produce, by a snowball effect, substantial differences in abilities (Renninger & Wozniak, 1985). One can imagine a scenario in which a child, for reasons that might involve temperament or perceptual sensitivity, spends slightly more time than other children attending to a particular category of events, and consequently remembers them more accurately and becomes more competent or successful at activities that involve events of that kind. Eventually, adults may begin to notice that the child has a "special" ability in that area of competence, and the resulting adult attention and praise may provide further encouragement for the child to become even more competent.

## ACKNOWLEDGMENTS

The authors gratefully acknowledge the extensive help and co-operation received from the headmaster, staff, and pupils of Chethams School of Music, Manchester, England. We are particularly grateful for the very generous aid given by Paul Andrews. The research was supported by a grant from the Nuffield Foundation.

## REFERENCES

Brady, P. T. (1970). The genesis of absolute pitch. *Journal of the Acoustical Society of America, 48*, 883–887.

Hargreaves D. J. (1986). *The developmental of music.* Cambridge: Cambridge University Press.

Hildesheimer, W. (1983). *Mozart* (translated by M. Faber). London: Dent.

Howe, M. J. A. (1982). Biographical evidence and the development of outstanding individuals. *American Psychologist, 37*, 1071–1081.

Howe, M. J. A. (1990a). *The origins of exceptional abilities.* Oxford: Blackwell.

Howe, M. J. A. (1990b). Children's gifts, talents, and natural abilities: an explanatory mythology? *Journal of Educational and Child Psychology, 7*, 52–54.

Howe, M. J. A., & Sloboda, J. A. (1991). Young musicians' accounts of significant influences in their early lives: 1. The family and the musical background. *British Journal of Music Education, 8*, 39–52.

Howe, M. J. A., & Sloboda, J. A. (1991). Young musicians' accounts of significant influences in their early lives: 2. Teachers, practising and performing. *British Journal of Music Education, 8*, 53–68.

Koldener, W. (1970). *Antonio Vivaldi: His life and work* (translated by W. Hopkins). London: Faber & Faber.

Kunkel, J. H. (1985). Vivaldi in Venice: an historical test of psychological propositions. *Psychological Record, 35*, 445–457.

Renninger, K. A., & Wozniak, R. N. (1985). Effect of interest on attentional shift, recognition and recall in young children. *Developmental Psychology, 21*, 624–632.

Shuter-Dyson, R., & Gabriel, C. (1981). *The psychology of musical ability* (2nd ed.). London: Methuen.

Sloboda, J. A. (1985). *The musical mind. The cognitive psychology of music.* London: Oxford University Press.

Sloboda, J. A. (1990). Musical excellence—how does it develop? In M. J. A. Howe (Ed.), *Encouraging the development of exceptional abilities and talents.* Leicester: The British Psychological Society.

Sloboda, J. A., & Howe, M. J. A. (1991). Biographical precursors of musical excellence: an interview study. *Psychology of Music*, *19*, 3–23.

Sosniak, L. A. (1985a). Learning to be a concert pianist. In B. S. Bloom (Ed.), *Developing talent in young people*. New York: Ballantine.

Sosniak, L. A. (1985b). Generalizations about talent develoment. In B. S. Bloom (Ed.), *Developing talent in young people*. New York: Ballantine.

Sosniak, L. A. (1990). The tortoise, the hare, and the development of talent. In M. J. A. Howe (Ed.), *Encouraging the development of exceptional abilities and talents*. Leicester: The British Psychological Society.

# 21

## The Critical Teens
### Musical Capacities Change in Adolescence

**Marianne Hassler**

*Tübingen, Germany*

Experimental data from an eight-year period in adolescence document the development of musical talent—measured with Wing's Standardized Tests of Musical Intelligence—and of creative musical behavior—assessed on the basis of original compositions or improvisations. Comparison of spatial and verbal test scores obtained at the same time with the musical data indicated that, although a complex interaction of social, cultural, and biological factors can be assumed to influence the course of development, possible hormonal influences—both prenatally and in adolescence—play a role in musical and cognitive performances.

### INTRODUCTION

Puberty is a crucial period of human development, both for the maturing capability of reproduction and also for musical talent and cognitive functioning. Musical abilities and spatial and verbal faculties seem to change in the course of adolescence in a sex-specific way. Before puberty no lasting sex differences have been observed on musical, spatial, or verbal tests. After puberty, however, males surpass females on some spatial tests and females surpass males on some verbal tests (Maccoby & Jacklin, 1974). Within the musical realm, the creative aspect seems to be especially vulnerable to influences occurring in adolescence.

Let me give some examples from the literature: In 1910, the psychologist Géza Révész met the musical prodigy Erwin N., and was able to follow the development of Erwin from his fifth to his thirteenth year of life (Révész, 1946). The five-year-old boy invented small melodies, and at the age of eleven found his own original musical style. Such musical development led people to expect him to become a great composer. Comparisons were made with Mozart and other child prodigies like Mendelssohn-Bartholdy. However, after the age of 11 Erwin gave up composing and concentrated exclusively on piano playing. He became a well known performer, but Révész was disappointed at this course of development. He was convinced that the young man had failed to work hard enough in order to develop his exceptional musical abilities to the full.

Changes of the creative aspect of musical talent seem to be the rule rather than the exception. This conclusion can be drawn from biographical materials collected by Hanslick in Vienna in the nineteenth century (see Wehmeyer, 1983) and from an extensive investigation of biographical data presented by Scott and Moffett (1977). These authors found that those who display early ability follow one of three variations in late adolescence. The first involves almost complete failure; music becomes just a hobby. At the other extreme, there are those whose early success continues into maturity, often to the final days of life. In between these extremes is the possibility of a life devoted to teaching or writing or to academic pursuits, or as a performer of greater or lesser merits (Scott & Moffett, 1977). Scott and Mofett described a very early experiment involving testing of musical prodigies: In 1764 Daines Barrington examined Mozart, who was visiting London at that time. He was given a test battery that was also administered to Charles and Samuel Wesley, to W. H. Crotch and to Lord Mornington. All five prodigies attained extraordinarily high test scores; however, only Mozart became a great composer. These examples were mostly concerned with male prodigies, although Hanslick included both boys and girls in his overview. With regard to the small number of female composers and conductors, it might be speculated that developmental changes in some aspects of musical talent may be even more dramatic in girls than in boys.

What happens in adolescence that can influence musical talent and cognitive functioning? Hoyenga and Hoyenga (1979) and Nyborg (1984) have argued that all sex dimorphic traits are based on sex hormones. What does this mean? It is necessary to distinguish two phases in human development when sex hormones exert their effects: First, they affect the developing brain during pre- and perinatal development. These effects are called "organizational," and are relatively enduring. Second, sex hormones work in adolescence and in adulthood, and their effects are activating and reversible.

Knowledge about sex hormone effects on the developing brain is still limited. According to Dörner (1985), so-called "sex centers" controlling female type and male type gonadotrophic secretion are organized by aromatized androgens, that is, by estrogens. So-called "mating centers" controlling sexual orientation are organized by androgens or by aromatized androgens (estrogens). Socalled "sex role centres" controlling female type and male type sex role behavior are organized only by androgens. The critical periods are not completely identical, but overlapping. They begin, as Dörner has argued, during the fourth month of gestation. The hormonal effects on the brain during the midtrimester of gestation have recently been questioned by Money (1988, p. 23), who reviewed findings of Abramovich, Davidson, Longstaff, and Pearson (1987). These authors undertook an extensive neurochemical search of tissues from fetal brains, aged 14–20 weeks of gestation, for evidence of receptors that would take up estrogenic, androgenic, or progestinic sex hormones. The evidence was nonexistent. Money concluded that the stage in development when hormones influence the differentiation of the human brain as dimorphically male or female remains to be discovered. It may be in the third trimester of pregnancy, or it may extend through the first three postnatal months.

The centers Dörner has postulated are located deep in the brain, and the hypothalamus plays an important role. In addition, structural changes of certain areas of the right hemisphere but also on the left have been suggested to be influenced by sex hormones (Geschwind & Galaburda, 1985; Waterhouse, 1988). The corpus callosum may be affected as well. These structural changes may provide the anatomical correlates of artistic talents and of exceptional cognitive abilities: However, it is still unknown exactly how gonadal hormones act on the developing brain. Among fascinating and surprising discoveries in the realm of human brain development, neuroscientists were able to show that degenerative processes play an important role. When the brain develops in its first phase neurons are produced in a much greater number than finally necessary. To form brain structures which function in the way seen in healthy subjects, many neurons must die. In this respect, development is a process whose necessary condition is cell death, and it is just this process that might be influenced by sex hormones that are able to prevent neurons from dying. As a result, some structures could become larger than normal and could provide the morphological substrate for special talents. Such developmental influences may begin after week 20 of gestation, and may continue into the fourth to seventh postnatal month.

The activating effects of sex hormones begin during puberty when androgens and estrogens rise dramatically in both sexes, and they continue into adulthood. How can musical and cognitive performance in adolescence be related to hormonal influences, and how can prenatal hormonal effects be recognized? These are the questions with which the empirical research presented here was concerned.

## METHOD

An eight-year longitudinal study focused on 120 children, 60 boys and 60 girls, who differed with respect to musical capacities: 20 boys and 20 girls were musically talented with the ability to compose or improvise, 20 boys and 20 girls were musically talented without the ability to compose–improvise and 20 boys and 20 girls were nonmusicians. All children were siblings, friends, or classmates. As a preliminary means of identifying children with musical talent, teachers at music schools, public schools and grammar schools judged those pupils to be musically talented who had played one or more instruments for several years. To be finally accepted as gifted these children had to score "A" on Wing's tests. Nonmusicians did not play musical instruments at the time of first testing.

The data to be presented here were obtained in a comprehensive study in which the relationship between musical and spatial ability, functional brain organization in musicians and nonmusicians, handedness, immune vulnerability, sex hormones, and androgyny were tested (Hassler, 1991; Hassler &

Birbaumer, 1988; Hassler, Birbaumer, & Feil, 1985). Musical, spatial, and verbal abilities were followed through adolescence using psychometric tests. Once a year children were tested with the same test battery. In addition to Wing's Standardized Tests of Musical Intelligence (Wing, 1968) which were used to assess general musical ability, the Spatial Relations Test from the PMA battery (Thurstone, 1962) and the Hidden Pattern Test from the ETS (Ekstrom, French, Harman & Derman, 1976) were administered to measure spatial ability, and a Verbal Fluency test was used as an indicator of verbal ability (Horn, 1962; German version of PMA). The creative aspect of musical talent had to be documented by performing at least two out of four pieces: 1. a written composition (score), 2. a composition *played* on instrument(s), 3. an extempore improvisation, or 4. an improvisation on an existing framework. These pieces were tape recorded and were later rated by four experts according to criteria which were elaborated by Feil (Hassler et al., 1985). All musicians in the study had had music training on one or more instruments and this information was included in the asssessment, because of interest in the question whether this variable would be connected with musical and cognitive performance.

## RESULTS

On the variable general musical ability, as measured with Wing's tests (Tests 1–3), the three female groups show only small changes over time; however, instrumentalists and nonmusicians showed a tendency to deteriorate towards the end of adolescence (see Figure 21-1). In males, there was no overall decrease in any of the groups (see Figure 21-2). There was, however, a peak in performance levels at midpuberty which was not found in girls. The results for males and females are compared in Figure 21-3.

While changes in general musical talent were small, the breakdown of the ability to compose–improvise was dramatic. As can be seen in Figure 21-4, this was true for both sexes, but girls showed an even greater decrease than boys. At stage 7 only two boys and one girl were willing to compose–improvise, and the expert raters were unable to evaluate these pieces in isolation. At stage 8—the last stage in the longitudinal study— all participants from group 1 were asked to provide a composition–improvisation even if they had given up composing, in

FIGURE 21-1.    Development of general music ability for females.

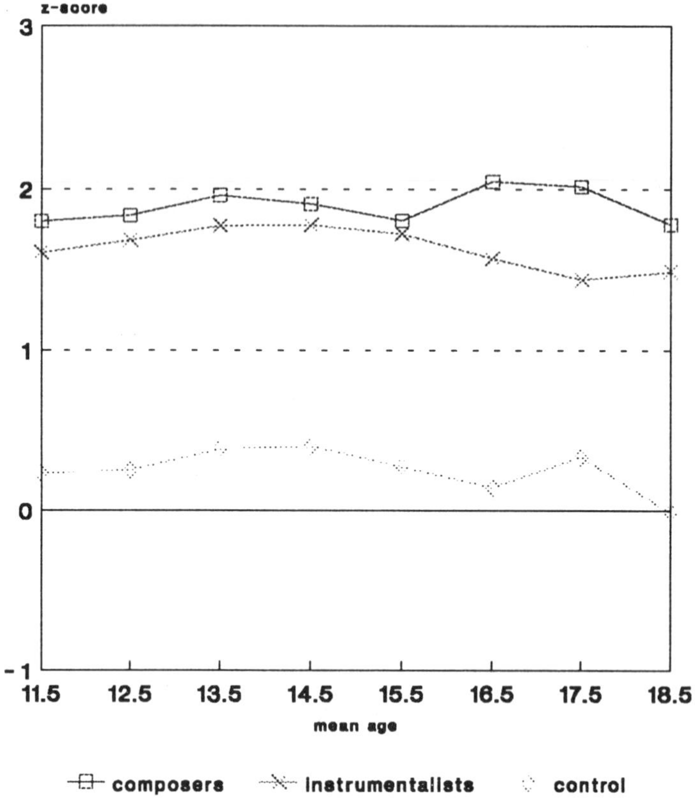

order to enable the musical experts to make a final comparison with pieces provided earlier in the study. All participants were willing to play pieces of well known composers for us, but most clearly stated that they had given up inventing music them-selves, because they felt unable to do so. Eventually, eight of them tried to play improvisations–compositions, but the musi-cal experts rated them very low. There was only one exception which was rated five points by three out of four music experts. If the method of searching out children with the ability to com-pose–improvise is kept in mind—they were not prodigies but children who expressed their feelings and thoughts by invent-ing music—the outcome is not surprising. Even among prodi-gies, only a small portion continue early success into maturity.

The developmental course of cognitive variables differed from that of musical talent. Spatial Relations (Figure 21-5), Hidden Patterns (Figure 21-6), and Verbal Fluency scores (Figure 21-7)

FIGURE 21-2.    Development of general music ability for males.

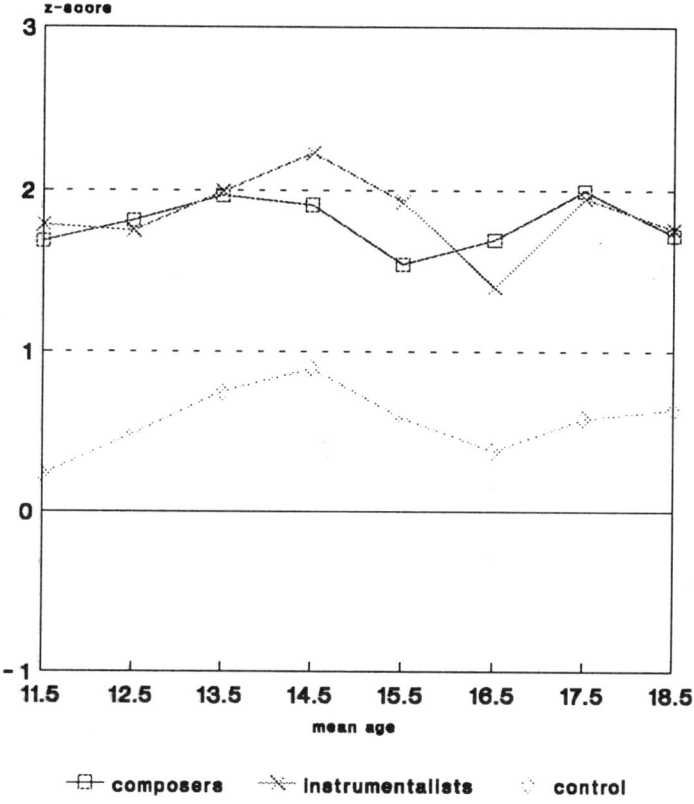

increased over time. Boys were somewhat better than girls on the Spatial Relations test. At the end of the study these sex differences in favor of males were significant. This spatial test has a rotational component and is especially sensitive to sex differences in spatial ability. On the Hidden Patterns test, girls outperformed boys most of the time; the same was true for verbal fluency. In verbal fluency, sex differences became significant at stage 7. Thus, towards the end of adolescence the well known picture of sex differences reported in the majority of studies with adults emerged (Maccoby & Jacklin, 1974).

The final data concern correlations between music training and performance tests (see Table 21-1).

Not surprisingly, strong relations were found between music training and Wing's tests. These connections became stronger with increasing age, that is, with increasing length of training.

FIGURE 21-3.    Development of general music ability for boys vs. girls.

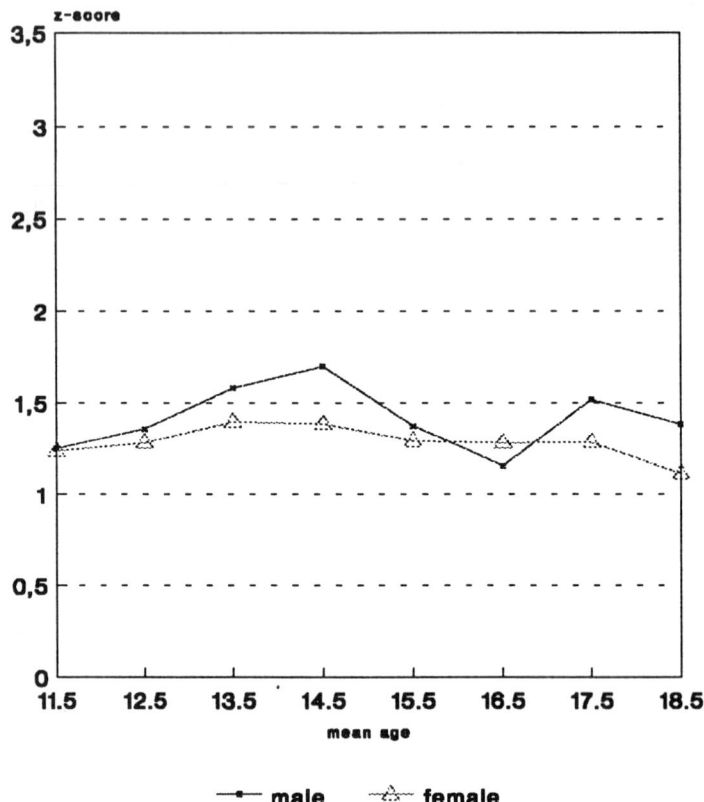

Cognitive performance also was positively influenced by music training. In boys, these positive influences were stronger on verbal fluency than on spatial tests, in girls, spatial ability was especially positively related. This can perhaps be interpreted as indicating that music training has positive effects on those abilities that tend to be lower in one or the other sex after puberty.

## DISCUSSION

The dramatic changes in the creative aspect of musical talent are reminiscent of the findings of Révész (1946). Did the participants fail to work hard enough to develop their extraordinary musical talents, as Révész suspected in Erwin N.'s case? Or did the teachers fail to change their teaching methods in a way con-

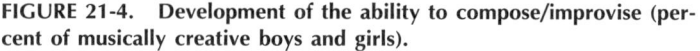

FIGURE 21-4.    Development of the ability to compose/improvise (percent of musically creative boys and girls).

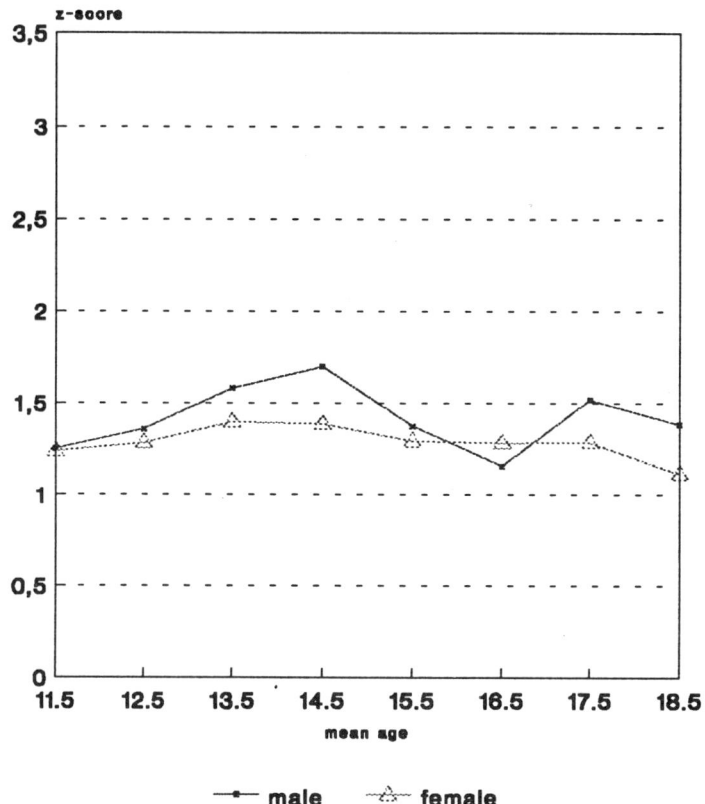

sistent with their students' changing needs? Or did the parents fail to support their children appropriately? Or was the breakdown attributable to school curricula that discriminate against music in favor of academic matters? The main purpose of this chapter is to draw attention to biological processes which seem to exert an influence on changes in musical and cognitive performance in adolescence, particularly the activating effects of sex hormones on sex-dimorphic abilities in adolescence and in adulthood.

One way to assess such relations between hormones and behavior is to measure sex hormones—especially the androgen testosterone, which is supposed to be especially important for musical and cognitive performance—and to relate the outcome to cognitive and musical test scores. Androgens can be mea-

FIGURE 21-5.    Developmental course of Spatial Relations (z-scores) for boys and girls.

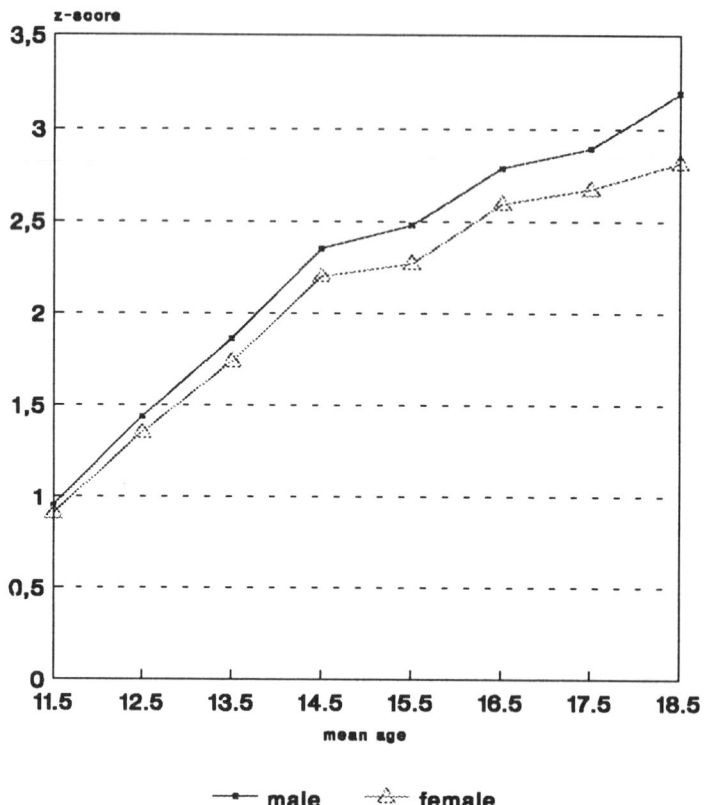

sured in blood serum or in saliva. The latter method is noninvasive and seems to be especially suitable for use with healthy subjects. However, the number of hormones detectable in saliva is limited. In the case of cognitive abilities, spatial faculties have been found to be related to sex hormones (Gouchie & Kimura, 1990; Nyborg, 1984). With respect to creative musical ability, testosterone in saliva was found to be significantly lower in male composers than in male instrumentalists and male nonmusicians, and to be significantly higher in female composers than in female instrumentalists and nonmusicians (Hassler, 1991a). With respect to development in puberty, this outcome seems to suggest that, in the course of adolescence, some boys who were able to compose in their early teens may exceed testosterone levels favorable for the expression of creative mu-

FIGURE 21-6.    Developmental course of Hidden Patterns (z-scores) for boys and girls.

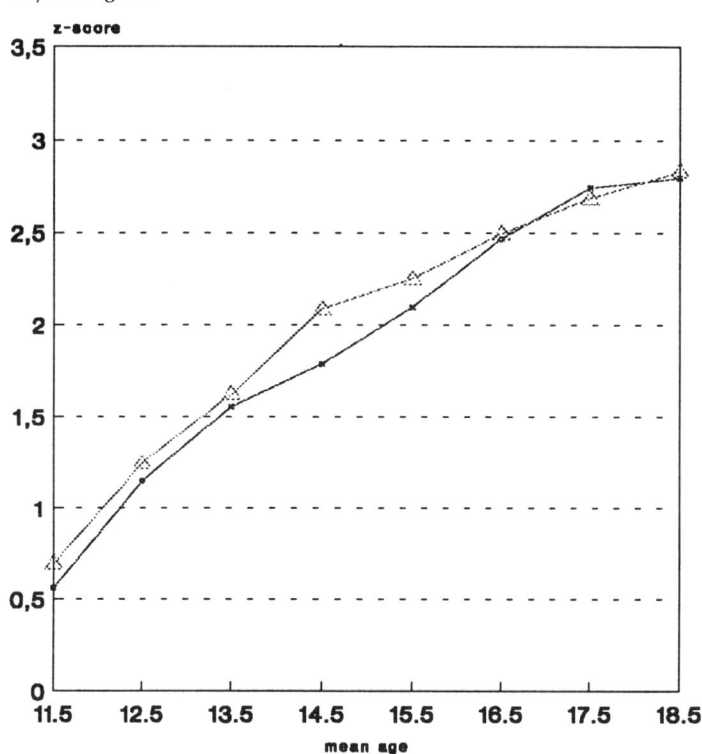

sical behavior. Among a complex interactional system of cultural, social, and biological variables, this may lead to a cessation of composing and/or improvising. Girls, on the other hand, may reach the high testosterone range only after puberty has come to an end. This means that there may be a sex difference with respect to the schedule of development of musical creativity. In the present investigation, the young male composers exceeded testosterone values obtained from adult composers at the mean age of 16 years. At that time a second dramatic decrease of composing–improvising occurred. The first dramatic decrease was found between 13 and 14 years, when testosterone measures were not included in the assessment. However, at that young age testosterone levels are not high enough to exceed adult composers' levels. This can be taken as an indicator

FIGURE 21-7.    Developmental course of Verbal Fluency (z-scores) for boys and girls.

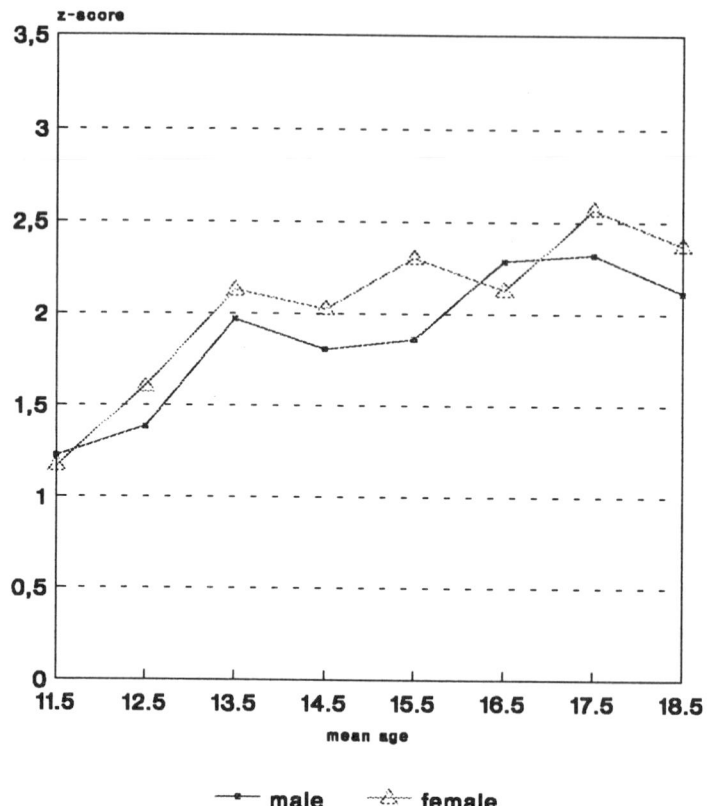

of the complex biological system, of which testosterone is only one component among others that may be related to changes in brain processes in adolescence.

There are indications from clinical data that current hormone levels must be viewed in relation to pre- and perinatal events (Hier & Crowley, 1982). The organizing effects of androgens or estrogens at that early stage of human development seem to have prepared the framework in which sex hormones will affect cognitive—and possibly musical—performance.

To open a window for assessing early organizing hormone influences on the developing brain, some researchers have compared early, mid, and late maturers on musical and cognitive tests (Hassler, 1991b; Waber, 1977). A relationship between maturation rate and spatial test performance was found, but no sig-

## TABLE 21-1
## Music Training of Boys and Girls. Correlation of Music Training with Musical and Cognitive Variables

| Year | Hidden Patterns | | Spatial Relations | | Verbal Fluency | | Wing | |
|---|---|---|---|---|---|---|---|---|
| | Boys | Girls | Boys | Girls | Boys | Girls | Boys | Girls |
| 1983 | .201 (n = 60) | .059 (n = 60) | .075 (n = 60) | .120 (n = 60) | .275* (n = 60) | .048 (n = 60) | .508** (n = 60) | .414** (n = 60) |
| 1984 | .351* (n = 51) | .211 (n = 52) | .104 (n = 51) | .249 (n = 52) | .272 (n = 51) | .132 (n = 52) | .444** (n = 51) | .546** (n = 52) |
| 1985 | .391 (n = 51) | .016 (n = 54) | .165 (n = 51) | .120 (n = 54) | .444 (n = 51) | .165 (n = 54) | .423 (n = 51) | .542** (n = 54) |
| 1986 | .304* (n = 50) | .321 (n = 53) | .199 (n = 50) | .204 (n = 53) | .427** (n = 50) | .338* (n = 53) | .571** (n = 50) | .540** (n = 53) |
| 1987 | .304* (n = 46) | .323* (n = 53) | .152 (n = 46) | .354** (n = 53) | .417** (n = 46) | .021 (n = 53) | .608** (n = 46) | .622** (n = 53) |
| 1988 | .251 (n = 46) | .286* (n = 48) | .170 (n = 46) | .406** (n = 48) | .421** (n = 46) | .184 (n = 48) | .642** (n = 46) | .607** (n = 48) |
| 1989 | .176 (n = 44) | .369** (n = 49) | .135 (n = 44) | .246 (n = 49) | .468** (n = 44) | .504** (n = 49) | .671** (n = 44) | .702** (n = 49) |
| 1990 | .155 (n = 45) | .474** (n = 48) | .229 (n = 45) | .261 (n = 48) | .228 (n = 45) | .418** (n = 48) | .660** (n = 45) | .775** (n = 48) |

* = $p < 0.05$; ** = $p < 0.01$.

nificant differences between the maturational groups emerged on the Wing tests. However, the sample was only small, and indications of the usefulness of such a procedure with a larger number of subjects were found.

In the field of hormones and behavior in humans, research is only at the beginning of the way. Many limitations of current research need to be overcome to improve knowledge: the restricted measurement of sex hormones must be overcome—that is, not merely one or two or three steroids but as many components of an interacting system as possible must be included; more must be learned about the interaction of hormones with other hormones, neurotransmitters or opioids in the brain, as well as about metabolization rates, and tissue sensitivity. Of course, it cannot be expected that complex abilities like musical or cognitive faculties have simple biological counterparts. Functional differences between musicians and nonmusicians in brain organization have been demonstrated repeatedly (Gordon, 1983; Hassler, 1990), and there are indications of structural differences as well (Meyer, 1977). They may be accompanied by biochemical differences, and adolescence seems to be a critical period for establishing them.

## ACKNOWLEDGMENTS

This research was supported by a grant from the German Research Council (DFG; Ha 1350). Prof. Dr. A. Feil, Institute of Musicology, University of Tübingen, is thanked for his cooperation, Dipl.-Psych. K. Kirschmann for statistical and graphical work.

## REFERENCES

Abramovich, D. R., Davidson, I. A., Longstaff, A., & Pearson, C. R. (1987). Sexual differentiation of the human midtrimester brain. *European Journal of Obstetrics, Gynecology, and Reproductive Biology, 25,* 7–14.

Barrington, D. (1781). *Miscellanies.* London: Nichols.

Dörner, G. (1985). Sex-specific gonadotropin secretion, sexual orientation and gender role behavior. *Experimental and Clinical Endocrinology, 86,* 1–6.

Ekstrom, R. B., French, J. W., Harman, H. H., & Dermen, D. (1976). *Manual for Kit of Factor-Referenced Cognitive Tests.* Princeton, NJ: ETS.

Geschwind, N., & Galaburda, A. M. (1985). Cerebral lateralization. Biological mechanisms, associations, and pathology: I. A hypothesis and a program for research. *Archives of Neurology, 42,* 428–459.

Gordon, H. W. (1983). Music and the right hemisphere. In A. W. Young (Ed.), *Functions of the right cerebral hemisphere* (pp. 65–86). New York: Academic Press.

Gouchie, C., & Kimura, D. (1990). Testosterone levels and cognitive ability. *Neuro-Endocrinology Letters, 12(4),* 296.

Hassler, M. (1990). Functional cerebral asymmetries and cognitive abilities in musicians, painters, and controls. *Brain and Cognition, 13,* 1–17.

Hassler, M. (1991a). Testosterone and artistic talents. *International Journal of Neuroscience, 56,* 25–38.

Hassler, M. (1991b). Maturation rate and spatial, verbal, and musical abilities: A seven-year longitudinal study. *International Journal of Neuroscience, 58,* 183–198.

Hassler, M., & Birbaumer, N. (1988). Handedness, musical abilities, and dichaptic and dichotic performance in adolescents: a longitudinal study. *Developmental Neuropsychology, 4,* 129–145.

Hassler, M., Birbaumer, N., & Feil, A. (1985). Musical talent and visual-spatial ability: A longitudinal study. *Psychology of Music, 13,* 99–113.

Hier, D. B., & Crowley, W. F. Jr. (1982). Spatial ability in androgen-deficient men. *New England Journal of Medicine,* May, 1202–1205.

Horn, W. (1962). *Leistungsprüfsystem.* Göttingen: Hogrefe.

Hoyenga, K. B,. & Hoyenga, K. T. (1979). *The question of sex differences.* Boston, MA: Little Brown Co.

Maccoby, E. E., & Jacklin, C. N. (1974). *The psychology of sex differences.* Stanford: Stanford University Press.

Meyer, A. (1977). The search for a morphological substrate in the brains of eminent persons including musicians: a historical review. In M. Critchley & R. A. Henson (Eds.), *Music and the brain* (pp. 255–281). London: Heinemann Medical Books.

Money, J. (1988). *Gay, straight, and in-between. The sexology of erotic orientation.* Oxford: Oxford University Press.

Nyborg, H. (1984). Performance and intelligence in hormonally different groups. In G. J. De Vries, J. P. C. De Bruin, H. B. M. Uylings, & M. A. Corner (Eds.), *Sex differences in the brain.* Amsterdam: Elsevier.

Révész, G. (1946). *Einführung in die Musikpsychologie* [Introduction to the psychology of music]. Bern: Francke Verlag.

Scott, D., & Moffett, A. (1977). The development of early musical talent in famous composers: a biographical review. In M. Critchley & R. A. Henson (Eds.), *Music and the brain* (pp. 174–201). London: Heinemann Medical Books.

Thurstone, T. G. (1962). *Primary Mental Abilities Test*. Chicago: Science Research Associates.

Waber, D. P. (1977). Sex differences in mental abilities, hemispheric lateralization, and rate of physical growth at adolescence. *Developmental Psychology, 13*, 29–38.

Waterhouse, L. (1988). Speculations on the neuroanatomical substrate of special talents. In K. Obler & D. Fein (Eds.), *The exceptional brain* (pp. 493–512). New York: Guilford Press.

Wehmeyer, G. (1983). Carl Czerny und die Einzelhaft am Klavier [Carl Czerny and solitary confinement at the piano]. Kassel: Bärenreiter Atlantis Musikbuch.

Wing, H. (1968). Tests of Musical Ability and Appreciation. Second Edition. *British Journal of Psychology, Monograph Supplements,* XXVII.

# 22

# Psychological Counseling in Music Schools in Poland

**Jolanta Kepinska-Welbel**

*Chopin Academy of Music, Warsaw, Poland*

The development of psychological counseling for students of music schools in Poland is presented. The author's counseling experience has shown that crises in music school students can be analyzed in terms of values, technology, and socioemotional factors. An important feature of psychological diagnosis is the analysis of musical achievement motivation (short-, medium-, and long-term).

## INTRODUCTION

In Poland there was an enormous upsurge of music schools after World War II. Elementary music schools for children, on a mass scale, starting with six-year-olds, advanced professional music schools, and eight music academies were opened. With this new proliferation of formalized music training, within a network of music schools teaching many thousands of children and adolescents, it became essential that the Polish educational system provide proper guidance for musically gifted children. Consequently, music school teachers invited psychologists to cooperate in the solving of many new problems.

The history of cooperation of psychologists and music school teachers in Poland dates a long way. In 1956 Maria Manturzewska inspired the establishment of the first psychological teams working in music schools in four different cities. New teams assembled in the years to follow, and they cared for more and more music schools. In the 1970s, psychological guidance clinics began to form in the music schools at different levels of advancement: In 1972, for instance, the Psychological Counselling Clinic was founded at the Frederic Chopin Music Academy in Warsaw. These clinics had the theoretical and methodological support of the Pedagogical Center for Artistic Schools until 1972, and of the Chair of Psychology of Music at the Frederic Chopin Music Academy from then on. The psychologists were trained in diagnostic techniques, adapted for use in Poland (first and foremost, musical ability and achievement tests), and music school teachers were trained, giving an outlet for discussion, exchange of experience, and research.

At first, both the teachers' and the psychologists' priority was selection of those wishing to study music and the provision of objective and comprehensive measures of candidates' musical abilities. The next objective was to diagnose the sources of difficulty and failure in studying music. The alarming dropout rate in music schools was becoming a real problem. Gradually, with experience, it became evident that the sources of failure in music school students could not be reduced to the problem of purely musical assessment. It became more and more apparent that the difficulties spring from a whole network of setbacks: insufficient intellectual, affective, and social maturity, maladaptive personality, lack of motivation, or unfavorable environment.

Gradually it became essential for psychologists to assist not only in recruitment to music schools and the diagnosis of sources of problems, but also to work in a focused way on guaranteeing each student optimal conditions for development at the music school. This implied close cooperation with the music teachers, and participation in the entire didactic process. During individual tutoring in playing an instrument, teachers can individualize their approach to the maximum; get to know the student's idiosyncratic personality make up, motives, aims, and interests; and can take these into account in the process of instruction. However, many teachers have their stiff and routine methods of teaching, which they apply to all students alike. Hence one of the most important tasks of the music school psychologist is to sensitize the teachers to the need for individual treatment of students, and to focus not only on their musical capacities, but also on development in general. The higher the level of education and the older the student, the more important his or her own aims, values, and ideals become. It must not be forgotten that at some point in the teaching of music, instruction becomes professional. At this point the student makes the decision to become a professional musician, and the decision affects his or her whole further life.

At earlier levels of instruction the family environment is paramount for the student's development and achievements. Research has shown that proper relationships within the family, and a good climate and atmosphere, are significant determinants of the entire development of the child, and hence also of school achievement. Parental ambitions not infrequently interfere with children's attitude to music school and their own achievements. Hence, contact and cooperation with the parents is the next task of the psychologist. Needless to say, the teacher more frequently than not has no time for such contact. Given the objectives and assignments of the psychologist in the music school system, it is appropriate that psychological counseling and guidance for music schools be separated from the general network of school guidance clinics. The psychologist in the music school must be well acquainted with and take into account the specifics of musical education, and also must be well aware of the specificity of the musical professions, their limitations, demands, contingencies, and opportunities.

I would like to make some comments based on my experience as a psychologist at the Music Academy Counselling and Guidance Clinic. The main aim of my work is to help students gain harmonious professional maturity and learn to steer their own lives and artistic and professional careers. They must learn to make the transition from the role of student to that of active professional musician.

In order to gain as much information as possible about the newly enrolled students at our academy, I scan their responses to tests given during the entrance exam and adaptive classes organized for first-year students. These include not only ability and musical achievement tests but also tests of intelligence, personality, neuroticism, and anxiety. In individual interviews I see both students and members of the faculty who have problems with their charges. When necessary I conduct long-term therapy using a variety of psychotherapeutic methods and techniques.

A detailed analysis of cases seen at the clinic has revealed that the critical years at our college are the first, third, and final. In the first year the problems reported center on difficulties in adaptation to the new environment and new methods of instruction and learning. In the third year the students establish their professional position, and hence the predominant problems are competition and fatigue. This is the year when they have the largest number of exams and compulsory classes. In the final year, apprehension about future jobs and further artistic development is predominant. Eight disjunctive categories of problems presented at the Psychological Counselling and Guidance Clinic can be distinguished (in fact, these problems frequently converge in the same patient).

1.  problems with learning;
2.  problems with artistic development and professional identification;
3.  problems with adaptation and interpersonal conflicts;
4.  stage fright;
5.  depression, anxiety, breakdowns, and stress;
6.  family problems;
7.  overload and burnout; and
8.  symptoms of psychotic disorders.

At the clinic the psychological problems presented by patients within the framework of their professional development are analyzed. This is primarily because the students are in the most important phase of their professional and artistic development. Most problems and complaints with which they report at the clinic are very dramatic and acute. Young people in this particular phase of development are extremely emotional, lacking in emotional control, prone to overgeneralization, and desperately seeking their own professional status. Therapy consists mainly in emotional support of their endeavors, increasing their experience of security, faith in their own capacities, and active participation in musical life.

In my therapeutic work the main objective is to help the patient develop a more realistic self-image (this usually consists in boosting self-esteem), to become more competent, not only musically but in all spheres of life, and to cope with difficult situations. I always try to encourage the patient to use his or her musical and intellectual abilities at college to the maximum, and to strive for set goals (usually a music academy diploma and becoming a professional musician). I often feel that the psychologist, in so doing, becomes a supplementary meaningful figure who frequently reinforces purely educational measures by showing the student that studying music not only focuses on a specific goal, great success, and so forth, but is first and foremost a means of self-realization, development of potential, and achievement of artistic satisfaction. It is a great impediment to therapeutic success when the patient feels inhibition and lack of developmental perspective, because he or she has no clearcut criterion of success or locates this criterion in purely external points that are irrelevant to total musical development.

Quite frequently the psychologist is asked for help by students of high achievement, winners of contests, with excellent grades in only musical and theoretical subjects. These students usually complain of great reluctance to complete their studies. Their breakdown can be analyzed on several levels.

## Values, Ideology, Meaning, and Goals of Studying, and Faith in the Musical Profession

Such students have lost their faith in musical production. Some complain that they find no satisfaction in music, others say that they cannot come to terms with the fact that in the future they will only be second rate and not first-class musicians. These patients are dissatisfied with their feeling of mediocrity and usually select a profession that is less competitive, with less clearcut divisions into first rate, mediocre, and poor (i.e., they switch from the piano department to sound control, or from the vocal department to musical education). Many students are apprehensive about their ability to make a living out of music, whereas others have doubts as to "whom exactly are we going to play for?" More and more frequently students find complete lack of an audience at and interest in concerts.

## Problems with Technique and Workshop

This group of patients complains of complete inability to overcome problems of technique or memory. They are unable to learn a large musical passage by heart; they have general deficiencies in musical education. (There are tragic examples of students near the end of their studies in the vocal department who are unable to sight read music well.) Deficiencies in "workshop" are often the complaint of players of instruments who must include modern composers in their repertoire for the first time, but are unable to assimilate their musical language.

## Social and Emotional Context—
## Loss of Emotional Support

The inhibition of the musical development of these patients has its source in maladaptive relationships in the social environment and impaired interpersonal relationships. These students frequently demonstrate great guilt toward people who "devoted" their whole lives to their careers and who are now being let down. "I've disappointed my parents," is a frequent complaint of students that often leads to depressive breakdowns. I would also be inclined to put into this category those students who complain of justified or unjustified feelings of being let down by their tutor. These students complain that their professor is quite oblivious to their musical development. This feeling of being let down is particularly dramatic when the student had previously been a favorite, and had been assessed very highly. (For instance, a student who, from the first year on did not have the qualifications to be a student, but "filled in" in a teacher's post then, having become redundant, was expelled just before his final year.)

Alongside these levels of breakdown I also frequently take into account, in my differential diagnosis and analysis of the sources and psychological mechanisms of symptoms, the problem of musical achievement motivation, and its previous development. It helps me a great deal to distinguish among three different types of musical achievement motivation.

1.  *short-term motivation*, which applies to duration, quality, and opportunities to practice, ability to concentrate on a given activity, and practice strategy;
2.  *medium-term motivation*, which is focused on more distant goals, such as preparing a piece, acquaintance with the literature, completing a year at college;
3.  *long-term motivation*, focused on imagined or envisaged roles as professional musician, dreams of winning contests, identification and accomplishment of artistic ideals.

Dysfunctions within these three types of motivation are found in students reporting at the clinic. Very gifted students with well-articulated long-term motivation often complain that they were unable to concentrate when practicing, and find it difficult to organize their time at college. Even if they get good grades they are dissatisfied with themselves and visit the psychologist in the hope of finding ways to practice more efficiently or concentrate better. I often feel that difficulties in concentration, that is, in short-term motivation, have their roots in a certain atrophy and vagueness of long-term motivation, or considerable disruption of medium-term motivation caused by overload at college and too many extracurricular activities.

If the student is to study music efficiently, he or she must achieve harmony in the functioning of all three levels of motivation and a deeper awareness of the need to set goals and assignments independently and actively and not to be steered from without. Teaching students of the music academy to be professionally competent requires that they learn not only to be technically efficient, to memorize their repertoire, and to accumulate musical experience, but also to plan and steer their own professional development, to be constantly ready to undertake musical assignments, to be prepared to practice and find satisfaction when they do as planned.

# 23

---

# Identification
# and Promotion
# of Musical Talent

---

**Maria Manturzewska**

*Akademia Muzyczna im. Fryderyka Chopina, Warsaw, Poland*

Research on musical giftedness in Poland has a long tradition. Looking back, these endeavors can be seen as a process of transformation and reorientation of the basic concepts, methods, and strategies of research, and of attitudes toward the problem of the psychology of talent. This process resulted from successive discoveries of new aspects of musical giftedness and new factors influencing its development. In the light of experience until now, musical giftedness can be seen as a lifelong process of music-related activity, with strong intrinsic motivation to improve both results and knowledge. Simultaneously, it is a stream, very sensitive to external and internal emotional pressures, a potential that cannot be realized without active and competent socioemotional support and tutoring—in all stages of the talented person's life. Research on this problem requires international cooperation among experienced researchers, counselors, music teachers, and parents of the musically gifted.

## INTRODUCTION

Psychological research on the problem of identification of the musically gifted has a long tradition in Poland. The first attempts concerned with validation and utilization of standardized musical tests began in the late 1930s, under the leadership of Professor Stefan Szuman at the Jagiellonian University (Pawlowski, 1938). Then, after a 10-year interval, caused by World War II German occupation, and the Stalinist regime, they were revived in 1956, when the first unit for research in the psychology of music, led by M. Manturzewska, was established at the Educational Centre for Schools of Arts and Music at the Ministry of Culture in Warsaw. The basic reason why this research unit was established and psychologists and music psychologists invited to cooperate with music schools and music teachers was the very high dropout rate of students from the special music schools in Poland.

The system of education of the musically gifted in Poland consists of three levels (elementary, secondary, and higher/university level). It is parallel to the general system of education and involves about 16–17 years of study (seven years at elementary school, five at secondary and four–five at the Music Academy). The schools are selective. The entrance examination at each school is competitive, and at each level musical and general abilities and musical performance are evaluated by musical experts: music teachers, usually working in teams (entrance examination committee). The number of candidates seeking entry to each type of school, particularly to the elementary schools, is usually much higher than the number of places available, sometimes 10–20 times higher.

In spite of the earnest endeavors of Polish music teachers to select the best candidates and the most promising musically gifted, the dropout rate at the elementary level of musical education (during the seven years of study) from one year's admittance in the late 1950s was more than 80%. This was a very frustrating situation, both for music teachers and the music school administration, as well as for the government, which was paying for the music schools and their entire equipment (music schools are free in Poland).

For this reason, music teachers turned to the university psychologists and to specialists in music psychology to help them solve this problem and to improve the methods of diagnosis of musical abilities. I was among those invited. Newly graduated in the psychology of music and experienced in musical study and performance, I was at the time full of enthusiasm for the psychology of music, fascinated by the books and works of Lundin (1953), Revèsz (1946), Schoen (1940), Schünemann (1930), Seashore (1938), Tieplov (1952) and deeply believing that contemporary science would improve music teachers' work and achievement in identifying the musically gifted.

In February 1956 the Educational Centre for Schools of Arts and Music at the Ministry of Culture in Warsaw, the first research unit for the psychology of music was established. As the only full time researcher at this unit, I started my job by organizing the first National Conference of music psychology, which took place in December 1956 in Warsaw. In all, 126 persons participated in this conference (professors of psychology from all Polish universities, professors and rectors of music academies, directors of music schools at different levels from different towns in Poland, outstanding musicians, and mass media representatives). After three days of papers and discussions a tentative program of research in the psychology of music was elaborated and the main directions of research and activities concerned with improvement of methods of identification and promotion of the musically gifted were proposed (*Szkola Artystyczna*, 1957, Nr. 1–2). In this way realization of the draft program commenced.

Looking back on the 35 years of endeavors, it is possible to distinguish four stages, differing in focus of main interests and research activity, as well as in the conceptualization of musical giftedness and the paradigms of research strategies and methods. Belief in the capacity of contemporary science to solve the problems of identification and fostering of the musically gifted has also evolved over the years. On the basis of Whitehead's (1929) and Sosniak's (1985) suggestions, the following stages can be identified: (1) The stage of romanticism and *exploration* of both literature and practice colored by naiveté and deep belief in the power of the psychology of music. (2) The stage of *perfectionism*, concerned with adaptation and restandardization of musical ability tests and the conscious application of achievements of world psychology of music and music psychometrics, with rigorous concern for all formal requirements of the theory of test construction and standardization. (3) The stage of *integration*, that is, the stage of designing our own multidimensional and multimethod research projects on the predictors of music achievements at school and the professional careers of musicians. (4) The stage of *scepticism*, that is, searching for new research paradigms, new methods and strategies, and new approaches to the problems of the musically gifted and their promotion.

In the first stage (1956–1959) the explorations were realized in three streams.

1. All the best (according to Buros' 1953, 1959 recommendations) tests of musical abilities at that time—Drake's (1954), Wing's (1948), Revèsz's (1946), Whistler and Thorpe's (1950), Farnum's (1953) and Seashore's (1919)—were imported to Poland, and an exploration of their applicability and utility for Polish schoolchildren began.
2. The methods of evaluation of musical ability used by music school teachers were studied, and the final examinations and criteria for evaluation of musical ability and achievement of elementary, secondary, and higher music school graduates by music teachers were observed.
3. Lectures for music teachers at different levels were implemented in an attempt to familiarize them with musical tests and the theory of test construction and standardization, as well as with the achievements of the psychology of music in the field of musical ability measurement and development.

At the time, the discoveries of Schünemann (1930) concerning stages in early musical development, the results of Revèsz's (1946) research and Drake's new methods of measurement of musical memory and sense of rhythm exerted a particular fascination. Attempts were made to make music teachers more interested in typical failures and disadvantages of the traditional approach to the identification of musical talent, and to show them the possibilities of the psychology of music and music psychometrics in the field by means of participation in many summer courses and national conferences for music teachers and music school directors, as well as through the conduct of special meetings and presentations on music tests for the staff of music academies. This was very successful, because the music teachers appreciated these endeavors very highly.

The second stage (1959–1966) was concerned with the adaptation, restandardisation and norming of two music ability tests, Drake's (1954) Musical Aptitude Tests, and Wing's (1948) Standardised Tests of Musical Intelligence, and two music achievement tests—Aliferis's Music Achievement Test (1954), and Farnum's Music Notation Test (1953). A network of teams of psychologists was involved in this research. These came from four different universities in Poland (Cracow, Wroclaw, Poznan, and Warsaw) that cooperated with local projects on validation and normalisation of chosen musical tests. In all, six different age levels were investigated: 10-, 12-, 14-, 16-, 18-, and 22-year-old students of music (elementary, secondary and university level schools), and parallel to this (matched for age and level of education) nonmusic students (Manturzewska, 1968a,b).

This research revealed:

1. Statistically significant differences in test scores between music and nonmusic students at all levels of age and educational development. This means that the tests measure traits connected with musical activity.
2. Stable intervals between music and nonmusic students at all levels of age and educational development, suggesting that the tests measure some musical potential independent of musical training.
3. A high level of musical ability of students at Polish music schools as compared with English norms for an unselected population.
4. Much higher scores for Polish music students on Drake's Musical Memory Test than the American norms. Students in Polish music schools are a more select group than music students abroad (Manturzewska, 1968b). The validation study yielded positive, statistically significant (but not as high as American and English) correlation coefficients of test scores with music teachers' ratings (for Wing's test $r = .41$ and for Drake's $r = .38$).

Parallel to the psychometric research connected with the adaptation, restandardization, and validation of musical ability tests, two independent psychological guidance centers for music school students in Warsaw (Manturzewska) and in Pozen (Horbulewicz) were organized. In these centers an attempt was made to use in counseling practice all musical tests that had been adapted and restandardized. All children who were about to drop out from music school in Warsaw and Pozen were sent to be tested. It was discovered that those who had to leave music schools because they were unable to fulfill the requirements sometimes had better music test results than those who finished music school successfully. This was observed at all levels of music education. At each level a different constellation of traits and factors was responsible. For first grade music school students the cause of the serious trouble in meeting school requirements was often "school immaturity syndrome." These children, in spite of a sometimes very high level of musical ability and intelligence, were socially and emotionally unable to sit in one place for one hour or longer. They were unable to concentrate their attention long enough during both individual music instrument instruction and group lessons in general music training (solfeggio, singing, eurhythmics, etc).

The most frequent causes of dropping out in older classes (above the fourth grade) were lack of proper support and stimulation from the parents (lack of musical tradition in the parental environment, conflict between parents, divorce, and so on, lack of emotional, volitional and cognitive support by parents, and lack of control by parents during individual practice hours at the beginning of music school studies). Sometimes the cause of dropping out was low level of general intelligence and inability to match the requirements of two parallel schools: musical and general education. Yet another reason for dropping out was a high level of neuroticism, lack of self-discipline, or a very immature (undemanding) personality and inability to work hard.

Stage III (1960–1974): Discussing with the music teachers all these problems and causes of dropping out of musical studies revealed a lack of consensus concerning problems and obstacles in the development of music achievement (high achievement) and ability. The problems of relative independence of school maturity from musical ability and intelligence were not noticed. The important role of the family environment and a favourable constellation of personality traits as factors determining musical achievement were also ignored. This controversy made it necessary to verify some of the hypotheses concerning the conditions of music achievement and professional development in research on adult musicians. It was decided to use as an experimental group in the research the group of participants at the international Chopin Piano Competition, Warsaw, 1960. Three control groups were used: a group of young pianists, a group of young musicologists, and a group of young psychologists. All groups investigated were of the same age, and the music groups had similar musical education (Manturzewska, 1963).

Three music tests were used: Drake's Music Aptitude tests, Wing's Standardised Tests of Musical Intelligence, and Aliferis's Music Achievement Test; one test of general intelligence (Raven's Progressive Matrices) and one questionnaire, especially constructed for this research by Professor Wronski (a very experienced music teacher and violin virtuoso, a professor of the Warsaw Academy and the Bloomington School of Music) and me. This questionnaire included both biographical questions and questions related to the family environment, style of work and musical practice, as well as personal and motivational questions. All groups were investigated with the same tests, but unfortunately the questionnaire was used only for the experimental group.

The results were analyzed both statistically and qualitatively. Results included:

1. Statistically significant differences between the experimental group and the other groups on Wing's tests and between the experimental group and musicologists and psychologists on Drake's Musical Memory Test and Aliferis's test.
2. Significant differences in the difficulty of the subtests of Raven's Progressive Matrices between the experimental group and nonmusicians, and differences between expert groups and other musicians in the speed of solving this test (Manturzewska, 1969). Correlation of the musical and intelligence test scores with the jurors' ratings were, for all musical tests with the exception of Drake's Rhythm test, positive, high, and statistically significant.

This research also revealed the very important role of environmental factors as a determinant of musical achievement. All of the competition prize winners were children of educated parents and had nonworking mothers; musical instruments were to be found in the family home when they were born. They had strong powers of concentration and the ability to focus energy in stress situations. Three quarters of the prize winners came from homes with musical traditions, and 20% of them were the children of professional musicians. Significant differences were found in the style of instrumental practice between prize winners and dropouts in the first stage of the Competition and between participants and music students (Manturzewska, 1969).

On completion of this research it was concluded that

> Musical talent seems to be a special constellation of psy-
> chophysiological factors, dynamic in its character and springing
> from interactions between biological possibilities (present and po-
> tential) and environmental requirements and rewards. The mean-
> ing and the weight (role) of each component (factor) as a predic-
> tor of musical achievement is relative, and should be evaluated in
> the context of other components in this constellation and with re-
> gard to the personal and emotional situation of the person being
> investigated. Musical talent should not be understood as the sum
> of independent specific musical abilities, but rather as a STREAM
> of present (status) and potential possibilities, which may reach
> realisation and fulfilment in different ways, according to the given
> personal situation of the artist (Manturzewska, 1969).

The study on the participants in the VIth International
F. Chopin Piano Competition was a pilot study. The report from
this study entitled "Psychological conditions of pianistic achievement" was published in Polish (Manturzewska, 1969). The hypotheses and conclusions of this study were verified in a later
project, a study on the predictors of success in music schools,
carried out in 1967–1968 on 300 music students from three different levels of music education: elementary, secondary, and
higher (Manturzewska, 1974). In this study 10 standardized tests
measuring four groups of factors—musical abilities, general intelligence, personality structure, and interest profile—were used.

This research revealed new aspects of musical giftedness.
There was a curvilinear relationship between almost all cognitive and noncognitive individual traits and music teachers' evaluations. The research also revealed age-related differences in
the structure of musical giftedness, and differences in requirements of different fields of music. In Drake's Musical Memory
Test the mean score for pianists was 10.54, for violinists 16.58,
and for wind instruments 24.40 (out of a possible score of 108)
(Manturzewska, 1970a). On Wing's Test the pianists achieved
110.42, the violinists 109.73, and wind instrument players
98.12 (out of a possible 136) (Manturzewska, 1972).

The quantitative results of this study were submited to statistical analyses testing differences in measured traits between

1.  music and nonmusic students;
2.  different levels of age and education;
3.  boys and girls;

4. different instrumentalists (pianists, violinists and wind instrumentalists);
5. different types of school (music schools with academic subjects and without); and
6. between best and worst students for each level of music education (5% of the best and 5% of the worst students).

Detailed results of this research have been published in Polish (Manturzewska, 1974). Comparisons of the scores of the best and worst students yielded statistically significant differences at all levels of education in musical abilities, general intelligence and personality.

Case study type analyses of the test score profiles of the good and poor students made it possible to distinguish three different types of good student, differing in the structure and profiles of cognitive and noncognitive traits, and three types of poor music student (Manturzewska, 1974). Statistically significant, although not very high correlations with external criteria (the mean of music school grades and evaluations by music teachers) were also found for all musical tests and a general intelligence test, for most of the interest scales, and for personality variables. The value of personality traits as predictors of musical school achievement was greater at higher levels of music education (increasing values of correlation coefficients) (Manturzewska, 1975).

The practical outcome of the studies on predictors of success in music schools consisted of 10 manuals for the 10 standardized tests used in the research. Each manual contained the following information:

1. brief information about the method and its application in research and educational practice in Poland and abroad;
2. information about the research project on the predictors of success in music studies;
3. results of the abovementioned analyses (the differences between music and nonmusic students, between girls and boys, levels of education, musical instruments and the scores of good and poor students);
4. evaluation of the test and its usefulness for Polish music schools; and
5. instructions and suggestions on how to use the scores for diagnosis and in counseling of the musically gifted. All manuals were published by COPSA between 1968–1975.

Simultaneously and parallel to the above mentioned research on the predictors of success in musical studies and career, and in very close connection with them, two other research projects were concerned with the reliability of evaluation of musical ability and achievement by music experts. These were studies on consistency in the evaluation of musical performances by musical experts, that is, international competition jurors (Manturzewska, 1966, 1970b) and on the stability and consistency of the evaluation of music students by music teachers (Manturzewska, 1974, 1990a; Manturzewska & Kotarska, 1981).

In 1974 the Ministry of Culture requested the organisation of a national symposium summarizing the achievements of research on the psychology of music and music education and on psychological counselling for music school students (*Zeszyty Naukowe PWSM w Warszawie*, Nr 5, I and II, 1977). By the end of that year the Institute for Research in Music Education (IRME) was established at the Academy of Music in Warsaw. This institute was responsible for the coordination of research in the fields of psychology, sociology of music, and music education. The establishment of the IRME opened new perspectives for researchers on musical giftedness and achievement, as well as new possibilities for international contact, exchange, and publication.

Stage IV (1975–1990): In the light of earlier experiences it was necessary to abandon the old paradigm of research based on traditional static trait and factor theory and traditional theory of test construction. The need for a new paradigm became obvious. The new approach to the problem of giftedness sees it as

1. A lifelong process of interaction between natural abilities and motivation and socioemotional and cultural environment.
2. A multidimensional process of transformation of both cognitive and noncognitive aspects (dimensions) of gifted persons.
3. A process which should be investigated and evaluated in large diachronic and synchronic environmental and biographical contexts.

During the fourth stage scientific activity began to develop in the following directions.

1. Biographical study of the lifespan development of professional musicians and musical talents (Manturzewska, 1977, 1980, 1986, 1990b).
2. Psychometric study of the construction and standardisation of objective and reliable tests and scales of music achieve-

ment that make it possible to study the process of acquiring musical excellence (Manasterska, 1980) and competence (Bogdan, 1973; Kotarska, 1976, 1983, 1986; Kotarska & Kaminska, 1984; Kaminska & Meyer, 1985; Kaminska, 1985a; Manturzewka, 1981; Manturzewska & Kotarska, 1986).

3. Experimental study of the process of learning in musical performance by professional musicians (Miklaszewski, 1982, 1989, 1990). It has been found that the strategy and style of work and learning have significant influence on musical achievement (Manturzewska, 1969; Wronski, 1965, 1979).

4. Study of the perception of music by professional musicians (Jordan-Szymanska, 1990).

5. Empirical study of early musical development (Kaminska, 1972, 1980; Manturzewska & Kaminska, 1990).

6. Study of the results of music education in secondary schools in Poland (Kaminska, 1985b).

7. Study of the usefulness of music achievement tests for improvement of methods of training professional musicians (Dobrzanska, 1988; Meyer, 1991; Moryk, 1988).

The results of these explorations and studies were presented during the First International Seminar for Researchers and Lecturers in the Psychology of Music, which took place in Radziejowice (Poland) on September 24–29, 1990. Proceedings are available in Polish from the Academy of Music, Warsaw.

## CONCLUSION

In the light of experience, both in research and counseling practice, the following tasks can be seen as the most important and urgent for music psychologists interested in the problems dealt with here.

1. To create and develop an international network of music talent researchers and counselors, and to include in this network experienced parents of the musically gifted, experienced music teachers, and outstanding musicians interested in the problems.

2. To organize an international summer school for researchers on musical giftedness and counselors—at the same place and time as the international music master's classes.

3. To design a comparative international and interdisciplinary study on the lifespan development of the musically gifted

and professional musicians, concerned with the following problems.

a.  the concept of musical giftedness—its dimensions, structure and observable characteristics;

b.  the characteristic parental environment of the musically gifted and outstanding musicians (the dimensions, aspects, variables, and factors involved in this problem);

c.  the lifespan development of professional musicians and musical talents and the stages in the process of learning and arriving at musical competence and excellence;

d.  the characteristics of a good teacher at each stage;

e.  the syndrome of burnout in the life of musicians and musical teachers and ways to avoid this;

f.  crises in the lifespan development of professional musicians and music teachers—their subjective and objective characteristics, internal and external course, and ways of overcoming them.

## ACKNOWLEDGMENT

I am grateful for personal contacts with Dr. Herbert Wing and Dr. Rosamund Shuter, who supported our research, and for our contacts with the Society for Research in the Psychology of Music and Music Education. Her book, *The Psychology of Musical Ability* (2nd ed., 1982) has been translated into Polish and was published by WSIP in 1986.

This chapter is based on a paper delivered at the International Conference of Experts on Research in Giftedness—Discovery and Promotion, Hadamar, November 21–24, 1990.

## REFERENCES

Aliferis, J. (1954). *Aliferis Music Achievement Test.* Minneapolis: University of Minnesota Press.

Bogdan, M. (1973). *The standardization of the Kielarzowska Solfeggio Test* [in Polish]. Unpublished M.A. Thesis. Academy of Music, Warsaw.

Buros, O. K. (1953). *The fourth mental measurements yearbook.* Highland Park, NJ: Gryphon Press.

Buros, O. K. (1959). *The fifth mental measurements yearbook.* Highland Park, NJ: Gryphon Press.

Dobrzanska, B. (1988). *Psychological tests as predictors of success in music study* [in Polish]. Unpublished M.A. Thesis. Academy of Music, Warsaw.

Drake, R. M. (1954). *Manual for the Drake Musical Aptitude Test.* Chicago: Science Research Association.

Farnum, S. F. (1953). *Farnum Music Notation Test.* New York: Psychological Corporation.

Jordan-Szymanska, A. (1990). Music perception. In M. Manturzewska & H. Kotarska (Eds.), *Wybrane zagadnienia z psychologii muzyki* [Selected issues in the psychology of music]. Warsaw: WSIP.

Kaminska, B. (1972). *On the possibilities of introducing preschool children to music structure* [in Polish]. Unpublished M.A. Thesis. Academy of Music, Warsaw.

Kaminska, B. (1980). Some remarks about listening to music in the preschool [in Polish]. *Poradnik Muzyczny, 4*, 3–5.

Kaminska, B. (1985a). Doreen Bridge's Australian Music Achievement Test tentative manual [in Polish]. Manuscript in IPM Archives.

Kaminska, B. (1985b). *Musical competence of secondary school students in Poland* [in Polish]. Unpublished PhD dissertation, Academy of Music, Warsaw.

Kaminska, B. M, & Meyer (1985). The candidates to the Academy of Music in Warsaw in the light of the Australian Test for Advanced Music Studies [in Polish]. *Zeszyty Naukowe AMFC, 11*, 144–150.

Kotarska, H. (1976). Standardised tests of music achievement as the method of evaluation of school achievement and progress in study [in Polish]. *Materialy Pomocrzicze COPSA*, Vol. 165. Warsaw: COPSA.

Kotarska, H. (1983). *Tests of musical competence and knowledge for music school students.* Warsaw: Academy of Music.

Kotarska, H. (1986). Entwicklungstendenzen und Leistungen der musik-psychologischen Diagnose in Polen. In *Materialien und Dokumente, Kieler-Woche-Kongress 1985.* Regensburg: Bosse.

Kotarska, H., & Kaminska, B. (1984). *Music achievement tests for students.* Warsaw: WSIP.

Lundin, W. R. (1953). *An objective psychology of music.* New York: Roland.

Manasterska, T. (1980). *The construction of a piano-performance scale.* Unpublished PhD dissertation. Academy of Music, Warsaw.

Manturzewska, M. (1963). *Psychological, biological and biographical conditions of piano achievement* [in Polish]. Unpublished PhD dissertation, Jagiellonian University, Cracow.

Manturzewska, M. (1966). The concordance of the evaluation of musical performance by musical experts [in Polish]. *Biuletyn Psychometryczny PAN, 1*, 111–115.

Manturzewska, M. (1968a). *H. Wing Standardised Tests of Musical Intelligence—A tentative manual* [in Polish]. Warsaw: COPSA.

Manturzewska, M. (1968b). *R. Drake Musical Aptitude Test—A tentative manual* [in Polish]. Warsaw: COPSA.

Manturzewska, M. (1969). *Psychological conditions of pianistic achievement* [in Polish]. Warsaw: Ossolineum.

Manturzewska, M. (1970a). *The results of research of Warsaw music students with Drake's Musical Aptitude Tests* [in Polish]. Warsaw: COPSA.

Manturzewska, M. (1970b). The reliability of evaluation of musical performance by musical experts [in Polish]. *Ruch Muzyczny, 21,* 3–8; *23,* 13–15.

Manturzewska, M. (1972). *The results of research on Polish music students with H. Wing's Test of Musical Intelligence* [in Polish]. Warsaw: COPSA.

Manturzewska, M. (1974). *Psychological determinants of success in music schools* [in Polish]. Warsaw: COPSA.

Manturzewska, M. (1975). *H. Gough California Personality Inventory— The results of research on music students.* Warsaw: COPSA.

Manturzewska, M. (1977). Das musikalische Talent als Gegenstand wissenschaftlicher Untersuchungen. In Probleme der Begabungsfindung und -förderung auf musikalischem Gebiet in der VR Polen und in der DDR. *Materialien der I. Rektorenkonferenz in Kraków, 1976.*

Manturzewska, M. (1980). Musical talent in the light of scientific research [in Polish]. In *Podstawy Ksztalcenia Muzycznego, T. II. z. 181,* 6–20.

Manturzewska, M. (1981). Theoretical foundations of psychomusical diagnosis [in Polish]. *Zagadnienia Wychowawcze a Zdrowie Pschiczne, 3–6,* 18–24.

Manturzewska, M. (1986). Musikalisches Talent im Lichte biographischer Forschung. In *Materialien und Dokumente, Kieler-Woche-Kongress, 1985.* Regensburg: Bosse.

Manturzewska, M. (1990a). Research on the evaluation of musical achievement by music teachers [in Polish]. In *Wybrane Zagadnienia z Psychologii Muzyki.* Warsaw: WSIP.

Manturzewska, M. (1990b). A biographical study on the lifespan development of professional musicians. *Psychology of Music, 18,* 112–139.

Manturzewska, M., & Kaminska, B. (1990). Musical development [in Polish]. In *Wybrane Zagadnienia z Psychologii Muzyki.* Warsaw: WSIP.

Manturzewska, M., & Kotarska, H. (1981). The development of psychomusical diagnosis in Poland [in Polish]. *Zagadnienia Wychowawcze a Zdrowie Pschiczne, 3–6,* 33–40.

Manturzewska, M., & Kotarska, H. (1986). Musikalische Fähigkeiten im Lichte psychometrischer Forschung. *Materialien und Dokumente, Kieler-Woche-Kongress, 1985.* Regensburg: Bosse.

Meyer, M. (1991). Candidates to Chopin Academy of Music as seen through the results of the Australian Test for Advanced Music Studies [in Polish]. *Proceedings of the International Seminar of*

*Researchers and Lecturers in the Psychology of Music.* Radziejowice, Sep. 24–29, 1990. Warsaw: Chopin Academy of Music Press.

Miklaszewski, K. (1982). *The process of preparation of musical performance by professional musicians* [in Polish]. Unpublished PhD dissertation. Academy of Music, Warsaw.

Miklaszewski, K. (1989). A case study of a pianist preparing a musical performance. *Psychology of Music, 2,* 95–109.

Miklaszewski, K. (1990). Learning of music [in Polish]. In M. Manturzewska & H. Kotarska (Eds.), *Wybrane zagadnienia z psychologii muzyki* [Selected issues in the psychology of music]. Warsaw: WSIP.

Moryk, M. (1988). The musical competence of candidates to the Chopin Academy of Music in Warsaw in the light of Australian Test for Advanced Music Studies scores [in Polish]. Unpublished M.A. Thesis. Academy of Music, Warsaw.

Pawlowski, L. (1938). *Kwalwasser-Dykema Music Tests as the method of measurement and evaluation of musical abilities of school children* [in Polish]. Warsaw: Wydawnictwe Naukowe Towarzstwa Pedagogicznego.

Revèsz, G. (1946). *Einführung in die Musikpsychologie.* Bern: Francke.

Schoen, M. (1940). *The psychology of music.* New York: Roland.

Schünemann, G. (1930). *Musikerziehung.* Leipzig: Kistner & Siegel.

Seashore, C. (1919). *Seashore's Measures of Musical Talent.* Chicago: Stoelting.

Seashore, C. (1938). *Psychology of music.* New York: McGraw-Hill.

Sosniak, L. (1985). Phases of learning. In B. Bloom (Ed.), *Developing talent in young people.* New York: Ballantine.

Tieplov, B. (1952). *Psychology of musical ability* [in Polish, translated from Russian]. Warsaw: Nasza Ksiegarnia.

Whistler, H. S., & Thorpe, L. P. (1950). *Whistler-Thorpe Musical Aptitude Test.* Los Angeles: California Test Bureau.

Whitehead, A. N. (1929). *The aims of education.* New York: Macmillan.

Wing, H. (1948). Tests of musical ability and appreciation. *British Journal of Psychology,* Monograph Supplement, Nr. 27.

Wronski, T. (1965). *The problems of violin playing. T. 3. Technology of musicians' learning* [in Polish]. Krakow: PWM.

Wronski, T. (1979). *The gifted and nongifted* [in Polish] . Krakow: PWM.

# 24

# Motivational and Influential Components of Musical Performance

## A Qualitative Analysis

**Roland S. Persson**

*University of Jönköping, Jönköping, Sweden*

**George Pratt**
**Colin Robson**

*University of Huddersfield, Huddersfield, England*

Fifteen pianists were asked to study the same piano piece for a period of time. They were then interviewed about motivation to pursue musical performance and factors that influence the generation of performance. Participants were encouraged to raise their own issues or refute the ones presented. The data were then subjected to a content analysis. It was assumed that emotion plays an important part in motivating a performer over a long period of time and also influences actual playing. Four main components common to the participants emerged as influencing performance generation. There also appeared to be four main components describing motives for pursuing music. The results suggest that emotion is intertwined with both performance generation and motivation for musical performance. Findings may have a bearing on the nurturing of musical talent, and imply that competitiveness could be detrimental rather than beneficial to an artistic endeavor.

## INTRODUCTION

"Let it not be forgotten that real musical feeling, through which one can find the appropriate character of a given page, can only truly come from within," argued the renowned cellist Paul Tortelier (Blum, 1977). A similar statement was made by the Russian violinist Yuri Bashmet: "Identify with the emotions and the notes—fearful as they are—will look after themselves" (Seckerson, 1991). For violinist Nigel Kennedy music is self-expression of feelings: ". . . music gave me a way to express my feelings when most of my other emotions were numb" (Kennedy, 1990). Accounts of emotion and music are numerous in contemporary and historical records of musicianship. It is generally, it appears, taken for granted that music and emotion go together. The extent and the way emotion and music interact has been a matter of debate for a long time. It is a debate that continues to challenge and intrigue music psychologists and philosophers. The major contributors to the field are Berlyne (1971), Cook (1959), Langer (1951), Mandler (1984), and Meyer (1956), whose investigations, however, have concentrated primarily on psychophysiological issues of perception and response. To our present knowledge there has been only a limited amount of research into motivational aspects of musical performance and even less—if any—into what might influence the generation of musical performance.

We assumed, on the anecdotal evidence of historic and contemporary biographical accounts, that emotion constitutes an important component in the makeup of an instrumentalist. Our investigation set out to gain insight into this relationship. In psychological theory the difference between motivation and emotion is vague and the two largely overlap. Motivation is often understood as a function of emotions proper—relating to the so-called basic emotions (Frijda, 1986; Leeper, 1970; Young, 1961). The two issues of motivation and generation of performance were dealt with separately in our study. Their assumed common denominator—emotion—was considered from two points of view: (a) as an intrapersonal *drive* to seek opportunity for creative expression through music over a long period of time; (b) as an *effector* having a direct impact on the actual playing.

## METHOD

Fifteen performers 18–63 years of age (10 males and five females), of whom 11 were music students and four professional musicians (one an active concert pianist), were asked to study a preselected piece of music (Gliére, 1920: *Prelude in E-flat Major*, Op 31, no. 1) over a period of time. At an agreed time participants were individually interviewed and the piece of music was performed and discussed. Participants were encouraged to make their own comments, adding to or refuting issues raised by the interviewing researcher. The issues that were brought up during the interviews were derived from observational data (Fetterman, 1989; Morison, 1986; Robson, 1993; Shipman, 1988); the structuring was guided by the researchers' own experience of music, music education, and performance—as recommended by Strauss.

> Experiential data are essential data . . . because they not only give added theoretical sensitivity but provide a wealth of provisional suggestions for making comparisons, finding variations, and sampling widely on theoretical grounds (Strauss, 1987, p. 11).

Two of the three researchers have a background as performing musicians, a fact that also seemed to facilitate achieving rapport with the musicians. They seemed to regard the interview as a discussion between colleagues, rather than as a scientific investigation. The data were later subjected to a content analysis where data were categorized in terms of the context of the investigation (Marton, 1986).

## RESULTS

### Influential Components of Performance Generation

Issues raised for discussion were: (a) tradition—the impact of traditional performance practices or particular schools of playing; (b) personal experiences in the past—whether past experiences somehow coloured the approach to interpretation and understanding. Other issues were: (c) present mood; (d) personal experience of the music while performing it—an issue that gave the participants a chance to confirm or deny the value of emotional involvement; (e) qualities inherent in the music itself—an issue that provided the opportunity to consider the importance of structural features in the music. Finally, participants were asked to comment on extramusical content as applied to the music, (f) allowing them to discuss the role of events and/or imagery in their conception of playing.

There seemed to be considerable agreement among the participants that the questions raised were well chosen. Although participants were invited to make other suggestions, this was rarely done. Three participants felt that the instrument used for the occasion was not up to standard. One of these three also mentioned "hall and location;" "heat, humidity, and comfort," and "general health and alertness" as influencing the performance. Only one performer acknowledged that the presence of the researcher made her slightly tense and nervous. The following group of components emerged from the content analysis (see Table 24-1).

The performers appeared to experience a discrepancy between the demands of performance tradition and what they felt was expected of them, and the feelings present either because of the situation or the moods associated with the piece of music. Performer A2 (male, music student, 18 years old) remarked: "When I am playing for an audience I play mainly for recognition. Otherwise I play because of a pure love of playing." Another participant—A10 (male, music student, 21 years old)—reported that "examinations . . . do not make me play well!" A third participant—B2 (male, lecturer, 52 years old)—made a clearcut distinction between a performance interpretation for personal satisfaction and an interpretation for satisfying jurors and examiners: "I really don't care what is done [to the piece] since it will not be done for an examination." It seems appropriate to label one influencing factor a component of conflict.

A second component relates to the emotional response generated by the music. The label—hedonic emotional reference— suggests that performers more or less accommodate their interpretation to give an optimal level of pleasure when playing. An interesting comparison to this suggestion is the concept of sensation seeking as "a trait defined by the need for varied, novel, and social risks for the sake of such experiences" (Zuckerman, 1979). Music and Art are also suggested by Zuckerman

TABLE 24-1
Main Components of Musical Performance Influence

| Label | Description/Function |
| --- | --- |
| Conflict component | Incongruity between intrinsic and extrinsic motives |
| Hedonic emotional reference | The accommodation of positive emotional experience |
| Noó-dynamic reference | The generation of metacognitive schemata of imagery and/or feeling |
| Music structural reference | Extrinsic cues to performance generation mainly from a score |

as a means for sensation seeking (Zuckerman, 1983). Performer A7 (male, music student, 26 years old) provided the following account when asked what he was thinking about during his performance.

> I can't really describe it in words. It is quite difficult. I can say little technical things I was thinking about. . . . [The performer fell into a pensive silence and then suddenly exclaimed:] Yes, I can! Around here [pointing in the score] there is a triumphant, sort of a joyful feeling when I recapitulate the main theme; hesitancy when I had ritardandi . . . and a tentative sort of feeling as I got to the end.

The importance of putting the musical performance into a descriptive framework where content is either fictional or derived from remembered events or impressions also seemed to constitute an essential means of influencing and generating performance. We adopted a term coined by Frankl (1962, 1969) in order to describe and label this phenomenon: Noódynamic reference. The term relates to applying a meaning to actions or events. Meaning in this respect has philosophical connotations rather than referring to cognitive psychobiological appraisals. Meaning in this context could also be understood as involving metacognitive schemata, where performers actively and consciously construct some type of descriptive context for the music; a framework that then directs how a certain piece of music is played (Adey, 1991; Swanwick, 1988). Our point is well exemplified by Performer B3 (male, lecturer/concert pianist, 49 years old) who quite elaborately described how he conceives an understanding of a piece of music.

> Oh, I apply images to the piece! I do that an awful lot when I'm playing music. I can apply pieces with scenes, events . . . whatever. Like if you play a sonata by Mozart you can imagine characters and things happening on stage. Beethoven—the same! Yes,

> I think that is certainly a part of my musical makeup anyway; using outside images to help colour and inflect music. That is a part of any musician's makeup, surely?

The noódynamic reference component seemed to be a psychological necessity rather than a mere interesting occurrence in the sample. Not all participants, however, made use of or experienced imagery. It seemed that the mood itself could provide a meaning.

> I find often that to get me into the mood of a piece, say, the *Pathétique Sonata* and the opening of that, you think of something sad. You think "sadly," not necessarily something that has happened to you, but you think of the experience of sadness before you play a chord (A10, music student, male, age 21).

A fourth component shared by the participants concerned the influence of the musical structure on the music to be performed. It surprised us that the score was seldom brought to attention. The experiences connected to the music and the playing of it seemed to have an overwhelming precedence over any kind of notated technicality. Musical structure, of course, is indispensable, but it seemed that when participants made the acquaintance of a new piece of music they usually started by creating a noódynamic framework for their interpretation, rather than concerning themselves with the technical difficulties. Performer A2 (male, music student, 18 years old) commented.

> I feel that if I take a new piece I take the bull by the horns and treat it as a 'new piece' despite the influence of tradition and shapes and so forth. I find it very, very, difficult to sit down and look at a piece of music and play it just as a piece of music. Trying to capture it as a scene makes me aware of—not necessarily only the emotion of the piece—but of all things around me.

The hedonic aspect of performance—the possible emotional conflict between conviction and expectation, and the creation of metacognitive schemata—are all likely to describe different ways in which emotion interacts with performance. The fact that music structure can provide stimuli which give cause for emotional response is already well established (Dowling & Harwood, 1986; Meyer, 1956). Hence, it seems that the influential components of performance generation involve and are dependent on emotions.

## Musical Performance Motivation

Participants were also invited to discuss issues assumed to be motivational in the pursuit of a musical career. Issues raised during the interviews fell into four categories. The first of these was the performance situation. Participants were asked whether performance examinations during their training were or had been motivating, and if the positive feedback of an audience was considered important. They were also asked how they regarded their ambition to be in the center of events, for example, if they valued being in the "limelight" in general. Participants were also invited to consider the possible motivating aspects of being a soloist or performing as a member of an ensemble or an orchestra.

It was thought conceivable that the will to achieve played an essential role, and that it was relevant to treat achievement as a separate concept. The second context category therefore considered some possible applications of achievement in musicianship. Performers were asked about their views on practising. Extrinsic motivation through the support of teachers, parents or others was also discussed. Performers were then invited to evaluate their own intrinsic motivation by commenting on the impact of their own obvious talent as an incentive to pursue music. In addition, participating pianists were asked to give their opinion on the importance of establishing a career, having success, being or becoming a recognized professional performer.

A third group of questions dealt with the social context, how important it was for performers to meet other musicians, to feel a kinship with a professional group, and whether or not a prospective teaching career was or could be motivating. The final group of issues considered the purely esthetic side of music, and sought to establish whether the pursuit of musicianship was based on the need for self-expression, the embodiment of a creative need, or if feelings and moods generated by music and the performance of music provide good and appropriate reasons for becoming a performer and pursuing such a career.

The analysis of the data suggested that four main categories of motives provide the motivational basis for a pursuit of musical performance, and these are shown in Table 24-2.

One component brings the hedonic features of making music and listening to it to the fore. All participants spoke of the pleasurable experiences involved in playing and listening to various

### TABLE 24-2
### Main Components of Musical Performance Generation

| Label | Description/Function |
| --- | --- |
| Hedonic motive | The search for positive emotional experience |
| Social motive | The importance of group identity and belonging |
| Achievement motives | |
| Independent | The means leading to achievement are secondary to success itself |
| Dependent | The means are important but do not constitute the ultimate target |
| Aesthetic | The means also provide the target itself |
| Supportive | Motives are extrinsically supplied, mainly by teachers and parents; this motive seems to be particularly important to children, and loses its impact as they grow older and become more independent |

types of music. Performer A6 (male, music student, 19 years old) describes his experience with the piece of music presented to him.

> I really like the piece. I really think it has something to do with feelings . . . someone who is sad; who has just lost his girl friend or a relative; a diresome thing that makes you want to sit in your room thinking about it . . . you can imagine a film where something like that happened: They had gone for a walk in the field, on their own—this music was playing. . . .

Performer B4 (female, lecturer/composer, 51 years old) appeared to enjoy performing the piece but did not appreciate the piece per se. Her conception and understanding of it seemed to be hedonic, and she imagined herself to have been removed in thought and time to the nineteenth century. ". . . hearing a pianist play through a drawing room window; French open windows. . . . There I heard this piece of music played." To the question, however, whether she liked the assigned piece or not, she answered.

> I have a problem with this because I am a composer more than a performer. I can look at a piece with two completely different sets of judgments. As a performer I liked it, but as a composer I would certainly know something better than this!

One participant made the following comment.

> Mood is a big one for me. You have to be in the right mood, because sometimes you can be in a sort of state where you can't exactly get yourself into how the music should be played. Some-

times you sit down and you play as if: . . . Ahhh! [The participant sighs profoundly]. You can really feel everything in the music (A1, male, music student, age 20).

Interestingly, not many of the participants liked to practice, and no one cared for examinations! Above all, examinations were construed as highly unpleasant in terms of emotional experience, but good as a means to "get things done." It seems to be the pressure and expectancy demanded by examinations and examiners that can subdue hedonic experience. The self-discipline of *having* to practice—the repetitive rigor of motor programming—also seemed at times to be construed as detrimental to a positive musical experience.

Also of considerable importance to the performers was the possibility of socializing and meeting other musicians; the need to be part of a group. Hence, it is appropriate to understand this component as a social motive. The feeling of kinship between musicians; obtaining the particular identity of being a musician and meeting other musicians were considered very motivating by most participants. Only Performer A9 (male, music student, 26 years old) disagreed. He construes himself as a "loner"—and it seems on the basis of frustration: "Chance were a fine thing . . . but I don't think so. I'm a loner!"

A third component concerns what we have termed an exhibitionistic motive. To some participants public performance and performing for an examination may be inhibiting rather than motivating. We suggest, however, that it is not being exposed to an audience or to adjudicators that poses a problem to some performers. It is rather the way the situation is construed by individual performers in terms of what they know or believe is expected of them that results in undesired tension (Burr & Butt, 1992; Kelly, 1963). Most, if not all, participants wanted to share and communicate their progress, their music and their understanding of it to others, for example, they do display an exhibitionistic motive. However, not all participating performers were able to put the worries of demand and extrinsic expectation aside. It seems that there is a certain tension between wanting to perform and being motivated by it, and at the same time not being able to cope with what is largely construed as adverse circumstances.

In our sample we also found that achievement, as we already suspected, was of importance to the participants in different ways, and needs to be added as an essential component of performance motivation. Achievement, however, did not necessarily have to do with music. What could be labeled *independent achievement* seemed to exist. Performer A3 (female, music student, 20 years old) made the remark.

> Basically, it is attention to yourself wanting to achieve something. Music is something I enjoy. . . . I have always had this drive in me to do well in whatever I do, so it is not necessarily just music but any other thing . . . I enjoy cooking . . . and I know I do it well because I enjoy doing it. It gives me a sense of achievement and satisfaction when my friends enjoy my cooking. It is basically self-motivation.

Where a will to independent achievement predominates, it appears, the means of achievement will be secondary to achievement itself.

We also found what could be termed *dependent achievement*; where musical performance is not construed as an end in itself, but as a means of reaching other subject related objectives. Performer A11 (female, music student, 20 years of age) explained.

> I've got this degree. That is motivating for me but I don't want to be famous by the end of it. I want to do something administrative which is not so much performance related really. . . .

Perhaps it is inevitable not to speak of *esthetic achievement* as a motive, where music is pursued for its own sake—which seemed to be relevant for a majority of participants. Participant A4 (female, music student, 20 years old) described the main reason for her involvement in music as "a compulsion, a love, a need for music . . . the love of music really!" Performer B1 (male, lecturer, 61 years of age) shared the same conviction. "Music making is for its own sake, isn't it? You want to feel that you have measured up to what the music demands." All of these three aspects of achievement seemed to be present in most of the participants. The will to aesthetic achievement, however, clearly dominated.

In the literature available on biographical research on musical talent, yet another aspect of achievement emerges, one that is developmental in nature (Bastian, 1989; Howe & Sloboda, 1991; Sloboda & Howe, 1991; Sosniak, 1985). Achievement (and inevitably motivation) was found to be very dependent on extrinsic support. It is feasible to assume that participants in these studies found it very important to satisfy the ones who provided the support by doing well, and in so doing also satisfy themselves.

Bastian (1989) phrased it thus, "That which must play a major role in practising is the enjoyment of, the love, and the appreciation of a particular individual: the parents, the teacher . . . ." (1989, p. 104 as translated by the present authors).

We found this only to a lesser extent in our sample, which was less extensive in number and covered a different age group with a larger age span than the studies referred to. One performer, however (B4, female, lecturer/composer, 52 years old), addressed the issue: "When you are a child it is difficult to separate out those [motivational aspects]. I was kind of forced into doing it then, but about the age of twelve I wanted to do it!" We suggest labeling this fourth aspect of achievement *supportive achievement*.

## GENERAL DISCUSSION

To speak of hedonism as an important issue in musical performance seems not to be farfetched. Our findings show that a positive emotional response in a hedonic sense is essential; this is important both where motivation to perform is concerned and also where direct influence on the actual playing is concerned.

A somewhat surprising but important finding is the component of conflict: the struggle between the way a performer wishes to understand and wants to perform a piece of music and the implicit directives of tradition and expectation. The advantage or disadvantage of performance competitions has been debated extensively (Bastian, 1987; European String Teachers Association ESTA, 1984; Renshaw, 1989), and that discussion perhaps is made relevant again by the emergence in our data of the conflict component. If it is assumed that extrinsic demand and expectation—which are currently inevitable issues for any performer wishing to launch a performing career—are incompatible with the positive emotional aspects of esthetic experience and creativity, this would imply a considerable rethinking in the music educational world. It would suggest that much of education and the way musical talent is handled could, in fact, be directly counterproductive. It may be that undue pressure is being created for the gifted sons and daughters of music; a pressure that perhaps moves their focus from the beautiful, although not necessarily successful, to the profitable. Although the concept of talent and giftedness is an extremely complex one, this assumption—as implied by our results—does find support from Amabile (1990) and Csikszentmihályi (1990). Amabile suggested (1990, p. 67):

> Intrinsic motivation is conducive to creativity, but extrinsic motivation detrimental. In other words, people will be most creative when they feel motivated primarily by the interest, enjoyment, satisfaction, and challenge of the work itself—and not by external pressures.

Pianist Jorge Bolet addressed the same issue—from the musician's point of view (Dubal, 1985, p.79).

> *Competitions*—I think they have done piano playing more harm than almost anything else. Look at it this way: A young pianist enters a big international competition. There are fifteen judges, roughly. The pianists have to get fifteen votes—or at least that is their aim. They cannot play anything that is going to antagonize any of those fifteen people in any way. They cannot do anything that can be considered controversial by any one of them; they cannot do anything that could be considered a personal idea. So, as a result, you hear one, ten, thirty young pianists and they are all alike. They have exactly the same approach. You never hear anything you haven't heard many times before.

In the light of this, we suggest that the emotional aspect of education in music is too often disregarded when talented students are trained to become performers. It is likely that emotional aspects are taken for granted and career moves are emphasized: the right contacts, the opportune repertoire and the technical brilliance and superiority which will win recognition and competitions. If competitiveness is defined as the prerequisite for recognition, then to what extent is artistic integrity (and perhaps quality) harmed if musicians are forced to compete to be the "best" in order to win opportunities and contracts?

If artistic integrity is being violated, how will this affect an artistic mind and talent? One subject, a touring professional singer (male, 40 years of age), and a member of a renowned European professional ensemble, gave the following account of how he always felt forced to maintain a competitive edge.

> The rehearsals with XX [a renowned conductor] are, however, high in quality. But, they make me lose *die Beziehung zur Musik* [a personal relationship to the music], as it is expressed in German. What is my relationship with that particular piece of music

that I'm rehearsing? He doesn't fill me in on that and I am not able to bring my own emotions into the framework he wants. We are constantly corrected in a technical way, and consequently one feels anxious at one point about not being able to live up to those standards, and one cannot think about anything but that. It's unpleasant. It's boring. It is in my view dangerous and—most of all—it isn't music!

The neglect of affective issues nurturing gifted individuals has recently been emphasized by Passow (1991), who observed that educators are keen on "accelerated intellectual development" but disregard "accelerated affective development." C. P. E. Bach (1778, p. 152), some 200 years ago, prescribed emotional involvement as a priority in studying and pursuing musical performance: "A musician cannot move others unless he too is moved. He must of necessity feel all the affects that he hopes to arouse in his audience." The question is, it seems, that of priorities in the promotion of musical talent.

We feel that emotion is an essential and inevitable part of musicianship, both with regard to motivational aspects and to the actual playing. We do not argue that a conflict always exists between the aesthetic and the extrinsic motives and pressures, nor that such motives are necessarily counterproductive. We do,, however, believe that extrinsic motivation, when construed by the performers as undue pressure, will in the long run be detrimental to both the performer and the music he or she plays. It may deprive the world of many a great artist; poetic voices that will never be heard unless provision is also made for artists driven by aesthetic achievement goals rather than by the desire for personal achievement in a competitive context. Interestingly, it has been suggested that the compelling need for competitive achievement is indicative of immaturity, whereas lack of competitiveness signifies maturity (Storr, 1960). This, we feel, is important to consider for anyone who takes the responsibility of nurturing the next generation of musical talents!

## REFERENCES

Adey, P. (1991). Pulling yourself up by your own thinking. *European Journal for High Ability, 2,* 28–34.

Amabile. T. M. (1990). Within you, without you: The social psychology of creativity, and beyond. In M. A. Runco & R. S. Albert (Eds.), *Theories of creativity.* London: Sage Publications.

Bach, C. P. E. (1778, reprinted 1974). *Essay on the true art of playing keyboard instruments.* London: Eulenburg.

Bastian, H. G. (1987). *Jugend musiziert—Der Wettbewerb in der Sicht von Teilnehmern und Verantwortlichen.* Mainz: Schott.

Bastian, H. G. (1989). Leben für Musik—Eine Biographie-Studie über musikalische (Hoch-)Begabungen. Mainz: B. Schott's Söhne.

Berlyne, D. E. (1971). *Aesthetics and psychobiology.* New York: Appleton-Century-Croft.

Blum, D. (1977). *Casals and the art of interpretation.* Berkeley: University of California Press.

Burr, V., & Butt, T. (1992). *Invitation to personal construct psychology.* London: Whurr Publishers Ltd.

Cook, D. (1959). *The language of music.* Oxford: Oxford University Press.

Csikszentmihałyi, M. (1990). The domain of creativity. In M. A. Runco & R. S. Albert (Eds.), *Theories of creativity.* London: Sage Publications.

Dowling, W. J., & Harwood, D. L. (1986). *Music cognition.* San Diego: Academic Press.

Dubal, D. (1985). *The world of the concert pianist.* London: Gollancz.

European String Teachers Association (1984). *Music competitions—A report.* London: ESTA/Alfred Russel.

Fetterman, D. M. (1989). *Ethnography step by step.* London: Sage.

Frankl, V. E. (1962). *Man's search for meaning—An introduction to logotherapy.* London: Hodder and Stoughton.

Frankl, V. E. (1969). *The will to meaning—Foundations and application for logotherapy.* London: Souvenir Press.

Frijda, N. H. (1986). *The emotions.* Cambridge: Cambridge University Press.

Glière, R. (1920). Prelude in E-flat Major, Op 31 No 1. In *Ten selected pieces for the piano.* London: J. W. Chester.

Howe, M. J. A., & Sloboda, J. A. (1991). Early signs of talents and special interests in the lives of young musicians. *European Journal for High Ability, 2,* 102–111.

Kelly, G. (1963). *A theory of personality—The psychology of personal constructs.* New York: Norton.

Kennedy, N. (1990). *Always playing.* London: Weidenfeld and Nicolson.

Langer, S. (1951). *Philosophy in a new key.* London: Oxford University Press.

Leeper, R. W. (1970). Feelings and emotions. In M. D. Arnold (Ed.), *Feelings and emotions: The Loyola Symposium.* New York: Academic Press.

Mandler, G. (1984). *Mind and body.* New York: Norton.

Marton, F. (1986). Phenomenography—A research approach to investigating different understandings of reality. *Journal of Thought, 21,* 28–49.

Meyer, L. B. (1956). *Emotion and meaning in music.* Chicago: University of Chicago Press.

Morison, M. (1986). *Methods in sociology.* London: Longman.

Passow, A. H. (1991). A neglected component of nurturing giftedness: Affective development. *European Journal for High Ability, 2,* 5–11.

Renshaw, P. (1989). *Competitions and the young musicians.* London: Rhinegold Publishing Limited.

Robson, C. (1993). *Real world research for social scientists and practitioner-researchers.* Oxford: Blackwell.

Seckerson, E. (1991). Yuri Bashmet as interviewed by Seckerson. In *Gramophon,* June, 26–27.

Shipman, M. (1988). *The limitations of social research* (3rd ed.). London: Longman.

Sloboda, J. A., & Howe, M. J. A. (1991). Biographical precursors of musical excellence: An interview study. *Psychology of Music, 19,* 3–21.

Sosniak, L. A. (1985). Learning to be a concert pianist. In B. S. Bloom. *Developing talent in young people.* New York: Ballantine Books.

Storr, A. (1960). *The integrity of the personality.* Oxford: Oxford University Press.

Strauss, A. L. (1987). *Qualitative analysis for social scientists.* Cambridge: Cambridge University Press.

Swanwick, K. (1988). *Music, mind and education.* London: Routledge.

Young, P. T. (1961). *Motivation and emotion.* New York: Wiley.

Zuckerman, M. (1979). *Sensation seeking: Beyond the optimal level of arousal.* Hillsdale, NJ: Erlbaum.

Zuckerman, M. (1983). A biological theory of sensation seeking. In M. Zuckerman. (Ed.), *Biological bases of sensation seeking, impulsivity, and anxiety.* Hillsdale, NJ: Erlbaum.

# 25

# Concert Musicians as Teachers

## On Good Intentions Falling Short

**Roland S. Persson**

*University of Jönköping, Jönköping, Sweden*

Teachers in institutions of higher musical training are experts in their field of performance, but frequently have limited knowledge of the dynamics of individual teaching and learning. Seven performance lecturers with little or no formal training as teachers, together with their students, took part in the present investigation. The seven cases were studied by means of participant observation and informal interviews. The qualitative data were subsequently submitted to a content analysis. The results showed that the lecturers' inflexibility, insensitivity to individual needs, unreasonable demands and dominance, along with an unsatisfactory balance in their instructional strategy were all potential inhibitors of artistic development, and were therefore also potential stressors for musicians to be.

## INTRODUCTION

In tertiary training programs for musical performers it is not uncommon that the leading teachers are eminent and well-known performers (Manturzewska, 1990). However, although such people are experts in their artistic field and are recognized as such, they often have little or no formal training as teachers. Hence, it could be expected that they would lack to some extent knowledge of teaching and learning processes as they apply to others rather than to themselves. It is feasible also to assume that lack of familiarity with the dynamics of individual teaching and learning could easily pave the way for difficulties in the teacher–student relationship and lead to considerable stress and frustration for both parties. In the case of the student, further artistic development with such a teacher could be impeded rather than promoted (cf., Hendrickson, 1986; Persson, 1993a).

Although it is implicit in most music-educational contexts, it is by no means always the case that musically gifted students who are admitted to performance training programs arrive with secure self-confidence in their own musical ability (Rovics, 1984). In fact, it could be argued with some certainty that a majority of musically very able performers seeking admission to tertiary training at about 17–18 years of age are still in the process of establishing their identity as musicians (cf., Erikson, 1977). The fact that Durrant (1992)—in a survey of the London colleges of music—found that most students are preoccupied with their potential failure rather than with their deep-rooted musical interest, would suggest that the need for individual support and encouragement is seldom met when it is most needed.

It is an often neglected fact that during adolescence music takes on a particularly personal (and affective) significance to the individual musician (Shuter-Dyson & Gabriel, 1980). The type of instruction that the musically gifted receive during tertiary training tends to be formal and teacher-centered rather than informal and student-centered (Sosniak, 1990; Tait, 1992); this strategy is well able to reinforce efficiency in the acquisition of practical skills, but is also sometimes applied at the expense of intrapersonal development. Manturzewska (1990) concluded her study of 165 Polish professional musicians by stating that

> one of the fundamental conditions for the development of artistic activity and for the development of creative musical talent in all stages of life seems to be the *musical dialogue* with someone

who believes in the talented individual's potential, who understands his or her musical ideas and accepts them, who supports him or her emotionally in these endeavours and helps to overcome the stresses of life (p. 138).

Skilled performers sometimes make unreasonable demands in instructing future generations of performers, and prevent insecure students from establishing their identity as musicians. Such teachers may cause undue pressure for students as a result of being experts in the field of performance but more or less ignorant in the field of teaching and learning. That musical performance training programs often result in high levels of stress and anxiety is well documented (e.g., Gelber, 1988; Pruett, 1991). This leads not only to an increasing number of cases of overuse injuries (Fry, 1986; Wagner, 1987), but also to psychological disorders that may be either triggered or worsened by a demanding musical environment (Fogle, 1982; Ostwald & Avery, 1991).

It is of great importance therefore to find some of the potential causes of such distress during the training of the musically gifted. Research in the field is to my knowledge virtually nonexistent. Although, for example, affective responses to musical stimuli are often studied, the significance of music-affective experience in music teaching and music making has received much less attention (Abeles, Hoffer, & Klotman, 1984). Yet affective targets, including affective musical experiences, are most probably paramount in intrapersonal and artistic development, because a performance teacher is more than likely to become a significant role model (Galbo, 1989; Kleinen, 1986). This is particularly the case if the musician to be has not experienced much understanding or support for his or her musical interest as a child (Rovics, 1984). The present investigation sampled the individual teaching styles of a number of esteemed and skilled performers with little or no formal training as teachers, in order to compare these styles and to assess their effectiveness as rated by students, for the purpose of identifying issues that are distressing and potentially inhibit creative endeavor.

## METHOD

The exploratory investigation was launched at a British university music department of good standing and reputation. Seven performance lecturers were selected largely on the basis of their own expressed interest. They represented different instruments or singing. With the exception of one participant who was an English teacher before going into professional performance, none had trained formally as a teacher (Table 25-1). All the participants, including the former English teacher, relied exclusively on their performance expertise in teaching performers-to-be. "Type" outlines the manner of researcher participation during lessons: "A" equals accompanying an instrumentalist during lessons, "D" equals discussions, and "S" denotes asking for second opinions in matters of performance–practice. T-tr refers to teacher training.

The investigation was conducted as seven case studies, where each case comprised one performance lecturer and his or her students. Of the 47 participating students, 26 were male and 21 were female, their mean age being approximately 20. The study was observational and participant observation and informal interviews were the methods by which data were gathered (Robson, 1993). Each case was studied for a period of about three weeks, during which time field notes were taken, rather than recording lessons on tape or video. The participating lecturers would not allow their lessons to be recorded by other means than by taking notes. To ensure the reliability of the transcripts, however, these were handed to the participating lecturers for validation (Guba & Lincoln, 1981) prior to the subsequent qualitative content analysis (Miles & Huberman, 1984). In addition, the potentially inhibiting and distressing issues that were identified by the analysis were to some extent validated by the participants. However, owing to the often sensitive nature of the find-

**TABLE 25-1**
**Participating Performance Teachers**

| Case | Sex | Age | T-tr | Designation | Type |
|------|-----|-----|------|-------------|------|
| B1 | M | 64 | Yes* | Lecturer in singing, a former opera singer | ADS |
| B2 | M | 52 | No | Lecturer in organ, concert organist, frequent recordings | -DS |
| B3 | M | 49 | No | Lecturer in piano, concert pianist, accomplished accompanist | -D- |
| B5 | M | 45 | No | Lecturer in the history of music, concert organist | -DS |
| B6 | F | 50 | No | Parttime lecturer in clarinet, experienced adjucator, limited performance experience | AD- |
| B7 | F | 50 | No | Lecturer in singing, concert singer | -D- |
| B8 | M | 30 | No | Parttime lecturer in piano, concert pianist | AD- |

*Not in music.

ings this was not possible with all of the participants, some of whom sought reassurance that they were indeed good teachers.

A comment on the presentation of the material in this chapter is appropriate here, since qualitative data are more difficult to present in a limited space than quantitative. The seven case studies are presented below as *summaries* of the extensive data that were gathered for each case. The study was *exploratory* in nature, which in this context by necessity means that the cases presented are different from each other. That is, their presentation is not based on preexisting unifying hypotheses. The objective has been to present teacher portraits derived from the data that, with exemplifying data, may yield an insight into a world of gifted teaching that is yet unknown in the field of giftedness research and education.

## CASE STUDIES

### Case One (B1): An Opera Singer

Lecturer B1 is high-spirited, accessible, informal, caring, and in general socially intelligent, all of which are qualities and characteristics that his students cherish. However, issues that impede the teaching process include the lecturer's utter reluctance to criticize his students. Just as eagerly as students commend his resourcefulness and the value of his knowledge and experience, they are alarmed by the lack of a systematic teaching method. The lecturer also has a tendency to deliver too much and too varied information in too short a time. For example, a male voice student speaks (and sings) in a heavy Scottish (Glaswegian) idiom. During the lesson, while singing, the student received the following instructions in rapid succession.

> A little less Glaswegian! . . . It should be like "thin tea biscuit" . . . Do you like the sound of what you are doing? . . . Use minimal covering. A bit more "pepper and salt"! . . . Keep it lyrical. Does it feel all right?

Such a series of instructions was difficult for the student, since he was prompted to take individual initiatives, while being asked to comply with common performance practices. B1 concluded his instructions to the student by asking if it "felt all right." The student did not answer this question. My guess is that he was still considering how to come to terms with his pronunciation. Sadly, the student failed his important first performance examination, and dropped out of the program.

## Case Two (B7): A Concert Singer

Lecturer B7 is a very systematic teacher who tends to be very dominant. She expects students to rebel against her dominance. "Rebellion" refers to a certain musical assertiveness, which the lecturer seeks to establish. With less assertive and extroverted students, however, this strategy tends to backfire and make timid students even more withdrawn. A majority of her students nevertheless see her as an understanding and knowledgeable friend. The lecturer is completely honest and speaks her mind at well chosen opportunities, which is a characteristic her students appreciate. However, the lecturer is probably not one to recommend for anyone with faltering self-confidence! The ever present dominance easily creates frustration. One male student supplied the following written description of a typical lesson with lecturer B7.

> Always when I sing, I'm waiting for her to stop me. When she doesn't stop me, I can't help but keep thinking why she didn't stop me. She often says so many things at once that I need to think about or consider. Then, when I start to sing again and don't succeed in changing whatever she commented on, she sometimes says that I think too much and forget to sing! It's impossible to remedy all things at once. . . . I feel quite patronised when she goes on like this, because she repeats comments several times during a lesson. I *know* when I make a mistake the first time. She is never interested in what *I* think; *my* understanding of a song. . . .

## Case Three (B2): A Concert Organist

Above all, lecturer B2 is honest and committed. He sets the goals for his students and decides what needs to be done to secure progress. The rapid pace and the high objectives, together with constant reference to the demands of "professional behaviour," appear to provide students with a considerable sense of purpose. However, the world of music to B2 and his students is one based entirely on right or wrong, correct or incorrect. For the most part, performance is taught through analysis, with little or no reference to the music-affective experience or individual interpretation. Students show an interesting ambivalence in their relationship toward this lecturer. Although he is highly esteemed and much liked, he manages to provide students with many a frustrating moment. It appears that the high demands, if conquered, provide a considerable sense of competence, which helps the students ignore their frustrations.

It is above all the innumerable interruptions that cause consternation. The following dialogue between B2 and one of his female performance students is typical. Bach's *Passacaglia* is on the agenda. Although the student has been studying it for some time, this is the first time the lecturer has allowed her to play it through without interruptions.

> B2: . . . Many good things and a few mistakes . . . . You appeared a bit nervous. Now, you may curse me like hell for this, but [one of the other students] was accepted to [one of the conservatories]. He can NEVER play well when he plays to me!! I really make him nervous. A good thing too! I put the fear of God into everyone!

> *Student:* [Hesitantly] Yes, I was terribly nervous playing both to you and to [the researcher]. . . .

> B2: Good! *You* tell *me* what mistakes you made! . . .

The lesson continues and there is a change of repertoire. The student plays Langlais' *Incantation*. She starts to play but is soon interrupted by the lecturer. There is a technical problem that needs to be attended to.

> B2: . . . Don't get a hitch on that! Just do the parts [without the pedals]. No mistakes! [The student plays]. Now together [She tries again] . . . and again! [She plays again] .

> B2:If the left hand is not secure, then you will not have synchronisation . . . *I'm* not worried [that you won't pass the final exam] to tell you the truth, but don't *you* become worried! You need bloody well to calm down for the examination. You do so many interesting things . . . you improvise a lot [referring derogatorily to the student's many mistakes]. . . .

## Case Four (B5): A Concert Organist

Lecturer B5 is a highly regarded scholar and his students much admire his learned comments, his organ playing, and his practical solutions to technical problems. He is versatile and seems to achieve a good balance between compliance and the objective of making students into autonomous musicians. However, the lecturer somehow fails to understand what the teacher–student relationship often entails. His inconsistency in behavior over time tends to discourage some students, who feel utterly rejected. The lecturer is very demanding and not prepared to lower his demands for less advanced or less self-assured students. It is not likely that a student with little self-confidence would benefit from his teaching. Although knowledge in abundance would be shared, the inconsistent relationship and the demand for speed and quality most probably would prevent a less confident student from benefiting.

I frequently and spontaneously obtained reports from a number of B5's students who felt rejected and discouraged, or even harassed, by what they described as the lecturer's "moods." In particular one of his students did not always feel comfortable with his teacher—which interestingly did not change the fact that he held his teacher in high regard. I ran into the student in the corridor after he had had a brief encounter with the lecturer. The student had been forced to cancel one of his organ lessons because of a master class given by a visiting lecturer, which the student had to attend. The student recalled the following exchange.

> *Student:* Could I have another rescheduled lesson since I'm attending the master class?

> *B5:* No! If *I* happen to miss a lesson, then it's OK to find another time. But if *you* miss a lesson, I have no obligation to give you another!

The student was very upset by the lecturer's reaction. He shook his head as he told me and added in profound dismay: "That's work affection for you!!!"

### Case Five (B3): A Concert Pianist

Lecturer B3 has an extraordinary imagination and is also able to put it into words that convey his musical ideas. Interestingly, his world of fantastic description and imagery is confusing to a majority of students. The fact that the lecturer always insists that students *should* be able to understand and assimilate his descriptions immediately adds to the confusion. His individual lessons could be described as a series of individual master classes. He does not seem to have a long term plan for how to develop a student's technique. Every lesson is more or less an independent unit focusing entirely on the artistic and the expressive. The lack of progression and clearly expressed objectives tends to discourage the students, who feel a general lack of technical progress and achievement. It is possibly true, as one of B3's students suggested, that B3 is an excellent teacher for students void of technical problems. If, on the other hand, a student needs to build up a technical skill progressively, then the lecturer would be less of a good choice. The following collection of expressions illustrates B3's imaginative teaching approach.

> Well . . . I don't think the lover and his lass had much fun, do you?! If a young girl and her boy go into the corn fields, they have other things in mind than playing cards surely?! (On singing Finzi's *It was a lover and his lass*).

> You forget to enjoy yourself! This is a neurotic, jolly, happy piece of music. When you play it you looked as if you were unravelling a complex knitting-pattern!

> There is the Gypsy violin, it needs to be more laid back . . . these men of evil . . . wild! . . . Somehow I don't think you have a mental picture in your mind. This for instance (pointing to the score) sounds like you are tuning a piano!! (The student plays again and B3 shouts): Cossacks!! When I say these things you look at me as if I were from outer space don't you!? (Or appropriate expression).

### Case Six (B8): A Concert Pianist

B8's teaching is very organized and is conveyed with patience when this is called for. He is also flexible and imaginative. The teaching strategy is explicit and based on meticulous motor programming, physical attitude (relaxation), and the quality of sound. References are often made to the music-affective experience. The lecturer appears to be an ideal teacher for students who are insecure and in need of a great deal of emotional support. As one student described the lecturer: "He is an equal and he is *sensitive* to his students' needs." B8's ability to be personal and self-disclosing without feeling forced to keep up the appearance of a mercilessly strict professional offers considerable security to many students. However, there is a difficulty in the student–teacher relationship, although it is not the result of the actual teaching. The lecturer is only part time and as a result only present in the music department one day per week. One of his students shared his frustration at not being able to meet or look up the lecturer during the week between lessons. To be taught by a part time lecturer could, it seems, under certain circumstances and to certain students, be the same as having a part time parent.

### Case Seven (B6): A Clarinetist

Lecturer B6 is highly consistent in everything she does. Her teaching follows clear and strict patterns. B6, too, is a very dominant teacher. Rather than flexibly altering her teaching in response to the individual student, the lecturer more or less makes the student fit into her pedagogical strategy. The students do not mind. On the contrary, they are overwhelmed by the lecturer's charismatic intensity. The sense of achievement as a result of progressively mastering the lecturer's proposals, supported by sincere encouragement, seems to make the students *suspend* taking any initiative on their own (cf., Luginbuhl, 1972). Whatever happens, B6's student is bound to learn a lot, regardless of level of skill and experience. However, it is perhaps of some importance to consider not only *that* students learn, but also consider *what* they learn. There is the possibility that such authoritarian teaching is applied at a cost, undesirable for musical performance and artistic development.

The lecturer's teaching strategy may be summarized as follows: A new piece studied from scratch is always first approached rhythmically. Rhythms are sorted out and the lecturer makes sure that timing is exact and according to the metronome, if this is given in the score. Then follows getting the written dynamics right, which in turn is followed by emphasizing key and pitch. That is, making sure that the student is well aware of the unfolding harmony and the intonation in relation to the harmonic progression. The next stage involves tone quality, fingering, and shaping. A substantial part of B6's lessons consists of finding a fingering yielding an acceptable tone quality. When these stages have been mastered sufficiently, the final stage follows: Students are encouraged to attempt "musical playing." In the lecturer's own words, the strategy may be briefly outlined as "control before shape."

I specifically asked B6 and several of her students what it means to play "musically," since this appeared to be such an essential part of her pedagogical strategy. The following replies were provided.

*B6:* To play musically ... (B6 takes a moment to reflect) that means simply that I want the students to *listen* to themselves. They tend to think too much.

*Student I:* [When] playing musically I try to ignore the technique [and its problems and shortcomings], and I imagine myself to be in concert [ignoring that I am in a small room].

*Student II:* It is to play "with feeling," to play expressively according to the markings [in the score]. It is something you've got or haven't got.

*Student III:* (the student is perplexed at my question) I don't know really! Shaping I suppose ... to play musically means to play things that you can't see in the score, to put things between what is already in the score. . . .

To play "musically" is not easy for B6's students it seems. After a long period of intense and meticulous instruction, a student is expected to leave the elaborate cognitive "scaffolding" of instructions behind and instantly terminate their influence. The result often is instant confusion rather than an inspired performance.

## DISCUSSION

It is well known that the more advanced in skill and knowledge a musician is, the better he or she can cope with a high pace and make good use of a vast amount of instructions delivered in a short period of time (Gruson, 1988). None among the participating lecturers, however, distinguished between different levels of their students' experience and practical skill. The temptation existed to teach *all* students as if they had no technical or artistic shortcomings.

According to the developmental model of gifted performers proposed by Sosniak (1990), the teacher–student relationship develops over time from the informal first teacher to the formal master teacher at the conservatoire. However, the model implicitly assumes that students reach master teachers with a high degree of self-confidence, *knowing* that they are already recognised as highly gifted. My observations are contrary to Sosniak's. Of the 47 participating students, only *one* did not seem to have to struggle with seeking the approval of her teacher. The remaining 46 students were *all* in need of an informal relationship with their teachers, one which perhaps ought to have established their identity as musicians and encouraged it to emerge (cf., Rovics, 1984). Rather, lecturers B2, B3, B5, B6, and B7 had a tendency to dominate their students completely, and seldom allowed them to have an opinion. The situation created a paradox, since most of the lecturers also complained that their students were not always able to express an opinion! Spoon feeding—to use lecturer B7's term—was a self-assigned task of every participating lecturer, and the teaching strategy of lecturer B6: "control before shape" was, with slight modifications, the approach favored by most participating lecturers.

In general, teaching mainly consisted of a series of instructions and analyses, which went on until a student had more or less mastered the particular repertoire at hand. At the stage of completing the technical work with a certain piece, not one of the lecturers considered the difficulty students had in suddenly ignoring the many, elaborate, and analytical instructions, for the purpose of finally playing "musically." It is not likely that the buildup of knowledge structures over a long period of time can be instantly undone or ignored. The piece of music studied has then inevitably taken on the form of a series of instructions rather than the meaning of an artistic expression. To demand that students should "stop thinking" or "not think too much" is indeed an unreasonable request. It should also be noted that there was no consensus among lecturer B6's students concerning what the instruction "to play musically" meant.

The students divided their performance teachers into two categories in a commonsense way, namely the "technical" ones and the "interpretational" ones. Students studying with a "technical" teacher (i.e., with lecturers B2, B7, and B6) sometimes complained about the little time spent on interpretational issues. Students studying with an "interpretational" teacher (i.e., lecturers B1 and B3), on the other hand, often complained about too much time being spent on interpretational issues, and felt the lack of progressive technical advancement. Lecturers B5 and B8 were exceptions. They were both more flexible and balanced in their strategy. No student had any adverse comments about lecturer B8. The students of lecturer B5, in contrast, praised his knowledge and his balanced teaching but, deplored his lack of support.

## CONCLUSION

The analysis of the data allows for the identification of some issues which are potential stress factors in the training of musical performers. These are insensitivity to lack of self-confidence, demands that in various ways exceed the limits of information processing, imbalance between instructional emphasis on technical problem solving and artistic problem solving (i.e., interpretation), and a not infrequent failure to encourage individual initiative.

However, although these are undeniably more or less damning findings, it is important to observe that each performance lecturer in the study taught with considerable commitment and effort. But commitment to the cause—and therein lies, most probably, the difficulty—does not seem to be sufficient. Although the participants were experts in their fields of performance, generally they lacked both flexibility in their pedagogical strategy and knowledge of the dynamic nature of teaching and learning. The results of the present study, therefore, emphasize the need for teacher training in musical performance. Although the training of teachers of the gifted is still in its infancy (Baldwin, 1993), there is a risk that as such training progresses the effort of special teacher training will emphasize other domains than the visual and performing arts. Art and music, in my experience, tend to be fields of interest that are often left unchallenged by anyone who is not a member of the musical community by means of being a qualified musician. I believe that this is an important obstacle that needs to be overcome. To be a formidable artist and a formidable pedagogue may well be attributes of the same individual, but they describe different *roles* as well as different *skills* in different contexts. It is probably in the interest of most musicians to be taught by a pedagogue rather than by a maestro, although the temptation for many students is invariably to choose the admired maestro.

For future research into musical giftedness and its nurture it is most probably essential to involve educational researchers who will be able to view the musical context unbiased by the dominating and often rigid traditions of Western art music. However, that is not to say that such a researcher can launch an investigation *insensitive* to the particularities of a musical setting. Musicians, by and large, regard scientific effort as the opposite to musical effort, since scientific behavior in the quest for objective generality by its methods poses a potential threat to the individuality of a performing musician (cf., Persson, 1993b; Persson & Robson, 1995).

## ACKNOWLEDGMENTS

This chapter was presented in part at the Tenth World Congress on Gifted and Talented Children and Adults, August 1993, Toronto, Canada.

## REFERENCES

Abeles, H. F., Hoffer, C. R., & Klotman, R. H. (1984). *Foundations of music education.* New York: Schirmer Books.

Baldwin, A. Y. (1993). Teachers of the gifted. In K. A. Heller, F. J. Mönks & A. Harry Passow (Eds.). *International Handbook of Research and Development of Giftedness and Talent* (pp. 621–629). Oxford: Pergamon.

Durrant, C. (1992, February). Those who can't . . . *Music Teacher.* 11–15.

Erikson, E. H. (1977). *Children and society* (2nd edition). London: Paladin Grafton Books.

Fogle, D. O. (1982). Toward effective treatment for music performance anxiety. *Psychotherapy: Theory, Research and Practice, 19,* 368–375.

Fry, H. J. H. (1986). Incidence of overuse syndrome in the symphony orchestra. *Medical Problems of the Performing Artists, 1,* 51–55.

Galbo, J. J. (1989). The teacher as significant adult: A review of the literature. *Adolescence, 24,* 549–556.

Gelber, G. (1988). Psychological development of the conservatory student. In F. L. Roehmann & F. R. Wilson (Eds.), *The biology of music making—Proceedings of the 1984 Denver Conference* (pp. 3–15). St. Louis, MO: MMB Music.

Gruson, L. (1988). Rehearsal skill and musical competence: does practice make perfect? In J. A. Sloboda (Ed.), "Generative processes in music: The psychology of performance, improvisation, and composition (pp. 91–112). Oxford: Clarendon.

Guba, E. G., & Lincoln, Y. S. (1981). *Effective evaluation: improving the usefulness of evaluation results through responsive and naturalistic approaches.* San Fransisco, CA: Jossey-Bass.

Hendrickson, L. (1986). A longitudinal study of precocity in music. In A. J. Cropley, K.K. Urban, H. Wagner, & W. Wieczerkowski (Eds.). *Giftedness: a worldwide challenge* (pp. 192–203). New York: Trillium Press.

Kleinen, G. (1986). Furtherance of the musically gifted: Pedagogical problems and perspectives. Effects on our society. (No editor). *Finding and promoting the musically gifted—Documentation of the Kiel-Week Congress 1985* (pp. 41–52). Regensburg: Gustav Bosse Verlag.

Luginbuhl, J. R. E. (1972). Role of choice and outcome on feelings of success and estimates of ability. *Journal of Personality and Social Psychology, 22,* 121–127.

Manturzewska, M. (1990). A biographical study of the life span development of professional musicians. *Psychology of Music, 18,* 112–139.

Miles, M. B., & Huberman, A. M. (1984). *Qualitative data analysis: a source book of new methods.* London: Sage Publications.

Ostwald. P., & Avery, M. (1991). Psychiatric problems of performing artists. In R. T. Sataloff, A. Brandfonbrenner, & R. Lederman (Eds.), *Textbook of performing arts medicine* (pp. 319–335). New York: Raven Press.

Persson, R. S. (1993a, August). *You have to conform! A closer look at the training of musical performers.* Paper presented at the Tenth World Congress on Gifted and Talented Children and Adults, Toronto, Canada.

Persson, R. S. (1993b). *The subjectivity of musical performance: An exploratory real world enquiry into the determinants and education of musical reality.* Unpublished doctoral dissertation, University of Huddersfield, England.

Persson, R. S., & Robson, C. (1995). The limits of experimentation: on researching musicians and musical settings. *Psychology of Music, 23,* 39–47.

Pruett, K. D. (1991). Psychological aspects of the development of exeptional young performers and prodigies. In R. T. Sataloff, A. Brandfonbrenner, & R. Lederman (Eds.), *Textbook of performing arts medicine* (pp. 337–349). New York: Raven Press.

Robson, C. (1993). *Real world research: A resource for social scientists and practitioner-researchers.* Oxford: Blackwell's.

Rovics, H. (1984). Musical development through personal growth. *Music Therapy, 4,* 39–46.

Shuter-Dyson, R., & Gabriel, C. (1980). *The psychology of musical ability* (2nd ed.). London: Methuen.

Sosniak, L. A. (1990). The tortoise, the hare, and the development of talent. In M. J. A. Howe (Ed.), *Encouraging the development of exceptional skills and talents* (pp. 149–164). Leicester: The British Psychological Society.

Tait, M. J. (1992). Teaching strategies and styles. In R. Colwell (Ed.), *Handbook of research on music teaching and learning* (pp. 525–534). New York: Schirmer Books.

Wagner, C. (1987). The evaluation of the musician's hand: an approach to prevention of occupational disease. In R. Spintge & R. Droh (Eds.), *Music in medicine: neurophysiological basis, clinical applications, aspects in the humanities* (pp. 333–341). New York: Springer-Verlag.

# Section IV

## Talent in Sport

# 26

# Sport Psychology and the Elite Athlete

**Ian M. Cockerill**

*University of Birmingham, Birmingham, England*

Five key factors contribute to success in competitive sport: technique, physical condition, psychological state, nutrition, and equipment. At the highest level, competitive pressures are as much psychological as physical, although attempts to describe the ideal personality for a competitive athlete have failed miserably. Recognition of women as sporting celebrities has generated interest in the so-called fear of success phenomenon, whereas some evidence suggests that fear of success may increasing among men. Players and coaches need to be aware that mood changes can be reflected in performance outcome and that precompetition mood can be used as one of several selection criteria. Mood measurement can help to monitor staleness and overtraining, producing a similar pattern to that illustrated among premenstrual syndrome sufferers. The sport psychologist can contribute positively to the attainment of goals that performers and coaches set, and psychological techniques can facilitate the preparation of high-ability sport performers.

## INTRODUCTION

The high aspiring, high achieving athlete of today needs to make use of all the legal means that sport science can offer in order to achieve a winning edge. There are also some individuals who are not averse to using illegal means, although a debate on such matters is beyond the scope of this chapter. The discussion will focus on those issues that affect the development of skill in sport which lead to success in competition, the essence of athletic endeavor. It is proposed that there are five key factors that contribute to the success of the elite athlete, namely technique, physical condition, psychological status, nutrition, and equipment. Although each has a crucial role to play in its own right and in being integrated with the other factors, it is psychology that plays a vital role in all branches of sport, and particularly at the highest levels of competition. As has been observed many times, the pressures on competitors, even at times self-inflicted pressures, are as much psychological as physical in nature.

The psychology of sport was first documented toward the end of the last century when Triplett (1898) observed that cyclists tended to pedal faster in the presence of an audience. Indeed, the effect of spectators on human performance still remains a fascinating and occasionally controversial area of study. Probably the most important area within sport psychology, however, is motivation and all its manifestations. Without the desire to work hard in order to attain a goal, whether it is merely to improve one's performance or to break a world record, everything else pales into insignificance. Sadly, many highly promising young athletes become lost to their sport in the early and mid-teens as a result of peer group pressure and the competing attractions that are presented to youngsters within this age group. For those who stay in sport, the increasing pressures of competition and the desire to keep one step ahead of the opposition can lead to acute anxiety, to problems of attention, concentration, and perhaps to increased aggression.

A major approach in sport psychology research over the past 30 years has involved studying the various relationships that are thought to exist between personality and athletic participation, and between personality and athletic achievement. Despite the large volume of published research in the area it is probably true that little more is known than a few general facts about the ways in which an athlete's personality can make a contribution to potential level of attainment. Attempts to describe the "ideal" personality of a champion athlete have failed miserably, and although successful individuals are unlikely to be neurotic, submissive, conforming, or group dependent, an all embracing theory of personality for sport has not yet emerged.

Although a difficult task in itself, some of the conditions which have militated against the establishment of such a theory have been associated with the procedures adopted by individual researchers. Their procedures usually have attempted to demonstrate differences between "sport" and "nonsport" groups, between successful and unsuccessful players of similar age and experience, or between sportsmen and sportswomen. Martens (1975) referred to a number of conceptual, methodological, and interpretative issues within sport personality research that illustrate clearly how difficult it has been to describe the kinds of psychological qualities that a champion athlete possesses. Perhaps it is Ryan's (1969) often quoted statement that best describes a situation that, by and large, still exists 20 years later.

The research in this area has been of the shotgun variety. By that I mean the investigator grabbed the nearest and most convenient personality test, and the closest sports group, and with little or no theoretical basis for their selection, fired into the air to see what they could bring down. It is not surprising that firing into the air at different times and at different places, and using different ammunition, should result in different findings. In fact, it would be surprising if the results were not contradictory and confusing. Many lessons from the past have been learned, and the sport psychologist is now seen to have a positive role to play in enhancing the performance of athletes of many standards, but especially for the elite player who demands that "little bit extra" in the transition from being very good to outstanding. But what does a sport psychologist actually do? He or she will perform a variety of functions, but a principal role includes that of counselor. It is useful for the athlete to have someone to share thoughts and aspirations, even problems with, someone who has knowledge of the sport but is also able to be a good listener, so that the athlete has an opportunity to verbalize ideas. Invariably, it is the athlete who will decide with very little prompting whether it is prudent to follow a particular course of action or not.

As an intermediary between player and coach the sport psychologist should not be perceived as someone who comes between the two principals. On the contrary, it is necessary that both player and coach integrate with the psychologist as part of a triangle. Sometimes a communication problem occurs because of a need for both athlete and coach to be in control of situations, or when neither wants to take charge. I have met both situations; they are quite common, but only honesty will overcome interpersonal difficulties. As a training analyst, issues such as time management—when to train and with whom—are important. If training is not going well and performance suffers as a result, is it owing to insufficient work or, more especially with the elite athlete, to overtraining? In other words, it is possible to identify and remedy problems that are often thought to be of a physical nature, when in fact they are of psychological origin.

The most frequent public perception of a sport psychologist is that of one who carries out psychological assessment. This means psychological testing, which may involve the athlete in completing questionnaires of various kinds. Some of them may appear simplistic and even irrelevant to the athlete, and I would not be speaking truthfully if I did not agree that this is so with some questionnaires. Fortunately, there are now a number of sport specific tests available that are reliable and have acceptable construct validity, although this is a comparatively recent development. Their predictive validity depends largely upon the context in which they are used, although once again matters are improving, with interesting and useful tests being made available. For example, it is possible to make reliable assessments of coach–athlete compatibility, anxiety proneness, capacity to concentrate, and self-image. Most of the past difficulty has been associated with issues of test interpretation, with some athletes being left with a sheet of data that are quite meaningless to them, or with a jargon filled report that is not much more informative.

In all matters, it is the athlete who is of prime concern, and it goes without saying that a good relationship between athlete, coach and sport psychologist is essential. Because of the physical and technical demands placed on top performers, it is often the case that both they and their coaches may fail to focus on the current situation. By this I mean that it is necessary to consider a number of questions: Are achievements compatible with objectives, and if not why not? How successful do you want to be? (This is a crucial question that demands an honest answer, yet surprisingly few athletes, even internationals, tend to consider it.) What are the necessary steps for attaining that goal in the short- and the long-term? Do you spend enough time on skill training, on physical conditioning, and on planning and thinking about your sport?

At the highest levels of sport some of the most frequently used words are "pressure" and "stress." A recent study of footballers has shown that there are five important factors that contribute to individual players' perceptions of stress. Top of the list is the situation, in other words the weather, waiting for an opponent to play—both of these could apply equally to golf and to tennis—and whether the game is played at home or away. Second, were opponents; was he or she a better player, stronger, slower, or perhaps lefthanded? Spectators tend to be important considerations as well as the size of the crowd. The composition of an audience and the presence or absence of parents, friends, or coach are quite likely to affect individual performance. Being the favorite can place untold pressure on a player, or on a team, because there is everything to lose and little to gain in defeat. Associated with others' expectations of you is your attitude to the competition. It is well known that negative thinking, or starting with an "I can't possibly win" attitude, will invariably fulfill the self-defeating prophecy.

A relatively new phenomenon in top level sport concerns an aspect of achievement motivation known as "fear of success." It was identified more than 40 years ago, but in the last 20 years, following work by Horner (1972), the incidence of fear of success among women has become a popular area for research. It has been claimed that social constraints have led to highly able women being resistant to seeking senior career positions. Because there are as many opportunities for women as for men to attain excellence in most sports, sport psychologists have, quite naturally, explored its incidence among potential high achievers, for men as well as for women. We know that a powerful agent of motivation is fear of failure, but fear of success is less well understood. Recent speculation has suggested that for some women athletes performances tend to improve markedly once they marry, and very often when they have had a child. The true reasons are unclear, and it has been claimed that changes in biochemistry following childbirth, the elimination of fear of being "unfeminine" as a successful athlete, or both, might contribute to the extinction of fear of success in some women.

A more recent suggestion is that the situation is changing somewhat and there is an increasing number of men who exhibit fear of success. This could be true, or it may be merely an artifact of research designs in this area that have tended, in the past, to focus more sharply on women than on men. An interesting perspective is to consider whether high achievers in sport have a lower fear of success (FOS) than those who play at a lower level. With colleagues I focussed on the youth team of an English first division football club and compared FOS scores with those of university footballers. Whereas the latter supported the findings of other researchers who have examined FOS in university athletes, the professional players' mean score was significantly lower. However, what was more interesting was the number of very low scores that the individual professionals produced. It could be suggested that a very low FOS is synonymous with a tendency to want to "win at all costs," and that such players may be predisposed to commit breaches of the laws of the game in order to achieve this end.

There appears to be almost as much printers's ink and television comment given to the injuries of elite athletes as to their actual performances. Great Britain sent a team of 386 athletes to the Seoul Olympic Games and a sum of 428,000 pounds (approximately $642,000) was reported to have been made available for sports medical services. Either a large number of injuries were expected or else some of them were likely to demand very expensive treatment. It has been claimed by the British Olympic Association that some team members traveled to Seoul while carrying serious injuries. If that were the case with the Great Britain team, there is no reason to think that they were unique in this respect; other countries may have also sent athletes who were not really fit enough to compete. In amateur, as well as in professional sport, the psychological and physical demands placed upon top performers often mean that being a success in sport tends to be synonymous with expecting to be injured for lengthy periods.

What, then, are the psychological antecedents of sports injuries? Indeed, do such causes actually exist? A growing interest in psychological aspects of sports injuries has identified a number of reasons why athletes of all standards might be injured. First of all, there is the obvious observation that an individual's skill level may not match enthusiasm. In other words, a young player might attempt to perform at a level that is incompatible with both skill and fitness. Marathon running provides a good example, where inexperienced runners are fired with enthusiasm after watching the London marathon, for example, on television, and then expect to run 42 km themselves without adequate preparation.

Regrettably it is true that the emphasis placed on winning in sport can easily lead to a loss of emotional control (Winters, 1987). Frustration and anger may be aimed at an opponent, an official, or at oneself. Very often the outcome is a loss of timing and coordination that only compounds the situation. Increased muscle tension and injury is a natural consequence in such an environment. A more subtle, yet nevertheless real, cause of injury is related to attention deficits. It has been well documented that an increase in anxiety will produce a narrowing of attention, a misperception of important situations, or both. In this context important visual and auditory cues can be missed, and players might fail to avoid serious collisions with, at best, other players and, at worst, with more solid objects. Finally, the player who has been injured and is now taking initial steps to be reintegrated into competition is naturally tentative for the first few days or weeks. Coaches in any sport will always emphasize the need for a high level of self-confidence and a positive attitude towards "taking charge of the situation," "making every tackle count," and "winning every ball." In potentially hazardous, high risk sports such as gymnastics, rugby or horse riding, a tentative approach often will lead to a further injury that may be even more serious than the original.

When athletes are injured, there appears to be a characteristic pattern to their behavior (Winters, 1987). Because of the many hours spent training for a forthcoming competition it is likely that an initial response will be to pretend that the injury does not exist. Having realized that there is cause for concern and that preparation for competition has to stop, the seriousness of the situation becomes apparent to the athlete, and it becomes impossible to train through the problem. Invariably the reaction will be one of anger that will not, of course, facilitate recovery. The athlete may begin to apportion blame and be critical of self, the coach, or both. Equipment, too, will sometimes be criticized as a potential cause of injury. Having expressed pent up emotions in the form of angry reactions, it is necessary for the athlete to begin to come to terms with the situation. Instead of a period of complete rest, accompanied by sound medical advice, the athlete will begin to enter into a form of negotiation. Very often this is internalized and is not always an attempt to "do a deal" with a coach or doctor. In the internalized negotiation state deals are struck with self in which decisions are made, for example to reduce the training load by, say, 25% or even more. Such negotiations are rarely successful, and the injury will continue to be troublesome. It is interesting that medical advice is seldom sought at this stage, because the athlete knows that a temporary embargo will be placed upon training. That is the last thing the elite athlete needs, because training leads to improved performance and that is the goal and purpose of training—or so the story goes. Eventually there is resignation to the injury and a way forward—or even a way out—is planned. There are very many instances of drop out at this stage or else a change to another sport, but it is not uncommon for a promising performer to be lost to sport altogether following an injury that is not treated promptly and sympathetically. The negative mood that accompanies the early stages of resignation is exacerbated when guilt feelings begin to be felt by the athlete. An awareness of the time that others have given in order to achieve this much are brought sharply into focus.

Thus, it can be seen that many responses to injury have important psychological implications and it is part of the sport psychologist's role to implement appropriate forms of behaviour modification and to structure the way forward. It is regrettable that having been given medical advice and treatment, most athletes are left to their own devices to find ways of self-counseling. A sport psychologist can facilitate rehabilitation by counseling athletes to think positively about the situation, to be pleased to have been afforded an opportunity to stand back, as it were, and to review the entire process and implications of sport participation for them. This is probably something the performer has neither considered nor felt willing to give time to. Instead of the all too common advice "rest it," the athlete needs to have the nature and extent of any injury explained clearly and simply.

Psychological skills such as relaxation and mental rehearsal can be taught and should be part of the injured athlete's rehabilitation program so that time is not wasted (Wiese & Weiss, 1987). Once again, it should be pointed out that this is an opportunity to acquire new skills and not merely to consider that existing ones will be lost. It has been demonstrated in the USA among professional footballers that injuries are associated with a player's emotional insecurity and related anxiety (Cryan & Alles, 1983). Concern about losing one's place in the team, family problems, and financial worries may be contributing factors to the incidence of injury. Thus, it may be prudent to explore some of these issues, provided that it is done sensitively.

Sport injuries are obvious, that is to say usually they can be seen. We can observe very easily the effects they have on an athlete and their clinical diagnosis and subsequent treatment is frequently straightforward. More recently, attention has been drawn to overtraining as an important factor contributing to performance decrement in elite athletes (Kuippers & Keizer, 1988). There are two important implications of overtraining. In one respect overtraining is necessary; a gradual increase in training load will produce a so-called "training effect" that leads to performance improvement. On the other hand, high intensity training can produce chronic fatigue and decrements in competition performance. Overtraining is the process, whereas the product is often referred to as staleness (Morgan, Brown, Raglin, O'Connor, & Ellikson, 1987). These researchers carried out a long term program that monitored psychological parameters in a group of competitive swimmers. The dependent variable was mood state disturbance as measured by the Profile of Mood States (POMS) inventory (McNair, Lorr, & Droppleman, 1971), a 65-item questionnaire that evaluates tension, depression, anger, vigor, fatigue, and confusion, as well as producing an overall Total Mood Disturbance (TMD) score. Morgan and his coworkers have used the POMS inventory with various sports groups, and in producing his Mental Health Model, Morgan (1985) has claimed that a positive mental health profile on the POMS—the "iceberg" profile—is associated with success in elite performers (Figure 26-1). Conversely, a "negative" profile (Figure 26-2) relates to poor performance that might not be diagnosed from conventional psychological indicators of stress.

The model has been tested with a female distance runner (Cockerill, 1988) and mood profiles were found to support Morgan's (1985) suggestion that an easing off in training usually will return the athlete to a more stable and controlled psychological

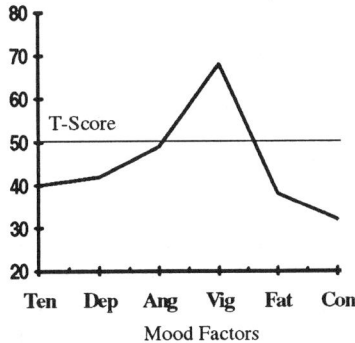

FIGURE 26-1.   The iceberg profile.

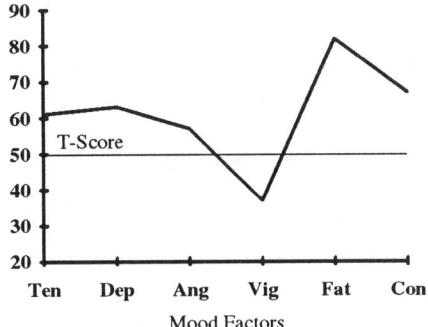

FIGURE 26-2.   Overtraining mood profile of a female middle distance runner.

state, with a commensurate renewal of enthusiasm for training and competition. If an iceberg profile is synonymous with a winner's profile, as Morgan suggests, then POMS would prove to be an appropriate criterion for the selection of athletes when used alongside track record, selection trials, and physiological measures. Clearly, it is necessary to include a range of criteria for selection purposes, and there is inevitably debate about the content of teams, as well as frequent criticism of those involved in their selection. However, tests such as the POMS, although valuable accessories, generally are subject to the social desirability factor—responding in a way that will place the individual in a favorable light—and the shrewd athlete readily can produce the sought after profile (Iso-Ahola & Hatfield, 1986).

An important consideration for sportswomen is the way in which the menstrual cycle might affect behavior; it has been estimated that up to 90% of women are affected in some way by Premenstrual Syndrome (PMS) (Bland, Goldstein, & Chatterjee, 1980). Interestingly, the words used to describe the psychological attributes of PMS are similar to those used to identify the six POMS factors. As a result of this observation my coworkers and I have carried out a number of preliminary studies to test the incidence and the influence of PMS on both athletes and nonathletes. Typically, POMS data are obtained during the two or three days before the onset of menstruation and again approximately 14 days later. Generally, it is found that there are significant differences between scores for all six mood factors when measures are obtained on the two occasions. Accordingly, the POMS inventory appears to be a useful device for investigating the incidence of PMS among competitive athletes. The next stage of research is to relate mood measures to performance on both laboratory tasks and in the field. If it can be shown that POMS is associated with PMS, which in turn is related to performance outcome, then this form of mood measurement will be especially useful in identifying an individual's "readiness to perform."

An investigation in progress at the present time has produced interesting data from high-level cross country runners. As pointed out already, although Morgan (1985) has argued that successful performance is associated with a precompetition iceberg profile, the present runners' data did not indicate that this is so. The relationship between finishing position in an important cross country race and TMD score was found to be nonsignificant. However, when a quadratic curve was fitted to the data the

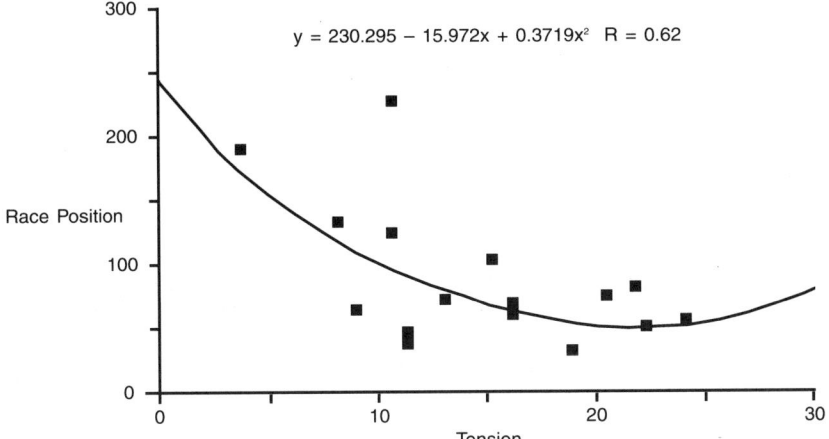

FIGURE 26-3.    Race position-tension relationship in crosscrountry runners.

$y = 230.295 - 15.972x + 0.3719x^2$    $R = 0.62$

V shape of the curve in Figure 26-3 suggests that prerace tension level might be an important parameter that influences finishing position. Both low- and high-tension scores tend to be associated with lower race positions, whereas the optimal T score for Tension lies somewhere between 20 and 25. If this finding is found to be robust in future studies, then tension level can be isolated as a potential predictor of performance in endurance sports, and possibly in other areas of skilled behavior as well. The value of using a dependent variable such as race position is that it provides an objective measure of performance, although obviously it is essential to ensure that data are not generated from elite athletes competing in "easy" races. In these instances a high race position could be associated erroneously with a low tension score.

In conclusion, today's elite athlete looks to many sources for help to improve performance and then to maintain it at a high level before developing further. Consequently, the sport psychologist is proving to be an important facilitator for the attainment of the goals that athletes and coaches set. "Be relaxed," "try to concentrate," and "don't worry" are heard with great frequency before a performer steps into the stadium, onto the concert platform, or into the interview room. It has been suggested that training intensity and the effects of the menstrual cycle are just two of the areas that can influence both behavioral and cognitive components of performance. The sport psychologist is able to work alongside the player and the coach in pursuit of a common goal, performance enhancement. Psychological research in the areas identified earlier is new, it is exciting, and its application has direct relevance to success in competitive sport. The implementation of psychological monitoring and preparation for high-ability sport performers can have positive benefits.

## REFERENCES

Bland, A. M., Goldstein, S. E., & Chatterjee, N. (1980). Premenstrual tension and mood change. *Canadian Journal of Psychiatry, 25,* 577–585.

Cockerill, I. M. (1988). *A case of overtraining in a female distance runner.* Unpublished paper. Department of Sport and Exercise Sciences, University of Birmingham.

Cryan, P. D., & Alles, W. F. (1983). The relationship between stress and college football injuries. *Journal of Sports Medicine, 23,* 52–58.

Horner, M. (1972). Towards an understanding of achievement-related conflicts in women. *Journal of Social Issues, 28,* 157–176.

Iso-Ahola, S. E., & Hatfield, B. (1986). *Psychology of sports: A social psychological approach.* New York: Wm. C. Brown.

Kuippers, H., & Keizer, H. A. (1988). Overtraining in elite athletes: Review and directions for the future. *Sports Medicine, 6,* 79–92.

Martens, R. (1975). *The psychology of physical activity.* New York: Harper & Row.

McNair, D. M., Lorr, M., & Droppleman, L. F. (1971). *Manual for the Profile of Mood States.* San Diego, CA: Educational and Industrial Testing Service.

Morgan, W. P. (1985). Selected psychological variables limiting performance: A mental health model. In D. H. Clarke & H. M. Eckert (Eds.), *Limits of human performance.* Champaign, IL: Human Kinetics Publishers.

Morgan, W. P., Brown, D. R., Raglin, J. S., O'Connor, P. J., & Ellikson, K. A. (1987). Psychological monitoring of overtraining and stalement. *British Journal of Sports Medicine, 21,* 107–114.

Ryan, E. D. (1969). Reaction to "Sport and personality dynamics," In *Proceedings of the National College of 1969 Physical Education Association for Men,* 70–75.

Triplett, N. (1898). The dynamogenic factor in pacemaking and competition. *American Journal of Psychology, 9,* 507–533.

Wiese, D. M. & Weiss, M. R. (1987). Psychological rehabilitation and physical injury: Implications for the sports medicine team. *The Sport Psychologist, 1,* 318–330.

Winters, G. (1987). Psychology and the injured athlete. *Excel, 3,* 16–18.

# 27

# High Ability in Sport

## A Case Study

**Ad Dudink**

*University of Amsterdam, Amsterdam, The Netherlands*

The purpose of this chapter is to explore the relationship between the concept of giftedness and sport. Generally the area of sport does not fit into the framework of contemporary models of intelligence. The neglect of the psychological aspects of exceptional development in physical abilities is a result of the historical cultural separation between body and psyche. A case study is given of a gifted girl in track and field. The present approach links up with Gardner's theory of multiple intelligences. Described and discussed is the influence of the variables family, exceptional drive and dedication, coaching, and schooling. It is proposed that research should concentrate more on the development and guidance of specific (sport) talents.

## INTRODUCTION

Why is that giftedness in sport is disregarded in psychological textbooks about giftedness? Why is it that psychological models about giftedness choose their favorite stars in the domains of science and arts? Why is it that psychological theories about the development of high ability often refer to winners of the Nobel Prize but never to winners of the Olympic Games? Why is it that research studies about giftedness in sport only exist in libraries of physical education? Here is one very simple explanation: There is no such thing as giftedness in sport! The view that giftedness in sport is overlooked may be proved by examining recent literature on giftedness (Freeman, 1985; Horowitz & O'Brien, 1985; Sternberg & Davidson, 1986). None of these books has a chapter about exceptional talent in sporting performances. The term "physical development" in the subject index does not refer to gifted athletes, but to the state of physical health of a young talent.

It is apparent that research interest in giftedness comes in waves. It is no coincidence that the first conference of the European Council for High Ability took place as late as 1988. Already at the beginning of this century an important European wave of publicity was rising. The centers of research were universities in Germany. In Berlin, schools for the gifted were founded during World War I ("Die Berliner Begabtenschulen"). Researchers such as Stern, Moede, and Piorkowski tried to develop instruments to identify gifted children. Their studies were an expansion of Binet's diagnosis of inferior states of intelligence (Binet & Simon, 1905). The renewed interest in the relationship between giftedness and education, however, is clearly non-European. On a morning in October 1957 Americans were shocked by a Russian satellite, Sputnik. The American technological supremacy was challenged. Was something wrong with American education? As a result educational policy changed, and money was made available to identify hidden creative talent. Several years ago another technological threat appeared.

> Now we are being awakened by the beepings of Japanese radios, phonographs and television sets, and Japanese wristwatch alarms, and again questions are being asked about American education, especially in science and mathematics (Skinner, 1984, p 947).

It is mainly within the context of science and mathematics that researchers address questions about the potential abilities of girls or ethnic minorities, but there is no interest in encouraging those groups to write poetry or to play Jazz music! When science is made top priority for fostering talent, then there will be a close association between giftedness and high intellectual ability. This perspective leads some to believe that a high level of intelligence is a prerequisite for giftedness (Renzulli, 1986). And what about art? Of course, the area of art is traditionally connected with outstanding creative behavior. Art is almost a synonym for creativity.

The concept of intelligence is less restricted today than at the beginning of this century. Neither Binet's nor Spearman's concept of intelligence included the domain of sport. One has to realize that sport in that period had completely different characteristics than at the present time. A professional career as a sports performer was out of the question. Later intelligence models also excluded physical abilities. Although Guilford included a behavioral content in his Structure of Intellect model, this refers only to mental operations (Guilford, 1967). Sternberg's triarchic model of intelligence differentiates exclusively among intellectual dimensions (Sternberg, 1988). The problem here is related to the scope of the concept of intelligence. If intelligence is split into specific domains, a choice should be made. Which ones? The Guinness Book of Records lists many domains where humans can excel. The diversity of possible human top achievements illustrates the danger that Spearman named "anarchic discipline" (Spearman, 1927). Fortunately, the current psychological literature in regard to this diversity is well outlined. This is explained to a large part by the norms that exist in society. Such an evaluation can be demonstrated by educational curricula. Feldhusen (1986) differentiates three areas.

1. Academic–intellectual areas (science, mathematics, social studies, etc.).
2. Artistic–creative areas (dance, music, drama, etc.).
3. Vocational areas (home economics, agriculture, business, etc.)

In many Western countries there is no specific schooling in areas such as chess, cricket, snooker, baseball, and so forth. Still it is my opinion that a fourth area, namely, the recreational area is legitimate. For many branches of sport it can even be said that the athlete has made a profession of his or her recreational activities. However, a career in sport is hardly ever long-lasting. Contrary to the gifted in science and art, the career of an internationally known athlete is very short-lived; Edwin Moses is an exception! The explanation is easily clarified: The relationship between age and performance in sport is dependent mainly on nonpsychological factors. The prediction criteria for giftedness in sport are for the most part limited to anatomical hardware. Athletes benefit from optimal size and physical prowess; small people do not play top basketball. The motoric aspects of sports skills are so apparent that there apears to be no connection with the psychological aspects. Sport psychology is a relatively new flower in the garden of psychology. Little by little the relationship between the psyche and body is being re-established.

There is another remarkable difference between giftedness in sport and other areas. Winners and losers, gifted and nongifted, are mainly determined by competition results. In many of these competitions the talent is not chosen by a jury but by an objective measurement, for example a time registered in 100ths of seconds. In art, on the other hand, talent is often discovered very late, sometimes even after death. Yet it must be said that many famous artists and scientists of the present day are only regarded as "gifted" during their life time. Contrary to art and science, predictions of gifted sport achievements are falsified easily. The previous arguments make it clear why a sports symposium within the First European Conference on Giftedness was regarded by many participants as a rarity. Considering that an athlete, Sebastian Coe, gave the opening keynote address, this conference was very exceptional at the least.

When I claim that the bodily skills are missing in books about intelligence, creativity, and giftedness, this does not mean that physical terms are not used. It is remarkable that so-called "thinking skills" often are explained metaphorically on the analogy of physical skills. A good example is the British psychologist Sir Frederic Bartlett, who gave much attention to the properties of skilled bodily performance. In his study of thinking he referred to skill properties such as "timing," "stationary phases," "point of no return," and "direction" (Bartlett, 1958).

However, a theory of intelligence recently has been advanced that offers space for talents such as those of Mohammed Ali and Sebastian Coe. I am referring to Gardner's theory of Multiple Intelligences (Gardner, 1985). According to Gardner, there are at least seven distinct "intelligences": linguistic, musical, logical–mathematical, spatial, bodily–kinesthetic, interpersonal, and intrapersonal. Gardner argues that the secondary status of bodily intelligence is a product of the Renaissance invention of rational humans.

A description of use of the body as a form of intelligence may at first jar. There has been a radical disjunction in our tradition between the activities of reasoning, on the one hand, and the activities of the manifestly physical part of our nature, as epitomized by our bodies, on the other. This divorce between the "mental" and the "physical" has not infrequently been coupled with a notion that what we do with our bodies is somehow less privileged, less special, than those problem-solving routines carried out chiefly through the use of language, logic, or some other relatively abstract symbolic system (pp. 207, 208).

At this time Gardner's theory is in the early stage of construction, and the research within his Frames of Mind is still in a period of dynamic development, so that it is too early to make a judgment. However, it offers a possibility for integrating case studies in the area of sports.

## A CASE STUDY

Most probably, most of the decisions to conduct case studies with gifted children stem from a pragmatic choice. The young athlete described here is an athlete in track and field whom I first noticed by chance while watching members of my family competing. The observations reported here started when she was 11 years old, and she is now 13. Everybody noticed the striking difference between this girl and the other competitors. Often there was a tremendous gap between D, the number one, and the other athletes. At this point the question arises: Is she really an extraordinary girl, or are the other athletes performing at a low level?

Track and field makes up a small percentage of sport in the Netherlands. Table 27-1 gives an impression. Athletes within the category Junior D are 12 and 13 years old. D has been top of her group for several years. As already mentioned, many sports performances can be measured very precisely: Not only the winner's name is known, but also the time and distance. Measurements in track and field provide the athlete with direct feedback. Athletes know exactly where they stand. Table 27-2 presents D's development. It also shows her position in a national perspective. One can see that already at the age of 10 she was the best. The numbers within the brackets give her rank order in her group. The results indicate that D dominates in the events of sprinting, jumping, throwing, and so forth—she is an all-round successful athlete. The last column (referring to six events) demonstrates this. The second athlete on this list has 600 fewer points!

TABLE 27-1
Sports in the Netherlands

| Organized Participants | 4,000,000 |
|---|---|
| Clubs | 35,000 |
| Soccer | 1,000,000 |
| Lawn tennis | 635,000 |
| Volleyball | 170,000 |
| Track and field | 60,000 |
| Women | 20,000 |
| Girl's Junior D | 2,392 |

TABLE 27-2
D's Results 1984–1988

|  | 60 m | 600 m | 1000 m | 60 m Hurdles | Long jump | High jump | Shotput | Javelin | Six* |
|---|---|---|---|---|---|---|---|---|---|
| 1984 | | | 3.40 | | 3.83 | 1.20 | 7.04 | | |
| | | | (3) | | (6) | (2) | (1) | | |
| 1985 | 8.8 | | 3.29 | | 4.32 | 1.35 | 8.07 | | |
| | (1) | | (3) | | (1) | (1) | (1) | | |
| 1986 | 8.2 | 140.8 | 3.09 | 9.9 | 4.69 | 1.51 | 10.35 | 27.28 | |
| | (1) | (1) | (1) | (3) | (3) | (3) | (9) | (8) | |
| 1987 | 8.1 | 140.1 | | 9.7 | 5.14 | 1.61 | 11.30 | 33.36 | 3535 |
| | (2) | (1) | | (1) | (1) | (1) | (5) | (1) | |
| 1988 | 7.8 | 139.0 | | 8.8 | 5.59 | 1.68 | 13.42 | 36.10 | 3820 |
| | (1) | (2) | | (1) | (1) | (1) | (2) | (1) | |

* = 60 m hurdles, long jump, shotput, jump, javelin, and 600 m.

If the factors explaining high ability in sport are categorized, then the biological category is one of them. Nowadays there is a great deal of discussion about racial differences in sports performance. Recently, the *Canadian Journal of Sport Sciences* published a review on this topic. Anyone who has followed the evolution of sports in the world has observed that athletes from different races excel in specific sport disciplines (e.g., Afro-American athletes in men's sprint events). Are there race linked physical or psychological characteristics? Samson and Yerlès (1988) present data on performance differentials between black and white athletes and comment on theories that have attempted to explain the observed differences. They conclude

Black athletes dominate the sport scene in a few events, whereas white athletes dominate a large spectrum of sports. Given the current state of knowledge, sociological factors seem best to explain the observed differences (p. 116).

The cultural category already has been mentioned. A good example of the cultural determination of sports performance is the history of women athletes participating in the Olympic Games. Track and field for women started in 1928 (Amsterdam). Twenty years later women were running the 200 meters and very recently it has been admitted that even women can run the marathon. If the performances of women winners of the Olympic Games high jump from 1928 until 1952 are compared to D's latest achievements, it becomes apparent that her present height would have been good for five gold medals. Were women not talented in those days? The explanation, of course, is the fact that the jumping style has changed. Since Fosbury surprised the audience with his spectacular technique in 1968, high jump performances have been characterized by a remarkable progression. Thus, three important categories relating to sports performance are: 1. cultural determinants; 2. anatomical and physiological determinants; and 3. technique determinants. What about the psychological determinants? Which psychological factors are needed to explain D's excellence?

Feldman (1980) proposes that in addition to an individual's talent, at least four forces must be recognized.

1. An exceptional drive and dedication in a specific domain;
2. The good fortune to grow up in an environment that will nurture this exceptional talent;
3. Outstanding instruction and mentorship in this field; and
4. The relative prestige and value placed on the field at a given time.

Mönks (1988) mentions three forces that are important for optimal development of motivation, intelligence, and creativity: family, school, and peers. The aspects mentioned by Feldman and Mönks were used as a frame of reference for several open interviews with D herself, her parents, and her coach.

## FAMILY

When one goes to a children's competition, one notices that there are no spectators. Only a few parents are there, usually the mothers of the young athletes. In D's case both her parents always are there, not only at the competition but also during training. D is the daughter of a very sports-minded family. When I asked her, "Where does your talent come from?" she laughed and said, "From my father." Her father was once a professional soccer player in one of the best teams in the Netherlands. Because of D's exceptional talents often she is put in a vulnerable and isolated position. Her father is the one who supports her at these times. At tournaments people always see her as the winner, even before the events start. This often leads to negative remarks. For example, if D has a false start parents of other athletes react in a negative fashion: "She is doing it on purpose, . . . she probably has a new tactic to win . . ." In reality it is D herself who loses concentration through a false start. Stressful situations like this sometimes make D want to lose on purpose. Her father talks her out of this and teaches her to cope with those situations. And the position of the mother? D's mother encourages her to compete in as many national and international tournaments as possible. Her coach often disagrees with the mother's wishful planning. To summarize: D's parents are exceptional in guiding her sporting career. Both of them hope and believe that D will participate in the next Olympics in Barcelona.

## EXCEPTIONAL DRIVE AND DEDICATION

"I want to be an athlete and that is all," is her comment for the future. An expression like this relates to the factor of motivation and commitment. "Every game, I hope to break my personal record." At home her room proves that she has won many times. Hundreds of trophies, medals, and certificates are gloriously displayed in two cupboards. The victories of the past are tidily kept in four scrapbooks illustrated with articles and pictures.

## THE COACH

The influence of the coach is very important. She is not qualified as a coach, but has a lot of experience in the athletic field. She herself was a top athlete in track and field. She sets a high value on social conditions. Athletes in her group are friends to each other. Although D's behavior is very much in the public eye, her coach does not give her special treatment. D is just one of them. Just like the others, D trains twice a week. Until now D's achievements have shown constant progress, but her coach predicts that soon there will be a period of stagnation. Within a few years her body will mature. "Then all you can do is work hard on your technique and your physical and mental condition." D is not a good loser, and her coach is anxious about the near future.

## THE SCHOOL

The opinion of the coach is, "D is not very intelligent." This opinion is based on her school achievements. Last year she did not pass her grade. Perhaps she is an underachiever because there is no motivation for school learning. Placing her on an academic intelligence dimension is not possible because no results on standardized tests are available.

What will happen with young talented athletes? Researchers in Belgium found that the proportion of youthful talents still successful after a period of five years is only 17%. Those who were successful had a better relationship with their parents, more ego strength, and less competition anxiety (Auweele, Parijs, & Vankerckhoven, 1988). The researchers concluded that these psychological factors demonstrate the importance of structured psychological guidance. In countries like Belgium, the Netherlands, the United Kingdom, and many others young talent is mainly dependent on the support of family and friends. What this ongoing case study has made very clear is that more field-specific approaches to giftedness are needed. More attention should be paid to knowledge and skills connected to specific disciplines or fields. The focus for identifying gifted individuals thus becomes children's specific talents, not their assumed general abilities. Even in the area of sports there are prodigies, but who cares about them?

## REFERENCES

Auweele, Y., Van den, Parijs, M. v., & Vankerckhoven, G. (1988). Topsport, hoe kom je er (niet) toe? *Sport, 30,* 19–26.

Bartlett, F. C. (1958). *Thinking: An experimental and social study.* London: Allen.

Binet, A., & Simon, T. (1905). Méthodes nouvelles pour le diagnostic du niveau intellectual des anormaux. *L'Année Psychologique, 11,* 191–244.

Feldhusen, J. F. (1986). A conceptions of giftedness. In R. J. Sternberg & J. E. Davidson (Eds.), *Conceptions of giftedness* (pp. 112–127). New York: Basic Books.

Feldman, D. H. (1980). *Beyond universals in cognitive development.* Norwood, NJ: Ablex.

Freeman, J. (Ed.) (1985). *The psychology of gifted children.* Chichester: Wiley.

Gardner, H. (1985). *Frames of mind.* New York: Basic Books.

Guilford, J. P. (1967). *The nature of human intelligence.* New York: McGraw-Hill.

Horowitz, F. D., & O'Brien, M. (Eds.) (1985). *The gifted and talented: Developmental perspectives.* Washington, DC: American Psychological Association.

Mönks, F. J. (1988). De rol van de sociale omgeving in de ontwikkeling van het hoogbegaafde kind. In G. Kanselaar, J. L. van der Linden, & A. Pennings (Eds.), *Begaafdheid: onderkenning en beinvloeding* (pp. 205–218). Amersfoort: Acco.

Renzulli, J. S. (1986). The three-ring conception of giftedness: a developmental model for creative productivity. In R. J. Sternberg & J. E. Davidson (Eds.), *Conceptions of giftedness* (pp. 53–92). New York: Basic Books.

Samson, J., & Yerlés, M. (1988). Racial differences in sports performance. *Canadian Journal of Sport Sciences, 13,* 109–116.

Skinner, B. F. (1984). The shame of American education. *American Psychologist, 39,* 947–954.

Spearman, C. (1927). *The abilities of man.* London: Macmillan.

Stern, W. (1920). *Die Intelligenz der Kinder und Jugendlichen und die Methoden ihrer Untersuchung.* Leipzig: Johann Ambrosius Barth.

Sternberg, R. J., & Davidson, J. E. (Eds.). (1986). *Conceptions of giftedness.* New York: Basic Books.

Sternberg, R. J. (1988). *The triarchic mind.* New York: Viking.

# 28

# Ability for Athletics

## Identification and Improvement of Talent

**László Harsányi**

*Budapest, Hungary*

In identification and improvement of talent for athletics, training practice is hindered by considerable errors of estimation. Sports sciences must wrestle with the problem of lack of an established theory to guide the search for talented people. Nevertheless, a theoretically and practically effective system was used in the former German Democratic Republic for 15 years. The existing elements of this system were integrated with pedagogical experience and other data from the literature in an attempt to outline a system to be used in athletics in the search for talented performers. In this novel concept the main means of identification of athletic talent is competition itself, the main indicator is competitive performance, and the most important stimulator of interest in a discipline is success in competition. Competitive performances, however, can be of prognostic value only if they are evaluated together with the factors of trainability, biological age, training age, and psychobiological, physiological, anthropometrical, and social characteristics.

## INTRODUCTION

Both pedagogical experience and the opinion of the medical geneticist Czeizel (1984) suggest that within a given population the proportion of those outstandingly gifted in a given ability complex (here sports) is extremely low (about 2.5%), from both statistical and practical points of view. Furthermore, the distribution of talented people within the whole population is random: Simply finding and identifying them requires laborious work and organization. The same holds true for the process of ability and talent development. On the other hand, both the individual and the nation justifiably wish that Plato's principle "the right person at the right place" should be met in the field of talent. Practical applications of the mentioned principle, however, have succeeded only in a controversial way so far.

Nevertheless, training practice solves continuously, although admittedly with considerable errors of estimate, the problems of identification and improvement of talent. The worldwide continuous improvement of athletic performances supports this opinion. Moreover, scientific efforts have been exerted for decades in order to decrease the errors of selection. Sports science, however, is unable to provide overall help for training practice, even today. This disability is owing to the fact that theory concerning talent for sports is only just developing, and the methods of identifying talent on the basis of test results have not yet proven sufficient (Gabler & Ruoff, 1979; Holz, 1988; Letzelter, 1981; Singer, 1981; Tschiene, 1974; Ulmer, 1988; Wendland, 1986). The situation is practically the same, as far as the problems of talent improvement and talent care in juveniles are concerned (Baursfeld & Schröter, 1980; Feige, 1978; Filin & Fomin, 1980; Hahn, 1982; Martin, 1982; Rossmann, 1987).

Although the whole world is confronted by these problems, among the 170 members of the International Amateur Athletics Association in 56% of the countries, just as in Hungary, there is no adequate system for selection of athletes. On the other hand, in a few countries, including the former German Democratic Republic (GDR) and Bulgaria (BUL), more efficient methods have been used for 15 years, especially for the identification but also for the care of talent. The efficacy of these methods was demonstrated year by year by the internationally outstanding performances of the GDR in sports, including athletics. The efficacy of the methods used can further be supported if results are related to the size of the population. The idea of De Solla Price (1963), namely that the scientific "greatness" of a given nation also depends on the size of the population, may serve as an analogy.

In the case of the first and second World Athletic Championships, Harsányi and Sebö (1988) evaluated the results of the first to eighth place winners by assigning points in the order 8-7-6-5-4-3-2-1, and referred these point values to one million inhabitants of a given country. This new index was considered to be fundamental for talent selection and talent care. The data shown in detail in Table 28-1 clearly indicate that the results of the GDR—and partly BUL—were, at least to some extent, superior to the results of countries with larger populations, which are better supplied with facilities for medical care, education, and culture, and where the living standard was higher. Moreover, not even national characteristics can be regarded as responsible for advantages in talent selection and talent care, since the results of the GDR exceeded those of the Federal Republic of Germany by 7.4- to 15.4-fold.

On the basis of these considerations, it can be assumed with reason that identification and improvement of talent for sports are determined mostly by both the rationality of the system used and the quality of the actual attempts made. The system used in the GDR also proves that experiences gleaned in training practice combined with new findings in sports sciences permit more accurate estimates than those made in other parts of the world. It is also true that it is not easy to gain proper knowledge about the elements of the system. Nevertheless, the works of Harsányi and Martin (1983), Hofman and Schneider (1985), Holz (1988), Kreutzer (1986), Lohman (1985), and Mocker (1988) make it possible for a good outline to be drawn.

For 15 years, that is, following the two-year experiment carried out in 1970 and 1971, extensive data were used in the GDR for screening the athletic abilities of 9- to 10-year-old children (Mocker, 1988). It can be assumed with reason that the prognostic value of these data is high. If these data and those mentioned in other papers cited earlier are supplemented both by Ágoston's thesis on talent (1985) and by the observations of Baursfeld and Schröter (1980), Feige (1978), Filin and Fomin (1980), Hahn (1982), Martin (1982), and Rossmann (1987) on the training of champions of the future, the profile of a more efficient system to be used in training can be outlined.

The present chapter is aimed at this purpose. Before data presentation, however, it is necessary to define, at least for present purposes, what athletic talent means.

TABLE 28-1
Efficacy of Selection and Development in Different Countries*

| Helsinki (1983) | | | Rome (1987) | | |
|---|---|---|---|---|---|
| Rank** | Country | points per 1 million inhabitants | Rank | Country | points per 1 million 1 million inhabitants |
| 2 | GDR | 13.86 | 2 | GDR | 16.93 |
| 4 | BUL | 8.86 | 4 | BUL | 7.48 |
| 10–11 | FRG | 1.88 | 13 | FRG | 1.10 |
| 13 | HUN | 1.31 | 21 | USSR | 0.97 |
| 17 | USA | 1.02 | 23 | USA | 0.90 |
| 20 | USSR | 0.87 | 24 | HUN | 0.58 |

*Based on Harsányi and Sebö (1988).
**In 1983, 39 countries and in 1987, 42 countries scored.

## ATHLETIC TALENT

Talented for athletics are those whose inherited physical, physiological, anthropometrical, motoric, and social abilities are at a level in a given period of ontogeny (under age matched environmental—primarily training—conditions) which ensures (with further training appropriate to the stage of psychobiological development) that at the period of peak performance (between the 20th and 30th years of life) the athlete will most probably reach the international level of athletic performances. In early childhood (from the ages of six to eight years) athletic talent can also be interpreted as general motor talent (Letzelter, 1981). In this period of life motor characteristics are determined only by five closely related factors; among these, general motor ability accounts for 45% of the variance. The number of dominant factors increases to eight by the age of 11 to 12 years, and to twelve by the age of 15 to 16 years. Moreover, in the latter period the factor of general motor ability has no importance at all (Filippovics & Turevskij, 1977). Therefore, with increasing age talent increasingly should be defined in a specific way related to a particular sports branch or specific event.

### Principles for the Identification and Improvement of Talent in Athletics

Human beings are born with characteristic features, but not with abilities or talents. These characteristic features are natural inherited prerequisites for any human action. The abilities and characteristics that may lead to talent evolve as a result of the interaction of the inherited features and the environment. Human abilities and characteristics develop not only nonsimultaneously, but also in an individually variable way. If, for any reason, the human being is deprived of the possibility of a given activity, his or her inherited features will not develop into abilities and characteristics. The level of the inherited features determines both the rate of development and the upper limits of the abilities and characteristics. It should be accepted as fact that, under similar conditions and levels of training, those with lower levels of inherited features will exhibit abilities and performances inferior to those of people with a higher level of inheritance. The younger the child, the more his or her performance is determined by inherited features rather than learned abilities.

Both decision making about aptitude as well as selection of the talented are processes that are bound to a certain branch of sport, in athletics first to several then to a decreasing number of athletic events. Both at the beginning (screening) and at every further stage of training, such elements should be taken into account for the identification of talent, which will determine performances even at the age of peak performances. It is necessary to face the fact, however, that at every stage of the process of long-term preparation only the ability for the next stage can be predicted with adequate certainty.

Both in childhood and in adolescence many-sided training and competition should be aimed not only at assuring development but also at measuring the efficacy of training and evaluating ability as well. Within a sports branch and event specific activities, identification of talent should consist of the estimation of abilities, dexterity, knowledge, motivation, interest, and tolerance of loads. Uncertainty in the prediction of talent decreases in parallel both with increasing biological and training ages and with accumulating theoretical and practical information. Performances and creativity at much higher levels than the average manifest themselves in event specific *performance*, which serves as the basic criterion for selection. Training and competition should develop step by step from the 50–50 proportion of comprehensive athletic and manysided general training (which is appropriate at the beginning of sport) to training in a particular sports branch and then event specific training that corresponds to the given stage of psychobiological maturation.

## Sports Branch Specific Characteristics of Athletics

Certain elements of athletics that can be performed even in early childhood mainly represent the interaction of conditional ability and disposition. The competition necessary for the evaluation of abilities is also possible at the ages of six to eight years. Performances in these events can reliably be measured by standardized instruments and methods, and the measurements can reliably be reproduced in situations of competition. Competition has motivating and rewarding effects. Finally, it is not necessary to verify the validity, reliability, objectivity, and economy of the procedures in order to use competitive performances as criterion, since these will be evaluated in real competition.

> In conclusion, the most effective practical way of selecting athletics is athletic competition.
>
> The primary and integrative criterion for selection is *athletic competitive performance*.
>
> The development rate of athletic competitive performance represents an indirect indicator of trainability.
>
> The most effective stimulator leading to selection of a given specialization is success in athletic competition.

### Evaluation of Performances

Competitive performances, even with their initial level and development rate, however, are not enough to predict talent (Letzelter, 1981). Mocker (1988) and Ulmer (1988) as well as others are of the opinion that on the basis of observations during training, the following parameters should be taken into consideration.

> *The extent of tolerance of loads.* Those young athletes can be regarded as able to tolerate loads who follow step-by-step vigorous increases in the amount of training (beginning in childhood with 50% all-round athletic and 50% general training, and always corresponding to the actual state of psychobiological maturation), do not lose their positive attitude to sport, and react to the increasing load by producing performance development rates that far exceed the average.
>
> *The ability to resist performance anxiety* (according to Helmke, 1983). This aspect involves a continuous state of alertness that manifests itself both in the ability to re-

sist the psychological, motor, and physiological effects (which are evoked by the training and competitive situations and perceived by the individual as threatening) and in higher than average and more stable performances.

*Anthropometrical characteristics.* Among these factors special attention should be paid to expected adult height, since this factor has considerable importance in the majority of athletic events. The method of Srámková, Prkopec, and Zelezny (1987) is recommended for predicting adult height.

Reliable evaluation of physical characteristics and actual performances is possible only if the *biological age* of the individual is taken into consideration, that is to say, physical dimensions and performance levels of athletes at the same chronological, but at higher or lower biological age (provided that the difference exceeds half a year) should be compared with data from the older or younger generation, and the actual level of abilities should be evaluated on this basis. In dealing with large numbers of people, as is necessary in selecting talented individuals, biological age cannot be determined by measuring bone age. Consequently, determination of morphological age seems to be a more practical approach. Morphological age can be estimated by the method of Mészáros, Mohácsi, and Szmodis (1984). This method was developed by means of investigation of young Hungarians: body height, body mass, and the so-called "plasticity index" (shoulder circumference + forearm circumference + hand circumference) should be measured for this calculation. It is also absolutely necessary to be aware of *training age*, including weekly training frequency, since of two young athletes with identical biological and performance ages, the one can be considered to have better abilities and to be more talented whose training age and training frequency is lower.

In addition to the primary factors of trainability and resistance to performance anxiety, speed of learning, will power, and attitude to sport represent additional factors that can scarcely be measured objectively. Nevertheless, although it is necessary to accept that these parameters cannot be measured for the purposes of training, it must be borne in mind that most of them are of decisive importance from the psychological and performance points of view. There are good reasons for assuming that competitive performances are determined to 50% by psychological factors (although this has not been directly proven so far). Consequently, on the basis of systematic pedagogical observations, the coach should also evaluate the competitor from the point of view of these factors. The young athlete can be classified as being excellent (5), good (4), moderate (3), weak (2), and inadequate (1).

The factors already outlined can be supplemented by data on frequency of illness and injury. If, in addition to the factors discussed earlier, the state of health of the young athlete is known, present knowledge suggests that sufficient information is available for the process of screening and selection.

## Follow Up of the Process of Selection

The results of measurements and observations should be recorded. These data can be evaluated by comparing the values recorded to standardized, performance related specific characteristics. Comparison of performances can also serve as a pedagogical method (Nádori, 1967). Moreover, the dynamics of the factors for selection can also be evaluated. For instance, in the case of a boy whose body height and performances in the high jump and 400-m flat race are compared with data for the Hungarian and international elite, it might become apparent that this child's performances in the high jump were closer to those of the international elite than his performances in the 400-m flat race. This means that within the field of athletics this sportsman is more likely to be successful in the jumping events than in events requiring endurance performance.

## The Process of Improvement

Basic questions in athletic talent care that are related to the process of development-maturation were summarized by Grosser, Brüggemann, and Zintl (1986). In connection with all-round athletic training and both subsequent discipline specific (sprint, hurdle, middle and long distance running, walking, jumps, and throws) and event-specific training, the question is not at what age specialization should begin, but how the process of specialization should be organized.

## REFERENCES

Ágoston, G. (1985). Theses on physical education in school (in Hungarian). *Pedagógiai Szemle*, 2, 137–142.

Baursfeld, K., & Schröter, G. (Eds.). (1980). *Grundlagen der Leichtathletik*. Berlin: Sportverlag.

Czeizel, E. (1984). *The value is inherent in us* (in Hungarian). Budapest: Gondolat.

De Solla Price, D. (1963). *Little science, big science*. New York: Columbia University Press.

Feige, K. (1978). *Leistungsentwicklung und Höchstleistungsalter von Spitzenläufern*. Schorndorf: Karl Hofmann.

Filin, V. P., & Fomin, N. A. (1980). Osnovü junoseskovo sporta. *Fizkultura i sport*. Moscow.

Filippovics, V. I., & Turevskij, I. M. (1977). Über die Prinzipien der sportlichen Orientierung von Kindern und Jugendlichen in Zusammenhang mit der altersspezifischen Veränderung in der Struktur der Bewegungsfähigkeiten. *Leistungssport, 6*, 503–508.

Gabler, H., & Ruoff, B. (1979). Zum Problem der Talentbestimmung im Sport. *Sportwissenschaft, 9*, 164–180.

Grosser, M., Brüggemann, P., & Zintl, F. (1986). *Leistungssteuerung in Training und Wettkampf*. München: BLV Verlagsgesellschaft.

Hahn, E. (1982). *Kindertraining. Probleme. Trainingstheorie. Praxis*. München: BLV Verlagsgesellschaft.

Harsányi, L. (1988). *Choice and selection of athletes in training practice*. Unpublished manuscript, Pécs.

Harsányi, L., & Martin, M. (1983). We have visited the GDR (in Hungarian). *Atlétika, 7/8*, 1–8.

Harsányi, L., Diósdi, L., Hirt, K. M., Martin, M., & Veres, L. (1985). Physical development and the maturity of motor functions (in Hungarian). *Testnevelés- és Sporttudamány, 3*, 17–32.

Harsányi, L., & Sebö, A. (1988). Novel method for the evaluation of the efficacy of choice and selection in sport. Unpublished manuscript, Pécs.

Helmke, A. (1983). Prüfungsangst. *Psychologische Rundschau, 34*, 193–211.

Hofman, S., & Schneider, G. (1985). Eignungsbeurteilung und Auswahl in Nachwuchsleistungssport. *Theorie und Praxis der Körperkultur, 1*, 44–52.

Holz, P. (1988). Praxisfragen zur Talentprognose—Ein Statement aus der Sicht der Sportpraxis. In H. de Marées (Ed.), *Die Talentproblematik im Sport* (pp. 187–196). Clausthal-Zellerfeld: dvs.

Kirsch, A. (1986). Die Grenzen des Menschen im Sport. *Leichtathletik, 40/41*, 1645–1649.

Kreutzer, A. (1986). Einheitliche Sichtung und Auswahl (ESA) als systematische Talentsuche in der DDR. *Leistungssport, 4*, 40–41.

Letzelter, M. (1981). Der Beitrag der Trainingswissenschaft zur "theorie des sportlichen Talents" (Problematik-Strategie-Lösungen). In D. Augustin & N. Müller (Eds.), *Leichtathletiktraining im Spannungsfeld von Wissenschaft und Praxis* (pp. 38–52). Niedernhausen: Schors.

Lohmann, W. (1985). *Leichtathletik Trainingsprogramme.* Berlin: Sportverlag.

Martin, D. (1982). *Grundlagen der Trainingslehre.* Teil II. Die Planung, Gestaltung, Steuerung des Trainings und das Kinder- und Jugendtraining. Schorndorf: Karl Hofman.

Martin, M., & Harsányi, L. (1987). Calculated characteristics of body dimension dynamics (in Hungarian). *Atlétika, 10,* 1–8, *11,* 11–16.

Mészáros, J., Mohácsi, J., & Szmodis, I. (1984). Determination of biological maturity on the basis of anthropometrical parameters (in Hungarian). *Hungarian Review of Sports Medicine, 4,* 263–268.

Mocker, K. (1988). Aspekte der Talentförderung in der DDR. In H. de Marées (Ed.), *Die Talentproblematik im Sport* (pp. 61–90). Clausthal-Zellerfeld: dvs.

Nádori, L. (1967). Performances as pedagogical method (in Hungarian). *A testnevelés tanítása, 5,* 80–84.

Rossmann, E. D. (1987). *Verhaltenskonzepte für das sportliche Training von Jugendlichen.* Schorndorf: Karl Hofmann.

Singer, R. (1981). *Allgemeine methodische Probleme der Talentbestimmung im Sport.* Schorndorf: Karl Hofmann.

Srámková, P., Prkopec, M., & Zelezny, J. (1987). Predicke telesné vysky. *Teoria Praxe Telené Wychowy, 4,* 226–234.

Tschiene, P. (1974). Das Problem aller Sportnationen: Talentbestimmung und Talentsuche. *Leistungssport, 4,* 270–273.

Ulmer, H. V. (1988). Zur Problematik der Talentsuche im Sport aus leistungsphysiologischer Sicht. In H. de Marées (Ed.), *Die Talentproblematik im Sport* (pp. 104–119). Clausthal-Zellerfeld: dvs.

Wendland, U. (1986). *Individuelle Leistungsprognosen im Spitzensport.* Schorndorf: Karl Hofmann.

# 29

# Rankings of Predictors of Athletic Performance by Top-Level Coaches

**Jacques H. A. van Rossum**

*Vrije Universiteit Amsterdam, Amsterdam, The Netherlands*

**Françoys Gagné**

*Université du Québec à Montréal, Montréal, Canada*

Two studies are reported in which coaches of Dutch top level athletes ranked 10 general factors recognized as predictors of athletic performance. In the first study, the coaching staff of the national teams in judo, speed skating, swimming, and table tennis were involved ($n = 50$), and in the second coaches in field hockey, golf, and track and field ($n = 65$); in track and field, two types of athlete were assessed: the "explosive" and the "endurance" types. Agreement among coaches within a sport appears to vary from rather high to quite low, indicating that they do not always rank the various factors in an identical way. In spite of these imperfect interjudge reliabilities, most of the groups of coaches made very similar group rankings, in which three factors were generally considered to be of primary importance: physical fitness, mental fitness, and natural endowment. These findings are discussed in the context of the emphasis that is often given to the effects of the immediate environment in the development of talented individuals.

## INTRODUCTION

Top-level coaches in most athletic disciplines dream of detecting at an early age and with a high degree of accuracy those who will become athletes of international stature. Researchers have been working for decades to make this dream come true. They have developed various predictive models and, with their help, have analyzed a large number of potentially valuable explanatory factors, including morphological characteristics, physiological factors, perceptual and motor skills, psychological traits, as well as various environmental influences. In a recent review of the literature on talent detection and talent development, Régnier, Salmela, and Russell (1993) presented many of the major models that have guided this research, as well as the results of the major predictive studies.

These explanatory models differ from each other in terms of the number and diversity of the predictors introduced, the structure of the detection process, and the relative importance attributed to each category of predictive factors. One particular characteristic stands out: the models proposed by specialists from Eastern Europe tend to give more emphasis to components with a high level of heritability, and thus more temporal stability. For instance, Régnier et al. (1993) presented a model proposed by Havlicek, Komadel, Komarik, and Simkova (1982, p. 298):

> There is a hierarchy of predictive factors, with stable and non-compensatory factors (e.g., height) of greatest concern. Second are more stable and compensatory factors, such as speed. Finally, unstable and compensatory factors, such as motivation, are considered.

Some of these models (e.g., Bompa, in Régnier et al., 1993) do not even consider psychological factors. The models proposed by researchers in the field of sport have many similarities with models of talent development found in the literature pertaining to intellectual giftedness and academic talent. For instance, Renzulli (1979, 1986) defined giftedness as the confluence of three traits: above-average abilities, creativity, and task commitment. For his part, Gagné (1985, 1993) proposed a differentiated model of giftedness and talent in which talent was defined as a complex set of skills characteristic of a field of human activity (e.g., science, geography, computers, art, music, mechanics, engineering, athletics, administration). These acquired skills are progressively developed from natural abilities having an important genetic underpinning, which are grouped in four domains: intellectual, creative, socio-affective, and sensorimotor. The long and systematic learning and training process through which natural abilities are transformed into the particular skills of a given talent domain is helped (or hindered) by two sets of moderator variables called catalysts: intrapersonal catalysts (motivation, temperament, character, etc.) and environmental catalysts (family, school, community, etc.).

Research in the field of sport using the detection models mentioned earlier has covered sports as diverse as wrestling, gymnastics, ice hockey, rowing, baseball, and diving. The results, in terms of the relationship between these predictors (alone or combined) and various indices of athletic performance, vary tremendously from study to study (Régnier et al., 1993). It seems that, in general, the studies with the more impressive results not only adopted a multidisciplinary approach, but also included many measures in each category. This scientific or empirical approach is "top down" (Régnier et al., 1993, p. 291), because it is based on hypotheses derived from accumulated scientific evidence. By contrast, the "bottom up" approach makes use of the knowledge, the anecdotal evidence and the language of sports performers.

This bottom up approach, also called "knowledge acquisition" (Boose & Gaines, 1988), can take many forms. It has been used to compare the strategies of experts and novices (e.g., Chi, Glaser, & Rees, 1982), to study how athletes perceive various training or competing situations and the coping strategies they adopt (e.g., Russell, 1990), as well as to analyze the development of the athlete's career from a more global perspective (e.g., Bloom, 1985; Hemery, 1986). Bloom's (1985) study examined career development through extensive interviews with 20 national (US) leaders in each of six talent fields, and with their parents. The six fields covered three general domains: concert pianists and sculptors in the arts, mathematicians and research neurologists in the cognitive domain, and olympic swimmers and tennis players in the psychomotor domain. Hemery's (1986) study considered 63 world-class level athletes in 21 sports, both team sports and individual sports, from 12 different countries. Each of the athletes was interviewed in person by the author himself. Hemery used the same list of questions in each interview, to arrive at conclusions about physical, social, psychological, and moral factors in the careers of highly talented athletes. Both Bloom's (1985) and Hemery's (1986) investigations must be considered reconstructions after the fact. In the case of some individual athletes, decades had passed between the end of the sporting career and the interviews about it. The findings from these investigations should therefore be interpreted with some caution, and be considered more than anything else as yielding interesting hypotheses about the athletes' careers. In these studies, the perspective of the talented individual was largely (Bloom) or solely (Hemery) taken into account as the information on which the sketch of the career was built.

Studies adopting a "bottom up" approach until now have focused on the athletes themselves as the source of information. But, in the world of sports, there is another particularly interesting source of information that has been largely ignored: the coaches. Coaches are placed at a very interesting crossroads: They have access to the scientific literature on talent detection and development in general, as well as in their particular disciplines, although also having daily access to concrete data from the athletes under their technical guidance. They are in a very good position to compare the more abstract data gathered in research situations with the concrete daily information obtained from their athletes. Being outside observers in the training process, they are in a good position to analyze the situation in a more objective way. It is surprising, in this context, that coaches have not been more frequently tapped as sources of information on the factors that make the difference between succeeding and failing in a given athletic domain. They might help not only to pinpoint variables that have been overlooked by scientists, but also to suggest different ways of measuring variables already known to play a significant role in the development of athletic talent.

The two exploratory studies described here have sought to assess how coaches rank various factors known to predict to some degree the performance of top level athletes. The studies differ essentially in the athletic domains sampled and the instrument used to obtain ranked judgments.

## STUDY 1

### Method

#### Subjects

The sample of 50 coaches came from four Dutch national teams: judo ($n$ = 11), speed skating ($n$ = 9), swimming ($n$ = 24), and table tennis ($n$ = 6). All were males, except for three swimming coaches. The ages of coaches varied from 32 to 65, with an average of 44.5 years (median age 47 years); experience (at the national team level) varied from one to 35 years, with an average of 6.5 years (median: five years). Following a telephone conversation in which the general aim of the investigation was discussed and their cooperation was obtained, the questionnaire was mailed to the coaches, who returned it by mail. Only 18% of the 61 coaches approached did not complete the questionnaire.

#### Instrument

The ranking carried out by the coaches was part of a longer questionnaire designed to gather information about strategies for coping with various mental or psychological problems encountered by athletes under their direction (see van Rossum, 1992a,b). Coaches were asked to rank eight general factors deemed to have at least a minimal impact on the performance of top-level athletes. These were identified from the literature, as well as through extensive interviews with a small group of experienced coaches. The eight factors are listed in the following in the order of presentation in the questionnaire (alphabetical order in Dutch):

1. *physical fitness* (physiological capacities such as strength, endurance, flexibility, speed);
2. *social recognition* (receiving recognition and appraisal at school, at work, in the athletic environment; i.e., how the athlete is recognized by society);
3. *social guidance* (support in educational affairs (school/college/job training; arranging things, financial or material support; i.e., what help the athlete receives regarding schooling, career planning, etc.);
4. *mental fitness* (psychological characteristics such as competitiveness, concentration, persistence, self-confidence);

5. *natural endowment* (innate physical, motor and/or mental qualities);
6. *motor skill* (the repertoire of sport–motor skills for the specific sport; i.e., the motor–technical aspect);
7. *tactical ability* (ability to "read the game;" changing strategy during a game; choosing the right move during play, or finding the appropriate solution to a game problem);
8. *quantity of training* (the number of hours spent to maintain and improve physical, motor or mental skills; that is, the product of the number of practice sessions multiplied by their duration).

Subjects were asked to assign rank 1 to the factor judged most important "to be successful as an athlete in their team" by the coach, rank 2 to the second most important factor, and so on. Equal ranks for two factors were accepted. Coaches could add factors to the list; five did so, introducing "working hard and being committed" ($n$ = 2), "professional guidance," "daily routine (diet, rest, sleep, school)," and "support of immediate social environment (parents, friends, school)."

## Results

Kendall coefficients of concordance were computed to assess agreement among respondents within a given sport. The values were .36 for judo, .86 for speed skating, .60 for swimming, and .30 for table tennis; they indicate satisfactory agreement in only two of the teams of coaches. However, despite the low level of agreement among coaches in judo and table tennis, the pooled rankings of these eight factors (i.e., the rank order based on the mean rank within a group) were almost identical in the four groups. The mean rankings are presented in Table 29-1. In fact, Spearman rank correlations between the first three sports were .93, .88, and .95, respectively, all statistically significant ($p <$ .01). Even when these three groups of coaches were compared with those in table tennis, the correlation coefficients were .68 ($p_{1-4} <$ .05), .68 ($p_{2-4} <$ .05), and .60 ($p_{3-4}$ .05). Natural endowment was ranked most important in three of the four sports, closely followed by motor skill; physical fitness and mental fitness were also judged to be very important in the four groups. The remaining four factors were judged to be less important by all four groups of coaches.

TABLE 29-1
Mean Rankings by Coaches in Four Sports of Eight Factors
Affecting the Performance of Top Level Athletes*

|  | Judo | Speed skating | Swimming | Table tennis |
|---|---|---|---|---|
| 1. Physical fitness | 2.65 (4) | 2.00 (3) | 2.63 (2) | 2.83 (3) |
| 2. Social recognition | 4.67 (8) | 5.13 (8) | 6.42 (8) | 5.00 (8) |
| 3. Social guidance | 3.60 (7) | 4.22 (7) | 5.29 (6) | 3.83 (7) |
| 4. Mental fitness | 2.09 (2) | 2.78 (4) | 3.17 (4) | 2.17 (2) |
| 5. Natural endowment | 1.60 (1) | 1.00 (1) | 1.79 (1) | 3.17 (5) |
| 6. Motor skill | 2.27 (3) | 1.89 (2) | 2.83 (3) | 1.50 (1) |
| 7. Tactical ability | 3.46 (6) | 4.17 (6) | 5.32 (7) | 3.17 (5) |
| 8. Quantity of training | 2.80 (5) | 3.88 (5) | 3.79 (5) | 3.00 (4) |

*The numbers in parentheses indicate the rank of the factor within a particular group of coaches.

## STUDY 2

### Method

#### Subjects

The sample of 65 coaches came from three different sports: field hockey ($n = 27$), golf ($n = 19$), and track and field ($n = 19$); they were all working at the highest level of competition in their respective fields. All but two coaches in both the field hockey and track and field samples were males. The ages of coaches varied from 25 to 61, with an average of 39.8 years (median age 39 years); experience at the highest competition level varied from one to 37 years, with an average of 6.8 years (median: four years).

#### Instrument

For the field hockey and the track and field coaches, a question similar to that in Study 1 was inserted in a short questionnaire designed to assess the coaches' views on the impact of various general and psychological factors on the development and performance of athletes in their disciplines. For the golf coaches, the question was included in a longer questionnaire devised to make an inventory of their views about various facets of talent development in Dutch golf. Two factors were added to the eight used in Study 1: (a) *contact with coaching staff* (social relationships with the members of the coaching staff), (b) *contact with team members* (social relationships with other athletes in the team). Respondents were asked to rate the importance of each factor "to be a successful athlete in their team," and think of a "typical" athlete in their field instead of one person in particular. Instead of ranking the factors as in Study 1, they were asked to distribute 100 points among the 10 factors so that the distribution would represent the relative importance of the various factors as contributors to the success of a top-level athlete.

### Procedure

For the field hockey and track and field coaches, the questionnaires were distributed and completed as part of a workshop on the psychology of sports given by the first author. Coaches in track and field were asked to assess two types of athletes: (a) the "explosive" athlete who participates in technical events (e.g., discus throw, high jump, etc.) or runs distances up to 400 m; and (b) the "endurance" athlete who runs middle- and long-distance events. Questionnaires were filled out on the spot and anonymously returned to the workshop leader. For the golf coaches, the questionnaire was mailed to coaches through the Dutch Golf Federation, and was returned directly to the first author. Only four (17%) of the 23 coaches approached did not return a completed questionnaire.

### Results

A minority of coaches (42%) distributed their 100 points among the 10 categories. The categories most often left unused were social recognition (in 41% of the cases), contact with team members (32%), contact with coaching staff (26%), social guidance (only in golf and in field hockey: 17%), and tactical ability (especially in track and field "explosive": 19%). Still, a large majority of the respondents used at least eight of the 10 categories, namely 67% in field hockey, 63% in golf, 84% in track and field "explosive" and 74% in track and field "endurance."

Kendall coefficients of concordance were computed to assess agreement among respondents. The values were .56 for field hockey, .48 for golf, .66 for track and field "explosive," and .52 for track and field "endurance;" these agreement indices are similar to those obtained in Study 1. Table 29-2 presents the average number of points attributed to the 10 factors by the three groups of coaches, as well as the average over the four athletic disciplines.

Mental fitness, natural endowment, and physical fitness came out clearly as the most important factors among these four ath-

TABLE 29-2
Mean Number of Points Attributed by Coaches to 10 Factors
Affecting the Performance of Top Level Athletes

|  | Field hockey | Golf | Track and field | | Average |
|---|---|---|---|---|---|
|  |  |  | Expl | Endu |  |
| 1. Physical fitness | 13.0 | 9.4 | 20.5 | 23.8 | 16.7 |
| 2. Social recognition | 2.2 | 3.5 | 5.3 | 4.6 | 3.9 |
| 3. Social guidance | 5.0 | 5.2 | 7.0 | 8.2 | 6.4 |
| 4. Mental fitness | 20.4 | 20.0 | 13.2 | 14.4 | 17.0 |
| 5. Natural endowment | 16.4 | 19.1 | 18.5 | 14.1 | 17.0 |
| 6. Motor skill | 13.3 | 14.7 | 13.6 | 4.6 | 11.6 |
| 7. Tactical ability | 11.7 | 8.8 | 2.0 | 6.4 | 7.2 |
| 8. Quantity of training | 8.3 | 10.2 | 12.4 | 15.4 | 11.6 |
| 9. Contact/training staff | 3.7 | 4.0 | 5.0 | 4.5 | 4.3 |
| 10. Contact/team members | 6.1 | 4.3 | 2.1 | 3.0 | 3.9 |
| Totals | 100.1 | 99.2 | 99.6 | 99.0 | 99.6 |

letic disciplines, with respective averages of 17.0, 17.0, and 16.7 points. Motor skill and quantity of training, with averages of 11.5 and 11.6 points, respectively, appear to be less important, whereas the remaining five factors were judged about equally to be of little importance in determining the success of top-level athletes in these three sports. Both disciplines within track and field were judged in a very similar way, except for the greater importance given to motor skills in the "explosive" domain. Field hockey and golf bore a strong resemblance to each other, although differing from both track and field disciplines in many ways. First, there was a reversal of importance between physical fitness and mental fitness, although both remained among the three most important factors. Second, tactical ability was perceived as much more important in field hockey, probably because it is a team sport. Finally, quantity of training was judged to be much less important in hockey and golf than in track and field. In spite of these differences, the four sets of rankings remain fairly well correlated with Spearman rank correlations of .95 ($p_{1-2} < .05$), .62 ($p_{1-3} < .05$), .48 ($p_{1-4} < .10$), .67 ($p_{2-3} < .05$), .58 ($p_{2-4} < .05$), .65 ($p_{3-4} < .10$).

## Discussion

The coefficients of concordance in both studies show clearly that agreement between coaches regarding their ranking of these general predictors of success was not always very high, and in some cases was rather low. These important individual differences indicate that coaches within a given sport do not share an identical frame of mind in terms of the relative weight they attribute to the various causal factors affecting the performance of their top level athletes. There is no uniform theoretical framework guiding the planning of the training regimens of the athletes. Nonetheless, despite these individual differences, certain general tendencies common to all the sports investigated in these two exploratory studies were visible, as well as certain emphases specific to individual sports. In this latter case, consider for instance the rather unimportant role attributed to natural endowment by coaches in table tennis as compared with the top ranking given by coaches in the three other sports involved in Study 1, the low importance of tactical abilities for "endurance" athletes in track and field, or the prime importance of physical fitness in the two track and field domains as opposed to the other sports. In assessing the very low ranking of the "social relationship" categories within track and field, golf and even field hockey, it should be remembered that the question to the coaches was formulated in such a manner that individual success was to be assessed, *not* the success of a team. Thus, in each of the seven sports considered, even in the team sport context of field hockey, the focus was on the performance of the *individual* athlete.

The different emphasis on some factors by coaches in particular sports does not prevent the presence of a general hierarchy common to all the sports examined in these two studies; this is confirmed by the generally high rank order correlations between the various series of rankings. First, the particular ranking technique used in Study 2 confirmed that none of the 10 proposed factors was completely ignored by the raters, even though some individual coaches did not use all the categories to distribute their 100 points. In Study 1, four factors shared the first four ranks, not necessarily in the same order: physical fitness, mental fitness, natural endowment, and motor skills. The first three reappear in Study 2, whereas motor skills and quantity of training are not too far behind, occupying the middle of the distribution. The three factors judged of less importance in Study 1, social recognition, social guidance, and tactical abilities, also occupy the lower ranks in Study 2, with contact with training staff and contact with team members. The lack of importance given to these factors indicates that coaches in the sports sampled do not consider environmental support to have a major impact on the success of their athletes.

This finding directly contradicts the thesis defended by Bloom (1985) in his study. Without formally negating the existence of natural abilities or aptitudes, Bloom (p. 544) emphasized overwhelmingly the role of the immediate environment (parents, peers and teachers) as a major influence in the development of the highly talented people he studied.

> We speculate that if the talented individuals we studied had been reared in a very different home environment, it is probable that their initial instruction and encouragement to learn would have been very different. And it is not likely that they would have reached the level or type of talent development for which they were included in this study (1985, p. 544).

This type of conclusion is not surprising because of the well known theoretical position of Bloom in favor of behaviorism, a position clearly affirmed in the very first pages of his 1985 book. In that book, Bloom continually downplayed the role of natural abilities, even when they appeared clearly in the interviews; not a single subsection of any chapter is devoted to the role of aptitudes as contributory factors to the development of talent. However, there could be many other explanations for the discrepancy in results between both studies, for instance diverging points of view between the sources of information, coaches in the present case, athletes and parents in Bloom's case. The method of data collection could also create differences, since the instrument in this study offered a list of possible causal factors, although Bloom's approach let the subjects' memories guide their answers. Moreover, Bloom did not describe his interview schedule; it could be that not a single question covered the subject of aptitudes. Aptitudes appear in many citations throughout the book, but they are rarely, if ever, dwelt upon as potential causal factors.

The three factors judged as most important by these seven groups of coaches, namely physical fitness, mental fitness and natural endowment, cover three different categories of factors: (a) natural abilities and their morphological and physiological substrate; (b) psychological characteristics that can be cognitive, conative (motivation and persistence) or affective (temperament and character); (c) regular and sustained physical training in order to develop and maintain the specific skills of the particular athletic domain. These three components fit well with Gagné's differentiated model of giftedness and talent described earlier: natural endowment, mental fitness and physical fitness correspond respectively to Gagné's natural abilities, intrapersonal catalysts and learning and practice. Only the environmental catalysts are left in the background by these groups of coaches.

In writing about the search for a champion, Sebastian Coe, a double Olympic gold medalist, emphasized (Coe, Teasdale, & Wickham, 1992) that champions are made not born. Dutch coaches of top level athletes in the present studies confirmed that the mental and physical facets certainly are important, but they also underlined the primary relevance of the genetic element. Long and hard years of skill development, effort, commitment, and help are certainly necessary, but do not appear to be sufficient. Instead of endorsing Coe et al.'s affirmation that "champions are made not born" (pp. 35–36), this large group of Dutch coaches of high level athletes was in fact saying that "champions are born *and* made".

## ACKNOWLEDGMENTS

The data for the first study were collected by Gitte Buitelaar, Maria Prins and Sandra van Rooij, and the golf data in the second study were collected by Rik Ruts, in each case as part of their doctoral theses.

The first study was financially supported by the Dutch organisation "Nederlandse Sport Federatie," whereas the Dutch Golf Federation has been very supportive in helping to obtain part of the data for the second study.

## REFERENCES

Bloom, B. S. (Ed.). (1985). *Developing talent in young people.* New York: Ballantine Books.

Bompa, T. O. (1985). Talent identification. *Science Periodical on Research and Technology in Sport* (February). Ottawa: Coaching Association of Canada.

Boose, J., & Gaines, B. (1988). *Knowledge acquisition tools for expert systems* (Vol. 2). Toronto: Academic Press.

Chi, M. T. H., Glaser, R., & Rees, E. (1982). Expertise in problem solving. In R. J. Sternberg (Ed.), *Advances in the psychology of human intelligence* (Vol. 1) (pp. 7–75). Hillsdale, NJ: Erlbaum.

Coe, S., Teasdale, D., & Wickham, D. (1992). *More than a game: Sport in our time.* London: BBC Books.

Gagné, F. (1985). Giftedness and talent: Reexamining a reexamination of the definitions. *Gifted Child Quarterly, 29*, 103–112.

Gagné, F. (1993). Constructs and models pertaining to exceptional human abilities. In K. A. Heller, F. J. Mönks, & A. H. Passow (Eds.), *International handbook of research and development of giftedness and talent* (pp. 69–87). Oxford: Pergamon Press.

Havlicek, I., Komadel, L., Komarik, E., & Simkova, N. (1982, June). *[Principles of the selection of youth talented in sport]*. Paper presented at the International Conference on the Selection and Preparation of Sport Talent. Bratislava, Czechoslovakia.

Hemery, D. (1986). *The pursuit of sporting excellence: A study of sport's highest achievers*. London: Willow Books.

Régnier, G., Salmela, J., & Russell, S. J. (1993). Talent detection and development in sport. In R. N. Singer, M. Murphey, & L. K. Tennant (Eds.), *Handbook of research on sport psychology* (pp. 290–313). New York: Macmillan.

Renzulli, J. S. (1979). *What makes giftedness: A reexamination of the definition of the gifted and talented*. Ventura, CA: Ventura County Superintendent of Schools Office.

Renzulli, J. S. (1986). The three-ring conception of giftedness: A developmental model for creative productivity. In R. J. Sternberg & J. E. Davidson (Eds.), *Conceptions of giftedness* (pp. 53–92). New York: Cambridge University Press.

Russell, S. J. (1990). Athletes' knowledge in task perception, definition and classification. *International Journal of Sport Psychology, 21*, 85–101.

van Rossum, J. H. A. (1992a). *Talent-ontwikkeling: Loopbaan en kenmerken van topsporters* [Talent development: Career and characteristics of top level athletes]. Arnhem: Nederlandse Sport Federatie.

van Rossum, J. H. A. (1992b). Talent in sport: Characteristics of top-level athletes according to their coaches. In E. A. Hany & K. A. Heller (Eds.), *Competence and responsibility* (Vol. 1) (pp. 173–175). Göttingen: Hogrefe & Huber.

# 30

# Imaginative Psychotherapy in the Psychological Care of Top Athletes

**Ferenc Süle**

*National Institute of Sports Medicine, Budapest, Hungary*

The way of life of top athletes imposes a burden exceeding the average not only on the biological but also on the psychological level. Apart from somatic problems, this may result in psychological disturbances that necessitate psychotherapeutic treatment. To achieve peak performance, both somatically and mentally superior levels of health and strength are needed. On the basis of this conviction, 50 first-class young sportsmen were prepared over a period of six to eight months, using procedures such as autogenic training, imaginative psychotherapy, imaginative mental training, and training on altered states of consciousness. Results indicated that these athletes suffered fewer injuries, were less often absent from training, obtained fewer competition results below their training performance, and showed more frequent improvement of performance. These findings show that psychotherapeutic work with top athletes can be a useful part of their preparation.

## INTRODUCTION

Sport basically is a good form of compensation for the civilized lifestyle of today, with its lack of physical activity. However, top athletes are overburdened by excessive activity. This is why increasing activity among sport psychologists is being observed, especially the clinically oriented: The method most frequently used by them involves different forms of relaxation therapy, but this supports the culture of passivity that is part of modern life. On the basis of previous experiments it can be said that the way of life of top athletes involves a burden exceeding the average not only in the biological but also in the psychological domain. This may result not only in somatic but also in psychological disturbances that require psychotherapeutic treatment. This is one of the reasons why psychotherapeutic methods need to be applied. The other main reason is that of achieving peak performance—both somatically and mentally above-average levels of health and strength are needed. For this work on the sports field, methods adopted from pedagogical and work psychology are not sufficient. My colleagues and I use different psychotherapeutic methods, most frequently imaginative psychotherapy, which is a deep psychological method, a dynamically oriented brief psychotherapy.

A number of theoretical considerations based on our experiences have emerged: The whole personality must be considered, not simply the conscious part but the unconscious too. This is a basic problem among coaches and sport psychologists, and is a frequent cause of ineffectiveness in their work with sportsmen and women—they take into consideration only the conscious part of personality or those parts that can be reached through the conscious ego. However, the more serious problems are located in the unconscious parts of the personality and these strata must be reached in order to reach the depths of the individual's personality and become effective. The better the inner psychic harmony and integration, the better the concentration of somatic and psychic energy. Imaginative psychotherapy has proved to be an excellent way of breaking down the resistance of athletes who do not accept psychotherapy.

In the course of routine personality examinations of top athletes, four practical diagnostic groups have been distinguished.

1.  Those showing psychiatric symptoms. In a year one or two psychotics and a large number of neurotics and alcoholics are seen.

2. Those having psychological problems or disturbances (observed by the athletes or their coaches) which do not reach the level of psychiatric illness; for instance, anxiety before performance, worse performance in competition than training.
3. Those with latent psychological disturbances; the athletes and coaches have no complaints but personality tests (Rorschach, Leary, Szondi, PFT, Lüscher, Wartegg, DAP, TAT) show serious psychic conflicts and disharmonies.
4. Those without complaints and serious latent problems: the healthy group.

Fifty first-class young sportsmen have undertaken the method described here and have completed it. The method of psychological preparation was the following: 1. Examination/in depth interview, personality tests, questionnaires during the first three days. 2. Preparation: once a week 1–1.5 hours of (a) Autogenic training; (b) Imaginative psychotherapy. In the first 12 sessions inductive pictures were general and constant (meadow, stream, mountain, house, cave, bottom of the sea, forest, childhood, good dream, bad dream, something startling, after 10 years). The following 7–20 pictures were sports specific and individual; (c) 7–12 sessions of imaginative mental training (= mental training on the altered states of consciousness of imagination).

The psychological preparation program was led by competent psychotherapists with long clinical practice—a psychiatrist and two clinical psychologists. The whole preparation period took at least six to eight months. Some of the athletes continued the psychological work beyond this period. The preparation always closed with an individual program that the sportsmen could practice independently and apply or develop autonomously if necessary. The best way of evaluating the program was its effectiveness in real life sport. It was difficult to conceive methods capable of grasping practical processes and values, but the criteria examined were

1. The number of sports injuries;
2. the number of days of absence from training and competition;
3. the number of cases of worse results in competition than in training;
4. the number of improved scores.

### TABLE 30-1
### Pre- and Post-Treatment Scores

| | Results | |
|---|---|---|
| | **Previous Three Months** | **Last Three Months** |
| Injuries | 47 | 6 |
| Absenses | 138 | 21 |
| Worse results | 83 | 7 |
| Score change | +22<br>=58<br>−83 | 93<br>39<br>15 |

+ = improved
= = no change
− = worse

The data were recorded for the three months before the treatment and the last three months of treatment, and relevant figures compared. Results of this comparison are shown in Table 30-1.

The results show that the psychotherapeutic work with top athletes helped their sports activity, but the more important consequence was their improved mental health and psychic stability. Clinical psychological methods and in depth psychological procedures can bring a qualitative improvement in the mental preparation of top athletes. Unfortunately, the education of experts working in the fields of sport in this way is insufficient. Applied psychotherapeutic methods, apart from their importance in preparation for peak performance, have a preventive effect for the future. The growing inner harmony stabilizes the development of the young personality.

# Section V

---

## Creativity
## and Curiosity

# 31

# Specific Intellectual Intentions and Creative Giftedness

**Larisa V. Shavinina**

*Institute of Psychology, Kiev, Ukvaine*

Intellectual giftedness is a complex psychological phenomenon. Further investigation of its essence requires study of unknown or little known phenomena, one of which is intellectual intentions. These can be considered the highest level of manifestation of the intellectual potentials of a personality. They can be defined as "subjective, internally developed standards of performance" and "norms of intellectually creative behaviour" (feeling of direction, beliefs, preferences, and so on). Understanding of intellectual intentions of gifted, creative, and talented persons will provide fundamental information about the nature of giftedness.

## INTRODUCTION

The phenomenon of intellectual intentions is seldom studied in the psychological literature. Despite this, biographical data on outstanding scientific geniuses show that their thinking processes are determined by a *specific feeling of direction*. For example, Einstein, in discussions with Wertheimer (1959) about the development of the theory of relativity and the way of thinking that led to it, said that

> during all those years there was the *feeling of direction*, of going straight toward something concrete. It is, of course, very hard to express that feeling in words; but it was decidedly the case, and clearly to be distinguished from later considerations about the rational form of the solution (p. 228).

Among the other   sorts of intellectual intention, the *specific beliefs* of intellectually gifted personalities connected with the manifestation of a feeling of necessity should also be considered. Simonton (1983) has shown in one of his studies of the relationship between external events and creative development of potential geniuses that they "adapt to the political environment by generating a set of philosophical *beliefs*" (p. 239). Zuckerman (1983), in her investigation of scientific elite (Nobel laureates), found that "the laureates, in their comparative youth, sometimes went to great lengths to *make sure* that they would be working with those they considered the best in their field" (pp. 241–242). This belief (i.e., confidence, which is very often explained as good fortune, fate or chance, etc.) led them to the outstanding masters of their craft—to the scientists of Nobel caliber. It is thus possible to confirm the existence of a feeling of direction in the scientific elite. For example, the biochemist Hans Krebs (1967) reflected

> If I ask myself how it came about that one day I found myself in Stockholm, I have not the slightest doubt that I owe this *good fortune* to the circumstance that I had an outstanding teacher at the critical stage in my scientific career (p. 1444).

The "good fortune" of Krebs is nothing else but the feeling of direction.

According to Kholodnaja (1991), belief in the existence of certain principles and standards, by which the nature of research is determined, and *a priori* confidence in the truth of a certain vision of things are other kinds of beliefs. Zuckerman (1983) found that *elevated standards of performance* (the methods and quality of first-rate research) are essential for Nobel Laureates. In addition, *specific scientific taste* is essential for them. "The prime criteria of it are a sense for the 'important problem' and an appreciation of stylish solutions. For them, deep problems and elegant solutions distinguish excellent science from the merely competent or commonplace" (p. 249). Finally, intellectual intentions can be found in *specific preferences*. For example, they exist in an inevitable choice of scientific field, in unusual kinds of investigations and in the development of new methods for obtaining information (Kholodnaja, 1991; Shavinina, 1993a,b).

Despite findings such as those just mentioned, scientific understanding of the nature of intellectual intentions is still at the beginning. Some further results will be presented here.

## INTELLECTUAL INTENTIONS IN THE CASE OF FULFILLED INTELLECTUAL GIFTEDNESS

The present research on intellectual intentions had two stages. In the first, a case study of the intellectual intentions of an outstanding and well-known Russian scientist—V. I. Vernadsky—was conducted. He was a prominent geologist, biochemist, geochemist, geobiochemist, philosopher, and historian of science. He was a founder of such sciences as geochemistry, biochemistry, geobiochemistry, and of many scientific theories like the theory of the biosphere, the theory of the noosphere, and so on. I have investigated Vernadsky's intellectual intentions by studying relevant biographical materials (letters, diaries, etc.).

There is considerable evidence of Vernadsky's *aspiration to harmony and beauty* in everything (in cognition, in science, and in life as a whole). Perhaps the difference between gifted and ordinary individuals is that gifted personalities are able to see more harmony in life than ordinary people do. Kholodnaja's (1991) definition of intellectual criteria in terms of "standards of work" and "norms of behavior" is not sufficient in the case of Vernadsky, because this definition is confined to work and behavior. His aspiration to harmony and beauty (and this should be especially underlined) had a general character, because it was directed to "life as a whole."

It is possible to assert that Vernadsky had a harmonious vision of reality and an esthetic vision of life. His aspiration to harmony and beauty is to be seen in various fields of his life and work.

1.  In the field of cognition, he wrote: ". . . Looking for clarity where there is scarcely *harmony*." . . . There is a strong

mathematical dependence in the shape of crystals; having measured four to five angles you can find out all the *harmony* . . ." "The idea is becoming clearer and clearer and I begin to recognise *the beauty—the harmony* . . . and I have a feeling that I will sort out everything soon. . . ." (Vernadsky, 1988, p. 105).

2. In the field of various interests, the scientist said: ". . . According to my present mood . . . I prefer theatre, rather than novels and tales. There is something in the former which is not worth looking for in the latter. . . . This is the *beauty of construction, the beauty of architecture.* You feel the real *whole beauty* in the shape of this creation as in good architecture or sculpture. . . ." (Vernadsky, 1988, p. 91).

3. In private life, he wrote, for example, to his wife: ". . . I greatly appreciate that you possess a *beautiful harmony of thoughts* and that you live *in harmony with thoughts.* . . ." (Vernadsky, 1988, p. 115).

4. In life as a whole, Vernadsky, admitting the fact that beauty and harmony exist, tried to understand what they are all about and tried to find in them something more general. Therefore, he asked himself, "Is it not the case that *beauty is in thought, in the belief in truth* . . . ?"

According to Vernadsky, the creation of harmony in the universe is only possible through the work of the mind. He wrote: "Thought is the background of personality. . . . It is deathless. . . . It is the *creator of harmony* in universal chaos. . . ." (Vernadsky, 1988, p. 78). He also wrote (Vernadsky, 1988, p. 113).

> How important is the purity of thought?! It seems to me that it is more important than anything else in life, because through it we experience the *desire to seek harmony.* The *feeling of harmony* is brought about this way. One must not think about the negative, or distract oneself with everyday problems and anxieties when all around there is so much space to think *more harmonic, more beautiful,* more important thoughts. . . .

The well-developed "feeling of style" of Vernadsky is related to his *harmonic vision of reality.* He said: "I am reading the books of *Marcus Aurelius* with great pleasure. They are so *wonderful,* there is so much humanity, strength. . . ." (Vernadsky, 1988, p. 63). ". . . What a *wonderful* book—*Don Quixote!* There is so much humanity!" (Vernadsky, 1988, p. 112).

The second manifestation of Vernadsky's intellectual intentions that should be considered is his *understanding of the value of mind work*, the consideration of Thought (Vernadsky wrote this word with a capital letter) as the most important thing in the life of human beings, of all humanity, and the very palpitating and inspired attitude to it. He wrote (Vernadsky, 1988, pp. 75–76)

> *Thought is the most important thing* in the whole life of human beings. It means everything. Goodness, dedication and feelings have a meaning for the life of individual persons. . . . Of course, it is impossible to live without that . . . But for the whole society and for all the people *Thought replaces everything*. I clearly and very strongly feel that it is very important and I am distressed and irritated by everything which could possibly restrict *Thought*. . . .

Vernadsky could not endure the fact, that *Thought is not yet accessible for everyone*. He wrote: ". . . There is no mental search, there are no doubts for the majority of people. They have a quiet family life . . . far from eternal, profound and excruciating, but at the same time beautiful problems, which are proposed by human history. . . ." (Vernadsky, 1988, p. 116). His strongly expressed *faith in the power of ideas* is the special case of this manifestation of intellectual intentions. He said: "There is one power and one strength—an idea. . . ." (Vernadsky, 1988, p. 115). ". . . I think, there is nothing more important than the power of the idea: It drives everything. . . ." (Vernadsky, 1988, p. 107).

The third manifestation of Vernadsky's intellectual intentions which should be considered is his *feeling of "the eternal."* He wrote: "It seems to me that I feel the pulse of eternity in each place and everywhere. . . ." (Vernadsky, 1988, p. 260). As was mentioned, Vernadsky also saw the beauty of life in its "eternal change." A special case of intellectual intentions of the feeling of eternity is Vernadsky's feeling of *"historical process."* He said: "I now have a very strong feeling . . . of historical process" (Vernadsky, 1988, p. 249). Vernadsky was interested in history as a whole and in the history of separate special subjects for a very long time. He tried to consider every single scientific event or problem from the historical point of view and in all aspects of its historical connections.

The fourth manifestation of Vernadsky's intellectual intentions is connected with his *aspiration to the "endlessness"* in scientific cognition: he tried to understand the essence of scientific cosmogony, biochemistry, and so on as the most synthetic events of the objective world. For example, he wrote: "It seems to me, I have a subconscious understanding of scientific cosmogony problems. *Once again, my mind longs for*" (Vernadsky, 1988, p. 230).

The fifth manifestation of Vernadsky's intellectual intentions is his *aspiration to see clarity* in everything. He said: "I often seek the clarity in there, where there is no harmony. . . ." (Vernadsky, 1988, p. 81). One of the distinctive peculiarities of Vernadsky's cognitive experience was his wish to understand the absolutely unknown puzzles of the world, of human origins, accompanied by his reflections about the obvious. For example, he wrote: "It seems to me so clear, that it is not worth writing about. However . . ., usually everything which is most clear is the source of delusions of all kinds, because the human mind thinks very little about these problems, because they seem lucid. . . ." (Vernadsky, 1988, p. 142).

## INTELLECTUAL INTENTIONS IN THE CASE OF DEVELOPMENT OF INTELLECTUAL GIFTEDNESS

In the second stage of the present research the intellectual intentions of three gifted, creative, and talented senior pupils in physics and mathematic were studied. The pupils (three boys) have made real life achievements like participation in local, national, and international Olympiads in physics and mathematics, winning first prizes in these Olympiads. They were studying in a physics–mathematics school, the only one in the Ukraine, and were evaluated by teachers as "the most gifted." They were in the ninth or tenth grade and were 15 or 16 years old.

Psychological methods for studying the phenomenon of intellectual intentions do not exist at present—it is well known that the initial research on any new scientific phenomenon lacks adequate methods. For this reason the method used by Wertheimer in his research on Einstein's way of thinking, which led to the theory of relativity, was adopted; conversations with gifted pupils were used in the same way Wertheimer used discussions with Einstein. During long conversations I questioned pupils about the peculiarities of their thinking and cognitive experience. None of my questions was directly related to intellectual intentions. These data arose indirectly during the conversations. The results of the research showed that the following intellectual intentions were characteristic of the gifted pupils.

In the first of the participants, there was a very significant manifestation of intellectual intention in his *aspiration to harmony*, which has a multidirectional character. For example,

1. In the field of his scientific interests, he said: ". . . Each physicist is . . . a lyric poet in the depths of the soul. . . . The physicist feels the *harmony in shape, in form and in a nice theory. . . .*"
2. Of his daily life he said: ". . . It is essential to try to *reach harmony.* . . . Daily life should not be very modest, but it should encourage activity and stimulate only the positive . . . . It should be *in harmony with a person. . . .*"

Two types of manifestation of intellectual intentions were found in the second gifted pupil. One of them can be classified as including "*beliefs.*" For example, to the question "Is it easy for you to get interested in new ideas?" he answered: "I get interested if *it seems to me* that the idea is correct. And I reject it if *I believe* that the idea is wrong. . . . Perhaps, it is not generally correct, but personally for me it seems correct. . . . A new idea is great if *I feel it in my heart. . . .*". The next manifestation of this senior pupil's intellectual intentions is his understanding of the value of the mind. In particular, he said: ". . . *Thought alone makes a human being.* If Thought dies, then the person will also die. . . ." His answer to a question about his life slogan also shows the extremely important status of Thought in his cognitive experience. He said: "*Think!* It is very simple, because if you think—you exist. If you do not think—you do not exist. . . ."

The third pupil's world of intellectual intentions consisted of:

1. the feeling of direction (for example, to the question: "Who is your ideal in science?" he answered: "I do not know . . . but *I feel* at the same time, that *I aspire* to something.");
2. the feeling of faith (for example, his answer to the question "What kind of feeling do you have, when new ideas come to your mind?" was the following: "When ideas come, I think about their practical realisation. Sometimes such ideas come into my mind, although I do not know how to put them into practice. . . . At the same time I very strongly want to do this. *I believe* that it *will happen in the future.* . . ;"
3. the feeling of truth, which is objectively correct and true (his answer to the question: "Is it easy for you to become inter-

ested in new ideas?" shows this manifestation of intellectual intentions: "I get interested easily, if the idea looks promising. *I get a feeling of whether it is correct or wrong. . . .*")

## CONCLUSIONS

The data show that the mind work of gifted, creative and talented personalities is determined by subjective, internally developed standards and orientations that are intellectual intentions. Their negative reaction to any attempts to impose external standards on intellectually creative behavior is not surprising. The results of the present research allow the conclusion that intellectual intentions play a significant part in the understanding of the nature of intellectually creative giftedness. The following three sorts of intellectual intentions are especially important in the understanding of this phenomenon.

1.  The gifted, creative, and talented personalities of all ages have a specific feeling of direction in their creativity and in their life as a whole. The study of intellectual intentions of such individuals is closely connected with present research on the subconscious and unconscious processes of creativity. The study of intellectual intentions should be regarded as one of the ways of studying creativity.
2.  Specific beliefs also belong to gifted, creative, and talented individuals. The world of these beliefs is very diverse and includes the feeling of truth, faith in the power of ideas, and so on. Intellectual intentions as a whole and especially beliefs determine the self-confidence of such personalities and the extraordinary stability of their intellectually creative work.
3.  These individuals are also characterized by specific preferences, including the aspiration to harmony and beauty, the understanding of mind work as very valuable and the consideration of Thought as an important aspect of human life. The feeling of the "eternal," the aspiration to "endlessness" and clarity in everything are among these preferences. Therefore, it can be said that intellectually creative personalities have very specific forms of cognitive direction (in the studying of problems, of themselves, of the world as a whole).

The data permit the conclusion that intellectual intentions are an important criterion of intellectually creative giftedness. It must be pointed out that research on the phenomena of the intellectual intentions of gifted, creative, and talented personalities is a new enterprise. Future research may reveal many more unknown manifestations of intellectual intentions.

## REFERENCES

Kholodnaja M. A. (1991). Psychological mechanisms of intellectual giftedness. *Voprosu psichologii, 1,* 32–39 (in Russian).

Krebs, H. (1967). The making of a scientist. *Nature, 215,* 1441–1445.

Shavinina L. V. (1993a). *Psychological peculiarities of the structure of cognitive experience of intellectually gifted personalities.* Unpublished doctoral dissertation, Institute of Psychology of Ukraine, Kiev (in Russian).

Shavinina L. V. (1993b, May). *Intellectual intentions of gifted and talented personalities.* International scientific-practical conference "Talented personality: family, school, state," Ukraine, Kiev (in Russian).

Simonton D. K. (1983). History and the eminent person. In R. S. Albert (Ed.), *Genius and eminence.* Oxford: Pergamon Press.

Vernadsky, V. I. (1988). *Diaries and letters.* Moscow: Molodaja Gwardia (in Russian).

Wertheimer, M. (1959). *Productive thinking.* Westport, CT: Greenwood Press.

Zuckerman H. (1983). The scientific elite: Nobel Laureates' mutual influences. In R. S. Albert (Ed.), *Genius and eminence.* Oxford: Pergamon Press.

# 32

# Nonverbal Aspects of Creative Thinking
## Studies of Deaf Children

**Anna Paszkowska-Rogacz**

*University of Łódz, Łódz, Poland*

Pictorial figural representations are of essential importance in the cognitive development of the deaf. Creative abilities of the deaf were studied with regard to five components of classroom behavior: motivation, socialization, antisocial behavior, passiveness, and level of intelligence. The subjects were a group of 22 deaf pupils aged 13–15 and a group of hearing children. The Test of Creative Thinking-Drawing Productions (TCT-DP), the Raven Standard Progressive Matrices, and the Pupil Behavior Inventory were used to examine main trends. Comparisons indicated that no significant difference was found between the school functioning of the hearing and the nonhearing in achievement motivation and antisocial behavior. However, in socialization and in intelligence level the nonhearing were significantly lower than the hearing. TCT-DP results showed that the number of thematic solutions and humor responses increased with deafness, and certain elements became more stereotypical, less individual, and less original. In addition, IQ in deaf pupils was related to the drawing of concrete objects, whereas in the hearing group intelligence level was related to use of abstractions.

## INTRODUCTION

Contemporary studies on the development of deaf children rarely concern themselves with creative thinking. In a few papers of this type (Furth, 1966; Kunicka-Kaiser, 1976; Stein, 1986) the authors stressed that a weak methodological basis and other substantial difficulties limit psychological analysis of this problem. In the field of psychology of deafness, particular difficulties are caused by defining many relations in the same way, such as relations between linguistic competence, level of abstraction, and operational thinking ability. Conceptual weakness among the deaf connected with their lack of linguistic experience is beyond doubt but, according to many authors (Furth & Younis, 1971; Myklebust, 1964; Oleron, 1972), whereas linguistic experience can increase the effectiveness of creation of ideas, it is not a necessary condition for developing elementary thinking ability. Undoubtedly, sensory deprivation of a deaf child alters in a fundamental way the effect of this experience on visual sensation. A defect of hearing adds to the severity of limitations of differentiating between symbols and makes the child dependent upon recognized contents.

On the other hand, research on the creative act by Shepard (Kozielecki, 1986) showed that in many cases a linguistic code plays a smaller role than a conceptual one. A hypothesis was even stated that the most original, unusual, and fantastic ideas are easier to perform in a mental picture than in a linguistic form. Abstract language is a very convenient form for transmitting conventional and stereotypical contents. Probably the indefiniteness and ambiguity of the term "creativity" are the cause of the tendency to use linguistic codes in opposition to mental pictures, and so it seems to be necessary to establish a proper criterion of creativity.

Recently some researchers (Necka, 1986; Urban, 1988, 1991) have tried to treat the process of creativity in a holistic way. Creativity is understood by them as the ability to create new, unusual, and surprising products, solving problems perceived intuitively or putting forward problems whose hidden meaning has been perceived intuitively. This process occurs thanks to conscious or unconscious understanding of the meaning of given data or purposful search for meaning. Data coming from experience and images are associated, analyzed, matched, and structured into a new form (gestalt). Conscious and unconscious processes are parallel. The product can be the subject of following recreations. Finally it can be presented to other people, who can learn its meaning by understanding or intuitive experience.

This approach, which stresses the role of images in creativity, is related in the present paper to data concerning the development of deaf children. The aim of the research is to solve two types of problem: the abilities and creativity of deaf children; interdependence between creativity and its intellectual and social correlates.

## METHOD

The subject was a group of 22 deaf pupils aged 13–15 (12 girls and 10 boys) and an equal-sized group of hearing children. The Test for Creative Thinking-Drawing Productions (TCT-DP) by Jellen and Urban, the Raven Standard Progressive Matrices and the Pupil Behavior Inventory (AZU) by Markowska and Szafraniec (1980) were used to obtain data. The tests were administered in two ways, verbally and using sign language with deaf children, verbally with hearing children. The children did the TCT-DP first, followed by the Raven scale. The AZU questionnaires were filled out by the tutors. All the tests were given and evaluated by the same trained person.

The groups of hearing and nonhearing children were compared on the Raven scale (scored in centiles), four AZU scales (motivation for school learning, antisocial behavior, passiveness, socialization) and particular criteria of the TCT-DP, using $t$-tests. Children obtaining results consistent with age standards were included in the study. Correlations (Pearson $r$) between particular variables within the groups were also calculated.

## RESULTS

The first differences between the groups were noticed during the instructions to the children. The hearing children were amused and eager to work. The nonhearing children demanded many explanations and arbitrariness in fulfilling the task appeared to be their biggest problem. They had to be assured many times that they could draw what they wished. The deaf children reacted in a quite different way to the intellectual test. That situation was felt to be neutral. They were concentrated and curious. The behavior of the hearing children during administration of the Raven test was similar.

The data showed that levels of intellectual abilities in the non-hearing group were more differentiated. The average number of correctly solved problems on the Raven scale ($M = 45.6$) was lower than in the hearing ($M = 59.5$) but this difference was not statistically significant. The comparison of social behavior on the four AZU scales indicated a significantly higher level among hearing children than among nonhearing ($M = 41$ vs. $M = 35$) only as far as socialization was concerned ($t (42) = 3.04; p < .01$). Other differences were not significant.

As far as particular categories of creativity were concerned, the hearing children were higher on most quantitative categories. Comparing their general results with test norms showed that the scores fell within average limits (girls $M = 35$; boys $M = 30$). Deaf boys were low in the average category ($M = 16$), deaf girls were in the group with low results ($M = 9.5$). Deaf children more often copied fragments ($t (42) = 2.11; p < .05$) and omitted details of the picture less frequently than the hearing ($t (42) = 3.28; p < .01$). A comparison of results obtained by girls and boys showed that in the hearing group sex is not a factor in creativity scores. In the nonhearing group, however, boys obtained better general TCT-DP test results than girls ($t (20) = 3.07; p < .01$). They also got more points in the categories of completion ($t (20) = 4.63; p < .01$), joining ($t (20) = 2.57; p < .05$) and putting fragments into concrete pictures ($t (20) = 3.90; p < .01$). Girls more often copied fragments ($t (20) = 2.23; p < .05$) and put them into abstract pictures ($t (20) = 3.43; p < .01$). In both groups boys and girls had the same Raven scale results.

Results of the tests were correlated in order to explain relationships between creativity and mental level and social behavior. It appeared that the general TCT-DP result of the deaf is negatively correlated with passiveness ($r = -.435; p < .05$); passiveness is associated with lower levels of creativity. Content relation or thematic composition and motivation to learn ($r = -.544; p < .01$) as well as intellectual level and abstraction in pictures ($r = -.484; p < .05$) were negatively correlated too. Statistically significant correlations appeared for sense of humor and antisocial behavior ($r = .553; p < .01$). Unconventionality was positively correlated with time spent on drawing productions ($r = .670; p < .01$) and sense of humor ($r = .461; p < .05$). Raven results were positively correlated with concrete drawing ($r = .532; p < .05$). In the hearing group there was a positive correlation between extension of small fragments and passiveness ($r = .499$; $p < .05$). Passiveness also appeared while drawing concretely ($r = .429$; $p < .05$). Raven scale results in the hearing group in comparison with the deaf had a reverse relationship with the way of drawing figures—abstract or concrete; they were positively correlated with abstraction ($r = .589$; $p < .01$) and negatively correlated with concreteness ($r = -.464$; $p < .05$).

The TCT-DP test does not analyse the content of the drawings. Some characteristic titles can be given, however, as examples. In the nonhearing group titles seldom appeared or small drawings were named "a house," "a vase," "a right angle," "geometry," "a game." The hearing children's titles were put into words for example, "A dream," "The Mirrors of Egypt," "The Goddess of Life," "The Unexpected Man." The theme of drawings was more often abstracted from the geometric form of the stimulus.

## DISCUSSION

The results concern both ways of carrying out the tasks and relations between variables. Deaf children were strongly subordinated to orders, girls more than boys, which is in line with cultural standards and developmental features of 13- to 15-year-olds. It is also a rather frequent effect of an institutional upbringing (boarding school) where these standards are more strongly stressed. Deaf children tried to carry out the task honestly, omitting no parts. If they had no idea for an original drawing, they simply copied the pattern.

Higher intelligence in the deaf was accompanied by a higher aptitude for the concrete in the case of the hearing for the abstract. This result is interesting, as the mental level measure was based on abstract stimuli. The concrete drawings of deaf children of higher mental level, however, were original and unconventional. The results undoubtedly are related to the development of language, but they are related to the dominant stimulation provided by the environment in which the children were brought up. Teaching deaf children aims at developing conceptual thinking, building analogies and synthesis, but it does this mainly on the basis of concrete material. This concrete material appeals to the imagination. According to the results of the analysis, it can be assumed that nonverbal creativity of the deaf is not lower than, but different from that of the hearing. In terms of psychoneurology, the right cerebral hemisphere is responsible for the creativity of the deaf, whereas in the case of the hearing the right cerebral hemisphere is not the only source of creativity. This conclusion calls for further studies on the creative thinking of deaf people, with the use of verbal and motor stimuli.

## REFERENCES

Furth, H. G. (1966). A review and perspective on the thinking of deaf people. *Volta Review, 68*, 35–36.

Furth, H. G., & Younis, J. (1971). Formal operations and language. A comparison of deaf and hearing adoescents. *International Journal of Psychology, 6*, 49–64.

Kozielecki, J. (1986). Mechanizmy dzialan tworczych [Mechanisms of creative activity]. *Kwartalnik Pedagogiczny, 31*, 11–22.

Kunicka-Kaiser, I. (1976). Charakterystyka procesów myslenia dzieci gluchych [The characteristics of deaf children's thinking processes]. In T. Galkowski & J. Smolenska (Eds.), *Psychologia dziecki gluchego* [The psychology of the deaf child] (pp. 120–143). Warsaw: PWN.

Markowska, B., & Szafraniec, H. (1980). *Testy psychologiczne w paradnictwie wychowawao-zawodowym* [Psychological tests in educational guidance]. Warsaw: PWN.

Myklebust, H. R. (1964). *The psychology of deafness.* New York: Grune and Stratton.

Necka, E. (1986). On the nature of creative talent. In A. J. Cropley, K. K. Urban, H. Wagner, & W. Wieczerkowski (Eds.), *Giftedness: A continuing worldwide challenge* (pp. 131–140). New York: Trillium Press.

Oleron, P. (1972). *Langue et developpment mental.* Bruxelles: Charles Dessart Editeur.

Stein, M. I. (1986). *Gifted, talented and creative young people: A guide to theory, teaching and research.* New York: Garland Publishing Inc.

Urban, K. K. (1988, November). Recent trends in creativity research and theory in Western Europe. Paper presented at the First ECHA Conference "High Ability—a European Persective," Zurich.

Urban, K. K. (1991). On the development of creativity in children. *Creativity Research Journal, 4*, 177–191.

# 33

# Creative Writing

## Fostering Verbal Gifts in Young People

**Joachim Schöpfel**

*Institut de l'Information Scientifique et Technique (C.N.R.S.),*
*Vandoeuvre-lès-Nancy Cedex, France*

In the context of German educational projects for gifted youth, an interdisciplinary model of identification and fostering of verbally gifted adolescents in an out of school course ("creative writing") was developed and carried out at Hamburg University from 1984 to 1990. The present chapter offers an introduction to its main objectives and to the identification and selection process, the curriculum and the results of an evaluation, with concluding remarks on redefining the concept of giftedness.

## INTRODUCTION

As a part of the "Hamburg Model" (Prado, Jansen, & Wieczerkowski, 1990; cf., Birx, 1988), an interdisciplinary research project was started in 1984 at the University of Hamburg (departments of psychology and education), with three objectives.

1. Development of a method of identification and selection of verbally gifted adolescents.
2. Development and evaluation of an adequate program for fostering the development of these adolescents.
3. Redefinition of the concept of verbal giftedness.

The project's results have previously been published (Fritzsche, 1988, 1990a; Fritzsche & Schöpfel, 1990; Schöpfel, 1992). The present chapter attempts an overall summary, dealing mainly with the program evaluation and possible consequences for redefining the concept of giftedness.

## IDENTIFICATION AND SELECTION

The sequential identification strategy integrated multivariate data covering most important domains of verbal giftedness.

Convergent verbal ability (verbal comprehension, verbal induction, analogical reasoning).
Divergent verbal ability (word fluency, fluency of association, fluency of expression).
Text production.

The convergent and divergent verbal ability factors were measured by means of an *ad hoc* test battery including subtests from intelligence, language ability and verbal creativity tests (IST-70, SASKA, VKT; Amthauer, 1971; Riegel, 1967; Schoppe, 1975) and informal, experimental subtests (literary ability, poetic competence). Measures of literary writing ability were taken from private free text production (novels, short stories, lyrics, etc.) and from an "exam text" (literary exercise) written under test conditions. In addition, a number of variables indicating level of motivation and extent of writing experience were assessed by a questionnaire.

Data processing of the different assessment methods may be described as an open, retroactive decision procedure, based on discussions in the identification and selection board (with psychologists and educational staff). In view of the intended program, the decision strategy in the selection process accorded more importance to the interrater judgment of free text production than to ability test scores. Because of the model character of the project, the error rate (estimated at 20%) reflected the intention to reduce false acceptances, most erroneous decisions involving nonselection of individuals who were probably gifted.

Participation in the selection process ("talent search") relied on the self-nomination of motivated and interested adolescents. Consequently, screening and identification largely depended in effect on the amount and the success of previous information among the target group and, further, on cooperation between university and school administration. From 1986 to 1988, 248 adolescents, most of them 12–13 years old and in grade six or seven (71% girls), took part in the project "talent searches." In all 33% ($N = 82$), were offered the possibility of voluntary participation in the program, free of charge.

## "CREATIVE WRITING"—THE PROGRAM

Three issues characterized the educational aspect of the research project.

1. Development and evaluation of an extracurricular out of school program that satisfied the needs of verbally gifted adolescents interested in creative (literary) writing.
2. Creation and evaluation of didactic material and methods.
3. Training of creative writing teachers.

The program's intentions may not be described in terms of mere skill training, but as an attempt at a general enhancement of verbal, esthetic, social, and cognitive abilities by promoting the pleasure of writing. The curriculum derived from a critical interpretation of comparable American models (Barnet & Stubbs, 1983; Kirszner & Mandell, 1983; Reynolds, Kopelke & Durden, 1984) and recent tendencies in German pedagogical discussion of composition and literature teaching (cf., Fritzsche, 1980; Waldmann, 1988; Winterling, 1984). Creative writing, considered as a problem-solving process (Flower, 1981; Hayes & Flower, 1980), was fostered by regular and frequent practice, by a series of exercises motivating idea production, and free writing of short stories, lyrics, journalism, essays, dialogues, and so forth ("learning by doing"). As important as writing were revision (rewriting) and evaluation processes, most of the texts being read and judged by the whole group. Further elements of the curriculum were creative language plays in order to increase verbal creativity and divergent thinking (cf., Torrance 1962, 1965), and presentation of literature likely to interest and motivate reading and writing.

Some remarks on organization and interaction (cf., Fritzsche, 1990b) are necessary here: The course took place in university rooms during term time on three Saturdays per month from 9.00 A.M. to 12.30 P.M. The group size was 10–15 pupils with two teachers, although much of the learning was done in small independent groups of two or three "creative writers." The program included literary workshops on weekends and in the holidays, public lectures, publication of an internal journal, and participation in literary competitions. All selected adolescents had the possibility of attending the program for a period of three years. The dropout rate was low: Only 6% left during the first year; after three years "creative writing," 67% were still coming to the university. Group ambience may be characterized as an environment of acceptance and fairness. This seems to be a most important condition for obtaining original efforts from talented adolescents (Rowe, 1967) and for enhancing the growth and development of creativity (Cropley, McLeod, & Dehn, 1988; Guilford, 1967). Selected course material has been published with appropriate commentary (Fritzsche, 1989; Waldmann & Bothe, 1990). During the project period, 15 teachers participated in training and supervision. Many more came as visitors, asked for course materials or discussed project didactics in educational meetings and conferences.

## PROGRAM EVALUATION

The evaluation of the individual program's effects was "hybrid" in nature (Scriven, 1966), integrating the analysis of the whole sample with in-group differentiation and case studies (George-Gonzalez, 1990), and combining formative issues with an overall summative evaluation. In order to cover a wide range of variables, multiple data sources were utilized and analyzed, including parents' and teachers' evaluation, adolescents' self-assessment, and text analysis. As comparison with an adequate control group was impossible for organizational reasons, the evaluation results may lay claim to a certain plausibility and probability (most of the results mentioned in this chapter were statistically significant with $p < .05$), but need confirmation by further research in order to distinguish course improvement from age or school factors. The main findings were

1. Course participation generally reinforced writing motivation. The amount and frequency of creative writing increased during the first year. Hereafter, private writing activity declined (because of changing interests and increasing school time), and creative writing was centered more and more on course sessions.
2. Stylistic change can be described as involving enhancement of literary competence, acquisition of specific new writing skills, and increasing consciousness of literary possibilities and effects.
3. The amount of planning processes and of "reflective planning" (Molitor, 1984) increased; the adolescents were better able to utilize, realize, modify, and create plans in the writing process.
4. In revision processes, an integration of "deeper revision levels" (Baurmann & Ludwig, 1985) was observed, for example, modification of text structure, changing action logic, and so on.
5. The range of literary forms and themes became broader. The adolescents learned to experiment with more and other text forms (dialogues, lyrics, journalistic articles, essays, or satires) and to write on "more serious" subjects, like personal conflicts, societal problems, historical events, and so on. The amount of pure fictional writing (SF, fantasy, crime fiction, etc.) decreased; more and more, own experiences, thoughts or feelings, and real events became—in realistic description or literary transformation—part of the creative writing.
6. At the same time, the function of creative writing changed. Writing became a "public affair," involving reflection on the production–reception relationship and thus anticipation of authors' intentions and readers' reactions. Course participation tended to differentiate and enrich motivational structures as a result of the integration of affective and cognitive motives, the reinforcement of desire for feedback and reflection on the possible future utility of writing competence (instrumental orientation). In the private writing of older adolescents, an increasing heuristic–epistemic motivation could be assessed.

7. Critical competence changed in three ways: increased self-critical attitude, more acceptance of others' critical judgment, and a better founded, more reflected and differentiated text evaluation in general.
8. Finally, program selection and participation seemed to reinforce self-confidence in writing and success expectation in general achievement behavior. (Increased self-confidence also could be observed in school. However, there were few effects on school achievement, the selected adolescents generally being good or excellent pupils in language subjects.)

In summary, program evaluation showed a wide range of effects involving the writers' long-term memory, including stored writing plans and knowledge of topic and audience, the cognitive "monitor" generating and controlling planning and review processes (cf., Hayes & Flower, 1980), and the subjective function of writing. Considering Bereiter's model of development in writing (Bereiter, 1980), some further statements are possible.

1. At the beginning of the program (after the selection process), almost all participants already showed high fluency ability in written language production and idea generation.
2. The program's effects mainly concerned three skill systems (cf., Bereiter, 1980): "Mastery of written conventions" (rules of style and mechanics), "social cognition" (communicative competence), and "literary appreciation and discrimination" (critical competence). Especially in the first year, a shift from "associative" and "performative" to "communicative writing" generally could be observed. The "integration of one's own evaluative reading skills with one's writing skills," the so-called "unified writing" level was attained by 50–70%.
3. Nevertheless, another skill system, the integration of reflective thought into an "epistemic" writing process, was relatively rare. Only a few older adolescents began, especially in private writing, to reflect and utilize the whole range of cognitive writing functions (Applebee, 1982), like structuring, modifying or generating knowledge in writing.

Although the discussed results concern the whole sample, cluster analysis and case studies provided evidence for differential program outcomes.

1. *Writing frequency and time.* The initial amount of private literary activity correlated with text and criticism quality and literary improvement.
2. *Writing importance.* The subjective consideration of creative writing seemed to have an impact on program participation, commitment, and achievement behavior (productivity). Furthermore, there was apparently a relationship between writing importance, interest in new subjects (personal experience, conflicts, etc.) and a self-conscious, self-critical writing attitude.
3. *Writing motivation.* Adolescents who started with an achievement and heuristic writing orientation and later integrated communicative, instrumental, and playful motives (a somehow typical course structure) generally scored higher in writing and learning assessment.
4. *Verbal ability.* Convergent verbal and nonverbal measures correlated with measures of literary and analytical quality, whereas divergent factors (verbal and ideational fluency) were related mainly to writing productivity.

According to these results, the effects of program participation and writing depended largely on three factors: verbal and cognitive abilities, a self-critical attitude (level of aspiration), and program-oriented achievement motivation. Convergent and divergent factors influenced learning improvement mainly during the first year of participation. They were obviously a necessary but not sufficient condition for learning success and writing quality in the long term. Later on, the impact of other variables increased, like self-confidence, achievement motivation, literary practice, or subjective measures of writing importance. All the same, only very few adolescents failed completely to profit or gained very little from course participation, a fact that emphasizes the program's capacity to integrate a large range of different ability and motivation structures, including latent abilities.

## CONCLUDING REMARKS

Nearly all those involved, parents as well as adolescents and teachers, considered the creative writing model beneficial for cognitive and creative training and personal growth. The main reasons were: the challenging and interesting exercises, the combination of writing and evaluation, the participants' motivation and ability level, and especially the learning climate and group interaction that created an authentic alternative to school, by fostering independence and self-responsibility (autonomy) of learning and working.

After the project period, the creative writing courses continued at Hamburg University for two further years, as part of the program of the William Stern Society. Since 1990 the Hamburg school administration has offered 10 literary workshops for sixth and seventh grade children. Since 1987, literary holiday workshops and summer camps have been organized each year (by the Foundation "Bildung und Begabung," Bonn) for young literary competition winners and other gifted and motivated adolescents. In both cases, didactic principles and materials from the Hamburg curriculum have been adapted to a new context. The writing model seems to be making a successful impact.

And the concept of giftedness? The research and identification strategy was based on a pragmatic multidimensional and interactional theory of giftedness, as proposed by Renzulli (1986), Wieczerkowski and Wagner (1985), and others. According to these models, the program evaluation integrated different approaches to verbal giftedness and creative writing, namely

Structural analysis of the writing process;
Functional analysis of writing motivation and intentions;
Developmental analysis of verbal behavior; and
Factor analysis of intelligence, verbal and ideational fluency, and nonverbal creativity.

Research results provided a solid basis for a typology of verbal giftedness in the different domains, for example, data clustering showed specific approaches of text planning or revision, typical verbal and literary development, and a set of motivation structures that reflected different writing practices and intentions (Schöpfel, 1992). There was strong evidence for an interactional development of verbal giftedness, with ability factors, achievement motivation, an enhancing verbal and cultural context (family, school), and a large range of creative and other out of school activities (cf., Trost, 1990).

Statistically, it was possible to combine the different approaches into a complex structure of giftedness clusters that integrated cognitive, affective, process, and learning variables. Such an atheoretical agglomeration of different data analyses allows an estimate of the degree and structure of ability in the sample, but accounting for the actual state of the art remains unsatisfying as long as there is no *a priori* conceptual integration of different research issues (such as creativity research, action process theory, writing models, and giftedness analyses).

Verbal giftedness, as part of creative-productive giftedness (Renzulli, 1986), cannot be considered as a one-dimensional variable, but has to be redefined as a multitrait concept including ability and performance factors as well as functional and action process variables. Only in this way will the giftedness concept reflect the individual, everyday reality of gifted children and contribute to an appropriate, personalized education and fostering program. What is needed, therefore, is a dialectic research strategy combining

a wide range, exploratory assessment methodology;
an integrating and differentiating data analysis; and
a theoretical concept elaboration.

This future concept will stress the functional (motivation, cf. Passow, 1991), structural (action), and dynamic (learning) aspects of ability, allowing concrete statements on their real relationship. The basis is there—a pragmatic ability concept, educational models, research perspectives, and methods—but much work remains to be done before it is possible to speak of a valid and useful theory of giftedness and high ability.

## ACKNOWLEDGMENTS

From 1986 to 1989, the research described here was supported by the Ministry for Education and Science, Bonn. I would like to thank Prof. Dr. Wieczerkowski and Prof. Dr. Fritzsche (project directors), Dr. Wagner, Dr. Schiebel and T. M. Prado for their assistance during data collection and analysis.

## REFERENCES

Amthauer, R. (1971). *Intelligenz-Struktur-Test (IST-70)*. Göttingen: Hogrefe.

Applebee, A. N. (1982). Writing and learning in school settings. In M. Nystrand (Ed.), *What writers know. The language, process, and structure of written discourse*. New York: Academic Press.

Barnet, S., & Stubbs, M. (1983). *Practical guide to writing.* Boston: Little, Brown.

Baurmann, J., & Ludwig, O. (1985). (Eds.). Texte überarbeiten. Zur Theorie und Praxis von Revisionen. *In D.* Boueke & N. Hopster (Eds.), *Schreiben-Schreiben* levnen (pp. 254–276). Tübingen: Narr.

Bereiter, C. (1980). Development in writing. In L. W. Gregg & E. R. Steinberg, (Eds.), *Cognitive processes in writing.* Hillsdale, NJ: Erlbaum.

Birx, E. (1988). *Mathematik und Begabung.* Hamburg: Krämer.

Cropley, A. J., McLeod, J., & Dehn, D. (1988). *Begabung und Begabungsförderung.* Heidelberg: Asanger.

Flower, L. S. (1981). *Problem solving strategies for writing.* New York: Harcourt Brace Jovanovich.

Fritzsche, J. (1980). *Aufsatzdidaktik.* Stuttgart: Kohlhammer.

Fritzsche, J. (1988). "Was ist literarische Begabung, und wie kann man sie fördern?" *Diskussion Deutsch, 19,* 347–365.

Fritzsche, J. (1989). *Schreibwerkstatt.* Stuttgart: Klett.

Fritzsche, J. (1990a). "Förderung sprachlich begabter Jugendlicher: Erfahrungen und Perspektiven." In H. Wagner (Ed.), *Begabungsforschung und Begabtenförderung in Deutschland 1980–1990–2000.* Bad Honnef: Bock.

Fritzsche, J. (1990b). "Soziale Kontextbedingungen des kreativen Schreibens." In H. Balhorn & H. Brügelmann (Eds.), 4. *Jahrbuch der Deutschen Gesellschaft für Lesen und Schreiben.* Konstanz: Faude.

Fritzsche, J., & Schöpfel, J. (1990). *Abschlussbericht. Forschungsprojekt "Identi-fikation und Förderung sprachlich besonders befähigter Schüler."* Unpublished research report, University of Hamburg.

George-Gonzalez, G. (1990). *Funktion und persönliche Bedeutung des Schreibens bei Jugendlichen.* Unpublished master thesis, University of Hamburg.

Guilford, J. P. (1967). Factors that aid and hinder creativity. In J. C. Gowan, G. D. Demos, & E. P. Torrance (Eds.), *Creativity: Its educational implications.* New York: Wiley.

Hayes, J. R. & Flower, L. S. (1980). Identifying the organization of writing process. In L. W. Gregg & E. R. Steinberg (Eds.), *Cognitive processes in writing.* Hillsdale, N.J.: Erlbaum.

Kirszner, L. G., & Mandell, S. R. (1983). *Patterns for college writing.* New York: St. Martin's Press.

Molitor, S. (1984). *Kognitive Prozesse beim Schreiben.* Tübingen: Deutsches Institut für Fernstudien, Forschungsbericht Nr. 31.

Passow, A. H. (1991). A neglected component of nurturing giftedness: Affective development. *European Journal for High Ability, 2,* 5–11.

Prado, T. M., Jansen, J., & Wieczerkowski, W. (1990). Hamburger Initiativen zur Begabungsforschung und Begabtenförderung. In

H. Wagner (Ed.), *Begabungsforschung und Begabtenförderung in Deutschland 1980–1990–2000*. Bad Honnef: Bock.

Renzulli, J. S. (1986). The three-ring conception of giftedness: A developmental model for creative productivity. In R.J. Sternberg & J.E. Davidson (Eds.), *Conceptions of giftedness* (pp. 53–92). New York: Cambridge University Press.

Reynolds, B., Kopelke, K., & Durden, W.G. (1984). *Writing instruction for verbally gifted youth. The Johns Hopkins Model.* Rockville, MD: Aspen Systems Corp.

Riegel, K. (1967). *Sprachlicher Leistungstest (SASKA).* Göttingen: Hogrefe.

Rowe, E. R. (1967). Creative writing and the gifted child. *Exceptional Children, 34*, 279–282.

Schöpfel, J. (1992). *Kreatives Schreiben. Identifikation und Förderung sprachlich-kreativ begabter Jugendlicher.* Unpublished doctoral dissertation, University of Hamburg.

Schoppe, K. J. (1975). *Verbaler Kreativitäts-Test (V-K-T).* Göttingen: Hogrefe.

Scriven, M. (1966). *The methodology of evaluation.* Social Science Education Consortium, Publ. 110. Boulder: University of Colorado.

Torrance, E. P. (1962). *Guiding creative talent.* Englewood Cliffs, NJ: Prentice-Hall.

Torrance, E. P. (1965). *Gifted children in the classroom.* New York: Macmillan.

Trost, G. (1990). Extracurricular activities of highly gifted and normal secondary school students. *European Journal for High Ability, 1*, 47–51.

Waldmann, G. (1988). *Produktiver Umgang mit Lyrik.* Baltmannsweiler: Pädagogischer Verlag Burgbücherei Schneider.

Waldmann, G. & Bothe, K. (1990). *Erzählen, Eine Einführung in Kreatives Schreiben und produktives Verstehen von traditionellen und modernen Erzählformen.* Stuttgart: Klett.

Wieczerkowski, W., & Wagner, H. (1985). Diagnostik von Hochbegabung. In R. S. Jaeger, R. Horn, & K. Ingenkamp (Eds.), *Tests und Trends. 4. Jahrbuch der pädagogischen Diagnostik* (pp. 109–134). Weinheim: Beltz.

Winterling, F. (1984). *Schreibweisen: Ein Arbeitsbuch für den Deutschunterricht der Sekundarstufe II. Teil I: Freies Schreiben.* Stuttgart: Klett.

# 34

# Cognitive Structures of Creativity

## Implications for Instructional Design

**Irena Yashin-Shaw**

*Griffith University, Brisbane, Australia*

While creativity of the order that produces paradigm shifts in a knowledge domain usually is the result of the efforts of creative experts, any novel outcome of the work of a problem solver can be referred to as "creative," be it process or product. Any individual, regardless of level of expertise, is capable of creativity if he or she employs the entire cognitive system differentially and synergistically. Consequently, the aim of instruction aimed at enhancing creativity should be to provide opportunities for learners to use all three knowledge orders for creative problem solving. This chapter provides various ways in which this may be done.

## WHAT IS CREATIVITY?

In this chapter creativity is taken to be any novel response on the part of a problem solver. A novel response may include a new combination of existing knowledge to solve a presented problem, identification, and subsequent solution of a previously unknown problem (problem finding), or a novel restructuring or definition of an existing problem. It will be argued that creativity may be displayed at any level of expertise, including that of the novice, the only criterion being that the solution is novel to the solver, even if it is known to others. However, creative outcomes that will be significant for a field of knowledge are most likely to be the result of the deep conceptual understanding, highly chunked knowledge, and automatized processing of the expert, and in particular the creative expert who can both identify and also solve novel problems.

Part of the mystique of creativity stems from the difficulty of defining it. A review of the literature reveals several definitions. Some researchers view it as expert problem solving (e.g., Weisberg, 1988), others as divergent thinking (e.g., Feldhusen, Treffinger, & Bahlke, 1970), others as the ability to apply heuristics across domains (e.g., de Bono, 1970, 1971; Edwards, 1991), and still others as the synergistic application of creative resources (e.g., Sternberg & Lubart, 1991). Clearly, no one definition is sufficient. It is necessary to acknowledge therefore that there are different kinds of creativity.

1. The creativity that results from domain specific expertise used in novel ways;
2. The creativity that yields novel solutions for any domain specific problem solvers, regardless of their level of expertise; and
3. Nondomain-specific creativity, where general heuristics may be applied to generate creative outcomes in domains in which the problem solver is not expert.

This chapter deals largely with the first two types of creativity that are domain specific. In each of these situations, problem solving is the central process. Problem solving and creative thinking are closely related. Some problem solving requires largely convergent thinking processes to arrive at a correct answer, for example, a mathematical or physics problem that does not challenge any existing rules or concepts. It may well be argued that such a problem provides little scope or necessity for creative thinking on the part of the solver. It may also be argued, however, that such a situation can hardly be called problem solving, as it may only require the application of an algorithm. If this is the case, then it cannot be considered creative. The exclusivity of algorithmization and creativity is discussed later in this chapter.

There are different degrees of creativity. It is posited (and will be elaborated on later) that creativity that requires both problem finding *and* problem solving is of a higher level than that which requires only problem solving as in the cited example. However, even a task that appears to be algorithmic may require heuristics, depending on the operator's existing knowledge base. If the person is not aware of the algorithm and arrives at a solution independently, then to the extent that the solution is novel for the individual it is creative (Amabile, 1983). Weisberg's (1988) definition of creativity is in accordance with the above reasoning. He defined creativity as all solutions to a problem so long as "they are novel as far as the problem solver is concerned, and solve the problem at hand" (p. 152).

Amabile (1983) presented two definitions of creativity—a consensual and a conceptual—arguing that one definition in itself is not sufficient for use in a theory of creativity. Her consensual definition caters for the subjective assessment of creativity (p. 31).

A product or response is creative to the extent that appropriate observers independently agree it is creative. Appropriate observers are those familiar with the domain in which the product was created or response articulated. Thus creativity can be regarded as the quality of products or responses judged to be creative by appropriate observers, and it can also be regarded as the process by which something so judged is produced.

The consensual definition is not entirely in accordance with the stance adopted in this chapter, which maintains that a product or response may be deemed creative as long as it is a novel outcome for the individual, even if it is not considered so by others who may be more expert. It is nonetheless appropriate when applied to the construct of the creative expert, which is dealt with later in this paper. Amabile's (p. 33) conceptual definition, however, is appropriate for the current argument.

A product or response will be judged as creative to the extent that (a) it is both a novel and appropriate, useful, correct, or valuable response to the task at hand, and (b) the task is heuristic rather than algorithmic.

An algorithm is a prescription determining operations to be performed, while a heuristic process is a "series of nonelementary operations (which a performer does not know beforehand how to perform) or of elementary operations that are not performed in a regular or uniform way" (Landa, 1983, p. 175).

It must be acknowledged that there are different degrees of creativity. The most creative outcomes in terms of contributions to a domain will be solutions produced by creative experts. These are most likely to produce a paradigm shift in a domain of knowledge and to be judged of value by other independent experts in that domain (consensual). Ghiselin, as early as 1964, suggested that "the more creative the contribution the more it restructures one's universe of understanding. Conversely, the less creative the contribution, the less it affects and requires any restructuring of our total universe of understanding" (Ghiselin, Rompel & Taylor, 1964, p.144). Isaksen and Parnes (1985, p. 8) define creative thinking as

> Making and communicating meaningful new connections; thinking of many possibilities; thinking and experiencing in various ways and using different points of view; thinking of new and unusual possibilities; and generating and selecting alternatives.

Each of the cognitive strategies for creativity implicit in the preceding definition may occur at any level of competence or expertise. However, the greatest relevance of this definition is to the discussion on instructional design for creativity that constitutes the final section of this chapter, because the processes and events described above are those advocated for the development of creative thinking.

From a review of the various definitions discussed, the question arises: Should creativity be considered more a product or a process? Both aspects are reflected in the definitions. Product predominates in Amabile's view, while Isaksen and Parnes emphasize process. In fact, for the purposes of this chapter both will be implicit in the term *creativity*.

## COGNITIVE STRUCTURES UNDERLYING CREATIVITY

From the model represented by Figure 34-1, knowledge is conceptualized as belonging to three orders.

First-order schemata represent familiar knowledge, skills, and procedures that have been mastered, chunked, automatized, and thoroughly assimilated into existing mental schemas.

FIGURE 34-1.    Cognitve structures underlying creativity.

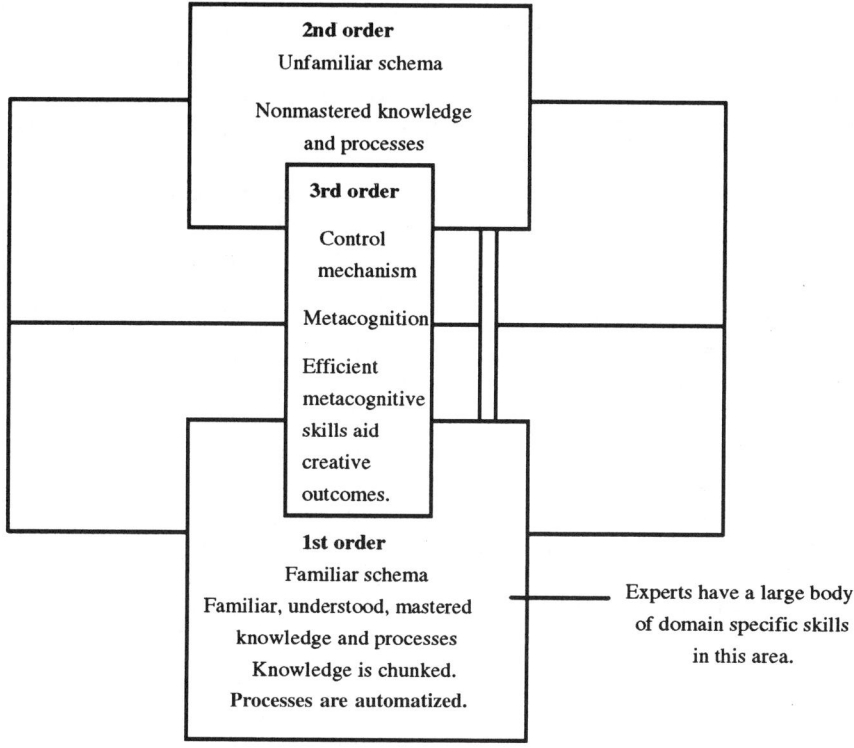

Knowledge located in this order is easily transformed and manipulated, and able to be utilized without imposing a heavy cognitive load. The second-order knowledge, skills, and procedures are those that are used for relatively unfamiliar schematas and need conscious control. Operation in this order poses a high cognitive load.

The location of processes within the first- and second-order boxes is not static. As people become familiar with and assimilate information, master knowledge and automatize procedures, cognitive processes for those tasks will be relocated from the second-order to the first-order domain. Using this logic, it is reasonable to infer that cognitive activity may also move from the first-order to the second-order domain for a short time if skills are rusty, until the practitioner hones them once more for routine utilization.

The third order represents metacognition, which is the cognition control mechanism enabling the operator to switch between knowledge orders as needed. The pathways connecting the various knowledge dimensions represent creative processes that may interact with and draw on all three orders differentially and synergistically. Creativity is not located in any one order, but results from a combination involving the three being utilized to various degrees. It is when the executive control effectively switches, monitors, and combines knowledge and processes both within and between cognitive orders that synergy occurs, that is, where the combined effect of the various parts exceeds the sum of their individual effects.

Good problem solvers and experts possess efficient metacognitive skills, that is they are able to reflect critically on the appropriateness of selected strategies, employ different ones where necessary, and monitor their progress while engaged in tasks (Glaser, 1985). An extension of the metacognitive process for creative activity is that of "metacreativity" proposed by Bruch (1988). The latter is referred to as an extension rather than a redefinition because it includes emotional and physiological experiences as well as cognitive ones. The affective states of creativity are a topic in themselves, and thus for the purposes of maintaining the cognitive focus of this chapter they will not be dealt with further.

## ALGORITHMIZATION AND CREATIVITY

If creativity is the ability to produce novel solutions through the combination and transformation of chunks of existing knowledge, then higher-order processes are being employed. However, once that pathway has been forged, to use that process or technique again in exactly the same way is not genuinely creative in accordance with the definition being used in this chapter. It may not be in the category of automaticity, but it is not new and original to the problem solver. If it is a good solution then the solver will keep it in his or her repertoire of strategies and use it or variations of it repeatedly. This ability will eventually become part of the automated knowledge domain. It follows therefore that there is a constant interaction of cognitive activity from the second to the first orders (see Figure 34-1), which is part of the process of going from competence to expertise. Experts will ultimately have a huge amount of unitarized and proceduralized knowledge in their first order domain. In this way a creative process that originally required a high level of cognitive activity may become algorithmized or semialgorithmized, and transformed into an automatic process that requires little cognitive load.

Landa (see Cook, 1980) argued that algorithmization produces a new and effective performance tool as well as grounds for effective and efficient instruction. Use of algorithms allows students to develop "master-level" (expert) problem-solving processes and decision making procedures. That algorithmization represses creative forces is a notion strongly contested by Landa (1974). On the contrary, he argued that automatized skills are a prerequisite for creative processes (p. 155).

> For example there can be no profound understanding and creative comprehension of a literary work, if a person reads poorly and if all his efforts and attention go into *penetrating the words* and into the technique of reading itself. No creative process is possible if these separate components of the processes are not highly automatized.

In this chapter a broader perspective has been adopted, proposing that creative thinking can take place regardless of level of knowledge or pool of algorithms at the disposal of the operator, and conversely a greater knowledge base does not indicate more creative activity. Any novel solution is a creative outcome. It stands to reason, however, that the more algorithms or chunked or proceduralized knowledge at a person's disposal, the more likely will be a creative outcome that makes a significant contribution to a field of knowledge, simply because of the greater number of permutations and combinations possible, combined with the deep conceptual understanding experts, by definition, have. Novices or neophytes are also capable of unitarising or combining existing knowledge. However, because they have less domain specific and strategic knowledge, that is, tacit knowledge underlying an expert's ability to make use of concepts, facts and procedures (Collins, Brown, & Newman, 1989) as a resource pool, the results will inevitably be less sophisticated and complex than those of the expert.

Algorithmization, chunking, proceduralization, and automatization are all convergent thinking processes. Given that creativity is usually associated with divergent thinking (Barron & Harrington, 1981), which follows tangential pathways, that is, the ability to make remote associations between topics (Mednick, 1962), how are they compatible? In fact, both convergent and divergent thinking are necessary for highly creative outcomes (Haley, 1984). Convergent thinking is essential for knowledge mastery, whereas divergent thinking is essential for making novel associations of that knowledge and identifying new uses to which it may be put (Sternberg & Lubart, 1991, p. 9).

> In short, creativity in a well developed area is likely to require some prerequisite knowledge of what is going in that area but also the ability to free oneself of the confines of that knowledge.

## CONVERGENT AND DIVERGENT THINKING IN EXPERTS AND NONEXPERTS

When confined to one domain, creativity becomes a matter of degree rather than of kind (Weisberg, 1988). Any solution to a problem may be considered creative as long as it is novel to the problem solver. According to this definition and model, creative outcomes are possible at any level of knowledge and performance, and are not confined to the expert.

Definitions of expertise and competence vary in the cognitive literature. For the purposes of this chapter competent practitioners may be differentiated from experts according to the difficulty level of problems they can solve (i.e., those who do well as compared to those who do very well). A competent chess player may have at his or her fingertips a number of effective strategies for board control, opponent capture, and so forth. However, he or she is differentiated from the expert in the structure and richness (quantity and quality) of networks and links within mental schemata. The expert has simply chunked more strategies and patterns and therefore possesses a knowledge base which allows generation of qualitatively superior moves (Bransford & Vye, 1989; deGroot, 1965). In this way, competence and expertise are delineated.

However, although experts may be able to solve difficult problems and think in terms of abstract principles, this does not necessarily mean that all experts are creative to the extent that they are able to make contributions to their field that extend the boundaries of their domain. Accumulation of knowledge by a person provides no assurance that he or she will be a producer of new knowledge beyond what is known (Taylor, 1988).

In fact, some studies (Simonton, 1983) have shown that experts may become increasingly inflexible in their thinking as they become firmly entrenched in their existing knowledge structures or procedures (Langer, 1978, 1989; Luchins, 1942). Familiarity with and mastery of the subject matter may tempt experts to coalesce solutions early (convergent thinking) rather than maintaining a divergent approach (Sternberg & Lubart, 1991, p. 10).

> . . . experts can essentially become mindless by applying standard solutions [algorithms] to tasks. Because [they] have a ready made way of viewing problems, they may have trouble seeing problems in a different way and become victims of set effects.

The early exclusion of ambiguity, the search for the least uncertain process and the apparent emphasis on closure are not likely to promote the creative process which tolerates ambiguity and multiple possibilities and delays closure. The notion of the creative expert is posited to account for the highest levels of creativity whence come the paradigm shifts in accepted knowledge, for example, Watson and Crick's conceptualization of the double-stranded helical model of the *DNA* molecule, which revolutionized molecular genetics, or Kekule's conceptualization of the ring structure of benzene. It is often claimed that such discoveries are accidental rather than the result of deliberate cognitive activity. After all, Watson and Crick were supposedly drunk when the model for the DNA molecule hit them; Kekule was asleep and saw in a dream a snake biting its tail. However, these people were grappling with a problem that consumed their thinking. Moments of insight, leaps of association may occur unexpectedly, but not without preparation, commitment, and effort (Torrance & Hall, 1980).

The creativity of a competent operator nonetheless is valid as a creative outcome for that particular person if it involves a novel response to a situation. However, it is of a lower order in terms of making an overall contribution to a field of knowledge. By contrast, the creative expert has not only the deep understanding and the substantial knowledge that provides the potential for rich associative networking for creativity (Sternberg & Lubart, 1991; Mednick, 1962) but takes advantage of the automaticity and proceduralization of knowledge (convergent thinking) to generate novel associations (divergent thinking) for creative outcomes. In this way, both convergent and divergent thinking processes are employed synergistically.

## CREATIVITY AND PROBLEM FINDING

The importance of problem finding for creative outcomes has been understated in recent creativity literature. Getzels and Csikszentmihalyi (1976) were the first to conduct major longitudinal research in this area, although the importance of problem finding has been recognized and described in various forms among psychologists for decades (Guilford, 1950; Wertheimer, 1959). According to Getzels and Csikszentmihalyi (1976, pp. 248, 250)

> . . . the formulation of a problem is more essential than its solution, and it is a more creative act . . . the rate and quality of discoveries depend on people who can articulate out of vague tensions the significant problems. Some individuals, like the copyist in art, the technician in science, the pedant in scholarship, the bureaucrat in government, deal with problems that have already been identified. The fine artist, the inventive scientist, the creative scholar, the innovative statesman, the self-actualising person are in addition aware of unformulated problems potentially present in the conflicts of their own experience.

A highly salient point in the research was that problem-finding scores among art students at the Art Institute of Chicago significantly predicted success as an artist seven years later. Problem-finding ability would appear to be not only an important component but also a predictive measure of creativity.

As with problem solving, problem finding is not restricted to the expert. A novice or competent operator also may perceive or discover problems through reflection and questioning, as Wakefield's (1985) study with children indicated. However, the novice's problem solutions are likely to be known to others with a greater degree of expertise (Sternberg & Lubart, 1991). In this way, although the outcome may be a creative process and or product for the novice, it is not so to an expert. Similarly, the difference between the expert and the creative expert is in the knowledge of the problem and its context. Has it already been formulated so that it is a presented problem, or does the problem itself need to be sought, identified or created? The latter situation, at the expert level, results in new inventions and discoveries, as it is the experts in a field of knowledge who have sufficiently deep understanding of that domain to be able to identify the gaps or potentials. People operating at this level are the so called geniuses of society. They produce high-quality solutions as a function of their high-quality questions (Getzels, 1975).

Problem finding may include not just identifying a previously undefined task, but reconstructing the way a question is asked so that it appears new or different. Problem definition affects problem solution (Sternberg & Martin, 1988). Defining a problem in a new way may in fact change the difficulty level of that problem (Hayes, 1989, p. 141).

Choosing to represent a problem visually rather than verbally or choosing to represent the problem by one metaphor rather than another, could make a sufficient difference in problem difficulty that one scholar may be able to solve the problem and another may not be able to. In some cases then, the creative person—the one who solved the problem when others could not–may be the person who chose the best representation of the problem.

## CREATIVITY AND CURRENT EDUCATIONAL PRACTICE

Much educational practice to date has centred on the learner's acquisition of content knowledge and procedures. The emphasis of this sort of curriculum stemmed from early twentieth century curriculum writers intent on providing good citizens for an industrialising work force (Isaksen & Parnes, 1985). Memorization and recall were the main objectives. In a world where total knowledge is doubling every 20 months (Naisbett & Aburdene, 1990), the acquisition of static knowledge is entirely inappropriate as an educational goal. Curriculum today must promote and provide creative learning and thinking in order to prepare the citizens of the twenty-first century for the rates of change which will inevitably define the context in which they will live.

As early as 1929 Whitehead (in Bransford & Vye, 1989) observed that schools were "especially good at producing inert knowledge" (p. 193). Subsequently, such claims have continued to be made (Gragg, 1940; Simon, 1980 in Bransford & Vye, 1989). Inert knowledge, which is nongenerative, is not readily activated and accessed for transfer, even when it is useful, nor is it readily combined with other mental components. Educational curricula at all levels—primary, secondary and tertiary— often fail to help students turn declarative knowledge into procedural knowledge, that is, not only knowing facts but when to apply them. For example, students may know about certain mathematical processes, but may not be able to translate that knowledge into a skill when faced with a real-life situation (Lave, 1990). Likewise, if thought processes are not directed by a well-developed executive control mechanism, existing knowledge may not be able to be applied creatively to unfamiliar circumstances. "Creative learning stresses the importance of *using* knowledge by focusing on analysis and synthesis" (Isaksen & Parnes, 1985, p. 6). Such learning does not invalidate the importance of information, but views it as a means rather than an end. However, "it is left largely to students to acquire the information that will help them to learn *when to use* various concepts, principles and strategies" (Bransford & Vye, 1989, p. 193).

This point is substantiated by the fact that school textbooks tend to fragment thinking skills (Sternberg & Martin, 1988). Analysis problems are differentiated from synthesis problems, and so on. In real life, however, problems are rarely soluble by the application of single processes or skills, yet students receive insufficient practice in combining them. The assumption still persists that if individuals have a fair mastery of knowledge and skills they will use them when the opportunity presents itself. This is not the case. Some students stumble onto strategies that help them use their entire cognitive system and think creatively, many do not. Is it in fact possible to teach this skill or at least enhance and access existing creative potential? If so, how?

## IMPLICATIONS FOR INSTRUCTIONAL DESIGN

Although research findings in this area tend to be mixed, there appears to be some basis for the belief that creative ability and thinking can be nurtured and enhanced through specially designed programs (Gehlbach, 1987; Isaksen & Parnes, 1985; Parnes & Noller, 1973; Torrance, 1972). Among the better known ones are *The Osborne-Parnes' Creative Problem Solving Program*, Covington's *Productive Thinking Program*, *Purdue Creative Thinking Program*, and *CoRT* (Cognitive Research Trust). Methodological limitations often weaken the convincingness of positive findings on the effects of creativity training. Subjects may simply be more persistent and expend more effort on post-tests than on pretests. They may also have a better idea of the sorts of responses required. Post-tests may be similar to training materials that would render the tasks algorithmic rather than creative. Furthermore, performance on creativity tests is not necessarily an accurate indicator of real-world creative performance (Amabile, 1983). New research that controls for all these limitations is needed in this field. The difficulties inherent in the experimental aspect of creativity research in no way diminish the importance of continued work in this area, nor do they invalidate or discredit existing research. Despite the limitations in measuring it, Torrance (1972) was vehement in his conviction that creative thinking could be taught.

If it is true (as discussed earlier) that all solutions to problems are creative as long as they are novel and meet the demands of the problem, then the capacity to think creatively must be a basic human capacity, and not the exotic trait or skill envisaged by the genius view. In fact, Gehlbach (1987) called creativity an everyday skill. This has potentially important implications for teaching creativity, as will be discussed in the following section.

Teaching for creativity is different from teaching for competence. The former implies a generative transformation of knowledge, while teaching for competence implies a more static condition. Langer's (1989) research showed that teaching facts in a conditional manner, that is, from the point of view that rather than being absolute entities they are probability statements that are true in some situations but not in others, produced more creative solutions among the subjects of the experimental group because they were more prepared to be flexible with their knowledge.

Current instructional designers and cognitive theorists (e.g., Anderson, 1982; Bransford & Vye, 1989) maintain that active use of knowledge to solve problems rather than reading about facts and concepts will enable students to instantiate their knowledge. That is, through "mental acts" (Lesgold, 1988, p. 198) students transform their declarative knowledge (knowledge that), into procedural knowledge (knowledge how). Creative thinking may be enhanced by encouraging a rich array of knowledge connections and divergent associations, the importance of which to creativity was dealt with earlier. This process will help students to become more expert in a domain as it promotes conceptual understanding and more complete schematas. Isaksen and Parnes (1985) surveyed a number of instructional designers in business and education as well as specialists in curriculum planning who had a demonstrated commitment to creative teaching and learning. It was found that 87% of those surveyed deliberately planned for the development of creative thinking and problem-solving skills rather than assuming that such skills would develop during the course of ordinary instruction. The latter assumption seems to be made often in much educational practice.

A simple model of instruction consists first of systematically exposing the learner to the knowledge or skill to be learned or incremented, second, engaging the learner in active practice and, finally, providing the learner with systematic feedback (Gehlbach, 1987). Teaching creativity needs a more flexible design, because a creative outcome is not specifiable in advance and evaluation of the outcome may be very subjective. One design that accommodated this flexibility is the "open process-open product" (OP-OP) approach which was tried and advocated by various artists and educators during the 1960s and 1970s (Kellogg, 1959). It provided vast amounts of freedom to the learner. The problem was that insufficient guidance was provided by the teacher, and opportunity for focused practice was negligible, the result being that it provided opportunities for those who were already operating creatively and little enhancement for those who were not. One solution proposed by Gehlbach (1987) is to adopt an "open process-fixed product" design, where an outcome must meet certain criteria or constraints but the process by which the product is arrived at is open to creative solutions. This is the process used by creative professional architects or engineers. A building, for example must fit onto a particular block of land, meet certain requirements, possibly even elicit certain aesthetic responses. It is up to the creator to reconcile disparate demands. Reconciling disparate demands is one way of providing learners with the opportunity of engaging in higher-order thinking activities requiring novel associations.

In their model of instructional design, Tennyson and Rasch (1988) proposed a learning environment in which students not only acquire knowledge but also enhance their cognitive abilities to employ and extend their knowledge, thus providing opportunity for convergent and divergent thinking, both of which, it has been argued earlier, are necessary for creativity. They recommended that nearly half of learning time be allocated to instructional strategies that utilize complex problem solving and creative methods of instruction that allow learners to employ their existing knowledge. The intention is to promote knowledge utilization rather than knowledge acquisition. Creativity is explained as the "ability to form new declarative and procedural knowledge as well as contextual knowledge by using the total cognitive system" (Tennyson & Rasch, 1988, p. 372). Declarative knowledge is "knowing that," procedural knowledge is "knowing how," whereas contextual knowledge implies "knowing when and why." In other words, declarative and procedural knowledge form the knowledge base, contextual knowledge determines its organization and accessibility. Creative processes make use of cognitive ability to create knowledge not already coded in memory.

To sum up, instructional design for creativity must provide students with opportunities to activate and associate existing knowledge that might otherwise remain inert. It would be hoped that the satisfaction arising from the experience of generativity of knowledge might prompt students to seek creative possibilities often. This is presumably what Perkins (1984, p. 21) meant when he wrote that teaching for creativity must involve "exposing students to the flavor and texture of creative inquiry and hoping they get hooked."

## REFERENCES

Amabile, T. M. (1983). *The social psychology of creativity.* New York: Springer-Verlag.

Anderson, J. R. (1982). Acquisition of cognitive skill. *Psychological Review, 89,* 369–406.

Barron, F., & Harrington, D. M. (1981). Creativity, intelligence and personality. *Annual Review of Psychology, 32,* 439–476.

Bransford, J. D., & Vye, N. J. (1989). A perspective on cognitive research and its implications for instruction. In L. Resnick & L. Klopfer (Eds.), *Towards the thinking curriculum: Current cognitive research.* 1989 Yearbook of the Association for Supervision and Curriculum Development. Pittsburg: ASCD Publications.

Bruch, C. (1988). Metacreativity: Awareness of thoughts and feelings during creative experiences. *Journal of Creative Behavior, 22*(2), 112–122.

Collins, A., Brown, J. S., & Newman, S. E. (1989). Cognitive apprenticeship: Teaching the crafts of reading, writing and mathematics. In L. Resnick (Ed.), *Knowing, learning and instruction. Essays in honor of Robert Glaser.* Hillsdale, NJ: Lawrence Erlbaum.

Cook, M. H. (1980). Algorithmization—A shortcut to learning. *Training and Development Journal, 34*(4), 4–8.

de Bono, E. (1970). *The thinking class.* London: Ward Lock Educational.

de Bono, E. (1971). *Lateral thinking for management*. Harmondsworth, Middlesex: Penguin Books Ltd.

de Bono, E. (1983). The Cognitive Research Trust (CoRT) Thinking Skills Program. In W. Maxwell (Ed.), *Thinking the expanding frontier* (pp. 115–28). Philadelphia, PA: The Franklin Institute Press.

deGroot, A. (1965). *Thought and choice in chess*. The Hague: Mouton.

Edwards, J. (1991). The direct teaching of thinking skills. In G. Evans (Ed.), *Teaching and learning*. Hawthorn, Vic.: Australian Council for Educational Research LTD.

Feldhusen, J. F., Treffinger, D. J., & Bahlke, S. J. (1970). Developing creative thinking: The Purdue creativity program. *Journal of Creative Behavior, 4*(2), 85–90.

Gehlbach, R. D. (1987). Creativity and instruction: The problem of task design. *Journal of Creative Behavior, 21*(1), 34–47.

Getzels J. W. (1975). Problem-finding and the inventiveness of solutions. *Journal of Creative Behavior, 9*(1), 12–18.

Getzels, J. W., & Csikszentmihalyi, M. (1976). *The creative vision*. New York: Wiley.

Ghiselin, B., Rompel, R., & Taylor, C. W. (1964). A creative process checklist: Its development and validation. In C. W. Taylor (Ed.), *Widening horizons in creativity*. New York: Wiley.

Glaser, R. (1985). *Thoughts on expertise*. ERIC document ED 264 301. Version of a talk gived at the Social Sceince Research Council conference on "The Study of Expertise as a Model for Life-Span Cognitive Development."

Gragg, C. I. (1940, Oct. 19). Harvard Alumni Bulletin.

Guilford, J. P. (1950). Creativity. *American Psychologist, 5*, 444–454.

Haley, G. L. (1984). Creative response styles: The effects of socioeconomic status and problem solving training. *Journal of Creative Behavior, 18*(1), 25–40.

Hayes, J. R. (1989). Cognitive processes in creativity. In J. A. Glover, R. R. Ronning & C. R. Reynolds (Eds.), *Handbook of creativity*. New York: Plenum Press.

Isaksen, S. G., and Parnes S. J. (1985). Curriculum planning for creative thinking and problem solving. *Journal of Creative Behavior, 19*(4), 1–29.

Kellogg, R. (1959). *What children scribble and why*. San Francisco: N-P Publications.

Landa, L. (1974). *Algorithmization in learning and instruction*. Englewood Cliffs, NJ: Educational Technologies Publications.

Landa, L. (1983). The algo-heuristic theory of instruction. In C. M. Reigeluth (Ed.), *Instructional design theories and models: An overview of their current status*. Hillsdale, NJ: Erlbaum.

Langer, E. J. (1978). Rethinking the role of thought in social interaction. In J. Harvey, W. Ickes, & R. Kidd (Eds), *New directions in atribution research*. Hillsdale, NJ: Erlbaum.

Langer, E. J. (1989). *Mindfullness*. New York. Addison-Wesley.

Lave, J. (1990). The culture of acquisition and the practice of under-standing. In J. W. Stigler, R. A. Shweder, & G. Herdt (Eds.), *Cultural psychology: Essays in comparative human development.* Cambridge: Cambridge University Press.

Lesgold, A. (1988). Problem solving. In R. J. Sternberg & E. E. Smith (Eds.), *The psychology of human thought.* New York: Cambridge University Press.

Luchins, A. S. (1942). Mechanisation in problem solving. *Psychological Monographs, 54,* No. 6.

Mednick, S. A. (1962). The associative basis of the creative process. *Psychological Review, 69,* 220–230.

Naisbitt, J., & Aburdene, P. (1990). *Megatrends 2000: Ten new directions for the 1990's.* New York: Morrow.

Parnes, S. J., & Noller, R. B. (1973). *Towards supersanity: Channeled freedom.* Buffalo, NY: D.O.K. Publishers.

Perkins, D. N. (1984). Creativity by design. *Educational Leadership, 42*(1), 18–25.

Perkins, D. N. (1991). Educating for insight. *Educational Leadership, 49*(2), 4–8.

Simon, H. A. (1980). Problem solving and education. In D. T. Tuma & R. Reif (Eds.), *Problem solving and education: Issues in teaching and research.* Hillsdale, NJ: Erlbaum.

Simonton, D. K. (1983). Formal education, eminence and dogmatism: The curvilinear relationship. *Journal of Creative Behavior, 17*(3), 149–162.

Sternberg, R. J., & Lubart, T. I. (1991). An investment theory of creativity and its development. *Human Development, 34*(1), 1–31.

Sternberg, R. J., & Martin, M. (1988). When teaching thinking does not work, what goes wrong? *Teachers College Record, 89*(4), 555–578.

Taylor, C. W. (1988). *Approaches to and definitions of creativity. The nature of creativity.* Cambridge: Cambridge University Press.

Tennyson, R. D., & Rasch, M. (1988). Linking cognitive learning theory to instructional prescriptions. *Instructional Science, 17,* 369–385.

Torrance, E. P. (1972). Can we teach children to think creatively? *The Journal of Creative Behavior, 6*(2), 114–143.

Torrance, P., & Hall, L. (1980). Assessing the further reaches of creative potential. *Journal of Creative Behavior, 14*(1), 1–19.

Wakefield, J. F. (1985). Towards creativity: Problem finding in a divergent-thinking exercise. *Child Study Journal, 15,* 265–270.

Weisberg, R. W. (1988). *Problem solving and creativity. The nature of creativity.* Cambridge: Cambridge University Press.

Wertheimer, M. (1959). *Productive thinking.* New York: Harper & Row.

Whitehead, A. N. (1929). *The aims of education.* New York: Macmillan.

# 35

# Curiosity in Small Children and the Childrearing Style of Their Mothers

**Sylwia Grzeskowiak**

*Philipps University of Marburg, Marburg, Germany*

The present study examines the connection between curiosity behavior of small children and their mothers' childrearing style. Twenty children from 2.5 years to 4.5 years in age were separately observed in free play with a toy set of the Sceno Test. For each child the amount of manipulated material was noted. It was found that the differences among the group were both sex and age independent. Subsequently, video observations of interactional play between mother and child in the home environment were carried out. By means of qualitative content analysis of the video recordings for all twenty mother–child pairs, the frequency of controlling behavior by the mothers was assessed. A very high correlation between curiosity behavior in a free play situation and controlling behavior of the mother in the mother–child interaction was established. Level of controlling behavior showed a U-shaped relationship to exploratory behavior in the children.

# INTRODUCTION

Curiosity, defined here as openness to experience, represents a crucial factor in creative development in human behavior. This is primarily obvious among small children, whose whole development is based on undisturbed observational and motor exploration of the environment. A certain continuity can be observed between openness to experience in small children and their creative capacity in the later years of life. This relationship is explained in various concepts of creativity. McCrae (1987) suggested two possible explanations.

1. The appreciation of novelty may be facilitated by the ability to think creatively.
2. People may develop their intellectual and especially divergent thinking capacity through exposure to rich and varied experiences.

In searching for the origins of creative activities, it is necessary to direct attention to the natural environment of small children. The ethological perspective in research in children (Cramer, 1987; Keller, Schölmerich, Miranda, & Gauda, 1987) on the development of behavioral systems states that exploratory behavior can only be investigated by considering mother–child relationships. Mother–child interactions in the natural environment are crucial in understanding the behavior of the child and its development. In this perspective, the present study examined the connection between the curiosity of small children and the childrearing style of their mothers. By means of several observations of 20 mother–child pairs a significant correlation was found between (1) the child's behavior in free-play situations, and (2) its position in interactional play with the mother.

# THE INVESTIGATION

## Measurement of Curiosity

A total of 10 girls and 10 boys from four different nursery schools in Hamburg and Berlin participated in the study. The children were 2.5–4.5 years old. Their mothers were middle class women who had a profession and a secure income. The study was carried out in the home of the persons being observed and in the nursery schools.

The curiosity of the children was determined in the following way: Each child was observed in free play with the Sceno Test (Staabs, 1985). This test contains small flexible puppets, figures of animals and symbolic figures, diverse cubes, and so on, in total approximately 130 objects. As a result it presents an unusual assortment of material for exploration. Because of this it fulfilled the conditions of complexity and novelty (cf., Voss & Keller, 1986) that are required in investigations of this kind (e.g., Hutt, 1970; Henderson & Moore, 1979; Hughes, 1987; Keller, Schölmerich, Miranda, & Gauda, 1987). This play material was also very attractive, and thus encouraged the children to play, even in the situation where they were being observed.

Observation of free play took place mostly in the morning in the nursery school, sometimes at home. The child and the observer sat separately in a room. At the beginning the wooden box with the toy set lay on the floor. If the child did not at once begin to play, the observer helped to open the box. At the same time she gave the information that her role was exclusively that of observer. Afterward she sat on the floor not far from the child with a pencil and notebook, and made notes on the number and kind of elements the child played with. Any invitation from the child to join in the play was refused. Questions raised by the child were answered as briefly as possible. The whole process of playing was observed in this way. Observation continued until the child said it did not want to play any more. In some rare cases the observation was interrupted by the observer after about 40 minutes' play.

The purpose of the evaluation was to define the extent of exploration the child displayed in relation to the toy set. The quantity of material explored was taken as a measure of curiosity. The assortment of material in the Sceno Test is arranged in seven different groups. Each of these groups has its own place in the wooden box. For the exploration of each group of playing elements, values on a scale of three (0-1-2) were assigned. Those children who investigated a group exhaustively were given two points for that group, those who did not explore so intensively received only one point for the particular group in question. If a child did not explore a group of items at all, it received no points for that group. Naturally, a child which explored more groups received more points (up to two per group, according to the intensity of exploration of that group). The scores actually obtained by the children ranged from four to 14 points.

## Measurement of Childrearing Style

The childrearing style of the mothers was evaluated in two different ways: by asking them about their views on bringing up their own child, on the one hand, through observation and microanalysis of their behavior in interactions with their own child, on the other. Setting limits on children's behavior versus supporting their autonomy were thought to be the most important categories for evaluating both the statements made by the mothers and the behavior they displayed.

Each mother–child pair was observed in interactive play in the following situation: a small table tennis table of 90 cm length, 50 cm width, and 20 cm height was installed. In its other aspects it did not differ from a normal table tennis table. Although separating the players, the table structured the observed situation, as did the rules of the game. Consequently, the play between mother and child could be regarded as a chain of consecutive interactions. The play was recorded for 15 minutes by video camera.

The observation was carried out in a familiar environment, mostly in the family at home, in three cases in the nursery school. All mothers whose cooperation had been requested expressed their acceptance and mostly their interest in playing with their own child while being video recorded. The children could not follow all rules of the game, and sometimes could not perform certain movements; for instance, they often missed the ball when it came from the other end. Nevertheless, the players overcame all difficulties in play creatively, for example, by rolling the ball on or under the table or dropping it. It sometimes happened that, shortly after the beginning, the play took an unusual course. It was assumed that the video camera installed in the room had no significant influence on the interactions observed.

In the next phase of the study, analyses of the mothers' behavior, as displayed in the interactions documented on the video recordings, were carried out. This means that the recordings became the actual object of investigation. This procedure has an important advantage by contrast with direct observation, in that it offers the possibility of repeated observation of a sequence. Through video recording, all dynamic, rapid, complex, and unique situations could be examined further with a high level of precision.

After the table tennis game, each mother was asked to express her views on raising her child. The researcher had prepared 21 small cards with various educational values, that is with character traits that would be expected from the child. The mothers had to rank these values according to their importance. This set of values was derived from earlier studies by Grüneisen and Hoff (1977). According to their factor analysis some of these values were characteristic of a childrearing style supporting the autonomy of children. High ranks on these values, that is "curiosity," "ability to criticize," "self-consciousness," "sexual naturalness," "imagination," "openmindedness" and "autonomy," were thought to be relevant for a style that supports free development of children. The ranks of these seven values were taken as revealing the role of autonomy in the mothers' views on childrearing.

In analyzing the interaction between mother and child, those behaviors of the mother were further scrutinized that directed or limited the activity of the child. For this purpose an appropriate system of categories from the *Münchener Trainingsmodell* [Munich training model] (Innerhoffer, 1977) were adopted. The changing elements in the behavior of both partners constituted a chain of interactions. Various distinct aspects in the behavior of the mothers were coded as units of controlling behavior. The system of categories defining controlling behavior included

> supportive controlling;
> oppositional controlling;
> nonsupportive controlling;
> obeying the child's control; and
> zero controlling (no control).

From each of the 20 recordings, three or four sequences were randomly selected and evaluated, each sequence of one minute's duration. The actual analysis of the recordings was preceded by the training of observers, and was then carried out on the original video recordings with the participation of two observers. The one-minute sections had first been described in a detailed way in everyday language. These descriptions were later encoded with the help of the categories outlined in the preceding. The classification was carried out by means of rules laid down in advance, and was based on repeated viewing of recordings. For each mother the frequency of controlling behavior was established: It was assumed that on the basis of this frequency it was possible to generalize about mother–child interactions—the frequency of controlling behavior in the experimental setting was regarded as a measure of the habitual behavior of the mother with her child.

## RESULTS

The two observations described in the preceding made it possible to test the relationship between exploratary behavior of the child and behavior of the mother during interactions with her child. In both cases, the data were expressed in ranks. On the scale for curiosity the highest rank was assigned to the child who scored the most points for exploration, succcessive ranks in order to those children with progressively lower scores. In the analysis of behavior, the highest rank was given to the mother who exhibited the lowest level of controlling behavior.

In the case of the mothers' views on childraising, it was found that all of the seven character traits mentioned were placed by all women without exception among the 10 most important ones, and moreover, at the top of the hierarchy. Thus, the inquiry revealed no significant differences in the opinions of the mothers regarding desirable characteristiscs of their children. These views, however, turned out to be relatively independent of the observed behavior of the mothers. A wide spectrum of actual childrearing behaviors was displayed by the mothers, despite the homogeneity of their theoretical views on this topic; this ranged from frequently setting limits on the child's behavior to displaying controlling behavior very rarely.

The curiosity ranks of the children were then compared with the rankings of the mothers on controlling behavior. The rank correlation ($r = .84$) was high ($p < .001$). In other words, high exploration values were shown by the children whose mothers displayed low levels of controlling behavior, whereas the mothers of the children who explored less frequently set stricter limits. However, the scatter diagram showed an approximate U shape (see Table 35-1); not those children whose mothers displayed the absolute lowest controlling behavior were the most curious, but those whose mothers exhibited a certain degree of control, low to be sure, but not nonexistent.

TABLE 35-1
Scatter Diagram of Children's Curiosity and Mothers' Controlling Behavior*

| R1 | 1 | 2 | 3 | 4 | 5 | 6 | 7 | 8 | 9 | 10 | 11 | 12 | 13 | 14 | 15 | 16 | 17 | 18 | 19 | 20 |
|-----|---|---|---|---|---|---|---|---|---|----|----|----|----|----|----|----|----|----|----|----|
| 2 | | | X | | | | X | X | | | | | | | | | | | | |
| 4 | | X | | | | | | | | | | | | | | | | | | |
| 6.5 | X | | | | X | X | | | | | | X | | | | | | | | |
| 10 | | X | | | | | | | X | X | | | | | | | | | | |
| 13 | | | | | | | | | | | X | | | X | X | | | | | |
| 15 | | | | | | | | | | | | | X | | | | | | | |
| 17 | | | | | | | | | | | | | | | | X | X | X | | |
| 19 | | | | | | | | | | | | | | | | | | | X | |
| 20 | | | | | | | | | | | | | | | | | | | | X |

*The rows indicate the curiosity ranks, the columns those for controlling behavior.

## DISCUSSION

This study was an attempt to investigate the relationship between the explorative behavior of small children and the childraising style of their mothers. The results showed that the stricter the limits set on the child's behavior by the mother, the less the independent exploration of the child in a new situation, that is, the less the curiosity behavior. In discussing these results, several factors need to be considered that have not yet been mentioned. Possibly, the high curiosity children, because of their temperament, tolerated no more than rare direction and control by their mothers. The observed variation in their behavior would then be more the outcome of individual temperament differences and less the consequence of the mothers' childraising style—the high rank order correlation indicates nothing about the direction of the influence.

In this study one special aspect of exploration was mainly considered, namely manipulative exploration. Some studies suggest that manipulation develops in contrast to other modes of exploration (Keller, Schölmerich, Miranda, & Gauda, 1987; Voss & Keller, 1986). If proximal exploration develops substantially differently to distal exploration, the present results would refer only to the first kind of curiosity behavior, perhaps exclusively to the special manifestation of it investigated here.

The group in this study involved mainly mothers who provided their children with more than minimal attention. Consequently, excessive controlling behavior was the main problem. Nevertheless, even in this group it was apparent that not only too much, but also too little control confines the exploration of the child (U-shaped relationship between control and exploration). If the observed group had included children who experienced a serious lack of controlling behavior, these children would probably have obtained only a minimal number of points for exploration. Thus, the present study does not seek to cast doubt on the worth of stimulation of small children by their mothers, but to focus attention on the difficulty of finding the narrow path that lies between insufficient attention from the mother and a permanent limiting of the child's behavior by excessive control, which inhibits the child from exploring its world itself. The positive attitudes toward curiosity, self-consciousness, imagination, open-mindedness, and autonomy declared by the mothers probably derive predominantly from widely propagated childrearing ideals—creativity and autonomy generally are thought to be very important in modern societies, and are declared aims of education nowadays. Decisive is, however, as shown by the present results, that this educational ideal is converted into appropriate behavior on the part of the childrearers.

## REFERENCES

Cramer, B. G. (1987). Objective and subjective aspects of parent-infant relations: An attempt at correlation between infant studies and clinical work. In J. D. Osofsky (Ed.), *Handbook of infant development* (pp. 1037–1057). New York: Wiley.

Grüneisen, V., & Hoff, E. (1977). *Familienerziehung und Lebenssituation*. Weinheim: Beltz.

Henderson, B., & Moore, S. G. (1979). Measuring exploratory behavior in young children: A factor-analytic study. *Developmental Psychology, 15*, 113–119.

Hughes, M. (1987). The relationship between symbolic and manipulative (object) play. In D. Görlitz & J. F. Wohlwill (Eds.), *Curiosity, imagination and play. On the development of spontaneous cognitive and motivational processes* (pp. 247–257). Hillsdale, NJ: Erlbaum.

Hutt, C. (1970). Specific and diversive exploration. In H. W. Reese & L. P. Lipsitt (Eds.), *Advances in child development and behaviour*, Vol. 5 (pp.120–180). New York: Academic Press.

Innerhoffer, P. (1977). *Das Münchener Trainingsmodell*. Berlin: Springer.

Keller, H., Schölmerich, A., Miranda, D., & Gauda, G. (1987). The development of exploratory behavior in the first four years of life. In

D. Görlitz & J. F. Wohlwill (Eds.), *Curiosity, imagination and play. On the development of spontaneous cognitive and motivational processes* (pp. 126–149). Hillsdale, NJ: Erlbaum.

McCrae, R. R. (1987). Creativity, divergent thinking and openness to experience. *Journal of Personality and Social Psychology, 52,* 1258–1265.

Staabs, G. v. (1985). *Der Scenotest. Beitrag zur Erfassung unbewusster Problematik und charakterologischer Struktur in Diagnostik und Therapie.* Bern: Huber Verlag.

Voss, H.-G., & Keller, H. (1986). Curiosity and exploration: A program of investigation. *German Journal of Psychology, 10,* 327–337.

# 36

# Creative Thinking as a Predictor of Achievement in Music

**Ewa Klimas-Kuchtowa**

*Jagiellonian University, Cracow, Poland*

One hundred twenty-seven students at a musical high school in Cracow completed the Test of Creative Thinking of Necka and Rychlicka and filled out a questionnaire on their musical achievements. They were rated also by their music teachers. The level of creative thinking increased with the age of subjects, but correlations between creative thinking and achievement in music were not significant. Further research on this apparent lack of relationship between musical and verbal creativity is important for music education and the counseling of music students.

## INTRODUCTION

Musical creativity is not an activity of the composer alone: The musical, aesthetic situation evokes three kinds of creativity—one is the composer's creativity, the second the creativity of the performer, and the third the creativity of the listener. Music, as an aesthetic phenomenon, needs all three kinds of creativity—

this is a *conditio sine qua non*—but they are different kinds of creativity. Different kinds of skills are needed in each of them, and different subjective functions are included in each of them. In all cases, however, the result is the creation of music. In this chapter, the listener's creativity (Klimas-Kuchtowa, 1986, 1987) will not be dealt with further.

Study of the relevant literature has led to the conclusion that there are five main groups of subjective correlates of musical creativity. These are

1. musical talent;
2. high level of general intelligence;
3. special cognitive traits, such as high levels of fluency and flexibility, superiority of divergent thinking over convergent thinking, a high level of imagination, broad knowledge, and large number of interests. In addition, there are specific cognitive skills connected with musical talent such as remarkable sensibility for pitch and timbre, sense of rhythm, musical memory, esthetic sensibility, and so on;
4. special personality characteristics such as high level of ego strength, susceptibility to personality deviations, introversion and rather poor socialization; and
5. particular motivational factors.

This chapter focuses on consideration of musicians' cognitive systems, especially those involved in many kinds of creative action.

Analysis of great musicians' biographies shows their pronounced disposition to uncommon, unusual associations and their tendency to go beyond the immediate sensory situation. This is made possible by fancy and intuition. Musicians have a rich imagination, especially for sounds. They have extensive interests, above all in arts and literature. They are very often linguistically and mathematically talented (Mursell, 1937). As in other creators, divergent thinking surpasses convergent thinking. This is the reason why findings relating to correlations among scores on tests of intelligence, talent, skills, and so on often are incompatible. In many studies subjects have not been musical geniuses or great composers, but gifted, talented musicians or students of music. There are many studies of this kind, but I will focus on some of them in which correlations between musical skills and verbal, spatial, and artistic skills or abilities were investigated.

Hanley (1956), for example, did not mention the correlation between verbal flexibility and results from Seashore's *Musical Talent Test*, but this correlation was reported by Solomon, Webster, and Curtis (1960). Karma (1975) obtained very interesting results using his own test of musical abilities. In his first study he reported higher correlations between musical and spatial abilities (0.33) than between musical and verbal abilities (0.09), but his later research showed higher correlations with verbal (0.45 and 0.47) than with spatial abilities (0.32 and 0.06). As Karma concluded, these differences reflect different levels of subjects' musical experience—limited experience leads to verbal processing of accoustic material. Karma anticipated that practice would influence this relationship and reduce the difference between verbal and spatial abilities. The strong relation between spatial and musical abilities was also reported in the research of Smith, Howes, and Shepard (1976) and Manturzewska (1979). Webster (1979) investigated three kinds of creative behavior in music—composition, improvization, and analysis—and reported significant correlations between all of them and musical achievement. However, figural creativity correlated significantly with improvization and analysis but not with composition, and verbal creativity correlated only with analysis but not with improvization and composition.

Of course, the studies just cited do not exhaust the long list of studies referring to relationships between musical and other abilities. They focus only on those that are relevant to the research discussed in this chapter. The present study is part of a larger research program ("Human creative activity") concerned with subjective correlates of musical achievements and using students of the musical high school in Cracow as subjects.

## METHOD

The hypotheses tested were

1. The level of creative thinking measured by fluency, flexibility, and metaphoricalness increases with the age of subjects.
2. Students with high musical achievement during their musical education and with favorable prognosis for their future musical career have higher levels of creative thinking.

Subjects were 127 students in the last four classes of high school (III class—31 persons, IV class—33 persons, V class—33 persons, and VI class—30 persons). The second hypothesis however was tested only with 96 students (the IV, V, and VI classes) because assessments from the music teachers were only available for these groups.

The students were tested with the *Test of Creative Thinking* by Necka and Rychlicka, and with a special questionnaire containing questions about the students' musical education and their musical achievements. Their music teachers were asked to prepare written opinions concerning the students' future musical careers.

## RESULTS

Results on the *Test of Creative Thinking* were analyzed first. This is a verbal test and measures creativity in terms of

1. fluency of thinking—the number of answers in the test;
2. flexibility of thinking—the number of kinds of answer in the test; and
3. metaphoricalness of answers.

Each of these traits was scored separately in sten scores. Arithmetic means are shown in Table 36-1.

As can be seen, in almost every case results were numerically higher than the average level of creative thinking (more than five stens). Statistical analysis using the $t$-test, however, indicated that only differences in flexibility between the youngest and oldest classes ($t$ (57) = 1.87; $\alpha$ < 0.05), in

TABLE 36-1
Creativity Test Mean Scores of the Four Classes

| Class | | Fluency | Flexibility | Metaphoricalness |
|-------|-----|---------|-------------|------------------|
| III   | M   | 5.663   | 5.733       | 3.800            |
|       | SD  | 1.691   | 1.929       | 2.483            |
| IV    | M   | 5.600   | 5.880       | 5.240            |
|       | SD  | 1.633   | 1.986       | 2.087            |
| V     | M   | 6.167   | 6.167       | 5.500            |
|       | SD  | 1.579   | 1.926       | 2.284            |
| VI    | M   | 6.333   | 6.704       | 6.148            |
|       | SD  | 1.981   | 2.949       | 2.852            |

metaphoricalness between the III and IV classes ($t$ (55) = 2.35; $\alpha$ < 0.05), and the III and VI class ($t$ (57) = 3.38; $\alpha$ < 0.01) were significant. All these results lead to conclusions verifying the first hypothesis.

The level of creative thinking of young musicians is higher than average students'. There is a significant increase in flexibility and metaphoricalness connected with the age of subjects.

The second part of the results involved qualitative analysis of teachers' opinions about the students, and of students' answers to the questionnaire. The whole group was divided into three subgroups.

1. highly skilled students with some musical achievements and very good prognosis for their future career (15 persons)—Group A;
2. average students; and
3. poorly skilled students without musical achievements and with low likelihood of a future musical career (14 persons)—Group B. Unfortunately, not all of these students participated in the entire investigation, and full data are available for only 11 persons.

Comparisions between the results on the *Test of Creative Thinking* for Group A and Group B were made. Table 36-2 shows the arithmetic means and standard deviations of the three parameters of creative thinking for Group A and Group B.

As can be seen (Table 36-2), there were no differences between groups. This allows the speculation that verbal artistic and musical creativity are separate mechanisms. Further research using creative musical, verbal and pictorial tasks is planned. It is hoped that this research will help to prepare a special test of musical creative thinking, something that is needed in music education and consulting.

**TABLE 36-2**
**Creativity Test Means of Students with Favorable and Unfavorable Job Prognoses**

|  |  | Fluency | Flexibility | Metaphoricalness | Total |
|---|---|---|---|---|---|
| Favorable Prognosis | M | 6.07 | 5.87 | 5.40 | 17.33 |
|  | SD | 1.94 | 2.42 | 2.77 | 6.26 |
| Unfavorable Prognosis | M | 5.91 | 6.18 | 5.36 | 17.46 |
|  | SD | 1.58 | 2.18 | 2.25 | 5.09 |

# REFERENCES

Hanley, C. N. (1956). Factorial analysis of speech perception. *Journal of Speech and Hearing Disabilities, 21*, 76–87.

Karma, K. (1975). The ability to structure acoustic materials as a measure of musical aptitude 2. Test construction and results. *Research Bulletin*, No. 43, Institute of Education, University of Helsinki.

Karma, K. (1980). The ability to structure acoustic material as a measure of musical aptitude 5. Summary and conclusions. *Research Bulletin*, No. 52, Institute of Education, University of Helsinki.

Klimas-Kuchtowa, E. (1986). O odbiorze muzyki z punktu widzenia teorii informacji [Music perception from the information processing point of view]. *Przeglad Psychologiczny, XXIX/2*, 335–344.

Klimas-Kuchtowa, E. (1987). Kreacja w percepcji muzyki [Creation in music perception]. In Z. Burowska & E. Gtwowacka (Eds.), *Z zagadnien zdolnoski, percepcji i ksztalcenia muzycznego* [About abilities, perception and music education] (pp. 59–72). Cracow: Zeszyty Naukowe Akademii Muzycznej.

Manturzewska, M. (1979). Results of psychological research on the process of music practice and its effective shaping. *Council for Research in Music Education*, Bulletin No. 59.

Smith, I. M., Howes, R., & Shepard, K. (1976). A study of the abilities and interests of overseas students. *Vocational Aspects of Education, 28*, 55–56.

Solomon, L. M., Webster, J. C., & Curtis, J. F. (1960). A factorial study of speech perception. *Journal of Speech and Hearing Research, 2*, 101–107.

Webster, P. R. (1979). Relationships between creative behaviour in music and selected variables as measured in high school students. *Journal of Research in Music Education, 27*, 227–242.

# Section VI

## School-Related Issues

# 37

# A Concept for Promotion of Gifts and Talents

**Wolfgang Steinhöfel**
**Siegfried Mescheder**

*Chemnitz, Germany*

Promotion of gifted people's talents can satisfy their humanistic values and their "productive" social character in the long run only if it is based on a systematic concept of education and training. This should integrate in a constructive and synthetic way the entire complex of challenges arising from social, scientific and technological progress. The concept should apply knowledge of biological, psychological, and social factors in personality development and link these to the educational process, taking into account the contents and form of the process. On the basis of such fundamental concepts, it is important to apply all educational reasoning and action to studying the development of talent in its relationship to level of development, challenges to be met, activities to be carried out, and strategy to be applied. It is also necessary to create a clear understanding of the objectives, contents, and processes of education, and to base promotion of talent on such understanding.

## INTRODUCTION

In fostering the development of talents, a strategy for teachers to use or, in simpler terms, a kind of philosophy, is of considerable importance. To avoid misunderstanding: What is being proposed are neither models created "from the top," nor organizational structures into which gifted students are to be "pressed." The aim of the present chapter is to help teachers develop concepts for their own development and for support of the self-realization of their students. What is proposed are concepts or models that are characterized by openness and permit wide individual variety.

What should be the place of such a strategy, which is to be integrated into a teaching concept? First, it is important to understand that

1. Any strategy is aimed at developing an image of the human being. If such an image is to be a humanistic one, the objective to be achieved is to shape the individual subjectivity of human beings in order to provide them with the ability for self-organization. This means that the strategy must focus its attention on people who are self-orienting and capable of self-control and the making of independent decisions and evaluations, that is, a human being who is mature and socially competent. This is highly compatible with the mission inherent in the promotion of talents.
2. Any strategy is embedded—and realizable—only within a given institutionalized framework, no matter how pluralistic it may be.

Aiming at the achievement of a humanist model of human beings, present day educational activities show that almost all efforts concerning training and school projects are basically directed at responding to the special characteristics of each individual, by flexibly providing individual education levels, passage from one level of training to another, and mandatory and optional training opportunities, and so on. Because of the paradigmatic change from an education of guidance to an education of development, which profoundly alters the educational system, educators are now faced with a culmination of talent promotion that will have to be shaped along new lines.

3. Any strategy is linked with a wide-ranging content concept which involves the essential structure and relationship of the branch of science concerned. Such a concept offers the possibility of developing all areas and suggests activities for the acquisition and preservation of children's metacognitive and mental competence, as well as of expert knowledge and skills (possibly in terms of artificial intelligence).

4. When considering points 1–3, it must be concluded that the only conception to be used is a teaching approach that is sufficiently open to leave enough room for the individual concerned, and within the framework of which the creation of a true human being is not only considered as acceptable but also as an obligation. Summing up what has been said until now, it can be said that the question to be answered in seeking solutions to the problem of high ability are similar to those to be solved in the educational process as a whole, while looking for the main elements contributing to improvement.

Such a comprehensive and complex, and at the same time dynamic, process concept should reflect the multidimensional structure of education and the course of personality development, as well as their reciprocal interaction, their profound dialectics, and their inherent dynamics, and should contribute to educational decision making at the different interfaces of the two processes. The development (identification, promotion, and genesis) of the gifted individual should take into account the challenges to be met, the activities to be accomplished, and the individual person to be promoted. Bearing in mind the implications of the challenges of society indicated, the theoretical concept adopted here reflects the following methodological and theoretical positions.

The concept starts from a basic paradigm involving the fixed features challenge, activity, personality (personality development), and the laws, theories, and principles that are behind these "supersigns."

The concept offers *a priori* an orientation toward the entirety of the personality and its development in a dialectical unity, with a comprehensive aproach to the educational process.

The concept considers all talent promoting activities deriving from it as immanent and integral components of the comprehensive educational processes aimed at achieving optimum development of the personality as a whole.

The concept links the promotion and genesis of scientifically and technologically gifted individuals (as in the case of personality development in general) with the solution of an optimization task, whose criterion is determined by the individual's abilities and ambition, and requires the creation of the best possible conditions and challenges for his or her development during ontogenesis, through the commitment and skill of teachers.

The concept regards the promotion of talents as an educational and specialized professional task that is to be solved in a spirit of responsibility and initiative by all teachers, educators, scientific workers, and other staff working in educational establishments (kindergartens, schools, universities, cultural, and educational centers, etc.), at all educational levels (preschool, primary and secondary school, vocational, training, advanced vocational and university level training), and in all fields of education (mandatory and optional courses, extracurricular and out-of-school activities, practical courses, general courses, special courses, seminars, etc.).

The concept recognizes that all those involved in the overall education process (in particular specialists in talent promotion) have to be included in the process, and that a coordinated effort both within the area of special promotion and beyond it is necessary.

Starting from this position, we will now specify the constituent elements ("modules") and process factors that yield the high degree of dynamics of the concept. Bearing in mind that the promotion of talents is a comprehensive, continuous, and long-term process involving the personality as a whole, it is evident that the basic modules of the concept have to be high quality objectives in personality and ability development, appropriate content, and educational processes, which are highly flexible and take into account the level of development achieved and the activities to be accomplished. Within the context of this optimization task, which occupies a central place in the concept, the following should be achieved: In addition to the goals for the personality development of all students derived from the humanist vision, basic and more special aims are to be achieved in the personality and talent development of scientifically and technologically gifted students.

These aims will be considered in greater depth. The goal is always acquisition and development of competence for action in each student personality. Competence for action in this context always involves the subjective preconditions for action (in particular the ability to act) and the objective requirements for action in their subjective form (readiness to act). The task of providing each personality with competence for action or, in other words, of organizing the process of development of the personality by educational guidance and independent activity so that competence for action is acquired, is two-dimensional from an educational point of view. The task is to guide all educational efforts toward the development of general competence for action in students, to enable them to tackle fundamental life processes in family, job, leisure, and day-to-day life in an individually unique manner. Based on this competence—and inseparably connected with it—education should strive for development of individually specific competence for action by deepening, enlarging, or developing general competence in such a way that individuals are able to respond to challenges in relatively restricted fields of activity. For the genesis of scientifically and technologically gifted individuals, the target function assumes a specific rôle, because it aims at developing competence in gifted students for action in the field of science and technology, or in selected spezialized fields of science and technology, as an immanent part of their all round personality development.

Questions now can be asked about the lines along which the process of acquisition of competence for action should be realized and the nature and structure of this process; this goes together with the requirement that the term as such should be characterized in a differentiated way. Methodologically, the answer can only be that competence for action can only be developed through the individual interaction of the personality with its environment. Educationally and psychologically, the answer will be that competence for action can be obtained only by intraindividually developing processes of information intake, processing, and storage, by their constant updating in relation to the challenges to be met, and by adequate action regulating mechanisms that are in permanent connection with the challenge meeting process.

The desired quality of competence for action is predominantly determined by the character and content of the challenge meeting process, in particular by the challenges that occupy a central position of particular importance in connection with these challenges. These are

> their *structure* (individual requirements, micro- and macrosequences of challenges, complex challenges, life related requirements, etc.);
> their *level* (development adequate requirements, open system of challenges of various difficulties);
> their specific *content* (content related to one specific subject, cross-disciplinary content, etc.);
> the *activities* required for the accomplishment of the task (type of action, complexity of actions and partial actions, qualities required for accomplishing the action);
> their multifactorially determined *condition complexes.*

In the final analysis, the results (partial results) obtained in and through the challenge meeting process (the acquisition of subject competence, metacognitive competence, and sensomotorically conditioned competence, the areas that determine competence for action) have their origin in the consciously selected or projected challenges (classes of challenges), in terms of *content* (challenges are always carriers of specific contents) and in terms of *process* (challenges can and must be arranged in a target–development oriented or in a process-oriented manner).

A more differentiated characterization of the term "competence for action in the scientific and technological field" is offered in the present chapter in order to improve theoretical understanding of the term, among other things. The realization, which has been proved many times in theory and practice, that the acquisition of competence for action is always a medium- or long-term process requiring activation of all areas of the personality (cognitive, motivational, volitional) shows that it is useful to delimit the described areas of competence. In this way, no area of competence is given a preferred place. The acquisition of subject competence (which is an extremely relevant target parameter for high ability in the scientific and technological field) is a dialectical process that mostly occurs simultaneously in time, a process that is aimed at creating a fundamental basis of knowledge. This requires a general scientific education, which alone is able to create in the long run fertile ground for the genesis of talent. This basic knowledge then will be enlarged and deepened and developed by the necessary expert knowledge, by wide-ranging problem specific knowledge which can be applied in a flexible manner, as well as by profound substantial insight into the differentiated problem fields of the area of high ability, in order to enable the gifted student to act successfully in his or her field of high ability.

The following are of special importance in shaping developmental processes affecting the acquisition of subject competence.

> stimulation of students to study special literature in a conscientious and comprehensive manner, and to take part in ensuing specialist discussion;
>
> active participation of the individuals concerned in various scientific and technological activities (Young Innovators' Fair, technical courses, student societies, student academies, teams of young research workers, etc.);
>
> study of the latest knowledge and trends in research, through continuous communication with outstanding scientific workers in the field of ability concerned (who should above all act as talent promoters), with a clear reference to teaching;
>
> elucidation of the wealth of problems in the particular subject field via study of the various aspects of this subject.

Subject competence only can be obtained by "focusing" attention on all elements of the field concerned. However, subject competence is not sufficient for competence for action. The body of knowledge, which can be used in a flexible way and should have a fundamental and at the same time subject specific character, must and should be suffused by metacognitive personality components. These have a decisive influence on the development—quality and quantity—of information processing and action regulating processes. The acquisition of metacognitive competence is linked with intraindividually specific integration and synthesis processes that aim at

> the further sensibilization of emotional excitability and responsiveness of gifted students with respect to outstanding scientific and technological problem fields;
>
> the consolidation of motivational and volitional conditions in these students;

the effective utilization and extension of mental capacities;
the further development of cognitive knowledge and skills;
and
further development of metacognitive knowledge structures
(in particular strategic knowledge and knowledge in the
fields of methods and planning) in scientifically and
technologically gifted students.

In order to elucidate the important place of metacognitive competence in the process of meeting challenges, it is necessary to mention the role of general and specific knowledge in the fields of planning and control, the role of cognitive skills in the fields of supervision and control (e.g., modeling, restructuring, etc.), and the role of knowledge in the fields of strategic thinking and methods that, according to recent cognitive psychological findings, can compensate for certain weak points in the body of specialist subject knowledge and favor the production of new and creative ideas. With regard to mental capacities, process qualities of information processing in gifted students, such as high information processing speed, the ability to process several pieces of information at the same time, well developed short- and long-term memory with high storage capacity, reversibility, and transformation ability, are of particular importance. These cannot be considered in isolation from the influences already mentioned. Stable motivational and volitional conditions are indispensable for the creation of the best possible internal development conditions in personality and ability genesis. What is meant here is the creation, stabilization, and further development of personality qualities such as striving for high performances and success, striving for more knowledge, sticking to principles, perseverance, persistence, courage to run a sound risk, optimism when it comes to exploring unknown fields of science, strength of character, and strong will in overcoming difficulties via increased effort. Also important are consolidation of interests, development of readiness to put a number of aspects of day-to-day life aside for some time and give priority to a more dominant task (objective), and the permanent consolidation of a long-term motivation to achieve high performances.

Another area of competence, which is of equal importance and determines competence for action, is sensorimotorically conditioned competence. In its totality it stands for the phenomenon of the "skilfull hand" that is characteristic of the practical and concrete aspects of technological ability, but has rarely been investigated until now. The close dialectical relationship of sensorimotorically conditioned competence with subject competence in the meeting of ambitious technical challenges (e.g., knowledge and experience concerning the technical object, the technical task, the technological problem, etc.), and with metacognitive competence (for instance, the mental anticipation of technical–technological solution strategies, of technical–functional solution concepts, of technical–economic solution variants, etc.) is uncontested. This is of vital importance for the implementation of scientific–technological innovation in practice (industry, craft, etc.). Theoretical findings now available show that the acquisition of sensorimotoric conditioned competence requires above all complex exercise and training sessions and a high time coefficient. Of equal importance for its genesis in the gifted student is encouragement by a real master of the trade (National Prize holder, distinguished technician, innovator, inventor, popular artist, etc.).

The progress and results of the activities of the gifted student are important criteria for ascertaining whether the person concerned has acquired competence for action in his or her field of ability during and through educationally guided challenge-meeting processes, as well as evaluating the level of quality of such competence. By establishing and evaluating such competence for action, it is possible to assess the personality growth achieved and to define new or more precise objectives in personality development for future work.

# 38

# Educating Gifted Pupils in Regular Schools

**W. van Dijk**
**W. A. M. Kok**
**G. T. M. Poorthuis**

*Utrecht, The Netherlands*

After introducing a differentiation model for the benefit of gifted pupils in regular schools, this chapter discusses some important findings of the research project "High giftedness in education," carried out at the ISOR, the Educational Research Department at the University of Utrecht. Data from survey research indicate what special provision has been made for gifted pupils in secondary schools in the Netherlands. Further data summarize experiences with the differentiation model at two different types of secondary school. Finally, some adaptations of the differentiation model are outlined.

## INTRODUCTION

The last few years have seen a growing awareness in the Netherlands that gifted pupils are given a raw deal in secondary education. Their special abilities are not sufficiently taken into account, and this can have negative consequences for their welfare and learning achievements. In global terms, the following two kinds of provision exist for meeting the needs of gifted pupils.

1. separation of gifted pupils from their peers, such as separate schools or classes; and
2. differentiated teaching for heterogeneous groups.

There is still considerable resistance to the first option in the Netherlands, the most important of which is that the early separation of gifted pupils leads to stigmatization. In addition, an exodus of gifted pupils means a serious erosion in the education of "normally" gifted children. To this should be added the fact that there are various forms of special education in the Netherlands for pupils with different learning or personality problems. For professedly sociopsychological, but in reality economic reasons, current policies are aimed at curbing the growth of this kind of special education. Pleas for separate schools for gifted pupils do not fit in with a policy of retrenchment. The second option, that is, provision within normal education, generally meets with approval. The ideal, at least for the first years of secondary education, is an education package for widely heterogeneous groups of pupils, including gifted pupils. The condition here should be that the package should offer possibilities for taking differences between pupils into account. The result is called internal differentiation. With regard to gifted pupils, the package should certainly include measures such as "acceleration" in combination with "enrichment." That is, gifted pupils should be enabled to complete the normal lessons in a short time, so that the time gained can be spent on the enhancement of knowledge already acquired.

Following the second option, a research project was started in 1988 at the ISOR, the Educational Research Department at the University of Utrecht. The aim of the project was to contribute to differentiated education for gifted children in the following two ways.

1. by developing exemplary teaching materials for gifted pupils that would meet the curriculum requirements mentioned in the literature; and

2. by gaining experience with a differentiation model as organizational framework for the use of materials especially developed for gifted pupils in heterogeneous groups.

In this chapter we will discuss in detail some of the findings of the ISOR project. In order to facilitate an understanding of these findings we shall first provide some information about the Dutch system of secondary education. Such information is necessary to determine whether certain educational provisions for gifted pupils would be possible or impossible. After this, we shall give some data from survey research carried out by us, which was aimed at finding out by means of a postal inquiry what special provisions had been made for gifted pupils in secondary schools. Subsequently we shall discuss experiences with the differentiation model used experimentally in two different types of secondary school. In the final section we shall take stock and again consider the two options mentioned earlier, which may be characterized in brief as the segregation or the integration of gifted secondary school pupils.

## DUTCH SECONDARY EDUCATION

There are two types of secondary schools in the Netherlands: combined schools and single category schools. Combined schools consist of different sections that teach courses at various levels. The division of pupils into these sections does not take place before the second or in some cases the third year. Until that time there are common courses for all pupils, regardless of level. Each section of a combined school can in theory stand on its own as a separate school to form a so-called single category school for relatively homogeneous groups of pupils. The gymnasium is an example of this type of school. Single category gymnasia do not by any means cater for gifted pupils alone. In the first year, in particular, the levels of pupils can differ widely. Because of these differences courses have to be differentiated—not least in order to meet the needs of gifted pupils—while keeping the existing year groups as they are. Not all gifted pupils go to the single category gymnasia. Most pupils in the Netherlands go to combined schools, including the gifted ones. Since these pupils end up in heterogeneous groups when they enter their school, courses have to be differentiated. The necessity for this is even greater than for the single category schools, since in general the differences between pupils are greater at the combined schools. Gifted pupils therefore are found mostly in schools with a more or less heterogeneous intake of pupils. Schools with differentiated courses that also fit in with the mental abilities of gifted pupils are naturally the most sought after. However, the question is whether there is special provision for gifted pupils at Dutch secondary schools. If so, what are these special provisions, and what do teachers think of them?

## EDUCATIONAL PROVISION FOR GIFTED PUPILS

In the period March to April 1990 we investigated, by means of a questionnaire, how far the special needs and abilities of gifted pupils are taken into account in Dutch secondary education. The questionnaire was sent to combined schools as well as single category schools, that is, to a total of 530 schools. The questionnaire consisted of two parts, a list of questions for the school management (the level of policy making) and a list for the teachers (the level of execution). Every school received six copies of the teachers' list, for the subjects history, geography, math, physics, Dutch, and English.

Responses were received from 207 schools (39%). The low response rate is not entirely unexpected. Inquiries in other areas of educational research have also achieved low response rates in the last few years. Many schools are not (are no longer) prepared to complete questionnaires. We cannot therefore state *a priori* that the schools which refused to cooperate give a lower priority to gifted pupils than the responding schools. Nonresponse research still to be carried out will have to show how far it is possible to rely on the general validity of the data: At present it is only possible to speculate about the 323 schools that did not respond.

The more types of education there are in a combined school, the more heterogeneous is the intake of pupils, and the more urgent the need to differentiate in the first years, not least to meet the needs of gifted pupils. It might be expected that differentiation occurs more often at these "broad" schools than at the single category schools or the combined schools with no more than two types of education, the "narrow" schools. The results showed that differentiation is a feature of 104 schools.

However, only in the case of 44 schools does this take the form of concrete measures to meet the needs of gifted pupils. These measures may be incidental in nature (e.g., referral to other school types) or structural (e.g., streaming). At 33 of the 44 schools, structural (sometimes including incidental) measures have been taken. In short, a relatively small number of responding schools attempt to effect improvements in the teaching of gifted pupils through differentiation.

As would be expected there are significantly more "broad" than "narrow" schools that practice differentiation (Chi-square = 10.51, $p < .001$). However, the differences between the two school types are nonsignificant as far as (structural) differentiation for gifted pupils is concerned. Even though there may be differentiation, at relatively many "broad" schools it is clear that the relevant measures are exclusively aimed at the weaker pupils.

At this point it is interesting to contrast the structural differentiation measures taken by schools to meet the needs of gifted pupils. Here a distinction must be made between combined schools and gymnasia, since not all measures mentioned are found at both types of school. The data showed that the structural measures taken by combined schools ($n = 29$) mainly involve the creation of homogeneous groups of pupils in the first year ($n = 14$). This measure implies that on entering school all pupils are distributed over the different forms of education contained within the combined school. For these schools the measure seems to be needed to guarantee effective education. The initial ideal of selection-free education in the first years is completely or partially abandoned. This results in what are called "bridging forms."

A possible measure for gymnasia that is comparable with the levelling effect of bridging forms in combined schools would be the formation of groups of pupils with roughly the same learning abilities. However, only one gymnasium had put this into practice. Besides or instead of the creation of heterogeneous classes, a number of schools (7 + 2 of each type)—both combined schools and gymnasia—chose to provide gifted pupils, either individually or in groups, with alternative assignments, exempting them from having to attend regular classes. These assignments may be free ranging or subject oriented. Other measures mentioned by the schools are the formation of a "gymnasium" class (at one combined school) and additional teaching in one subject. It may be concluded that the creation of homogeneous groups is the most frequent structural measure for meeting the needs of gifted pupils. However, this measure is not confined to gifted pupils, since it concerns the redistribution of all pupils in the same year. Even though some exclusive measures are taken, such as exemptions in order to carry out different assignments, these measures are few and far between.

A shortage of measures in favor of gifted pupils does not necessarily mean that these pupils are neglected in the actual practice of teaching the different subjects. The relevant data covering this aspect of the inquiry come from subject teachers representing history, geography, math, physics, Dutch, and English. Only a few teachers have not (ever) come across gifted pupils. A remarkably large number of these teachers, however, do not see any reason why they should take special measures in such cases. The differences between the various subject departments are considerable. The departments of math, geography, and English were in the vanguard with around 40%, compared to other departments. Further data provide answers to the question of what measures are taken by separate subject departments for the benefit of gifted pupils. A relatively large number of teachers select special textbook items aimed at gifted pupils. Geography and math have the highest scores in this respect. The reason for this has to do with the nature of the textbooks available for these subjects. Beside textbooks, some teachers use additional items for gifted pupils. The less suitable a textbook is deemed to be by the teacher as a source of teaching items for gifted pupils, the greater will be the need for additional materials. Indeed, teachers of physics and English use textbooks relatively infrequently as a source of teaching material, while making use of additional items relatively frequently.

Generally speaking, half of the teachers use gifted pupils to help others, history being the exception. It is also relatively rare for teachers in this subject to make gifted pupils do homework, no doubt due to the fact that they have many stories to relate. Maths, being an action subject par excellence, is different. In class only a small part of the time is spent on teaching. The rest of the time is spent on doing sums or math homework, the most radical measure for unsupervised activity. There are relatively few teachers who apply this measure. In the great majority of cases gifted pupils are given the opportunity to work on their own projects during supervision periods.

In conclusion it can be said that teachers who want to optimize the education of gifted pupils usually choose special teaching materials. All the measures mentioned earlier are, however, either not confined to gifted pupils, or are applied by only a few teachers. The teaching materials option is for the most part determined by the textbook used for a particular subject. In particular, teachers of geography and math tend to use textbooks with provisions for differentiated teaching. The provision in textbooks consists in nearly all cases of additional items in the sense of revision or enhancement items, expansion or free choice items. Where there are provisions for differentiated teaching in the textbook these usually take the form, according to the teachers, of enhancement and/or expansion items, and to a lesser extent of free choice items. The differences between the subjects are negligible except in the case of English, which uses markedly different textbooks with relatively many free choice items and relatively few enhancement items.

The data indicate that about 40% of the teachers of geography, math, and English use differentiated teaching for gifted pupils. The percentage for history, physics, and Dutch is much lower. To a large extent this difference can be traced back to the textbooks used by the teachers. Geography and maths in particular often use textbooks that contain enhancement or expansion items. In these subjects it is, of course, relatively easy to differentiate the teaching according to subject matter. In the other subjects teachers, who often do not have differentiated teaching items at their disposal, have to make greater effort to meet the needs of gifted pupils. The readiness and expertise to do this seem to be greatest for English.

## THE BRE MODEL

### Nature of the Model

Nearly all textbooks with provision for differentiated teaching are based on the BRE model. The subject matter in these textbooks is divided into a number of units. Each unit consists of basic concepts, revision items, enhancement, or expansion items. The assumed working method for pupils is represented schematically in the following. The first component is Basic concepts (B). The relevant learning targets (basic targets) must be attained by all pupils. The second component is the Diagnostic test. It follows after the basic concepts have been dealt

FIGURE 38-1.  The BRE model.

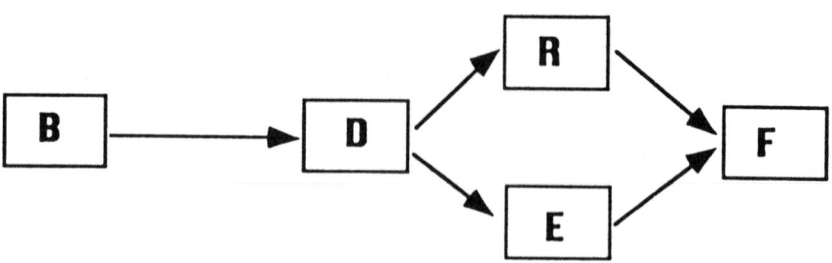

with and internalized by the pupils. The test provides a diagnosis of the pupils' attainment of the basic targets. Depending on the test scores there are Revision items (R) or Enhancement items (E). Revision items are meant for pupils who have shown gaps in their attainment of the basic targets. They receive extra (varying forms of) teaching and extra time to reach the target previous missed. The enhancement items are for pupils whom the test has shown to have a sufficient mastery of the basic concepts. As a follow up to the basic targets additional goals are set and different subject matter is presented accordingly.

In an earlier project the BRE model was introduced in two schools, a combined school and a single category gymnasium. This model was chosen because it fits in with current teaching practice better than other options such as cooperative learning, and offers teachers a more or less familiar and well ordered organizational framework within which heterogeneous group teaching can be carried out. In two tryouts of about one month each, various teachers of math and Dutch applied the principles of the BRE method. With the gifted student in mind data were gathered, by means of interviews with teachers and classroom observations, concerning the advantages and disadvantages of the BRE model as a form of internal differentiation.

## TESTING THE BRE MODEL

### The Teaching Materials

In math the subjects of "triangles" and "powers" were dealt with. For Dutch a grammatical topic was chosen (nominal predicates) and the topic of "critical reading" (the distinction be-tween facts and opinions). The basic concepts and revision items that went with these subjects were taken from the rele-vant textbooks. By contrast, the enhancement items were de-veloped from within the project, because the sections of the textbooks that contained these items were in general not up to the standards set in the literature. Unfortunately there was no time to try out the enhancement items with a small number of pupils. As a result, not only the BRE model but also the mate-rials developed had to be tested.

After the tryout it became clear that the enhancement items varied in quality. The main problem was the degree of difficulty. Some problems were too difficult, whereas others were too easy for pupils who had mastered the basic concepts. As regards maths, the enhancement items for "triangles" proved more sat-isfactory than those for "powers." For most pupils who got that far the additional material for "triangles" proved an interesting challenge, whereas the subject of "powers" proved much more problematic. Since many pupils, often including the relatively gifted ones in the class, found "powers," difficult at the basic level, having to face enhancement problems proved even more confusing and frustrating. The enhancement material was most valuable only for those pupils who had a complete mastery of the basic concepts.

What happened with math and the subject "powers" also hap-pened with Dutch and the subject of "nominal predicates." In general, pupils found it hard going at the basic level. The en-hancement items proved to lead not so much to greater insights as to numerous misunderstandings. The other component, "critical reading" (facts and opinions), appealed more to the pupils and teachers. However, it was difficult to distinguish be-tween basic concepts on the one hand and enhancement items on the other. Differentiation manifested itself mainly in learn-ing achievements. Gifted pupils were given an opportunity to shine, whereas their less gifted classmates were not automati-cally excluded.

**Classroom Organization**

Once the pupils had been divided after the diagnostic test into a "revision group" and an "enhancement group," the BRE model became more difficult to handle in proportion to the number of times the pupils appealed to the teacher for help. During the project the pupils who were doing the enhancement items, including the gifted ones, continually asked for supplementary instructions. This lack of independence partly was induced by the items themselves: Some instructions were unclear and not completely free of ambiguity, the presentation of some problems differed strongly from what the pupils were used to, such as working with diagrams, and, as mentioned earlier, some items were of a high degree of difficulty, alternating with relatively simple ones. To this should be added the fact that independent work was not a daily routine at the project schools. In general, the pupils were not used to following written instructions, whereas the teachers were unfamiliar with differentiated teaching. All this resulted in a majority of the teachers experiencing considerable problems in organizing their classes while applying the BRE model.

## Selection of Pupils

Pupils were allowed to start on the enhancement items if they had passed the diagnostic test. This, of course, was true also for those pupils who, on the basis of tests and teacher assessments, had been selected as gifted. However, the norms applied by teachers during the project were not strict enough. The result was that a number of pupils started on the enhancement items while their mastery of the basic concepts was insufficient. This too led to organizational problems in the classrooms. In contrast to the combined school, the division into groups after the diagnostic test caused some difficulties. Pupils who were made to do the revision items felt that they were being treated unfairly. They started with the idea that pupils who were allowed to do the enhancement items were better prepared for the final test. In addition, compulsory participation in the revision was seen as a sign of incompetence rather than as a second chance. At the combined schools there were hardly any critical comments on this point. For gifted pupils the learning of basic concepts is in many cases straightforward. The danger is that they underestimate their task and work superficially, with undesirable consequences for subsequent learning of more exacting items. Within the framework of the BRE model they are persuaded by means of an interim test to take the basic items seriously. They too have to show that they have mastered the basic concepts before they can start on the enhancement items.

The project distinguished four groups of pupils.

1. pupils selected as gifted on the basis of tests and teacher assessments;
2. pupils selected as gifted on the basis of teacher assessments alone;
3. pupils selected as gifted on the basis of tests alone; and
4. pupils not selected as gifted.

Table 38-1 shows how many pupils from each of the groups mentioned completed the revision as well as the enhancement items.

In the first tryout all "gifted" pupils completed the enhancement items, together with 57 nonselected pupils. In the second tryout, however, some of the gifted pupils had to do the revision items. It is clear that they had worked below their level of ability. A similar pattern can be detected for math. The BRE model is therefore anything but a panacea for the persistent problem of underachievement that exists for a number of gifted pupils.

## DISCUSSION

There is an increase in readiness in the Netherlands to improve the education of gifted pupils. For the time being, solutions are not being sought in the establishment of special schools. The majority view is that segregation of gifted pupils is undesirable. This puts a heavy onus on school management and teachers to cater for the special needs of gifted pupils in more or less heterogeneous groups. This means that solutions are bound to be confined to applying differentiation within and between groups of pupils. A nationwide inquiry has shown that most secondary schools pay attention to the problem of the gifted pupil, but that this attention is accompanied by concrete and exclusive measures for gifted pupils at few schools. The readiness is

**TABLE 38-1**
**Participants in the Dutch Teaching Program**

| Selection | 1st rev | Tryout enh | 2nd rev | Tryout enh |
|---|---|---|---|---|
| Test + teacher | 0 | 2 | 0 | 2 |
| teacher | 0 | 7 | 3 | 4 |
| Test | 0 | 7 | 2 | 2 |
| not selected | 112 | 57 | 135 | 34 |

there, but through lack of time, expertise, experience, supervision and suitable teaching materials, changes in teaching that benefit gifted pupils are extremely slow in coming. On the other hand, the subject of "highly gifted pupils" has been all but taboo for the last 10–15 years. Seen in that light, the inquiry results provide plenty of reasons for optimism.

The BRE model provides a well-tried method of differentiated teaching for gifted pupils. The advantage of this model is that the measures taken fit in with many textbooks used in secondary schools. Another advantage is that there is no total break with current forms of classroom teaching. Both these advantages increase the chance of successful implementation of the model in practical education. Other positive aspects include the diagnostic element, the systematic nature of the model and the room it leaves for the inclusion of enhancement items that might benefit not only gifted pupils but also others. However, the model has its limitations. Its usability is highly dependent on subject, teaching material, type of school, and learner characteristics. Generally speaking, the BRE model seems too rigid to be able to function as the differentiation model for gifted pupils. Alternative, more flexible forms of differentiation also should be considered. These might include tempo differentiation and exemption for pupils who are exceptionally fast in attaining basic targets. The available extra time might then be used for enhancement or for projects connected in subject matter with the normal curriculum. The inquiry showed that these forms of differentiation are feasible in practice. However, it is of paramount importance that the problem of shortages of available teaching materials for independent use by gifted pupils be solved.

# 39

# Predicting (Under)achievement of Gifted Children

**Ton Mooij**

*Catholic University of Nijmegen, Nijmegen, The Netherlands*

Gifted children may perform worse or achieve much less than expected: How can this happen and how can such underachievement be prevented? To answer this question it is theorized that personal variables (e.g., identity, cognitive, and motivational factors) and environmental variables (e.g., home and school) influence or interact with each other. The environmental variables may occur at different levels, for example, the individual level or the group level. Mutual influences or interactions between variables at different levels can be integrated within an interactional multilevel theory. A first example of such a theory is constructed with the aid of four consecutive developmental models. With a child's increasing age the number of variables in a model increases because of the child's growth in cognitive complexity and the accumulating differentiation in meaningful environmental levels and situations. With these models it is possible to explain a gifted child's underachievement in certain situations and its simultaneous high achievement in others. It is also possible to predict that by changing certain environmental characteristics underachievement can be turned into high achievement.

## INTRODUCTION

Research shows that (highly) gifted children may achieve very badly compared to what can be expected of them (Freeman, 1983; Heinbokel, 1988). Although this "underachievement" has been widely recognized as a serious problem (Butler-Por, 1987; Davis & Rimm, 1985), its explanation and in particular the way to circumvent it are subject to various interpretations (Rost, 1990). Theoretical clarification of the phenomenon of giftedness and its relationships with achievement and underachievement therefore may provide the ground for a more consistent attack on the problem of underachievement. In this chapter this will be done by using recent developments in interactional multilevel theorizing and analysis with respect to education in particular (cf., Aitkin & Longford, 1986; Goldstein, 1987; Mooij, 1987, 1991a).

Mehlhorn (1988) states that giftedness has a genetic basis, influences the environment but is also influenced by the environment, and is expressed through a specific individual set of inner characteristics with six dimensions (general intellectual skills, specific intellectual skills, social communicative skills, creative skills, emotional skills, athletic skills). Comparable distinctions are used rather often in theory and research on giftedness (e.g., Davis & Rimm, 1985; Khatena, 1982). According to Mehlhorn (1988), giftedness is present when the existing societal highest norms on one or more of the dimensions are approached or surpassed through actual achievement.

The inner characteristics of a person therefore represent a *potential* that the person may use or not use in order to behave, perform, or achieve in a certain environment (cf., also Rost, 1990). With respect to the explanation or prediction of achievement or underachievement of gifted children, it is important to realize that a child can choose whether or not to behave or perform in the required ways. This decision is based on personal cognitive and motivational variables concerning experiences with and results of former performances, expectations and evaluations of possible effects of the actual behavior, and expectations of alternative behavior possibilities (Bowerman, 1978). Environmental or situational variables operate either to facilitate or to hinder the actual performance or achievement according to certain criteria. The decision whether or not to apply potential in a certain situation is thus influenced by learning and evaluational experiences in (comparable) situations, and by situational characteristics themselves.

The goal of this chapter, then, is to clarify processes and effects concerning the (under)achievement of gifted children, in education in particular. The two main topics of concern are

1. When will a gifted child achieve below his or her potential, and why?
2. How could an underachieving gifted child be (re)motivated to achieve according to his or her capacities?

## THREE APPROACHES

Three general approaches exist to explain or predict a person's behavior. First, within a *personality or psychometric approach* the theorist concentrates on personality dimensions or variables that are assumed to be invariant across situations. Butler-Por (1987), for example, is surprised by the fact that, parallel to "dependent" achievement variables, personality variables used as covariates also change as a side effect of experimental variation in environmental variables. Furthermore, the personality theorist often uses a person's "motivation" as the explanatory source for the person's behavior that neglects potentially relevant environmental conditions (see Heckhausen (1980) for a detailed treatment of this topic).

Second, in the *environmental approach* only environmental variables function in an explanatory or predictive way. To give an example: Regular education in many countries does not differentiate between potential capacities of young children in kindergarten. This seems to be responsible for the sudden increase in behavioral and motivational problems of gifted children at this age (cf., Mooij, 1991a). More generally, concentrating only on situational conditions while neglecting the specific features of the gifted personality may lead to cognitive, motivational, emotional, and social problems of a gifted child in many different situations (Khatena, 1982).

In a third approach attention is given to the reciprocal influences or interaction between personal and environmental variables. This *interactional approach* can be defined in the terms used by Pervin and Lewis (1978): "The essence . . . is the view that the variables of interest are constantly influencing one another, the action of one affecting another variable that in turn affects the nature of the first variable" (p. 15). The emphasis is on: ". . . the interaction (i.e., reciprocal action) between parts of

the organism and between the organism and its environment"
(p. 15). Essential is the use of a time orientation or time dimension in order to specify adequately cause–effect relationships between variables.

Early examples of this interactional approach were offered by
Rosenthal and Jacobson (1968), who suggested that the
teacher's expectation of a pupil's potential high achievement
stimulated the development of the actual achievement (the "Pygmalion effect"). Rubovits and Maehr (1971) discovered that: ". . .
gifted students were called upon more and were praised more
than nongifted students" (p. 202). Many other kinds of example
can be given (cf., Magnusson & Allen, 1983a,b; Mooij, 1987).

## The Interactional Multilevel Approach

Compared to the personality approach and the environmental approach, the interactional approach to explaining a person's behavior seems most adequate, for several reasons. First, it seems to be
the most realistic approach because underachievement events experienced by gifted children show that both personal and environmental variables are relevant (Fransen, 1988; Gallagher, 1975; Heinbokel, 1988; Mooij, 1991a,b,c). With the interactional approach
these different kinds of variable can be integrated theoretically.
This approach also functions as a safeguard in a psychodiagnostic
setting: It prevents concentration on personality variables only,
which may distort psychodiagnostic advice in the case of school
problems of highly gifted children.

Second, the interactional approach seems to be the most
comprehensive, because of its longitudinal character and its
"completeness": It considers both personal and environmental
variables. If appropriate, the researcher can study the effects of
only (some) personal or only (some) environmental variables on
the person's development or behavior. This means that both
other approaches are subsumed in the interactional approach.
If either one of these kinds of variable falls short of confirmation in research, this informs the researcher about the possible
theoretical and empirical irrelevance of either kind.

Third, it is the approach with the widest scope: It can probably cover any problem that is associated with dynamic aspects
of personal, social, and societal variables related to a person's
development or behavior in specified environments.

Fourth, in this approach the development of a person's behavior can also be explained by characteristics of the others in a group to which the person belongs. In particular, achieving or scoring either high or low in comparison to the others in a group may influence the individual's feeling of competence, which stimulates or hinders the person's subsequent achievement (the "frog-pond effect": Davis, 1966; Werts & Watley, 1969). Such comparison effects are typically "interactional effects."

The interactional approach is therefore clearly to be favored in order to predict the achievement level of a gifted child. However, interactional theorizing is not easy. First, it has to be based on detailed knowledge of relevant personal and environmental variables and their causal relationships in the course of time (Magnusson & Allen, 1983a,b). Second, confirmation of interactional theories necessitates the use of "interactional" research, which means doing longitudinal research with respect to personal and environmental variables (see also Heckhausen, 1980). Such research is relatively costly and has to be carried out by especially well qualified researchers. Third, the environmental variables have to be "real" and "meaningful" to the person, that is they have to be ecologically valid (Frijda, 1981; Jackson, 1968; Mooij, 1982). This may complicate the measurement of such variables. Fourth, taking the environment into account also requires looking at the different possible groupings of persons in this environment. These groupings may refer to different environmental or system levels with their own system variables; within the education system for example the pupil level, the group level, the school level, the regional level, and the national level seem most relevant. Each level can be characterized by variables that may involve level specific but also cross-level processes and effects relevant to development in the pupil's behavior. This grouping or multilevel aspect is studied in multilevel theorizing and research (Aitkin & Longford, 1986; Goldstein, 1987).

From an interactional multilevel point of view, personal variables and environmental variables on two or more different levels may influence each other, which leads to complex processes and effects. Multilevel interrelationships and longitudinal effects on the (development in the) person's behavior are the main focus. For this reason, interactional multilevel theorizing seems most promising in clarifying complex developmental processes, for example, the prediction of (under)achievement of a gifted child.

## INTERACTIONAL MULTILEVEL THEORY
## ON (UNDER)ACHIEVEMENT

The relevance of personal (cognitive, motivational, emotional, social, creative) and environmental (home, kindergarten, school) variables to development in achievement changes during infancy and childhood. This process also influences the possible interactions between the different kinds of variables. With increasing age the numbers of potentially relevant levels and variables in the environment increase, so that the theoretical models have to become more complex as the child grows older. Therefore, different interactional models with different but related theoretical specifications have to be constructed, as is shown in the following.

### Preschool Development

In early infancy gifted children are very eager to do a lot of different things (Freeman, 1979, 1983; Gallagher, 1975). Compared to their peers they usually do very well on for instance cognitive–intellectual, musical, motoric, or social activities, but they do not need to be ahead in all kinds of task. No doubt exists about the genetic or hereditary basis of their qualities, but exact specification of the role of either genetic or learning conditions is still lacking (De Leeuw, 1986).

The individual genetic basis can be seen as a starting point influencing the dimensions given by Mehlhorn. The scores of a child on these dimensions can be seen as indicators of the "identity" of the child. In the preschool period the development of these individual qualities furthers the identity formation of the child. The development of these "identity dimensions" can be explained by the interaction with environmental home variables. Four home variables may be relevant here.

> stimulation of the child by the parent(s): a supporting attitude taken by the parent(s) or caretaker(s) with respect to the diverse demands and expressions of a child will strengthen the underlying identity dimensions and, consequently, the child's resulting development. This seems especially true for a gifted child who may become deeply involved in one kind of behavior but, after some time, may turn toward another activity with comparable eager-

ness and intensity. Parents who take the child seriously let this happen, provide interesting resources and materials and, if required, help or cooperate with the child. Such a supporting parent attitude will generally stimulate the development of the child.

the parents' level of education, in particular the mother's educational level, is of crucial importance to the child's early development (e.g., Meijnen, 1977). If the parents' level of education is higher, this will foster the general and specific intellectual and creativity conditions usually needed by gifted children.

siblings' characteristics: If siblings are older than the gifted child, this may positively stimulate the development of this child because it can easily play and work with the siblings. However, if siblings are younger this may block a gifted child's cognitive–intellectual development but stimulate its social communicative, creative, and emotional skills. If there are no siblings this may promote intellectual and creative skills but hinder the development of social communicative and emotional skills. This may cause serious problems when the child starts in regular kindergarten. Because of its social sensitivity and relatively underdeveloped social–communicative and emotional skills, such a gifted child may feel threatened continuously by its peers, in particularly if it is not allowed to realize its own interests.

parents' economic level: it is reasoned that more wealthy parents have greater capacity to give the child a more enriched home environment. Such an environment supplies the material conditions for a more favorable development of the intellectual and creativity identity dimensions.

This interactional preschool theorizing is represented in the model in Figure 39-1. The model shows the genetic basis of the identity dimensions; the development of the identity dimensions from time 1 (e.g., the age of two months) to time 2 (e.g., the age of three years) is influenced interactionally by the home variables. To avoid too complex theorizing at this moment, all variables lie at the individual or child level. When relevant longitudinal data are available the model can be statistically analyzed quite easily.

FIGURE 39-1.    Preschool development (one level model).

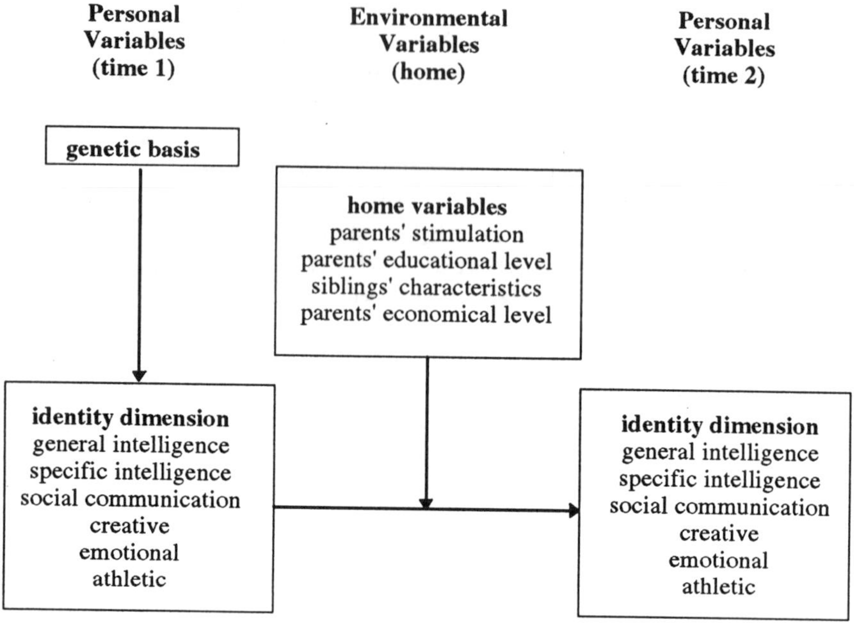

| Personal Variables (time 1) | Environmental Variables (home) | Personal Variables (time 2) |
|---|---|---|

**genetic basis**

**home variables**
parents' stimulation
parents' educational level
siblings' characteristics
parents' economical level

**identity dimension**
general intelligence
specific intelligence
social communication
creative
emotional
athletic

**identity dimension**
general intelligence
specific intelligence
social communication
creative
emotional
athletic

## Kindergarten

At home a child usually has a lot of things to play with or to concentrate on, whereas assistance, if required, is given by an adult who has a close and trusting relationship with the child. In kindergarten, however, a lot of children may stumble or play around doing lots of different things for short periods of time. Entering kindergarten thus means encountering many "new" situations within a play group, which requires adjustments in the cognitive–motivational maps of the child about the surrounding world and its meaning (cf., Kuhl, 1986; Neisser, 1976). In other words: New concepts and new meanings arise and have to be integrated within the child's cognitive–motivational internal representations of the outer world.

After some time a "new" child will be able to direct and give meaning to his or her own behavior in the play group, carry out and evaluate play or task activities, and evaluate its own achievement according to certain norms (in particular, the norms of the teacher). Moreover, the child will compare its own play processes or their results with processes or results of the other children. If its own activities and achievement are considered to be relatively high, the child feels competent (Bowerman, 1978) and will feel attracted or oriented toward the processes and activities.

The reverse, however, also occurs. This may happen to children who are either relatively highly or relatively low gifted compared to the other children in the group. In regular kindergarten the gifted child is generally not able to carry out his or her own favored activities: The necessary materials or conditions are not present because the play situation is meant to comfort the modal four- and five-year-olds. Within days or weeks after entrance, a gifted child may therefore experience cognitive and motivational stress, which in the long run may result in emotional, social, and behavioral problems. A gifted child may then not want to go to kindergarten any more, or may only say it likes to go there, whereas its behavior shows that this is not true.

Because of the transition into kindergarten the "preschool identity" of the child changes into what may be called a "kindergarten identity." Two kinds of environmental characteristics may influence this process: kindergarten variables and home variables. Kindergarten variables that seem important to the identity development and positive growth of the behavior, achievement, competence, and orientation of a gifted child in kindergarten can be based on the individual level and on the play group level. At the individual level, a higher degree of individualization in instruction, a higher differentiation in content complexity in play or learning processes, and a higher degree of discovery processes in the content of play or learning processes can be assumed to promote behavioral processes that are more adjusted to the learning characteristics of gifted children (cf., Mooij, 1991a). At the same time, however, variables on the play group level also play a role. Six potentially relevant group level conditions fostering the development of gifted children are.

> a high degree of "openness" or orientation of the teacher towards the real development of each child in the group (Mooij, 1991c,d);
> a high degree of alertness or "with-it-ness" of the teacher during play and learning processes (Kounin, 1970);
> a high degree of directness in the teacher's management behavior (cf., Mooij & Jansen, 1990);

a high mean development of the pupils in the group;

a low degree of heterogeneity in development or achievement between the pupils in the group;

a low degree of disciplinary problems of the pupils in the group (Kounin, 1970).

Concerning home variables, the parents' expectation of the functioning of the child in kindergarten and school will be relevant. First, this expectation influences the choice of kindergarten the child will attend. If parents believe that their gifted child needs a more individualized play group situation with more complex contents and discovery processes, they will choose a kindergarten offering such situations. If the kindergarten or school actually available has only a uniform modal system, parents may try to change these kindergarten practices. Usually, however, teachers are immune to proposals to change their practices in the interest of only one or a few of the children. Second, because of kindergarten entrance the parents will mentally prepare and coach the child. If the parents expect the child to function well in kindergarten because of its preschool identity, they will share this positive feeling with the child, which will positively influence the necessary adjustment processes. Parental expectation will then have a positive effect on the further development and balanced identity growth of the child. On the other hand, when parents are relatively insecure or anxious about the child's transition to and functioning in kindergarten and school, the child may also become anxious. This may happen, for instance, when the child is able to read and write and is eager to do such things at home, whereas this is not allowed or not really integrated into kindergarten activities. In this case the child's identity growth, and its kindergarten identity in particular, may become disturbed.

Figure 39-2 gives a schematic representation of this interactional theorizing. In the model the environmental home variable is considered at the individual level; the environmental kindergarten variables are situated at the individual and the play group level. The long term interaction between the personal preschool identity dimensions and the environmental variables both at home and at school affects the development of the identity as a kindergarten child. In the course of time the transition process from home to kindergarten is expressed in specific changes in the identity dimensions and in the emergence of rel-

FIGURE 39-2.    Home–kindergarten transition (two-level model).

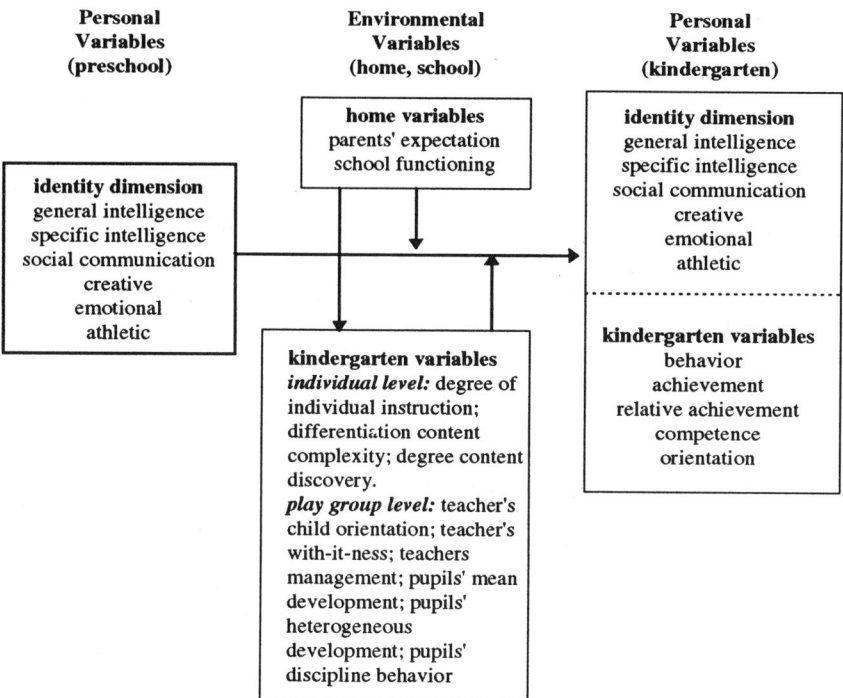

**Personal Variables (preschool)**

**identity dimension**
general intelligence
specific intelligence
social communication
creative
emotional
athletic

**Environmental Variables (home, school)**

**home variables**
parents' expectation
school functioning

**kindergarten variables**
*individual level:* degree of individual instruction; differentiation content complexity; degree content discovery.
*play group level:* teacher's child orientation; teacher's with-it-ness; teachers management; pupils' mean development; pupils' heterogeneous development; pupils' discipline behavior

**Personal Variables (kindergarten)**

**identity dimension**
general intelligence
specific intelligence
social communication
creative
emotional
athletic

**kindergarten variables**
behavior
achievement
relative achievement
competence
orientation

evant personal variables: kindergarten behavior, kindergarten achievement, kindergarten relative achievement, kindergarten competence, and kindergarten orientation (see Figure 39-2).

It is now possible to explain that, for example, a gifted child may do well at home (cf., Figure 39-1). However, the transition to kindergarten may bring the interaction of the child's personal variables with a number of environmental kindergarten variables (cf., Figure 39-2), which may block or even reverse its development. The more extremely gifted the child, the more serious this setback may be. On the other hand, Figure 39-2 also suggests which environmental kindergarten variables could be used in order to change the interaction with personal variables in such ways as to produce positive kindergarten effects on weakly functioning or underachieving gifted pupils (see Mooij, 1991c,d). For instance, these children usually need to be able to read and write in kindergarten.

## Elementary School

In many ways the transition from kindergarten to elementary school is less disruptive than the transition from home to kindergarten. The child is older and has already had to get used to spending many hours with a teacher and a crowd of other children in the classroom. The most important change is from playful developmental activities in kindergarten toward the more planned and compulsory learning activities in elementary school, which become coordinated within specific school subjects like native language and mathematics/arithmetic. These school subjects gradually become more or less specific learning processes characterized by school subject bound behaviors, achievements, relative achievements (compared to the achievements of the other pupils in the classroom), competences, and orientations.

In elementary school the child's cognitive–motivational differentiation and complexity is still growing. The child becomes able to distinguish experiences with respect to a specific school subject from the more generalized behavior, achievement, relative achievement, competence, and orientation involved in attending school. For example, although the child may reject one school subject, it may still like going to school, or vice versa (cf., Lens, 1987; Mooij, 1987).

Instances of home variables promoting the transition to elementary school are parents' educational level and parents' economic level. Both variables may influence the choice of the actual elementary school, but may also influence the development of the "kindergarten identity" into an "elementary school identity" that is characterized by the personal identity dimensions and school subject specific behavioral, cognitive, and motivational processes and effects (cf. *Arbeitsgruppe Schulforschung*, 1980; Cattell & Child, 1975; Krampen & Mory, 1982). The relevant environmental school variables are more or less the same as in kindergarten (although they have to be operationalized in other ways). Information about these variables and their functioning can be found in Davis and Rimm (1985), Gallagher (1975), Khatena (1982), and Mooij (1987), among others.

The teacher, the other pupils and the parents react upon the school subject specific learning processes, products, and achievements of a child. Positive reactions or relatively high school marks affect cognitive, motivational and social variables, which in turn may cause the pupil to select the same or more difficult learning activities; negative reactions or inadequate school marks usually block the (same kind of) learning activities, and the child starts looking for other or undesirable (disturbing) ways to behave.

An example of a gifted child illustrating these processes and effects is Jos (in Mooij, 1991a). In his preschool period this highly gifted boy was doing very well at home. In traditional regular kindergarten he was extremely unhappy and developed psychosomatic problems. After starting elementary school he did better, because his learning processes and the results revealed to the teacher that he was able and wanted to do much more than his classmates. The teacher actually provided Jos with more individualized instruction and learning activities with more complex contents during the lessons. His problems were reduced considerably (although he also had to skip two of the six elementary school classes). The transition process from kindergarten to elementary school, and the possible effects of the elementary school variables on the personal variables in particular, are schematized in the model in Figure 39-3.

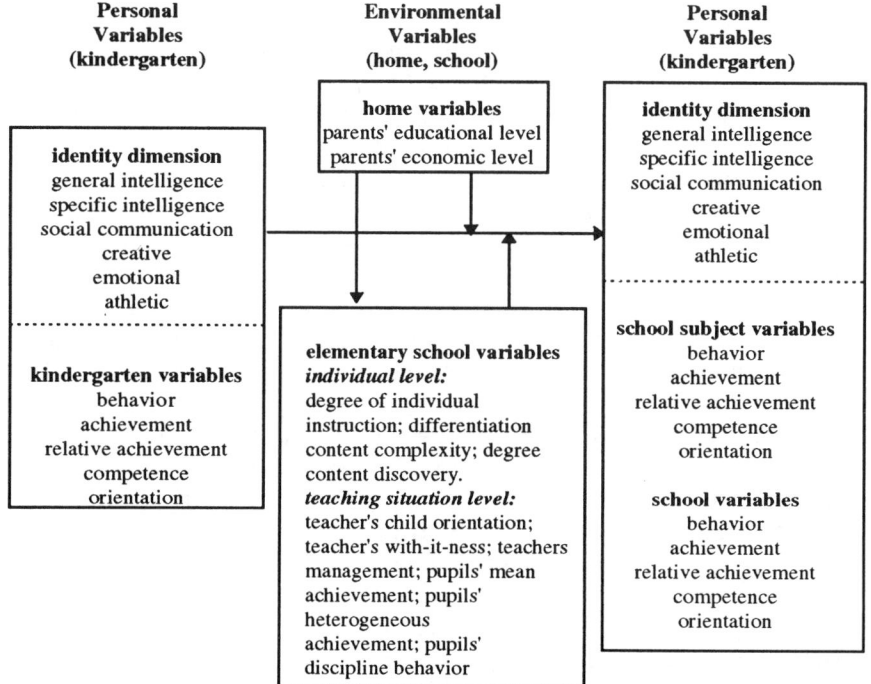

FIGURE 39-3.   Kindergarten–elementary school transition (two-level model).

## Secondary School

In secondary education a pupil is able to discriminate between his or her own characteristics and those of a classroom, a school, or education as such. This implies that a pupil gradually learns to distinguish variables and their meanings on the individual level, the teaching situation level, the school level, and the educational system level.

Variables characterizing education on the individual level and teaching situation level have already been dealt with in previous sections. At the school level "school flexibility" can be defined as the degree of adjustment of the schooling processes to the requirements of individual pupils in school. In particular in (Dutch) secondary education, school flexibility seems to be rather low nowadays: During the last 15 years most attention in secondary school development has been given to school management and to individual pupils' school anxiety problems. Hardly any or no progress seems to have been made on topics such as curriculum differentiation and educational psychology in relation to individualization within classrooms. A lack of school flexibility seems responsible for a lot of school problems of gifted children in secondary education (cf., Hargreaves, 1967; Mooij, 1991a). Analogous to the variables on the teaching situation level, on the school level "pupils' mean achievement in school" and "pupils' heterogeneity in achievement in school" may also influence the formation of a pupil's "school identity." In fact, comparison of achievement between students on the campus was the original impetus for the "frog-pond phenomenon" (Davis, 1966), in which achievement scores of other students on the campus were used to direct one's own behavior.

In the course of secondary education a pupil's own functioning with respect to the educational system becomes crystallized in the concepts of educational behavior, educational achievement, relative educational achievement, educational competence, and educational orientation (see Mooij (1987) for the respective definitions). The growth and development of these cognitive–motivational concepts and their meanings are recognized by the pupil, and the advantages and disadvantages of education are weighed with respect to one's own future and societal position. The pupil can do this—among other things—by evaluating earlier experiences in elementary and secondary education and by anticipating the consequences of one's own choices concerning going to school or, for instance, leaving school early. These experiences can be based on a number of different schools in elementary or secondary education. For gifted pupils these experiences usually are not positive. In Mooij (1991a) the girl Sofieke leaves a Montessori elementary school because of understimulation. She does somewhat better in a traditional regular elementary school; in secondary education understimulation problems resurface. The boy Harmen has serious "authority problems" in elementary education and in secondary education in particular: Therefore he changes to another high school. This has positive consequences for his behavior and achievement. If he had not changed secondary school he certainly would have become a dropout.

A theoretical model of the relevant levels and variables is given in Figure 39-4. This model is an extension of the former models.

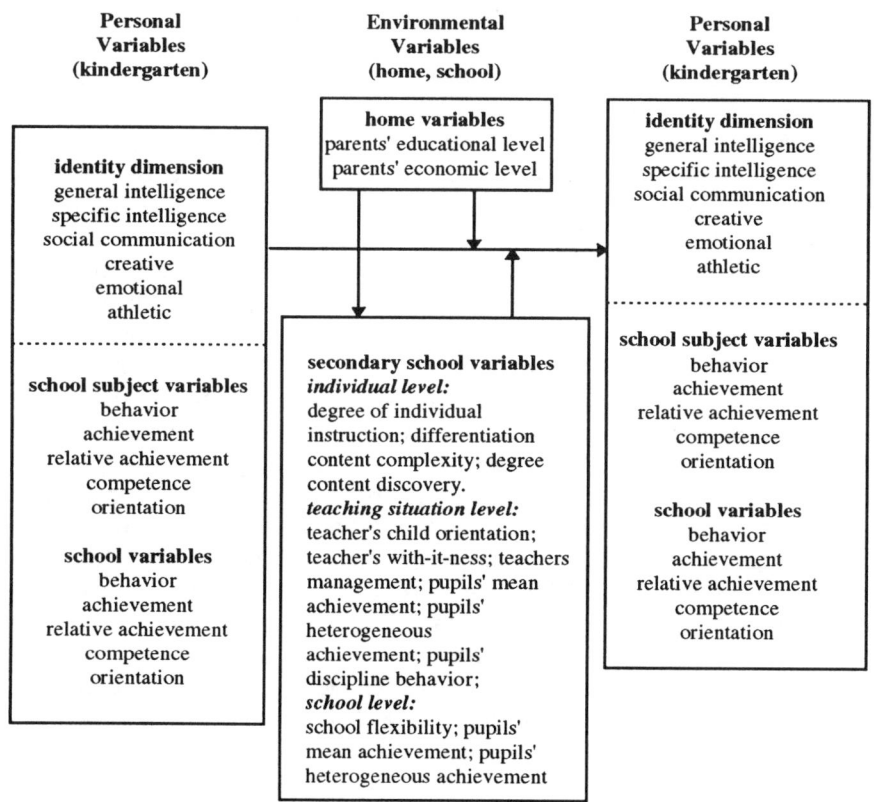

FIGURE 39-4.    Elementary–secondary school career (three-level model).

## DISCUSSION

A set of four theoretical models has been developed in order to explain or predict (under)achievement of gifted children. The models refer to different consecutive life stages: preschool, kindergarten, elementary school, and secondary school. Very important in the models is the longitudinal aspect, which allows explicit theorizing about the effects of personal or environmental (home, school) variables on the development of personal variables. These personal variables are separated into identity dimensions and different kinds of school related variables, so that scores on the identity variables characterizing a person may diverge from the relevant scores on the school variables. In this way it is possible to explain or to predict cognitive, motivational, behavioral, and achievement problems of a gifted child either at home or at school, within school but not at home, conflicts within one school subject but not in the other school subjects, and early school leaving processes (Mooij, 1980; Tinto, 1975), and so on. Moreover, it can be demonstrated how an underachieving gifted child could be remotivated to achieve according to its capacities in school. Taken together, the models represent the structure of a coherent interactional multilevel theory predicting (under)achievement of a gifted child at home or at school.

The genetic factors are included only in the model depicted in Figure 39-1. The reason for this is that, although genetic factors are relevant throughout life, it is very difficult to measure them adequately. Moreover, although genetic factors are important they cannot be manipulated: Their influence is stable despite (possible) environmental changes. It can also be assumed that their influence is represented in the early measurement of the identity dimensions. In going from Figure 39-1 (preschool period) to Figure 39-4 (secondary education), the models become more complicated because of the increase in a child's cognitive–motivational complexity and the increases in relevant educational levels and variables. The number of potentially relevant variables in the interactional multilevel models becomes relatively large, as is shown in Figure 39-4. However, research may prove some of the variables to be of less relevance or irrelevant in combination with other variables. From a theoretical point of view, the models function as a heuristic device, which has already been used in some small scale qualitative research (Mooij, 1991d). Quantitative research in particular will reveal more about the usefulness and validity of the models. If such research is carried out from the models in Figures 39-1 or 39-2 onward, this may facilitate the variable reduction process considerably. First steps to check the models in a quantitative procedure have been made: Mooij (1991c) operationalized the identity dimensions and the expectation about the school functioning of a child. Operationalizations of most of the other variables already exist (Mooij, 1987, 1990).

## REFERENCES

Aitkin, M., & Longford, N. (1986). Statistical modelling issues in school effectiveness studies. *The Journal of the Royal Statistical Society, 149*, 1–43.

Arbeitsgruppe Schulforschung (1980). *Leistung und Versagen.* München: Juventa.

Bowerman, W. R. (1978). Subjective competence: the structure, process and function of self-referent causal attributions. *Journal for the Theory of Social Behavior, 8*, 45–75.

Butler-Por, N. (1987). *Underachievers in school: issues and intervention.* Chicester: Wiley.

Cattell, R. B., & Child, D. (1975). *Motivation and dynamic structure.* London: Holt, Rinehart and Winston.

Davis, G. A., & Rimm, S. B. (1985). *Education of the gifted and talented.* Englewood Cliffs: Prentice-Hall.

Davis, J. A. (1966). The campus as a frog pond: an application of the theory of relative deprivation to career decisions of college men. *The American Journal of Sociology, 40*, 1–10.

Fransen, G. (1988). Het verhaal van Jan, een hoogbegaafd kind. *Tijdschrift voor Orthopedagogiek, Kinderpsychiatrie en Klinische Kinderpsychologie, 13*, 101–110.

Freeman, J. (1979). *Gifted children.* Lancaster: MTP Press.

Freeman, J. (1983). *Clever children.* Middlesex: Hamlyn.

Frijda, N. H. (1981). Menselijke natuur en informatie als determinanten van gedrag. *Nederlands Tijdschrift voor de Psychologie, 36*, 135–150.

Gallagher, J. J. (1975). *Teaching the gifted child.* Boston: Allyn and Bacon.

Goldstein, H. (1987). *Multilevel models in educational and social research.* New York: Oxford University Press.

Hargreaves, D. H. (1967). *Social relations in a secondary school.* London: Routledge & Kegan Paul.

Heckhausen, H. (1980). *Motivation und Handeln: Lehrbuch der Motivationspsychologie.* Berlin: Springer.

Heinbokel, A. (1988). *Hochbegabte. Erkennen, Probleme, Lösungswege.* Frankfurt: Deutsches Institut für Internationale Pädagogische Forschung.

Jackson, P. W. (1968). *Life in classrooms.* New York: Holt, Rhinehart and Winston.

Khatena, J. (1982). *Educational psychology of the gifted.* New York: Wiley.

Kounin, J. S. (1970). *Discipline and group management in classrooms.* New York: Holt, Rhinehart and Winston.

Krampen, G., & Mory, M. (1982). *Zur kognitiv-emotionalen Verarbeitung schlechter Zensuren bei Schülern.* Trier: Universität Trier, Trierer Psychologische Berichte.

Kuhl, J. (1986). Motivation and information processing. In R. N. Sorrentino & E. T. Higgins (Eds.), *The handbook of motivation and cognition: foundations of social behavior* (pp. 404–434). Berlin: Springer.

Leeuw, J. de (1986). Individuele verschillen en ongelijkheid. Enige historische achtergronden van het IQ-debat. In J. Dronkers & I. Prinsen (Eds.), *Sociale ongelijkheid* (pp. 45–61). Muiderberg: Coutinho.

Lens, W. (1987). Motivatie op school: een theoretische benadering. *Pedagogisch Tijdschrift, 12,* 280–300.

Magnusson, D., & Allen, V. L. (1983a). An interactional perspective for human development. In D. Magnusson & V. L. Allen (Eds.), *Human development. An interactional perspective* (pp. 3–31). New York: Academic Press.

Magnusson, D., & Allen, V. L. (1983b). Implications and applications of an interactional perspective for human development. In D. Magnusson & V. L. Allen (Eds.), *Human development. An interactional perspective* (pp. 369–387). New York: Academic Press.

Mehlhorn, H.-G. (1988). *Persönlichkeitsentwicklung Hochbegabter.* Berlin: Volk und Wissen Volkseigener Verlag.

Meijnen, G. W. (1977). *Maatschappelijke achtergronden van intellektuele ontwikkeling.* Groningen: Wolters-Noordhoff.

Mooij, T. (1980). Schoolproblemen en uitval in het voortgezet onderwijs. *Pedagogische Studiën, 57,* 369–382.

Mooij, T. (1982). Onderwijsleersituatie en lesondergravend gedrag van lto-leerlingen. In E. Diekerhof (Ed.), *Leren, wat moet je ermee?* (pp. 39–52). Muiderberg: Coutinho.

Mooij, T. (1987). *Interactional multilevel investigation into pupil behavior, achievement, competence, and orientation in educational situations.* 's-Gravenhage: SVO.

Mooij, T. (1990): Effecten van computerprogramma's op ontwikkeling in leesprestaties. *Tijdschrift voor Onderwijsresearch, 15,* 285–300.

Mooij, T. (1991a). *Schoolproblemen van hoogbegaafde kinderen. Richtlijnen voor passend onderwijs.* Muiderberg: Coutinho.

Mooij, T. (1991b) (Ed.). *Onderwijs aan hoogbegaafde kinderen.* Muiderberg: Coutinho.

Mooij, T. (1991c). *Instrument bepaling beginsituatie leerlingen.* Nijmegen: Katholieke Universiteit, Instituut voor Toegepaste Sociale wetenschappen.

Mooij, T. (1991d). Begaafd (onder)presteren in groep of klas. Ontwikkeling van een interactionele multi-niveau theorie. In A. Collot d'Escury- Koenigs, T. Engelen-Snaterse, & L. Tijhuis (Eds.), *Gelukkig of school?* Amsterdam/Lisse: Swets & Zeitlinger.

Mooij, T., & Jansen, R. (1990). Theory and analysis of multilevel processes and effects: A two level example on pupil achievement, competence, and orientation. In P. van den Eeden, J. Hox, & J. Hauer (Eds.), *Theory and model in multilevel research: convergence or divergence?* (pp. 35–54). Amsterdam: SISWO.

Neisser, U. (1976). *Cognition and reality.* San Francisco: Freeman.

Pervin, L.A., & Lewis, M. (1978). Overview of the internal-external issue. In L. A. Pervin & M. Lewis (Eds.), *Perspectives in interactional psychology* (pp. 1–22). New York: Plenum Press.

Rosenthal, R., & Jacobson, L. (1968). *Pygmalion in the classroom.* New York: Holt, Rinehart and Winston.

Rost, D. (1990). Identificatie van hoogbegaafdheid. *Nederlands Tijdschrift voor Opvoeding, vorming en onderwijs, 6,* 122–151.

Rubovits, P. C., & Maehr, M. L. (1971). Pygmalion analyzed: Toward an explanation of the Rosenthal-Jacobson findings. *Journal of Personality and Social Psychology, 19,* 197–203.

Tinto, V. (1975). Dropout from higher education: a theoretical synthesis of recent research. *Review of Educational Research, 45,* 89–125.

Werts, C. E., & Watley, D. J. (1969). A student's dilemma: Big Fish–little pond or little fish-big pond. *Journal of Counseling Psychology, 16,* 14–19.

# 40

# School Adjustment of High Ability Students

**Leon Niebrzydowski**
**Grazyna Poraj**

*University of Lodz, Lodz, Poland*

This chapter investigates interpersonal relations of high-ability children with peers in the same class. Subjects were eighth grade students who, eight years earlier, had started school at the age of six (i.e., one year in advance of agemates), because they had demonstrated outstanding abilities while in nursery school. Of the 51 students from 40 elementary schools in the industrial town of Lodz, 27 were girls and 24 were boys. Research instruments included the Chart of Students' Behavior, Raven's Matrices, Choynowski's TZT, the sociometric technique of J. L. Moreno, and school records including marks. The majority of the students tested displayed high or very high achievement and appropriate interpersonal relations with peers. However, a small group of about one-quarter of the total group displayed low achievement and low social acceptance, although they were of high ability. This finding is of considerable interest in view of conflicting conclusions in the relevant literature.

## INTRODUCTION

For many years the problem of school adjustment has been an issue of special interest to psychologists and educators in Poland, as well as worldwide. Researchers have mostly concentrated on the school situation of students with low intellectual, cognitive, and psychomotor abilities, or those suffering from behavior disorders. Most of the research work is directed toward analyzing the reasons behind school failure and searching for ways of preventing it. However, another group of students exists—high ability children who start school earlier than usual.

A school may make provision for high ability students in various ways. In Polish schools it is most common to form classes of selected, particularly intelligent pupils, to provide individualized instruction in those subjects in which students display high levels of skill, to organize individual teaching or to transfer students of outstanding ability to higher forms if all teachers give their consent. However, the most popular form of special provision for high ability children is one (or sometimes two) years advancement of their schooling.

While at school, a student is expected not only to acquire the required information and develop certain abilities and habits, but also to acquire some experience as a result of assuming two important roles connected with school life: those of a pupil, on the one hand, a classmate on the other. The first is conditioned by school regulations and requires from a student high achievement in learning, proper behavior, and obedience to the code of the school. The second is concerned with students' attractiveness, broadly understood, to their classmates. Successful adjustment to those roles may determine the school adjustment of a child.

In the process of putting into practice its didactic and educational programs school becomes the second most important—next to the family—educational environment. It is effective only as long as the mutual relationships between teachers and students, and among students, are created on its territory. In such a situation the child belongs to the educating environment and it belongs to the child. This is a bilateral bond. At the same time, the feeling of security and confidence in teachers and schoolmates develops; the child believes that their attitude is friendly. Functioning in a group of peers—that is, in a school class—fulfills those social needs of a child that cannot be fulfilled in relationships with tutors, because they represent the generation of adults. Children need to coexist with a group of peers, members of the same school class, who assume different but equal roles. They need to be able to establish friendly relations and exchange views and opinions without any help from adults. The membership of a group as realized and understood in this way reinforces the feeling of self-value and social usefulness.

It is possible to classify pupils into five social positions in their class: full acceptance, average position, polarization, isolation and rejection. Fully accepted by the class are those students who are attractive partners in various social contacts. Those pupils who enjoy average acceptance may not occupy important positions in the structure of the group, but they are liked. Students who polarize opinions are accepted by some but rejected by others, and are regarded as attractive partners by a few friends only. Children who are classified as isolated are unimportant for others, they exist outside the class. Those students who are rejected by their peers have only negative social experiences, because they can sense the dislike and hostility of the group. The popularity of a student among classmates depends on many factors and determines the course of his or her socializing. Acceptance, respect, and a friendly attitude on the part of classmates and teachers help children to solve problems and develop cognitive abilities, and motivate them to study. Disapproval may restrain almost all spheres of a child's development.

## PROCEDURE

This study should be regarded as an attempt to estimate students' adjustment and capacity to participate in school life and their ability to fulfil the social role of a school child. The research concerned students in the eighth form who, because of their high skills, were able to start school one year in advance. This was the result of a decision to advance their elementary education taken by education authorities at the beginning of their schooling. The aims of this research are presented in the following questions.

1. What is the degree of school adjustment among the students concerned?
2. Is there any difference in school adjustment depending on sex?

3.  What are the interpersonal relations in the group? Are they different for boys and girls?
4.  Do the achievement scores of the students reflect their high intellectual potential?

The empirical part of this research was based on the results of the following tests and procedures.

the Charter of Student's Behavior;
Raven's Matrices;
the sociometric technique of Moreno; and
the analysis of school records.

In addition, interviews were conducted with teachers about the students' situation at school and at home.

The Charter of Student's Behavior (Markowska & Szafraniec, 1980) was used to investigate social adjustment in terms of behavior at school. Possible emotional and social disorders were taken into account. This method is based on a standardized scale of 50 features of observable behavior classified into five dimensions of adjustment: motivation to study, antisocial behavior, retardation, socialization, and sexual interests. Moreno's classic sociometric technique was used to examine social relationships and position of students in the study. Two criteria were applied: positive or negative with regard to sympathy (liking) and cooperation (studying together), with the number of choices restricted to three. In order to estimate intellectual and cognitive abilities of the tested teenagers the nonverbal perception test by Raven and the Knowledge of Vocabulary Test by Choynowski (1980) were administered. The detailed analysis of school documentation (i.e., registers, records of grades, and health in the last three years of schooling) was carried out in order to determine the results achieved by the students in fifth to eighth grades.

The subjects in this research were 51 students in the eighth grade, 27 girls and 24 boys born in 1975. The research was pursued in 40 elementary schools in Lodz—an industrial city of more than one million inhabitants. One criterion for qualifying for the test was that a student started attending school one year in advance: Eight years earlier, 93 children born in 1975 had been tested in education counseling centers for possible early school entry. Only 67 of those children actually started school early, and these youngsters were observed throughout elementary school. We were able to find only 51 of those children in the eighth form; the rest of them had left Lodz.

## RESULTS

Table 40-1 presents results on the Charter of Students' Behavior—five items were tested. The majority of the students reached an average level of motivation to study (mean = 3.95), antisocial behavior (mean = 1.7), and sexual interest (mean = 2.2), a very high level of socialization (mean = 4.0), and a low level of retardation (mean = 2.1).

The fact that the degree of socialization was generally high was largely determined by the favorable results of the girls, who had a significantly higher mean in this category than boys ($t$ = 5.33; $p < .01$). The detailed comparative analysis of 12 features of socialization showed that girls were more helpful than boys ($t$ = 2.11; $p < .05$), more sensitive to feelings of others ($t$ = 4.93; $p < .01$), more protective ($t$ = 4.88; $p < .01$), and more willing to do civic work ($t$ = 4.23; $p < .01$). Although the indices of antisocial behavior and of sexual interests were average, in both cases there were considerable sex differences: The boys had significantly higher results in antisocial behavior ($t$ = 3.50; $p < .001$) and sexual interests ($t$ = 4.54; $p < .01$), whereas the girls were able to control their behavior better and were less preoccupied with sexual matters. Although the level of motivation to study was more or less the same in both groups, the girls were more diligent ($t$ = 3.52; $p < .01$) and looked after educational equipment better ($t$ = 3.17; $p < .01$). Both groups had a similar low index of retardation, which means that they were resistant to stresses, sporadically reacted fearfully, and felt depressed.

TABLE 40-1
Results of the Charter of Students' Behavior
Grouped According to Sex

| Items | Girls | Boys | Total | $t$ |
|---|---|---|---|---|
| Motivation to study | 4.05 | 3.83 | 3.95 | 1.46 |
| Antisocial behavior | 1.60 | 1.90 | 1.70 | 3.50** |
| Retardation | 2.12 | 2.12 | 2.10 | 0.15 |
| Socialization | 4.20 | 4.20 | 3.70 | 5.30** |
| Sexual interests | 2.00 | 2.40 | 2.20 | 4.54** |

Summing up this part of the research, it may be said that the students were, according to their tutors, generally well adjusted to school conditions. However, they were expected to achieve better results, the level of their motivation to study was merely average, they were not very willing to meet the requirements set by their schools, they were moderately diligent and persevering, and concentrated on their tasks. The girls turned out to fit the stereotypical role of a student better than the boys.

The analysis of achievements in learning in fifth to eighth grades was interesting. The average scores of the students during the last three years of education are presented in Table 40-2. An average of 4.1–5.0 is good or very good. As can be seen in Table 40-2, achievement was lower in the sixth grade than in the fifth—in the case of the girls by 3.7%, the boys as much as 20%. In the seventh grade the majority of the girls had high achievement again (92.6%), whereas the school achievement of the boys did not improve much when compared with the sixth grade. Achievement dropped again in the eighth grade in both groups—girls by 3.7%, boys by 4.2%. The majority of children (68%) had very good and good scores throughout their studies. However, there was a difference between the boys and the girls: 62% of these students were girls. Twenty-six percent of tested students obtained average marks: nearly 80% of these were boys. The group of students with low marks was smallest, only 6%, of whom two-thirds were boys.

Although 68% of the pupils obtained good marks in fifth to eighth grades, the question remained open why 32% of students who had been allowed to start schooling one year in advance because of their high intellectual potential had only average, low, or even unsatisfactory achievement. In order to find an answer to this question we tried to look for the link between school

**TABLE 40-2**
**Percent of Students Obtaining High Grades in Grades 5-8**

| School Grade | Achievement (grades) | | | |
| | Girls | | Boys | |
| | 3.0–4.0 | 4.1–5.0 | 3.0–4.0 | 4.1–5.0 |
|---|---|---|---|---|
| 5 | 7.4 | 92.6 | 16.6 | 83.4 |
| 6 | 11.1 | 88.9 | 37.4 | 62.6 |
| 7 | 7.4 | 92.6 | 29.1 | 70.9 |
| 8 | 11.1 | 88.9 | 33.3 | 66.7 |

achievement and the scores on intellectual efficiency tests: the Raven Scale and Choynowski's TZN. The results achieved by the students concerned are presented in Table 40-3.

Generally, the largest group consisted of children who achieved very high results in the tests, the second largest of students who achieved high results. Girls were in the majority in both groups. Of the students who had good and very good marks, the majority were classified as very highly or highly intelligent according to the Raven Scale and Choynowski's TZS. Although students who obtained high scores in both tests were in the majority, a number achieved low results—14% according to Raven's Scale and 2% according to Choynowski's. Moreover, a substantial percentage of students obtained merely average results: 18% according to the first scale and 29% according to the second. It can be hypothesized that these students should not have started school early, as the criteria for early school entry had not been met—they were not qualified for early entry. Another hypothesis is that in the process of schooling circumstances emerged that influenced the children's development unfavorably, and finally resulted in low intellectual efficiency, low interest in studying, and little need for school achievement.

In order to test the described hypotheses the study was rounded out with an analysis of interpersonal relations within school classes, taking into account the criteria of sympathy and cooperation. On the criterion of sympathy the majority of students (52.9%) did not have positive relationships with their classmates. They were isolated and rejected by the group. The number of children who were not accepted by their peers was lower (43.2%) on the criterion of cooperation. At the same time, the girls were better accepted than the boys on both criteria. When the results of the tests for both criteria were compared, it became apparent that a selected group of students existed, who were not accepted in either area. In this group of 27% of students the number of boys and girls was equal. Detailed analysis of the results of their other tests showed that they were students with low marks, although most of them achieved very good results according to Raven's Scale and Choynowski's TZS. Their levels of motivation to study and socialization were average, but some of them exhibited antisocial behavior, whereas some were retarded. Because of their tendency to aggression, their passivity and fearful reactions, these children were not regarded as attractive partners by their peers. This finding is of considerable help in reconciling conflicting find-

## TABLE 40-3
### Raven and Vocabulary Scores Grouped According to Sex

| | Girls | | | | Boys | | | | Total | | | |
| | Raven | | Vocabulary | | Raven | | Vocabulary | | Raven | | Vocabulary | |
| Results | N | percent | N | percent | N | percent | N | percent | N | percent | N | percent |
|---|---|---|---|---|---|---|---|---|---|---|---|---|
| Very high | 12 | 23 | 1 | 2 | 7 | 14 | 2 | 4 | 19 | 37 | 3 | 6 |
| High | 10 | 19 | 14 | 28 | 6 | 12 | 18 | 35 | 16 | 31 | 32 | 63 |
| Average | 2 | 4 | 11 | 22 | 7 | 14 | 4 | 7 | 9 | 18 | 15 | 29 |
| Low | 2 | 4 | 1 | 2 | 2 | 4 | — | — | 4 | 8 | 1 | 2 |
| Unsatisfactory | 1 | 2 | — | — | 2 | 4 | — | — | 3 | 6 | — | — |
| Total | 27 | 52 | 27 | 52 | 24 | 48 | 24 | 48 | 51 | 100 | 51 | 00 |

ings about social adjustment of gifted pupils, which sometimes report difficulties in this area, sometimes excellent and "healthy" adjustment.

## ACKNOWLEDGMENTS

The investigation was conducted by Beata Nawrot, a participant in Prof. Niebrzydowski's master's level seminars.

## REFERENCES

Choynowski, M. (1980). Podrecznik do "Testu Znajomosci Slow." In *Testy psychologiczne w poradnictwie wychowawczo-zawodo-wym*. Warsaw: PWN. [Handbook for "Knowledge of Vocabulary Test." In *The use of psychological tests in educational and career consulting.*]

Markowska, B., & Szafraniec, H. (1980). Podrecznik do Arkusza Zachowania sie Ucznia. In *Testy psychologiczne w poradnictwie wychowawczo-zawodowym*. Warsaw: PWN. [Handbook for the "Charter of Student's Behavior." In *The use of psychological tests in educational and career consulting.*]

# 41

# The Connection between Motivational and Cognitive Components of the Personality of Gifted Pupils

**Helga Joswig**

*University of Rostock, Rostock, Germany*

This chapter introduces results of empirical research in connection with motivational and cognitive components of gifted pupils. In all 250 pupils in the seventh and eighth grades were included in this experiment. Of these pupils, 177 applied for entrance to a special school for mathematics, natural sciences and technology (research), whereas 73 formed the control group. The cognitive components were tested—using the Raven Matrices as well as the results of the entrance exams of the special school applicants. The motivational components were measured with tests of striving for knowledge and motivation for physics. There were significant differences between the two groups in terms of cognitive and motivational components, which favored the special school applicants. The pupils also showed a positive correlation between the mathematics and physics exam results and the extent of primary motivation and striving for knowledge.

## INTRODUCTION

In this chapter, "giftedness" includes the individual cognitive, motivational and social properties for successfully completing activities in one or more given areas. This covers an inner complex of prerequisites for successful task completion, not their origins. These prerequisites open up the possibility—but not the certainty—of successful task completion. The multidimensional model of giftedness arising from the approach includes the personality conditions and indicators listed in Figure 41-1.

The (noncognitive) personality factors include

    primary motivation;
    self-concept;
    social, including moral behavior or traits; and
    temperament.

Among the cognitive individual prerequisites are

    general mental ability (intelligence); and
    special abilities.

Major environmental characteristics are

    encouragement in the home;
    parental demand for achievement;
    educational level of parents;
    number of siblings and position; and
    classroom environment, and so on.

The empirical investigation reported here focused on the connection between the cognitive individual prerequisites and the noncognitive personality factor of primary motivation. The other noncognitive personality factors and the environmental properties will not be mentioned here. As portrayed in Figure 41-1, the cognitive individual prerequisites include general mental ability (intelligence) and special abilities. The term "primary motivation" denotes the "independent, subjective focusing on the ob-

FIGURE 41.1.    Model of conditions of giftedness.

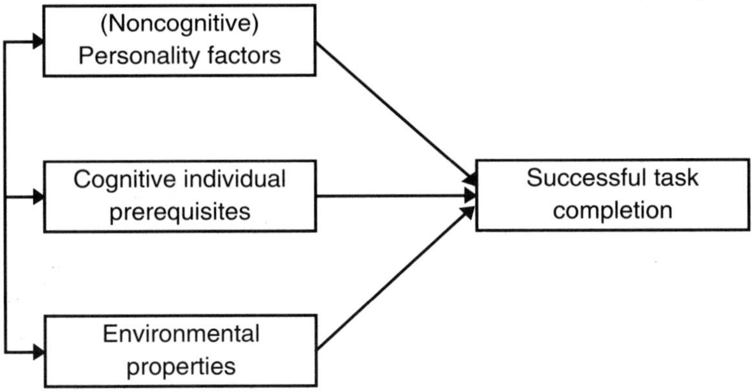

ject without outside guidance" (Wiese, 1983). The theoretical construct of primary motivation includes three dimensions.

> object related initiative;
> finding a personal meaning for an activity; and
> the ability to regulate oneself.

Indicators of these dimensions are

> for object related personal initiative;
>> the attraction to objects,
>> striving for and interest in general and specialized knowledge,
>> the sense of joy in thought processes, in advancing knowledge, and in the activity.
> for finding personal meaning;
>> task commitment and a commitment to others and to oneself,
>> professional motives,
>> social motives.
> for the ability to regulate oneself;
>> self-concept,
>> level of demand,
>> volitional traits.

The empirical investigation was oriented toward a clarification of the relation between cognitive and motivational personality components of gifted pupils; the relationship between intelligence, primary motivation for physics, and striving for knowledge was particularly emphasized. This striving for knowledge was taken to be a significant indicator of primary motivation.

## METHOD

The participants in the study were 12- and 13-year-old pupils who had applied for admission to a special school for mathematics, natural sciences, and technology in Rostock in the years 1990 and 1991. A control group was composed of children of the same age from a regular school. These children had been in the same class as the special school applicants through eighth grade, and had obtained good marks also in mathematics, natural sciences and technology, but did not apply to the special school.*

Pupils were only admitted to the special school after attending a socalled "examination camp" during summer holidays between the seventh and eighth grade. During the examination period pupils were given tests in mathematics, physics, or chemistry, and asked to solve technical problems as well as completing psychological tests on general mental ability and selected personal variables. Admission to the special school took place starting in ninth grade. The composition of the various samples is shown in Table 41-1.

The cognitive realm was assessed by means of the following instruments.

the Advanced Progressive Matrices (APM), SET II from Raven, 1962 (German version: Kratzmeier, 1980);

the results of the entrance exams in mathematics, physics, or chemistry or the results of work on a complex task in math, natural science, or technical content (tested during the summer camp);

school records (marks) in mathematics, physics, and technical subjects in the first half year of ninth grade after being accepted into the special school.

---

*The educational system of East Germany had supported gifted children by founding special schools. After German unification, Rostock's special school was taken over by the *Jugenddorf Christopherus*, which has committed itself to the support of gifted education (especially for underachievers). Our investigations were done at the special school before it was taken over.

TABLE 41-1
Composition of the Samples*

| | Number of special school applicants | | | | | | Control group | | |
| | 1990 | | | 1991 | | | | | |
| | m | f | total | m | f | total | m | f | total |
|---|---|---|---|---|---|---|---|---|---|
| Grade 7 | 100 | 31 | 131 | — | — | — | — | — | — |
| Grade 8 | 49 | 13 | 62 | *49** | *11* | *60* | 33 | 40 | 73 |
| | | | | 128 | 49 | 177 | | | |
| Number of those accepted to the special school | 30 | 7 | 37 | *35* | *7* | *42* | — | — | — |
| | | | | 34 | 8 | 42 | | | |

*Figures in **boldface italics** indicate the number of participants who took the post-test in 1991.

In the motivational realm the questionnaire to indicate the level of striving for knowledge and the level of demand (FES) (Lehwald, 1975) and a questionnaire developed by Rust (1992) to measure primary motivation for physics (PMP) were administered.

## RESULTS

### Cognitive Realm

Testing with Raven's Matrices yielded three fundamental results.

1.  All three samples of special school applicants showed clear, significant differences from the control group in dealing with the cognitive demands of the test. These are summarized in Table 41-2.

In comparison with pupils from regular schools (CG), all groups of special school applicants showed a significantly higher level of ability. The differences in carrying out these cognitive tasks between special school applicants (1990) as well as the post-examinees (1991), who took part in the examinations twice, and the control group were significantly in favor of the special school applicants. These differences could be confirmed with the new applicants in 1991. This leads to the conclusion

**TABLE 41-2**
**Mean Differences between Special School Applicants (SPA)**
**and the Control Group (CG)**

| Population | n | Mean | SD | Probability |
|---|---|---|---|---|
| SPA-1990, | | | | |
| grade 7 | 129 | 22.37 | 5.59 | $t = 5.61$ |
| (new applicants) | 35 | 16.25 | 6.19 | $< 0.1$ |
| CG | | | | |
| SPA-1991 | | | | |
| (post-examination) | 60 | 24.90 | 3.80 | $t = 7.52$ |
| CG | 35 | 16.25 | 6.19 | $< 0.1$ |
| SPA-1991 | | | | |
| (new applicants) | 171 | 18.57 | 6.18 | $t = 2.02$ |
| CG | 35 | 16.25 | 6.19 | $< 0.5$ |

that those invited by the special school to participate had been accurately identified.

Furthermore, there were also significant differences in eighth grade between the "post-examinees" and the new applicants in favor of the post-examinees, which cannot be seen in Table 41-2. It must be mentioned here that these "post-examinees" had already been tested in seventh grade, and that they had been tutored by correspondence courses throughout the year by the special school. They had registered for the exam based on encouragement from their teachers. The new applicants did not have this teacher recommendation, as they had applied on their own. Interpretations of these results are that the pupils taking the exam the second time around were more comfortable with the testing situation or that the teacher evaluation in the seventh grade had been quite reliable. It could also be assumed that the year long correspondence had a training effect on the "post-examinees," which would not apply to the new applicants.

2. Testing with Raven's Matrices made it clear that special school applicants solved problems that were well above the average of their age group. Table 41-3 compares the values quoted by Kratzmeier (1980) for the APM for different age groups with those of the special school applicants (age 12–13 years).

This table shows clearly that the special school applicants had above average intellectual ability. They exceeded comparable norms even when compared with 20-year-olds.

3.   There were no gender differences in test scores, although it must be said that the female applicants were far outnumbered by the male applicants. This unequal distribution of the sexes among the applicants points to gender specific giftedness in reference to mathematics, natural sciences, and technology.

A comparison of the results of the Raven's test with the results of the entrance exams showed a significant correlation between Raven's scores and mathematics scores. No strong tie was found between the Raven's results and the physics scores, although there were clear parallels between the mathematics and physics exams. There were also connections between the Raven's results and the teacher evaluations (1990). In sum, the analysis of the cognitive realm of special school applicants showed that intellectual preconditions were developed to a well above average level.

The close relationship between intelligence and giftedness in mathematics points to the connection of intellectual and mathematical giftedness in the ability structure of personality discussed in gifted research, or else it raises questions about test construction. There are also correlations between special giftedness in mathematics and physics. There seems to be a connection among areas involving chiefly theoretically oriented thought processes. A gender specific intellectual difference could not be determined in special school applicants. Intelligence shows itself in the ability to move flexibly between different levels of abstract thought and in analogical deduction in the processing of information. Research by van der Meer (1990) shows that the mathematically gifted approach analogical deduction processes in a less complicated manner, owing to their more strongly formed sense of perception of structures. Intelligence tests which examine more analytical-synthetic aspects of

TABLE 41-3
APM Scores at Various Percentiles Compared with Special School Applicants (SPA)

| Age Percentile | 12 | 12.5 | 13 | 13.5 | 20 | 12–13 (SPA) |
|---|---|---|---|---|---|---|
| 95 | 17 | 18 | 19 | 20 | 20 | 29 |
| 90 | 14 | 15 | 16 | 17 | 21 | 28 |
| 75 | 10 | 11 | 12 | 13 | 14 | 24 |
| 50 | — | — | 8 | 9 | 9 | 21 |

perception, such as Raven's (see Friedrich & Henning, 1975), are more easily solved by the mathematically gifted, which in turn results in their higher scores. The connection between special giftedness in mathematics and physics shown in the research could be interpreted in this manner.

## Motivation

In the motivational realm, however, gender specific differences became clear. They mainly had to do with motivational orientation toward physics. Male special school applicants had a significantly stronger orientation on almost every item (1, 3, 4, 6, 7, 8, 9, 10, 11, 12, 14, 15, 17, 19, 20, 22) of Rust's (1992) questionnaire *Primary Motivation for Physics*. These gender specific differences were also clear in the control group.

The girls' self-evaluations were significantly lower than the boys' in regard to their abilities and achievements in physics (see Hoffmann, 1990). The sex specific differences determined by Pollmer (1989) and Hoffmann (1990) were also confirmed in the present observations. Explanations for these gender-specific differences can be found in Beermann, Heller, and Menacher (1992), as well as in biological, personality–psychological and socialization–theoretical or pedagogical theories. Testing with Lehwald's questionnaire on striving for knowledge revealed no differences between the sexes, so that the difference just reported apparently involves a specific orientation of males in favor of physics.

Testing with the FES (Lehwald, 1975) showed significant differences between special school applicants and pupils from the regular school. This instrument measures a general motivational orientation to the areas of mathematics, natural sciences, and technology. It involves important motivational components such as the will to exert oneself, orientation toward the problem, interest in independent acquisition of knowledge, and high expectations for the level of mental activity, which play a special role in giftedness for physics (see Balla, 1989). The special school applicants had an explicit striving for knowledge.

Results of both evaluations of the motivational realm (FES and PMP) showed significant positive correlations between striving for knowledge and primary motivation for physics in special school applicants (see Table 41-4). All coefficients are statistically significant.

These correlations allow the following conclusions.

Striving for knowledge and primary motivation for physics are closely connected.

The validity of the integration of striving for knowledge into the theoretical construct of primary motivation by Wiese (1983) and of the questionnaire developed by Rust (1992) was demonstrated.

## Connection between Cognitive and Motivational Components

The following table (Table 41-5) shows the correlations among various dimensions (see Rust, 1994, p. 25).

Significant correlations were found between primary motivation for physics and the results of the physics entrance exam. This concentrated specifically on solving physics–arithmetic problems at a high level, as well as on logical conclusive explanations of physical processes, events, and principles. This leads to the idea that a specific motivational orientation toward certain areas, in this case toward physics, goes along with the activity itself and success in it. Motivation and cognition interact in turn, and are interwoven with each another. To test this connection further, marks for the first semester of special school were compared with PMP scores. The results showed that the PMP has high prognostic ability. The positive correlations between the mathematics and physics exams verify the re-

**TABLE 41-4**
Correlation between Primary Motivation for Physics
and Striving for Knowledge in Special School Applicants

| Group | Sex | n | Correlation Coefficient |
|---|---|---|---|
| SPA 1990 | Male | 128 | 0.49 |
| | Female | 36 | 0.71 |
| | Total | 164 | 0.52 |
| SPA 1991 | Male | 46 | 0.49 |
| post examinees | Female | 8 | 0.82 |
| | Total | 54 | 0.54 |
| SPA 1991 | Male | 125 | 0.31 |
| new applicants | Female | 48 | 0.34 |
| | Total | 173 | 0.31 |

TABLE 41-5
Correlations among the APM, PMP, FES, and the Mathematics and Physics
Entrance Exams (1990 examination, grades 7/8, $n$ = 189)

| | 1. | 2. | 3. | 4. | 5. |
|---|---|---|---|---|---|
| APM (Raven, 1962) | — | — | — | — | — |
| Physics exam | 0.10 | — | — | — | — |
| Mathematics exam | 0.30* | 0.38* | — | — | — |
| PMP (Rust, 1992) | 0.05 | 0.38* | 0.38* | — | — |
| FES (Lehwald, 1975) | 0.08 | 0.30* | 0.26* | 0.52* | — |

*$p$ < .01.

lationship between mathematics and physics found in the literature. According to Pollmer (1989), general mathematical giftedness is seen as important for the formation of giftedness in physics, both pure and applied.

In sum, it can be said that the relations between cognitive and motivational components of gifted personalities can be seen as a further indicator of the high general psychological level portrayed in the literature (Klix, 1978). Primary motivation for physics is an important factor for achievement in physics. The PMP questionnaire developed by Rust aided in clearing up the question of the relevance of the motivational conditions for specific cognitive abilities.

## REFERENCES

Balla, J. (1989). *Zur Ausprägung und Diagnostik des Merkmals "Lernen aus eigenem Antrieb" bei für Physik begabten Schülern* [Extent and diagnosis of the characteristic "Learning on one's own" of pupils gifted in physics]. Unpublished doctoral dissertation, Pedagogical College of Güstrow, Germany.

Beermann, L., Heller, K. A., & Menacher, P. (1992). *Mathe: Nichts für Mädchen? Begabung und Geschlecht am Beispiel von Mathematik, Naturwissenschaft und Technik* [Maths: Not for girls? Giftedness and gender in relation to mathematics, natural science, and gender]. Bern: Huber.

Friedrich, W., & Henning, W. (1975). *Der sozialwissenschaftliche Forschungsprozess* [The research process in the social sciences]. Berlin: Deutscher Verlag der Wissenschaften.

Hoffmann, L. (1990). Mädchen und Physik—ein aktuelles, ein drängendes Thema. [Girls and physics—a current, a pressing topic]. In *Naturwissenschaften im Unterricht—Physik-Chemie, 38th yr.* IPN Kiel 1990, Vol. 1.

Klix, F. (1978). *Information und Verhalten* [Information and behavior] (4th ed.). Berlin: Deutscher Verlag der Wissenschaften.

Kratzmeier, H. (1980). *Manual for Raven Matrices Test.* Weinheim: Beltz

Lehwald, G. (1975). *Zur Diagnostik des Erkenntnisstrebens bei Schülern* [On the diagnosis of striving for knowledge in pupils]. In *Beiträge zur Psychologie*, Vol. 20. Berlin: Volk und Wissen

Pollmer, K. (1989). *Zur Bedeutung von Fähigkeiten, Motiven und Interessen für den Leistungserfolg von Spezialschülern mathematisch-naturwissenschaftlich-technischer Richtung* [On the significance of ability, motives and interest for success of pupils in special school in the fields of mathematics, natural sciences, and technology]. Unpublished doctoral dissertation, University of Rostock, Germany.

Rust, H.-M. (1992). Fragebogen zur Erfassung primärer Motivation für Physik [Questionnaire for measuring primary motivation for physics]. In H. Wiese. *Motivation und Begabungsentwicklung* [Motivation and development of ability]. University of Rostock, Unpublished manuscript.

Rust, H.-M. (1994). *Zur Zusammenhang von kognitiven, motivationalen und dynamischen Komponenten der Persönlichkeit bei Bewerbern für Spezialschulen mathematisch-naturwissenschaftlich-technischer Richtung* [On the connection between cognitive, motivational and dynamic components of the personality of applicants to a special school in the fields of mathematics, natural sciences, and technology]. Unpublished doctoral dissertation, University of Rostock, Germany.

van der Meer, E. (1990). *Wissensdynamik: Mechanismen und Erscheinungen* [Knowledge-dynamic: Mechanisms and phenomena]. In D. Frey (Ed.), Bericht über den 37. Kongress der Deutschen Gesellschaft für Psychologie in Kiel 1990, Vol. 2. Göttingen: Hogrefe.

Wiese, H. (1983). *Bedeutung primärer Motivation für das Lernen bei Schülern der Oberstufe* [The meaning of primary motivation for learning in high school pupils]. Unpublished doctoral dissertation, Pedagogical College of Güstrow, Germany.

# 42

# The Effect of Identification and Differential Treatment of Gifted Elementary School Pupils

## Vladimir Kolesaric

*University of Zagreb, Zagreb, Croatia*

## Ivan Koren

*University of Zagreb, Zagreb, Croatia*

Within the framework of a comprehensive research project entitled "The effects of identification and specific treatment of gifted pupils," this chapter deals with the problem of the effects of such a procedure on the attitudes of pupils, their parents, and teachers regarding giftedness and gifted individuals. Attention was mainly directed toward the effects of identification on the development of personality characteristics of the gifted pupils, on relations between gifted and other pupils, on the characteristics of teachers necessary for work with the gifted, on the controversy about separation of the gifted into special classes or schools, and on society's obligations to the gifted. The results of this two year follow-up study are based on a comparison of the data from the initial and the final surveys of an experimental and a control group of subjects.

## INTRODUCTION

Most authors reviewing research on the effects of identification and special treatment of gifted individuals have drawn attention to the relative scarcity of such studies, as well as the controversial nature of their results, because some of them indicated smaller or greater positive, and the others smaller or greater negative outcomes of such interventions.

Attention was drawn to the problem of effects of the identification and labeling of the gifted—based on results obtained by a number of authors—by Freeman and Urban (1983). They emphasized the importance of the identification procedure and the cultural background in which the development of the gifted takes place. They also stressed the possible negative outcomes of segregation, especially in smaller children, and favored the inner differentiation of the educational process, that is, the individualization of procedures within the normal educational environment.

On the basis of his own results, and the studies by Guskin, Tannenbaum, Morgan, and other authors whose results indicated predominantly positive outcomes of the identification of the gifted, as well as on the basis of studies by Fisher, Cornell, and other authors whose results indicated the opposite, Robinson (1986) concluded the following.

> The effects of the public identification of children as gifted are unclear up to date . . . In any case, the identification of the talented children and their subsequent naming as the gifted remains an interesting and a controversial area of research.

Freeman (1986), reviewing the results of the Gulbenkian project for gifted children in England, emphasized the statistically significant findings of emotional disturbances in children treated in such a way, as compared with the control sample. Guskin and Zimmermann (1986) spoke of the acceptance of the identified gifted by their peers, but also of the apprehensions related to their separation into some sort of elite groups. Colangelo and Brown (1987), investigating the effects of identification on other members of the family, endorsed the distinction between the short-term, prevailingly negative, and the long-term effects, in which the negative outcomes become neutralized. Cornell (1989) showed that gifted children whose parents publicly call them gifted are significantly more poorly adapted than gifted children whose parents refrain from the use of the term.

Various dilemmas and controversies in these empirical findings regarding the effects of labeling and special treatment of gifted pupils led us to organize a wide scale study, the first of this kind in Croatia (Koren, 1990). The study was conceived as a two-year follow-up study with experimental and control groups. A representative sample was formed, including seven experimental and seven control elementary schools from the Republic of Croatia, the subjects being all sixth grade pupils of those schools in the school year 1988/89 (initial survey), and eighth grade pupils in the school year 1990/91 (final survey).

The study included three groups of variables: (1) subjects' cognitive characteristics; (2) their personality characteristics; and (3) attitudes toward giftedness and the gifted. Cognitive characteristics studied encompassed: verbal ability, ability to identify problems, creative thinking, and the amount of general information attained. The set of personality characteristics surveyed included: achievement–directedness, introversion–extraversion, dogmatism, aggressiveness, optimism–realism–pessimism, neurotic tendencies, and the hierarchy of work values. The attitudes towards giftedness recorded in the early study consisted of a series of value judgments comprehensively covering various aspects of giftedness related subject matter. All the variables in the study were measured by use of appropriate standardized instruments.

At the beginning of the study the initial status of the subjects on all variables was recorded, and two years later their final status in all those dimensions was also determined. The differences in the development and change of subjects' characteristics in both experimental and control groups were analyzed in relation to the independent variable, that is, the identification and special two-year educational treatment of the gifted pupils in the experimental group.

This chapter reports on only a portion of the results of the whole study, namely on the data regarding the structure, development, and change of subjects' attitudes to giftedness and the gifted. The purpose of the whole study was to collect data and to articulate knowledge regarding the positive or negative effects of identification and labelling of the gifted and the organization of formal public support for them both on their personality development and on their immediate (family) and remote (school) environments.

The aim of the portion of the study reported here was determination of the effects of labeling and special treatment of gifted pupils on the formation and development of their attitudes, as well as the attitudes of their parents and teachers, to various aspects of giftedness, especially regarding the following issues: (a) identification and special treatment of gifted pupils; (b) influence of the gifted on their classmates; (c) characteristics of teachers successful in work with the gifted; (d) separation of the gifted into special classes and schools; and (e) the obligations of the community in fostering development of gifted children and youth.

## METHOD

### Subjects

In the initial survey (September, 1988) the subjects were 1389 sixth grade elementary school pupils, aged on average 11.5, 1099 of their parents, and 342 of their teachers. The final survey (September, 1990) included a repetition of the testing procedures in the same sample, whose numbers now were somewhat decreased, and encompassed 1215 pupils, aged on average 13.5, 932 parents, and 300 teachers. Only those subjects were included in the final analysis for whom a complete set of data had been gathered.

### Instruments

In addition to the measuring instruments for personality and cognitive characteristics (eight tests and questionnaires), three compatible attitude scales were constructed: SNAD-U (for pupils), SNAD-R (for parents), and SNAD-N (for teachers). Each of the scales, in addition to motivational and technical instructions, included 20 statements covering different aspects of giftedness; for each statement the subjects had to determine their level of agreement on a four-point scale, ranging from "I agree completely" to "I disagree completely." Every fourth statement in each of the forms was identical, allowing for a valid comparison of attitudes of pupils, parents, and teachers on the most important issues in this area.

## Procedure

Immediately following determination of the initial status of the subjects on the basis of their results in four tests of cognitive ability, the identification of intellectually gifted pupils in both experimental and control groups was carried out by selecting approximately the top 10% of the total sample of pupils. In the experimental group such pupils were publicly declared to be gifted (in the class, in the school, in parents' conferences). Subsequently they were divided into various additional groups (science groups, competitions groups, research groups, etc.) during a period of two years. The results were not publicized in the control group, nor were there any specially organized activities for the gifted members of this group. In order to increase their motivation, the subjects of the control group were told that their results would be used in the process of individual vocational guidance, which indeed was done afterwards. The final survey was carried out using the same, only slightly reduced, set of measurement instruments.

## Data Analysis

All the data collected in the initial and final survey were stored in a computer, and subsequently statistically analyzed by use of analysis of variance and of regression analyses based on the relationships shown in Figure 42-1.

## RESULTS AND DISCUSSION

In this chapter the five statements identical in content, appearing in all three attitude measurement scales (measuring attitudes of pupils, parents and teachers) were analyzed. All the other statements, whose content is specific to individual categories of subjects, were analyzed in the overall project report (Koren, 1991).

FIGURE 42.1.   Model of relationships among variables employed in the regression analyses.

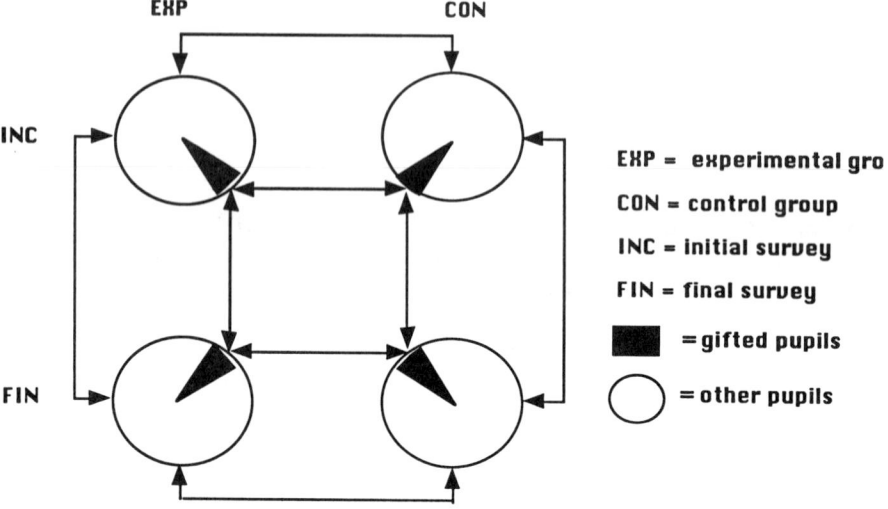

EXP = experimental gro

CON = control group

INC = initial survey

FIN = final survey

■ = gifted pupils

○ = other pupils

## Means of All Subjects

The distribution of the results, as shown in Table 42-1, and the testing of mean differences showed that, with minor exceptions, the recorded attitudes of the experimental and control groups within individual categories did not differ (neither in the initial nor in the final survey). However, significant differences were found when the results of the initial and final surveys were compared, and especially between the individual categories of subjects. Only those differences significant at the .01 level and beyond will be discussed here.

In the final, as compared to the initial survey, the pupils in the overall sample emphasized the importance of the favorable influence of the gifted on other pupils, which could be ascribed to their extended knowlege on the issue of giftedness. Contrary to this, the parents and the teachers of the experimental group did not assign such importance to the gifted, which, in our opinion, defies logical explanation. However, the teachers in the experimental group notably played down the extent of the unfavorable effects of identification on the development of gifted pupils' character traits, which probably stems from their personal two-year experience of immediate work with such pupils.

The difference in virtually all recorded attitudes between cat-

TABLE 42-1
Group Means on Attitudes

| Statement | | | | | | Group | | | | | |
|---|---|---|---|---|---|---|---|---|---|---|---|
| 1    2    3    4 | | | | | | | | | | | |
| I___I___I___I___I | | | | | | | | | | | |
| Disagree        Agree | | | | | | Pupils | | Parents | | Teachers | |
| completely     completely | | | | | | | | | | | |
| 1. Identification brings about | | | | INC | | 2.39 | 2.38 | 2.05 | 2.13 | 1.45 | 1.45 |
| negative personality | | | | FIN | | 2.26 | 2.47 | 2.05 | 2.11 | 1.59 | 1.54 |
| characteristics in gifted pupils | | | | | | | | | | | |
| 2. Gifted pupils favorably | | | | INC | | 2.41 | 2.41 | 3.10 | 2.94 | 2.94 | 3.07 |
| influence their classmates | | | | FIN | | 2.62 | 2.68 | 2.91 | 2.95 | 2.81 | 3.05 |
| 3. Only the most qualified | | | | INC | | 1.82 | 1.80 | 2.10 | 2.20 | 2.08 | 2.11 |
| teachers can teach gifted pupils | | | | FIN | | 1.53 | 1.53 | 2.19 | 2.16 | 2.22 | 2.05 |
| 4. Gifted pupils should be | | | | INC | | 1.81 | 1.82 | 1.98 | 1.91 | 2.81 | 2.72 |
| separated into special classes | | | | FIN | | 1.71 | 1.77 | 2.04 | 2.06 | 2.80 | 2.68 |
| and schools | | | | | | | | | | | |
| 5. Society must lend special | | | | INC | | 2.20 | 2.17 | 2.67 | 2.57 | 3.17 | 3.22 |
| support to gifted pupils | | | | FIN | | 1.98 | 2.04 | 2.61 | 2.45 | 2.98 | 3.10 |

egories of subjects proved to be statistically significant and quite substantial. The pupils in the overall sample, as compared to teachers and parents, both in the initial and in the final survey, were more convinced of the negative effects of identification on the gifted, attributed less importance to the favorable influence of the gifted on other pupils, showed more confidence in every teacher's aptitude for work with the gifted, more frequently believed that the gifted should not be separated into special schools and classes, and favored to a lesser degree society's special support for the gifted. Such a trend in their attitudes can be explained by the poorer insight of pupils into the specific characteristics of the gifted, when compared to their teachers and parents. Bearing in mind their chronological age, this is quite understandable. The teachers, as compared to the parents, attributed less unfavorable effects to the identification, were more in favor of separate treatment for the gifted, and believed to a greater extent in society's obligation to lend special support to the gifted. The parents, therefore, seem to be more cautious in these matters. The other attitudes did not differ significantly in the two categories.

All the relationships commented on here are based on analyses of means. However, in all subgroups there was a certain number of completely contrary and extreme attitudes, naturally.

## Differences and Change of Attitudes

By means of three-way analysis of variance an attempt was made to establish whether attitudes, as expressed in the responses to the five statements listed in the following, changed differentially in the experimental and control groups of pupils, parents, and teachers.

**Statement 1.**    Labeling some pupils as gifted and treating them specially regularly leads to conceitedness and other negative character features.

**Statement 2.**    Gifted pupils exert a positive influence on other pupils in the class, encouraging the whole class to learn better.

**Statement 3.**    As gifted teachers only can work successfully with gifted children, not all teachers are capable of dealing with them.

**Statement 4.**    Special schools should be set up for gifted children and young people, or they should at least be set apart in special classes where they would work according to special curricula.

**Statement 5.**    Since society is bound to profit most from gifted children, it must make better provision for their development than for other children's.

We were especially interested in the existence of interactions that would indicate such differential changes in attitudes. Such an interaction was recorded in pupils for Statement 1 (labeling some pupils as gifted and treating them in a special way regularly leads to conceitedness and other negative character features). The gifted pupils in the experimental group showed a more favorable attitude (agreed to a lesser extent with the statement on the negative influence of identification) in the final survey, whereas the gifted pupils in the control group proved to be somewhat more in favor of such a claim in the final survey. This interactive effect was statistically significant ($p < 0.01$).

Apart from this, no other second order interaction in the analysis of variance reached statistical significance. The first-order interactions in the pupil sample proved to be significant in relation to Statement 5, both in experimental and control group (since society is bound to profit most from gifted children, it must make better provision for their development than for other children's). The gifted pupils in the final survey agreed significantly more with the statement of society's obligation to support the gifted.

The existence of an interaction in relation to Statement 1 in pupils and its lack in parents documents, in our opinion, the sensitivity of talented children to the procedures they are subjected to and the rigidity of their parents as well. This result has implications for work with talented children, and especially with their parents.

## Stability of Attitudes in the Two Year Period

Retesting of the subjects (after an interval of two years) by use of the judgment scales provided the data regarding the stability of their attitudes toward giftedness. Table 42-2 presents contingency coefficients (C) and correlation coefficients (r) for initial and final data for the various groups. The data in the table reveal some facts and regularities concerning changes of opinion in pupils, their parents, and their teachers during the follow-up period.

First, if the magnitude of correlation coefficients is considered, the most stable proved to be the attitudes of teachers (average correlation = .42), followed by parents (average correlation = .32), whereas the attitudes of pupils changed the most (average correlation = .20). This finding is in line with the expected rank of the extent of attitude consolidation, which is, naturally, dependent on the extent of acquaintance with and knowledge of the problem itself. In this framework a generally low level of attitude stability in all subject categories should be noted.

Secondly, the gifted pupils, as compared with their peers, showed greater stability of attitudes, which, on the one hand, could represent the effect of their deeper understanding of the content of statements as early as the first survey, and, therefore, of a more realistic judgment. On the other hand, it could stem from the development of attitudes to the matter in the family environment, for Table 42-2 clearly shows that the gifted pupils' parents expressed attitudes of greater stability than parents in general.

However, the differences in correlation coefficients between the experimental and the control group in all subject categories failed to show trends so straightforward as to allow the conclusion that there was a substantial influence of the experimental factor on changes in attitudes in any subject category as a whole. Similarly, the congruence of attitudes of children and their parents, both in the initial and the final survey, proved to be very small, with a mild tendency toward more congruence in the final survey, which indicates poor children–parents communication in these matters, whether caused by children's chronological age or a lack of importance attributed to such matters by parents.

## GENERAL CONCLUSIONS

1.  The attitudes of pupils toward giftedness and the gifted differ in some aspects from those of teachers and parents, for instance, when the pupils agreed more with the proposition that identification of the gifted may unfavorably influence their personality development. The pupils were also not in favor of separation of the gifted into special schools, as opposed to the teachers (and parents, to some extent), who proved to be more willing to endorse such treatment of the gifted.
2.  The differences in attitudes between the initial and the final survey did not, in general terms, show any dramatic changes either in the experimental or the control group. There was, however, a significant change in attitudes of the gifted in the experimental group, which proved to be opposite in direction to the change of attitudes of the gifted in the control group: The gifted in the treatment group agreed less with the proposition of unfavorable effects of identification, whereas the control group gifted tended to accept it more in the final survey.
3.  Parents and teachers, as compared to pupils, showed more stability in their attitudes. Such a result seems to be reasonably predictable, and need not suggest rigidity of teachers and parents.

Even these partial results on the effects of labeling and treatment of the gifted show, in our opinion, at least two things: gifted pupils have well formed attitudes toward giftedness, which are subject to change relative to the presence or absence of differential educational treatment; and the rigidity of attitudes of teachers and parents suggests that in further attempts at organization of care of the gifted special attention should be paid to work with teachers and parents.

## TABLE 42-2
### Stability of Attitudes Over the Period of Two Years

| Statement | | Pupils | | | Parents | | | Parents/Pupils | | Teachers | | |
|---|---|---|---|---|---|---|---|---|---|---|---|---|
| | | EXP $n = 651$ | CON $n = 552$ | ALL $n = 203$ | Gifted $n = 125$ | All $n = 838$ | of gifted children $n = 93$ | INC/INC $n = 1091$ | FIN/FIN $n = 912$ | EXP $n = 128$ | CON $n = 92$ | ALL $n = 220$ |
| 1. | C | 0.19 | 0.23 | 0.20 | 0.38 | 0.31 | 0.46 | 0.13* | 0.13 | 0.45 | 0.57 | 0.52 |
| | r | 0.11 | 0.16 | 0.13 | 0.32 | 0.26 | 0.38 | 0.03* | 0.09 | 0.29 | 0.36 | 0.31 |
| 2. | C | 0.25 | 0.27 | 0.24 | 0.30 | 0.30 | 0.41 | 0.11* | 0.14 | 0.39 | 0.45 | 0.41 |
| | r | 0.23 | 0.24 | 0.24 | 0.22 | 0.26 | 0.26 | 0.05* | 0.09 | 0.34 | 0.44 | 0.39 |
| 3. | C | 0.30 | 0.24 | 0.25 | 0.32 | 0.39 | 0.35* | 0.15 | 0.13 | 0.58 | 0.44 | 0.51 |
| | r | 0.24 | 0.21 | 0.23 | 0.17 | 0.35 | 0.19* | 0.09 | 0.11 | 0.59 | 0.34 | 0.51 |
| 4. | C | 0.23 | 0.17 | 0.17 | 0.35 | 0.37 | 0.50 | 0.15 | 0.20 | 0.41 | 0.57 | 0.47 |
| | r | 0.16 | 0.10 | 0.13 | 0.14 | 0.33 | 0.46 | 0.10 | 0.16 | 0.41 | 0.55 | 0.47 |
| 5. | C | 0.21 | 0.25 | 0.21 | 0.37 | 0.35 | 0.37 | 0.11 | 0.12 | 0.35 | 0.38 | 0.35 |
| | r | 0.17 | 0.17 | 0.17 | 0.31 | 0.32 | 0.21 | 0.07 | 0.10 | 0.29 | 0.31 | 0.30 |

*All coefficients except those with an asterisk are statistically significant.

## ACKNOWLEDGMENTS

This chapter is based on a lecture held at the IXth World Conference on Gifted and Talented Children (The Hague, 1991).

## REFERENCES

Colangelo, N., & Brown, P. (1987). Labelling gifted youngsters: Long-term impact of families. *Gifted Child Quarterly, 31*, 75–78.

Cornell, D. G. (1989). Child adjustment and parent use of the term "gifted." *Gifted Child Quarterly, 33*, 59–64.

Freeman, J. (1986). Emotional aspects of giftedness. In J. Freeman (Ed.), *The psychology of gifted children* (pp. 247–264). Chichester: Wiley.

Freeman, J., & Urban, K. K. (1983). Über Probleme des Identifizierens und Etikettierens von hochbegabten Kindern. *Psychologie in Erziehung und Unterricht, 30*, 67–73.

Guskin, S. L., & Zimmermann, E. (1986). Being labeled gifted or talented: Meanings and effects perceived by students in special programs. *Gifted Child Quarterly, 30*, 61–65.

Koren, I. (1990, August). *Some filial and parental attitudes to talent.* Paper presented at the Second ECHA Conference, Budapest, 1990.

Koren, I. (1991). *Posljedice javnog proglasavanja i specificnog tretmana nadarenih ucenika* [The consequences of labelling and specific treatment of gifted pupils]. (Manuscript prepared for publication).

Robinson, A. (1986). The identification and labelling of gifted children. What does research tell us? In K. A. Heller and J. F. Feldhusen (Eds.), *Identifying and nurturing the gifted.* Bern: Huber.

# Section V11

## Counseling and Family

# 43

# Parental Fears and Expectations from the Point of View of a Counseling Center for the Gifted

**Wilhelm Wieczerkowski**
**Tania M. Prado**

*University of Hamburg, Hamburg, Germany*

During the last five years the counseling center in Hamburg has dealt with the identification, counseling, and offering of special provision to gifted children aged from five to 17. More than 300 children and their parents have been individually interviewed, particular attention being paid to the childrens' motivational, social, and emotional difficulties in school. Various counseling strategies have been adopted, whereas a number of concerns and expectancies of parents, according to the children's different IQ levels, have become apparent. Early identification and special provision for the gifted are of particular importance.

## INTRODUCTION

A five-year-old boy sits sullen and uncommunicative under his kindergarten table, and stubbornly refuses to come out and join in a game with the other children. Neither the persuasiveness of the teacher nor the strictness of the mother have any effect on the behavior of the boy. At home, however, he is open, curious, and capable of concentrated work. An eight-year-old, also a boy, disturbs his teacher with his far-fetched ideas and the way in which he demands attention during lessons, is impatient, and asks questions that have nothing to do with the actual lesson. One day he asks the teacher for a photograph of her, and when asked why explains that he is starting a collection of photos of natural disasters! When he climbed onto his desk in the middle of a lesson and refused to climb down again, the teacher had had enough. The boy's parents were confronted with a long list of complaints. This took them by surprise, as they had regarded their son as friendly, helpful, and interested in everything; until this moment they had had no idea that there were problems at school. A fifteen-year-old boy, who finished elementary and junior high school with outstanding grades, receives steadily worsening marks, and slips more and more into a disaster situation. He has lost all interest in school, and even his hobbies fail to attract him any more. His parents have no idea what to do, and fear the worst for his school career.

To be sure, these are only three single cases, each with its own history, but all have one common element: All the youngsters possess exceptional intellectual potential; they belong to the group of potentially gifted children. In order to eliminate a possible misunderstanding right at the start, it is not being proposed here that giftedness is to be equated with learning difficulties, that all gifted individuals are disadvantaged, or that gifted students have more problems than others. It goes without saying that there are young people who distinguish themselves by their exceptional achievements and, in many cases, by their varied interests, without ever experiencing any difficulties with themselves or the surrounding world. However, sometimes there really are problems associated with giftedness, and teachers (and also many parents) often, or even usually, fail to relate these to exceptional ability. One additional preliminary comment: The fact that the youngsters in the three examples—who were all referred to the center by their parents—were all boys is no coincidence. Of the nearly 350 children and young people seen so far in Hamburg, a mere 24% have been girls.

## THE COUNSELING CENTER

Even though the project "Counselling Centre for Identification and Guidance of the Gifted" started in the late autumn of 1984, the counseling center began its work in February, 1985 with a limited staff: a full-time director and a part-time secretary. Additional members of the counseling group included colleagues from the division of educational and developmental psychology of the University of Hamburg, so that, with the passage of time, the team came to be of an appropriate size. The centre is operated by the William Stern Society for Research and Development on Giftedness.

What are the tasks of such a center related to the special situation in Germany? Essentially there are five.

1. Giving diagnostic information, counseling, and guidance to parents and students on all educational and psychological problems associated with giftedness.
2. Helping teachers confronted with behavior difficulties on the part of gifted children to plan differential treatment in the framework of the regular classroom.
3. Providing information to interested parents.
4. Planning and carrying out seminars and courses for psychologists and teachers.
5. Keeping in touch with and informing pediatricians and child guidance centers (cf., Feger & Prado, 1986).

In its first five years of work the center concentrated mainly on the first three tasks. This is a result of the fact that the counseling contacts in the center are extremely time-consuming—in fact, interviewing, testing, counseling, and documenting a case typically requires about 18 hours.

## TWO BASIC CONSIDERATIONS

Before presenting a number of practical results of the work of the counseling center, preliminary remarks need to be made on two basic points.

the importance of giftedness as a phenomenon; and
the theoretical background of identification and counseling
    strategies.

## Identification and Counseling of the Gifted
## as Special Tasks within the General Framework
## of School Guidance

Identification and counseling of the gifted are to be understood
as special tasks within the general framework of school guidance. This view involves three assumptions.

1. *Giftedness is not an end in itself.* The existence of gifts and
   talents places an obligation on both the individual and society to develop them for the benefit of all.
2. *Being gifted is not a state that is the opposite of being
   ungifted.* It is not a matter of being either gifted or not, but
   a matter of being somehow different, that is, gifted. Explaining this to parents, children, and teachers seems to be
   essential both for understanding of the phenomenon and
   for development of realistic expectations of gifted children.
3. *Giftedness is not simply a cognitive phenomenon.* It also
   involves a complex of motivational, emotional, and volitional factors. Understanding this point is essential if gifted
   children and their parents are to be offered the help they
   need.

Innate potentials do not realize themselves automatically, independent of the circumstances of life. Gifts and talents need to
be fostered in everyday life. The emergence of giftedness has
been shown to be a developmental process in which an outstanding performance in one or more areas of human activity—
in science, technology, music, the arts, and so on—will only
occur if facilitating conditions such as motivation, concentration, persistence, and environmental stimulation come together
in a favorable constellation. The interaction among the different
elements of this constellation are still largely undetermined. As
a result, predictions about individual biographies or future life
events contain a good deal of uncertainty (Gallagher, 1986).

Five years' observation in the counseling center indicate that
parents of blue collar families have difficulty in coping with a
gifted child. These parents express, above all, two concerns.

1.  That the child's talents will demand too much from the parents.
2.  That friends and acquaintances will regard them as excessively ambitious if they attempt to provide their child with special help.

For these reasons, they avoid—to a greater degree than parents possessing traditional, middle class cultural values—encouraging and stimulating their offspring in what are, in their eyes, strange activities. As a result, they tend to try to make their children conform to "normality." One consequence of this is that the population of children seen in the counseling center has a bias, not only in the distribution of boys and girls, but also in the socioeconomic status of the families.

## An Identification and Counseling Strategy

It is necessary to start by explaining what is understood under the term "counseling." This involves intensive work on a problem that parents and children have identified as relatively serious (see Feger, 1988). An integral part of our counseling strategy is the filling out by parents of a preliminary questionnaire that permits initial structuring of the counselling contact. This questionnaire requests

> background information on the parents;
> information about the child and its position in the family;
> description of the problem;
> parents' expectations of counseling;
> behavioral characteristics and "disturbances" of the child in kindergarten or school;
> the child's contacts with others;
> special interests of the child; and
> behavioral problems: when these were first noticed.

As a rule, parents and children come to the initial session together. While the child is being interviewed, and in most cases being tested, the parents take part in an interview. Naturally, considerable emphasis is given during this first contact with the child to

> Spontaneity and openness versus withdrawal during the interview;

The reaction to a new and unknown situation; and

The degree of willingness to discuss personal matters. In this first stage of the work with the youngster, identifying possible intellectual potential is of particular importance.

In the event that the results of the interview and tests indicate the existence of exceptional potential, it is important to carry out a diagnosis that identifies the reasons for low levels of achievement or behavioral disturbances. Figure 43-1 provides an insight into the nature of the decision process.

The situation is more difficult when the interview provides no clear evidence of gifts or talents. It is well known that understimulation continuing over a number of years, especially at the elementary school level, can lead to substantial disruptions of the developmental process. This is especially true when access to compensatory activities, both in and out of school, is limited. The consequences are often lack of interest in school, loss of motivation, and unwillingness to make the necessary effort. These factors frequently affect children's behavior in the interview and test situation (see also Wieczerkowski & Cropley, 1986).

What the parents really expect of their children is not always clear. As Strategy 2 (see Figure 43-2) shows, careful consideration of this factor is necessary from the start, in order to meet the needs of both children and parents.

Identification without subsequent special provision is merely an empty promise, and should be avoided. In the present educational situation in Germany possibilities are very limited. Measures available within the framework of conventional schools are: early admission to school, skipping grades, participation in special group activities, and cluster grouping. Among the out of school activities which are available are courses and summer camps organized by parents or institutions.

As Feger (1987) pointed out, the decision to recommend particular special procedures to parents involves a number of steps (see Figure 43-3).

The option of making no recommendation to the parents may seem surprising at first glance, and may even lead to dissatisfaction with the strategy. However, it is necessary in every specific case to consider carefully whether the expectations of parents and children can be fulfilled, or whether these could have negative consequences for the outcome of special provision. As

FIGURE 43-1.   Strategy 1 (of identification and counseling).

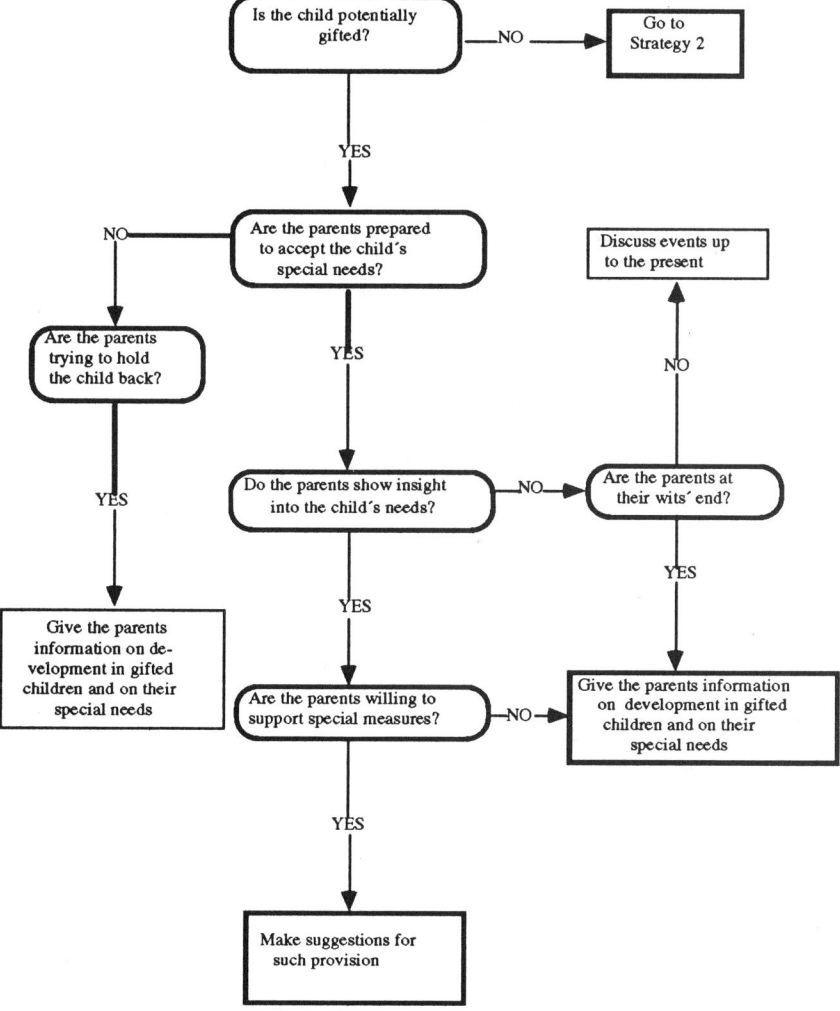

Feger (1987) pointed out, the younger the child the more important it is to find a qualified supervisor.

The supervisor is simultaneously coordinator, confidant and source of information. Where there are grounds for believing that the supervisor has physical, psychological or intellectual limitations which restrict the likelihood of success, it is better not to start the provision at all.

FIGURE 43-2.   Strategy 2 (of identification and counseling).

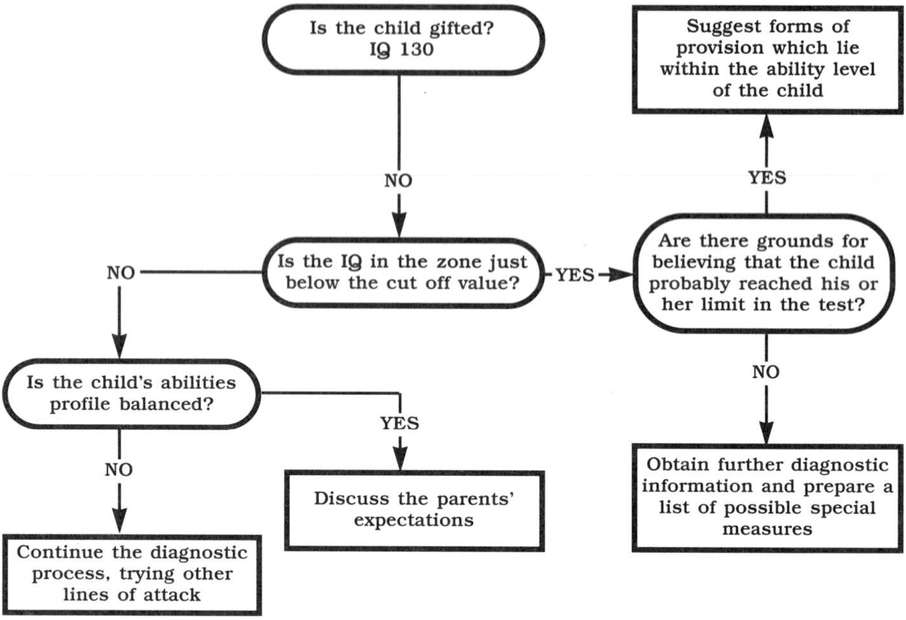

Is the child gifted?
IQ 130

Suggest forms of
provision which lie
within the ability level
of the child

NO

YES

NO ———— Is the IQ in the zone just
below the cut off value?  ⟩-YES→

Are there grounds for
believing that the child
probably reached his or
her limit in the test?

Is the child's abilities
profile balanced?

YES

NO

NO

Obtain further diagnostic
information and prepare a
list of possible special
measures

Discuss the parents'
expectations

Continue the diagnostic
process, trying other
lines of attack

## PRACTICAL ISSUES

### The Clientele

As mentioned earlier, the clientele of the counseling center is
strongly biased in two aspects—the sex of the children and the
social status of the parents. Table 43-1 offers an overview of the
situation with regard to parental occupation.

Of the total group, 232 (76.3%) were boys, 72 (23.7%) girls. In
all, 40 children (13.2%) were aged five or below, 180 (59.6%) between six and 11, and 84 (27.6%) 12 or above.

Three important points can be seen from these tables.

> Families with parents having an academic background or
> in white collar occupations are strongly overrepresented
> in our sample, as has already been mentioned. The cen-
> ter serves, above all, children from better off families;
> blue collar workers make relatively little use of it.

We can only speculate about the reasons for this. Since it is
assumed that the distribution of ability to master abstract sym-

FIGURE 43-3.    Steps involved in the decision to recommend special provision for the gifted.

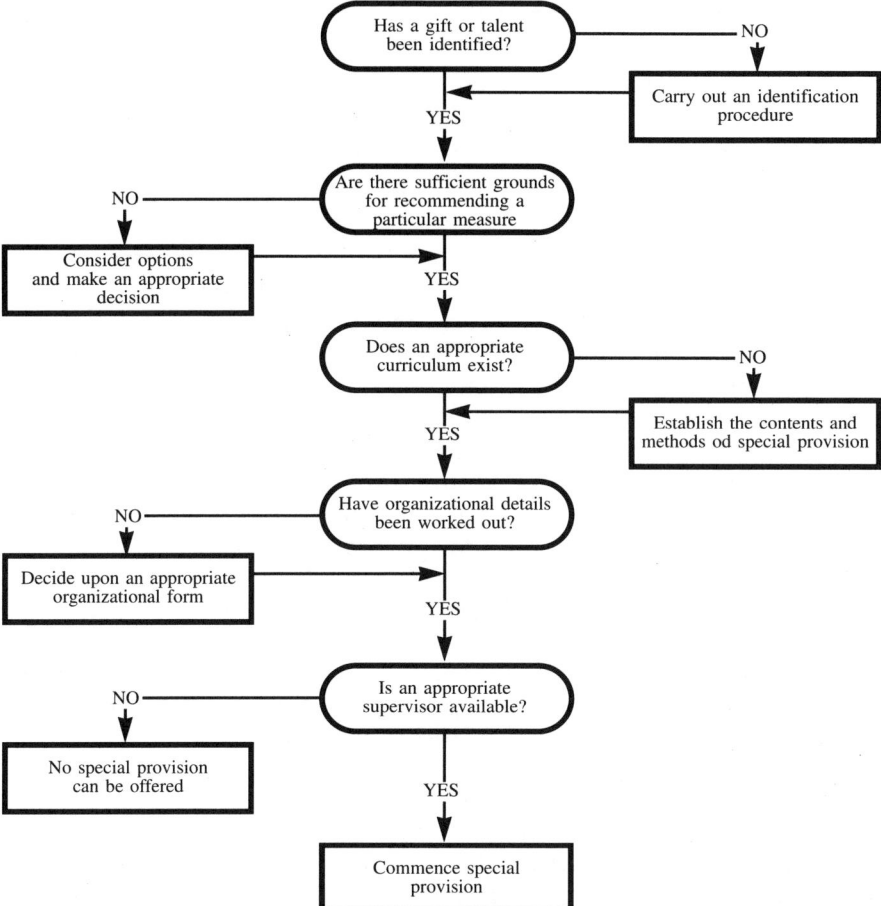

bol systems is independent of social class, the explanation of
the social class bias in use of the center seems likely to lie,
above all, in the different values placed on intellectual activity
by various social groups. In view of the fact that attending a
counseling center occurs on a voluntary basis, measures for altering the imbalance in clientele (e.g., articles in magazines, TV,
and radio programs) seem unlikely to be very successful. However, it is precisely through these media that the center has become known in recent years. Perhaps the situation could be
changed through more intensive cooperation with teachers, although this would take considerable time.

TABLE 43-1
Educational/Occupational Status of the Father (Mother)

|                    | IQ ≥130 | IQ 115–129 | IQ <115 |
|--------------------|---------|------------|---------|
| University Graduate | 23.1%*  | 20.7%      | 9.2%    |
| White collar       | 10.4%   | 13.5%      | 11.9%   |
| Blue collar        | 2.8%    | 2.4%       | 6.0%    |

*These percentages refer to the total group.

The sex imbalance is very striking. Since we cannot assume that intellectual ability in girls differs from that in boys, it is necessary to look at other possible reasons. Feger and Prado (1986) pointed out that there are at least three possibilities.

1. Sex role expectations may be important. Some parents consider success in school more important for boys than for girls. When problems arise they look for help sooner for their sons than for their daughters.
2. Girls have a tendency to adjust more easily to social situations: They are more willing to compromise and show self-denial.
3. Girls tend to be more extensively involved in extracurricular activities in the arts, music, and dance. These serve as a compensation for frustrations in school.

The children whose parents brought them to the counseling center were mainly still in the lower elementary grades. Apparently it is at this level that the strongest pressure to conform is experienced by substantial numbers of gifted children. At this age a number of the children had obviously not yet developed coping strategies with the help of which problems could have been avoided.

**The Parents**

The parents making contact with the center are usually those whose children are experiencing educational problems. They are concerned about the child and its future. The motives of the parents to make contact with the center are complex and by no means always clearly discernable. Our experience indicates that four motives for bringing a child to the counseling center can be distinguished.

1. Concern about behavior atypical for the child's age group (unsual interests, lack of contact to children of the same age group, no interest in children's games, etc.).
2. Uncertainty about how to provide the child with an appropriate upbringing (counseling on the possibilities both within and outside schools).
3. Concern about difficulties the child is experiencing in school (failure, lack of interest in learning, behavioral problems, etc.).
4. The need to establish what potentials the child possesses (information about the level of intelligence or special talents).

Are these motives—and they are ones that predominate in parents' decisions to come to the center—to be dismissed as merely an expression of their vanity? Our practical experience indicates that parents are very frequently correct in believing that their children have at least above average ability: No fewer than 72.4% of children tested had an IQ of 115 and above, 36.0% of 130 or more.

## Concerns of Parents

An overview of children's problems, as stated by parents, is shown in Table 43-2.

The problems most frequently mentioned by parents are

1. boredom and underachievement;
2. lack of progress in class which is too slow for the children; and
3. total lack of challenge.

The children's difficulties with formal schooling (institution "school") can be classified into four aspects (see Table 43-2).

Lack of motivation (boredom, loss of interest, rejection, etc.);

School problems (problems of concentration, lack of support, inadequate stimulation, etc.);

Problems with teachers (lack of understanding, no special provision for special abilitites, etc.); and

Socioemotional problems (adaptation problems, isolation, aggressiveness, behavioral disorders, etc).

The incidence of these unspecific symptoms within the three intelligence groups (IQ <115, IQ 115–129, IQ ≥130) shows a tendency similar to that seen in the "expectations of parents." The

**TABLE 43-2**
**School-Related Concerns of Parents**

| IQ <115<br>Motivation | IQ 115–129<br>Motivation | IQ ≥130<br>Motivation |
|---|---|---|
| Loss of the joy of learning<br>Blockage of unrealized abilities<br>Loss of interest in school | Unsatisfied hunger for knowledge<br>Rejection of school<br>Loss of interest in school learning<br>Resignation<br>Boredom<br>Loss of ambition<br>Disappointment<br>Unwillingness to learn | Listlessness, pretended illnesses<br>Unwillingness to go to school, no interest in school<br>Unwillingness to learn<br>Refusal to learn<br>Lack of interest in lessons<br>Boredom and dissatisfaction<br>No opportunity to satisfy the thirst for knowledge |
| **Social and emotional problems** | **Social and emotional problems** | **Social and emotional problems** |
| Difficulties in contacts<br>Unhappiness<br>Difficulties of adaptation<br>Negative self-image | Social isolation<br>Loss of psychological balance<br>Adoption of a loner role<br>Execessive self-confidence<br>Reduced self-confidence (possibility of suicide)<br>Permanent sense of frustration<br>Adoption of the black sheep role<br>Aggression/behavioral disturbance | A loner role/impatience with others<br>Problems in getting along with others<br>Difficulty in getting on in a group<br>Disturbance of contact with others, underdeveloped social skills<br>Aggression including aggression against oneself<br>Lack of discipline<br>Inadequate or deviant personal development<br>Isolation and antisocial behaviour<br>Behavior problems |

**TABLE 43-2 (Cont.)**
**School-Related Concerns of Parents**

| School problems | School problems | School problems |
|---|---|---|
| Problems in concentration | Failure to learn how to learn | Loss of learning ability |
| Lack of support | Lack of support/ | Inadequate stimulation |
| Limited challenge | Understimulation | Failure to develop learning |
| Lack of challenge | Misdirection of effort | strategies |
| Inadequate workload | A friction-filled school career | Lack of diligence |
| Failure | Failure/rejection of school | Understimulation |
| | Lack of progress in school | |

| Problems with teachers | Problems with teachers | Problems with teachers |
|---|---|---|
| Lack of understanding | Lack of understanding and sympathy (e.g., no fostering of logical thinking, etc.) | |

children from group 1 (IQ <115) are more "passive" in their behavior and may suffer socioemotional problems (unhappiness, negative self-image), whereas in groups 2 (IQ 115–129) and 3 (IQ ≥130) the children more often display "active" forms of opposition.

The list of observed symptoms, also based on parents' reports, shown in Table 43-2 is too undifferentiated to permit relating school and personal problems to level of intellectual giftedness. Our experience shows that parents who come to our counseling center mainly are searching for causes for their problems. They are worried about remarkable behavior and reactions of their children, and want to understand the children better. They hope for answers to questions such as

Why does the child refuse to go to school?
Why does the child show a lack of motivation and display resignation?
Why does the child have difficulties in contacts with others (peer group)?
Why does the child show difficulties of adaptation?

Observable symptoms such as difficulties in contact with others, a weak self-concept or declining self-confidence, and refusal to learn can only be interpreted by counselors after they have investigated the etiology of the case. A professional differential diagnosis is necessary in order to identify the origins of complex problems in their various ramifications, and to design appropiate corrective measures. A differentiated diagnosis incorporating all available diagnostic data must be followed by differentiated treatment proposals. Therefore, the preconception of some psychologists that, in a counseling center for gifted children, giftedness would be offered almost exclusively as an explanation of school problems reflects nonpsychological ways of thinking.

## Parents' Expectations

Child related concerns of parents lead to a focus on the question of what the counseling center can do for them. After initial contact, such as a phone call and filling out a questionnaire, parents come to the center with feelings of uncertainty, insecurity, and concern. The issues with which they need help can be classified into five aspects.

> general questions about education;
> level and structure of ability;
> information about future development;
> advice about school development and how to treat the teachers; and
> information about intellectually challenging activities outside the school.

Table 43-3 lists these aspects and concerns of the parents according to the different IQ levels. The task is a challenging one, not least because there is no simple way of dealing with the individual cases seen in the center. Gifted individuals—with or without personal, emotional, social, or cognitive problems—do not form a homogeneous group. It should be borne in mind that in Table 43-3 (1) the frequency of the nomination of a problem is not considered; (2) the division and weighting of the problems varies with each set of parents. There are similarities in the interests of parents whose children fall into a particular IQ group, but there are also important differences, which must be kept in mind in the counseling situation.

All parents who visit the counseling center are mainly interested in answers to and information about three questions

> Is the child unusually able?
> Is it possible to identify specific interests, capabilities and structures of ability?

How certain and objective are diagnostic analyses of "intelligence"?

At the first IQ-level (IQ <115) a clear interest in counseling dealing with special problems of high ability can be found, which contrasts with the expectations of parents with children who are identified as having an IQ ≥130. Parents with children belonging to the latter group seek advice on eliminating school problems such as dislike of school and lack of concentration. They want advice on establishing a better relationship with teachers, and educational ideas that will solve or reduce the problems of their children. Parents of children belonging to the middle group hope for help in solving the socioemotional problems of their children. These problems obviously cause a dis-

TABLE 43-3
Parents' Expectations of the Counseling Center

| IQ <115<br>General | IQ 115–129<br>General | IQ ≥130<br>General |
|---|---|---|
| How to treat the child | Suggestions for promoting | Counseling and support |
| Specific suggestions on | the child's ability | Suggestions for promoting |
| child rearing practices | Advice on social problems | the child's ability |
| Information on the help | Counseling for single parents | |
| that the center can offer | Advice for parents for whom | |
| | the child is too great | |
| | a challenge | |
| | Elimination of parents' | |
| | uncertainty | |
| **Level and<br>structure of ability** | **Level and<br>structure of ability** | **Level and<br>structure of ability** |
| Is the child really | Information on high | Is the child gifted or not? |
| unusually able? | intelligence or other | Objective analysis of child's |
| Precise information on | source of problems | situation (diagnosis) |
| abilities | Accurate information on | Structure of abilities and |
| Accurate information on its | its "intelligence" | Information on its |
| "intelligence" | Is the child gifted or not? | "intelligence" |
| Information on special | IQ | |
| aptitudes and abilities | | |
| **Prognosis** | **Prognosis** | **Prognosis** |
| Suggestions for promoting | Recommendations for | Information on how to |
| development | therapy | facilitate the further |
| Hints on how to avoid | How to help the child | development of the child |
| school problems | make friends | |

TABLE 43-3(Cont.)
Parents' Expectations of the Counselling Center

| School | School | School |
|---|---|---|
| Advice on how to improve instruction<br>Advice on how to work with teachers | Advice on school problems<br>Alternative school possibilities<br>Material for the teacher<br>Suggestions on how obtain cooperation from the school<br>Better cooperation with the school | Choosing an appropriate school<br>Forms of special provision<br>Advisability of changing classes<br>Counseling on school problems<br>Counseling on change of school<br>Suggestions on how to improve school situation<br>Information on alternative school possibilities |

| Out of school | Out of school | Out of school |
|---|---|---|
| Achieving a balance | How to help the child pass its time constructively | Counseling and information on available possibilities<br>Advice on sensible ways of promoting the child's development<br>Information on courses and other out of school activities |

like of school and the parents anticipate therapeutic help. Parents of gifted children (IQ ≥130), on the other hand seek specific advice on how to improve the school situation for their children. They seek exact information on the choice of school, the consequences and possibilities of a school or class change, and the usefulness of skipping a grade.

Different expectations are mainly found in the search for advice on out of school activities.

1.  compensation for school;
2.  significant leisure activities; and
3.  general possibilities of promoting the child's development.

Primarily the parents of children who are identified as gifted think about how to satisfy the children's curiosity and improve their interests, and are motivated to relieve the child's boredom at school.

## CONCLUDING REMARKS

Fears and expectations, the central topics of this paper, can both be explained in terms of three psychological aspects.

1.  *Uncertainty* of the parents about atypical attitudes of the child, for example refusal to play age-appropriate games, or having only poor contact to peers, or either showing need of such contacts or having developed coping strategies for managing them;
2.  *Insecurity* of the parents regarding their own capability to support the child in a helpful way; and
3.  *Uneasiness* about reported difficulties of the child within and outside the family, in particular in school.

Of course, these three aspects are closely linked with five expectancies that form the basis for counseling contacts with the center. These are

1.  General advice on educational matters and procedures for promoting the development of gifts and talents;
2.  Questions about the level of giftedness or about the structure of talents;
3.  Prognostic information about the further development of the child;
4.  Advice about the further scholastic development of the child and parental contact with teachers; and
5.  Information about ways of challenging the child outside school.

Experience during the counseling center's years of operation supports the assumption that counseling and guidance for the gifted and their parents is a very important, responsible, and time-consuming procedure that involves detailed interviews as well as extensive diagnostic procedures. Furthermore, the work in such a center should not be solely a practical task (helping gifted students and their parents to deal with typical problem areas), but should include systematic study of problems of the gifted, their individual characteristics and development, and, at the same time, an implementation–analysis of counseling concepts. Consequently, an evaluation process is no less important than the practical work. At present, counseling and guidance of gifted students in Germany are conducted in specialized centers, most of them in close cooperation with a local university (i.e., Hamburg, Munich, Tübingen).

It has also become apparent that the professional competence of the counseling personel is of essential importance (cf., Feger & Prado, 1986). Even though efforts have been made to increase professional awareness and to awaken public consciousness, there is still a lack of comprehension of and information about the needs of gifted children. Planning and carrying out seminars and courses for teachers, school psychologists, and psychologists in regular child guidance centers are important aims of the center's work, as are in addition, not only building professional and public support for the gifted, but also promoting an exchange of professional experiences.

In the discussion of early cognitive support of the gifted child, one critical point has often been emphasized: Will the challenge to his or her intellectual potentials lead to deterioration of the child's emotional and social development? Five years' experience have shown that a sensitive, understanding, and appreciative encounter with the special needs and the unique challenge of the particular abilities of, in general, highly motivated children has positive effects on their development, not least of all in the social area. This seems to be quite reasonable: Equal interests and the same "language" are important aspects in each social activity. This is true even for intellectually accelerated children. In the kindergarten and in elementary school they seldom experience appreciation of their intellectual interests and their performance in grasping the subject matter in class. Therefore, they often slip into a state of "splendid isolation."

Practical experience indicates that the preschool period is of special importance for the development of exceptional abilities. During this time actual interests have to be stimulated. For some psychologists, special provision has often been regarded as giving one-sided preference to narrow intellectual (cognitive) stimulation, which sometimes has negative effects on a child's development. In the present conceptualization, a fostering strategy should not exclusively promote intellectual development. However, children should not be compelled to participate in a sports or music program against their will. Fostering development at preschool or elementary school age, in particular, means promoting the interests of the child within the family environment. Procedures such as early admission to school or skipping grades should not be routinely adopted without reference to the complete diagnostic process. It may seem reasonable to let a child skip one or two grades for two reasons: (1) to reduce the stress that the child suffers because the lessons offer no new and interesting information, (2) to offer contents that challenge the child's capacity. This intervention should never be carried out in isolation, independent of diagnostic information, and it should be kept in mind that it has a therapeutic value for only a limited space of time. In some cases it seems more reasonable to give the child the opportunity to sit in on specific lessons for students in a higher grade.

It is not proposed here that giftedness or (even) a potential for high achievement is necessarily connected with learning difficulties or socioemotional problems, in short with disadvantages of one kind or the other. On the other hand, the fact cannot be neglected that there are young persons who suffer severe problems and need help—in all age groups. Practical observations have given rise to the conviction that such help has to begin as early as possible. The prognosis for 15-year-old youngsters already involved in a *spiral of disappointment* is in many cases not good. Having experienced a lack of understanding of their special needs—cognitive as well as emotional—many of them display a distrust of authority that is not easy to eliminate. It seems disastrous when a previously eager and happy child who grasps ideas rapidly, concentrates at a high level, and effectively organizes information becomes, after years of frustration, an unhappy, indifferent person. This is not the fate of all children with high potential, but many such youngsters come to the counseling center. Not only the children need help—the parents need it too. Instead of being proud of an outstanding child they often do not know how to handle the problems arising with the passage of the years. The experience of having their uncertainties, fears, and expectations taken seriously, that someone takes time to listen to them and work out how to treat the child within and outside the family, or give advice on how to talk with teachers has—as experience has shown—a beneficial effect in their relationship with their children, and helps in coping with difficulties.

## REFERENCES

Feger, B. (1987). Förderprogramme für Hochbegabte—Uberlegungen zur Planung und Durchführung. *Psychologie in Erziehung und Unterricht, 34,* 161–170.

Feger, B. (1988). *Die Beratungsstelle für Hochbegabtenprobleme in Hamburg.* In H. Bartenwerfer (Ed.). (1988). *Besondere Begabun-*

*gen in der normalen Schule. Forschung, Beratung, pädagogischer Auftrag.* Frankfurt/Main: GFPF-Materialien Nr. 18, pp. 109–123.

Feger, B., & Prado, T. (1986). The first information and counselling centre for the gifted in West Germany. In K. A. Heller & J. F. Feldhusen (Eds.), *Identifying and nurturing the gifted. An international perspective* (pp. 139–148). Bern: Huber.

Gallagher, J. J. (1986). The conservation of intellectual resources. In A. J. Cropley, K. K. Urban, H. Wagner, & W. Wieczerkowski (Eds.), *Giftedness: A continuing worldwide challenge* (pp. 21–30). New York: Tillium Press.

Wieczerkowski, W., & Cropley. A. J. (1986). Preface. In K. A. Heller & J. F. Feldhusen (Eds.), *Identifying and nurturing the gifted: An international perspective* (pp. 11–18). Bern: Huber.

# 44

# Spiral of Disappointment

## Decline in Achievement among Gifted Adolescents

**Wilhelm Wieczerkowski**
**Tania M. Prado**

*University of Hamburg, Hamburg, Germany*

The view that the pattern of development and the scholastic performance of potentially highly gifted children are as prone to disturbances as those of less gifted youngsters now is accepted widely. The emergence of giftedness and the unfolding of talent has been shown to be a developmental process, in which a variety of cognitive, noncognitive, and ecopsychological preconditions are involved. Whether the observed developmental patterns of a young person are harmonious or disruptive depends on what has been described in the literature as a favorable (vs. unfavorable) constellation of facilitating factors. With the help of a dynamic model, case studies of failure and refusal to perform in school among young underachievers are analyzed and related to previous school experiences.

## THE HAMBURG COUNSELLING CENTER

Since its foundation in 1985, the Counselling Center for the Gifted in Hamburg has primarily concerned itself with identifying gifted children and youths aged 5–17, as well as with counseling parents. More than 400 parents have made use of the diagnostic and counseling services offered since the center's inception.

The sample of children seen in the counseling center shows in comparison to the normal population of young people, of course, bias in three repects. First, age groups are unequally represented: The proportion of those of preschool age (up to the ages of 5–6) is about 12%, elementary school children (aged 6–7 to 10–11) account for 53%, those between the ages of 11–12 to 15 make up 27% and those over 16 6%. Second, the proportion of girls and boys is also asymmetrical: 77% of those interviewed were boys. (This ratio corresponds, however, with the usual distribution of gender at general educational counseling centers [Feger, 1988]). Third, the IQ groupings arrived at were predominantly at the upper end of the scale: IQ <115 (24%), IQ = 115–129 (39%), and IQ ≥130 (36%). Children and youths brought to the counseling center were mainly of above average or even superior intelligence.

## REASONS FOR VISITING THE CENTER

Parents who had found out about counseling available for the gifted through acquaintances, teachers, counselors, or the media are the ones who most commonly initiate contact with the center. As a rule, they feel compelled to bring their children to the center for various reasons, depending on the child's age and school circumstances.

At preschool age, parents are often at a loss concerning how to deal with their child's learning needs and precociousness. There is uncertainty whether to meet and support these needs or to remain aloof. Often it is a practical question of whether they should or should not fulfill the child's desire to learn how to read, write, and perform mathematical problems before reaching school age. Uncertainty concerning "adequate" parental behavior often is compounded by admonitions from friends and relatives, preschool workers, and elementary school teachers who advocate not stimulating the child intellectually too soon, but rather challenging the child according to the emotional and social stage of development.

Parents often report their child's elementary school years as a source of disappointment because the degree of learning is not only far below the child's cognitive ability, but also involves content areas far distant from his or her cognitive interests. The intense drive to know more exhibited by pupils who persistently ask questions or are capable of answers well ahead of the set syllabus often is not recognized or is discouraged, or the pupil is asked to refrain from such behavior in the interest of slower pupils and the time alloted for the subject. In elementary school, the precocious pupil must take part for long periods of time in basic exercises that she or he has already mastered. The reaction of the child to such an unsatisfying learning environment then in many cases is withdrawal, lapses in concentration, or aggressiveness, although the level of marks almost always remains excellent.

In secondary school, sharply declining performance and lack of motivation combined with inability to concentrate and apply oneself to a goal can be observed after a year or two in school, along with a growing general lack of interest in the curriculum reaching a peak at the age of 13 to 14. The practical concern of parents when their child is in danger of being held back or has indeed been held back for the cited reasons frequently gives rise to a visit to the counseling center.

What percentage these cases of at-risk pupils represent within the normal (or the highly gifted) population cannot be stated exactly, and can at best be ascertained only very roughly. Because of the unavoidable bias in a sample of the type seen at the center (e.g., children of blue collar families make up only 18.9% of all cases), and the regionalized use made of the service, any estimation (e.g., of a "risk factor" in gifted development) capable of wider application obviously cannot be obtained. It can only be stated that the young people under consideration are of either above average or unusual giftedness and that their requirements are fully met neither by their schooling nor their immediate (social) environment, rendering counseling inevitable.

## SPIRAL OF DISAPPOINTMENT

More strongly manifested emotional, motivational, and behavioral disturbances accompanied by social difficulties and refusal to perform scholastically, as well as a decline in achievement, are all daily symptoms among young people brought to the counseling center. As a rule, these experiences are rooted in early childhood, only surfacing for the various reasons given for seeking advice within each of the three age groups.

The disturbed developmental patterns of youths brought to the center reveal various related phases where the child's expectations and willingness to act were hardly being catered for by the curriculum. The discrepancy that results from this breeds the basic elements of a *spiral of disappointment*. These are

1.  *A discrepancy between learning expectations and curriculum.* The preschool child who is eager to learn and primed to recognize and assimilate the environment (in the sense of Piaget) frequently is given hope that school will be an "adventure and challenge," only to have these great expectations frustrated by the limitations of elementary school, in which the organizational form and structure are not able to meet the needs of highly able children.
2.  *A discrepancy between learning ability (learning speed) and curriculum.* Placed in a classroom heterogeneous with regard to both learning prerequisites and ability, the child must adapt to the slower pace. Primarily this involves exercises covering content the child has already mastered.
3.  *A discrepancy between willingness to exert effort and the need to act.* The willingness of a highly gifted child to take up the challenge of cognitive tasks is held in check by the necessity of maximizing the learning of all pupils in the class. Inevitably, a pupil's willingness to go beyond the predetermined curriculum is met with disapproval or is regarded as a nuisance.

The spiral of disappointment results from protracted hindrance of elementary cognitive needs among particularly capable and willing learners. The long-term effects of this state can be detected in the motivational, emotional, and social lives of these young people as seen in individual case studies. Childhood disappointments and setbacks often go unnoticed for long periods among children of above average potential. Furthermore, this state is commonly underestimated when conclusions are made concerning a child's behavior. Inadequate coping strategies adopted by a child in a relatively unsympathetic environment that also provoke resistance and rejection are also frequently misread, and the signals being given are not always properly understood in terms of their differential diagnostic content. The spiral is presented graphically in Figure 44-1.

FIGURE 44-1.   Spiral of disappointment.

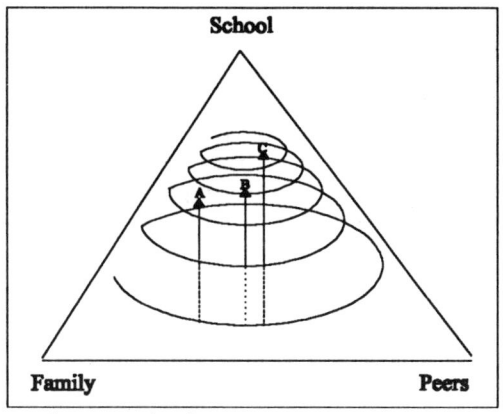
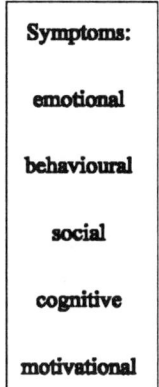

A = pre-school age
B = elementary school age
C = from the beginning of secondary school age

The given structure of ecopsychological circumstances within a child's surroundings is as formatively and interactively involved in that which constitutes the distinct nature of a particular spiral of disappointment as are the personal characteristics of the young person in question. Each young person's willingness to act and have new experiences at a given time—itself attracting the attention of other people in the surrounding environment and apparently prompting a given educational measure—depends on the one hand on the child's active and reactive behaviorial patterns, and on the other on how others react to them, either as patterns to be disapproved of or as signals from a child whose needs are not being met. Within this model based on a needs orientation, different stages of psychic states are assumed from preschool age on into secondary school in which the child's range of action appears to have been severely curbed and can be widened, if at all, only to a limited extent owing to rational objections or disciplinary measures in school or at home.

Insufficient gratification of the need for a general cognitive orientation has occurred, as well as lack of challenge of abilities. Resulting problems become obvious as early as the first years of elementary school, and take the form of aversion to school and frequently, mostly in the case of boys, in disruptive behavior in class and otherwise ostentatious behavior, all generally leading to reprimands. Since the scholastic achievements of such children, who exert little effort while learning minimally, are generally good or even better, they obtain in early years a self-concept with respect to their ability that, in the later school career, can lead to problems of performance and task commitment. If willingness to exert themselves is poorly developed and there is an unrealistic conception of how much concentration is called for in "unpopular" tasks and subjects, the result is disappointment over scholastic achievement, the cause for which is often attributed to external factors. Young people fall into a *circulus vitiosus*, from which they are unable to extricate themselves by their own effort in most cases.

## THE CLIENTELE OF THE HAMBURG COUNSELING CENTER AND THEIR PARENTS

The following section reports data for 53 young people aged 12–17. No cases with severe emotional disturbances or need for clinical therapy were considered. The group was distributed as follows: 34 youngsters aged 12–14 years (64.2%) and 19 aged 15–17 (35.8%). Of these 24.5% were girls. Among the fathers of these young people, 27.7% were academics, 35.8% were white collar employees without a university degree, and 18.9% were artisans and blue collar workers. In all, 34% of the mothers were homemakers. A total of 84% of the youths attended a German *gymnasium*, 12% were at a secondary school concluding in the tenth grade (*Realschule*) and 4% attended a comprehensive preparatory school. A total of 34% obtained an IQ of <115, 32% scored between 115–129, and 34% had an IQ ≥130. A major problem is that disturbances of the developmental process frequently also depress actual test scores. This was taken into account.

## PROBLEM AREAS AMONG CLIENTS

Reasons for visiting the center and asking for advice can be found in four areas of parental concern after the child's transition into secondary school (see Table 44-1).

Decline in learning behavior and motivation includes minimal interest in school, disinterest in subjects, defective work attitude, discrepancies between achievement in and out of school,

## TABLE 44-1
## Four Problem Areas Considered by Parents to be Problematic
## for Their Troubled Children

Problems in learning behavior (lack of concentration [15.1%], drop in achievement [8.9%])

Decline in learning motivation [49.1%]

Difficulties with teachers (unsympathetic attitude [15,1%], unwillingness to adapt instruction [11.3%])

Social problems in the classroom (adjustment, "fitting in," isolation [5.7%], interactive difficulties [30.2%], disruptive behavior [18.9%])

lack of participation in discussions, poor concentration and lack of diligence, wavering concentration, decline in achievement, varying levels of marks, decline in desire to undertake activities, and lack of attentiveness in "uninteresting" subjects.

Difficulties with teachers include lack of support, lack of recognition, requirements too slack, lack of challenge and unutilized capacity.

Social problems within class include being an outsider, mobbing by classmates, isolated position among class members, lack of friends, feeling of exclusion, communication difficulties, disturbance in social behavior, frequent disruptiveness, and disregard of school rules.

## POSITIVE AND NEGATIVE ASPECTS
## OF SCHOOL SETTING

Warning signs are seen. Feedback from school (from the classroom teacher, in report cards) indicates a steady decline in achievement level, accompanied and caused by apathy, withdrawal and, finally, not only refusal to take part in class instruction but also lack of interest in challenging intellectual activity and resistance to any scholastic demands. These warning signs are accompanied by more serious social problems, such as difficulty in integrating, introverted self-sufficiency, or the brash and impatient, sometimes arrogant snubbing of peers.

In developmental psychological research, surface symptoms such as those cited are often treated as concomitant to a particular vulnerability and insecurity during a search for identity in puberty. Lack of interest in "imposed" subject matter having little to do with life or interests at the time, aloofness toward or even rejection of adults (sometimes going as far as open aggressiveness and provocation followed by withdrawal into one's own world) all characterize the decisive reorientation underway in a young person's life. Ambivalence toward school and school routine, characteristic of puberty, of course, is common in the present risk group. This becomes clearly visible when important aspects of a (desired) positive ecopsychological environment are expressed, and, conversely, when other (undesired) counterproductive aspects are brought up with negative connotations (see Table 44-2).

Regardless of whether these observations are real or distorted, the impressions represent a subjective experience of reality that each individual reacts to uniquely, and that the people will not be willing to alter, either in their perception of it or their behavior toward it.

The perception of self in a school setting is experienced by a young person in five areas: social relationships, classroom atmosphere, teacher personality, general curriculum, and additional class offerings. Since the outward, physical, and organi-

TABLE 44-2
Overview of Positive and Negative Aspects of the School Setting

### Positive aspects

*Social components:* closely knit grade/class, contact with peers, time spent with friends

*Classroom atmosphere:* interesting class instruction, room for creativity, open interchange between teacher and pupils, feeling secure, achievement without pressure

*Teachers:* competent in subject, sympathetic toward pupil's problems, fair minded, friendly, nice, less authoritarian in attitude

*General curriculum:* stimulating to the mind, experiencing and learning new and interesting things, acquiring wideranging knowledge

*Electives:* foreign language courses, natural sciences, applied science, music, drama, extracurricular events

### Negative aspects

*Social components:* lack of cameraderie, attitude of some other students, envy

*Classroom atmosphere:* ponderous and unimaginative instruction, course contents, subjects, monotonous instruction, frequent repetition, self-centered striving to achieve, excessive rote learning, drive to succeed, confusing course structure, insufficient presentation of course materials

*Teachers:* little interest in teaching, lack of educative intervention, impatience, chicanery (tormenting pupils), strictness, unsympathetic attitude, authority, lack of fairness, unpedagogic attitude, disagreeable personality

*General curriculum:* no learning objective spoken of, instruction "runs on the spot," lack of new material in favorite subjects, insufficient scholastic challenge

*Electives:* Courses canceled, time-consuming homework

zational circumstances apparently play a lesser role, overly large school buildings, limited space in the schoolyard or gym in breaks, large class size, too many canceled periods and the long hours at school seem to be severely disturbing. The contrary poles found in the statements made by the adolescent clientele make it unmistakably clear what they feel school should be like, as opposed to how the large majority of them experience it. The statements delineate a reality that in its distortions is, despite some partial aspects, a subjectively biased representation of it. It is striking that the picture of experienced reality drawn by youths nearly always precludes any active role being taken by them in the ecopsychological web of relations, their part in the main being passively experienced and described as such in an interview.

## SOME ASPECTS IN THE HISTORY OF RISK PRONE

It is often the case that an unfavorable school situation, whether it be failing a grade or impending expulsion from school, motivates parents to seek advice at the counseling center. Disturbances in the development of the child (see Table 44-1) are preeminent because of this. As a retrospective analysis of earlier patterns of development shows, some earlier observations are seen in a new light given the most recent changes in the child. Thus, parents of 52% of our clientele reported having had difficulties as early as the beginning of elementary school and on into the first grades, with 24.3% experiencing these difficulties at the onset of junior high school, without there being an immediately noticeable drop in school achievement. Those parents who could recall a decline in achievement only in the most recent past—and were very surprised by it—made up only 9.4% of our clientele. In all 13.2% made no comment on their children's school career.

As to the history of the gifted pupils, drawing both from statements by parents as well as school report cards, the following picture takes shape.

The first years of elementary school are handled with no apparent problems by the children. In most cases they are at the head of their class or near this level. They are distinguished both by their ability to learn and by minor to more serious behavioral problems and violations of school norms. A sampling from report cards reveals instances of thoughtlessness, lapses in concentration, sloppy handwriting, and disruption of classes.

Praise can be found in almost all cases for the level of involvement in academic tasks and their input into subject matter. The children, however, complain at an early stage about boredom in school, and frequently must be made to complete homework assignments and only do so dispiritedly.

The coping strategies used in elementary school are readily apparent: On the one hand, these children are only willing to confront the demands placed on them in class with a modicum of effort. On the other, they break the behavioral rules at school in a clumsy effort to gain attention. The obvious signals stemming from this, for the child, unsatisfactory situation remain outside the scope of teachers' and parents' awareness for the moment. It is much more likely that comments about the scholastic achievement and conduct of a child remain in the area of a naive cause and effect model, accounting for events with such pat statements as "Because . . . it follows that . . ." or "Whenever . . . then . . ." That such reasoning on the part of teachers and parents could not have brought about the desired change in conduct is, of course, not surprising considering the innate shortsightedness of the "diagnosis" of giftedness.

The observations made by children as well as parents and teachers include one distinct contrast: Although the youths mostly account for their problems by pointing out external locus of control (boredom, unsympathetic teachers, and classmates, etc.), adults tend to see internal traits (greater attentiveness, improved work attitude, better social integration in the class, etc.) as the necessary components that should be improved or changed in order to succeed in school.

## CASE STUDIES

The following cases illustrate the spiral of disappointment from its first appearance to when it becomes a recurring pattern.

### John

John came to the counseling center when he was seven years old. The reason for seeking advice was the discrepancy between his interests, atypical for his age, his advanced intellectual skills since kindergarten, and his performance and behavior in the school setting. When he was 13 years old, he again came to the center, this time with enormous difficulties in school.

### Some aspects in preschool development

As a child John was always a perceptive, insightful, and active boy. At four and a half he displayed a strong interest in numbers and sums, and asked for more and more tasks in this area. At the age of five he taught himself how to read without parental assistance. In kindergarten he encountered no problems; he was always friendly and helpful to others. Although it was acknowledged by the kindergarten teacher that John was cognitively far ahead of his peers and should have an earlier start in elementary school, the parents decided not to do so because of a strong recommendation of the prospective elementary school.

### First visit to the center

After John's entrance into the first grade in school, the mother noted more and more lethargic signs in his behavior. No longer did he show interest in arithmetic or ask for additional assignments. He became more rambunctious in school, was often bored, and completed assignments at a fast pace and well ahead of the others. When playing with other children he had become wilfull in his behavior, and showed less interest in social contacts with peers. Although John's teacher was aware of his superior level of ability she felt unable to meet his learning needs, despite being asked to do so by John's mother.

Testing with the HAWIK-R (a revised version of the German WISC) indicated that John's IQ was 135, thus indicating his extraordinary memory and powers of logical reasoning. After a comprehensive counseling interview with John's mother, and based on his developmental background and an interview with him at the centre, it was recommended that John skip a grade.

According to the mother's report five years later, skipping a grade had not been a real success, partly because of the teacher's resistance to the move and to an accompanying stigmatization of John within the school's social setting. Nevertheless, John gained high scores in the fourth grade of elementary school, which led to entrance into an academic secondary school (*Gymnasium*).

### Second visit to the center

Five years later, when John was in the eighth grade of a *gymnasium*, he came to the center, again accompanied by his mother, because his school achievement had drastically declined and he was in danger of being held back. John now categorically refused to talk about school at all. When tested with the IST-70 (Intelligence Structure Test, Amthauer 1970), he achieved an IQ of 133, based on a relatively stable profile with strengths in three subtests (memory, arithmetic, number series). The primary goal of John's counselling was, of course, to instill renewed positive attitudes toward school work, which had declined dramatically during the last two years, and to counteract further isolation and increasing refusal to involve himself in scholastic activities.

In order to halt the cycle of John's disastrous *circulus vitiosus*, the intensive support of a counselor seemed to be urgently needed to discuss his personal problems in a semitherapeutic (rational) encounter.

## Oliver

Oliver came to the counseling center when he was 16 years old. The apparent reason for the visit was to establish what kind of school would be best for his needs and what therapeutic measures would help him. Oliver's main problems appeared to be difficulty in communicating with some of his teachers and resulting inattentiveness, mainly in the subjects they taught (German, English, Latin).

### Some developmental aspects in Oliver's elementary school career

Oliver had already experienced problems in dealing with classmates in elementary school, which he felt to be too simple-minded for his interest in astronomy and technical problems. Entering elementary school at the age of five, he took part in certain subjects only grudgingly, and refused to do assignments that he felt were too simple. As a result, his school records showed an apparent discrepancy in scholastic achievement between linguistic and scientific subjects as early as the third grade. This difference, now more marked than earlier, could still be observed when Oliver came to the center.

### Visit to the center

Six months before Oliver came to the centre he had not passed the ninth grade because of unsastisfactorily low grades in German, English and Latin, as well as because of unsatisfactory grades in subjects whose teachers he could not relate to. By contrast, his achievements in mathematics, chemistry, art, physical education, and ethics were good. School records showed that his task commitment was only weakly developed: He showed interest only in subjects and topics of particular interest to him.

Repeating the ninth grade was of no special benefit to Oliver's overall achievement. His grades did not show any radical change in the dichotomy of learning results: Weak to very weak grades in the less favored subjects and good grades in the others. At the time of his visit he was more frequently inattentive and deeply resigned in the classroom. His self-esteem in mathematics and science were very highly developed and stood in obvious and striking contrast to his lack of an *internal locus of control* related to the humanities. In his self-confident estimate of his scholastic and social problems with his peers, conducted in a diagnostic interview at the center, he denied having any motivation to alleviate his situation by his own efforts, and blamed his incompetent teachers and unfriendly classmates and an overall low intellectual and achievement level of the school for it. Furthermore, he claimed to possess a particular talent for mathematics and sciences as determined by a school counseling service during his third year of elementary school.

On the IST-70 Oliver achieved a score of 137, which places him at the 99th percentile. Although he was in the upper range in almost all subtests, his strengths were indeed in the mathematical–logical area. In the German version of the SAT-M (Scholastic Aptitude Test-Mathematics) he achieved a score of 660, which places him in the upper third of the distribution.

Though Oliver's development reveals an almost exclusive interest in mathematics and natural sciences, the obvious discrepancy between potential and school performance cannot solely be explained by a one-sided, unique talent. In spite of his distaste for and difficulties in concentrating on tasks without special interest for him, his general intellectual abilities, observed in the IST, are more than sufficient for coping successfully with the scholastic expectations in the unstimulating humanistic subjects as well. His "weakness" and his lack of interest in these areas, already observable in elementary school to some degree, became more and more marked compared with his level in sciences after his entrance to the *gymnasium*, culminating in failure in the ninth grade. Obviously, in the scholastic developmental processes the humanities had become less interesting and attractive to him. Because of the absence of special measures involving challenging experiences in early education, he was unable to develop coping habits as prerequisites for a successful secondary school career.

In his case, too, a tutorship was set up to support him over some time, to discuss his unfavorable view of unchallenging scholastic surroundings, and to lead to a change in his subjective locus of control. In the same way, he was nominated for a course for mathematically precocious youth in order to provide him with a challenge by means of competition with peers of equally high ability.

## Tomas

Tomas was 12 years old when he came to the counseling center with his parents. The reason given for the visit was the discrepancy between well above average intellectual ability determined in two independent tests (revised version of the German WISC when he was nine and a German version of the Cattell CFT when he was 11) and, in the eyes of the parents, only average academic achievement. They wanted to find out whether their son was at an appropriate school, and they wished to be be informed about special measures that could be implemented to foster his development.

### Some developmental aspects

Tomas's scholastic development was not characterized by unusual occurrences on the surface. The school records from the first to the fourth grade painted the picture of a school child with no particular problems. Tomas possessed the academic prerequisites and was regarded by his teachers as a good (but not particularly gifted) pupil. Throughout the four years he received rather good but by no means extraordinarily good grades, which were relatively low when compared with his high level of abilities. Beneath the surface he developed a dwindling interest in school, which from the fourth grade onward was striking, manifesting itself in unstable behavior as early as the transition from elementary to secondary school. Although his social interaction in the classroom was friendly and good, Tomas was on the way to becoming an outsider among his classmates with whom he could not establish close friendships. His contacts with peers in and outside the school were very loose.

### Visit to the center

Tomas's above average abilities were confirmed by an IST-70 score of 140. The test profile did not reveal remarkable instability. Except for a weak score on memory and lower scores in verbal analogies and arithmetic, his IST scores fitted in well with the outstanding test result. The interview gave evidence that this highly able young student was responding to the absence of adequate academic challenge in a twofold way: In school he applied himself only to topics of special interest. Outside school and in the privacy of his home he displayed wideranging activities: model building, collecting rocks and fossils, working at a personal computer, participating in science projects as well as in young artist competitions, in which he had already won awards.

At the time of consultation, Tomas had seemingly succeeded in compensating for his disappointment about a lack of challenge in school by engaging in numerous satisfying out-of-school activities. Although he is working at half speed in school, his most recent report is still quite fair, and not yet noticeably worse than previous reports. However, there are strong symptoms of unfavorable attitudes to schoolwork, for example, unstable interest and declining motivation in school and a growing view of the *gymnasium* setting as very distracting. For Tomas it seems to be important to experience a more challenging school setting, either by skipping a grade or by the change to a more stimulating *gymnasium*. His weak contacts to peers seem to involve divergent operational strategies and intellectual interests. As a result, it was recommended that he participate in advanced courses for precocious students, in order to experience highly challenging activities and contact with equally able young students of his own age.

## Susan

Susan was twelve when she was brought to the counseling center by her mother. Susan's mother sought counseling because she feared that Susan was not adjusting to school and was being intellectually starved by the curriculum.

### Some aspects of development

In the course of elementary school, Susan achieved at a level well above the average. She displayed an early and intense interest in music and literature, producing some of her own stories and poems. Because of her clear predilection for languages and the arts, and also because she was not gaining acceptance at her original school because of her marked musical interests, her parents decided to enroll her in a Waldorf School (Rudolf

Steiner School). The transition period at the new school proved to be rich in positive experiences for Susan. She was being readily accepted for the first time, and felt happy and at ease because of this. Nevertheless, after a short time, warning signals emerged: Susan suddenly stopped writing stories and poems. She began to experience more and more severe attacks (fits) in the classroom, making her leave class more and more frequently. A thorough physical examination revealed nothing. During this phase her concerned mother saw her cheerful grade-school daughter become an indifferent, lethargic, and indolent child.

### The visit to the counseling center

Testing on the IST-70 confirmed that her language and general intellectual abilities were far above average. Her overall IQ was 130. During discussion of her difficulties at the Waldorf School, it became evident that her unusual potential and advanced thinking skills apparently were not being met with a great deal of support (for the most part because of the philosophy of this kind of school). In the opinion of her teachers, she was much too "intellectual." Beside this, Susan felt that the ambitions of parents were too strongly present in the school, for, in one example, she felt that winning first prize in a youth music contest could be achieved only as a result of pressure by parents. Her critical reaction to arbitrary essay topics did not go over well with faculty. When she answered the question "How does a wolf hunt a gazelle?" in biology class by saying "Not at all," she was severely reprimanded and criticized: "Susan shows no fantasy and creativity."

The instructional policy of Susan's school had every appearance of not being able to meet her special needs, and it became apparent that, in this case, there was a clear discrepancy between the pedagogical ideals of the school and Susan's individuality, the eventual result of which could only adversely affect the gifted girl. Two recommendations were made as result of this. It was advised that she not only transfer to a secondary school (*gymnasium*) with special emphasis on music studies, but also that she enroll in a special course on creative writing. Her parents followed the advice and since then Susan's mother reports that her daughter has become more cheerful and is apparently happy in school.

Two aspects are common to these four children: an early feeling of disappointment associated with difficulties in peer relationships, lack of cognitive challenge in the classroom (they had been cognitively underchallenged and kept from fulfilling cognitive competence, as is particularly apparent in Susan's case). Of course, the reaction of a child to profoundly unsatisfactory stimulation cannot be predicted exactly, but there are three particular responses which can be observed: assimilation to the extreme in fulfillment of the school's expectations, rebellious behavior, and disruption in class, and withdrawal into psychosomatic symptoms. In all cases, it is very striking that a child's problem is only rarely attributed to its unusual learning ability, and that teachers are scarcely able to find any adequate way of meeting such a child's needs.

## CONCLUDING REMARKS

The emotional health and psychological stability of highly gifted children runs all through the discussion of the highly controversial topic of giftedness, being looked at in either an optimistic or pessimistic vein. Giftedness has raised many questions, such as whether it is rooted in a harmonious or unharmonious personality, or whether the highly gifted are psychologically, emotionally, and socially stable or generally less stable and prone to risk (see Becker, 1978; Freeman, 1979; Mönks, 1981; Rost, 1993; Schmidt, 1977, 1981).

Hypotheses on giftedness and personality development of gifted children (harmony/disharmony, convergence/divergence, psychological durability, and stability vs. lability) have been arrived at using varying methodological approaches. Terrassier (1982), for example, derived the concept of "inner asynchrony," that is, of a discrepancy between intellectual and socioemotional development in early childhood, from interviews and observations of highly gifted children at a counseling center, whereas Rost (1993), because of his screening and interviewing method, could not make use of such data. Based on observational data obtained in a special sample with behavioral problems, general statements about giftedness are, of course, restricted to this sample. However, it is possible to maintain that risk groups calling for particularly close attention exist within the gifted population (see Feger, 1988; Wieczerkowski & Prado, 1991). Underachievement, emotional disruptions, and developmental discontinuities encountered at the Hamburg Centre and elsewhere provide evidence of disharmony that results from affective and ecopsychological developmental conditions (Boe-karts, 1991). The heuristic model of a spiral of disappointment presented in this chapter describes a form of childhood development that can be stumbled into by both highly and also normally gifted children.

Establishing what causes underlying behavior and reaction patterns that have developed in an unwanted direction is a complex matter calling for diagnostic expertise employing differential methods. There is a close relationship between the spiral of disappointment and, in the case of the gifted, long-term lack of special measures. Given their intellectual abilities, these children frequently underachieve, lagging behind their scholastic potential. The effects of further variables can lead in various degrees to children not being given the opportunity to test their potential. For this reason underachievement is a component of the spiral of disappointment.

It can be concluded from this that the time before schooling begins as well as the period of elementary schooling are of importance for trying out special gifts. Already at this point basic interests come to the fore, whose fulfillment is crucial in preventing the experience of frustration or restriction and ensuring that the first phase of development is harmonious. Finally, it is of great importance that difficulties encountered by the highly gifted be recognized as intrinsically individual in nature, and that they can only truly be understood in the particular set of circumstances in which the child finds him- or herself.

# REFERENCES

Becker, G. (1978). *The mad genius controversy. A study in the sociology of deviance.* Beverly Hills: Sage.

Boekarts, M. (1991). The affective learning process and giftedness. *European Journal for High Ability, 2,* 146–160.

Feger, B. (1988). *Hochbegabung.* Bern: Huber.

Freeman, J. (1979). *Gifted children.* Lancaster: MTP Press.

Gallagher, J. J. (1985). The conservation of intellectual resources. In A. J. Cropley, K. K. Urban, H. Wagner, & W. Wieczerkowski (Eds.), *Giftedness. A continuing worldwide challenge* (pp. 21–30). New York: Trillium Press.

Mönks, F. J. (1981). Entwicklungspsychologische Aspekte der Hochbegabten-forschung. In W. Wieczerkowski & H. Wagner (Eds.), *Das hochbegabte Kind* (pp. 38–51). Düsseldorf: Schwann.

Rost, D. H. (1993). Persönlichkeitsmerkmale hochbegabter Kinder. In D. H. Rost. (Ed.), *Lebensumweltanalyse hochbegabter Kinder* (pp. 105–137). Göttingen: Hogrefe.

Schmidt, M. H. (1977). *Verhaltensstörungen bei Kindern mit sehr hoher Intelligenz*. Bern: Huber.

Schmidt, M. H. (1981). Psychiatrische Aspekte der Hochbegabung. In W. Wieczerkowski & H. Wagner (Eds), *Das hochbegabte Kind* (pp. 110–119). Düsseldorf: Schwann.

Terrassier, J. Ch. (1982). Das Asynchronie-Syndrom und der negative Pygmalion-Effekt. In K. K. Urban (Hrsg.), *Hochbegabte Kinder* (pp. 92–97). Heidelberg: Schindele.

Wieczerkowski, W., & Prado, T. M. (1991). Parental fears and expectations from the point of view of a counselling centre for the gifted. *European Journal for High Ability*, 2, 56–72.

Wieczerkowski, W., & Wagner H. (1985). Diagnostik von Hochbegabung. In R. S. Jäger, R. Horn, & K. Ingenkamp (Eds.), *Tests und Trends 4. Jahrbuch der Pädagogischen Diagnostik*. Weinheim: Beltz.

# 45

# Parental Attitudes and Type A Behavior Patterns in High and Low Creative Adolescents

**Waldemar Swietochowski**
**Grazyna Poraj**

*University of Lodz, Lodz, Poland*

Research presented in this chapter deals with the specific category of human behavior known as type "A" behavior pattern (ABP). The authors studied the interaction between creative abilities, educational influences (including parental attitudes), and type A behavior. In order to estimate the level of creative abilities in 249 teenagers, the Test for Creative Thinking—Drawing Production was administered. The data indicated the existence of significant differences between ABP profiles of high and low creative individuals. Parental attitudes were important mediating variables in this relationship.

## INTRODUCTION

It is generally agreed that a high level of creative ability is accompanied by special features of personality characterizing the so-called creative personality. The features most frequently mentioned are impulsiveness, independence, introversion, self-acceptance, intuition, strong motivation, diligence and stubbornness, critical attitude, and nonconformism. Urban (1991) regarded need for novelty as the main feature of creative individuals; according to him this is associated with a high need for external stimulation. When this is lacking, creative individuals show intense activity based on looking for problems and finding new solutions. Thus, it can be said that the level of creativity has an influence on behavior in different situations. Creativity probably involves special mechanisms, the effects of which are as follows.

1.  The creative personality is guided not only by motivation focused on the result, but also by so-called imminent and inner motivation, which may modify the hierarchy of values and thus the structure and strength of motives.
2.  The more highly motivated attitude of creative individuals means that frustration is less likely to appear in difficult situations, which should reduce the frequency and intensity of aggressive reactions.
3.  The basis of creative behavior is instrumental abilities that include features of reasoning that favour generation of a large number of solutions (imagination, flexibility and fluency of thinking, evaluative autonomy, and so on).

The research presented in this chapter deals with the specific pattern of behavior known as the type A behavior pattern (ABP). Treated as a behavior syndrome, it is regarded as one of the factors that cause coronary disease. ABP is a heterogeneous syndrome, which is composed of behavior patterns closely connected with temperament, for example, haste or high activity. In addition, ABP involves other factors that are most probably the result of upbringing, such as need for achievement or domination in interpersonal relations. Well-known research has shown that emotional reactions of individuals with high ABP in stressful situations are different from those of people with low ABP. It thus seems reasonable to interpret ABP as resulting from the desire to achieve the greatest number of goals without taking account of limitations resulting from situational or personal conditions, for example temperamental ones. It could thus be said that ABP is a form of application of ineffective ways of handling the problems of life. It may be assumed that one of the reasons for this is lack of ability to find more effective solutions in difficult and new situations.

It has also been shown that educational influences, mainly those exercised by the parents, are very important in the development of A patterns (Glass, 1977). They have a great impact on the creation of the hierarchy of values and the level of aspiration. Parents' reactions to successes or failures of children are the basis for children's self-estimation and their attitudes to other people and to themselves. Educational processes also create specific habits and expose children to models of behavior in specific situations. Consequently, in investigating the relationship between creative abilities and features characteristic for ABP, the role of parental attitude cannot be neglected.

The role of the educational attitudes of parents is not confined to their influence on ABP. According to contemporary research on creativity, the home environment has a decisive impact on the development of creative potential in a child. Among other things, parental attitudes can serve as stimulators or inhibitors of creative attitudes. This is why, in the present research, parental attitudes to children were regarded as a very important mediator crucial for both main variables: the type A pattern as well as the level of creative ability.

Few empirical studies have dealt with the influence of creative abilities in normal life situations. The research discussed in this article is a preliminary attempt at exploring this issue. The present results are the first stage of a much wider plan. For this reason, no specific research hypothesis was formulated. The second reason is the lack of significant empirical findings as well as the very complex and heterogeneous character of the variables investigated.

## METHOD

In order to determine the level of creative ability in a sample of teenagers, a Polish adaptation of the Test for Creative Thinking-Drawing Production (Urban & Jellen, 1986) was applied at the Institute of Psychology of the Jagiellonian University. Research on behavior patterns was carried out with the help of the "ABP" test by Wrzesniewski (Eliasz & Wrzesniewski, 1988). This is a questionnaire consisting of 20 items. Basically the test measures ABP as a global factor. However, it is so constructed that five homogeneous sections deal with different elements of ABP: need for achievement, aggression, domination, energy, and haste (each of these is tested by four statements of the questionnaire). In a validation study the test reached a high rate of accuracy and reliability, but only as far as general ABP was concerned. The components of ABP mentioned above have no assured status; consequently, results concerning them should be treated only as suggestive. It should be added that the ABP test is suitable for testing teenagers, the age group from which the subjects came.

A questionnaire was also used to test parents' attitudes in the estimate of the teenagers: The-Parent-Child Relations Questionnaire (PCR, Roe & Siegelman), adapted by Kowalski (1984). It was assumed that the way in which children perceive and interpret their parents' behavior is more important for the development of the child's personality than objectively manifested behavior patterns of the parents (Kowalski, 1984; Schaefer, 1965). The sample consisted of 249 students at a Secondary Music School in Lódz, aged 13–19. There were 135 girls and 114 boys. They were divided into two subgroups: high creative and low creative, according to the criterion half a standard deviation above or below the mean. Parents' attitudes were measured on five dimensions: love, demand, attention, rejection, and permissiveness.

## RESULTS

The results showed tendencies toward a change of the value of the A pattern. The graphs in Figures 45-1 and 45-2 depict differences statistically significant at or beyond the .05 level. The significance of differences was calculated for three levels of parents' behavior patterns according to the polish normalization of the PCR Questionnaire (Kowalski, 1984). In many cases, a significant difference of the ABP value for one of the parental variables (aggression, energy, etc.) refers only to one of the behavior pattern poles. In this case the level of statistical significance is written only at the one pole.

Figure 45-1 includes results for persons who achieved high results on Urban and Jellen's test. They are creative individu-

FIGURE 45-1.    Results for highly creative subjects (*n* = 35).

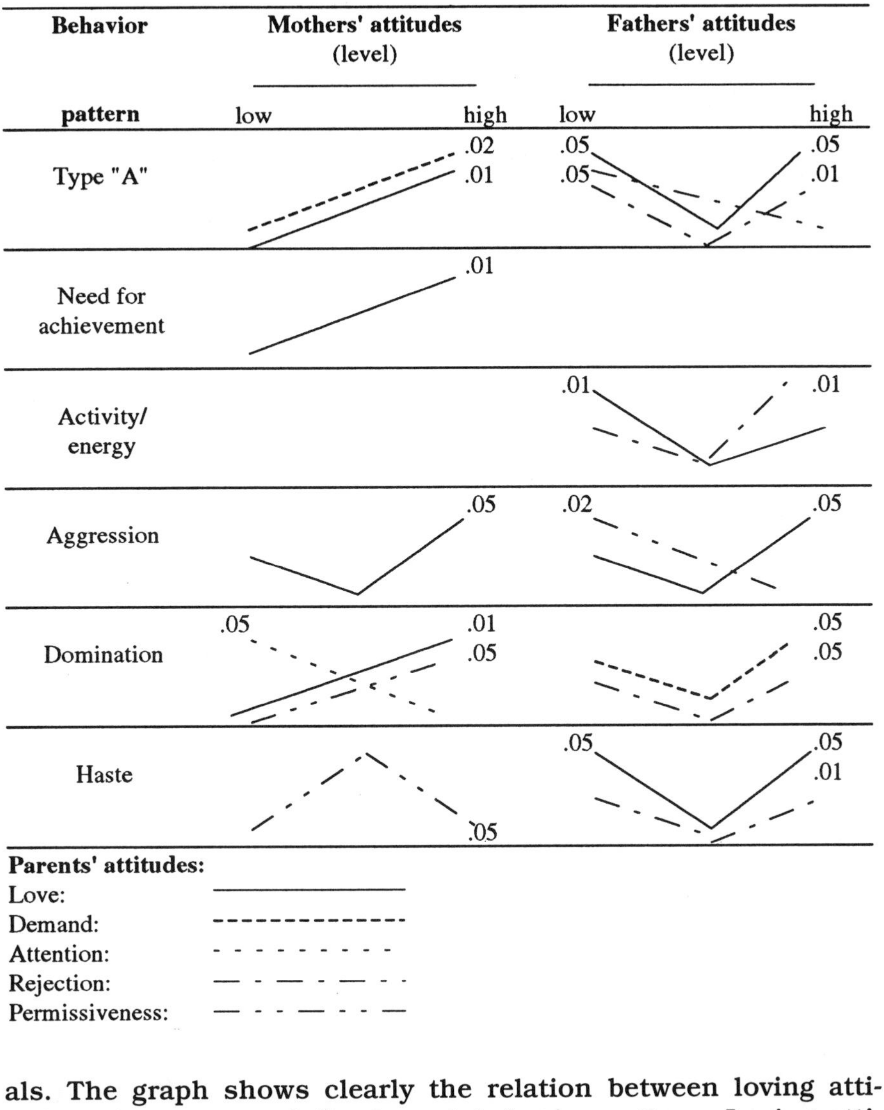

| Behavior | Mothers' attitudes (level) | | Fathers' attitudes (level) | |
|---|---|---|---|---|
| **pattern** | low | high | low | high |
| Type "A" | | .02 .01 | .05 .05 | .05 .01 |
| Need for achievement | | .01 | | |
| Activity/ energy | | | .01 | .01 |
| Aggression | | .05 | .02 | .05 |
| Domination | .05 | .01 .05 | | .05 .05 |
| Haste | | .05 | .05 | .05 .01 |

Parents' attitudes:
Love:
Demand:
Attention:
Rejection:
Permissiveness:

als. The graph shows clearly the relation between loving attitudes of parents and the type A behavior pattern. Loving attitudes of mothers correspond with high results for general ABP (*p* < .01). As far as influence of fathers' attitudes is concerned, these relations are not generally so explicit: High results for ABP are high both at high and low values of loving fathers—this difference is statistically significant (*p* < .05). A rejecting attitude evidently is connected with high ABP (*p* < .01), whereas

FIGURE 45-2.   Results for less creative subjects ($n = 85$).

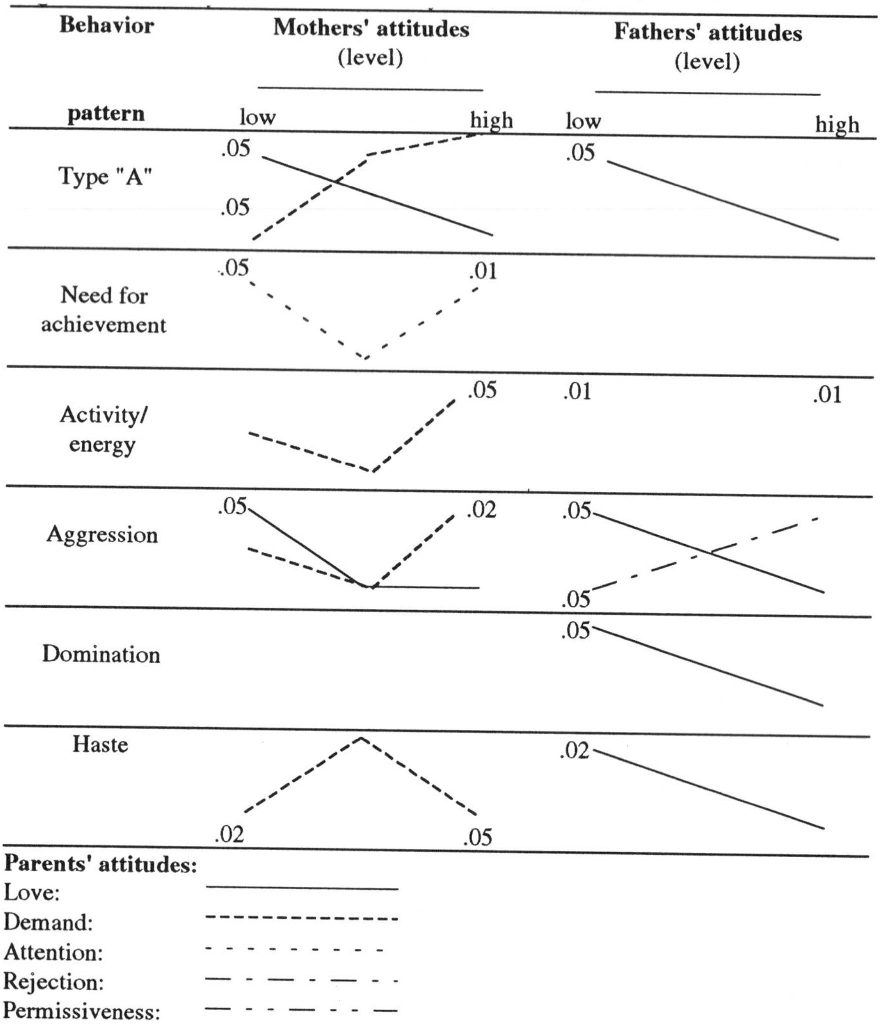

low ABP corresponds to a permissive attitude of fathers ($p <$ .05). Demanding attitudes of mothers, like their loving attitudes, go with high ABP. Without discussing obvious differences in detail, it should be noted that for creative individuals rejecting and demanding attitudes of mothers are not significantly related to components of ABP, but significantly higher coefficients in respect of domination, haste and energy are seen with rejection by fathers. Generally speaking, a loving attitude on the part of both parents is the most important factor, and a rejecting attitude the least important.

Figure 45-2 presents analogous results for the subjects who showed low levels of creativity. In general, less influence of parents' attitudes on behavior typical of ABP was seen (12 significant differences against 21 in the case of creative individuals). The conclusion can be drawn that parents' attitudes influence the behavior of low creatives to a lesser degree than highly creative individuals. Particularly striking is the influence of a loving attitude, which is completely different in the case of creative individuals. Children of both loving mothers and fathers obtained considerably lower ABP coefficients than children of parents regarded as less loving.

Loving attitudes of parents were similarly related to several other ABP factors: aggression, domination, and haste (in the latter two cases attitudes manifested by fathers). A demanding attitude of mothers is connected with high coefficients of general ABP ($p < .05$) as well as energy ($p < .05$) and aggression ($p < .05$). In the group of less creative persons, a considerably higher level of aggression is related to rejecting attitudes of fathers. Fathers' attitudes (attentive, permissive, and demanding) do not differentiate ABP results at all in this group of subjects.

## CONCLUSIONS

1.  The profiles of creative and noncreative individuals are significantly different. This finding is consistent with the view that creativity determines behavior in different situations, and also shows that attitudes of parents play a part in this relationship.
2.  A loving attitude of parents is important (in the sense of the present study) in the case of creative individuals, but not for noncreative subjects. This result is unexpected and difficult to explain. It requires more detailed analysis.
3.  In both groups of subjects, high ABP coefficients go with too demanding attitudes of mothers.
4.  Apart from the loving attitude discussed earlier, there are two further attitudes of fathers connected with general ABP: A rejecting attitude is related to high ABP and a permissive one to low ABP.

# REFERENCES

Eliasz, A., & Wrzesniewski, K. (1988). *Ryzyko chorob psychosomaty-cznych: srodowisko, temperament a wzwor zachowania A* [The risky agents of psychosomatic diseases: environment, temperament and pattern A behavior]. Wrockaw: Zakkad Narodowiy im. Ossolinkich.

Glass, D. C. (1977). *Behavior patterns, stress and coronary disease.* Hillsdale, NJ: Erlbaum.

Kowalski, W. S. (1984). *Kwesionariusz stosunkow miedzy rodzcami a dziecmi* [Parent-children Relationship Questionnaire]. Warsaw: Polkie Towarzysto Psychologiczne.

Schaefer, E. S. (1965). Childrens' reports of parental behavior: an inventory. *Child Development, 34.*

Urban, K. K. (1991). On the development of creativity in children. *Creativity Research Journal, 4,* 177–191.

Urban, K. K., & Jellen, H. G. (1986). Assessing creative potential via drawing production: The Test for Creative Thinking—Drawing Production (TCT-DP). In A. J. Cropley, K. K. Urban, H. Wagner, & W. H. Wieczerkowski (Eds.), *Giftedness: A continuing worldwide challenge* (pp. 163–169). New York: Trillium Press.

# 46

# Attitudes of Parents and Development of Creativity

**Grazyna Mendecka**

*Siemianowice Slaskie, Poland*

Biographical surveys of 65 inventors employed in the mining industry were contrasted with those of a control group of men of similar age, education, and period of employment who had failed to display inventiveness in their work. The following variables were taken into account: family life, course of learning, origin and development of interests, financial status, health and physical fitness, and course of professional work. It was shown that positive parental attitudes had influenced the development of certain features in these people as children, which later resulted in their adult life in a creative approach to their professional work. In a similar way, negative parental attitudes were restrictive and made development of such features difficult.

## DEFINITIONS OF VARIABLES AND HYPOTHESES

Four types of attitude thought likely to influence technical inventiveness were defined in this study. They are stated here as bipolar dimensions (Tyszkowa, 1985; Ziemska, 1980): (1) acceptance versus rejection; (2) cooperation versus avoidance; (3) freedom versus overprotection; and (4) recognition of the child's rights versus an excessively demanding attitude.

When children are accepted they are loved no matter what their faults and virtues. By contrast, rejection means withholding of love and expression of the view that the child has failed to meet parental expectations, as well as lack of interest in the child and its problems. Parental cooperation means fostering of partnership and introducing the child to all family matters, being interested in its problems and helping with their solution. Avoidance, on the other hand, means isolating the child from the parents' problems and only sporadically intervening in the child's problems. Leaving a child reasonable freedom means recognizing his or her autonomy and uniqueness and interfering in private matters only when necessary. This may be contrasted with overprotection, which is based on raising barriers to the child's freedom in almost every sphere of activity, thus inhibiting personality development and limiting the child's dignity. Respecting the child's rights means allowing it to make mistakes and to make an independent choice of goals and the ways to reach them. The other extreme involves an attitude of demandingness and pressure on the child to meet excessive goals, imposed by the parents through a strict system of control that disregards the child's own interests and talents.

The following hypotheses were established. They were based on the assumption that an individual's creativity is strongly related to the parents' attitudes toward childrearing.

1.  Positive parental attitudes advantageously influence development of certain features in children that later result in their adult life in a creative approach to their professional work.
2.  Negative parental attitudes prove to be restrictive, and make development of such features impossible.

## METHOD

### Subjects

The group of creative inventors consisted of people employed in the mining industry who had worked out by themselves a minimum of one invention and had applied for a patent. The average number of inventions was calculated by dividing the total number of inventions and applications reported during the five years preceding the survey by the number of inventors (the majority of applications were made by teams of inventors). The inventors were employees of the Central Mining Institute (27 men) or were technical supervisors in various coal mines (38 men). The sample from the Central Mining Institute was selected at random from among the inventors who had registered the highest number of patents. The remaining group was chosen by drawing lots from among the most prolific and creative employees in two coal mines with the highest number of registered patents. The control group consisted of volunteers. Data comparing the samples are shown in Table 46-1.

Mental and temperamental characteristics greatly influence creative work (Barron & Harrington, 1981; Guilford, 1978). These factors were taken into account in this survey by using Raven's Progressive Matrices (Raven, 1960), the Square Test (Vernon, 1940), and the Maudsley Personality Inventory (MPI) (Choynowski, 1977). If the members of the control group had been negatively selected in regard to their mental and neurotic features, then conclusions about any interdependence between creativity and the course of life of the subjects would not have been justified.

TABLE 46-1
Comparison of Experimental and Control Groups

|  | Creative group | | Noncreative group | | Chi square (df = 1) |
|---|---|---|---|---|---|
|  | N | % | N | % |  |
| **Level of education** |  |  |  |  |  |
| DSc. or technical science | 17 | 26 | 11 | 16 | 1.92 |
| MA | 25 | 38 | 31 | 48 |  |
| BSc | 14 | 22 | 14 | 22 |  |
| Technician | 9 | 14 | 9 | 14 |  |
| Total | 65 | 100 | 65 | 100 |  |
| **Age** |  |  |  |  |  |
| Up to 40 | 21 | 32 | 26 | 40 | .83 |
| 41 and over | 44 | 68 | 39 | 60 |  |
| Total | 65 | 100 | 65 | 100 |  |
| **Years of employment** |  |  |  |  |  |
| Up to 25 | 19 | 29 | 22 | 34 | .32 |
| 26 and over | 46 | 71 | 43 | 66 |  |
| Total | 65 | 100 | 65 | 100 |  |

The results showed that the creative and control groups were similar. In the creative group 40 persons (62%) successfully solved over 50 problems on Raven's test, whereas in the noncreative group 48% achieved this ($\chi^2$ = 2.51; n.s.). On the Square Test all 65 creators scored 100% whereas in the noncreative group this result was achieved by 42% ($\chi^2$ = 2.49; n.s.). Neurotic attitudes measured by the MPI seemed to have no connection with creativity, but in the creative group 51% were classed as introverts, whereas in the control group the figure was 28% ($\chi^2$ = 7.85; df = 1; $p$ < .01).

## Procedure

The interview was the basic method in this survey—many hours were spent talking to subjects, during which they had a chance to talk freely about various aspects of their life. These interviews yielded complete biographies of the subjects (Denzin, 1970), which were written down and then analyzed in detail, in order to examine parental attitudes reported by the subjects. The biographies were evaluated by three qualified judges who were familiar with the definitions of the variables and could categorize statements accordingly. Statements of the subject about whether the relationship between their parents in their marriage was of a partnerlike character or whether one of them used to dominate the other were also taken into consideration. In the case of true partnership in these marriages, the attitudes of both parents were taken into consideration, but in the case of one partner's dominance, only this person's attitudes were examined.

## RESULTS

In the creative group, 50 out of 65 subjects indicated that one parent had been dominant in the marriage, 37 fathers and 13 mothers. In the noncreative group 51 out of 65 indicated that one parent was dominant (19 fathers and 32 mothers). These data are summarized in Table 46-2. Table 46-2 shows the distribution of dominance of the father or of the mother. In the creative group, fathers were more often dominant, in the noncreative group, mothers.

Table 46-3 contains data referring to the hypotheses about interrelationships between attitudes of parents and the development of their children's creative abilities.

TABLE 45-2
Dominance of One Parent in the Marriage

| Dominance | | Creative group | | Noncreative group | | Chi square (df = 1) |
|---|---|---|---|---|---|---|
| | | N | % | N | % | |
| Father | Yes | 37 | 57 | 19 | 29 | |
| | No | 28 | 43 | 46 | 71 | 10.16; $p < .01$ |
| Mother | Yes | 13 | 20 | 32 | 49 | |
| | No | 52 | 80 | 33 | 51 | 12.26; $p < .001$ |

## DISCUSSION

The "meaning" of various attitudes can be demonstrated by citations from actual interviews, and a number of examples are listed in the following.

### Acceptance

Our parents loved us dearly and we loved them. We never had to lie to them. I have never met anyone better than they were (creative group, physicist, PhD, age 36).

### Rejection

When I was nine my father, who was a well-known and respectable physician, fell in love with some woman and left my mother. He got married again and was the best possible father for the two daughters of his wife from her first marriage, although I stopped existing for him. He did not even show he cared about me when I needed him most because my mother died and I was left alone in the world (noncreative group, miner, MSc, head of the production section, age 36).

### Cooperative Attitude

When my father found out that I wanted to go to university he was upset. He was a skilled worker, loved his job and wanted me to follow his example and hoped to teach me his trade. He finally agreed on one condition—that I would work in his team during every holiday. I agreed and never regretted it—it was great to work with my dad and his colleagues. I learned a lot from them and it has been beneficial for me up to now (creative group, mechanic, MSc, chief mechanic in a mine, age 41).

**TABLE 46-3**
**Parental Attitudes in Creative and Control Groups**

| Attitude | | Creative group N | % | Noncreative group N | % | Chi square (df = 1) |
|---|---|---|---|---|---|---|
| Acceptance | Yes | 61 | 94 | 49 | 75 | |
| | No | 4 | 6 | 16 | 25 | 8.50; $p < .01$ |
| Cooperation | Yes | 35 | 54 | 14 | 22 | |
| | No | 30 | 46 | 51 | 78 | 14.44; $p < .001$ |
| Freedom | Yes | 39 | 60 | 30 | 46 | |
| | No | 26 | 40 | 35 | 54 | 2.50; n.s. |
| Recognizing children's rights | Yes | 40 | 62 | 20 | 31 | |
| | No | 25 | 38 | 45 | 69 | 12.33; $p < .001$ |
| Rejection | Yes | 4 | 6 | 16 | 25 | |
| | No | 61 | 94 | 49 | 75 | 8.50; $p < .01$ |
| Avoidance | Yes | 14 | 22 | 23 | 35 | |
| | No | 51 | 78 | 42 | 65 | 3.06; n.s. |
| Over-protection | Yes | 3 | 5 | 4 | 6 | |
| | No | 62 | 95 | 61 | 94 | .15; n.s. |
| Excessive demands | Yes | 5 | 8 | 20 | 31 | |
| | No | 60 | 92 | 45 | 69 | 11.13; $p < .001$ |

## Avoiding the Child

My father was an alcoholic and he always had a band of his pals; they made terrible rows and started fighting in the local district. He did not like his children to see it, though, and he tried to get rid of us whenever he could, beating us or swearing with dirty words. I remember only one thing: To be on guard most of the time, not to get in my father's way (noncreative group, miner, MSc, head of section, age 38).

In the case of one positive parental attitude—leaving the child reasonable freedom—there were no significant quantitative differences between the creative and control groups. There was, however, a qualitative difference in the contents of this attitude—representatives of the control group stated that their parents allowed them considerable freedom, but this referred only to the way they spent their free time and being allowed to stay outdoors, whereas the inventors treated the concept of freedom as referring to many spheres of life; they reported that their parents allowed them great freedom and independence, and they were allowed to correct their own mistakes. Thus it is possible to say that the data confirm the hypothesis that positive parental attitudes favor development of creative abilities leading to technological inventiveness.

Numerical data referring to negative parental attitudes showed that, only in two cases out of four, the control group scored significantly higher than the creative subjects. An overprotective attitude turned out to be rare in both groups. Avoidance of the child was not quantitatively different in the groups, but the reasons for such an attitude varied. The creative group stressed that their parents were so absorbed with problems of their adult, most often professional life, that they had no time for close contacts with their children. In the noncreative group, parents avoided cooperation with their children, assuming that they should be kept away from their parents' problems, which should be censored for them because of the parents' authority and need to set a good example. The results are not unanimous in reference to negative parental attitudes. They suggest, however, that avoidance of the child or making excessive demands inhibits development of the child's personality. If more precise instruments for measuring parental attitudes were used, it might be possible to show the influence of negative attitudes on the development of the creative abilities of their children.

The inventors had parents who expressed the attitudes of wise love (Roe, 1968), who accepted their children, cooperated with them, and respected their subjectivity and autonomy. These features, typical of healthy family attitudes, are regarded as essential for the development of creative abilities according to the psychological literature (Dreyer & Wells, 1966; MacKinnon, 1978; Solowiej, 1980; Strzalecki, 1968).

## REFERENCES

Barron, F., & Harrington, D. M. (1981). Creativity, intelligence, and personality. *Annual Review of Psychology, 32,* 439–476.

Choynowski, M. (1977). Podrecznik do Inventarza Osobowosci [Manual for H. J. Eysenck's Personality Inventory]. In M. Choynowski (Ed.), *Testy psychologiczne w poradnictwie wychowawczo-zawodowym* [Psychological tests in educational-vocational guidance]. Warsaw: PWN.

Denzin, N. K. (1970). *The research act.* Chicago: Aldine.

Dreyer, A. S., & Wells, M. B. (1966). Parental values, parental control and creativity in young children. *Journal of Marriage and Family, 28*(1), 83–88.

Guilford, J. P. (1978). *The nature of human intelligence.* New York: Mc-Graw Hill.

MacKinnon, D. W. (1978). *In search of human effectiveness: Identifying and developing creativity.* Buffalo: Creative Education Foundation Inc.

Raven, J. C. (1960). *Guide to the Standard Progressive Matrices set A, B, C, D, E.* London: H. K. Lewis.

Roe, A. (1968). Parent child relation and creativity. In F. E. Williams (Ed.), *Report of the conference on child rearing practices for developing creativity.* St. Paul: Macalaster College.

Solowiej, J. (1980). Rodzina a rozwój zdolnosci twórczych [Family and development of creativity abilities]. In M. Ziemska (Ed.), *Rodzina i dziecko* [Family and child]. Warsaw: PWN.

Strzalecki, A. (1968). *Wybrane zagadnienia psychologii twórcozsci* [Selected problems of the psychology of productiveness]. Warsaw: PWN.

Tyszkowa, M. (1985). Badania nad uspolecznieniem i osobowoscia dzieci jedynych i majacych rodzenstwo [Research on socialization and personality of only children and those who have brothers and/or sisters]. In M. Tyszkowa (Ed.), *Rozwój dziecka w rodzinie i poza rodzina* [Development of the child in the family and outside it]. Poznan: Wydawnictwo Naukowe, Seria Psychologia i Pedagogika, 60.

Vernon, P. E. (1940). *The measurements of abilities.* London: London University Press.

Ziemska, M. (1980). Postawy rodzicielskie i ich wplyw na osobowosc dziecka [Attitudes of parents and development of the child's personality]. *Rodzina i dziecko* [Family and child]. Warsaw: PWN.

# 47

# Diagnosing and Treating the Problems of Able Maladjusted Children

**Ludwig F. Lowenstein**

*Allington Manor, Fair Oak, England*

Current research demonstrates that maladjusted children can be treated successfully if skilled and timely help is brought to bear on their needs. The methods used to assist in this program of rehabilitation and sometimes prevention of maladjustment are delineated in the chapter. Of the 100 children treated to date, 90% achieved higher levels of performance in school and later in society and, most especially, vocationally. Of the 100 able children who acted as a control group, only 20% achieved such success. Many became maladjusted adults and in some areas also suffered from difficulties with personal relationships, including a lack of success in their marriage and in parenting.

## INTRODUCTION

The identification of maladjusted children has not always proved to be an easy matter. Frequently it has been left either to parents or teachers to identify such youngsters, usually by their performance or appearance. Much of the judgment is subjective and frequently is not based on an intellectual diagnosis of the child. Lowenstein (1972) noted the difficulties teachers frequently had in identifying gifted children. This was owing to the fact that the bright child or bright looking child who had some particular ability in the area of reading or writing was often deemed to be advanced for his or her age when, in fact, this was owing to excessive coaching at home or resulted from a specific area of ability which did not necessarily match with other intellectual functions.

Another booklet by Lowenstein (1976) noted that there were certain personality characteristics likely to be influential in whether a child achieved or not. Intellectual ability as measured by intelligence tests naturally was one of these. Other aspects identified through the literature as well as through observations of able children were

1. Reducing the likelihood of depression;
2. Parental attitudes;
3. Removing the need for immediate gratification and hence seeking long-term goals;
4. Developing perseverance, reducing emotional, and psychological problems;
5. Reducing hostility toward others;
6. Receiving effective teaching for a particular ability;
7. Developing the capacity to conform to school discipline and rules;
8. Developing powers of concentration; and
9. Developing general motivation toward learning.

Giftedness or high intellectual ability is of special importance in less technologically developed countries in promoting these nations and their human resources to the maximum. Lowenstein (1979) identified numerous children as gifted in the Sudan, this being the largest country in Africa and the tenth largest in the world. He suggested that it was important to do the following in these particular countries, where the development of ability was of paramount value.

1. Organize courses for teachers to develop an understanding of the psychology of child development.
2. Set up a school psychological service to deal with emotional and educational needs of problem children.

3.  Promote the growth of special education for the education-
    ally handicapped and disadvantaged as well as for those of
    high ability.
4.  Develop an assessment technique whereby the intellectually
    able were identified as early as possible so that their edu-
    cation could be promoted in every way. It was, of course,
    vital to gear the intellectual assessment techniques to the
    culture, and current methods being used in the West were
    unlikely to be altogether relevant for such populations.

More recent studies (e.g., Hollinger, 1985) indicated that self-
esteem was an important factor in gifted children. Emotional
problems also affected the development of gifted children and
their potential, according to Roedell (1986). Typical problems included myths surrounding giftedness, unrealistic expectations,
pressure to perform, constant criticism or praise, and difficulties in finding friends.

Underachievement, especially with able children, frequently
resulted in internal conflicts as reported by Janos, Sanfilippo,
and Robinson (1986). These symptoms, in turn, affected further
academic achievement. The fact that able children engaged in
abstract thinking early (Thornburg, Adey, & Finnis, 1986) indicated that special approaches at an early age may well be required, to cater to such development. As was frequently pointed
out, it is vital to identify gifted children as early as possible in
order to develop educational strategies that are in line with
their needs (Heller, 1986). Among the methods frequently considered were an enriched or accelerated program, opportunities
for individualization, and introduction of some degree of structure and flexibility in the program (Kitano, 1986). Lowenstein
(1980) emphasized the importance of segregation as an additional measure for very able children in order to provide them
with a program that was tailor made for their personal needs.

The parenting of able children also must be relatively specialized. Such children often are difficult to treat as ordinary
children in the home. They are often quite active, require little
sleep, and need a great deal of individual attention, especially
in connection with learning. Failure to provide such individual
care and learning experiences leads to pressures on gifted children (Silverman, 1986). Needless to say, both parents of such
children and the gifted children themselves suffer from the
stressfulness of life unless their individual needs are somehow
met. The fact that such children are labeled as gifted should not

lead to greater stress for them (Karnes & Oehler-Stinnett, 1986). Parents of gifted children need a considerable amount of information on how best to deal with such youngsters, but first of all there is a need for psychological assessment and an increased understanding of giftedness (Freeman, 1986).

Much research still needs to be done to examine giftedness in its sociocultural context. Most common approaches, as already mentioned, use enrichment and acceleration as a model (Horowitz & O'Brien, 1986). Many investigators who have worked with able children agree with Lowenstein (1982), that there should be education for the intellectually and emotionally different.

Despite the fact that intelligence tests are not the only way of assessing able children, or anyone for that matter, there are positive features to such an objective assessment (Kaufman & Harrison, 1986). Indeed, it is important to use such tests and other measures as early as possible in order to identify such young persons, as there are many benefits to be derived from early identification (Edwards & Edwards, 1986; Robinson & Chamrad, 1986).

The social and emotional adjustment of talented adolescents was studied by Brody and Benbow (1986). They investigated self-esteem, locus of control, popularity, depression, and discipline problems in 300 highly verbally or mathematically talented adolescents with a mean age of 13.7 years. Compared to a group of 111 students of approximately the same age, who were much less gifted, the highly gifted youngsters perceived themselves as less popular, but no differences were found in self-esteem, depression, or the incidence of discipline problems. The gifted youngsters reported greater internal locus of control. Comparisons between the highly mathematically talented and the highly verbally talented children suggested that the latter group perceived themselves as less popular. Within both groups there were slight indications that higher verbal ability was related to social and emotional problems. Naturally, much depended on the type of environment in which the able children resided, as did their signs of adequacy. Providing for the special needs of gifted youngsters, for instance, by providing diversity of reading matter, was likely to make them feel more adjusted, as they could learn and practice larger vocabularies and their heightened curiosity and sensitivity was also likely to be satisfied (Greenlaw & McIntosh, 1986).

The speed of learning of able children makes it possible for them to learn complex materials. Lajoie and Shore (1986) found this speed to be both a handicap and an asset, depending on the type of teaching that was provided. It was likely to be a handicap rather than an asset when ordinary teaching in the classroom was available, but an asset when more advanced and speedier teaching was available. Despite this fact, gifted children frequently suffered from certain deficits that made it almost impossible to identify them through the teaching process. Warkany (1986) presented examples of precocious and slow children who became outstanding scientists such as Blaise Pascal, Albert Einstein, and others. The inability of some of these children to express themselves despite high intelligence suggested that researchers and practitioners were perhaps failing to recognize faculties that existed beneath the superficial surface of academic performance in the classroom. Certain characteristics of mathematically and verbally precocious students were studied by Benbow (1986) using the College Board Scholastic Aptitude Test. Three physiological characteristics were found with high frequencies: left- or mixed-handedness, asthma and other allergies, and myopia.

Gifted children were described as a heterogeneous group with its own set of strengths and weaknesses by Hillyer (1989). She noted that different societies had contradictory treatments for gifted children. This gave rise to a number of crises facing gifted children, especially when there were gaps between intellectual and social skills or when unrealistic goals and expectations or perfectionism were stressed, leading to anxiety and possible depression when there was a failure in achieving success. One of the major problems that gifted children have, according to Gross (1989), is the dilemma concerning interaction of psychosocial drives toward intimacy with desire for achievement. If the gifted child chooses to satisfy the drive for excellence, she or he risks forfeiting the attainment of intimacy with age peers; if the choice is intimacy, she or he is forced into a pattern of deliberate underachievement to retain membership in a social group. It was for this reason that homogeneous grouping of gifted pupils was suggested as a partial solution to this dilemma.

Gifted pupils, despite their ability, sometimes suffer from suicidal ideation, according to Farrell (1989). He reviewed the literature on incidents and causes of suicide in gifted pupils. The incidence of suicide and suicide attempts among youth in the United States increased every year during the past decade. Although evidence of giftedness among suicide victims was difficult to document in the literature, it was likely that there would be a corresponding increase in that subgroup. In addition to the usual stressors, gifted teenagers also confronted such issues as perfectionism, societal expectations to achieve, differential development of intellectual and social skills, and impotence to effect real-world change. For this reason it was recommended that a preventive counseling intervention strategy was necessary as part of every program, to address these issues and others.

## THE PRESENT STUDY

The research to be reported here is a 16-year study of 200 consecutively referred boys who were diagnosed via the Wechsler Intelligence Test for Children (Short Form) (WISC) as able or gifted with an intelligence level of 125–135+. The children ranged in chronological age from 7–14+ when first referred and assessed. Those below that age or above it, for various reasons, were not included in the study. Children suffering from specific learning difficulties such as those commonly termed dyslexia, dysgraphia, or mathematics blocks also were excluded from the study. Many of the youngsters were underachieving academically. There were also problems in such categories as behavior and emotional problems and withdrawing from the educational system (see Table 47-1). Academic underachievement was diagnosed on the basis of whether a child's attainments in reading, spelling, or mathematics were at least two years behind chronological age and intellectual ability. The question that needed to be answered was, "Do able maladjusted children benefit from treatment or alternative forms of education including an enriched program, acceleration, or segregation?"

Of the highly able youngsters, 100 were placed into a control group on the basis of their not being able or willing to receive therapeutic input or education commensurate with their ability or needs. The study concerned itself with boys only, as these appeared to present themselves more often than girls, although there were numerous girls but an insufficient number for this study. A number of problems in school, at home or in both settings were manifested among these high ability boys, who, on the whole, appeared to be frustrated by their inappropriate earlier and later learning experiences. They had frequently attended a number of schools, and were referred to the psychologist from a number of sources with the following general problems.

**TABLE 47-1**
**Description of Experimental and Control Groups**
**on the Basis of Age and Problems Assessed**

| Age when Assessed | Experimental | Control |
|---|---|---|
| 7–10 | 26 | 20 |
| 11– 4 | 47 | 46 |
| 14+ | 27 | 34 |
| Total | 100 | 100 |
| **Problems Assessed** | | |
| Lower than expected academic achievement | 54 | 43 |
| Behavioral / emotional problems | 65 | 57 |
| Withdrawal from educational system, emotionally or otherwise | 35 | 43 |
| **Intelligence of Experimental and Control Sample** | | |
| IQ  125–135 | 61 | 57 |
| IQ  135+ | 39 | 43 |

1.   Poor academic achievement.
2.   Behavior–emotional problems.
3.   An apparent wish to withdraw from the educational setting.

In addition to the WISC, the children were assessed on the following.

1.   Standardized tests of reading, spelling and mathematics;
2.   The Mooney Problem Checklist (Junior);
3.   The MPI (The Maudsley Personality Inventory); and later
4.   The EPQ (Eysenck Personality Questionnaire).

The objective was to verify both the severity and number of symptoms related to maladaptive behavior and emotional problems as measured through the neuroticism and psychoticism scales of the tests. In order to validate observed behavior by teachers and parents, the objective personality testing was supplemented by

5.   The Sentence Completion Test; and
6.   Selected cards from the Thematic Apperception Test (TAT).

Both the experimental and the control groups were followed up 10 years later.

In the case of the control group, nothing was done because very often nothing could be done for various reasons, except to follow up their academic, vocational, and other development 10 years later. This essentially was owing to the fact that there was no cooperation for special provision either by the school or the parents or other agencies. Consequently, such children did not receive an enriched program, acceleration or segregation, or any other specific help based on their personal needs. This was despite advice from one or more educational psychologists that something should have been provided. In all cases, however, the intellectual and educational as well as personal assessment was carried out by the psychologist. In the case of the experimental group, there was pressure from parents that something positive had to be done to help their able children, and the school was influenced by such pressure. In some cases, the help was provided by the school without such pressure. The nature of the help provided is summarized in Table 47-2.

## FOLLOW-UP STUDY

Follow-up studies are fraught with difficulties, especially when a long period of time has passed since the assessment. Only 74 members of the experimental and 68 of the control group responded to telephone calls or letters. The letters were purposely kept short and contained specific questions as well as an opportunity to respond to structured questions. A letter

TABLE 47-2
Predominant Types of Therapeutic Remedial Interventions
Following the Diagnosis and Assessment

| Intervention Technique | Number of Children Receiving this Help (Experimental Group Only) |
|---|---|
| Enriched curriculum provided in own school | 67 |
| Acceleration (move up one or more terms) | 7 |
| Segregation | |
| (Taught by tutor at home | 2 |
| Attending special schools or classes compromised of able children | 11 |
| Receiving outpatient treatment in child guidance centers or private centers in addition to remedial education intervention | 6 |

based on another follow-up study assessed the development of children diagnosed as maladjusted who had attended Allington Manor School and Therapeutic Community (Lowenstein, 1989). In telephone conversations, the same questions were asked as in the letter. The questions touched on the following issues: post-secondary education, examinations successfully completed, work history, and respondent's opinion about educational measures that would have provided a better start in life.

## RESULTS

Answers to the various questions are summarized in Table 47-3.

TABLE 47-3
Outcomes of Experimental and Control Groups on Certain Criteria
of Positive Development

|  | Experimental | Control |
| --- | --- | --- |
| **Continuing education after** | 69 | 43 |
| secondary school |  |  |
| Passing 1 0 level | 63 | 41 |
| Passing 2–3 0 levels | 59 | 38 |
| Passing 4+ 0 levels | 57 | 27 |
| Passing 1 or more A levels | 48 | 19 |
| Attending university | 36 | 16 |
| Obtaining a degree | 34 | 9 |
| Obtaining subsequent degrees | 21 | 1 |
| **Vocational achievement** |  |  |
| Unskilled work | 3 | 19 |
| Semiskilled work | 7 | 16 |
| Skilled work | 19 | 13 |
| Own business | 17 | 12 |
| Professionals | 28 | 8 |
| **Personal relationship with life** |  |  |
| Very contented with life | 59 | 27 |
| Moderately contented | 7 | 13 |
| Not contented | 6 | 13 |
| Very discontented with life | 2 | 15 |
| **Close personal relationships** | 64 | 29 |
| **What actions retrospectively assessed would** |  |  |
| **have helped able children** |  |  |
| Education based on personal needs | 13 | 61 |
| Smaller classes | 54 | 59 |
| Being with others of the same ability and interest | 54 | 59 |
| Better teachers | 44 | 37 |
| Being less bored with my education | 12 | 52 |
| Other reasons | 9 | 36 |

## CONCLUSIONS

There was value in providing these able boys with special educational provision, such as enriched curriculum, acceleration and segregation in some instances. Manifestations of improvement occurred in the area of educational performance in the future, vocational success and personal contentment with life. This was not the case for the control group, which proved to be considerably less positive in its development.

## REFERENCES

Benbow, C. P. (1986). Physiological correlates of extreme intellectual precocity. *Neuropsychologie, 24*, 719–725.

Brody, L. E., & Benbow, C. P. (1986). Social and emotional adjustment of adolescents extremely talented in verbal or mathematical reasoning. *Journal of Youth and Adolescence, 15*, 1–18.

Edwards, D., & Edwards, S. (1986). A parent's I-view. *Roeper Review, 8*, 172–173.

Farrell, D. M. (1989). Suicide among gifted students. *Roeper Review, 11*, 134–139.

Freeman, J. (1986). Up-Date on gifted children. *Developmental Medicine and Child Neurology, 28*, 77–80.

Greenlaw, M. J., & McIntosh, M. E. (1986). Literature for use with gifted children. *Childhood Education, 62*, 281–286.

Gross, M. U. (1989). The pursuit of excellence or the search for intimacy? The forced choice dilemma of gifted youth. *Roeper Review, 11*, 189–194.

Heller, K. A. (1986). Psychological problems in giftedness research. *Zeitschrift für Entwicklungspsychologie und Pädagogische Psychologie, 18*, 335–361.

Hillyer, K. (1989). Problems of gifted children. *Journal of the Association for the Study of Perception, 21*, 10–26.

Hollinger, C. L. (1985). The stability of self perceptions of instrumental and expressive traits and social self-esteem among gifted and talented female adolescents. *Journal for the Education of the Gifted, 8*, 107–125.

Horowitz, F. D., & O'Brien, M. (1986). Gifted and talented children: State of knowledge and directions for research. *American Psychologist, 41*, 1147–1152.

Janos, P. M., Sanfilippo, S. M., & Robinson, N. M. (1986). "Underachievement" among markedly accelerated college students. *Journal of Youth and Adolescence, 15*, 303–313.

Karnes, F. A., & Oehler-Stinnett, J. J. (1986). Life events as stressors with gifted adolescents. *Psychology in the Schools, 23,* 406–414.

Kaufman, A. S., & Harrison, P. L. (1986). Intelligence tests and gifted assessment: What are the positives? *Roeper Review, 8,* 154–159.

Kitano, M. K. (1986). Evaluating program options for young gifted children. *Journal of Children in Contemporary Society, 18,* 3–4.

Lajoie, S. P., & Shore, B. M. (1986). Intelligence: The speed and accuracy tradeoff in high aptitude individuals. *Journal for the Education of the Gifted, 9,* 85–104.

Lowenstein, L. F. (1972). The teacher and the gifted child. *Association of Educational Psychology Journal, 3,* 2.

Lowenstein, L. F. (1976). Helping children to achieve. *Journal of the Parents National Union, 2,* 1, 2.

Lowenstein, L. F. (1979). Discovering gifted children in a Third World nation. *School Psychology International, 1,* 27–29.

Lowenstein, L. F. (1980). Is there a case for the segregation of the gifted? *The Journal of the Gifted Child, 1,* 23–24.

Lowenstein, L. F. (1982). Should there be special education for the intellectually and emotionally different? *School Psychology International, 3,* 65–84.

Lowenstein, L. F. (1989). Follow up of maladjusted academically children in a therapeutic community. *International Journal of Rehabilitation Research, 12,* 297–305.

Robinson, N. M., & Chamrad, D. L. (1986). Appropriate uses of intelligence tests with gifted children. *Roeper Review, 8,* 160–163.

Roedell, W. C. (1986). Socio-emotional vulnerabilities of young gifted children. *Journal of Children in Contemporary Society, 18,* 17–29.

Silverman, L. K. (1986). Parenting young gifted children. *Journal of Children in Contemporary Society, 18,* 73–87.

Thornburg, H. D., Adey, K. L., & Finnis, E. (1986). A comparison of gifted and non-gifted early adolescents movement towards abstract thinking. *Journal of Early Adolescence, 6,* 231–245.

Warkany, J. (1986). Unusual children. *Developmental Neuropsychology, 2,* 147–154.

# Notes on Authors

**Manfred von Ardenne** is one of the most senior and highly respected living scientists of the former German Democratic Republic, as is witnessed by the large number of awards and citations he still continues to receive. He is probably the last surviving person present at Max Planck's lecture in which he introduced his famous ideas on thermodynamics. Despite his retirement Prof. Dr. von Ardenne continues to write on both educational and natural science topics, leading to publications such as his recent book on creativity in physics.

Contact address: Prof. Dr. Manfred von Ardenne, Zeppelinstraße 7, 01324 Dresden, Germany.

**Philip Adey** is a researcher at the Kings College (London University) Centre for Educational Studies. For nearly 20 years he has been concerned with students' difficulties in learning, especially in science. While initially working with a model for matching the cognitive demand of the curriculum with students' apparent levels of cognitive development, he has in the last 5 years become much more concerned with the distinction between learning and development, and in particular with the question how cognitive development may be maximised in ordinary high school students.

Contact address: Dr. Philip S. Adey, Centre for Educational Studies, Kings College, University of London, Cornwall House Annex, Waterloo Road, London SE1 8TX.

**László Balogh** lives in Debrecen, where he is head of the Department of Educational Psychology. He has been doing research for two decades, his main subject matter being the development of intellectual abilities within the framework of school learning. Recently he has been examining the possibilities for intensive development of talented children at the ages of 13–14. Simultaneously he has been studying longitudinally the relationship of the development of thinking to the level of mother tongue acquisition at the ages of 6–14. He has published several books and nearly 50 papers.

Contact address: Dr. László Balogh, Senior Lecturer, Psychological Institute, Kossuth Lajos University, H-4010 Debrecen 10, Pf. 28 Hungary.

**Gerard M. Brugman** works in the department of developmental psychology of the State University of Utrecht, Holland. His scientific interests include (high) ability over (the second half of) the lifespan, cognitive plasticity, developmental tasks, wisdom, and autobiography as a tool for creating developmental models.

Contact address: Gerard M. Brugman, Rijksuniversiteit Utrecht, Department of Developmental Psychology, Transitorium II, P.O. Box 80140, 3508 TC, Utrecht, Holland.

**Ian Cockerill** is a chartered psychologist and a lecturer in the school of Sport and Exercise Sciences, University of Birmingham, England, where he teaches courses in motor development, skill acquisition, and sport psychology. His research interests include visual factors in sport and the visual control of movement, laterality and human performance, and mood measurement. For a number of years he has advised high level sport performers on mental preparation methods for performance enhancement.

Contact address: Dr. Ian Cockerill, School of Sport and Exercise Sciences, University of Birmingham, P.O.B. 363, Birmingham B15 2TT, England.

**Sebastian Coe** was Vice-Chairman of the United Kingdom Sports Council at the time he wrote this chapter. His authority to write on society's responsibility for the promotion of excellence derives, to some extent at least, from the fact that he is former holder of several world records in middle distance running and an Olympic Gold Medal holder.

Contact address: Mr. Sebastian Coe, Vice-Chairman, The Sports Council, 16 Upper Woburn Place, WC1H OQP, England.

**Harry T. Conrad** was, until his recent untimely death, a teacher of classical song, a concert singer, and an active participant in the Schleswig Holstein Festival 1988 and the summer university, Mozarteum Salzburg in 1989.

**Ornella Andreani Dentici** is the Director of the Institute of Psychology of the University of Pavia (Italy), where she has been teaching since 1962 as a lecturer, since 1965 as full professor of Psychology. She is also responsible for the courses of Ph.D. and the post-graduate School of Specialization in Psychology. In the first period her interests were centered on educational and vocational problems, and she published books on the gifted and on disadvantaged children. In recent years the focus of her research has been on memory, imagery and mental abilities in a lifespan perspective. Recently she has started a large study on the development of intellectual potential. She is author of 150 academic papers.

Contact address: Prof. Ornella Andreani Dentici, Istituto di Psicologia dell'Università, p.zza Botta 6, 27100 PAVIA—Italy.

**Wim van Dijk** is a researcher at the ISOR, the Educational Research Department at the University of Utrecht. His main fields of interest and research are curriculum development and implementation, reading, (second) language acquisition and the use of computers (LOGO) in education. He also concentrates his attention on the study of gifted pupils and has published several articles on this topic.

Contact address: Dr. Wim van Dijk, ISOR-Afdeling Onderwijsonderzoek, Heidelberglaan 2, 3584 CS Utrecht, The Netherlands.

**Ad Dudink** is associated with the Department of Developmental Psychology, University of Amsterdam. His research and lectures are centered around developmental applications in education. He has published books in Dutch on the concept of creativity and the instruction of intelligence. He is especially interested in the development of giftedness in the areas beyond academic skills such as writing, reading and arithmetic.

Contact address: Dr. Ad Dudink, Department of Developmental Psychology, University of Amsterdam, NL—Amsterdam, The Netherlands.

**Jan Elshout** is professor of cognitive psychology at the University of Amsterdam. His research interest in the past decade has been the computer modeling of growing expertise in physics problem solving.

Contact address: Prof. Dr. J. Elshout, Department of Psychology, University of Amsterdam, NL—Amsterdam, The Netherlands.

**Joan Freeman** is the author of a considerable body of internationally published research and presentations on the development of highly able children's abilities. She received her doctorate in Educational Psychology from the University of Manchester, England, and is now at the Institute of Education in London. She has been honoured with a Fellowship of the British Psychological Society. She was elected first President of the European Council for High Ability (ECHA).

Contact address: Prof. Joan Freeman, 21 Montagu Square, GB—London W1H 1RE.

**Françoys Gagné** is a full professor of Educational Psychology in the Department of Psychology at l'Université du Québec à Montréal. His main research interests in the field of gifted education include: definitions and models, accelerative enrichment and its impact, identification through peer nominations, and the phenomenon of polyvalence (i.e., persons with wide multiple abilities in various areas).

Contact address: Prof. Françoys Gagné, Ph.D., Department of Psychology, Université du Québec à Montréal, P.O. Box 8888, Station Downtown, Montréal, QC, Canada H3C 3P8.

**Lidia A. Germikova** Ph.D. is the senior scientific worker of the Institute of Psychology and Law of the Academy of Sciences, TSSR. For 25 years she has been concerned with the problems of the child and social psychology, especially the problem of abilities. She has about 100 published works. She is a member of the International Association on Personality Psychology. Her recent publications are devoted to the psychological aspects of the personality of the renewing society, cross-cultural investigations.

Contact address: Dr. Lidia A. Germikova, Academy of Sciences, Institute of Psychology, 24-4, Vostochny Bulvar, Ashkhabad—744025 Turkmenia, CIS.

**Sylwia Grzeskowiak** studied at the University of Poznan (Poland), the University of Berlin (FU) and the University of Hamburg, and is currently lecturer in psychology at the University of Marburg. Her theoretical and practical studies have focused on early child development.

Contact address: Dr. Sylwia WilbergMarburg, University of Marburg, Gutenbergsvt. 18, 35032 Marburg, Germany.

**László Harsányi** works for the National Office for Physical Education and Sport. Formerly he was managing trainer of the athletics section of BÅZIS Sport Club (Pécs, Hungary). He managed 400 athletes—10 years and older—with the assistance of 15 trainers, and directed an athletics sports ground. After obtaining degrees in Education and Sport he completed his PhD in 1984, and in 1989 was awarded the "Master trainer" title. He has taught physical training in primary and secondary schools and worked on sport methodology and on the training of athletes. He has taken part in teaching trainers and sports teachers at the school of Physical Training of Hungary and the "Janus Pannonius" University of Pécs since the 1960s. He is interested in the development of sports performance, selection, and prognostics in athletics. His research on sports science since the 1960s has led to 98 published studies, a number of them in German, English, Italian and Russian.

Contact address: Dr. László Harsányi, OTSH Tudományszervezési Osztály, H-1054 Budapest, Hold u.1, Hungary.

**Marianne Hassler** is a researcher at the University of Tübingen, Department of Clinical and Physiological Psychology. In an interdisciplinary approach she has been concerned with developmental, neuropsychological, endocrinological, and immunological aspects of special talents, such as musical and spatial faculties, for nearly 10 years. She is author of numerous articles on these subjects. She is also a lecturer and psychotherapist.

Contact address: PD Dr. Marianne Hassler, Hausserstr. 114, 72076 Tübingen 1, Germany.

**Kurt A. Heller** is professor of psychology and Director of the Institute of Educational Psychology and Psychological Diagnostics at the University of Munich. He received degrees in education and psychology, and his Ph.D. at the University of Heidelberg. After teaching posts in high and special educational schools (for the deaf and speech disordered) and as a professor in psychology for special education at the Teachers College/University of Heidelberg, he became full professor at the Universities in Bonn (1971-1975) and Cologne (1976-1981) before he accepted a post at the University of Munich in 1981. He has published approximately 250 books, psychological tests, chapters, and articles in the fields of psychology and (special) education. In the last decade his major research area has been high ability, for which he has received substantial grants. He has conducted projects on metacognition, technical creativity (including cross-cultural perspectives) and gifted counseling. Currently he is involved in several evaluation studies related to enrichment and acceleration programs, as well as several international cooperative studies.

Contact address: Prof. Dr. Kurt A. Heller, University of Munich, Department of Psychology, Leopoldstr. 13, 80802 München, Germany.

**Michael Howe** is reader in human cognition in the Department of Psychology at Exeter University. He has a broad interest in human accomplishments and his most recent books deal with exceptional abilities, "hothouse children" and the feats of idiots savants.

Contact address: Dr. Michael J. A. Howe, Department of Psychology, University of Exeter, Exeter EX4 4QG, England.

**Helga Joswig** is a lecturer in learning and developmental psychology in the Institute of Educational Psychology at the University of Rostock. In 1979 she completed her doctorate in Educational Psychology and in 1984 she did her habilitation on the topic "The meaning of primary motivation for learning in high school pupils." For ten years she has examined the motivation of gifted children and youths. Results of her research have been presented in international publications and lectures (until 1993 under the name Helga Wiese).

Contact address: Dr. Helga Joswig, University of Rostock, Department of Psychology, August-Bebel-Straße 28, 18051 Rostock, Germany.

**Jolanta Kepinska-Welbel** obtained her M.A. in psychology at the University of Poznan in 1968. She worked as a clinical psychologist at the Institute of Psychiatry and Neurology in Warsaw from 1968 to 1978. She specializes in psychological counselling for professional musicians. Her main research area is stage fright in musicians.

Contact address: Jolanta Kepinska-Welbel, Chopin Academy of Music, Chair of Psychology of Music, Okólnik 2, 00-368 Warzawa, Poland.

**Karl Josef Klauer** is professor of education at the Technical University of Aachen, Germany. His main topics of research include:

Cognitive fostering through training, instructiorial design theory, criterion-referenced tests and measurement.

Contact address: Prof. Dr. K.J. Klauer, University of Aachen, Department of Education, Eilfschornsteinstraße 7, 52062 Aachen, Germany.

**Ewa Klimas-Kuchtowa** is a psychologist in the Institute of Psychology of the Jagiellonian University, Cracow. She submitted her doctoral dissertation in 1979 on the topic "Some problems of rembering. Comparison between recall and recognition". Her main interests are the psychology of music and, in this field, perception of music, musical creativity and personality of musicians. She is the co-author of two psychological handbooks, as well as several articles and papers.

Contact address: Dr. Ewa Klimas-Kuchtowa, ul. Zygmunta Augusta 9/12, 31-504 Kraców, Poland.

**Wil. A.M. Kok** is a senior researcher at the Department of Educational Research of the Interdisciplinary Research Institute for the Social Sciences in Utrecht, the Netherlands. His main area of activity is research on learning and instruction. He manages several research and development projects on special provision for gifted students in secondary education. Other fields of interest are information processing, reading and learning to read and computer assisted instruction.

Contact address: Dr. Wil. Kok, ISOR-Afdeling Onderwijsonderzoek, Heidelberglaan 2, 3584 CS Utrecht, The Netherlands.

**Vladimir Kolesaric** is professor of experimental psychology and head of the Department of Psychology, University of Zagreb. On behalf of the Ministry of Education of the Republic of Croatia he directs a team of experts on the systematic care of gifted children in primary and secondary schools. He also supervises a small number of young researchers in the field of giftedness.

Contact address: Prof. Dr. Vladimir Kolesaric, University of Zagreb, Department of Psychology, Salajeva 3, 41000 Zagreb, Croatia.

**Ivan Koren** is currently a lecturer in the Department of Pedagogy of the Faculty of Philosophy, University of Zagreb. He is an educational psychologist and spent over 20 years in an employment office offering vocational guidance services. He received his M.A. and Ph.D. for theses on the structure and dynamics of professional interests of youth. His major research works include studies of identification and education of gifted children, and he has he has published 110 works including numerous articles, monographs and handbooks, as well as 20 books.

Contact address: Dr. Ivan Koren, Trg J. Broza 15, 44000 Sisak, Croatia.

**Ludwig F. Lowenstein** obtained his M.A. and Doctorate in psychology and education at London University. His background includes work in mental hospitals, child guidance clinics and residential centres for maladjusted adolescents in New York City. He has served as a teacher, a welfare officer, and, in Australia, as a probation officer, and has been a visiting staff member at universities in UK, USA and Sudan.

Contact address: Prof. Dr. L.F. Lowenstein, Allington Manor, Fair Oak, Hampshire SO5 7DE, Great Britain.

**Maria Manturzewska** is head of the Department of Psychology at the Academy of Music in Warsaw. She graduated from the Jagiellonian University in 1953, and obtained her Ph.D. and habilitation from the same university. For more than 35 years she has been involved in research on musical abilities and predictors of musical achievement, in close cooperation with music schools in Poland. She is also interested in counselling for the musically gifted and organised from 1957-1961 the first network of counselling units for music schools in Poland. Since 1972 she has been in charge of a psychological research unit at the Academy of Music in Warsaw. She has published two books and more than 50 papers and research reports concerning cognitive, personality and socio-environmental determinants of musical achievement. Her present areas of interest are the biographical study of lifespan development of professional musicians in Poland and noncognitive determinants of professional careers.

Contact address: Prof. Dr. Maria Manturzewska, Akademia Muzyczna im. Fryderyka Chopina, Department of Psycology, ul. Okólnik 2, 00-368 Warszawa, Poland.

**Alexey Matyushkin** is director of the Institute of General and Educational Psychology of the Academy of Pedagogical Sciences of the USSR. He is also director of the National Center of Creative Giftedness. He is National Correspondent of ECHA and Chief Editor of the Journal "Questions of Psychology", the main journal of professional psychologists in the Soviet Union. His publications are mainly in the area of the psychology of creative thinking, education based on creative problem solving, dialogical forms of educational practices and the psychology of giftedness.

Contact address: Prof. Alexey Matyushkin, Director, Institute of General and Educational Psychology; Prospect Marxa 20, b. "W", Moscow 103 009, CIS.

**Grazyna Mendecka** obtained her Ph.D. from the Faculty of Philosophy of the Jagiellonian University of Cracow in 1986. Her present areas of interest are familiar correlates of creativity. She has published several papers on these topics.

Contact address: Dr. Grazyna Mendecka, Wladyslawa Jagielly 13 b m 48, 41-106 Siemianowice Slaskie, Poland.

**Siegfried Mescheder** worked as educator and researcher on giftedness at the Technical University of Chemnitz. A variety of teaching assignments on classroom instruction, coupled with practical work in a counselling centre, enabled him to focus his research activity on fostering giftedness in the classroom, with particular emphasis on instruction in mathematics, science and technology in both regular schools and also special schools for the gifted. He received his Ph.D. in 1986 for research on special provision for the gifted in mathematics lessons. He is author or co-author of a large number of papers, research reports and articles in national and international journals.

Contact address: Dr. Siegfried Mescheder, Tschaikowskistraße 40, 09130 Chemnitz, Germany.

**Ton Mooij** is a senior researcher in education at the Catholic University of Nijmegen, Institute for Applied Social Sciences. His main interest lies in longitudinal reciprocal relationships between characteristics of pupils (like giftedness, behaviour, motivation, achievement) on the one hand and characteristics of educational situations (on different levels) on the other, and in the effects of personal and situational characteristics on the development of personal characteristics. Special interest is devoted to discovering educational conditions which favour the learning processes and learning effects of pupils of varying capacities. He has published books and articles, and has co-operated in making relevant movies.

Contact address: Dr. Ton Mooij, Catholic University of Nijmegen, Institute for Applied Social Sciences, Toernooiveld 5, NL 6525 ED Nijmegen, The Netherlands.

**Kálmán Nagy** is headmaster of an elementary school in Hungary. For over 10 years he has led a staff consisting of about 50 teachers. During this time several different attempts have been made to foster development of talented children: special music classes have been launched, a second foreign language has been introduced and at present the main program is concerned with the development of talented children aged 13-14.

Contact address: Kálmán Nagy, Headmaster, Bethlen Gábor Elementary School, Törökszentmiklós, Hungary.

**Edward Necka** graduated from the Jagiellonian University in 1977. Four years later he obtained his Ph.D. from the same university, with which he has been connected from the beginning of his professional career. His present position is Associate Professor of Psychology. His research interests include intelligence and creativity. He is presently supervising a series of studies on the cognitive processes connected with intelligence. Earlier he published two monographs on creativity.

Contact address: A/Prof. Dr. Edward Necka, Jagiellonian University, Institute of Psychology, ul. Golebia 13, PL-31-007 Kraków, Poland.

**Colleen Neitzke** obtained a Bachelor of Arts degree from the University of South Africa in 1983 and her diploma in psychology at the University of Bonn in 1988. After completing a research project on gifted adults, which was sponsored by the Federal Ministery of Education and Science, she is currently working towards her Ph.D. in the field of achievement motivation and high performance in gifted adults.

Contact address: Dipl.-Psych. Colleen Neitzke, Im Nesselbornfeld 11, D-6380 Bad Homburg v.d.H., Germany.

**Leon Niebrzydowski** completed his undergraduate studies at the Catholic University in Lublin in 1956. In 1968 he obtained the degree of doctor of psychology from Maria Curie-Sklodowska University in Lublin, and in 1974 the habilitation from the University of Gdansk. He has been a professor since 1975. In 1980 he was appointed head of the Department of Psychology at the University of Lodz, and has retained this position until today. He has published several books and about 140 articles in educational and psychological journals and edited ten or more books.

Contact address: Prof. Dr. Leon Niebrzydowski, Department of Psychology, University of Lodz, Metylowa 7 m 33, zam. 90-360 Lódz, Poland.

**Adriano Pagnin,** was born in Padova in 1946. Since 1972 he has been an assistant, and since 1983 associate professor in Developmental Psychology at the University of Pavia, Italy. He is also lecturing in social psychology and developmental psychology courses in postgraduate schools in Psychology and in Neuropsychiatry. He has published more than 50 articles and some books, mainly in the areas of adolescent psychology, attitude formation, and creativity. He is presently working in the areas of moral and logical thinking in adolescence, social representation of war (about which he is editing a volume) and attitude change.

Contact address: Prof. Adriano Pagnin, Istituto di Psicologia dell'Università, p.zza Botta 6, 27100 PAVIA (Italy).

**Anna Paszkowska-Rogacz** PhD graduated from Jagiellonian University in 1978. She obtained her Ph.D. in the field of psychology in 1986. The subject of her thesis was: "The influence of family on social adjustment of partially seeing children". She is presently working in the Department of Psychology at the University of Lodz. Her present areas of research are the creativity of physically diabled children.

Contact address: Dr. Anna Paszkowska-Rogacz, University of Lódz, Department of Psychology, ul. Smogowa 10/12, 91-433 Lódz, Poland.

**Christoph Perleth** works in the Institute for Empirical Pedagogics and Educational Psychology (Munich University) where he has been with Prof. Heller on the Munich Longitudinal Study on the Highly Gifted. His fields of interest include research methods, cognitive abilities and meta-memory, as well as research on giftedness, his interest in the latter field already having been documented by a number of publications.

Contact address: Dr. Christoph Perleth, University of Munich, Department of Empirical Pedagogic and Educational Psychology, Leopoldstraße 13, 80802 München, Germany.

**Roland S. Persson** is a former researcher of the RAMP-Unit (Research Into Applied Musical Perception) of the University of Huddersfield, UK. Research interests and publications concern the concepts musical talent, educational policy, socio-affective development, qualitative research methodology as an alternative psychological method, and student-teacher interaction.

Contact address: Dr. Roland S. Persson, College of Education and Communication, Division of Pedagogy and Psychology, University of Jönköping, S-51111 Jönköping, Sweden.

**G.T.M. Poorthuis** is a researcher at the ISOR, the Educational Research Department at the University of Utrecht. She is doing research on the effects of writing tasks on knowledge acquisition and on curriculum materials for gifted students in secondary education. An other field of interest is computer assisted instruction.

Contact address: Dr. G.T.M. Poorthuis, ISOR-Afdeling Onderwijsonderzoek, Heidelberglaan 2, 3584 CS Utrecht, The Netherlands.

**Grazyna Poraj** completed her undergraduate studies at the University of Lodz in 1978. In 1986 she obtained the degree of doctor of psychology from this university under the supervision of Prof. Dr. Leon Niebryzdowski. She teaches Educational Psychology in the Faculty of Psychology at the University of Lodz. Her research centers on the topics of the only child at home and at school and school adjustment of high ability students. She has also published a number of articles in these fields.

Contact address: Dr. Grazyna Poraj, Faculty of Psychology, University of Lodz, Smugowa 10-12 Str., 91-433 Lodz, Poland.

**Tania M. Prado** is a research assistant at the University of Hamburg, Department of Developmental and Educational Psychology. Her research interests include diagnosis of high ability, in particular cognitive abilities, and development and evaluation of counselling strategies for the gifted. Results of her work are documented in a number of publications. In addition she is a board member of the Counselling Centre for Gifted Children in Hamburg, which is supported by the William Stern Society for Research on Giftedness.

Contact address: Tania M. Prado, Department of Psychology II, University of Hamburg, Von-Melle-Park 5, 20146 Hamburg, Germany.

**George Pratt** is professor of music at the Department of Music of the University of Huddersfield. He also founded the RAMP (Research into Applied Musical Perception) unit at Huddersfield in 1985. Course development work in aural training at undergraduate level has recently been published in book form. Other current areas of investigation in the RAMP unit include musical memory, emotion and the musical performer, and the perception of extended musical structure.

Contact address: Prof. George Pratt, Department of Music, University of Huddersfield, Queensgate, Huddersfield HD1 3DH, W. Yorkshire, England.

**Colin Robson** is director of postgraduate programmes at the University of Huddersfield and professor in the University of Huddersfield School of Human and Health Sciences. He is a psychologist with interests in combining quantitative and qualitative approaches to various types of inquiry in non-laboratory settings.

Contact address: Prof. Colin Robson, Department of Behavioural Sciences, University of Huddersfield, Queensgate, Huddersfield HD1 3DH, W. Yorkshire, England.

**Una M. Röhr-Sendlmeier** is Professor of Educational Psychology in the Department of Education, University of Bonn. Her main academic research interests are focused on cognitive development, language acquisition and diagnostics in a mono-cultural and cross cultural perspective.

Contact address: Prof. Dr. Una M. Röhr-Sendlmeier, Institute of Education, University of Bonn, Am Hof 3–5, D-5300 Bonn 1, Germany.

**Jacques H.A. van Rossum,** is a developmental psychologist in the Department of Psychology of the Faculty of Human Movement Sciences at the Vrije Universiteit (Amsterdam, The Netherlands). He holds a Ph.D. in human movement sciences (topic: variability and motor learning). In addition to a research interest in top level athletics, he is active in the area of motor development.

Contact address: Dr. J.H.A. van Rossum, Vrije Universiteit, Human Movement Sciences, Dept. of Psychology, v.d. Boechorststraat 9, 1081 BT Amsterdam, The Netherlands.

**Anna Rychlicka** works at the Jagiellonian University in Poland. Contact address: Anna Rychlicka, Jagiellonian University, School of Public Health, ul. Grzegórzecka 20, Kraków, Poland.

**Joachim Schöpfel** graduated from the University of Hamburg in 1984. A research assistant and lecturer at the University of Hamburg, Department of Developmental and Educational Psychology, from 1985 to 1990, he obtained his Ph.D. from the same university in 1992. He is presently working in the Department of Psychology at the French Interdisciplinary National Information Centre and teaches Culture and Society, Department of Educational Science, at the University of Nancy II, France.

Contact address: Dr. Joachim Schöpfel, Institut de l'Information Scientifique et Technique (C.N.R.S.), 2 allée du Parc de Brabois, 54514 Vandoeuvre-lès-Nancy Cedex, France.

**Larisa V. Shavinina** is a senior researcher in the laboratory "Creative giftedness" at the Institute of Psychology, Kiev, Ukraine. Her major scientific interest is the nature and fundamental mechanisms of intellectual-creative giftedness (such as cognitive experience, objectivity of cognition, specific intellectual intentions, intellectual control, etc.). The development of new psychodiagnostic procedures for the identification of gifted, talented and creative individuals and the intellectual technologies for the development of their intellectual-creative potential are also in the field of her scientific interest.

Contact address: Dr. Larisa V. Shavinina, Str. Tretya-2-3, 142432 Chernogolovka, Moscow region, Russia.

**John Sloboda** is Senior Lecturer in Psychology at Keele University. The psychology of music has been his major research interest for 20 years. He is an active performer and the author of *The Musical Mind* (Oxford University Press, 1985).

Contact address: Dr. John A. Sloboda, Department of Psychology, University of Keele, Staffordshire ST5 5BG, England.

**Karl Steffens** teaches at the University of Cologne, Department of Education, where he focuses on social and educational psychology (attitude measurement and change, socialization, cognitive abilities, problem solving, giftedness, artificial intelligence) as well as on research methodology (statistical methods, programming, computer training, philosophy of science). He has also published a number of articles in these fields.

Contact address: Dr. Karl Steffens, University of Cologne, Department of Education, Albertus-Magnus-Platz, 50931 Köln, Germany.

**Wolfgang Steinhöfel** was professor of teaching methods in the Faculty of Education of the Technical University of Chemnitz. He has been president of the German Educational Society and leader of a research group on fostering ability as well as of a school project in the same area. He has been working in the area of research on giftedness for over 10 years: as specialist for instruction in mathematics and educational researcher he has focused his work on gifted education. He has articulated his call for better gifted education in over 40 theoretical and empirical papers in national and international journals.

Contact address: Prof. Dr. Wolfgang Steinhöfel, Drosselweg 6, 09130 Chemnitz, Germany.

**Ferenc Süle** is a psychotherapist and psychiatrist who has been working since 1982 as the chief doctor of the Sports Mental Hygiene Department of the Hungarian National Institute of Sports Medicine. Previously he had been a member of the Psychotherapeutic Methodological Centre of Budapest for 8 years, and later led a psychiatric and psychotherapeutic department for 6 years. He is the leader of the Complex-psychotherapeutic Section of the Hungarian Psychiatric Association and is a member of the British Association of Group Analysis and the American Group Psychotherapeutic Association.

Contact address: Dr. Ferenc Süle, National Institute of Sports Medicine, Alkotás 48, Budapest, Hungary 1123.

**Waldemar Swietochowski** graduated from the University of Lódz in 1978. He specialized in clinical psychology. His Ph.D. was obtained from the Polish Academy of Science in 1989. He is now a researcher in the Department of Psychology at the University of Lódz. He has conducted research on interpersonal communication and temperament. Presently, his main areas of activity are research on the personality and motivational aspects of creativity.

Contact address: Dr. Waldemar Swietochowski, Department of Psychology, University of Lódz, ul. Smugowa 10/12, 91-433 Lódz, Poland.

**Dorien J. de Tombe** is assistant professor at the Delft University of Technology in the Faculty of Systems Engineering, Policy Analysis and Management. Her main areas of activity are in the field of learning and instruction and computer science. She has published several articles on manager training and complex societal problems. Her special focus is on the use of computers in problem solving. She is coordinator of a Special Interest Group of the European Association of Learning and Instruction (EARLI) on the subject of manager training and complex problems, and is coordinator of the East West Exchange Centre of the University of Utrecht, which focuses on scientific exchange with East-European scientists in the areas of manager training and the use of computers in science and education.

Contact address: Dr. Dorien J. de Tombe, Delft University of Technology, Faculty of Systems Engineering, Policy Analysis and Management, Jaffalaan 5, P.O. Box 5015, 2600 GA Delft, The Netherlands.

**Wilhelm Wieczerkowski** is emeritus professor of developmental and educational psychology in the Faculty of Psychology, University of Hamburg, where he initiated and directs the Counselling Centre for Gifted Children. He is former chairman of the William Stern Society for Research on Giftedness. Among his many publications are books and articles in the fields of cognitive and linguistic (bilingual) development and on gifted children.

Contact address: Prof. Dr. Wilhelm Wieczerkowski, Department of Psychology II, University of Hamburg, Von-Melle-Park 5, 20146 Hamburg, Germany.

**Irena Yashin-Shaw** is a research student in the Education faculty of Griffith University, Brisbane. Her current research is concerned with the cognitive processes and procedures employed by adults engaged in authentic tasks requiring creative outcomes. Her research, publications and presentations have dealt with topics as diverse as creative thinking, classroom teachers' immediacy behaviours and the impact of government policy on Queensland schools and teachers.

Contact address: Irena Yashin-Shaw, Faculty of Education, School of Adult and Vocational Education, Griffith University, Brisbane 4111, Queensland, Australia.

# Author Index

# Subject Index